THE CULTURAL LANDSCAPE

AN INTRODUCTION TO

HUMAN

GEOGRAPHY

This book belongs to Mari Ramoz
a very poor student.
(H) 510-595-7127

THE CULTURAL LANDSCAPE

AN INTRODUCTION TO

HUMAN

GEOGRAPHY

Fifth Edition

JAMES M. RUBENSTEIN

Miami University, Oxford, Ohio

PRENTICE HALL, UPPER SADDLE RIVER, NJ 07458

Library of Congress Cataloging-in-Publication Data

Rubenstein, James M.
    The cultural landscape: an introduction to human geography /
James M. Rubenstein. — 5th ed.
       p. cm.
    Includes bibliographical references and indexes.
    ISBN 0-13-386418-9
    1. Human geography. I. Title.
GF41.R82 1996
304.2—dc20   95-24280
                                      CIP

Acquisition editor: Ray Henderson
Editor-in-chief: Paul Corey
Production editor: Edward Thomas
Development editor: Fred Schroyer
Editor-in-chief of development: Ray Mullaney
Marketing manager: Leslie Cavaliere
Director of production and manufacturing: David W. Riccardi
Managing editor: Kathleen Schiaparelli
Supplements editor: Wendy Rivers
Manufacturing buyer: Trudy Pisciotti
Creative director: Paula Maylahn
Art director: Heather Scott
Text and cover designer: Patrice Fodero
Page layout and text composition: Molly Pike Riccardi/Lido Graphics
Art manager: Patrice Van Acker
Photo editor: Melinda Reo
Photo research: Terri Stratford
Editorial assistant: Pamela Holland-Moritz
Art studio: Maryland Cartographics
Copy editor: Margo Quinto
Cover photo: Gary Brettnacher/Tony Stone Images

Additional photograph credits: World map used on chapter openings is provided courtesy of The Granger Collection. The world photo used in starburst logo is provided courtesy of NASA. The 13 images that appear in the People, Places, and Change boxes are provided courtesy of the B.B.C., The Open University, and the Annenberg/C.P.B.

©1996 by Prentice-Hall, Inc.
Simon & Schuster/A Viacom Company
Upper Saddle River, New Jersey 07458

Previous editions ©1994, 1992, 1989, and 1983 by McMillan Publishing Company.

Printed in the United States of America
10 9 8 7 6 5 4 3 2 1

ISBN 0-13-386418-9

Prentice-Hall International (UK) Limited, *London*
Prentice-Hall of Australia Pty. Limited, *Sydney*
Prentice-Hall Canada Inc., *Toronto*
Prentice-Hall Hispanoamericana, S.A., *Mexico*
Prentice-Hall of India Private Limited, *New Delhi*
Prentice-Hall of Japan, Inc., *Tokyo*
Simon & Schuster Asia Pte. Ltd., *Singapore*
Editora Prentice-Hall do Brasil, Ltda., *Rio de Janeiro*

CONTENTS

1

BASIC CONCEPTS 3

2

POPULATION   57

3

MIGRATION   99

4

LANGUAGE   147

5

RELIGION   193

6

SOCIAL CUSTOMS ON THE LANDSCAPE 245

7

POLITICAL GEOGRAPHY 287

8

DEVELOPMENT 347

9

AGRICULTURE 387

10

INDUSTRY   427

11

SETTLEMENTS AND SERVICES   473

12

URBAN PATTERNS 519

13

RESOURCE PROBLEMS 563

PREFACE

What is geography? Geography is the study of where things are located on Earth's surface and the reasons for the location. The word *geography*, invented by the ancient Greek scholar Eratosthenes, is based on two Greek words. Geo means "Earth," and *graphy* means "to write." Geographers ask three simple questions: Where? Why? and So what? Where are people and activities located across Earth's surface? Why are they located in particular places? What is the significance of the distribution?

Geography as a Social Science

Recent world events lend a sense of urgency to geographic inquiry. Geography's spatial perspectives help relate political unrest in Eastern Europe, the Middle East, and other regions to the spatial distributions of cultural features such as languages and religions, demographic patterns such as population growth and migration, and natural resources such as energy and food supply.

Does the world face an overpopulation crisis? Geographers study population problems by comparing the arrangements of human organizations and natural resources across Earth. Given these spatial distributions, geographers conclude that some locations may have more people than can be provided for, whereas other places may be underpopulated.

Similarly, geographers examine the prospects for an energy crisis by relating the spatial distributions of energy sources and consumption. Geographers find that the users of energy are located in places with different social, economic, and political institutions than the producers of energy. Geographers seek first to describe the distribution of features such as the production and consumption of energy and then to ex-

plain the relationships between these distributions and other human and physical phenomena.

The main purpose of this book is to introduce students to the study of geography as a social science by emphasizing the relevance of geographic concepts to human problems. It is intended for use in college-level introductory human or cultural geography courses. The book is written for students who have not previously taken a college-level geography course and have had little, if any, geography in high school.

Divisions within Geography

Because geography is a broad subject, some specialization is inevitable. At the same time, one of geography's strengths is its diversity of approaches. Rather than being forced to adhere rigorously to established disciplinary laws, geographers can combine a variety of methods and approaches. This tradition stimulates innovative thinking, although students who are looking for a series of ironclad laws to memorize may be disappointed.

Human versus Physical Geography. Geography is both a physical and a social science. When geography concentrates on the distribution of physical features, such as climate, soil, and vegetation, it is a natural science. When it studies cultural features, such as language, industries, and cities, geography is a social science. This division is reflected in some colleges, where physical geography courses may carry natural science credit, and human and cultural geography courses carry social science credit.

While this book is concerned with geography from a social science perspective, one of the distinctive features of geography is its use of physical science concepts to help understand human behavior. The distinction between physical and human geography reflects differences in emphasis, not an absolute separation.

Topical versus Regional Approach. Geographers face a choice between a topical and a regional approach. The topical approach, which is used in this book, starts by identifying a set of important cultural issues to be studied, such as population growth, political disputes, and economic restructuring. Geographers using the topical approach examine the location of different aspects of the topic, the reasons for the observed pattern, and the significance of the distribution.

The alternative approach is regional. Regional geographers start by selecting a portion of Earth and studying the environment, people, and activities within the area. The regional geography approach is used in courses on Europe, Africa, Asia, and other areas of the world. Although this book is organized by topics, geography students should be aware of the location of places in the world. A separate index section lists the book's maps by location. One indispensable aid in the study of regions is an atlas, which can also be used to find unfamiliar places that may pop up in the news.

Descriptive versus Systematic Method. Whether using a topical or a regional approach, geographers can select either a descriptive or a systematic method. Again, the distinction is one of emphasis, not an absolute separation. The descriptive method emphasizes the collection of a variety of details about a particular location. This method has been used primarily by regional geographers to illustrate the uniqueness of a particular location on Earth's surface. The systematic method emphasizes the identification of several basic theories or techniques developed by geographers to explain the distribution of activities.

This book uses both the descriptive and systematic methods because total dependence on either approach is unsatisfactory. An entirely descriptive book would contain a large collection of individual examples not organized into a unified structure. A completely systematic approach suffers because some of the theories and techniques are so abstract that they lack meaning for the student. Geographers who de-

pend only on the systematic approach may have difficulty explaining important contemporary issues.

Features

This book is sensitive to the study needs of students. Each chapter is clearly structured to help students understand the material and effectively review from the book.

Outline. The book discusses the following main topics:

- **What basic concepts do geographers use?** Chapter 1 provides an introduction to basic geographic concepts, as well as a brief summary of the development of the science of geography. Geographers employ several concepts to describe the distribution of people and activities across Earth, to explain reasons underlying the observed distribution, and to understand the significance of the arrangements.
- **Where are people located in the world?** Chapters 2 and 3 examine the distribution and growth of the world's population, as well as the movement of people from one place to another. Why do some places on Earth contain large numbers of people or attract newcomers while other places are sparsely inhabited?
- **How are different cultural groups distributed?** Chapters 4 through 7 analyze the distribution of different cultural traits and beliefs and the problems that result from those spatial patterns. Important cultural features include political systems, languages, religions, and daily customs, such as the choice of food, clothing, shelter, and leisure activities. Geographers look for similarities and differences in the cultural features at different places, the reasons for their distribution, and the importance of these differences for world peace.
- **How do people earn a living in different parts of the world?** Human survival depends on acquiring an adequate food supply. One of the most significant distinctions in the world is whether people produce their food directly from the land or buy it with money earned by performing nonagricultural types of work. Chapters 8 through 12 look at these ways of earning a living. These chapters describe the

economic activities people undertake in different regions of the world and the factors that account for the distribution of agriculture, industry, and services. Chapter 12 and a portion of Chapter 11 concentrate on cities, the centers for economic as well as cultural activities.

- **What problems result from using Earth's resources?** The final chapter is devoted to a study of three issues related to the use of Earth's natural resources: energy, pollution, and food supply. Geographers recognize that cultural problems result from the depletion, destruction, and inefficient use of the world's natural resources.

Chapter Organization. Each chapter is organized with these study aids:

- **Case Study.** Each chapter opens with a case study that illustrates some of the key concepts presented in the text. The case studies are generally drawn from news events or from daily experiences familiar to residents of North America.
- **Key Issues.** Each chapter contains a set of three or four key issues around which the chapter material is organized. These questions reappear as major headings within the chapter.
- **Key Terms.** The key terms in each chapter are indicated in bold type when they are introduced. These terms are also defined at the end of each chapter.
- **Geography in Action Box.** Each chapter has a one- or two-page box that explores in depth a particular topic related to the subject of the chapter. The Geography in Action boxes relate principles and concepts to applied, practical issues.
- **Summary.** The key issues are repeated at the end of the chapter with a brief review of the important concepts covered in detail in the text.
- **Case Study Revisited.** Additional information related to the chapter's case study may be used to reinforce some of the main points.
- **Thinking Geographically.** This section offers five questions based on concepts and themes developed in the chapter. The questions help students apply geographic concepts to explore issues more intensively.
- **Further Readings.** A list of books and articles is provided for students who wish to study the subject further.

- **People, Places, and Change Box.** Each chapter concludes with an excerpt from a video series on human geography being prepared by the Corporation for Public Broadcasting and the Annenberg Project in conjunction with the British Broadcasting Corporation and the Open University, based in England. These videos will play on some Public Broadcasting System stations and will be available for instructors to show in classrooms.

Appendix. A special appendix on scale and major projections enhances the discussion of the subject in Chapter 1 of the text. We are grateful to Phillip C. Muehrcke, Professor of Geography at the University of Wisconsin-Madison, and former president of the American Cartographic Association, for his clear explanation of the subject.

Ancillaries Materials: Annenberg/CPB Video Series

We are pleased to announce that this text has been selected as the companion text for a new video series co-produced by Annenberg/CPB, The Open University, and the BBC. *Human Geography: People Places and Change* provides on-location footage from all over the globe. The series contains eleven professionally produced tapes which average 30 minutes in length. This edition contains optional boxes referring to appropriate segments from the series. The tapes may be purchased at low cost directly from Annenberg/CPB by phoning (800)-LEARNER. Complementary copies of video tapes and a comprehensive *Annenberg Series Faculty Guide* are available free to qualified adopters. An *Annenberg Series Student Guide* will also be available at low cost for courses that intend to maximize use of the video. For information about these or the supplements listed below, please contact your local Prentice Hall representative.

- Study Guide (0-13-459504-1)
- Instructor's Resource Manual (0-13-392465-3)
- Slide Set (0-13-393463-2)
- Acetate Transparencies (0-13-392754-7)
- Test Item File (0-13-392523-4)
- IBM Test Manager (0-13-393448-9)
- Mac Test Manager (0-13-393455-1)
- New York Times Geography Supplement

Suggestions for Use

This book can be used in an introductory human or cultural geography course that extends over one semester, one quarter, or two quarters. An instructor in a one-semester course could devote one week to each of the chapters, leaving time for examinations.

In a one-quarter course, the instructor might need to omit some of the book's material. A course with more of a cultural orientation could include Chapters 1 through 8, plus Chapter 13. If the course has more of an economic orientation, then the appropriate chapters would be 1 through 3 and 7 through 12, or if time permits, 13.

A two-quarter course could be organized around the culturally oriented Chapters 1 through 7 during the first quarter and the more economically oriented Chapters 8 through 13 during the second quarter. Topics of particular interest to the instructor or students could be discussed for more than one week.

Changes

Until the late 1980s, geography textbooks were revised infrequently. Thematic concepts seemed timeless, and world economic and political structures static. During the 1990s, the rapid rate of world changes can make geography texts seem outdated quickly.

A few years ago, geography books had to cope with the creation of two dozen new countries in a couple of years, primarily as the result of the fall of communism in Eastern Europe and the resulting breakup of the Soviet Union, Yugoslavia, and Czechoslovakia. Until recently, geographers could delineate the boundaries of the new countries, but they possessed few statistics about these new countries' peoples and economies. As more data become available, geographers are able to understand the deep cultural and economic differences underlying the pressures to create new countries.

Material once central to a human geography course is now relegated to historical geography: the Soviet Union no longer exists, and South Africa no longer practices apartheid. In a rapidly changing world, an introductory human geography text must decide how much history to retain. This book retains maps of the former Soviet Union and segregated South Africa. Overall, the book probably contains more examples of history than many students prefer and less than many instructors prefer.

Geographic changes in the mid-1990s are less visible on world maps than the delineation of new countries, but they have more profound impacts on our culture, economy, and environment. This edition of the book is organized around a tension between two important themes in the 1990s—globalization and cultural diversity. In many respects we are living in a more unified world economically, culturally, and environmentally. The actions of a particular corporation or country affect people around the world. At the same time, people are taking deliberate steps to retain distinctive cultural identities. They are preserving little-used languages and fighting fiercely to protect their religions.

An important change in this edition is the allocation of more space to the service sector of the economy. Two-thirds of North Americans work in the services, but this sector of the economy receives minimal treatment in introductory (or even intermediate-level) geography books. Part of the problem in introducing this material at the introductory level is that geographers have not settled upon an authoritative typology. This book adopts a format used by the United Nations of dividing services into five types—transport (along with communication and utility) services, producer services, retail and wholesale services, consumer services, and government services. It is hoped that, by giving service the position of prominence it deserves, this book can contribute to the development of a widely accepted geographic framework.

Critical to delivery of up-to-date information is minimizing the time between completion of changes in the text and maps and distribution of the printed book. For example, maps incorporate data published by the Encyclopaedia Britannica in May 1995. This edition reflects world changes through mid-June 1995, and copies of the book were available in some bookstores by August 1995.

Maps have also been added to reinforce the tension between globalization and cultural diversity. For example, maps have been added to illustrate transnational corporations and the changing hierarchies of cities in the world and within the United States according to the type of services they perform. Increasing cultural diversity is represented in new maps of Fez and Ho Chi Minh City, immigration to the

United States from Latin America and from Asia, immigration of African-Americans within the United States, and differences in population characteristics among six U.S. communities. Charts have been added to illustrate such points as changes over time, sources of migrants to the United States, relative size of world languages and language families, distribution of energy reserves, divergence between Malthus's theory of overpopulation and contemporary reality, and relationship between a country's income and level of pollution.

In the past, maps were drawn to illustrate only a narrow or precise idea. But maps have been redrawn to include information of interest to the reader that may not be absolutely central to the map's precise purpose.

Finally, given the enormous amount of material now available electronically, through CD-ROM, networking, and so on, why should an instructor continue to make students buy an expensive textbook? In the computer age, is a textbook an anachronism? A book is a slow way to communicate: by the time this book is in your hands, something in it will be outdated, perhaps a new war, peace treaty, or United Nations member.

The information superhighway is filled with information that can be retrieved quickly, but the information is poorly organized and written. In contrast, a high-quality book is crafted carefully by the author, editors, and publishers. For example, the author rewrote this sentence five times to convey a precise meaning. Editors then change many of the words and punctuation to assure that the author's intended meaning is successfully communicated. A book allows an author to lay out a more careful and clear route to explanation and understanding than is possible electronically. For now, computers are tools for retrieval of facts and for advanced analysis, but they cannot yet compete with books in explaining a discipline's basic concepts and themes.

Acknowledgments

The successful completion of a book like this requires the contribution of many people. I gratefully acknowledge the help I received.

A number of people reviewed portions of the manuscript at various stages in the revision process and offered excellent suggestions. These reviewers included:

- Arthur Steele Becker, University of Nebraska at Kearney
- Henry W. Bullamore, Frostburg State University
- Satish K. Davgun, Bemidji State University
- Fiona M. Davidson, University of Arkansas
- Paul B. Frederic, University of Maine at Farmington
- Douglas Heffington, Middle Tennessee State University
- William C. Jameson, University of Central Arkansas
- John C. Lowe, George Washington University
- John Milbauer, Northeastern University
- Roger Miller, University of Minnesota
- Woodrow W. Nichols, Jr., North Carolina Central University
- Thomas M. Orf, Prestonsburg Community College
- Yda Schreuder, University of Delaware
- Paul Shott, Plymouth State College
- Gerald R. Webster, University of Alabama

This book was produced shortly after Macmillan Publishing Company and Prentice Hall Publishing Company completed a merger that has created the country's dominant publisher of geography books. From the author's perspective, the transition has been seamless and invigorating. Ray Henderson, geography editor for the combined company, is filled with fresh, new ideas for nudging the book and the company's entire geography program into the multimedia age. Ed Thomas has been a sensitive, articulate production editor, who kept the project flowing smoothly. Ray Mullaney, editor-in-chief in charge of development, set up a clear timetable that we have all been able to meet. Paul Corey, once geography editor at Macmillan, and now editor-in-chief of the combined company, has maintained a strategic interest in this book, which he was instrumental in nursing to success in the past. This edition benefited enormously from work done by the development editor Fred Schroyer, who has a natural science background. Fred brought a fresh perspective to the book's social science framework and strengthened both the natural science material, such as in Chapter 13, and the integration of natural and social sciences, which is at the core of geography. Other dedicated people at Prentice Hall deserve thanks, especially the design directors—Paula Maylahn and Heather Scott.

Outside Prentice Hall, the production staff at Maryland CartoGraphics, under the leadership of John Radziszewski, continue to produce outstanding maps and line drawings for this book. For speed, accuracy, and attractiveness they continue to set the standard in introductory geography texts. Terri Stratford produced an outstanding collection of photographs, and Molly Pike Riccardi of Lido Graphics did a fantastic job with page design. At Miami University, I especially want to thank Andrew Johns for his dedicated work over a two-year period assisting with the development of fresh material for this edition; the two-year life of this edition coincides with Andy's two years of service in the Peace Corps in Chile. Thanks also for the help from other Miami students, including Kelly Cooney, Kenneth Guttman, Kevin Leeson, and Nicole Monroe.

Finally, I thank my introductory geography students and my family for all of their support over the years. I would like to dedicate this book to my wife, Bernadette Unger, who, as a city planner, does an outstanding job of practicing what I preach.

James Rubenstein
Oxford, Ohio

ABOUT THE AUTHOR

Dr. James M. Rubenstein received his Ph.D. from Johns Hopkins University in 1975. His dissertation on French urban planning was later developed into a book entitled **The French New Towns** (Johns Hopkins University Press). In 1976 he joined the faculty at Miami University, where he is currently Professor of Geography. Besides teaching courses on Urban and Human Geography and writing textbooks, Dr. Rubenstein also conducts research in the automotive industry and has a recently published book on the subject entitled **The Changing U.S. Auto Industry: A Geographical Analysis** (Routledge). Originally from Baltimore, he is an avid Orioles fan and follows college lacrosse.

The world map at right reveals one of the most significant elements of the cultural landscape—the political boundaries that separate its five billion inhabitants. The numerous states range in size from Russia, which occupies one-sixth of the world's land area, to microstates such as Singapore, Malta, or Grenada. The names of these states evoke images of different environments, peoples, cultures, and levels of well-being. However, the political boundaries are only one of the many patterns that geographers observe across the earth's surface. Geographers study the distribution of a wide variety of cultural and environmental features—social customs, agricultural patterns, the use of resources—many of which transcend political boundaries. As scientists, geographers also try to explain why we can observe these patterns on the landscape. The facing map and chapters that follow are intended to begin the student on a journey toward understanding our exciting and complex world.

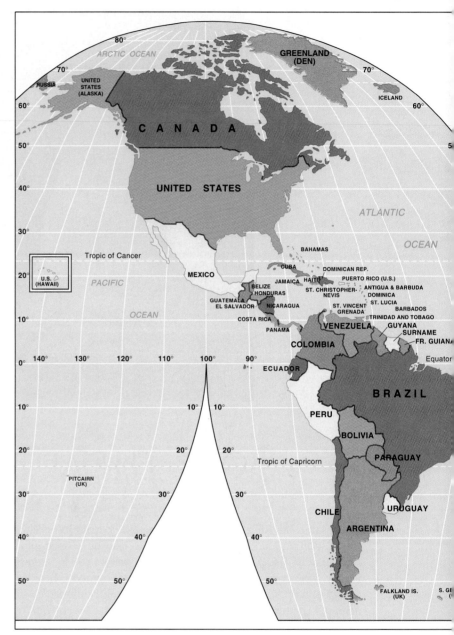

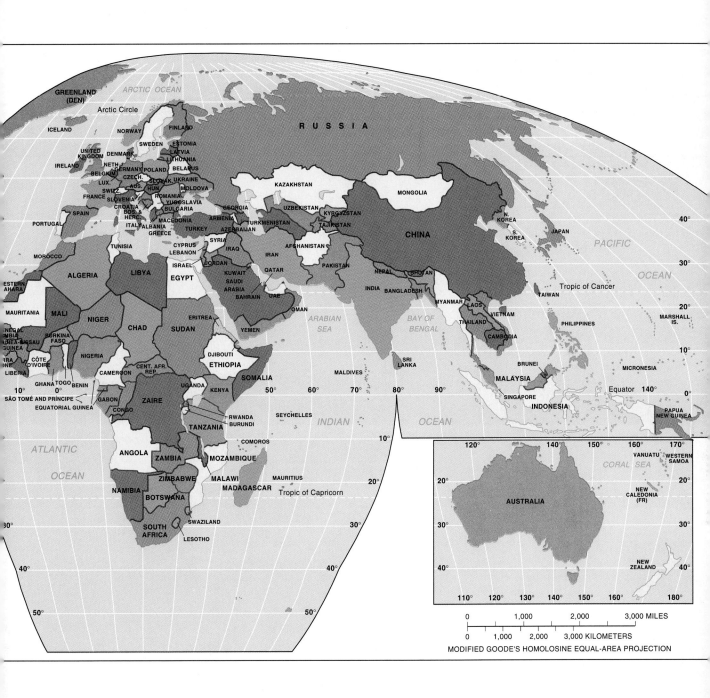

GREENLAND
(DEN)

ARCTIC OCEAN

Arctic Circle

ICELAND

NORWAY

FINLAND

R U S S I A

SWEDEN

ESTONIA
LATVIA
LITHUANIA

UNITED
KINGDOM

DENMARK

IRELAND

NETH.
BELGIUM
GERMANY
POLAND
BELARUS

LUX.

KAZAKHSTAN

MONGOLIA

40°

SWITZ.
AUS.
SLOVAK
UKRAINE
MOLDOVA

N.
KOREA

PACIFIC

FRANCE

SLOVENIA

CZECH.

HUN.

UZBEKISTAN

KYRGYZSTAN

S.
KOREA

JAPAN

SPAIN

CROATIA
BOS.&
HERC.
ROMANIA
YUGOSLAVIA

GEORGIA

TAJIKISTAN

CHINA

30°

OCEAN

PORTUGAL

ITALY
ALBANIA
GREECE

MACEDONIA
BULGARIA

ARMENIA
TURKMENISTAN

AZERBAIJAN

TURKEY

MOROCCO

TUNISIA

CYPRUS
LEBANON

SYRIA

IRAQ

IRAN

AFGHANISTAN

PAKISTAN

BHUTAN

Tropic of Cancer

TAIWAN

20°

ISRAEL

JORDAN

NEPAL

MARSHALL
IS.

ALGERIA

LIBYA

EGYPT

KUWAIT

SAUDI
ARABIA

QATAR

UAE

INDIA

BANGLADESH

MYANMAR

LAOS

VIETNAM

PHILIPPINES

WESTERN
SAHARA

BAHRAIN

OMAN

ARABIAN
SEA

BAY OF
BENGAL

THAILAND

10°

MAURITANIA

MALI

NIGER

CHAD

SUDAN

ERITREA

YEMEN

CAMBODIA

BRUNEI

MICRONESIA

SENEGAL
GAMBIA
GUINEA-BISSAU
GUINEA

BURKINA
FASO

NIGERIA

DJIBOUTI

ETHIOPIA

MALDIVES

SRI
LANKA

MALAYSIA

SIERRA
LEONE
LIBERIA

CÔTE
D'IVOIRE

GHANA
TOGO
BENIN

CAMEROON

CENT. AFR.
REP.

SOMALIA

UGANDA

KENYA

50°

60°

70°

80°

90°

SINGAPORE

Equator 140°

0°

SÃO TOMÉ AND PRÍNCIPE

EQUATORIAL GUINEA

GABON

CONGO

ZAIRE

RWANDA
BURUNDI

SEYCHELLES

INDONESIA

PAPUA
NEW GUINEA

ATLANTIC

TANZANIA

COMOROS

INDIAN

OCEAN

10°

ANGOLA

ZAMBIA

MOZAMBIQUE

MALAWI

MAURITIUS

OCEAN

ZIMBABWE

NAMIBIA

BOTSWANA

MADAGASCAR

Tropic of Capricorn

20°

SWAZILAND

30°

SOUTH
AFRICA

LESOTHO

40°

50°

CORAL SEA

VANUATU
WESTERN
SAMOA

120°

140°

150°

160°

170°

20°

AUSTRALIA

NEW
CALEDONIA
(FR)

20°

30°

30°

NEW
ZEALAND

40°

40°

110°

120°

130°

140°

150°

160°

180°

| 0 | 1,000 | 2,000 | 3,000 MILES |

| 0 | 1,000 | 2,000 | 3,000 KILOMETERS |

MODIFIED GOODE'S HOMOLOSINE EQUAL-AREA PROJECTION

1

BASIC CONCEPTS

KEY ISSUES

- How do geographers answer the "where" question?
- How do geographers answer the "why" question?
- How do geographers explain the significance of geographic patterns?

What do you expect from this geography course? You may think that geography involves memorizing lists of countries and capitals, climates and crop types, or exports and imports. Perhaps you associate geography with photographic essays of exotic places in popular magazines.

But contemporary geography is much more. It is a fascinating science, and one in which everyone can participate. Geography is the scientific study of the location of people and activities across Earth's surface and the reasons for their distribution. Geographers ask where things are, why they are there, and why their geographic arrangements are significant.

Like all sciences, geography requires you to understand some basic concepts. For example, the definition of geography in the previous paragraph included the words *location* and *distribution*. We use these words commonly in daily speech, but geographers give them precise meanings. This first chapter is a short tour through the interesting basics of geography.

YOUNG BUDDHIST MONKS LOOK THROUGH TELEPHOTO LENS OF A CAMERA, SYRIAM, MYANMAR (BURMA). (BUSHNELL•SOIFER/TONY STONE IMAGES)

Where Is Miami?

Consider the following conversation between two students during winter vacation:

First student: Where do you go to school?

Second student: Miami University.

First student: I'll bet you enjoy the warm weather and nearby ocean.

Second student: No way. I don't go to school in Florida. We have snow and hills.

First student: Then where is your Miami?

Second student: In Oxford, Ohio.

First student: Where is Oxford, Ohio?

Second student: About 35 miles northwest of Cincinnati and 2 miles from the Indiana border.

First student: [overwhelmed]: Oh.

Second student: [conversation gets more technical]: Not only that, Miami, Ohio, is located at 39°30´40″ north latitude and 84°44´40″ west longitude, in township T5N R1E.

The conversation between the two students presents a key question that geographers ask: Where is something located? Geographers study the arrangement of people and activities across Earth's surface. But geography is much more than a description of place-names. It is a scientific study of the reasons why people and activities are arranged in a particular way. Further, geographers seek to know the significance of where something is located. Like other scientists, geographers try to solve problems, in this case those that arise from the location of people and activities.

Geography's most fundamental principle is location, because the location of people, activities, and environments can help explain human behavior and can help solve human problems. Just as historians study the logical sequence of human activities in time, so do geographers study the logical arrangement of human activities in space.

On a tiny scale, geography can explain daily behavior, such as the distribution of students in a classroom. Some students sit in the front of the room for maximum interaction with the instructor. Students near the front can more easily read the chalkboard, hear what the instructor and other students say during lectures and discussions, and make eye contact with the instructor. Other students choose a location in the rear of the room to avoid interaction with the instructor. Perhaps they have not done the assignment, or they wish to spend class time doing other things. Whether in the front or rear, students quickly acquire a sense of place in the classroom: Having selected seats at the beginning of the term, they tend to sit in or near the same location every day, even if the instructor does not require it.

On a regional and national scale, geography is a way of thinking about far more urgent problems than where to perch in a classroom. Geographers study human characteristics, such as where and why population is skyrocketing in Africa. Geographers examine where and why petroleum resources are being depleted in the United States, and the consequences. Geographers look at disputes among followers of different religions worldwide.

On a global scale, geographers look at the worldwide distribution and movement of

- Languages, religions, and other cultural and social values
- Money, corporations, information, and other economic values

- Pollution, resources, hazards, and other environmental values

Geography is divided broadly into two categories: human geography, which includes cultural, social, and economic features, and physical geography, which includes climate, landforms, vegetation, and other environmental features. Because geographers are trained in a broad range of topics, they are particularly well equipped to understand interactions between people and their environment. This book focuses on human geography, but never forget Earth's atmosphere, land, water, vegetation, and other living creatures.

Geographers also study how different characteristics of places are related. For example:

- To explain the problem of hunger in Somalia and neighboring countries in Africa, geographers examine relations among population growth, drought, farming practices, environmental degradation, and political unrest.
- To explain unrest in the Middle East, geographers study the distribution of energy resources, differences in religious beliefs, and alternative strategies for modernizing economies.

This chapter presents basic concepts that help geographers describe where people and activities occur, why they occur where they do, and the significance of the observed geographic arrangements. The basic "where," "why," and "so what" questions are fundamental to human geography. Subjects found in subsequent chapters, such as demographic, cultural, political, and economic patterns, make use of the basic concepts presented here.

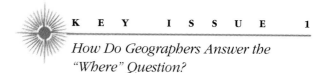

K E Y   I S S U E   1

How Do Geographers Answer the "Where" Question?

- Maps: Scale Models That Show Where Something Is
- How Geography Grew as a Science by Answering "Where?"
- Location: Where Something Is

ou want to know where something is, how do you find out? To find the way to a restaurant, you could ask someone or phone the restaurant for directions. But if you want to find out where San Salvador Island is (the place where Christopher Columbus first made landfall), or where drought is occurring in Africa, or where shipping routes to Singapore are located, you need a map.

Geography is immediately distinguished from other disciplines by its reliance on maps. For centuries, geographers have worked to perfect the science of mapmaking, called **cartography.** The first geographic concept we need to examine is geography's most important tool, the map.

Maps: Scale Models That Show Where Something Is

A **map** is a two-dimensional (flat) scale model of Earth's surface or some portion of it. Maps are scale models of the real world, just like a model automobile or ship, made small enough to work with on a desk or display on a wall. Maps are normally made flat because three-dimensional models are expensive and difficult to reproduce. Maps range from hasty sketches ("here's how to get to the party") to precise, sophisticated, computer-generated works of art.

A map is both a pathfinder and a tool for learning. We consult maps to learn where in the world something is found, especially in relation to a place we know, such as a town, body of water, or highway. Maps help us find the shortest route between two places and avoid getting lost along the way. Maps often are the best way to present information, such as population density.

Geographers not only draw maps, but interpret them as well, extracting information to explain patterns of human behavior (vacation travel) or physical phenomena (hurricane paths). A series of maps of the same area over several years can reveal dynamic processes at work, such as soil erosion or human migration or the spread of a disease. Patterns on maps may suggest interactions among different features of Earth.

Geographers also use maps to communicate their research results or explanations of human or physical processes. Placing information on a map is a principal way that geographers share data or critical analysis of patterns.

A map is different from a photograph because it is a less-literal representation of Earth, an artistic creation constrained by scientific principles. To communicate geographic concepts effectively through maps, cartographers must design them properly and assure that users know how to read them. To create an accurate map, the cartographer must make several decisions. The two most important are scale and projection.

Scale

The first decision a cartographer faces is how much of Earth's surface to depict on the map. Is it necessary to show the entire globe or just one continent, or a country, or a city? To make a scale model of the entire world, the cartographer must omit many details because there simply is not enough space. Conversely, if a map shows only a small portion of Earth's surface, as would a street map of a city, it can provide a wealth of detail about a particular place.

The level of detail and the amount of area covered on a map depend on its scale. The scale of a map is the same concept as the scale of a model car or boat: **Scale** is the relation of a feature's size on a map to its actual size on Earth's surface. For example, if 1 inch of roadway on a map is actually 24,000 inches on the ground, the map scale is 1:24,000.

Cartographers usually present scale in one of three ways: a fraction (1/24,000) or ratio (1:24,000), written statement ("1 inch equals 1 mile"), or graphic bar scale (Figure 1-1).

A fractional scale shows the numerical ratio between distances on the map and Earth's surface. A scale of 1:24,000 or 1/24,000 means that one unit (inch, centimeter, foot, finger length) on the map represents 24,000 of the same unit (inch, centimeter, foot, finger length) on the ground. The unit chosen for distance can be anything, as long as the units of measure on both the map and the ground are the same. The 1 on the left side of the ratio always refers to a unit of distance on the map, and the number on the right always refers to the same unit of distance on Earth's surface.

The written scale describes this relation between map and Earth distances in words. For example, the statement "1 inch equals 1 mile" on a map means that 1 inch on the map represents 1 mile on Earth's surface. Again, the first number always refers to map distance, and the second to distance on Earth's sur-

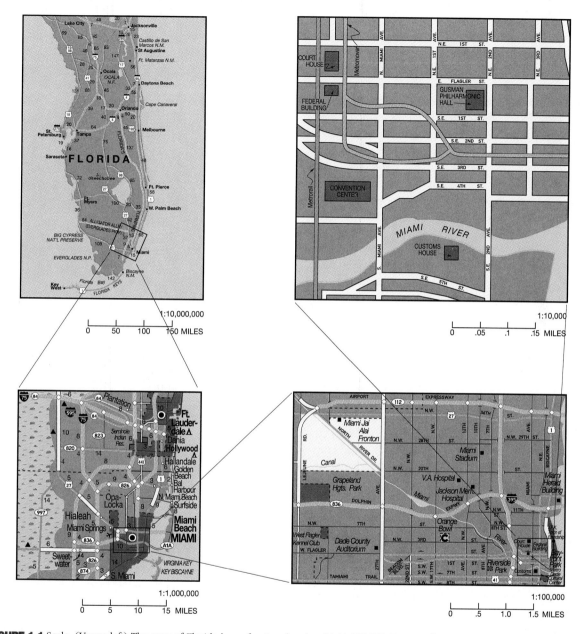

FIGURE 1-1 Scale. (Upper left) The map of Florida has a fractional scale of 1:10,000,000. Expressed as a written statement, 1 inch on the map represents 10 million inches (about 158 miles) on the ground. The bar line below the map displays the scale in a graphic form. (Lower left) The map of South Florida has a scale of 1:1,000,000; 1 inch on the map equals 1 million inches on the ground, or about 16 miles. (Lower right) The map of the Miami metropolitan area in the lower right has a scale of 1:100,000; 1 inch on the map equals 100,000 inches, or about 1.6 miles. (Upper right) The map of downtown Miami has a scale of 1:10,000; 1 inch on the map equals 10,000 inches, or about 0.16 miles, or 833 feet.

face. (Here the units are different—inch and mile—for ease of use.)

A graphic scale usually consists of a bar line marked to show distance on Earth's surface. To use a bar line, first determine with a ruler the distance on the map in inches or centimeters. Then hold the ruler against the bar line and read the number on the bar line opposite the map distance on the ruler. The number on the bar line is the equivalent distance on Earth's surface.

A map's scale can be any ratio the mapmaker desires. Here are three examples.

1. A flower bed could be mapped at 1:1 scale by drawing the flower bed at its actual size on a huge sheet of paper.
2. A state could be mapped at 1:250,000 scale, where 1 inch on the map represents 250,000 inches (about 4 miles) on the ground.
3. Earth could be mapped at 1:42,000,000 scale, where 1 inch on the map represents 42,000,000 inches (about 665 miles) on the ground. This is the scale of a common world globe.

When comparing map scales, remember that the smaller the fractional scale, the larger the overall area represented (example 3 above), and the larger the fractional scale, the smaller the area covered (example 1 above). A world map uses a smaller scale than a city map, because it covers a larger area. A large-scale map is suitable for detailed information about a small area.

Projections

Earth is very nearly a sphere, and therefore it is quite accurately represented in the form of a globe. A globe, however, is an extremely limited tool to communicate information about Earth's surface. A small globe doesn't have enough space to display detailed information, whereas a large globe is too cumbersome to use. And a globe is difficult to write on, photocopy, mail, or carry in the glove box of a car!

Consequently, most maps are flat. This feature poses a dilemma to cartographers: When drawing a spherical Earth on a flat piece of paper, some distortion is unavoidable. The act of transferring locations on Earth's surface to a flat map is called **projection.** Cartographers have invented hundreds of clever projections, but none is free of distortion.

The problem of distortion is especially severe for world-scale and small-scale maps. Four types of distortion can result:

1. The shape of an area can be distorted, so that it appears more elongated or squat than it really is.
2. The distance between two points may become increased or decreased.
3. The relative size of different areas may be altered. One area may appear larger than another on a map but in reality be smaller.
4. The direction from one place to another can be distorted.

Most of the world maps in this book, such as Figure 1-19 on page 43, are *equal area* projections. The primary benefit of this type of projection is that the relative sizes (areas) of the land masses on the map are the same as in reality. The projection also minimizes distortion in the shape of most land masses, although areas toward the North and South poles—such as Greenland and Antarctica—become more distorted. Those areas are sparsely inhabited, so distorting their shape usually is not important.

Preservation of the size and shape of land masses, however, requires that the map be forced into other distortions:

- The Eastern and Western hemispheres are separated into two pieces, a characteristic known as interruption.
- The meridians (the vertical lines), which in reality converge at the North and South poles, do not converge at all on the map. Also, they do not form right angles with the parallels (the horizontal lines).

In contrast, we use uninterrupted projections to display information in the time zone map in the Geography in Action box on page 22. This figure also uses the Mercator projection, one of the most common. It has several advantages: Shape is distorted very little, direction is consistent, and the map is rectangular. But, its greatest disadvantage is that area is grossly distorted toward the poles, making high-latitude places look much larger than they actually are. For example, compare the sizes of Greenland and South America in the time zone map and in Figure 1-19, which shows their size accurately.

The Appendix presents some of the decisions that must be made when developing a map.

Contemporary High-Tech Mapping

Having largely completed the great task of accurately mapping Earth's surface, which required several centuries, geographers have turned to new technologies to learn more about the characteristics of places. Two important technologies that have been developed during the past quarter-century are remote sensing from satellites (to collect data) and geographic information systems (computer programs for manipulating geographic data). These technologies help geographers create more accurate and complex maps and measure changes over time in the characteristics of places.

Remote Sensing. The acquisition of data about Earth's surface from a satellite orbiting Earth or other long-distance methods is known as **remote sensing.** Geographic applications of remote sensing include mapping of vegetation and other surface cover, gathering data for large unpopulated areas such as the extent of winter ice cover on the oceans, and monitoring changes such as weather patterns and deforestation.

Remote sensing satellites scan Earth's surface, much as a television camera scans an image in the thin lines you can see on a TV screen. At any moment, a satellite sensor records the image of a tiny area, an area called a picture element, or pixel. A map created by remote sensing is essentially a grid containing many rows of pixels.

The smallest feature on Earth's surface that can be detected by a sensor is the resolution of the scanner. Some scanners can sense objects as small as 10 meters across. Future satellites will improve resolution to 1 meter or less.

Weather satellites take a broader view, looking at several kilometers at a time, so they can rapidly map a large area such as a continent. Weather forecasters need data about large areas very quickly, because weather systems change so rapidly.

GIS. A **geographic information system (GIS)** is a high-performance computer system that processes geographic data. Many pieces of information about a location are stored in computer files. Each type of information (topography, political boundaries, population density, manufacturing, soil type, earthquake faults, and so on) is stored as an "information layer." A single layer can be displayed by itself, but the GIS is most powerful when it is used to combine several layers to show relations among different kinds of information (Figure 1-2). Powerful desktop microcomputers, now commonplace, have speeded the diffusion of GIS technology worldwide.

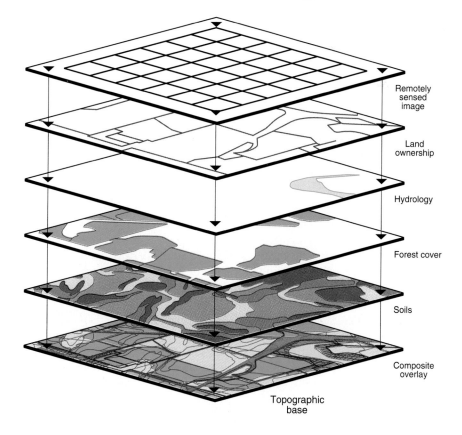

FIGURE 1-2 A geographic information system (GIS) involves storing information about a location in layers. Each layer represents a different piece of human or environmental information. The layers can be viewed individually or in combination.

Remotely sensed image

Land ownership

Hydrology

Forest cover

Soils

Composite overlay

Topographic base

Geographers use GIS to analyze both environmental and social phenomena. A human geography example is combining a street map with a population map to determine the number of people living within walking distance of a proposed bus route.

GPS. The ***Global Positioning System (GPS)*** is an example of applying new technology to an old human habit: consulting a map to get to a desired destination. The GPS navigation system takes signals from a series of satellites that can pinpoint the current location of a car within 15 meters (50 feet). As a cross-check, sensors in the wheels pinpoint movement of the car.

The driver programs the desired destination, and the monitor calls up the appropriate map, stored on CD-ROM. An antenna receives signals from GPS satellites and feeds them into a computer stored in the trunk of the car. The navigation system provides oral instructions for where to turn, because reading the map while driving can be dangerous. Hand-held GPS units also are available.

How Geography Grew as a Science by Answering "Where?"

The first "geographer" probably was the unknown ancient person who crossed a river or climbed a hill, observed what was on the other side, returned home to tell about it, and scratched a rough "map" in the dirt. The second "geographer" probably was the person who used the rough map to find a way from one place to another—in other words, to navigate.

Historical Development of Geography

In early history, geography was synonymous with navigation. As early as 800 B.C., Mediterranean sailors and traders made charts of useful information for finding their way, noting distinctive landmarks such as rock formations, islands, and the direction of ocean currents. For millennia, Polynesian peoples navigated thousands of kilometers over the South Pacific islands, using three-dimensional maps, called stick charts, made of strips from palm trees and seashells. The shells represented islands, and the palm strips represented patterns of waves between the islands (Figure 1-3).

Geography in the Ancient World. The ancient Greeks were concerned with geographic concepts for hundreds of years before the name *geography* was invented. In the sixth century B.C., the philosopher Thales of Miletus applied principles of geometry to measuring land area. (Miletus was an ancient port city in Turkey.) Thales' student Anaximander argued that the world was shaped like a cylinder and made a world map based on information from sailors.

Aristotle (384–322 B.C.) was the first to demonstrate that Earth was spherical, noting that matter falls together toward a common center, that during an eclipse Earth's shadow on the moon is circular, and that the groups of stars visible at night change as one travels north or south. The Greek astronomer and geographer Pytheas sailed to Iceland in 325 B.C. and worked out a method for determining latitude by observing the position of stars. Hipparchus (190?–125? B.C.) drew lines on maps of Earth's surface to create reference points for the location of places. To this day, we depend on his concept of north-south meridians and east-west parallels (longitude and latitude).

The first person of record to use the word *geography* was another Greek, Eratosthenes (276?–195? B.C.). He not only accepted that Earth was round, as few did in his day, but also calculated its circumference within an amazing 0.5 percent accuracy. In one of the first geography books, he described the known world and correctly divided Earth into five climatic regions—a torrid zone across the middle, two frigid zones at the extreme north and south, and two temperate bands in between. He also prepared one of the earliest maps of the known world.

Roman geographers made their contribution, too. Strabo (63? B.C.–A.D. 24?) exhaustively described the known world in his seventeen-volume work *Geography*. Strabo regarded Earth as a sphere at the center of a spherical universe. In the second century A.D., the Roman Empire controlled an extensive area of the known world, including much of Europe, northern Africa, and western Asia. Taking advantage of information collected by Roman merchants and soldiers, another Greek, Ptolemy (A.D. 100?–170?), wrote an eight-volume *Guide to Geography*. He prepared numerous maps that were not improved upon for more than a thousand years.

Geography also developed in China, independent of European studies. The oldest Chinese geograph-

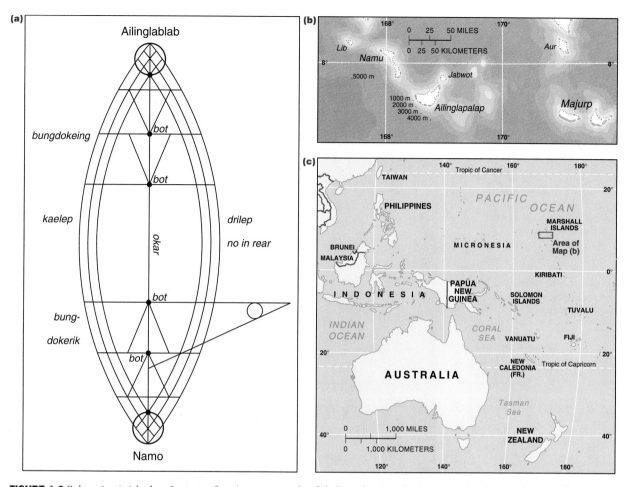

FIGURE 1-3 Polynesian "stick chart," a type of ancient map, made of shells and strips of palm trees. Islands were shown with shells, and patterns of swelling of waves with palm strips. Curved palms represented different wave swells than straight strips. This ancient example depicted the sea route between Ailinglapalap and Namu, two islands in the present-day Marshall Islands, in the South Pacific.

ic writing, from the fifth century B.C., describes the economic resources of the country's different provinces. Phei Hsiu (or Fei Xiu), the "father of Chinese cartography," produced an elaborate map of the country in A.D. 267.

Geography in the Middle Ages and the Age of Exploration. After Ptolemy, little progress in geographic thought was made in the ancient world. After the collapse of the Roman Empire in the fifth century A.D., the word *geography* disappeared from European vocabulary. Beginning in the seventh century, Muslim armies controlled much of northern Africa and southern Europe and eventually reached as far

east as present-day Indonesia in Southeast Asia. Muslim writers such as Edrisi (1099?–1154), ibn-Batuta (1304?–1378?), and ibn-Khaldun (1332–1406) gathered accurate data on the location of coastlines, rivers, and mountain ranges in the conquered areas. During the Middle Ages (roughly A.D. 1100–1500), geographic inquiry continued outside of Europe.

Europeans did continue to explore portions of Earth's surface previously unfamiliar to them. Vikings sailed westward from Scandinavia to Iceland in 860. Erik the Red, banished from Iceland, sailed to Greenland in 981, returned to Iceland to collect colonists, and established a permanent settlement on Greenland in 984. Bjarni Herjolfsson left Iceland in 985 to

(Top) A world map drawn in 1607 by Pieter van den Keere. The relative accuracy of the east coasts of North and South America compared with the west coasts, or the relative accuracy of the coastlines of Africa as compared with the South Pacific, indicates the knowledge of the time, based on the extent of exploration (The Granger Collection).

(Bottom) Compare the accuracy of coastlines on the old map with the recent image of the world based on satellite photographs. The composite picture was assembled by the Geosphere Project of Santa Monica, California. Thousands of images were recorded over a ten-month period by satellites of the National Oceanographic and Atmospheric Administration. The images were then electronically assembled, much like a jigsaw puzzle (Tom Van Sant/The Stock Market).

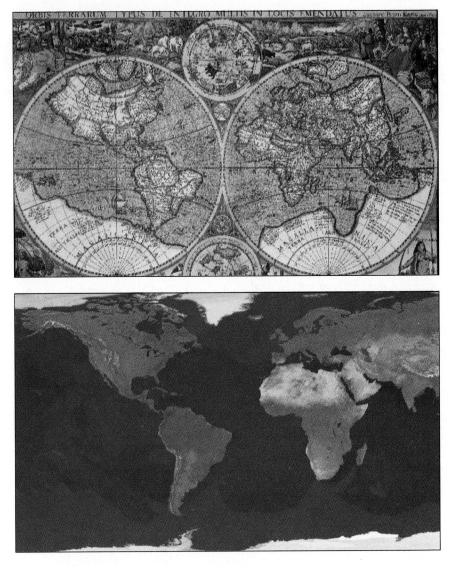

join Erik's colony, but he sailed too far south and reached Newfoundland instead, probably the first European to reach the Western Hemisphere. Herjolfsson did not land in Newfoundland, preferring to find his way eventually to Greenland. In 995, Leif Eriksson, son of Erik the Red, bought Herjolfsson's ship and sailed to Newfoundland, where he landed and set up a camp.

The 1492 voyage of Christopher Columbus led him westward across the Atlantic to discover a sea passage between Europe and Asia that would eliminate the long, difficult trip around the southern tip of Africa. Columbus made four voyages across the Atlantic and died in 1506 believing that he had reached Asia. But other explorers soon realized Columbus's error, and within a year of his death, the first European map was published showing the existence of a land mass in the Western Hemisphere.

The first European explorer to see the Pacific was Vasco Núñez de Balboa, who viewed the great ocean from a mountain in Panama in 1513. The first ship to sail around the world was the *Victoria,* captained for most of its voyage by Ferdinand Magellan. The ship left Spain in 1519, passed from the Atlantic to the Pacific through what is now known as the Estrecho de Magallanes (Strait of Magellan) in southern Chile, and reached the Philippines in 1521. Magellan was killed in battle with inhabitants of the Philippines, but another member of the crew, Juan Sebastián del Cano, sailed across the Indian Ocean and around the southern tip of Africa, to complete the round-the-world voyage back to Spain in 1522.

Geographic thought enjoyed a resurgence in Europe in the seventeenth century, inspired by exploits of European explorers to establish trading routes and gain control of resources elsewhere in the world. *Geographia Generalis,* written by the German Bernhardus Varenius (1622–1650), stood for more than a century as the standard treatise on systematic geography. Varenius also wrote a description of Japan, but he died before he could complete a more comprehensive work on regional geography.

How Geography Grew as a Science

German philosopher Immanuel Kant (1724–1804) placed geography within an overall framework of scientific knowledge. He argued that all knowledge can be classified logically or physically. For example, a *logical classification* organizes plants and animals into a systematic framework of species, based on their characteristics, regardless of when or where they exist. A *physical classification* identifies plants and animals that occur together in particular times and places. Descriptions according to *time* constitute *history,* and descriptions according to *place* constitute *geography.* History studies phenomena that follow one another chronologically, whereas geography studies phenomena that are located beside one another.

As modern geography developed, two major approaches emerged. One group of geographers believed that our physical environment causes human behavior. Another group believed that everything in the landscape is interrelated, but physical factors do not necessarily cause human actions. Let us look at each school of thought.

Does the Physical Environment Cause Human Actions? Modern geography began with two nineteenth-century German geographers, Alexander von Humboldt (1769-1859) and Carl Ritter (1779-1859). Prior to their work, geographers described the physical and social characteristics of places in great detail but did not explain their observations systematically. Humboldt and Ritter argued that geography should move beyond describing Earth's surface to explaining *why* certain phenomena were present or absent. This is the origin of our "where," "why," and "significance" approach.

Humboldt and Ritter urged human geographers to adopt the methods of scientific inquiry used by natural scientists. They argued that the scientific study of social and natural processes is fundamentally the same. Natural scientists have made more progress in formulating general laws than have social scientists, so an important goal of human geographers is to discover general laws.

According to Humboldt and Ritter, human geographers should apply laws from the natural sciences to understanding relationships between the physical environment and human actions. This geographic approach to the "why" question is sometimes known as "cultural ecology" and in the past was insensitively called the "man-land" tradition. Humboldt and Ritter concentrated on how the physical environment *caused* social development, an approach called **environmental determinism.**

Other influential geographers adopted environmental determinism in the late nineteenth and early twentieth centuries. Friedrich Ratzel (1844–1904) and his American student, Ellen Churchill Semple (1863–1932), claimed that geography was the study of the influences of the natural environment on people. Another early American geographer, Ellsworth Huntington (1876–1947), argued that climate was a major determinant of civilization. For instance, according to Huntington, the temperate climate of maritime northwestern Europe produced greater human efficiency as measured by better health conditions, lower death rates, and higher standards of living.

Geographers no longer regard environmental determinism as a viable way to explain the relationship between human activities and the physical environment. Instead, the concept of *possibilism* (discussed later in the chapter) now is widely accepted. This whole school of geographic thought is identified today as the *human-environment approach.*

In a Region, Everything Is Related. A second school of geographic thought, regional studies, developed in France during the nineteenth century. The regional studies approach—sometimes called the cultural landscape approach—was initiated by Paul Vidal de la Blache (1845-1918) and Jean Brunhes (1869-1930). It was later adopted by several American geographers, including Carl Sauer (1889-1975) and Robert Platt (1880-1950).

These geographers rejected the idea that physical factors simply determine human actions. Instead, they argued that each place has its own distinctive landscape that results from a unique combination of social relationships and physical processes. Therefore, geographers should start by closely observing the physical and social characteristics of a place.

They called this the regional studies approach, stating that the work of human geography is to discern the relationships among social and physical phenomena in a particular study area. Everything in the landscape is interrelated, so physical factors do not simply cause human actions, as environmental determinists had argued.

Today, contemporary geographers reject the extreme position of the environmental determinists that the physical environment causes human actions. They also have considerably modified the regional studies approach. But, these two traditions of geographic thought—human-environment relationships and regional studies—remain fundamental to the scientific study of geography.

Location: Where Something Is

The most fundamental concept in geography is **location,** which is *the position that something occupies on Earth's surface.* Geographers identify the location of something in four ways—by place-name, site, situation, and mathematical location—to answer the "where" question.

The dialogue about Miami that opened this chapter illustrates all four methods. The student's first response to the "where" question was the *place-name* "Miami." When this response failed to accurately indicate the location of Miami, the student then referred to its *site* characteristics, such as vegetation, topography, and climate. The next response drew on Miami's *situation,* in the city of Oxford and the state of Ohio and near the city of Cincinnati and the state of Indiana. Finally, the student gave two examples of Miami's *mathematical location.*

Place-names

Because all inhabited places on Earth's surface have been named, the simplest way to describe a particular location is by referring to its name. Geographers call the name given to a portion of Earth's surface its **toponym** (literally, place-name).

The name of a place may give us a clue about its founders, physical setting, social customs, or political changes. Some communities take the name of an otherwise obscure founder or early leader, such as the West Virginia communities of Jenkinjones (named for a mine operator) and Gassaway (named for Senator Henry Gassaway Davis). Others adopt the name of a famous person who had no connection with the community. George Washington's name has been selected for one state, counties in thirty other states, and dozens of cities, including the national capital. Most states also contain places named after James Madison and Thomas Jefferson.

Places may be named after important historical events. One of the most straightforward is found in England. The key victory in the Norman (French) conquest of England in 1066 was the Battle of Hastings. The actual battle site, 10 kilometers (6 miles) from the town of Hastings, is now simply known as "Battle." After the assassinations of President John F. Kennedy in 1963 and the Rev. Martin Luther King, Jr., in 1968, many communities renamed streets, parks, and other places after them.

Some place-names derive from features of the physical environment. Trees, valleys, bodies of water, and other natural features appear in the place-names of most languages. The capital of the Netherlands, called *'s Gravenhage* in Dutch (in English, The Hague), means "the prince's forest." *Aberystwyth,* in Wales, means "mouth of the River Ystwyth," and 22 kilometers (13 miles) upstream lies the tiny village of *Cwmystwyth,* which means "valley of the Ystwyth." The name of the river, *Ystwyth,* in turn is the Welsh word for "meandering," descriptive of a stream that bends like a snake.

The name of a place can tell us a lot about the social customs of its early inhabitants. Some settlers select place-names associated with religion, such as Saint Louis, while other names derive from ancient history, such as Athens, Attica, and Rome. A place-name may also indicate the origin of its settlers. Place-names commonly have British origins in North America and Australia, Portuguese origins in Brazil, Spanish origins elsewhere in Latin America, and Dutch origins in South Africa.

Repeated use of the same name can cause confusion, as in the introductory case study. Dozens of streets in London, England, are called High Street, a relic of medieval times, when each neighborhood was an independent town. The most important shopping street in each town was known as the High Street.

Confusion and Name Changes. Confusion may also arise if local residents commonly use names other than the official ones. New York City has an abundance of unofficial names for its streets and structures. The Avenue of the Americas is almost universally known by its former name, Sixth Avenue, and the Queensboro Bridge is generally called the 59th Street Bridge. A place having two or more local names presents a quandary to cartographers who need to give the place a label.

The Board of Geographical Names, operated by the U.S. Geological Survey, was established in the late nineteenth century to be the final arbiter of names on U.S. maps. In recent years, the board has been especially concerned with removing offensive place names, such as racial or ethnic slurs.

Places can change names. The city of Cincinnati was originally named Losantiville. The name was derived as follows: *L* is for Licking River; *os* is Latin for mouth; *anti* is Latin for opposite; *ville* is Latin for town—hence, "town opposite the mouth of the Licking River." The name was changed to Cincinnati in honor of a society of Revolutionary War heroes named after Cincinnatus, an ancient Roman general.

Names can also change as a result of political upheavals. For example, after World War II, Poland gained control over territory that was formerly part of Germany and changed many of the place-names from German to Polish. Among the larger cities, Danzig became Gdańsk, Breslau became Wrocław, and Stettin became Szczecin.

Names associated with communism throughout Eastern Europe have been changed, in many cases reverting to those used before the Communists gained power in 1917. For example, in Olomouc, a Czech city of 100,000, Lenin Street has been changed to Liberty Street, Red Army Square to Lower Square, and Liberation Street to Masaryk Street (for the first president of democratic Czechoslovakia between 1919 and 1935). Gottwaldov, a Czech city named for a communist president of Czechoslovakia, reverted to its former name Zlín, and Leningrad, the second largest city in the former Soviet Union, reverted to St. Petersburg, Russia.

Someone unfamiliar with foreign languages might have difficulty in identifying the English name for these European countries: Civitas Helvetia, Österreich, Magyarország, and Suomi. These are the official names for Switzerland, Austria, Hungary, and Finland, respectively.

Money and Politics. Pioneers lured to the American West by the prospect of finding gold or silver placed many picturesque names on the landscape. Place-names in Nevada selected by successful miners include Eureka, Lucky Boy Pass, Gold Point, and Silver Peak. Unsuccessful Nevada pioneers sadly or

bitterly named other places Battle, Disaster Peak, and Massacre Lake. In 1959 the Elko, Nevada, county commissioners gave the name Jackpot to a town near the Idaho state border, in recognition of the importance of legalized gambling to the local economy.

What may be the longest community name in the world has an economic origin—the Welsh town of *Llanfairpwllgwyngyllgogerychwyrndrobwllllantysiliogogogoch*. The fifty-eight-letter name means "the Church of St. Mary's in the grove of the white hazelnut tree near the rapid whirlpool and the Church of St. Tisilio near the red cave." The town's name originally encompassed only the first twenty letters (*Llanfairpwllgwyngyll*), but when the railway was built in the nineteenth century, the townspeople lengthened it. They decided that signs with the longer name in the railway station would attract attention and bring more business and visitors to the town.

Sometimes a place-name is so symbolic that its use can cause great political difficulty—and lost revenue. When Yugoslavia's southernmost republic declared independence in 1991, its leaders wished to call the new country *Macedonia,* the same name it had as a local government within Yugoslavia. But Greece felt threatened by this use of the name, because Macedonia is also the name of Greece's northernmost region. As the home of Aristotle and Alexander the Great, ancient Greek Macedonia was an important cultural hearth for Greece and Western civilization. Further, older Greeks recalled that the communists had promised that, if their side won the civil war in Greece in 1948–49, they would transfer Greek Macedonia to a new federation comprising the neighboring countries of Yugoslavia and Bulgaria.

Greece suggested that the new country be called the Slavic Republic of Macedonia, but this name was rejected because only 64 percent of the inhabitants of the new country were Slavs. Using the word *Slavic* would offend Albanians and Turks, who accounted for 21 percent and 5 percent of the new country's population, respectively. The consequence was more than just a quibble over naming real estate: Lack of agreement on a name for the new country delayed diplomatic recognition by other countries and financial support to help it achieve economic development.

Site

The second way to indicate location is by **site,** which is the physical character of a place. Important site characteristics include climate, water sources, topography, soil, vegetation, latitude, and elevation. The combination of physical characteristics gives each location a unique character.

Site factors always have been essential in selecting locations for settlements, although people have disagreed on the attributes of a good site, depending on cultural values. Some have preferred a hilltop site for easy defense from attack. Other people located settlements near convenient river-crossing points to facilitate communication with people in other places.

An island combines the attributes of both hilltop and riverside locations, because the site provides good defense and transportation links. The site of the country of Singapore, for example, is a small, swampy island approximately 1 kilometer (.63 miles) off the southern tip of the Malay Peninsula at the eastern end of the Strait of Malacca. The city of Singapore covers nearly 20 percent of the island.

In general, the characteristics of a site do not change over time, but human preferences do. The warmer, humid climate in the southeastern United States traditionally retarded population growth, but in recent years it has become an attraction. People increasingly prefer the climate in the Southeast because they can participate in outdoor recreational activities throughout the year and do not have to shovel snow in winter. At the same time, technological change, especially the invention of air conditioning, has increased the Southeast's attractiveness by enabling people to escape the high heat and humidity.

Human actions can modify the characteristics of a site. The southern portion of New York City's Manhattan Island is twice as large today as it was in 1626, when Peter Minuit bought the island from its native inhabitants for the equivalent of $23.75 worth of Dutch gold and silver coins. The additional land area was created by filling in portions of the East River and Hudson River. In the eighteenth century, landfills were created by sinking old ships and dumping refuse on top of them.

Because of poor health conditions, the city decided in 1797 to cover all the landfills with soil and gravel and to lay out a new street, called South Street, to halt further dumping in the river. Today, South Street is two blocks from the river. More recently, New York City permitted construction of Battery Park City, a 57-hectare (142-acre) site designed to house more than 20,000 residents and 30,000 office workers (Figure 1-4). The central areas of Boston and Tokyo have also been expanded through centuries of landfilling in nearby bays, substantially changing these sites.

Situation

Situation is the location of a place relative to other places. Situation is a valuable way to indicate location, for two reasons—finding an unfamiliar place and understanding its importance.

First, situation helps us find an unfamiliar place by comparing its location with that of a familiar one. We give directions by referring to the situation of a place: "It's down past the court house, on Locust Street, after the third traffic light, beside the yellow brick bank." We identify important buildings, streets, and other landmarks to direct people to the desired location.

For example, even long-time residents of Paris might have difficulty finding the Marmottan Museum by its address, 2 rue Louis-Boilly, because the street is only one block long. The museum, which contains one of the world's largest collections of paintings by Claude Monet, can be found by referring to its situation: one block east of the city's largest park, the Bois de Boulogne, near the Muette stop on the métro (subway).

Second, situation helps us understand the importance of a location. Many locations are important because they are accessible to other places. For example, because of its location, Singapore has become a center for the trading and distribution of goods for much of Southeast Asia. Singapore is situated near the Strait of Malacca, which is the major passageway for ships traveling between the South China Sea and the Indian Ocean (Figure 1-5).

Mathematical Location

Sometimes it is necessary to locate something more precisely. In using an atlas, you probably have used the familiar "A-1" system of finding a place on a map. Typically, a row of numbers runs across the top of the map, and a column of letters runs down the side. When you look up Cactus, Texas, in the atlas, its map coordinates are given as C-7. You simply find C in the column and look across under the 7, and there is Cactus. But, this general location is accurate only within several kilometers.

Latitude and Longitude. The location of Cactus, or any other place on Earth's surface, can be described precisely by drawing an imaginary grid on the globe and then describing the place's location

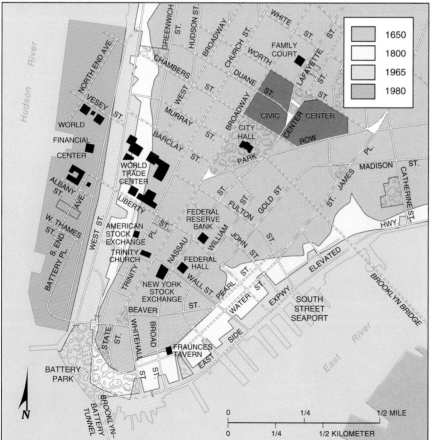

FIGURE 1-4 Site of New York City. Much of the southern part of New York City's Manhattan Island was built on landfill. Several times in the past 200 years, the waterfront has been extended into the Hudson River and East River to provide more land for offices, homes, parks, warehouses, and docks. Battery Park City and the 110-story World Trade Center towers (at left in photo) were built on landfill in the Hudson River. The office buildings at right, were built on landfill in the East River. (Manfred Gottschalk/West Light)

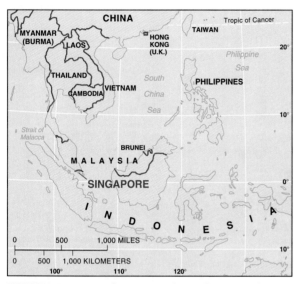

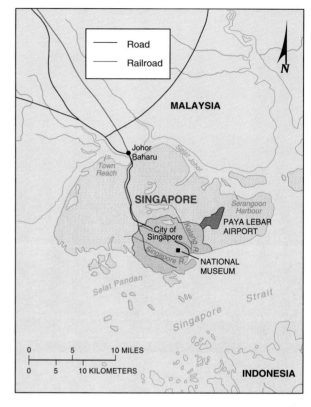

FIGURE 1-5 Situation of Singapore. The small country of Singapore, less than one-fifth the size of Rhode Island, has an important situation for international trade. The country is situated at the confluence of several straits that serve as major passageways for shipping between the South China Sea and the Indian Ocean. Downtown Singapore is situated near where the Singapore River flows into the Singapore Strait. In the foreground, the dome at right is the National Museum; the spire at center is St. Andrew's Cathedral.

on the grid, using a set of numbers called latitude and longitude. The universally accepted numbering system of latitude and longitude consists of imaginary arcs drawn on the globe.

A **meridian** is an arc drawn between the North and South poles. All meridians have the same length and the same beginning and end points. The location of each meridian is identified on Earth's surface according to a numbering system known as **longitude.** One meridian, which passes through the Royal Observatory at Greenwich, England, has been designated by international agreement as the "starting point" for numbering the meridians. It is labeled as *0 degrees longitude* and is also called the **prime meridian** (Figure 1-6).

The meridian on the opposite side of the globe from the prime meridian is 180° longitude. All other meridians have numbers between 0° and 180° and are designated "east" or "west" to show that they are either east or west of the prime meridian. For example, New York City is located at 74° west longitude, and Lahore, Pakistan, is 74° east longitude. San Diego is located at 117° west longitude, Tianjin, China, at 117° east longitude.

The second set of imaginary arcs drawn on Earth's surface are **parallels.** These are circles drawn around the globe parallel to the equator at right angles to the meridians. The numbering system used to indicate the location of parallels is called **latitude.** The equator is 0° latitude, the North Pole 90° north, and the South Pole 90° south. New York City is located at 41° north latitude, whereas Wellington, New Zealand, is at 41° south. San Diego is located at 33° north latitude; Santiago, Chile, at 33° south. Latitude and longitude are used together to identify locations. For example, Cactus, Texas, is at the intersection of 36° north latitude and 102° west longitude.

We can determine the mathematical location of a place even more precisely, if necessary. Each degree is divided into 60 minutes ('), and each minute in turn is divided into 60 seconds ("). For example, the official mathematical location of Paris, France, is 48°51' north latitude and 2°20' east longitude. The Observatory building in Paris is located at 48°50'11" north latitude and 2°20'14" east longitude. The latitude-longitude system is especially useful for navigation on the sea. (See the Geography in Action box: Time Zones and the International Dateline, page 23.)

U.S. Land Ordinance of 1785. In addition to the global system of latitude and longitude, other math-

ematical indicators of locations are used in different parts of the world. In the United States, the **Land Ordinance of 1785** divided much of the country into a system of townships and ranges to facilitate the sale of land to settlers in the West. The initial surveying was performed by Thomas Hutchins, who was appointed geographer to the United States in 1781. After Hutchins died in 1789, responsibility for surveying was transferred to the Surveyor General.

In this system, a **township** is a square 6 miles on each side. Some of the north-south lines separating townships are called **principal meridians,** and some east-west lines are designated **base lines** (Figure 1-7). Each township has a number corresponding to its distance north or south of a particular base line. Townships in the first row north of a base line are called T1N (Township 1 North), the second row to the north is T2N, the first row to the south is T1S, and so on. Each township has a second number, known as the *range,* corresponding to its location east or west of a principal meridian. Townships in the first column east of a principal meridian are designated R1E (Range 1 East). The Tallahatchie River, for example, is in township T23N R1E, north of a base line that runs east-west across Mississippi and east of a principal meridian along 90° west longitude.

FIGURE 1-6 Geographic grid. Meridians are arcs that connect the North and South poles. The meridian through Greenwich, England, is the prime meridian, or 0° longitude. Parallels are circles drawn around the globe parallel to the equator. The equator is 0° latitude, and the North Pole is 90° north latitude.

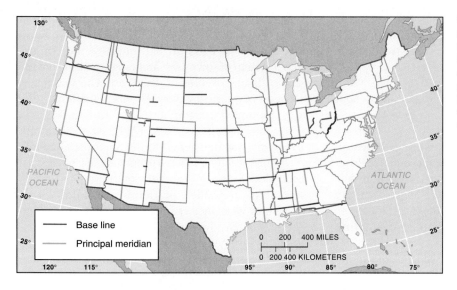

FIGURE 1-7 Principal meridians and base lines. To facilitate the numbering of townships, the U.S. Land Ordinance of 1785 designated several north-south lines as principal meridians and several east-west lines as base lines. As territory farther west was settled, additional lines were delineated.

A township is divided into thirty-six **sections,** each of which is 1 mile by 1 mile (Figure 1-8). Sections are numbered in a consistent order, from 1 in the northeast to 36 in the southeast. Each section is divided into four quarter-sections, designated as the northeast, northwest, southeast, and southwest quarters of a particular section. A quarter-section, which is 0.5 mile by 0.5 mile, or 160 acres, was the amount of land many western pioneers bought as a homestead. The Tallahatchie River is located in the southeast and southwest quarter-sections of Section 32.

The township and range system is still important in understanding the location of objects across much of the United States. It explains the location of highways across the Midwest, farm fields in Iowa, and major streets in Chicago.

K E Y   I S S U E   2

How Do Geographers Answer the "Why" Question?

- Regional Analysis
- Spatial Analysis

You have seen how geographers answer the "where" question with maps and location—placenames, site, situation, and mathematical coordinates. Geographers also ask *why* things are located in particular places, rather than being distributed randomly. Two geographic approaches help answer this "why" question: area analysis and spatial analysis.

Geographers approach the "why" question through **spatial association,** the concept that the distribution of one phenomenon across the landscape is scientifically related to the location of other phenomena. For example, the distribution of livestock in Africa's Sahel results from the distribution of watering holes. All geographers collect and analyze geographic information, but they focus on different topics and employ different analytic strategies. Contemporary geographers employ two analytic strategies:

Regional analysis, or area analysis, integrates the geographic features of an area or place.

Spatial analysis, or locational analysis, emphasizes interactions among places.

Regional Analysis

Neighboring places can be combined into a **region,** which is an area of Earth defined by one or more distinctive features or trends, such as climate, agriculture, industry, religion, or language. Geography's **regional analysis tradition** is a way of organizing the study of Earth's peoples and environments through identification of regions and description of similarities and differences among them. Certain human activities and environments give regions their unified character and distinguish them from other areas of Earth's surface.

(a)

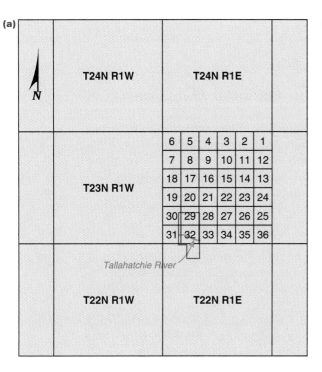

(b)

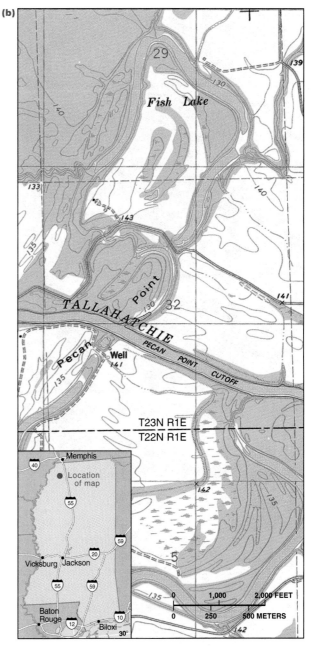

FIGURE 1-8 (Left) Townships. Townships are typically 6 miles by 6 miles, although physical features, such as rivers and mountains, result in some irregularly shaped ones. The Tallahatchie River, for example, is located in the twenty-third township north of a base line that runs east-west across Mississippi, and in the first range east of the principal meridian, at 90° west longitude. Townships are divided into thirty-six sections, each 1 square mile. Sections are divided into four quarter-sections. The Tallahatchie River is located in the southeast and southwest quarter-sections of Section 32, T23N R1E. (Right) Topographic map. This map, published by the U.S. Geological Survey, has a scale of 1:24,000. Expressed as a written statement, 1 inch on the map represents 24,000 inches on the ground (2,000 feet). The map displays portions of three townships, shown on the diagram at left. The brown lines on the map are contour lines, which show the elevation of any location.

In the past, geographers who used the old regional studies approach identified an area of Earth's surface and described in careful detail as many of its characteristics as they could uncover. When Julius Caesar wrote that "All Gaul is divided into three parts," he gave an example of the traditional regional studies approach to geographic explanation. Some introductory geography courses still emphasize the old regional studies approach by organizing much of the syllabus around regions of the world, such as Latin America, East Asia, and Sub-Saharan Africa. This approach selects a portion of Earth and studies the environment, people, and activities within the region. Although this book is organized by key issues rather than regions, you should be aware of the importance of location and characteristics of places in the world.

Today, regional analysis may start by identifying an important characteristic, such as population growth, level of wealth, or energy consumption. Then, geographers search for reasons to explain why that char-

Time Zones and the International Dateline

Longitude plays an important role in calculating time. Time obviously is very important to us, for we all live by schedules. We could divide the daily cycle into any number of units, but our practice of dividing it into 24 hours comes from some simple arithmetic. Earth as a sphere is divided into 360 degrees of longitude (the degrees from 0 to 180 west longitude, plus the degrees from 0 to 180 east longitude). As Earth rotates daily, these 360 imaginary lines of longitude pass beneath the cascading sunshine. If we let every fifteenth degree of longitude represent an hour, and divide the 360 by 15, we get 24 hours.

By international agreement, the time at the prime meridian or 0° longitude is designated *Greenwich Mean Time* (GMT). It is the master reference time for all points on Earth. Earth rotates eastward, so any place to the east of you always passes "under" the sun earlier. Thus, as you travel eastward from the prime meridian, you are "catching up" with the sun, so you must turn your clock ahead from GMT, by 1 hour for each 15 degrees. If you travel westward from the prime meridian, you are "falling behind" the sun, so you turn your clock back from GMT, by 1 hour for each 15 degrees.

The eastern United States, which is near 75° west longitude, is therefore 5 hours earlier than Greenwich Mean Time (the 75° difference between the prime meridian and 75° west longitude, divided by 15 per hour, equals 5 hours). Thus, when the time is 11 A.M. GMT, the time in the eastern United States is 5 hours earlier, or 6 A.M. (Figure 1).

For convenience, each 15°-band of longitude is assigned to a standard time zone. The forty-eight contiguous U.S. states and Canada share four standard time zones, known as Eastern, Central, Mountain, and Pacific.

- The Eastern Standard Time Zone is near 75° west longitude, which passes close to Philadelphia, and is 5 hours earlier than GMT.
- The Central Standard Time Zone is near 90° west longitude, which passes through Memphis, Tennessee, and is 6 hours earlier than GMT.
- The Mountain Standard Time Zone is near 105° west longitude, which passes through Denver, Colorado, and is 7 hours earlier than GMT.
- The Pacific Standard Time Zone is near 120° west longitude, which passes through Lake Tahoe in California, and is 8 hours earlier than GMT.

Most of Alaska is in the Alaska Time Zone, which is 9 hours earlier than GMT; Hawaii is in the Hawaii Time Zone, which is 10 hours earlier than GMT. Canada has an Atlantic Time Zone, which is 4 hours earlier than GMT, and a Newfoundland Time Zone, which is 3 1/2 hours earlier than GMT.

The concept of standard time zones is rather recent. They were established in the United States in 1883 and in the rest of the world after a conference in Washington, D.C. in 1884. Before standard time zones were created, each locality set its own time, usually that kept by a local jeweler. Railroads were the main cross-country transportation of the time, and each rail company kept its own time, normally that of the largest city it served. Train timetables listed two sets of arrival and departure times, one for local time and one for railroad company time. Railroad stations had one clock for local time and a separate clock for each of the railroad companies using the station.

At noon on November 18, 1883, time stood still in the United States so that each locality could adjust to the new standard time zones. In New York City, for example, time stopped for 3 minutes and 58 seconds to adjust to the new Eastern Standard Time. For many years, however, Chicago resisted the change and continued to be 17 minutes ahead of Central Standard Time.

Suppose today is Sunday. Is it Sunday all over the world? No. The role of the International Date Line is the trickiest part of understanding time zones. The *International Date Line* generally corresponds to 180° longitude. (It deviates in several places to avoid dividing land areas.) When you cross the International Date Line heading eastward (toward America), the clock moves back 24 hours, or one entire day. When you go westward (toward Asia), the calendar moves ahead one day.

To see the need for the International Date Line, try counting the hours around the world from the time zone in which you live. As you go from west to east, you add 1 hour for each time zone. When you return to your starting point, you will reach the absurd conclusion that it is 24 hours later in your locality than it really is.

Therefore, when the time in New York City is 2 P.M. Sunday (as shown in the figure), it is 7 P.M. Sunday in London, 8 P.M. Sunday in Rome, 9 P.M. Sunday in Jerusalem, 10 P.M. Sunday in Moscow, 3 A.M. Monday in Singapore, and 5 A.M. Monday in Sydney, Australia. Continuing farther east, it is 7 A.M. *Monday* in Wellington, New Zealand—but when you get to Honolulu, it is 9 A.M. *Sunday,* because the International Date Line lies between New Zealand and Hawaii.

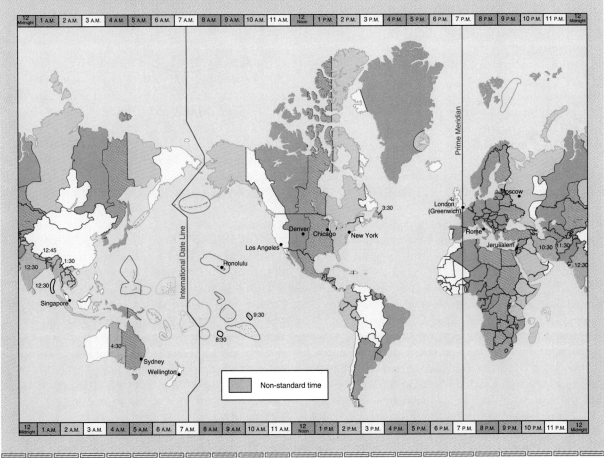

acteristic is greater or more intense in one area than elsewhere. Geographers recognize that the distribution of a characteristic results from a process of movement of people and activities across Earth's surface.

In building a model of explanation, geographers identify regions that are distinguished by one or more unique characteristics and document characteristics that are integrated and interrelated within and among regions.

Region

Geographers employ the concept of region to summarize what is distinctive about an area of Earth's surface. Within a region, the people, activities, and environment will display similarities and regularities. A region's cultural, economic, and physical characteristics will differ in some way from those of other regions. Geographers identify three types of regions: formal, functional, and vernacular. We will now see how these three types of regions help explain why characteristics are distributed as they are.

Formal Region. A **formal region** is an area in which the selected feature or trend is present throughout. The people, activities, and environment in the region share one or more distinctive characteristics. (It is also called a uniform region or homogeneous region.)

Geographers typically employ formal regions to explain broad patterns. A formal region may display a distinctive cultural characteristic, such as a language, religion, or social custom, or an economic characteristic, such as level of development, predominant type of agriculture practiced, or average income. The characteristic selected to distinguish a formal region often illustrates a general concept, rather than representing a precise mathematical distribution (although it may be quantifiable as well).

Some formal regions are easy to identify, such as countries or local government units within them. Montana is an example of a formal region, characterized by a government that passes laws, collects taxes, and issues license plates with equal intensity throughout the state. We can easily identify the formal region of Montana, because it has clearly drawn and legally recognized boundaries, and everyone living within them is, legally, a Montanan.

In other kinds of formal regions, not everyone necessarily possesses the identifying characteristic. Not every farmer living in the U.S. or Canadian wheat belt grows wheat, nor does every farmer living in the U.S. ranching area raise cattle. Nonetheless, we can distinguish the wheat belt as a region in which the predominant agricultural activity is growing wheat. Similarly, we can distinguish formal regions within the United States characterized by a predominant voting for Republican candidates. Republicans may not get 100 percent of the votes in these regions, nor in fact do they always win. In a presidential election, however, the candidate with the largest number of votes receives all of the electoral votes of a state, regardless of the margin of victory. Consequently, a state that usually has Republican electors can be considered a Republican state.

The previous examples reveal a cautionary step that must be taken in identifying formal regions: The *diversity* of cultural, economic, and environmental factors, must be recognized even while making a generalization. Problems may arise because a minority of people in a region speak a language, practice a religion, or possess resources different from those of the majority. People in a region may play distinctive roles in the economy and hold different positions in society on the basis of their gender or ethnicity.

Functional Region. A **functional region** is an area in which an activity has a focal point. The characteristic chosen to define a functional region dominates at a central focus, or node, and diffuses outward with diminishing importance. Geographers often use functional regions (also known as nodal regions) to display information about economic characteristics. The region's node may be a shop or service, and the boundaries of the region mark the limits of the trading area of the activity. People and activities may be attracted to the node, and information may flow from the node to the surrounding area.

An example of a functional region is the circulation area of a newspaper. A newspaper dominates circulation figures in the city in which it is published. Farther away from the city, fewer people read that newspaper, whereas more people read a newspaper published in a neighboring city. At some point between the two cities, the circulation of the newspaper from the second city equals the circulation of the newspaper from the first. That point is the boundary between the nodal regions of the two newspapers.

A more contemporary example is television broadcasting. The United States is divided into several hundred functional regions based on television networks. Every television market has an *area of dominant influence (ADI),* the region in which the preponderance of viewers are tuned to that market's stations. The United States is divided into several hundred functional regions, according to the distribution of the ADIs. The culture disseminated by television stations diffuses to the surrounding region.

An ADI is a good example of a functional region, because the characteristic—people who are viewing a particular station—is dominant at the center and declines toward the periphery. For example, everyone in Des Moines, Iowa, who wishes to watch a program on NBC tunes to Channel 13. In Omaha, Nebraska, 225 kilometers (140 miles) to the west, everyone watching NBC is tuned to Channel 6. With increasing distance eastward from Omaha, Channel 6's signal gets weaker and Channel 13's gets stronger. The percentage of people watching NBC declines for Channel 6 and increases for Channel 13 (Figure 1-9).

The boundary between the Omaha and Des Moines ADIs is the point where an equal number of people

watch Channel 13 and Channel 6, near the Cass-Adair county line. Other functional regions in Iowa centered around NBC affiliates include Sioux City's Channel 4 to the northwest, Davenport's Channel 6 to the east, Waterloo's Channel 7 to the northeast, and Rochester, Minnesota's, Channel 10 to the north.

Vernacular Region. A **vernacular region,** or perceptual region, is one that people believe to exist as part of their cultural identity. Such regions emerge from concepts that people use informally in daily life, rather than from scientific models developed through geographic thought. (In language, the term *vernacular* means everyday language that is used by ordinary people.)

An example of vernacular regions is Americans' frequent use of the terms *sunbelt* and *frostbelt* or *rustbelt* to distinguish two regions in the country. Sunbelt refers to the southern and western parts of the United States. Frostbelt or rustbelt refers to the northern and eastern parts. Several important characteristics distinguish the sunbelt from the frostbelt,

The sunbelt and frostbelt are vernacular regions distinguished by a number of features, such as differences in winter climate. In a frostbelt city like Philadelphia, average winter temperatures are generally 40°F (22°C) lower than in sunbelt communities of South Florida. **(Robert Landau/West Light)** (Joseph Nettis/Photo Researchers, Inc.)

including more temperate climate and higher levels of population and economic growth in the sunbelt.

Analysts have difficulty fixing the precise boundary between the two regions. At a conference called "The Sunbelt: A Region and Regionalism in the Making?" participants were given blank outline maps of the United States and asked to delineate the sunbelt. Respondents most frequently cited southern California, from Los Angeles to San Diego, as part of the sunbelt. Other areas of the United States that most participants considered part of the sunbelt included southern Texas, southern Florida, and south-central Arizona. A few considered the sunbelt to reach as far north as Oregon or Virginia (Figure 1-10). Similar studies have been done to identify the Midwest and other vernacular regions.

Vernacular or perceptual regions can play a critical role in organizing daily life. For example, students at one university were shown a map of their campus divided into squares. They were asked to indicate in which squares they felt safe walking alone at 10:30 P.M. When combined, the responses portrayed a campus divided into regions that were widely regarded as safe and regions that were widely regarded as dangerous. Such studies can also determine whether perceptions of safety are uniform among groups of students or vary by age, gender, and ethnicity.

Regional Integration

A region gains uniqueness, not from possessing a single human or environmental characteristic, but a combination of them. Not content merely to identify these characteristics, geographers seek relationships among them. Geographers recognize that, in the real world, characteristics are integrated.

For example, geographers divide the world into formal regions that are more developed economically and those that are less developed. Regions of **more developed countries (MDCs),** such as Europe, North America, and Japan, are located primarily in the northern latitudes. Regions of developing countries, or **less developed countries (LDCs),** are concentrated in the southern latitudes. This north-south regional split underlies many of the world's social and economic problems.

A variety of characteristics—such as per capita income, literacy rates, televisions per capita, and hospital beds per capita—distinguish more developed from less developed regions. Geographers demonstrate that the distribution of one characteristic of development is associated with others.

The geographer's job is to sort out the associations among various social characteristics, each of which is uniquely distributed across Earth's surface. For example, geographers conclude that political un-

FIGURE 1-9 Functional regions of television stations. The map shows the regions of dominance for different television stations within Iowa. These areas are known as areas of dominant influence (ADIs). In several cases, the node of the functional region—the location of the television station—is in an adjacent state. Functional regions frequently overlap state or national boundaries.

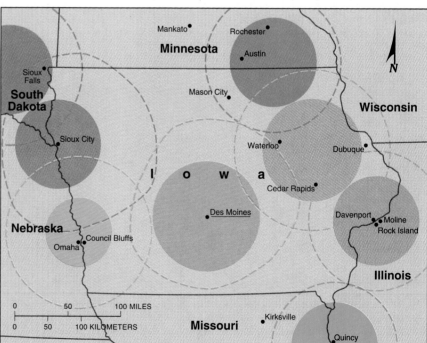

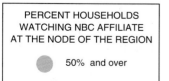

PERCENT HOUSEHOLDS WATCHING NBC AFFILIATE AT THE NODE OF THE REGION

50% and over

25-49%

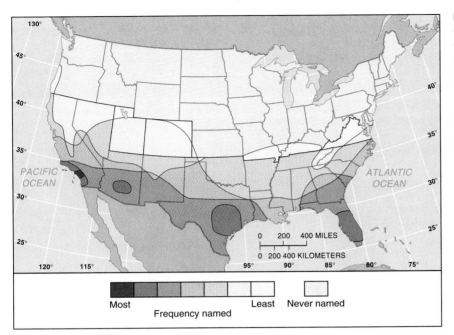

FIGURE 1-10 Defining the sunbelt. Geographers at a recent conference disagreed on the definition of the sunbelt. Respondents most frequently mentioned southwestern California between Los Angeles and San Diego, followed by south Florida and south-central Arizona between Phoenix and Tucson. Some geographers cited areas as far north as Oregon or Virginia.

rest in the Middle East, Eastern Europe, and other areas derives in large measure from the fact that the spatial distributions of important cultural and physical characteristics, such as language, religion, and resources, do not match the political boundaries of individual countries.

In some cases, geographers can build models to prove that the distribution of one characteristic causes the distribution of another. For example, we shall see in Chapter 2 that differences among regions in the rate of population growth are caused primarily by differences in the crude birth rates. But, geographers often hedge their bets: They recognize that one characteristic must be associated across Earth's surface with others, even if the relationship cannot be modeled precisely. Geographers may have difficulty in constructing exact models of cause and effect, because they must integrate many cultural and physical characteristics to explain a region's distinctiveness.

Integrating Cancer Information. Recognizing that the distributions of various cultural and physical characteristics are integrated helps us understand important social problems. For example, the percentage of people who die each year from cancer differs among regions in the United States. The mid-Atlantic region has the highest level, with Maryland ranked first among the fifty states, followed by Delaware. The rate in Washington, D.C., which is adjacent to Maryland, is higher than in any state.

Why does Maryland have the highest cancer rate among the fifty states? Mapping the distribution of cancer among Maryland's major subdivisions (twenty-three counties plus the independent city of Baltimore), as well as the District of Columbia, shows sharp internal variations. The cancer rate in Baltimore City is more than 50 percent higher than in westernmost Garrett County (Figure 1-11).

The map of cancer rates by county in Maryland does not communicate useful information to someone who knows little about the distribution of people, activities, and environments within the state. By integrating other spatial information, we can begin to see factors that may be associated with regional differences in cancer.

We can divide the state into two groups of counties: those that comprise part of the region's large metropolitan area, Washington-Baltimore, and those that do not. (See Chapter 11 for details on how counties are classified as metropolitan or nonmetropolitan.) Thus far, this division does not appear helpful in explaining the distribution of cancer, because we can find high and low rates among both metropolitan and nonmetropolitan counties. Within the metropolitan area, however, a pattern emerges: The highest cancer rates are in the cities of Baltimore and Washington, whereas the suburban counties surrounding the two cities have lower rates.

Once we recognize that the cities have higher cancer rates than the suburbs, we can integrate that in-

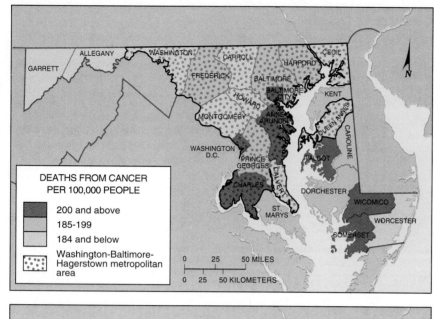

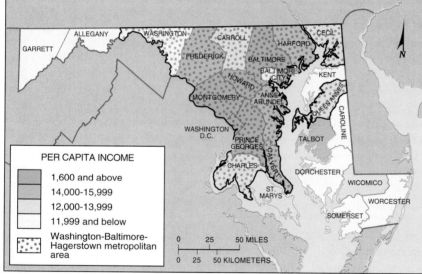

FIGURE 1-11 Integrating information about cancer. Maryland has the highest incidence of cancer in the United States, although the rate varies widely within the state (top). The highest rates are in areas of lowest income, including the large cities and rural Eastern Shore counties (bottom).

formation with a variety of other characteristics. People in Baltimore City and Washington are more likely than suburbanites to have low incomes and low levels of education. As a result of these characteristics, people living in the cities may be less aware of the risks associated with activities such as smoking and consuming alcohol and less able to afford medical care to minimize the risk of dying from cancer.

Among nonmetropolitan counties, Maryland shows a sharp division between the west, where rates are relatively low, and the east, where rates are relatively high. Income and education do not explain the difference, because levels are lower in most of the nonmetropolitan counties than in the metropolitan areas. Instead, we must attempt to integrate other economic and environmental factors into our explanation.

People living in counties on the Chesapeake Bay's Eastern Shore may be especially exposed to cancer-causing chemicals, because higher percentages are engaged in fishing and farming than are people living in the mountainous western counties. The nearby Chesapeake Bay is one of the nation's principal sources of shellfish, and many Eastern Shore residents work in seafood-processing industries. But the Chesapeake Bay also suffers from runoff of chemicals from Eastern Shore farms, which make heavy use of pesticides, as well as discharges of waste from factories, for the most part located in the metropolitan counties on the western side of the bay. Prevailing winds also carry pollutants eastward from industries in the metropolitan areas.

Spatial Analysis

While accepting that each place or region on Earth is unique, geographers recognize that specific human activities and environmental processes rarely are confined to one location. Rather, they are spread spatially. Thus, a second approach to geographic inquiry is spatial analysis (also known as locational analysis). Spatial analysis looks worldwide for patterns in the distribution of human actions and environmental processes.

The distribution of a human activity or an environmental condition changes over time. Consequently, geographers study the *movement*, or diffusion, of people, goods, ideas, energy, and natural materials (such as water) across Earth's surface. Any place is connected to all other places through these processes of human and environmental movement. Examples abound: People in one place originate an idea and then "move" it—communicate it—to people in another place. Humans ship their products from one place to another. People move themselves from place to place for work, pleasure, or survival. The movement of energy influences a region's climate. The movement of water carves distinctive landforms. All are subject to the geographer's spatial analysis.

Distribution

The regular arrangement of a phenomenon across Earth's surface is known as its **spatial distribution.** Geographers seek patterns in the spatial distribution of people and activities, measure them, and place them on a map. Spatial distribution has three important properties: density, concentration, and pattern.

Density. The frequency with which something exists in a measured area is its **density.** The phenomenon being measured could be people, build-

ings, dwelling units, cars, volcanoes, or anything. Areas can be measured in square kilometers or miles, hectares, or acres (Figure 1-12).

The *arithmetic density* is the total number of objects, such as people, in an area. The arithmetic density of the United Kingdom, for example, is 242 persons per square kilometer (627 persons per square mile). This is simply the total population (about 58 million people) divided by the United Kingdom's area (241,595 square kilometers or 93,280 square miles). Arithmetic density is a useful measure of living arrangements in different places.

Remember that a large *population* does not necessarily lead to a high *density*. Arithmetic density involves two measures: the number of people and the area. The most populous country in the world, China, with approximately 1.2 billion inhabitants, by no means has the highest density. The arithmetic density of China is approximately 126 persons per square kilometer (317 persons per square mile), only one-half as high as that of the United Kingdom. Although China has about twenty times as many inhabitants as the United Kingdom, it also has nearly forty times as much land.

High population density is also unrelated to poverty. The Netherlands, one of the world's wealthiest countries, has an arithmetic density of approximately 453 persons per square kilometer (1,173 persons per square mile). One of the poorest countries, Mali, has an arithmetic density of only 7 persons per square kilometer (19 persons per square mile).

Geographers measure density in other ways, depending on the subject being studied. Geographers concerned with the relationship between population growth and food supply often calculate two other densities. *Physiological density* is the number of persons per unit of area suitable for agriculture. *Agricultural density* is the number of farmers per unit area of farmland.

Urban geographers frequently use housing density, which is the number of dwelling units per unit of area.

Concentration. How something is spread over an area is its **concentration.** If the objects in an area are close together, they are considered to be *clustered*. If they are farther apart, they are considered to be *dispersed*. To compare the level of concentration clearly, one must have two areas with the same number of objects and the same size area, or else the areas must be adjusted to correspond.

Density	Concentration	Pattern

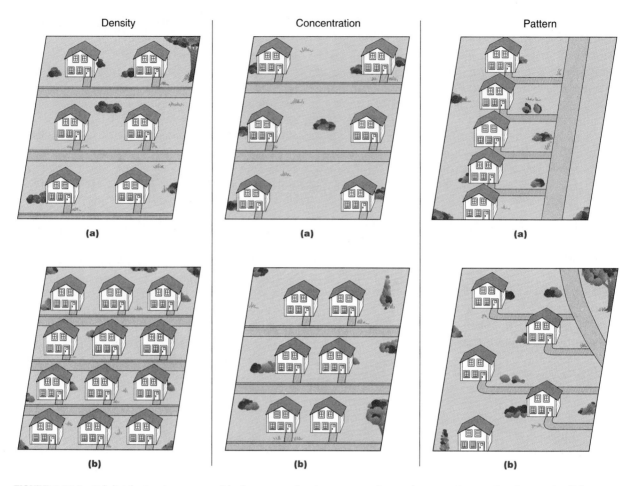

(a)   **(a)**   **(a)**

(b)   **(b)**   **(b)**

FIGURE 1-12 Spatial distribution is represented in three ways: density, concentration, and pattern. Assume that the area in all figures represents 1 acre. The density (left) is six houses per acre in (a) and twelve houses per acre in (b). The houses (center) are dispersed in (a) and clustered in (b). Note that, although the concentration in (a) is different from that in (b), the density is the same in the two figures. Five houses (right) are arranged in a linear pattern in (a) (right) and form a staggered pattern in (b).

Geographers use the concept of concentration in several ways. For example, one of the major changes in the distribution of the U.S. population is greater dispersion. The total number of people living in the United States is growing slowly—less than 1 percent per year—and the land area is essentially unchanged. But the population distribution is changing from *relatively clustered* in the Northeast to more *evenly dispersed* across the country.

Concentration is not the same as density. One area with higher density could have a dispersed population, while another area with the same density could have a clustered population. We can illustrate the difference between density and concentration by the change in the distribution of major league baseball teams in North America (Figure 1-13). In 1900,

the major leagues had sixteen teams, a distribution that remained unchanged for more than half a century. Beginning in 1953, the following six of the sixteen teams moved to other cities:

Braves: Boston to Milwaukee in 1953, then to Atlanta in 1966

Browns: St. Louis to Baltimore (Orioles) in 1954

Athletics: Philadelphia to Kansas City in 1955, then to Oakland in 1968

Dodgers: Brooklyn to Los Angeles in 1957

Giants: New York to San Francisco in 1957

Senators: Washington to Minneapolis (Minnesota Twins) in 1960

These moves resulted in a more dispersed distribution. Before the moves, seven teams were clustered in the three northeastern cities of Philadelphia, New York, and Boston, compared with only three teams after the moves. In 1953, no team was located south or west of St. Louis, but after the moves, teams were located on the West Coast and in the Southeast for the first time.

In addition to the shifts by established teams, the major leagues expanded between 1960 and 1993 from sixteen to twenty-eight teams. The new teams selected the following locations:

Angels: Los Angeles in 1961, then to Anaheim (California) in 1966
Senators: Washington in 1961, then to Dallas (Texas Rangers) in 1972
Mets: New York in 1962
Astros: Houston in 1962
Expos: Montreal in 1969
Padres: San Diego in 1969
Pilots: Seattle in 1969, then to Milwaukee (Brewers) in 1970
Royals: Kansas City in 1969
Blue Jays: Toronto in 1977
Mariners: Seattle in 1977
Marlins: Miami (Florida) in 1993
Rockies: Denver (Colorado) in 1993

Thus, the density of major league teams in North America increased from 16 to 28, and at the same time the distribution became more dispersed.

Pattern. The third property of distribution is the **pattern,** which is the geometric or regular arrangement of the objects. Some phenomena are organized in a regular (geometric) pattern, whereas others are distributed randomly. Geographers observe that many objects form a linear distribution, such as the arrangement of houses along a street or stations along a subway line.

Objects frequently are arranged in a square or rectangular pattern. Many American cities contain a regular pattern of streets, known as a grid pattern, which intersect at right angles at uniform intervals to form square or rectangular blocks. The system of townships, ranges, and sections established by the Land Ordinance of 1785 is another example of a square or grid pattern.

The distribution of baseball teams also follows a regular pattern. With the addition of expansion teams in the Tampa and Phoenix areas, the 30 teams are located in North America's 26 largest metropolitan areas (four metropolitan areas have two teams each).

Not all objects are distributed in a regular pattern. The streets in the older parts of European cities are arranged in a random pattern, following centuries of haphazard development.

Diffusion

Diffusion is the process by which a feature or trend spreads or moves, across the landscape. A characteristic originates at a hearth or node and diffuses from there to other locations. Geographers doc-

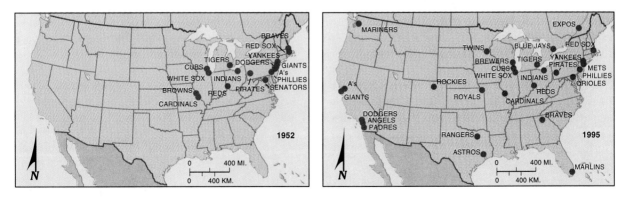

FIGURE 1-13 Density and concentration of baseball teams. The changing distribution of North American baseball teams illustrates the difference between density and concentration. The figures show that density of baseball teams in North America has increased from 16 teams in North America (1952) to 28 (1995). At the same time, the distribution has changed from a clustered arrangement in the northeastern part of the United States to a more dispersed arrangement across the United States and southern Canada.

ument the location of a node and the process by which diffusion carries the characteristic elsewhere.

Hearths. The region from which a phenomenon originates is called a **hearth**. How might a hearth emerge? A cultural group must be willing to try something new and be able to allocate resources to nurture the innovation. To develop a hearth, a group of people must also have the technical ability to achieve the desired idea and the economic structures, such as financial institutions, to facilitate implementation of the innovation.

We will discuss in subsequent chapters how geographers can trace the dominant languages, religions, economic systems, political institutions, and other important elements of the contemporary U.S. and Canadian landscape primarily to hearths in Europe and the Middle East. But other areas of the world also contain important hearths. In some cases an idea, such as an agricultural practice, may originate independently in more than one hearth. In other cases, hearths may emerge in two regions because two cultural groups modify a shared concept in two different ways.

Once a phenomenon appears in a region, it may diffuse to other locations. Geographers observe two basic types of diffusion: relocation and expansion.

Relocation Diffusion. Relocation diffusion is the spread of a feature or trend by the bodily movement of people from one region to another. We shall see in Chapter 3 that people migrate for a variety of political, economic, and environmental reasons. When they move, they carry with them their cultural characteristics, such as language, religion, and social customs. The most commonly spoken languages in North and Latin America are Spanish, English, French, and Portuguese, primarily because several hundred years ago, Europeans who spoke those languages accounted for the largest number of migrants. Thus, these languages spread via relocation diffusion. We will examine the diffusion of languages, religions, and other social customs in Chapters 4 through 6.

The process of relocation diffusion helps us understand the distribution of AIDS (acquired immunodeficiency syndrome) within the United States. During the early 1980s, New York, California, and Florida were the nodes of origin for the disease within the United States. Half of the fifty states had no reported cases, and New York City, with only 3 percent of the nation's population, contained more than one-fourth of the AIDS cases. In the neighboring state of New Jersey, the number of AIDS cases dropped with increasing distance from New York City. A decade later, the disease had spread to every state, although California and the New York City area remained the focal points (Figure 1-14).

Even within cities, such as New York, the distribution of AIDS cases varied sharply among neighborhoods. At the beginning of 1993, rates of AIDS exceeded 1,500 cases per 100,000 people in Manhattan's Lower West Side, compared with fewer than 400 in most of Queens, Staten Island, southern Brooklyn, and northern Bronx (Figure 1-15).

Expansion Diffusion. Expansion diffusion is the spread of a feature or trend among people from one area to another in a snowballing process. This expansion may result from one of three processes:

- Hierarchical diffusion
- Contagious diffusion
- Stimulus diffusion

Hierarchical diffusion is the spread of a feature or trend that originates at a node within a region. That node may consist of a particular place in the region, such as a large urban center. For example, ideas generated in a large city may follow communications channels and bypass isolated rural areas until much later. Hierarchical diffusion may also result from the spread of ideas from political leaders, socially elite people, or other important persons to others in the community. The idea may bypass other persons or areas.

Contagious diffusion is the widespread diffusion of a feature or trend throughout the population. As the term implies, this form of diffusion is analogous to the spread of a contagious disease, such as influenza. Contagious diffusion spreads like a wave among fans in a stadium, without regard for hierarchies.

Stimulus diffusion is the spread of an underlying principle, even though a specific characteristic itself apparently is rejected. As discussed in Chapter 9, the early diffusion of agriculture may have taken place according to stimulus diffusion. According to the geographer Carl Sauer, the earliest form of agriculture to diffuse may have been vegetative planting, involving such practices as cutting stems and dividing roots. The specific practice of vegetative

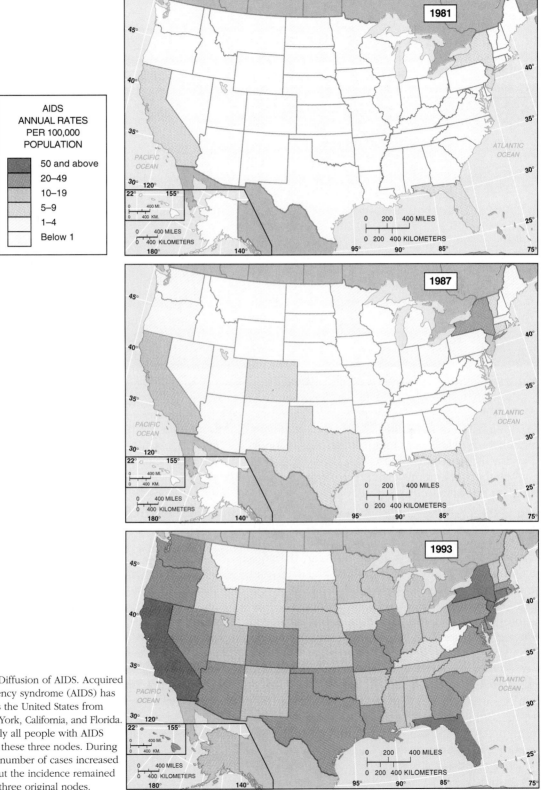

FIGURE 1-14 Diffusion of AIDS. Acquired immunodeficiency syndrome (AIDS) has diffused across the United States from nodes in New York, California, and Florida. In 1981, virtually all people with AIDS were found in these three nodes. During the 1980s, the number of cases increased everywhere, but the incidence remained highest in the three original nodes.

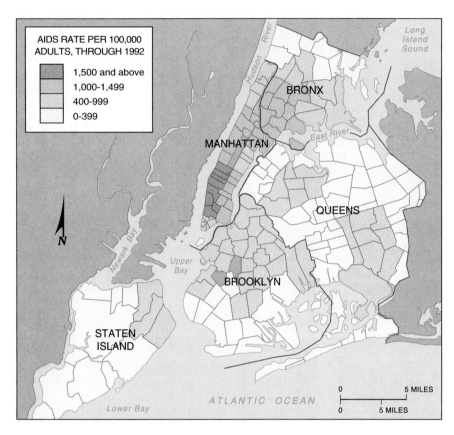

FIGURE 1-15 Distribution of AIDS within New York City. The state-by-state distribution in Figure 1-14 masks an extremely high local variability of AIDS cases. In the Lower West Side of Manhattan, AIDS rates exceed 1,500 cases per 100,000 people, but only a couple of miles away, in other neighborhoods of New York City, such as Queens, AIDS rates are closer to levels in midwestern states. Geographers conclude that these differences are related to differences in other social and economic characteristics of people, as discussed in Chapter 12.

planting may not have diffused, but the underlying principle of deliberately transforming vegetation to provide food was accepted.

Whether important cultural concepts diffuse through relocation or expansion diffusion is a very real issue for many countries today. How should today's less developed countries promote development? One alternative—the international trade approach—assumes that a country's economy develops as a result of diffusion of economic practices from more developed to less developed countries. A second alternative—the self-sufficiency approach—assumes that economic development is achieved through a process of innovation inside a country. The health and welfare of a people are vitally affected by the ability of a country's leaders to judge which alternative best suits its region. These alternatives are discussed in more detail in Chapter 8.

Expansion diffusion occurs much more rapidly in the contemporary world than in the past. Modern methods of communications, such as computers, fax machines, and e-mail systems have encouraged more rapid diffusion of a cultural idea or an economic ac-tivity from one place to another. As a result, diffusion can be instantaneous in time, even if the physical distance between two places—as measured in kilometers or miles—is large. Geographers apply the term *space-time compression* to describe the reduction in the time it takes to diffuse something to a distant place.

Interaction

The diffusion of ideas and characteristics fosters cultural integration because people in different regions interact. To achieve interaction, one group must be accessible to the other; interaction fails to occur when the two groups are isolated. The movement of people, goods, and ideas within and among regions is called **spatial interaction.**

Interaction takes place through *networks,* which are chains of communication that connect places. Today, ideas that originate in one area diffuse rapidly to other areas because of our sophisticated communications and transportation networks. As a result of this rapid diffusion, interaction in the contemporary world is complex. People in more than one re-

The AIDS quilt on display in Washington, DC. The quilt was assembled as a memorial to people who have died of AIDS. By increasing awareness of AIDS, the creators of the quilt hope to slow diffusion of the disease. (Alon Reininger/Contact Press Images/The Stock Market)

gion may improve and modify an idea at the same time but in different ways.

A well-known example of a network in the United States is the television network (ABC, CBS, FOX, NBC, PBS). Each comprises a chain of stations around the country simultaneously broadcasting the same program, such as a football game. Transportation systems also form networks that connect places. Airlines in the United States, for example, have adopted distinctive networks known as "hub-and-spokes." Under the hub-and-spokes system, airlines fly planes from a large number of places into one hub airport within a short period of time and then a short time later send the planes to another set of places. In principle, travelers originating in smaller towns can reach a wide variety of destinations by changing planes at the hub airport.

Local differences in farming, clothing, settlements, language, and religion arise through centuries of isolation from inhabitants of other regions. Typically, the farther away one group is from another, the less likely the two groups are to interact. Contact diminishes with increasing distance and eventually disappears. This trailing-off phenomenon is called **distance decay.**

Interaction among groups can be retarded by barriers. These can be physical, such as oceans and deserts, or cultural, such as language and legal systems. We regard the landscape as part of our inheritance from the past. As a result, we may be reluctant to modify it unless we are under heavy pressure to do so. A major change in the landscape may reflect an upheaval in a people's culture.

Acculturation. When two groups interact, the more dynamic and powerful culture is likely to dominate the weaker one. The modification of one culture as a result of contact with a more powerful one is called **acculturation.**

One of two things may happen to the weaker culture through acculturation. First, the weaker culture may be obliterated. For example, most immigrants to the United States quickly lost touch with most of the cultural characteristics of their former home and adopted the cultural traits of their new community. Second, the weaker culture may be transformed into a new culture, in which a new set of characteristics may coexist with older ones. New patterns emerge through the integration of the two cultures, but elements of the older culture remain.

Cargo Cult. The diffusion of cultural elements from Europe and North America may transform rather than destroy local cultural beliefs. For example, people on the Pacific island of Tana, part of the country of Vanuatu, worship Prince Phillip, the husband of Britain's Queen Elizabeth, as a god. According to local customary belief, Prince Phillip is a messiah who grew up on Tana Island, and Queen Elizabeth broke with her great council of chiefs to marry him. Prince Phillip was added to the collection of local gods a few years ago when he visited the country, formerly the British colony of New Hebrides. His advance person apparently distributed photographs, which the people regard as holy icons.

The introduction of Prince Phillip as a god in Vanuatu is an example of a **cargo cult.** A cargo cult is a belief that the arrival of a ship or airplane in a locality has spiritual meaning. Several hundred years ago, some American Indians regarded Europeans who arrived on ships as gods.

Belief in a cargo cult persists in Papua New Guinea and other Pacific Ocean islands because American ships and airplanes brought new technology and equipment during World War II. Some residents believe that if they remain faithful, the planes will return with vast wealth. People in Papua New Guinea prepare large wooden planes as female sirens to lure male planes and their cargo from the sky.

☀ **K E Y   I S S U E   3**

How Do Geographers Explain the Significance of Geographic Patterns?

- Globalization of Culture
- Globalization of Economy
- Our Global Environment

Globalization refers to actions or processes that involve the entire world and result in making something worldwide in scope. The globalization concept helps human geographers explain why distributions and movements of people, goods, and ideas within and among regions are important.

Globalization means that the world is "shrinking"— not literally in size of course, but in the time it takes for a person, good, or idea to get from one place to another. People are plugged into a global culture, economy, and environment, and the world has become more uniform, integrated, and interdependent.

But globalization has not destroyed the uniqueness of an individual place's culture, economy, and environment. Human geographers understand that many contemporary social problems result from a tension between forces promoting global culture, economy, and environment on the one hand and preservation of local economic autonomy, cultural traditions, and physical conditions on the other hand.

For geographers, globalization has three important dimensions: globalization of culture, globalization of economy, and globalization of environment. Each of the three is addressed below.

Globalization of Culture

Culture is a concept that can embody the entire spectrum of human behavior. According to geographer Peirce Lewis, "the cultural landscape is our un-

witting autobiography," because it reflects in tangible form our tastes, values, aspirations, and fears.

Culture Defined

To understand how culture has globalized, we must first define culture. Webster's *Third New International Dictionary* offers this definition of **culture:** the body of customary beliefs, social forms, and material traits constituting a distinct complex of tradition of a group of people.

Customary Beliefs. The customary beliefs of a people produce a distinctive culture. Customary beliefs particularly affect population growth, religion, and food. Why do some people have many children, while others choose to have none? Why do some believe in a particular religion, while others follow another? Powerful customary beliefs are at work. We examine differences in population growth rates among cultural groups in Chapter 2 and different religious beliefs in Chapter 5.

Social Forms. A second element of a people's culture is social forms and institutions. A critical social form for any culture group is language, which is the communication of ideas through written symbols, sounds, and gestures. People live and work together and remember the same past by sharing a common language. Facial expressions and other nonverbal communication also carry meaning within a cultural group. Language patterns are discussed in Chapter 4.

Material Traits. The third element of a culture is its material traits, especially food, clothing, and shelter. All people consume food, wear clothing, and build shelter, but different cultural groups provide these necessities in different ways. Distinctive material traits derive in part from a cultural group's technical knowledge. Some cultures have the capacity to transform the natural environment considerably, whereas others do not.

Elements of Globalization of Culture

The trend toward a common global culture, based on shared beliefs, social forms, and material traits, results from several elements, which we will explore in more detail.

- People in different places are displaying less difference in their cultural preferences.
- Increased uniformity in cultural preferences is made possible through enhanced communications.
- Although consumers in different places express increasingly similar cultural preferences, they do not share the same access to them.

The desire of some people to retain their traditional cultural elements, despite increased globalization of cultural preferences, has led to political conflict and market fragmentation in some regions.

Uniform Consumption Preferences. The survival of a culture's distinctive beliefs, forms, and traits is threatened by global diffusion of social customs: wearing jeans and Nike shoes, consuming Coca-Cola and McDonald's hamburgers, and other preferences in food, clothing, shelter, and leisure activities. Regardless of cultural traditions, people around the world aspire to drive an automobile, watch television, and own a house. The globalization of culture is based primarily on diffusion of lifestyles and products from more developed countries, especially the United States.

Geographers observe that increasingly uniform cultural preferences produce a "global" landscape that is uniform in appearance. Fast-food restaurants, service stations, and retail chains deliberately create a visual appearance that varies little among locations, so customers can recognize them regardless of where in the world they happen to be. Houses built on the edge of one urban area very much resemble houses built on the edge of urban areas in other regions.

Enhanced Communications. Cultural groups in different regions share beliefs, forms, and traits through enhanced communications. Today, we know a great deal about events around in the world, and we know quickly. Distant places now seem less remote and more accessible to us than they did a few decades ago. We can reach into the everyday lives of people in far-off places.

In the past, most interaction among cultural groups required relocation diffusion—the physical movement of settlers, explorers, and plunderers from one location to another. As recently as A.D. 1800, people traveled in the same ways and at about the same speeds as in 1800 B.C.—they walked or were carried by an animal or sailboat.

Today, travel by motor vehicle or airplane is much quicker (Figure 1-16). But we need not travel to know about another place. We receive images and messages worldwide at the touch of a button. We communicate instantly with people in distant places through computers and telecommunications, and we instantly see people in distant places on television.

This diffusion of global communication has encouraged globalization of beliefs, social forms, and material traits. Africans, in particular, have moved away from traditional religions and have adopted Christianity or Islam, religions shared with hundreds of millions people throughout the world. People still speak thousands of different languages, traditionally a people's most distinctive social form. But English has become increasingly important as the language of international communication; more than three-fourths of college-age Europeans have learned to speak English.

People living in different places increasingly share tastes in food, clothing, and shelter. The globalization of communication and culture gives a sense that barriers among groups of people have been broken.

Unequal Access to Cultural Elements. People in more developed countries take for granted watching distant events on television, speaking across oceans by telephone, and traveling to distant places by motor vehicle and aircraft. Elsewhere in the world, people may regard such devices as novelties, perhaps recently experiencing them for the first time. The world still contains a handful of people who are so isolated and sheltered that they have never seen television, used a telephone, or ridden in a motor vehicle. Even these people are aware that such devices exist, but access to them is a distant aspiration. Knowledge of these devices is global, but the ability to purchase them is not.

Access to communication and transportation is restricted by an uneven division of wealth worldwide. Even within a region, access may be restricted because of uneven distribution of wealth or because of discrimination against women or minorities.

Maintaining Local Traditions. As more people become aware of global culture and aspire to possess its elements, extinction threatens local cultural beliefs, social forms, and material traits. Yet, despite globalization, differences among places not only per-

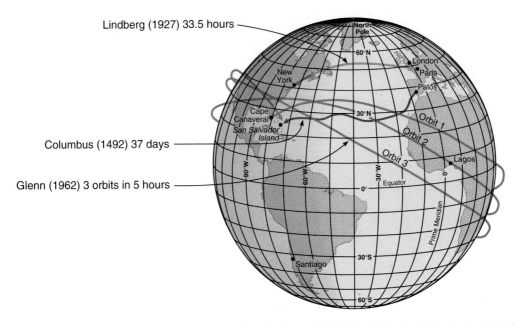

Lindberg (1927) 33.5 hours

Columbus (1492) 37 days

Glenn (1962) 3 orbits in 5 hours

FIGURE 1-16 Transportation improvements have "shrunk" the world. In 1492, Christopher Columbus took 37 days (nearly 900 hours) to sail across the Atlantic Ocean from the Canary Islands to San Salvador (Watling) Island. In 1927, Charles Lindberg was the first pilot to fly an aircraft alone across the Atlantic, taking 33.5 hours. In 1962, John Glenn, the first American to orbit in space, circled around the world three times in 5 hours; he crossed over the Atlantic in about 15 minutes.

sist but flourish in many places. After all, global standardization of products does not mean that everyone wants them. And when the same message or image is transmitted simultaneously around the world, people in different places may not derive the same meaning from it.

The communications revolution that promotes cultural globalization also permits preservation of cultural diversity. Television, for example, is no longer restricted to a handful of channels displaying one set of cultural values. With the distribution of programming through cable and satellite systems, people in many countries have a choice of hundreds of programs rather than a handful. The proliferation in programming enables people in English-speaking countries to watch programs in other languages, such as Spanish in the United States, Welsh in the United Kingdom, or Gaelic in Ireland.

Local cultural traditions may be transmitted around the world. Chinese, Ethiopian, Greek, Italian, Mexican, and Thai restaurants may coexist side by side along a single street in Chicago, London, or Toronto.

It is ironic that, with the globalization of communications, people in Oregon and South Africa can watch the same soccer game, yet with the fragmentation of broadcasting, two people in the same house can watch different programs. Groups of people on every continent may aspire to wear jeans, but jeans buyers may live with someone who prefers khakis. In a global culture, companies can target groups of consumers with similar tastes in different parts of the world.

Strong determination to retain cultural traditions in the face of globalization can lead to intolerance of people who display other beliefs, social forms, and material traits. Political disputes, unrest, and wars erupt in places such as southeastern Europe, East Africa, and the Middle East, where different cultural groups have been unable to peacefully share the same space (see Chapter 7).

Globalization of Economy

The trend toward global cultural sameness is a product of the *world economy*. Companies and workers that once were unaffected by events elsewhere now share a single economic world with other companies and workers. The fate of an autoworker in Detroit is tied to investment decisions made in Mexico City, Seoul, Stuttgart, and Tokyo.

Globalization of the economy, in which national borders and differences become less important, has resulted from several trends:

- Instantaneous global movement of money by companies
- Increasing control of investment by large transnational corporations
- Global investment flows from three more developed core regions—North America, Western Europe, and Japan
- Specialization in the location of production

We will look at each of these briefly here and in more detail in Chapters 8 through 10.

Global Movement of Money

Historically, people and companies had difficulty moving even small sums of money from one country to another. International monetary transfer involved cumbersome procedures, and funds could be frozen for several weeks until all the paperwork cleared. Most governments prohibited the removal of large sums of money beyond their borders, and in the case of communist countries, no money at all could be removed without government approval.

Modern communication and transportation provide the technical means to easily move money—as well as materials, products, technology, and other economic assets—around the world. Thanks to the electronic superhighway, companies can now organize economic activities across vast distances.

Banks, corporations, and other financial institutions can operate worldwide in part because the decision centers that command the global economy—New York, London, and Tokyo—are located in different time zones. When Tokyo's stock market closes, at 3 P.M. local time, it is 6 A.M. in London, only 3 hours before the opening of the day's trading there. The stock market opens in New York at 9:30 A.M., while London's is still open. When the market closes in New York at 4 P.M., it's 6 A.M. the next morning in Tokyo, only 3 hours before the opening of the Tokyo market the next day. Consequently, investors can react immediately to changes in the value of gold, the rate of exchange between the dollar and the yen, and other constantly shifting elements of the global economy (refer to the time zone map in the Geography in Action box).

Transnational Corporations

Globalization of the economy has been led primarily by transnational corporations, sometimes called multinational corporations. A transnational corporation conducts research, operates factories, and sells products in many countries, not just where its headquarters are located.

Most transnational corporations have their headquarters in one of three regions—North America (especially the United States), Western Europe (especially the United Kingdom, Germany, and France), and Japan. Transnational corporations also locate most of their factories and markets within these three regions. The United Nations reports, however, that in 1994, transnational corporations employed 61 million people in the core regions and 12 million elsewhere.

An increasing percentage of investment reaches Latin America, Africa, and Asian countries outside Japan (Figure 1-17). U.S. transnational corporations are most likely to invest in Latin America. Western European transnationals are most likely to invest in Eastern Europe and Africa. Japanese transnationals are most likely to invest in Asia.

Since the 1980s, governments in the three regions where transnational corporations are based have changed tax codes and regulations that hindered transnational operations. Other countries where transnational corporations wish to invest have changed laws and bureaucratic procedures that prevented transnationals from operating within their borders.

Investment Flows from Three Core Regions

Although transnational corporations have increased investment worldwide, improved communication has enabled them to concentrate their key decision makers in North America, Western Europe, and Japan. The global economy is increasingly centered in these three core regions. From "command centers" in New York, London, and Tokyo, orders are sent instantly to factories, shops, and research centers around the world.

Meanwhile, "nonessential" employees of the companies can be relocated to lower-cost offices outside the major financial centers. For example, Fila maintains headquarters in Italy but has moved 90 percent of its production of sportswear to Asian countries. Mitsubishi's corporate offices are in Japan, but all of its VCRs are produced in other Asian countries.

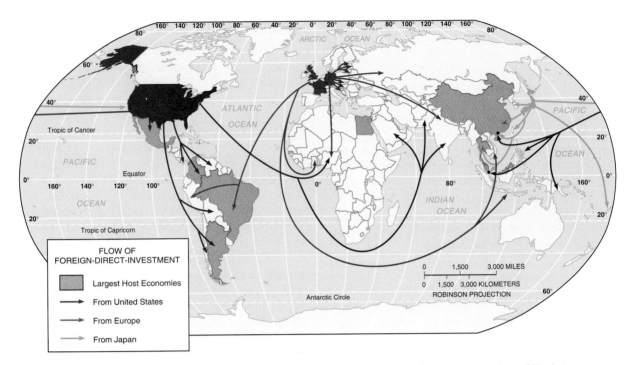

FIGURE 1-17 Majors flows of foreign investment. Most transnational companies invest in the three core regions of North America, Western Europe, and Japan. Outside the core regions, the largest amount of investment by transnational corporations is in Latin America (especially by transnationals based in the United States) and in Asia (especially by Japanese transnationals).

Countries in Africa, Asia, and Latin America contain three-fourths of the world's population and nearly all of Earth's population growth, but they find themselves on a periphery, or outer edge, of global investment decisions made by transnationals. As a result, the global economy has increased the disparity between the levels of wealth and well-being in the core and in the periphery. This widening gap is logically called **uneven development.**

Specialization in the Location of Production

Every place on Earth is part of the global economy, but each plays a distinctive role, based on its particular assets. A place may be near valuable minerals, or it may be inhabited by especially well-educated workers. Transnational corporations assess the economic assets of each place.

A place may be especially suited to conducting research, to developing new engineering systems, to extracting raw materials, to producing parts, to storing finished products, to selling them, or to managing operations. In a global economy, transnationals remain competitive by correctly identifying the optimal location for each of these activities. Suitable places

for each activity may be clustered in one country or region, or they may dispersed around the world.

As a result, globalization of the economy has heightened economic differences among places. Factories are closed in some locations and opened in others. Some places become centers for technical research, whereas others become centers for low-skilled tasks. Changes in production have led to a spatial division of labor, in which a region's workers specialize in particular tasks. Transnationals decide where to produce things in response to characteristics of the local labor force, such as skill level, prevailing wage rates, and attitudes toward unions. Transnationals may close factories in regions with high wage rates and strong labor unions (Figure 1-18).

Our Global Environment

We regard the physical environment as a large collection of resources. **Resources** are substances that have value or usefulness. We can deplete some resources, such as energy, and endanger the survival of living things. Through pollution, humans can alter or damage other resources, especially air and water.

Some of these effects are local, some regional, and some global.

Some human impacts on the environment seem trivial or even contradictory: Why do we plant our front yards with grass, water it to make it grow, then mow it to keep it from growing tall, and impose fines on those who fail to mow often enough?

Other human impacts on the environment are based on deep-seated cultural values: Why does one group of people consume the fruit from deciduous trees and chop down the conifers, while another group chops down the deciduous trees for furniture while preserving the conifers as religious symbols?

Possibilism

Nineteenth-century environmental determinists believed that the physical environment caused human actions, but modern geographers reject this environmental determinism in favor of possibilism. According to **possibilism,** the physical environment may limit some human actions, but people have the ability to adjust to their environment. People can choose a course of action from many alternatives in the physical environment.

For example, the climate of any location influences human activities, especially food production.

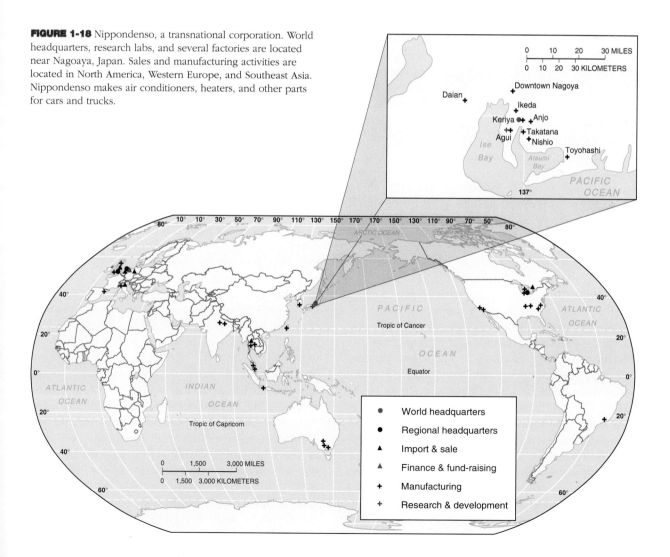

FIGURE 1-18 Nippondenso, a transnational corporation. World headquarters, research labs, and several factories are located near Nagoaya, Japan. Sales and manufacturing activities are located in North America, Western Europe, and Southeast Asia. Nippondenso makes air conditioners, heaters, and other parts for cars and trucks.

From one generation to the next, people learn that different crops thrive in different climates—rice requires plentiful water, whereas wheat survives on limited moisture, and it actually grows poorly in very wet environments. On the other hand, wheat is more likely than rice to be grown successfully in colder climates. Thus, under possibilism, it is possible for people to choose the crops they grow, to be compatible with their environment.

A people's level of wealth can influence their attitude toward modifying the environment. A farmer rich enough to possess a tractor may regard a hilly piece of land as an obstacle to avoid while plowing vast expanses of flat land, whereas a poor farmer with little land may regard hilly land as the only opportunity to produce food for survival through hand cultivation.

This human-environment approach explains many global issues. For example, world population growth is a problem if the number of people exceeds the capacity of the physical environment to produce food. But people can adjust to the capacity of the physical environment by controlling their numbers, adopting new technology, consuming different foods, migrating to new locations, and other actions.

Physical Processes

Human geographers need some familiarity with global environmental processes to understand the distribution of human activities, such as where people live and how they earn a living. Important physical processes include climate, vegetation, soil, and landforms.

Climate. Climate is the long-term average weather conditions at a particular location. Geographers frequently classify climates according to a system developed by German climatologist Vladimir Köppen. The modified Köppen system divides the world into five main climate regions, which are identified by the letters A through E, as well as by names (Figure 1-19).

A Humid low-latitude climates: The average temperature of the coldest month exceeds 18°C (64.4°F). Some A climate regions receive heavy precipitation throughout the year; others have sharp seasonal variations.

B Dry climates: The amount of evaporation equals or exceeds precipitation. B climate regions are classified as desert if they receive less than 4 centimeters (1.6 inches) of precipitation per year and steppe if they receive more than 4 centimeters.

C Warm mid-latitude climates: The average temperature of the coldest month is between 0°C (32°F) and 18°C (64.4°F); in addition, the average monthly temperature exceeds 10°C (50°F) at least eight months of the year.

D Cold mid-latitude climates: The coldest month averages below 0°C (32°F), and four of the months have an average temperature above 10°C (50°F). Precipitation is generally lower in D climates than in C climates.

E Polar climates: The average temperature of every month is less than 10°C (50°F).

The modified Köppen system divides the five main climate regions into several subtypes. For all but the B climate, the basis for the subdivision is the amount of precipitation and the season in which it falls. For the B climate, subdivision is on the basis of temperature and precipitation.

Humans have a limited tolerance for extreme temperature and precipitation levels and thus avoid living in places that are too hot, too cold, too wet, or too dry. Compare the map of global climate with the distribution of population (see Figure 2-1). Fewer people live in the dry (B) and polar (E) climates than in the tropical (A) and mid–latitude (C and D) climates.

The climate of a particular location has a great influence on the lives of the people who live there. People in parts of the A climate region, especially southwestern India, Bangladesh, and the Myanmar (Burma) coast, anxiously await the annual monsoon rain, which is essential for successful agriculture and provides nearly 90 percent of India's water supply. For most of the year, the region receives dry, somewhat cool air from the northeast. In June, the wind direction suddenly shifts, bringing moist, warm southwesterly air, known as the *monsoon,* from the Indian Ocean. The monsoon rain lasts until September.

In years when the monsoon rain is delayed or fails to arrive—in recent decades, at least one-fourth of the time—agricultural output falls and famine threatens in the countries of South Asia, where nearly 20 percent of the world's people live. The monsoon rain is so important in India that the words for "year," "rain," and "rainy season" are identical in many local languages.

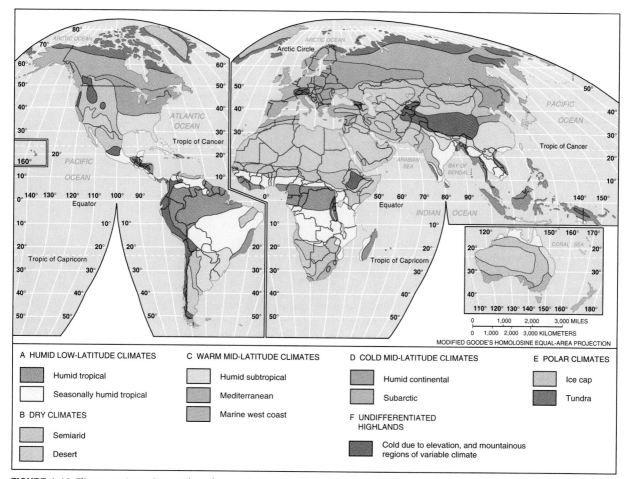

FIGURE 1-19 Climate regions. Geographers frequently classify global climates according to a system developed by Vladimir Köppen. The modified Köppen system divides the world into five main climate regions, indicated on the map by the letters A, B, C, D, and E.

Vegetation. Nearly the entire land surface of Earth supports some kind of vegetation. Earth's land vegetation includes four major forms of plant communities, called **biomes.** Their location and extent are influenced by both climate and human activities. Vegetation and soil, in turn, influence the types of agriculture that people practice in a particular region. The four main biomes are forest, savanna, grassland, and desert.

In the *forest biome,* trees form a continuous canopy over the ground. Although trees are the dominant vegetation, grasses and shrubs may grow beneath the cover. The forest biome covers a large percentage of Earth's surface, including much of North America, Europe, and Asia, as well as tropical areas of South America, Africa, and Southeast Asia.

The *savanna biome* is a mixture of trees and grasses. The trees do not form a continuous canopy, and the resultant lack of shade allows grass to grow.

Savanna covers large areas of Africa, South Asia, South America, and Australia.

As the name implies, the *grassland biome* is covered by grass rather than trees. Few trees grow in the region because of low precipitation. Early explorers from northern Europe and eastern North America regarded the American prairies—the world's most extensive grassland area—to be uninhabitable, because of the lack of trees with which to build houses, barns, and fences. But modern cultivation of wheat and other crops has turned the grasslands into a very productive region.

The *desert biome* is not completely bereft of vegetation. Although many desert areas have essentially no vegetation, the region contains dispersed patches of plants adapted to dry conditions. Vegetation is often sufficient for the survival of small numbers of animals.

Soil. The material that forms on Earth's surface, in the thin interface between the air and the rocks, is **soil.** Soil is not merely dirt; it contains the nutrients necessary for successful growth of plants, including those useful to humans.

The U.S. Comprehensive Soil Classification System divides global soil types into ten *orders,* according to the characteristics of the immediate surface soil layers and the subsoil. The orders are subdivided into suborders, great groups, subgroups, families, and series. More than 12,000 soil types have been identified in the United States alone.

Human geographers are concerned with the destruction of the soil that results from a combination of natural processes and human actions. Two basic problems contribute to the destruction of soil: erosion and depletion of nutrients. Erosion occurs when the soil washes away in the rain or blows away in the wind. To reduce the erosion problem, farmers reduce the amount of plowing, plant crops whose roots help bind the soil, and avoid planting on steep slopes.

Nutrients are depleted when plants withdraw more nutrients than natural processes can replace. Each type of plant withdraws certain nutrients from the soil and restores others. Repeated harvesting of the same type of crop year after year can remove certain nutrients and reduce the soil's productivity.

To minimize the depletion problem, farmers in more developed countries sometimes plant crops that offer no economic return but restore nutrients to the soil and keep the land productive over a longer term. Farmers also restore nutrients to the soil by adding fertilizers, either natural or synthetic. Farmers in less developed countries may face greater problems with depletion of nutrients because they lack knowledge of proper soil management practices and funds to buy fertilizer.

Landforms. Geographers find that some human actions can be explained through **geomorphology,** the science that studies the shape of Earth's surface and the processes that modify it. Some parts of Earth's surface are relatively flat; other areas are mountainous. **Relief** is the difference in elevation between any two points, and it measures the extent to which an area is flat or hilly. The steepness of hills is measured by **slope,** which is the relief divided by the distance between two points.

Relief and slope angle help to explain the distribution of population and the choice of economic activities at different locations. People prefer living on flatter land, which generally is better suited for agriculture. Great concentrations of people and activities in hilly areas—in other words, land with high relief and steep slopes—may require extensive effort to modify the landscape.

Geographers use **topographic maps** to study the relief and slope of localities. These maps are published for the United States by the U.S. Geological Survey (USGS). Figure 1-8 shows a portion of a topographic map for northern Mississippi, at the scale of 1:24,000. The brown lines on the map are **contour lines,** which connect points of equal elevation above sea level (or below). Contour lines are closer together to show steeper slopes and farther apart in flatter areas.

Topographic maps show a remarkable detail of physical features, such as bodies of water, forests, mountains, valleys, and wetlands. They also show cultural features, such as buildings, roads, parks, farms, and dams. Topos, as they are called, are used by engineers, hikers, hunters, people seeking a homesite, and anyone who really needs to see the lay of the land.

How People Change the Environment

Modern technology has altered the historical relationship between people and the environment. Humans now can modify the physical environment to a greater extent than in the past. For example, air conditioning has increased the attractiveness of living in warmer climates, and better insulation now permits living in colder climates.

Geographers are concerned that people sometimes use modern technology to modify the environment insensitively. The following stories from the Netherlands and Florida relate a contrast in sensitive and not-so-sensitive environmental modification.

The Netherlands: Sensitive Environmental Modification. Few lands have been as thoroughly modified by humans as the Netherlands. Because more than half of the Netherlands lies below sea level, most of the country today would be under water if it were not for massive projects to modify the environment by holding back the sea. The Dutch have a saying that "God made Earth, but the Dutch made the Netherlands." The Dutch have modified their environment with two distinctive types of construction projects: polders and dikes (Figure 1-20).

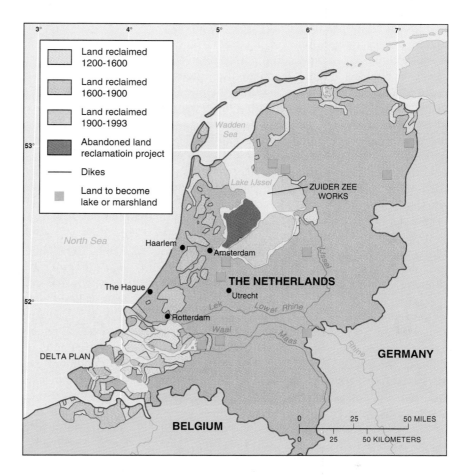

Land reclaimed
1200-1600

Land reclaimed
1600-1900

Land reclaimed
1900-1993

Abandoned land
reclamatioin project

Dikes

Land to become
lake or marshland

ZUIDER ZEE
WORKS

Wadden
Sea

Lake IJssel

North Sea

Haarlem

Amsterdam

THE NETHERLANDS

The Hague

Utrecht

Lek

Lower Rhine

Rotterdam

Waal

Maas

Rhine

IJssel

GERMANY

DELTA PLAN

BELGIUM

0   25   50 MILES

0   25   50 KILOMETERS

FIGURE 1-20 Location of polders and dikes in the Netherlands. The Dutch people have considerably altered the site of the Netherlands through creation of polders and dikes. Since the thirteenth century the Dutch have reclaimed more than 6,500 square kilometers (2,600 square miles) of polders, more than three-fourths of which have been reclaimed in the past 200 years. The Zuider Zee and Delta Plan have altered the coastline of the Netherlands and enabled the Dutch to reduce the amount of destruction caused by flooding. (Benelux Press/West Light)

A **polder** is a piece of land that is created by draining water from an area. Polders, first created in the thirteenth century, were constructed primarily by private developers in the sixteenth and seventeenth centuries and by the government during the past 200 years. Altogether, the Netherlands has 6,500 square kilometers (2,600 square miles) of polders, comprising 16 percent of the country's land area.

The first step in making a polder is to build a wall encircling the site, which is still under water. Then the water inside the walled area is pumped from the site into either nearby canals or the remaining portion of the original body of water. Before the invention of modern engines, windmills performed the pumping operation. Many of these windmills remain as a picturesque element of the Dutch landscape, although they were originally built for a practical purpose (Figure 1-20).

Once dry, the site—now known as a polder—can be prepared for human activities. The Dutch government has reserved most of the polders for agriculture, to reduce the country's dependence on imported food. Some of the polders are used for housing, and one contains Schiphol, one of the busiest airports in Europe.

The second distinctive modification of the landscape in the Netherlands is the construction of massive dikes to prevent the North Sea, an arm of the Atlantic Ocean, from flooding much of the country. The Dutch have built dikes in two major locations, the Zuider Zee project in the north and the Delta Plan project in the southwest.

The Zuider Zee, an arm of the North Sea, once protruded into the heart of the Netherlands. For centuries, the Dutch unsuccessfully attempted to prevent the Zuider Zee from flooding much of the country. Then, in the late nineteenth century, a Dutch engineer named Cornelis Lely proposed an ambitious project to seal off the Zuider Zee permanently from the North Sea, the ultimate source of the flood waters.

In accordance with Lely's plan, a dike was built, 32 kilometers (20 miles) long, across the mouth of the Zuider Zee to block the flow of North Sea water. When completed in 1932, the dike caused the Zuider Zee to be converted from a saltwater sea to a freshwater lake. The newly created body of water was named the IJsselmeer, or Lake IJssel, because the IJssel River now flows into it. Some of the lake has been drained to create several polders, encompassing an area of 1,600 square kilometers (620 square miles).

A second ambitious project in the Netherlands is the Delta Plan in the southwestern part of the country. Several important rivers flow through the Netherlands, including the Rhine (Europe's busiest river), the Maas (known as the Meuse in France), and the Scheldt (known as the Schelde in Belgium). As these rivers flow into the North Sea, they split into many branches and form a low-lying delta that is vulnerable to flooding.

After a devastating flood in January 1953 killed nearly 2,000 people, the Delta Plan called for the construction of several dams to close off most of the waterways from the North Sea. Together these dams shorten the coastline of the Netherlands by approximately 700 kilometers (435 miles). Because Rotterdam, Europe's largest port, is located nearby, some of the waterways were kept open. The project took 30 years to build and was completed in the mid-1980s.

With these two massive projects finished, attitudes toward modifying the environment have changed in the Netherlands. The Dutch have scrapped plans to build additional polders in the IJsselmeer, in order to preserve the lake's value for recreation. A plan adopted in 1990 calls for returning 263,000 hectares (650,000 acres) of farms to wetlands or forests. Widespread use of insecticides and fertilizers on Dutch farms contributes to contaminated drinking water, acid rain, and other environmental problems. The Dutch are deliberately breaking some of the dikes to flood fields.

But modifying the environment will still be essential to the survival of the Dutch. Global warming could raise the level of the sea around the Netherlands by between 20 and 58 centimeters (8 and 23 inches) within the next 100 years. Severe flooding in 1995 sent the Dutch a warning about the consequences of neglecting their dikes. Without expensive maintenance, the dikes will not continue to protect the Dutch people from floods.

Florida: Not-So-Sensitive Environmental Modification. Humans do not always modify the environment as sensitively as the Dutch. In Florida, the rechanneling of the Kissimmee River and construction on coastal barrier islands demonstrate the negative consequences that result from ill-conceived human actions to modify the environment.

In 1961, the state of Florida asked the U.S. Army Corps of Engineers to straighten the course of the Kissimmee River, which meandered for 160 kilometers (98 miles) from near Orlando to Lake Okee-

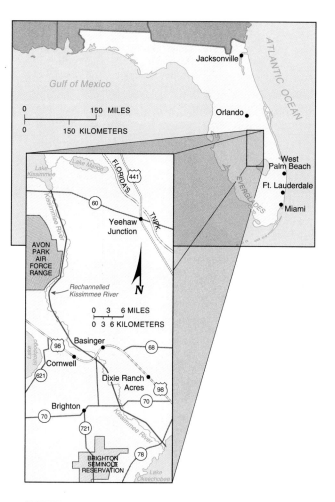

FIGURE 1-21 Kissimmee River. The U.S. Army Corps of Engineers straightened the course of the Kissimmee River to control flooding in central Florida. After the canal, known as C-38, opened in 1971, millions of gallons of polluted water—mainly runoff from cattle grazing—began pouring into Lake Okeechobee, which is the major source of fresh water for about half of Florida's population. Now the state wants the corps to return the river to its original course.

chobee (Figure 1-21). In years with heavy rains, the river flooded 115,000 hectares (45,000 acres) of nearby land, creating an obstacle to cattle grazing and construction of buildings in areas with potential for rapid population growth. The Corps channeled the river into a canal 90 meters (300 feet) wide and 9 meters (30 feet) deep, which ran in a straight line for 84 kilometers (52 miles).

The opening of the canal in 1971 changed the region's environment. Tens of thousands of gallons of

polluted water, mainly from cattle grazing along the banks, ran into the canal and flowed into Lake Okeechobee, which is the source of fresh water for half of Florida's population. Fish in the lake began to die from the high levels of mercury, phosphorus, and other contaminants. The polluted water then continued to flow south, from Lake Okeechobee to the Everglades, where wildlife habitats were also disturbed.

The Corps is now spending hundreds of millions of dollars to restore the Kissimmee River to its meandering course and to buy the nearby grazing land, which will again be subject to flooding. In an ironic reminder of the Dutch saying quoted earlier, Floridians say "God made the world in six days, and the Army Corps of Engineers has been tinkering with it ever since."

The rechanneling of the Kissimmee River is not the only example of insensitive environmental management in Florida. Barrier islands extend for several hundred kilometers along Florida's east and west coasts, as well as the rest of the Atlantic coast and Gulf coast between Maine and Texas. These barrier islands are essentially large sandbars that shield the mainland from flooding and storm damage. They are constantly being eroded and shifted from the force of storms and pounding surf, and after a major storm large sections can be washed away and disappear.

Despite the fragile condition of the barrier islands, hundreds of thousands of people live on them. They are increasingly attractive locations for constructing homes and recreational facilities to take advantage of proximity to the seashore. Two-thirds of the barrier islands are linked with the mainland by bridge, causeway, ferry service, or airplane flights.

To fight erosion along the barrier islands, people build sea walls and jetties, which are structures extending into the sea, but these projects result in more damage than protection. A sea wall or jetty can prevent sand from drifting away, but by trapping sand along the up-current side, it causes erosion on the barrier islands on the down-current side.

Human actions can deplete scarce environmental resources, destroy irreplaceable resources, and use resources inefficiently. The refrigerants in the air conditioners that have increased the comfort of residents of warmer climates have also increased the amount of chlorofluorocarbons in the atmosphere, damaging the ozone layer that protects living things from X-rays and contributing to global warming. We explore the consequences of such use, abuse, and misuse of the environment in more detail in Chapter 13.

Beach-front homes in Fort Lauderdale, Florida. The strip of land in the foreground is a barrier island. Most of the beaches in this part of Florida are eroding, and sand must be imported to replace what is lost to the waves. (Alese and Mort Pechter/The Stock Market)

Summary   Here again are the key issues for Chapter 1:

1. How do geographers answer the "where" question?

The most fundamental concept in geography is location, which is the position on Earth's surface that something occupies. Geographers use maps to display the location of objects and to extract information about places. Early geographers drew maps of Earth's surface based on exploration and observation. During the past century, geographic inquiry has become more scientific.

2. How do geographers answer the "why" question?

Geographers employ two approaches to analyze the location of things. First, geographers identify regions and explain the integration among features within and between regions. Second, geographers analyze how diffusion affects the distribution of features across Earth.

3. How do geographers explain the significance of geographic patterns?

Geographers explain the underlying significance of observed spatial arrangements through the concept of globalization. Cultural, economic, and environmental features have been increasingly worldwide in scope, although diverse local cultural, economic, and environmental conditions remain important.

CASE STUDY REVISITED
Why Is More Than One Location Named Miami?

The case study that opened this chapter described some of the differences between two places, Miami, Ohio, and Miami, Florida. After describing these differences, geographers then work to explain the reasons underlying the observed pattern, such as the repeated use of the name Miami. Two processes that you learned about in this chapter, diffusion and spatial interaction, help in the explanation.

The name *Miami* originated with the Miami people, a Native American tribe belonging to the Algonquin family. When European explorers first encountered them, the Miami people lived in northeastern Wisconsin's Door County peninsula, near Sturgeon Bay. The word *Miami* means "people on the peninsula," a reference to the tribe's Wisconsin homeland.

In the late seventeenth century, the Miamis migrated southward and settled along the St. Joseph River (today in southwestern Michigan) and the Wabash River (northeastern Indiana). Pushed out of the southern Lake Michigan area by other tribes, the Miamis then migrated eastward to present-day Ohio, where they were living when the territory became part of the United States. Early nineteenth-century settlers from the East Coast retained the name Miami on the landscape to identify rivers, towns, and a university. Maumee, a river in northern Ohio, is a variant spelling of Miami.

Settlements called Miami were established in several other states by migrants from Ohio or members of the Miami tribe. For example, most of the Miamis were forced to migrate from Ohio to eastern Kansas between 1832 and 1840. The present-day town of Miami, Kansas, is located near the land that the government gave to the tribe. In 1867, the tribe relocated with the Illinois Indians farther westward to Oklahoma, then known as Indian Territory. In 1891, Miami chief Thomas P. Richardville and Colonel W. C. Lykins established a town in the northeastern corner of Oklahoma that they named Miami. In the late nineteenth century, settlers from Ohio established a settlement in Gila County, Arizona, also named Miami. Settlements called Miami were likewise established in Missouri, New Mexico, Texas, and West Virginia.

In Florida, the name *Miami* apparently derived from a completely different source. The first recorded European to live near present-day Miami, Florida, was a Spaniard, Hernando d'Escalante Fontañeda. After a shipwreck, he became a prisoner of the Tequesta Indians, a branch of the Calusa people, between 1545 and 1562. In his 1575 memoir, Fontañeda used the Calusa Indian word *mayaimi* to describe Lake Okeechobee, as well as a river that flowed from the lake to the Atlantic Ocean. He translated the word *mayaimi* as "very large."

Around 1830, Richard R. Fitzgerald established a plantation at the future site of the city of Miami. He named the plantation Miami, the first time that the Ohio spelling rather than the Spanish-Calusa version was used in Florida. Born in Columbia, South Carolina, Fitzgerald may have encountered the Ohio spelling Miami, but had no known connection with the Miami in Ohio.

The army took over the Miami plantation from the late 1830s until the early 1850s and renamed it Fort Dallas. After its abandonment as a fort, the site was sparsely inhabited until the 1890s. Henry M. Flagler started to build shops and hotels on the site in March 1896 and extended his Florida East Coast Railroad to the settlement one month later. By

July 1896, the new settlement had 1,500 inhabitants and was incorporated as a city. Given a choice in naming the new settlement, the voters selected the former plantation name Miami instead of Flagler or Fort Dallas. The choice may have been influenced in part by the presence of several former Ohio residents in the new settlement.

Thus, the name Miami originated with Native Americans in northeastern Wisconsin and diffused to other locations in the United States as a result of the tribe's migration. The name Miami originated independently in Florida, the sort of coincidence that occurs when groups of people live in isolation from one another. When south Florida became part of the United States, the process of spatial interaction produced a modified spelling in conformance with the northern Indian tribe.

Key Terms

Acculturation The modification of a culture as a result of contact with a more powerful culture.

Base line An east-west line designated in the Land Ordinance of 1785 to facilitate the surveying and numbering of townships.

Biome A large region of Earth's surface characterized by particular plant and animal types.

Cargo cult A belief that the arrival of a ship or airplane in a locality has spiritual meaning.

Cartography The science of making maps.

Climate The long-term average weather conditions at a particular location.

Concentration The spread of something over a given study area.

Contagious diffusion The widespread diffusion of a feature or trend throughout a population.

Contour lines Lines on a topographic map connecting points of equal elevation above sea level (or below).

Culture The body of customary beliefs, social forms, and material traits of a group of people.

Density The frequency with which something exists within a given unit of area.

Diffusion The process of spread of a feature or trend across the landscape.

Distance decay The diminishing in importance and eventual disappearance of a phenomenon with increasing distance from its origin.

Environmental determinism A nineteenth- and early twentieth-century approach to the study of geography that argued that the general laws sought by human geographers could be found in the physical sciences. Geography was therefore the study of how the physical environment caused human activities.

Expansion diffusion The spread of a feature or trend among people from one area to another in a snowballing process.

Formal region (or uniform or homogeneous region) An area in which the selected trend or feature is present throughout.

Functional region (or nodal region) An area in which an activity has a focal point. The characteristic dominates at a central node, diffuses toward the outer part of the region, diminishes in importance, and eventually disappears.

Geomorphology The study of the shape of Earth's surface and the processes that modify it.

GIS (Geographic Information System) A computer system that stores, organizes, analyzes, and displays geographic data.

Globalization. Actions or processes that involve the entire world and result in making something worldwide in scope.

Greenwich Mean Time (GMT) The time in the time zone that encompasses the prime meridian, or 0° longitude.

Hearth The region from which a phenomenon originates; a center of innovation.

Hierarchical diffusion The spread of a feature or trend from one key person or node of innovation to another through bypassing of other persons or areas.

International Date Line An arc that for the most part follows 180° longitude, although it deviates in several places to avoid dividing land areas. When you cross the International Date Line heading east (toward America), the clock moves back 24 hours, or one entire day. When you go west (toward Asia), the calendar moves ahead one day.

Land Ordinance of 1785 A law that divided much of the United States into a system of townships to facilitate the sale of land to settlers.

Latitude The numbering system used to indicate the location of parallels drawn on a globe and measuring distance north and south of the equator (0°).

Less developed countries (LDCs) Countries that are not well developed economically; also called *developing countries*. Most are in the southern latitudes.

Location The position of anything on Earth's surface.

Longitude The numbering system used to indicate the location of meridians drawn on a globe and measuring distance east and west of the prime meridian (0°).

Map A two-dimensional, or flat, representation of Earth's surface or a portion of it.

Meridian An arc drawn on a map between the North and South poles.

More developed countries (MDCs) Countries that are well developed economically; also called *relatively developed countries*. Most are in the northern latitudes.

Parallel A circle drawn around the globe parallel to the equator and at right angles to the meridians.

Pattern The geometric or regular arrangement of something in a study area.

Polder Land created by the Dutch by draining water from an area.

Possibilism The theory that the physical environment may set limits on some human actions, but people have the ability to adjust to the physical environment and choose a course of action from many alternatives.

Prime meridian The meridian, designated as 0° longitude, that passes through the Royal Observatory at Greenwich, England.

Principal meridian A north-south line designated in the Land Ordinance of 1785 to facilitate the surveying and numbering of townships.

Projection The system used to transfer locations from Earth's surface to a flat map.

Region An area defined by one or more distinctive trends or features.

Relief The difference in elevation between two points; measures the extent to which an area is flat or hilly.

Relocation diffusion The spread of a feature or trend through bodily movement of people from one region to another.

Remote sensing The acquisition of data about Earth's surface from an orbiting satellite or other long-distance method.

Resource A substance that has value or usefulness.

Scale The relationship between the size of an object on a map and the actual size of the same feature on Earth's surface.

Section A square normally 1 mile long and 1 mile wide under the Land Ordinance of 1785; townships were normally divided into thirty-six sections.

Site The physical character of a location.

Situation The location of a place relative to other places.

Slope Relief divided by the distance between two points; measures the steepness of hills.

Soil The material that lies on Earth's surface between the air and rocks.

Space-time compression The reduction in the time it takes to diffuse something to a distant place.

Spatial association The distribution of one phenomenon across a landscape is scientifically related to the location of other phenomena.

Spatial distribution The regular arrangement of a phenomenon across Earth's surface.

Spatial interaction The movement of people, goods, and ideas within and among regions.

Stimulus diffusion The spread of an underlying principle, even though a specific characteristic is rejected.

Topographic maps Maps published (in the United States) by the U.S. Geological Survey that display a variety of physical features, such as relief and slope, as well as cultural features, such as buildings and roads.

Toponym The name given to a portion of Earth's surface.

Township A square normally 6 miles on a side. The Land Ordinance of 1785 divided much of the United States into a series of townships.

Uneven development The widening gap between more developed and less de-

veloped countries as a result of the globalization of the economy.

Vernacular region (or perceptual region) An area that people believe to exist as part of their cultural identity.

Thinking Geographically

1. Cartography is not simply a technical exercise in penmanship and coloring; nor are decisions confined to scale and projection. Mapping is a politically sensitive undertaking. Look at how maps in this book distinguish between the territories of Israel and its neighbors, the locations of borders in South Asia and the Arabian peninsula, the relationship of China and Taiwan, and the status of countries in Eastern Europe. Are there other logical ways to draw boundaries and distinguish among territories in these regions? What might they be?

2. Imagine that a transportation device (perhaps the one in *Star Trek*) would enable all humans to travel instantaneously to any location on Earth's surface. What impact would that invention have on the distribution of peoples and activities across Earth's surface?

3. When earthquakes, hurricanes, or other environmental disasters strike, humans tend to blame nature and see themselves as innocent victims of a harsh and cruel nature. To what extent do environmental hazards stem from unpredictable nature, and to what extent do they originate from human actions? Should victims blame nature, other humans, or themselves for the disaster? Why?

4. The construction of dams is a particularly prominent example of human-environment interaction in regions throughout the world. Turkey is building the Ataturk Dam on the Euphrates River, a move opposed by Syria and Iraq, the two downstream countries. Egypt, which operates the Aswan Dam on the Nile River, has blocked loans to Ethiopia that could be used to divert the source of the Nile. Some Russians oppose construction of the Gorskaya Dam in the Gulf of Finland near St. Petersburg. Similarly, the Balbina Dam on the Uatuma River, a tributary of the Amazon, has generated considerable opposition in Brazil. Why do some governments push the construction of dams so forcefully, and why do others oppose their construction so passionately?

5. Geographic concepts, such as the human-environment and regional studies traditions, are supposed to help explain contemporary issues. Are there any stories in your newspaper to which geographic concepts can be applied to help understand the issues? Discuss.

Further Readings

Andriot, John L., ed. *Township Atlas of the United States*. McLean, VA: Andriot Associates, 1979.

Bennett, John W. *The Ecological Transition: Cultural Anthropology and Human Adaptation*. Oxford: Pergamon Press, 1976.

Blaut, J. M. "Diffusionism: A Uniformitarian Critique." *Annals of the Association of American Geographers* 77 (March 1987): 48–62.

Bodman, Andrew R. "Weavers of Influence: The Structure of Contemporary Geographic Research." *Transactions of British Geographers New Series* 16 (1991): 21–37.

Brown, Lawrence A. *Innovation Diffusion: A New Perspective*. London: Methuen, 1981.

Brunn, Stanley D. "Sunbelt USA." *Focus 36* (Spring 1986): 34–35.

Carlson, Helen S. *Nevada Place Names: A Geographical Dictionary.* Reno: University of Nevada Press, 1974.

Claval, Paul. "The Region as a Geographical, Economic and Cultural Concept." *International Social Science Journal* 39 (May 1987): 159–72.

Cohen, Saul B., and Nurit Kliot. "Place Names in Israel's Ideological Struggle over the Administered Territories." *Annals of the Association of American Geographers* 82 (December 1992): 653–80.

Constandse, A. K. *Planning and Creation of an Environment.* Lelystad, The Netherlands: Rijksdienst voor de IJsselmeerpolders, 1976.

Eldridge, J. Douglas, and John Paul Jones III. "Warped Space: A Geography of Distance Decay." *Professional Geographer* 43 (November 1991): 500–11.

Entrikin, J. Nicholas, and Stanley D. Brunn, eds. *Reflections on Richard Hartshorne's "The Nature of Geography."* Washington, D.C.: Association of American Geographers, 1989.

Espenshade, Edward B., Jr., ed. *Goode's World Atlas.* 19th ed. Chicago: Rand McNally, 1995.

Forman, R. T. T., and M. Godron. *Landscape Ecology.* New York: John Wiley, 1986.

Freeman, Donald B. "The Importance of Being First: Preemption by Early Adopters of Farming Innovations in Kenya." *Annals of the Association of American Geographers* 75 (March 1985): 1–16.

Gaile, Gary L., and Cort J. Willmott, eds. *Geography in America.* New York: Merrill/Macmillan, 1989.

Gardner, Lytt I., Jr., et al. "Spatial Diffusion of the Human Immunodeficiency Virus Infection Epidemic in the United States, 1985–87." *Annals of the Association of American Geographers* 79 (March 1989): 25–43.

Goliber, Thomas J. "Sub-Saharan Africa: Population Pressures on Development World Population in Transition." Washington, D.C.: Population Reference Bureau. *Population Bulletin* 40, no. 1 (1985).

Gould, Peter R. *The Geographer at Work.* Boston: Routledge and Kegan Paul, 1985.

Gritzner, Charles F., Jr. "The Scope of Cultural Geography." *Journal of Geography* 65 (January 1966): 4–11.

Gross, Jonathan L., and Steve Rayner. *Measuring Culture.* New York: Columbia University Press, 1985.

Hägerstrand, Torsten. *Innovation Diffusion as a Spatial Process.* Chicago: University of Chicago Press, 1967.

Hamm, Bernd, and Martin Lutsch. "Sunbelt v. Frostbelt: A Case for Convergence Theory?" *International Social Science Journal* 39 (May 1987): 199–214.

Hartshorne, Richard. *The Nature of Geography.* Lancaster, PA: Association of American Geographers, 1939.

Jackson, John Brinckerhoff. *American Space.* New York: W. W. Norton, 1972.

James, Preston E. *All Possible Worlds: A History of Geographical Ideas.* New York: Bobbs-Merrill, 1972.

Janelle, Donald G., ed. *Geographical Snapshots of North America.* New York: Guilford, 1992.

Johnson, Hildegard B. *Order upon the Land.* New York: Oxford University Press, 1976.

Johnston, R. J. "A Place for Everything and Everything in Its Place." *Transactions of British Geographers New Series* 16 (1991): 131–47.

_____. *Philosophy and Human Geography.* 2d ed. London: Edward Arnold, 1986.

_____, ed. *The Dictionary of Human Geography.* 2d ed. Oxford: Basil Blackwell, 1985.

Kramer, A. *Hawaii, Ostmikronesien und Samoa.* Stuttgart: Strecker and Schroder, 1902.

Leighly, John, ed. *Land and Life: A Selection from the Writings of Carl Ortwin Sauer.* Berkeley: University of California Press, 1963.

Lewis, David. *Voyaging Stars.* New York: W. W. Norton, 1978.

Macgill, Sally M. "Environmental Questions and Human Geography." *International Social Science Journal* 38 (August 1986): 357–76.

Meinig, D. W., ed. *The Interpretation of Ordinary Landscapes.* New York: Oxford University Press, 1979.

Mikesell, Marvin W. "Tradition and Innovation in Cultural Geography." *Annals of the Association of American Geographers* 68 (March 1978): 1–16.

Monmonier, Mark. *How to Lie with Maps.* Chicago: University of Chicago Press, 1991.

Noronha, Valerian T., and Michael F. Goodchild. "Modeling Interregional Interaction: Implications for Defining Functional Regions." *Annals of the Association of American Geography* 82 (March 1992): 86–102.

Norton, William. *Explorations in the Understanding of Landscape: A Cultural Geography.* Westport, CT: Greenwood Press, 1989.

Peet, Richard. "The Social Origins of Environmental Determinism." *Annals of the Association of American Geographers* 75 (September 1985): 309–33.

Penning-Rowsell, Edmund C., and David Lowenthal, eds. *Landscape, Meanings and Values.* London: Allen and Unwin, 1986.

Reed, Michael, ed. *Discovering Past Landscapes.* London: Croom Helm, 1986.

Rice, Bradley R. "Searching for the Sunbelt." *American Demographics* 3 (March 1981): 22–23.

Rowntree, Lester B., and Margaret W. Conkey. "Symbolism and the Cultural Landscape." *Annals of the Association of American Geographers* 70 (December 1980): 459–74.

Salter, Christopher L. *The Cultural Landscape.* Belmont, CA: Duxbury Press, 1971.

_____. "What Can I Do with Geography?" *Professional Geographer* 35 (August 1983): 266–73.

Santos, Milton. "Geography in the Late Twentieth Century: New Roles for a Theoretical Discipline." *International Social Science Journal* 36 (November 1984): 657–72.

Sauer, Carl O. "Morphology of Landscape." University of California Publications in Geography 2 (1925): 19-54.

Sawers, Larry, and William K. Tabb, eds. *Sunbelt/Snowbelt: Urban Development and Regional Restructuring.* New York: Oxford University Press, 1984.

Shannon, Gary W., and Gerald F. Pyle. "The Origin and Diffusion of AIDS: A View from Medical Geography." *Annals of the Association of American Geographers* 79 (March 1989): 1–24.

Shannon, Gary W., and Rashid L. Bashshur. *The Geography of AIDS.* New York: Guilford Press, 1991.

Shortridge, James R. *The Middle West: Its Meaning in American Culture.* Lawrence: University of Kansas Press, 1989.

Solot, Michael. "Carl Sauer and Cultural Evolution." *Annals of the Association of American Geographers* 76 (December 1986): 508–20.

Tuan, Yi-Fu. "Cultural Pluralism and Technology." *Geographical Review* 79 (July 1989): 269–79.

Wagner, Philip L., and Marvin W. Mikesell, eds. *Readings in Cultural Geography.* Chicago: University of Chicago Press, 1962.

Also consult the following journals:

Annals of the Association of American Geographers, Area, The Canadian Geographer (Géographe Canadien), Focus, Geographical Analysis, Geographical Review, Geography, Journal of Geography, Professional Geographer, Progress in Human Geography, Transactions of the Institute of British Geographers.

The Annenberg
CPB Project

PEOPLE, PLACES AND CHANGE
Water is for Fighting Over

Cultural differences underlie conflicts over scarce environmental resources, such as water in the western United States.

Commentator	Pyramid Lake is the home of the Pyramid Lake Tribe, Paiute Indians known historically as the "fish-eaters," or "cui-ui eaters."
Mervin Wright, Jr. [member of Pyramid Lake Tribe]	The cui-ui itself is the foundation of our culture. That's the basis for what we believe in when we talk about our traditions, our customs.
Commentator	The tribe is seeking more water for Pyramid Lake and in particular for the cui-ui fish spawning runs.
Terry Hardesty [Reporter, KTVN-TV, Reno]	Fishing at Stampede Reservoir will never be the same, once 85 percent of the water is gone. The U.S. Fish and Wildlife Service decided it will need to take this water now at 170,000 acre-feet down to 20,000 acre-feet to save the endangered cui-ui fish at Pyramid Lake.
Commentator	The people of the nearby town of Truckee see the water in Stampede Reservoir as an essential resource that sustains this economy.
Kathleen Eagen [Mayor of Truckee, Nevada]	Almost every level of our economy relates in one way or another to the environment. Certainly, most directly recreation and tourism is a key element of our economy, and the health of our environment here relates strongly to the attractiveness of our region to people coming to visit.
Mervin Wright, Jr.	They don't really understand the importance of the environment, the resources that are here. I don't have sympathy for them for the fact that they are losing money. Money isn't everything.

2

POPULATION

KEY ISSUES

- How is the world's population distributed?
- How has the world's population increased?
- Why is population increasing at different rates in different countries?
- Does the world face an overpopulation problem?

How many brothers and sisters do you have? How many brothers and sisters did your parents or grandparents have? Did they have more, fewer, or the same number of siblings as yourself? How many children do you have, or intend to have? Is that figure larger, smaller, or the same number as your parents and grandparents had? In North America and Europe today, most people have fewer or the same number of siblings than their parents and grandparents had. And the average number of children current college–age people will have will probably be even fewer.

In other regions of the world, the number of children per household tends to be much higher than in the more developed countries (MDCs). The ability of less developed countries (LDCs) to provide food, clothing, and shelter for their people is severely hampered by the continued rapid growth of their populations.

A study of population is the basis for understanding a wide variety of issues in human geography. To study the challenge of increasing the food supply, reducing pollution, and encouraging economic growth, geographers must know the size and distribution of a region's population. Therefore, our study of the cultural landscape begins with a study of population.

RUSH HOUR, HO CHI MINH CITY, VIETNAM (PAUL CHESLEY/TONY STONE IMAGES)

Population Growth in India

The Phatak family lives in a village of 600 inhabitants in India. At age 40, Indira Phatak has been pregnant five times. Four of her children have survived; they are aged 5 to 18.

When the two Phatak daughters marry a few years from now, how many children will each of them bear? The Indian government hopes that they will choose to have fewer children than their mother. India's population is growing by more than 19 million people per year and is projected to exceed 1 billion in the year 1999. Unless attitudes and behavior drastically change in the next few years, India's population could exceed 2 billion a century from now.

Three-fourths of Indians live in rural settlements that have fewer than 5,000 inhabitants. For many of these people, children are an economic asset, because they help perform chores on the farm and are expected to provide for their parents in their old age. The high percentage of children who will die before they reach working age also encourages large families. Nearly one out of every ten infants in India dies within one year of birth.

In recent years, India has made significant progress in diffusing modern agricultural practices, building new industry, and developing natural resources, all of which have increased national wealth. In a country with a rapidly expanding population, however, much of the newly created wealth must be used to provide food, housing, and other basic services for the additional people. With more than one-third of the population under the age of 15, the government must build schools, hospitals, and day-care centers. Therefore, the growing wealth is going primarily to provide a reasonable standard of living for an expanding population. Further, will employment be available to these 350 million children when they are old enough to work?

The study of population is critically important for three reasons:

1. More people—nearly 6 billion—are alive at this time than at any point in Earth's long history.
2. The world's population has increased at a faster rate during the past 50 years (since the end of World War II) than ever before in history.
3. Virtually all global population growth is concentrated in the less developed countries.

Those facts lend urgency to the task of understanding the diversity of population problems in the world today.

The scientific study of population characteristics is **demography.** Demographers look statistically at how people are distributed spatially and by age, gender, occupation, fertility, health, and so on. Some demographers worry that the world may become overburdened with people in the future. Will the world's population exceed the capacity of Earth to support people? Will there be large-scale starvation, poverty, and revolution? Geographers who specialize in demography cannot offer a simple yes or no answer. Geography's focus on answering the where, why, and significance questions, however, helps to explain the global population problem and to suggest solutions.

Using the human-environment approach, geographers argue that the so-called **overpopulation** problem is not simply a matter of the total number of people in the world, but the relationship between the number of people and the availability of resources. Problems result when an area's population exceeds the capacity of the environment to support them at an acceptable standard of living.

Using the regional analysis approach, geographers find that overpopulation is a threat in some regions of the world but not in others. The capacity of Earth as a whole to support human life may be high, but some regions have a favorable balance between people and available resources; others do not. Further, the regions with the most people are not necessarily the same as the regions with an unfavorable balance between population and resources.

This chapter examines the distribution and growth of world population. Subsequent chapters look at the other side of the overpopulation equation—the availability of resources (energy, food, water, land, and material goods).

KEY ISSUE 1

How Is the World's Population Distributed?

- Population Concentrations
- Sparsely Populated Regions
- Density

Human beings are not distributed uniformly across Earth's surface. Specifically where we are, and why, and the significance of our distribution can be understood by examining two basic properties: concentration and density. Geographers identify regions of Earth where population is concentrated and regions where it is sparse. We also construct several density measures to help explain the relationship between the number of people and available resources.

Population Concentrations

Approximately three-fourths of the world's population live on only 5 percent of Earth's surface; the balance of Earth's surface consists of oceans (about 71 percent) and less intensively inhabited land.

The world's population is clustered in five regions: East Asia, South Asia, Western Europe, Southeast Asia, and Eastern North America (Figure 2-1). These five regions display some similarities. Most of their people live near an ocean or near a river with easy access to an ocean, rather than in the interior of major land masses. In fact, approximately two-thirds of the world's population lives within 500 kilometers (300 miles) of an ocean, and 80 percent lives within 800 kilometers (500 miles). The five population clusters occupy generally low-lying areas, with fertile soil and temperate climate. The regions all are located in the Northern Hemisphere between 10° and 55° north latitude, with the exception of part of the Southeast Asia concentration. Despite these similarities, we can see significant differences in the pattern of occupancy of the land in the five concentrations.

East Asia

Approximately one-fourth of the world's people live in East Asia, the largest cluster of inhabitants. The region, bordering the Pacific Ocean, includes eastern China, the islands of Japan, the Korean peninsula, and the island of Taiwan.

FIGURE 2-1 Population distribution. People are not distributed uniformly across Earth's surface. This map illustrates the use of both density and concentration to describe the regularities in the distribution of population.

In Chapter 1, we defined density as the frequency of occurrence of a phenomenon within a given unit of area. On this map, the phenomenon is people and the unit of area is square kilometers (or square miles). The density of population in much of Asia and Europe exceeds 50 persons per square kilometer (125 persons per square mile). In contrast, the density in most of the Western Hemisphere is fewer than 30 persons per square kilometer (75 persons per square mile).

Concentration is the extent of spread of a phenomenon, such as people, over a given area. More than three-fourths of the world's population is clustered in these five regions, listed according to number of people: (1) East Asia—eastern China, southern Korea, and Japan; (2) South Asia—India, Pakistan, and Bangladesh; (3) Europe—from southern United Kingdom to western Russia; (4) Southeast Asia— especially the island of Java, Indonesia; and (5), Eastern North America (northeastern United States and southeastern Canada).

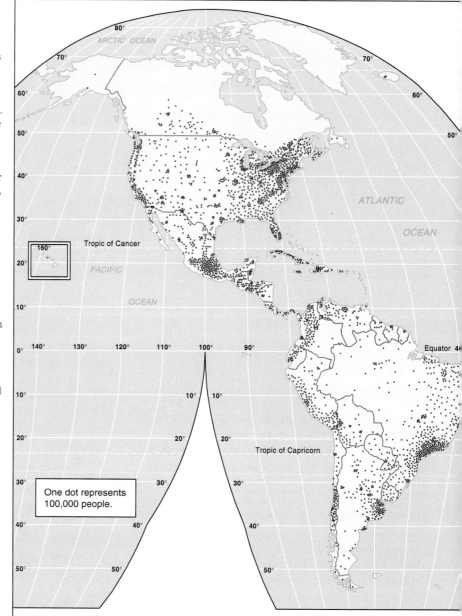

PERCENT OF WORLD POPULATION BY REGION

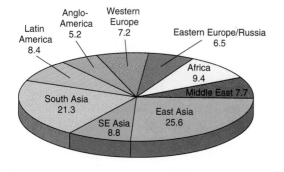

Five-sixths of the people in this concentration live in the People's Republic of China, the world's most populous country. China is the world's third largest country in land area, but much of its interior is sparsely inhabited mountains and deserts. The Chinese population is clustered near the Pacific coast and in several fertile river valleys that extend inland, such as the Huang and the Yangtze. Although China has eight cities with more than 2 million inhabitants, three-fourths of the people live in rural areas where they work as farmers.

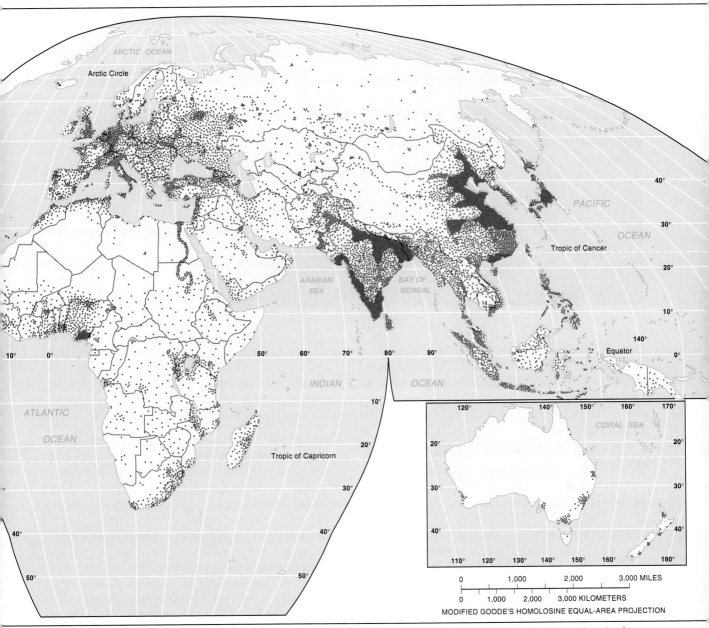

MODIFIED GOODE'S HOMOLOSINE EQUAL-AREA PROJECTION

In Japan, population is not distributed uniformly either. More than one-fourth of the people live in two large metropolitan areas—Tokyo and Osaka—that cover less than 3 percent of the country's land area. In sharp contrast to China, more than three-fourths of the Japanese live in urban areas and work at industrial or service jobs.

South Asia

The second largest concentration of people, more than 20 percent, is in South Asia, which includes India, Pakistan, Bangladesh, and the island of Sri Lanka. India, the world's second most populous country, contains more than three-fourths of the South Asia population concentration.

The most important concentration of people within South Asia lives along a 1,500-kilometer (900-mile) corridor from Lahore, Pakistan, through India and Bangladesh to the Bay of Bengal. Much of this area's population is concentrated along the plains of the Indus and Ganges rivers. Population is also heavily concentrated near India's two long coastlines—the Arabian Sea to the west and the Bay of Bengal to the east.

Women washing and collecting water at a river in India. Millions die in India each year from diseases such as diarrhea, carried by inadequately treated water. (Ken Heyman/Woodfin Camp & Associates)

Like the Chinese, most people in South Asia are farmers living in rural areas. The region contains ten cities with more than 2 million inhabitants, but only one-fourth of the total population lives in an urban area.

Southeast Asia

A third important Asian population cluster, and the world's fourth largest, is in Southeast Asia. Nearly 500 million people live in Southeast Asia, mostly on a series of islands that lie between the Indian and Pacific oceans. These islands include Java, Sumatra, Borneo, Papua New Guinea, and the Philippines. The largest concentration is on the island of Java, inhabited by more than 100 million people.

Indonesia, which consists of 13,677 islands, including Java, is the world's fourth most populous country. Several islands that belong to the Philippines contain high population concentrations, and population is also clustered along several river valleys and deltas at the southeastern tip of the Asian mainland, known as Indochina. Like that of East and South Asia, the Southeast Asia concentration is characterized by a high percentage of people working as farmers in rural areas.

The three Asian population concentrations together encompass more than half of the world's total population, but together they live on less than 10 percent of Earth's land area. The same held true 2,000 years ago, when approximately half of the world's population was found in these same regions.

Europe

Much of Europe, from the United Kingdom to western Russia forms the world's third largest population cluster, which approaches 14 percent of the world's people. The region includes more than two dozen countries, ranging from Monaco, with 1 square kilometer (0.7 square miles) and a population of 30,000, and San Marino, with 62 square kilometers (24 square miles) and a population of 20,000, to Russia, the world's largest country in land area when its Asian part is included.

In contrast with the three Asian concentrations, three-fourths of Europe's inhabitants live in cities, while less than 20 percent are farmers. A dense network of road and rail lines links settlements. The highest concentrations in Europe are near the coal fields of England, Germany, and Belgium, historically the major source of energy for industry.

Although the region's temperate climate permits cultivation of a variety of crops, Europeans do not produce enough food for themselves. Instead, they import food and other resources. The search for additional resources has been a major incentive for Europeans to explore and colonize other parts of the world during the past six centuries. Today, Europeans turn many of these imported resources into manufactured products.

Eastern North America

The largest population concentration in the Western Hemisphere is in the northeastern United States and southeastern Canada. This cluster extends along the Atlantic coast from Boston to Newport News, Virginia, and westward along the Great Lakes to Chicago. Approximately 150 million people live in the area. Like the Europeans, most Americans are urban dwellers; fewer than 5 percent are farmers.

Sparsely Populated Regions

Human beings avoid clustering in certain physical environments. Relatively few people live in regions that are too dry, too wet, too cold, or too mountainous for activities such as agriculture. But it is instructive to examine the reasons why people avoid those areas, for some of the factors can operate selectively to control population size in more populous areas.

Dry Lands

Areas too dry for farming cover approximately 20 percent of Earth's land surface. The two largest desert regions in the world lie in the Northern Hemisphere between 15° and 50° north latitude and in the Southern Hemisphere between 20° and 50° south latitude. The largest desert region, extending from North Africa to Southwest and Central Asia, is known by several names, including the Sahara, Arabian, Thar, Takla Makan, and Gobi deserts. A smaller desert region, in the Southern Hemisphere, comprises much of Australia. Earth's desert regions are shown on Figure 1–19. Regions where desert conditions are advancing appear in Figure 13-16.

Deserts generally lack sufficient water to grow crops that could feed a large population, although some people survive there by raising animals, such as camels, that are adapted to the climate. By constructing irrigation systems, people can grow crops in some parts of the desert. Although dry lands are generally inhospitable to intensive agriculture, they may contain natural resources useful to people—no-

tably, much of the world's oil reserves. The increasing demand for these resources has led to a growth in settlements in or near deserts.

Wet Lands

Lands that receive very high levels of precipitation may also be inhospitable for human occupation. These lands are located primarily near the equator between 20° north and south latitude in the interiors of South America, central Africa, and Southeast Asia. Rainfall averages more than 1.25 meters (50 inches) per year, with most areas receiving more than 2.25 meters (90 inches) per year. The combination of rain and heat rapidly depletes nutrients from the soil, thus hindering agriculture.

Precipitation may be concentrated into specific times of the year or spread throughout the year. In seasonally wet lands, such as those in Southeast Asia, enough food can be grown to support a large population (see the rice production map, Figure 9-4).

Cold Lands

Much of the land near the North and South poles is perpetually covered with ice, or the ground is permanently frozen (permafrost). The polar regions receive less precipitation than some Central Asian deserts, but over thousands of years the small annual snowfall has accumulated into thick ice. Consequently, the polar regions are unsuitable for planting crops, few animals can survive the extreme cold, and few human beings live there.

High Lands

Finally, relatively few people live at high elevations. The highest mountains in the world are steep, snow-covered, and sparsely settled. For example, approximately half of Switzerland's land is more than 1,000 meters (3,300 feet) above sea level, and only 5 percent of the country's people live there.

We can find some significant exceptions, especially in Latin America and Africa. People may prefer to occupy higher lands if temperatures and precipitation are uncomfortably high at lower elevations. In fact, Mexico City, one of the world's largest cities, is located at an elevation of 2,243 meters (7,360 feet).

Counting our Numbers

The most important source of knowledge about the growth and composition of a country's population is the **census.** A simultaneous global census has never been held, but individual countries generally undertake a census on a regular basis. In the course of counting inhabitants, governments normally require a member of every household to answer questions about the family and its dwelling. Important information includes when people were born, where they live and work, and with whom they live. In some countries, people must answer more detailed questions concerning the characteristics of the dwelling and the people living in it.

Obtaining an accurate census is critical in most countries because a portion of the national budget is turned over to localities in proportion to their population. Congressional and parliamentary districts are adjusted in many countries after a new census, to promote equal representation. Officials of large U.S. cities claim that their populations have been undercounted because they contain high concentrations of people who do not participate in the census. As a result, the cities may be receiving less funding and fewer state and federal representatives than they should.

Rulers counted their subjects to assess taxes and raise an army as far back as the fourth century B.C. in such places as present-day Korea and Pakistan. In general, though, we must estimate the past population of the world from fragmentary information, such as reports compiled in ancient Rome and China and parish church records of baptisms, marriages, and burials.

The first comprehensive, modern census of any country took place in Sweden in 1745. In the United States, Article 1, Section 2 of the Constitution requires that a census be taken every 10 years, beginning 3 years after the first meeting of Congress in 1787. In accordance with the Constitution, the U.S. census has been taken in every year ending in zero since 1790. People in many African and Asian territories were counted during the 1800s by their European colonial rulers. After gaining independence in the twentieth century, taking an accurate census has become a priority for many countries.

Canada, the United Kingdom, and other countries once ruled by the British take the census every 10 years, but in years ending in the numeral one rather than zero, as is done in the United States. The French average 7 years between censuses, but the government decrees exactly when each will be done.

Successfully counting a country's population frequently depends on the cleverness and resourcefulness of census takers. In some countries, census takers must communicate with people who live in isolated locations that lack modern services, such as electricity, telephones, and mail delivery. Surveyors in such countries as India must count millions of people who have no permanent address and live on sidewalks. Sometimes a census brings surprises: a census worker in Rio de Janeiro, Brazil, opened an icebox in a butcher shop and discovered that it provided access to a street unknown to officials, where people lived.

Securing a complete count of a country's population is difficult. To undertake a census in November 1991, the government of Nigeria ordered shops and factories to close and millions of people to remain at home for 3 days. The 1991 census was the first one completed in Nigeria since 1963, when Christians and animists living in the east and west of the country accused Muslims of inflating the totals in the north, where their followers were clustered. A census was begun in 1973, but the count was nullified after reports that some census takers had been beaten or kidnapped and others bribed to inflate figures. Different ethnic groups within Nigeria wanted higher census figures in order to increase their representation in the government and their share of public investment.

The accuracy of Nigeria's 1991 census has been questioned, because the total population—88.5 million—was 20 percent lower than estimates made by the World Bank, United Nations, and other organizations, an indication that the census takers missed many people. The value of the census was also reduced: to minimize controversy, it avoided questions about religion, language, and other critical cultural characteristics. By not asking those questions, the government of Nigeria was unable to document the extent of the country's cultural diversity.

Nigeria's situation displays a major difficulty in computing changes in global population over time. The Population Reference Bureau—one of the most authoritative sources of data about global population—reported Nigeria's population as 122.6 million in 1991 but only 90.1 million in 1992.

Many people do not participate in the census because they are unable to read the forms. Even in the United States, with its relatively high degree of literacy and few isolated communities, not everyone is counted. Many undocumented aliens fail to complete a census form because they fear that the government will discover and deport them. Other people simply ignore the census, even though noncompliance is illegal.

Despite the hazards and uncertainties, a person-by-person count is normally the most accurate method of obtaining precise information about a population. Unless we take a census periodically, our understanding of people is based on speculation or old data, rather than on current facts. The census is also a prominent symbol of the fact that most people do not live in complete isolation but must be counted as part of a global society.

One of India's 1.5 million census takers questions a family in a poor section of Delhi, as the government tries to find out how many people actually live in the country. (Reuters/Bettmann)

Density

The concept of density helps geographers measure the relationship between population and available resources. Density was defined in Chapter 1 as the frequency with which something exists in an area. We can compute density in several ways, including arithmetic density, physiological density, and agricultural density.

Arithmetic Density

Geographers most frequently use **arithmetic density,** which is the total number of people divided by total land area. (This measure also is called *population density*.) Geographers rely on the arithmetic density to compare conditions in different countries because the two pieces of information needed to calculate the measure—total population and total land area—are easy to obtain.

For example, to compute the arithmetic, or population, density for the United States, we can divide the population (approximately 262 million people) by the land area (approximately 9.2 million square kilometers or 3.5 million square miles). The result

shows that the United States has an arithmetic density of 29 persons per square kilometer (74 persons per square mile). By comparison, the arithmetic density is much higher in South Asia. In Bangladesh, it is approximately 900 persons per square kilometer (2,320 persons per square mile) and 307 (794) in India. On the other hand, the arithmetic density is only 3 persons per square kilometer (8 persons per square mile) in Canada and 2 (6) in Australia (Figure 2-2).

Arithmetic density varies even more within individual countries. In the United States, for example, New York County (Manhattan Island) has a population density of approximately 21,000 persons per square kilometer (53,000 persons per square mile), whereas Esmeralda County, Nevada, has a population density of approximately 0.15 person per square kilometer (0.38 per square mile). In Egypt, the arithmetic density is only 59 persons per square kilometer (153 persons per square mile) overall, but it is nearly 2,000 persons per square kilometer (5,000 persons per square mile) in the delta and valley of the Nile River.

Arithmetic density enables geographers to make approximate comparisons of the number of people

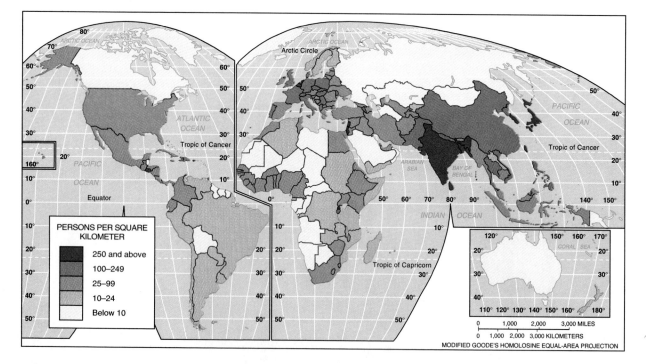

FIGURE 2-2 Arithmetic or population density is the total number of people divided by the total land area. The highest population densities are found in Asia, Europe, and Central America; the lowest are in North and South America and Australia.

trying to live on a given piece of land in different regions of the world. Thus, arithmetic density answers the "where" question. Other density measures are more useful, however, for explaining *why* people are not uniformly distributed across Earth's surface.

Physiological Density

A more meaningful population measure is afforded by looking at the number of people per area of a certain type of land in a region. Land suited for agriculture is called *arable land*. The number of people supported by a unit area of arable land in a region is called the **physiological density.** For example, in the United States, the physiological density is about 153 persons per square kilometer (396 per square mile); in Egypt it is about 1,967 persons per square kilometer (5,095 persons per square mile). This large difference in physiological densities demonstrates that crops grown on a hectare of land in Egypt must feed far more people than in the United States (Figure 2-3).

The higher the physiological density, the greater is the pressure that people place on the land to pro-

duce food. Physiological density provides insights into the relationship between the size of a population and the availability of resources in a region.

Comparing physiological and arithmetic densities helps geographers to understand the capacity of the land to yield enough food for the needs of its people. In Egypt, for example, the large difference between physiological density (1,967 people per square kilometer) and arithmetic density (59 persons per square kilometer over the entire country) indicates that most of the country's land area is unsuitable for intensive agriculture. In fact, all but 5 percent of the Egyptian people live in the Nile River valley and delta, because it is the only area in the country that receives enough moisture (by irrigation from the river) to allow intensive cultivation of crops (Table 2-1).

Agricultural Density

Two countries can have similar physiological densities, but they may produce significantly different amounts of food because of different economic conditions. **Agricultural density** is the ratio of the num-

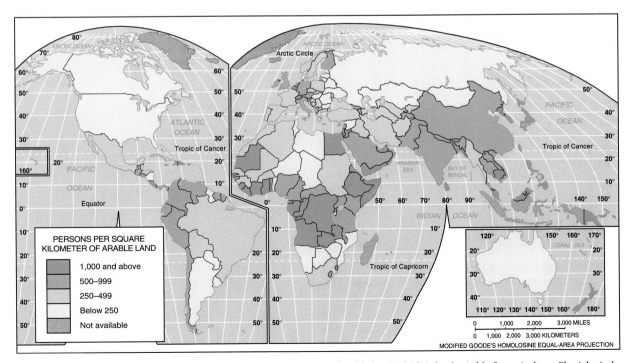

FIGURE 2-3 Physiological density is the number of people per unit area of arable land, which is land suitable for agriculture. Physiological density is a better measure than arithmetic density of the relationship between population and the availability of resources in a society.

ber of farmers to the amount of arable land. This density measure helps us account for economic differences. For example, the United States has an extremely low agricultural density (5 farmers per square kilometer of arable land), whereas Egypt has a very high density (708 farmers per square kilometer of arable land). MDCs have lower agricultural densities because technology and finance allow a few people to farm extensive land areas and feed many people. Consequently most of the MDC population work in factories, offices, or shops, rather than in the fields.

To understand the relationship between population and resources in a country, geographers examine its physiological and agricultural densities together. As Table 2-1 shows, the physiological densities of both Egypt and the Netherlands are high, but the Dutch have a much lower agricultural density than the Egyptians. Geographers conclude that both the Dutch and Egyptians put heavy pressure on the land to produce food, but the more efficient Dutch agricultural system requires many fewer farmers than the Egyptian system.

Similarly, the Netherlands has a higher physiological density than India, but a lower agricultural density. This difference demonstrates that, compared with India, the Dutch have extremely limited arable land to meet the needs of their population. (Recall from Chapter 1 how the Dutch have built dikes and created polders, areas of land made usable by draining water from them.) The highly efficient Dutch farmers can generate a large food supply from a limited resource.

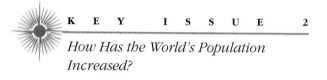

K E Y   I S S U E   2

How Has the World's Population Increased?

- Three Revolutions That Increased World Population
- Measuring How Population Changes

For most of human history, geographers estimate that Earth's population was virtually unchanged, at perhaps one-half million people. The species multiplied in some regions, declined in others, and remained sparse throughout the world. During this period, people lived as nomadic hunters and gatherers of food.

Cairo, Egypt. Population is not distributed within Egypt. Egyptians are highly clustered in the delta and valley of the Nile River, including Cairo. The remainder of the country consists of sparsely inhabited desert lands. (Dilip Mehta/Contact Press Images)

TABLE 2–1

Measures of density in selected countries, expressed as number of people per square kilometer

Country	Arithmetic Density	Physiological Density	Agricultural Density	Percent Farmers	Percent Arable
Bangladesh	900	1,636	933	57	55
Canada	3	61	2	4	5
Egypt	59	1,967	708	36	3
India	307	640	422	66	48
Japan	332	2,767	194	7	12
Netherlands	453	2,157	86	4	21
United Kingdom	242	896	18	2	27
United States	28	153	5	3	19

TABLE 2-2

World population and growth rates

Year	Estimated Number of People	Percent Average Yearly Growth in Prior Period	Number of Years in Which Population Doubles at Current Growth Rate
400,000 B.C.	500,000	—	—
8000 B.C.	5,000,000	0.001	59,007
A.D. 1	300,000,000	0.05	1,354
1750	791,000,000	0.06	1,250
1800	978,000,000	0.43	163
1850	1,262,000,000	0.51	136
1900	1,650,000,000	0.54	129
1950	2,517,000,000	0.85	82
1994	5,607,000,000	1.78	38

Three Revolutions That Increased World Population

The global rate of population growth sharply increased during three distinct periods: around 8000 B.C., A.D. 1750, and 1950. Each of these population spurts resulted from technological advances that gave people greater control over their physical and social environments. In turn, these technological improvements increased the capacity of Earth to support human population.

Agricultural Revolution (circa 8000 B.C.)

For several hundred thousand years before about 8000 B.C., global population had increased very modestly, at an average of only a couple of dozen people per year. Then, around the year 8000 B.C., the annual growth rate surged to fifty times higher than in the past, and world population grew by several thousand per year. Between 8000 B.C. and A.D. 1750, global population increased from approximately 5 million to almost 800 million (Table 2-2).

What caused the burst of population growth around 8000 B.C.? Scientists point to the **agricultur-**

al revolution, which is the time when human beings first domesticated plants and animals and no longer relied entirely on hunting and gathering. By growing plants and raising animals, human beings created larger and more predictable sources of food, so more people could survive.

The agricultural revolution involved a series of accidents and experiments over a period of several hundred years. Plant and animal domestication apparently originated independently in several hearths in Africa, Asia, and South America, but major advances in agriculture occurred in the Fertile Crescent, an area that extends from the eastern edge of the Mediterranean Sea to present-day Iran (see Chapter 9).

Industrial Revolution (circa A.D. 1750)

For nearly 10,000 years after the agricultural revolution, world population grew at a fairly steady pace. After around A.D. 1750, the world's population suddenly began to grow ten times faster than in the past. The average annual increase jumped from several thousand in the early eighteenth century to several hundred thousand in the late eighteenth century. Global population tripled from approximately 800 million in 1750 to 2.5 billion in 1950, an average annual increase of 0.6 percent per year.

This second spurt in the rate of population increase resulted from the **industrial revolution,** which began in England in the late eighteenth century and spread to the European continent and North America during the nineteenth century. The industrial revolution was a conjunction of major improvements in industrial technology (invention of the steam engine, mass production, powered transportation) that transformed the process of manufacturing goods and delivering them to market. The result of this transformation was an unprecedented level of wealth, some of which was used to make communities healthier places to live.

New machines helped farmers increase agricultural production and feed the rapidly growing population. More efficient agriculture freed people to work in factories, producing other goods and generating enough food for the industrial workers.

The wealth produced by the industrial revolution was also used to improve sanitation and personal hygiene. Sewer systems were installed in cities, and food and water supplies were protected against contamination. As a result of these public improvements, people were healthier and lived longer (see Chapter 10).

Medical Revolution (circa 1950)

The third dramatic increase in global population began in the late 1940s, after World War II. At this time, the population increase rate jumped from an average 0.5 percent early in the twentieth century to nearly 2 percent by the end of the twentieth century. Thus, instead of adding 8 million people per year, as was the case at the beginning of the twentieth century, the world has grown by more than 70 million per year since the late 1940s. During the 1990s, world population is increasing by about 90 million people per year.

This most recent population growth has been caused by the **medical revolution.** Medical technology invented in Europe and North America has diffused to the poorer countries of Latin America, Asia, and Africa. Improved medical practices suddenly eliminated many of the traditional causes of death in poorer countries and enabled more people to have longer and healthier lives. Penicillin, vaccines, and insecticides effectively and inexpensively controlled many infectious diseases, such as malaria, smallpox, and tuberculosis. Current mortality rates in Africa, Asia, and Latin America are 60 to 80 percent lower than they were in the late 1940s.

Measuring How Population Changes

Each birth and each death changes Earth's population. Put in demographic terms, the worldwide rate of population growth is controlled by *fertility* and *mortality*. In the case of individual countries, which "contain" people, a third factor operates—migration. The population of a country increases because of births and in-migration of people from elsewhere, and the population declines as a result of deaths and out-migration of people. In this section we look at fertility and mortality. Migration is discussed in detail in chapter 3.

Natural Increase

The rate of **natural increase** is the percentage by which a population grows in a year. It is computed by subtracting the crude death rate from the crude birth rate. The term *natural* means that a country's growth rate excludes migration. The word *crude* means that we are concerned with society as a whole, rather than a refined look at particular individuals or groups.

During the 1980s and 1990s, the world rate of natural increase has been 1.7, meaning that world population grows in one year by 1.7 percent. For many things in life, such as an examination grade, the difference between 1 percent and 2 percent may not be important. For population, however, the difference is critical.

The rate of natural increase affects the **doubling time,** which is the number of years needed to double a population, assuming a constant rate of natural increase. At the current rate of natural increase, 1.7 percent per year, world population will double in about 40 years. Should the natural increase rate decline to 1.0 percent, global population would double in approximately 70 years. People in the twenty-first century definitely would notice the difference between these two natural increase rates. The current rate would place global population in the year 2100 at approximately 35 billion, but if the natural increase rate during the next century declines to 1.0, the world's population would be less than 20 billion in 2100.

Very small changes in the natural increase rate dramatically affect the size of the population, because the base population from which we derive the percentage is so high. For example, when we mul-

tiply the natural increase rate of 1.7 percent by the current global population base of more than 5 billion, the result is an annual increase of more than 90 million people. If the natural increase rate immediately dropped to 1.0 percent, then the annual population increase would decline to approximately 55 million. As the base continues to grow in the twenty-first century, a change of only one-tenth of 1 percent would produce very large swings in population growth.

The distribution of natural increase rates shows very large regional differences (Figure 2-4). The natural increase rate exceeds 3.0 percent in much of Africa and southwestern Asia. At the other extreme, the United States, Canada, and Europe (except Albania, Iceland, and possibly Macedonia) have natural increase rates below 1.0 percent. Japan, Australia, and a handful of smaller countries also have natural increase rates below 1.0 percent. Several European countries even have negative rates of natural increase, meaning that in the absence of net in-migration, population actually is declining.

Not only is world population increasing faster than ever before, but virtually all the growth is concentrated in poorer countries. Over the past decade,

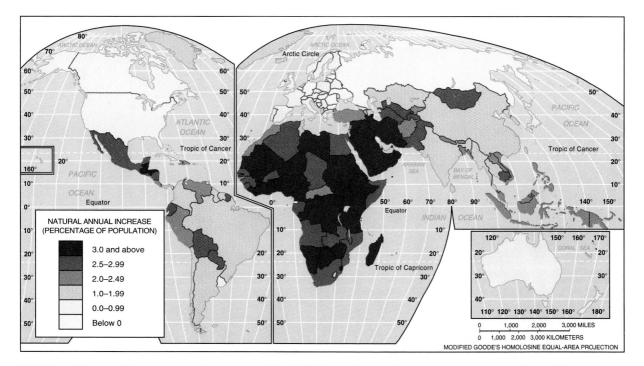

FIGURE 2-4 The natural increase rate is the percentage by which the population of a country grows in a year. The world average in recent years has been approximately 1.7 percent per year. The countries with the highest natural increase rates are concentrated in Africa and southwestern Asia.

approximately 66 percent of the world's population growth has been in Asia, 19 percent in Africa, and 9 percent in Latin America. The more developed countries of Europe and North America account for only 6 percent of global population growth. Regional differences in natural increase rates mean that virtually all the world's additional people live in the countries that are least able to maintain them. To explain these differences in growth rates, geographers point to regional differences in fertility and mortality rates.

Fertility

To study the number of births at the national or global scale, geographers most frequently refer to the **crude birth rate (CBR),** which is the total number of live births in a year for every 1,000 people alive in the society (Figure 2-5). A crude birth rate of 20 means that for every 1,000 people in a country, 20 babies are born over a one-year period. (Remember that *crude* in this context means we are concerned with society as a whole, rather than individuals or groups. In communities with an unusually large number of people of a certain age—such as a college town—we may study separate birth rates for women of each age. These numbers are *age-specific* rather than crude birth rates.)

Geographers also use the **total fertility rate (TFR)** to measure the number of births in a society. The total fertility rate is the average number of children a woman will have throughout her childbearing years (roughly ages 15 through 49). To compute the TFR, scientists must assume that, a woman reaches a particular age in the future will be just as likely to have a child as are women of that age today. Therefore, the crude birth rate provides a picture of a society as a whole in a given year, whereas the total fertility rate attempts to predict the future behavior of individual women in a world where customs are rapidly changing.

The world map of crude birth rates mirrors the distribution of natural increase rates (compare Figures 2-4 and 2-5). As was the case with natural increase rates, the highest crude birth rates are in Africa and the lowest are in Europe and North America. Most African countries have a crude birth rate over 40, and some exceed 50. Crude birth rates over 30 are common in Asia and Central America. On the other hand, the United States, Canada, and every European country except Albania have crude birth rates

In Iraq, where this family lives, the average woman gives birth seven times. (Reuters/Bettmann)

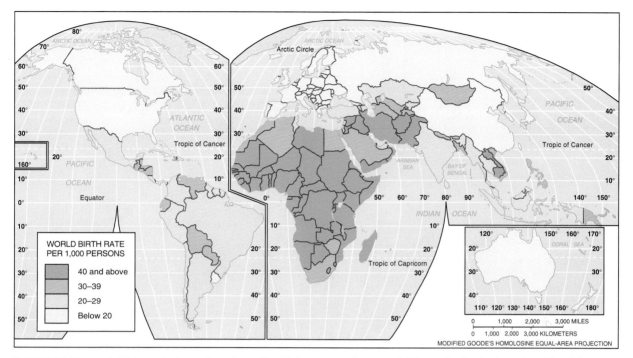

FIGURE 2-5 The crude birth rate is the total number of live births in a year for every 1,000 people alive in the society. The global distribution of crude birth rates parallels that of natural increase rates. Again, the highest crude birth rates are found in Africa and Southwest Asia, whereas the lowest are in Europe.

below 20. Japan, Australia, New Zealand, and a handful of smaller countries also have crude birth rates below 20.

Mortality

One useful measure of mortality is the **infant mortality rate (IMR),** which is the annual number of deaths of infants under 1 year of age, compared with total live births. The infant mortality rate is usually expressed as the number of deaths among infants per 1,000 births.

The global distribution of infant mortality rates follows the pattern that by now has become familiar. The highest rates are in the poorer countries of Africa and Asia; the lowest rates are in Europe, North America, and other wealthier societies. Infant mortality rates exceed 100 in many African and Asian countries, meaning that more than 10 percent of all babies die before reaching their first birthday. Infant mortality rates are less than 10 in most European countries, the United States, Canada, Japan, Australia, and New Zealand (Figure 2-6).

In general, the infant mortality rate reflects a country's health-care system. We find lower infant mortality rates in countries with well-trained doctors and nurses and large supplies of hospitals and medicine. Ironically, although the United States is well-endowed with medical facilities, it suffers from somewhat higher infant mortality rates than Canada and many European countries. African-Americans and other minorities in the United States have infant mortality rates that are twice as high as the national average. Some health experts attribute this difference to the fact that many poor people in the United States, especially minorities, cannot afford good health care for their infants.

Life expectancy at birth measures the average number of years a newborn infant can be expected to live at current mortality levels. Like the rates for infant mortality, crude birth, and natural increase, life expectancy varies sharply among regions. Babies born today can be expected to live into their early fifties if they are African and into their late seventies if they are European or North American (Figure 2-7).

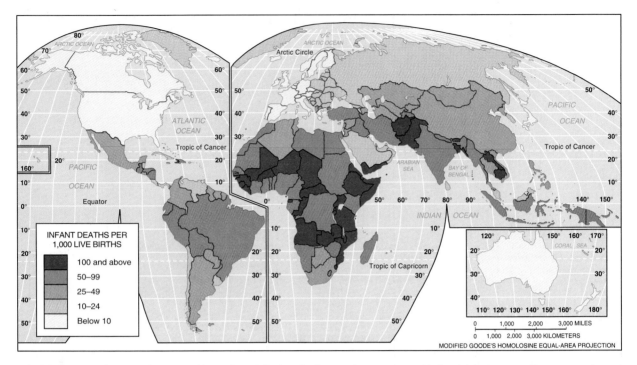

FIGURE 2-6 The infant mortality rate is the number of deaths of infants under age 1 per 1,000 live births in a year. European and North American countries generally have infant mortality rates of under 10 per 1,000, whereas rates of more than 100 per 1,000 are common in Africa.

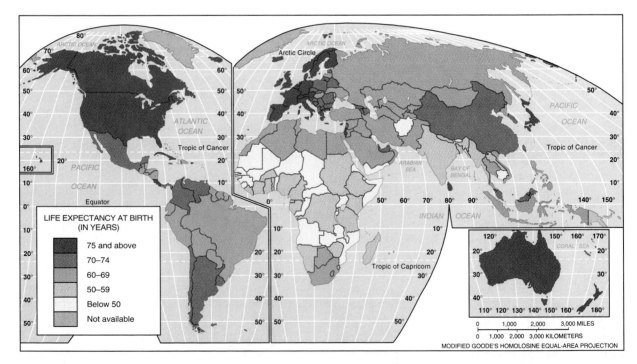

FIGURE 2-7 Life expectancy at birth. Babies born this year are expected to live on average until their mid-sixties. Life expectancy for babies, however, ranges from the low forties in several African countries to the late seventies in much of Europe, Australia, North America, and Japan.

The **crude death rate (CDR)** compares the total number of deaths with the total number of people living in a country in one year. Comparable to the crude birth rate, the crude death rate is expressed as the annual number of deaths per 1,000 population. Geographers also compute specific death rates for different age groups or for males and females.

The global distribution of crude death rates does not follow the pattern of other mortality and fertility variables. Consistent with the other demographic characteristics, the highest crude death rates are in Africa. But, perhaps unexpectedly, the lowest crude death rates are in Latin America and Asia, rather than in the wealthy countries of North America and Europe (Figure 2-8).

Furthermore, the spread among different countries between the highest and lowest crude death rates is relatively low. Crude *birth* rates for individual countries range from about 10 to 50, a spread of more than 40. However, the highest crude *death* rate is only in the low 20s, and the difference between the highest and lowest rates is around 20.

Why does Sweden, one of the world's wealthiest countries, have a higher crude death rate than the Philippines, one of the poorest? The United States, with its extensive system of hospitals and physicians, has a higher crude death rate than Belize, Costa Rica, or Panama. Why? The answer is that the populations of different countries are at various stages in an important process known as the *demographic transition,* upon which we focus in the next section.

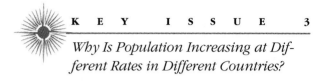

K E Y   I S S U E   3

Why Is Population Increasing at Different Rates in Different Countries?

- The Demographic Transition
- Population Pyramids
- Countries in Different Stages of Demographic Transition
- Demographic Transition and World Population Growth

Over time, every country has experienced changes in its natural increase, fertility, and mortality rates. These demographic changes have followed

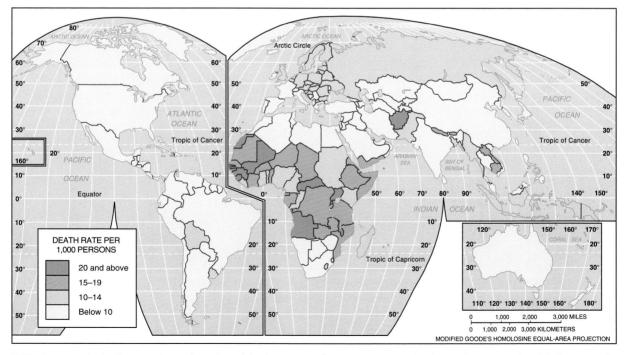

FIGURE 2-8 Crude death rate is the total number of deaths in a year for every 1,000 people alive in the society. The global pattern of crude death rates varies from those for the other demographic variables already mapped in this chapter. First, although Europe has the lowest natural increase, crude birth, and infant mortality rates, it has relatively high crude death rates. Second, the variance between the highest and lowest crude death rates is much lower than was the case for the crude birth rates. The concept of the demographic transition helps to explain the distinctive distribution of crude death rates.

similar patterns in different countries, but they have not happened at the same time or at the same rate in every country. The difference is explained by the several stages through which countries evolve.

The Demographic Transition

The process of change in a society's population is called the **demographic transition.** It is a process with several stages, and every country is in one of them. The process has a beginning, middle, and end, and—barring a catastrophe such as a nuclear war—it is irreversible. Once a country moves from one stage of the process to the next, it does not revert to an earlier stage. The four stages are shown in Figure 2-9.

Stage 1: Low Growth

In stage 1 of the demographic transition, crude birth and death rates are both generally high. These rates may vary considerably from one year to the next, but over the long term they are roughly comparable. As a result, the natural increase rate is very low.

Survival is unpredictable in a stage 1 society. The population may depend on hunting and gathering for food. When food is easily obtained, the population increases, but it declines in times of shortage. People who practice settled farming prosper during abundant harvests and suffer when unfavorable climatic conditions result in low output. Wars and diseases also take their toll in a stage 1 society.

Most of human history was spent in stage 1 of the demographic transition, but there is no stage 1 country today. Every country has moved on to at least stage 2 of the demographic transition and with that transition has experienced profound changes.

Stage 2: High Growth

In stage 2 of the demographic transition, the crude death rate suddenly plummets, but the crude birth rate remains roughly the same as in stage 1. Because the difference between the crude birth rate and crude death rate is very high, the natural increase rate is also very high, and population grows rapidly.

Some demographers divide stage 2 of the demographic transition into two parts. The first part is the period of accelerating population growth. During the second part the growth rate begins to slow, although the gap between births and deaths remains high.

Countries in Europe and North America entered stage 2 of the demographic transition in the late eighteenth or nineteenth century. The stage 2 transition has come in the twentieth century for countries in Africa, Asia, and Latin America. New technology, which permits increases in the permanent food supply and control of diseases, accounts for the rapid decline in the crude death rate.

Stage 3: Moderate Growth

A country moves from stage 2 to stage 3 of the demographic transition when the crude birth rate begins to drop sharply. The crude death rate continues

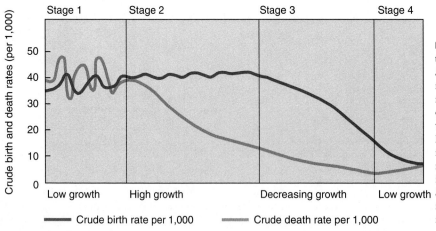

FIGURE 2-9 The demographic transition consists of four stages: *Stage 1*—very high birth and death rates produce virtually no long-term natural increase. *Stage 2*—rapidly declining death rates combined with very high birth rates produce very high natural increase. *Stage 3*—birth rates rapidly decline, while death rates continue to decline; natural increase rates begin to moderate. *Stage 4*—very low birth and death rates produce virtually no long-term natural increase.

to fall in stage 3 but at a much slower rate than in stage 2. Consequently, the population continues to grow because the crude birth rate is still greater than the crude death rate. The rate of natural increase is more modest in stage 3 countries than in stage 2, however, because the gap between the crude birth and death rates narrows.

European and North American countries generally moved from stage 2 to stage 3 of the demographic transition during the first half of the twentieth century. Some countries in Africa, Asia, and Latin America have moved to stage 3 in recent years, but others remain in stage 2.

The sudden drop in the crude birth rate during stage 3 occurs for different reasons than the rapid decline of the crude death rate during stage 2. The crude death rate declines in stage 2 following introduction of new technology into the society, but the crude birth rate declines in stage 3 because of changes in social customs.

A society enters stage 3 of the demographic transition when people choose to have fewer children. The decision is partly a delayed reaction to a decline in mortality, especially the infant mortality rate. In stage 1 societies, the survival of any one infant could not be confidently predicted, and families typically had a large number of babies to improve the chances of some surviving to adulthood. Medical practices introduced in stage 2 societies greatly improved the probability of an infant's surviving, but many years elapsed before families reacted by conceiving fewer babies.

Economic changes in stage 3 societies also induce people to have fewer babies. People in stage 3 societies are more likely to live in cities rather than the countryside and to work in offices, shops, or factories rather than on farms. Farmers often consider a large family to be an asset because children can do some of the chores. In contrast, children living in cities are generally not economic assets to their parents, because they are prohibited from working in most types of urban jobs. In addition, urban homes are relatively small and may not have space to accommodate large families.

Stage 4: Low Growth

A country reaches stage 4 of the demographic transition when the crude birth rate declines to the point where it equals the crude death rate, and the natural increase rate approaches 0. This condition is called **zero population growth (ZPG),** a term often applied to stage 4 countries.

Zero population growth may occur when the crude birth rate is still slightly higher than the crude death rate, because some females die before reaching childbearing years, and the number of females in their childbearing years can vary. To account for these discrepancies, demographers frequently express zero population growth as the total fertility rate that results in a lack of change in the total population over a long term. At this time, a TFR of approximately 2.1 produces ZPG. A country experiencing a high level of net in-migration, however, may need a lower total fertility rate to achieve ZPG.

Several countries in Western and Northern Europe have reached stage 4 of the demographic transition, including Sweden, Germany, and the United Kingdom. The United States has not completely moved into stage 4 because birth rates remain higher among some groups, such as recent immigrants from Latin America. In several European countries, including Denmark, Germany, and Hungary, the crude birth rate slips below the crude death rate in some years. But the total population has not declined (at least not in Denmark and Germany) because people have been immigrating from other countries.

Social customs again explain the movement from one stage of the demographic transition to the next. Increasingly, women in stage 4 societies enter the labor force rather than remain at home as full-time homemakers. When most families lived on farms, employment and child rearing were conducted at the same place, but in urban societies most parents must leave the home to work in an office, shop, or factory. An employed parent must arrange for someone to take care of preschool children during working hours.

Changes in lifestyle also encourage smaller families. People who have access to a wider variety of birth-control methods are more likely to use some of them. With increased income and leisure time, more people participate in entertainment and recreation activities that may not be suitable for young children, such as attending cultural events, traveling overseas, going to bars, and eating at upscale restaurants.

A country that has passed through all four stages of the demographic transition has in some ways completed a cycle—from little or no natural increase in stage 1, to little or no natural increase in stage 4. Two crucial demographic differences underlie this process, however. First, at the beginning of the demographic transition, the crude birth and death rates are high—35 to 40 per 1,000—while at the end of the process the rates are very low, approximately 10 per

1,000. Second, the total population of the country is much higher in stage 4 than in stage 1.

The Demographic Transition in England

England provides a good case study of the long-term impact of the demographic transition, for several reasons. England has reached stage 4, and at least fragmentary information on its population is available for the past 1,000 years. Further, unlike the United States and many other countries, England has not changed its boundaries, nor has it been affected by migration of enough people to affect national trends.

Stage 1: Low Growth until 1750. In 1066, when the Normans invaded England, the country's population was approximately 1 million. Seven hundred years later, the population was only 6 million, and the country was still in stage 1 of the demographic transition (Figure 2-10).

During that 700-year period, population rose in some years and fell in others. Crude birth and death rates averaged more than 35 per 1,000 but varied considerably from one year to the next. For example,

England's population declined from 4 million in the year 1250 to 2 million a century later, after the Black Death (bubonic plague) and famines swept the country. As recently as the 1740s, the crude death rate skyrocketed following a series of bad harvests.

Stage 2: High Growth (1750–1880). In 1750, the crude birth and death rates in England were both 40 per 1,000. In 1800, the crude birth rate remained very high at 34, but the crude death rate had plummeted to 20. This 50-year period marked the start of the industrial revolution in England. New production techniques increased the nation's food supply and generated money that was spent on improvements in public health.

England remained in stage 2 of the demographic transition for about 125 years. During that period the population rose from 6 million to 30 million, an average annual natural increase rate of 1.4.

Stage 3: Moderate Growth (1880–early 1970s). Crude birth and death rates changed little in England during most of the nineteenth century. In 1880 the crude birth rate was 33 per 1,000 and the

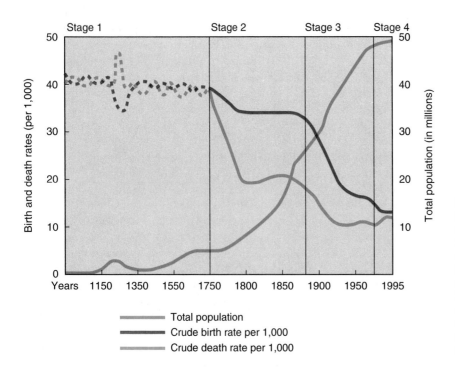

FIGURE 2-10 Demographic transition for England. Demographers must estimate birth and death rates before 1750, because precise records are not available. Church parish records of births, baptisms, marriages, and burials help in making estimates. England entered stage 2 of the demographic transition in the mid-eighteenth century, stage 3 in the late nineteenth century, and stage 4 in the mid-twentieth century.

crude death rate 19, in both cases only 1 per 1,000 lower than in 1800. After 1880, England entered stage 3 of the demographic transition. The crude death rate continued to fall somewhat over the next century, from 19 per 1,000 in 1880 to 12 in 1970. However, the crude birth rate declined sharply, from 33 per 1,000 in 1880 to 18 by 1930 and 15 in 1970. The population increased between 1880 and 1970 from 26 to 49 million, about 0.7 percent per year.

Stage 4: Low Growth (early 1970s–present). Since the early 1970s, England has been in stage 4 of the demographic transition. The population has increased only 1 million since 1970, an average natural increase rate of 0.1. The crude death rate has consistently rested at 12 per 1,000 since the 1970s, while the crude birth rate has varied between 12 and 14. The crude birth rate increases slightly in some years because the number of women in their childbearing years is greater, not because women decide to have more children.

When England began to progress through the demographic transition around 1750, the country had 6 million people, crude birth and death rates of 40 per 1,000, and a record of little population growth over the previous 700 years. England has recently entered another period of little population growth. The difference is that the crude birth and death rates are now around 12 rather than 40, and the country has 50 million inhabitants instead of 6 million.

Population Pyramids

As you might expect, the stage of demographic transition in which a country exists gives it a distinctive population structure. A country's population varies in two ways: the percentage of the population in each age group and the distribution of males and females.

We can display the distribution of a country's population by age and gender groups on a bar graph called a **population pyramid.** A population pyramid normally shows the percentage of the total population in 5-year age groups, with the youngest group (0 to 4 years old) at the base of the pyramid and the oldest group at the top. The length of the bar represents the percentage of the total population contained in that group. By convention, males are usually shown on the left side of the pyramid and females on the right (Figure 2-11).

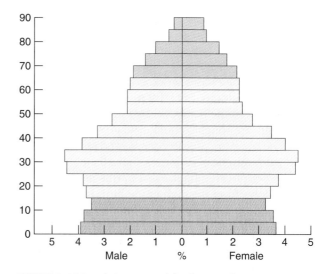

FIGURE 2-11 Population pyramid for the United States, 1992. The length of the bar shows the percentage of males and females in each 5-year age group. People under age 15 and over age 65 are considered dependents. The graph is not precisely in the shape of a pyramid. The indentation at the base shows that the crude birth rate has declined sharply in the United States since the mid-1960s, when the people in their thirties were born.

The shape of a pyramid is determined primarily by the crude birth rate in the country. A country with a high crude birth rate has a larger number of young children than of elderly people, making the base of the population pyramid very broad. On the other hand, if the country has a relatively large number of older people, the top of the pyramid is wider, and the graph looks more like a rectangle than a pyramid.

Age Distribution

The age structure of a population is extremely important in understanding similarities and differences among different countries in the world. The most important factor is the **dependency ratio,** which is the number of people who are too young or too old to work, compared with the number of people in their productive years. The larger the percentage of dependents, the greater is the financial burden on those who are working to support those who cannot.

To compare the dependency ratios of different countries, we can divide the population into three age groups: 0 to 14, 15 to 64, and 65 and older. People who are 0–14 and 65-plus normally are classified as dependents. Approximately one-half of all people living in countries in stage 2 of the demographic transition are dependents, compared with only one-third in stage 4 countries. Consequently, the dependency ratio is nearly 1:1 in stage 2 countries, whereas in stage 4 countries the ratio is 1:2 (1 dependent for every 2 workers). Young dependents outnumber elderly ones by ten to one in stage 2 countries, but the numbers of young and elderly dependents are roughly equal in stage 4 countries.

In nearly every African country, and in many Asian and Latin American countries, more than 40 percent of the people are under age 15. This high percentage follows from the high crude birth rates in these regions. In contrast, in European and North American countries, which are at or near stage 4 of the demographic transition, the percentage of children under 15 is only around 20 percent (Figure 2-12).

In Africa, Asia, and Latin America, the large percentage of children strains the ability of poorer countries to provide needed services, such as schools, hospitals, and day-care centers. When children reach the age of leaving school, jobs must be found for them, but the government must continue to allocate scarce resources to meeting the needs of the still-growing number of young people.

As countries pass through the stages of the demographic transition, the percentage of elderly people increases. The higher percentage partly reflects the lower percentage of young people produced by declining crude birth rates. Older people also benefit in stage 4 countries from improved medical care and higher incomes. People over age 65 exceed 15 percent of the population in several European countries, such as Denmark, Sweden, the United Kingdom, and Germany, compared with less than 5 percent in most African countries. In some cities in Florida, more than one-third of the people are over age 65. The graph of population by age and sex resembles an upside-down pyramid (Figure 2-13).

Older people must receive adequate levels of income and medical care after they retire from their jobs. The "graying" of the population places a burden on European and North American governments

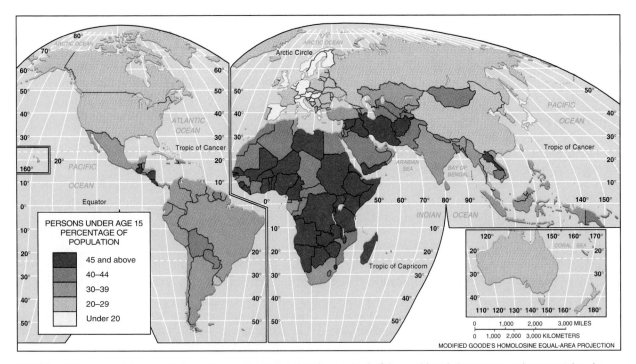

FIGURE 2-12 Percent of the population under age 15. Approximately one-third of the world's inhabitants are under age 15, but the percentage varies from over 40 percent in most African countries to less than 20 percent in many European countries. A map of the percentage of people over age 65 would show a reverse pattern, with the highest percentages in Europe and the lowest in Africa.

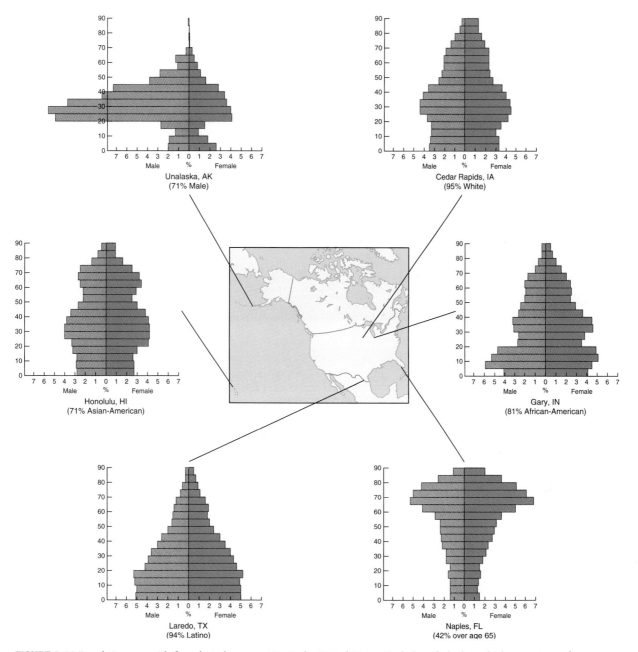

FIGURE 2-13 Population pyramids for selected communities in the United States. Unalaska, Alaska has a high percentage of young males in military service. In contrast, Naples, Florida, has a high percentage of older females, who have retired there. African-Americans in Gary, Indiana, and Latinos in Laredo, Texas, have high percentages of young people.

to meet these needs. More than one-fourth of all government expenditures in the United States, Canada, Japan, and many European countries go to social security, health care, and other programs for the older

population. Because of the larger percentage of older people, countries in stage 3 or 4 of the demographic transition, such as the United States and Sweden, have higher crude death rates than stage 2 countries.

In countries in stage 4 of the demographic transition, care for older people takes up an increasing share of national wealth. These elderly women are receiving care at the Geriatric Department of Charles Richet Hospital, near Paris, France. (J. Pavlovsky/Sygma)

Sex Ratio

The number of males per hundred females in the population is the **sex ratio.** It varies among countries, depending on birth and death rates. In general, slightly more males than females are born, but males have higher death rates. In Europe and North America, the ratio of men to women is about 95:100 (that is, 95 men for each 100 women). In the rest of the world, the ratio is 102:100.

In the United States, males under 15 exceed females 105:100. Women start outnumbering men at about age 30 and constitute 60 percent of the population over age 65. In poorer countries, high mortality rates during childbirth partly explain the lower percentage of women. The difference also is related to the age structure, because poorer countries have a larger percentage of young people—where males generally outnumber females—and a lower percentage of older people—where females are much more numerous.

Societies with a high rate of immigration typically have more males than females because males are more likely to undertake long-distance migration. Frontier areas and boom towns typically have more men than women. For example, 71 percent of the population is male in the town of Unalaska, in Alaska's Aleutian Islands (Figure 2-13). On the other hand, Naples, Florida, a retirement community is 60 percent female, because women have longer life expectancies than men.

Countries in Different Stages of Demographic Transition

Countries display distinctive population characteristics depending on their stage in the demographic transition. No country today remains in stage 1 of the demographic transition, but it is instructive to compare countries in each of the other three stages. Let us look at three case studies of countries in stages 2, 3, and 4.

Cape Verde: Stage 2 (High Growth)

When the world's countries were in stage 1, they experienced wide fluctuations in the crude birth and death rates from one year to the next, depending on economic and environmental conditions. Cape Verde, a collection of twelve small islands in the Atlantic Ocean off the coast of West Africa, moved from stage 1 to stage 2 nearly fifty years ago. As a Portuguese colony, Cape Verde kept unusually good demographic records when it was still in stage 1. (Cape Verde attained independence in 1975.)

During most years, the crude birth rate in Cape Verde ranged between 40 and 45 per 1,000; the crude death rate was generally between 20 and 30.

Although the population increased in most years, Cape Verde remained in stage 1 of the demographic transition until the late 1940s. Between 1900 and 1949 its population actually declined, from 147,000 to 137,000. Although births exceeded deaths in most years, the country was hit several times by severe famines that dramatically disrupted the typical pattern. Famine made the crude death rate rocket to 74 per 1,000 in 1941 and 101 in 1942. Because fewer babies were conceived at the height of the famine in 1942, the crude birth rate fell in 1943, to only 22. Population also declined during periods of famine because survivors migrated to other countries.

This long-term pattern of demographic uncertainty suddenly ended in the late 1940s, when an anti-malarial campaign was launched. The crude death rate dropped by more than one-third between 1949 and 1950, from 27 to 17 per 1,000. It further declined during the 1950s and 1960s to around 10 per 1,000. Since the 1970s, the crude death rate has remained just under 10 for most years, although a drought in 1971 and a famine in 1986 temporarily lifted the rate above 10 (Figure 2-14).

Meanwhile, the crude birth rate increased in the early 1950s to a maximum of 53 per 1,000 in 1954. The crude birth rate declined during the 1960s and dipped below 30 in the early 1980s; a major contributing factor was the smaller number of women in childbearing years, as a result of the low birth rates during the 1940s. The crude birth rate, however, has increased since the

mid-1980s, and during the 1990s has averaged nearly 40 again, the highest level since the 1960s.

Since Cape Verde entered stage 2 of the demographic transition around 1950, its population has nearly tripled, to approximately 400,000. Natural increase has averaged nearly 3.0 percent per year since 1950. Recent increases in the natural increase and crude birth rates show that Cape Verde remains in stage 2 of the demographic transition.

Chile: Stage 3 (Moderate Growth)

Chile provides an example of a country outside Europe and North America that has reached stage 3 of the demographic transition but is likely to take some time before continuing to stage 4. Chile has changed from a predominantly rural society based on agriculture to an urban society, in which most people now work in factories, offices, and shops. Many Chileans, however, still prefer to have large families.

Like most countries outside Europe and North America, Chile entered the twentieth century still in stage 1 of the demographic transition. Population had grown modestly during the nineteenth century, at a natural increase rate of less than 1 percent per year. But much of Chile's population growth—as in other countries in the Western Hemisphere—resulted from European immigration.

Chile's crude death rate declined sharply in the 1930s, moving the country into stage 2 of the demographic transition. As in other Latin American

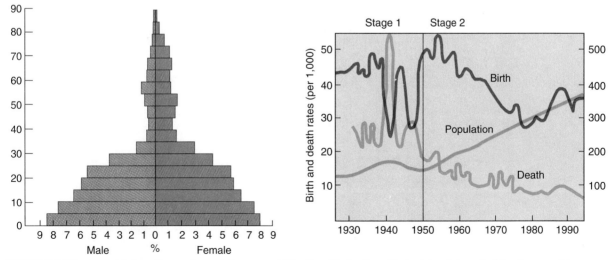

FIGURE 2-14 Demographic transition and population pyramid for Cape Verde. Cape Verde entered stage 2 of the demographic transition in approximately 1950, as indicated by the large gap between birth rates (in red) and death rates since then. As is typical of countries in stage 2 of the demographic transition, Cape Verde has a population pyramid with a very wide base.

countries, Chile's crude death rate was lowered by the infusion of medical technology from MDCs such as the United States, bringing under control such diseases as smallpox, malaria, and dysentery. During the 1940s and 1950s, Chile's rate of natural increase exceeded 2 percent per year, and the crude death rate dropped from the mid-30s to less than 15 (Figure 2-15).

Chile has been in stage 3 of the demographic transition since about 1960. The crude death rate declined further during the 1960s and 1970s to less than 10, while the crude birth rate dropped sharply, from around 35 in the early 1960s to around 20 by the late 1970s. However, Chile has failed to make further progress over the past 15 years in reducing the gap between births and deaths. The natural increase rate has remained around 1.5 percent per year since the 1960s.

Chile moved into stage 3 of the demographic transition primarily because of a vigorous government family-planning policy, initiated in 1966. Reduced income and high unemployment at that time also induced couples to postpone marriage and delay childbearing.

Although Chile's natural increase rate is lower today than in the 1950s, the country is unlikely to move into stage 4 of the demographic transition in the near future. By 1979, Chile's government reversed its policy and renounced support for family planning. The government policy was that population growth could help promote national security

and economic development. Further reduction in the crude birth rate is also hindered by the fact that most Chileans belong to the Roman Catholic church, which opposes the use of what it calls artificial birth control techniques.

Denmark: Stage 4 (Low Growth)

Denmark, like several other northern and western European countries, has reached stage 4 of the demographic transition. Denmark's history is similar to that of England's. The country entered stage 2 of the demographic transition in the nineteenth century, when the crude death rate began its permanent decline. The crude birth rate then dropped in the late nineteenth century, and the country moved into stage 3 (Figure 2-16).

Since the 1970s, the crude birth and the crude death rates have been roughly equal, about 12 per 1,000. The country has reached zero population growth, and the population is unlikely to increase from the current level of just over 5 million.

Denmark's population pyramid shows the impact of the demographic transition. Instead of a classic pyramid shape, Denmark has a column, demonstrating that the percentages of young and elderly people are nearly the same. With further medical advances, the number of elderly people may actually exceed the number of young people in a few years. Denmark's crude death rate has actually increased somewhat in recent years because of the increasing

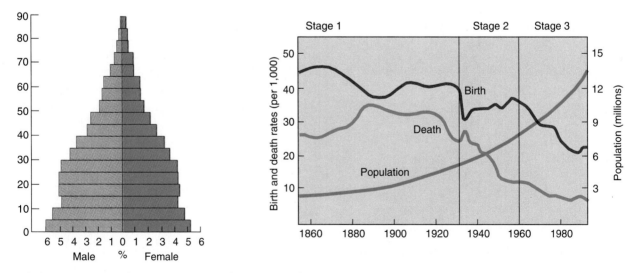

FIGURE 2-15 Demographic transition and population pyramid for Chile. Chile entered stage 2 of the demographic transition in the 1930s, when death rates (in blue) declined sharply, and stage 3 in the 1960s, when birth rates declined sharply. Since the mid-1980s, however, birth rates have no longer declined, and Chile's natural increase rate has remained over 1.5.

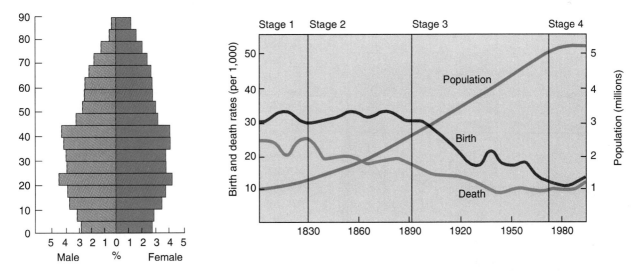

FIGURE 2-16 Demographic transition and population pyramid for Denmark. Denmark has been in stage 4 of the demographic transition and has experienced virtually no change in total population since the 1970s. The population pyramid is much straighter than those of Cape Verde and Chile, a reflection of the relatively large percentage of elderly people and small percentage of children.

number of elderly people. The CDR is unlikely to decline unless another medical revolution, such as a cure for cancer, keeps older elderly people alive much longer.

Demographic Transition and World Population Growth

Having used case studies to see the patterns of the demographic transition in individual countries, we now are ready to take the global view. Why is worldwide population increasing rapidly today? Because few countries are in the two stages of the demographic transition that have low population growth—no country remains in stage 1, and few have reached stage 4. The overwhelming majority of countries are in either stage 2 or stage 3 of the demographic transition—stages with rapid population growth—and only a few are likely to reach stage 4 in the near future.

The four-stage demographic transition is characterized by two big breaks with the past. The first break—the sudden drop in the death rate that comes from technological innovation—has been accomplished everywhere. The second break—the sudden drop in the birth rate that comes from changing social customs—has yet to be achieved in many countries. If most countries in Europe and North America

have reached—or at least are approaching—stage 4 of the demographic transition, why aren't countries elsewhere in the world? The answer is that fundamental problems prevent other countries from replicating the experience in Europe and North America.

The first demographic change—the sudden decline in crude death rate—occurred for different reasons in the past. The nineteenth-century decline in the crude death rate in Europe and North America took place in conjunction with the industrial revolution. The unprecedented level of wealth generated by the industrial revolution was used in part to stimulate research by European and North American scientists into the causes and cures for diseases. These studies ultimately led to medical advances, such as pasteurization, X-rays, penicillin, and insecticides.

In contrast, the sudden drop in the crude death rate in Africa, Asia, and Latin America in the twentieth century was accomplished by different means, and with less internal effort by local citizens. For example, the crude death rate on the island of Sri Lanka (then known as Ceylon) plummeted 43 percent between 1946 and 1947. The most important reason for the sharp drop was the use of the insecticide DDT to control the mosquitoes that spread malaria.

European and North American countries invented and manufactured the DDT and trained the experts to supervise its use. The spraying of Sri Lankans' houses and other medical services, which cost only

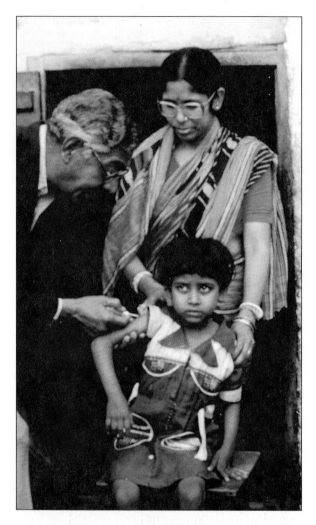

Inoculations reduce the crude death rates in less developed countries and move the countries into stage 2 of the demographic transition. (Steve Maines/Stock Bostson)

$2 per person per year, were paid for primarily by international organizations.

Thus, Sri Lanka's crude death rate was reduced by nearly one-half in a single year with no change in the country's economy or social system. Medical technology was injected from Europe and North America instead of arising within the country as part of an economic revolution. This pattern has been repeated in dozens of countries in Africa, Asia, and Latin America.

Having caused the first break with the past through diffusion of medical technology, European and North American countries now urge other countries to complete the second break with the past by reducing the birth rate. But reducing the crude birth rate is difficult. A decline in the crude death rate can be induced through introduction of new technology by outsiders, but the crude birth rate will drop only when people decide for themselves to have fewer children.

Many people in Africa, Asia, and Latin America may be unprepared for this second break with the past, plus they are being urged to move through the demographic transition rapidly. In Europe and North America, stage 2 of the demographic transition lasted for approximately 100 years. During that time, global population increased by about 1 billion. If stage 2 of the demographic transition in Africa, Asia, and Latin America also lasts for 100 years—from around 1950 to 2050—15 billion people will be added to the world during that time.

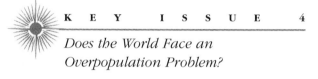

K E Y I S S U E 4

Does the World Face an Overpopulation Problem?

- Malthus on Overpopulation
- Debate Over How to Reduce Natural Increase

In view of the current size of Earth's population, and the natural increase rate, will there soon be too many of us? Will continued population growth lead to global starvation, war, and lower quality of life?

Malthus on Overpopulation

English economist Thomas Malthus (1766–1834) was one of the first to argue that the world's rate of population increase was far outrunning the development of food supplies. Malthus's views remain influential today.

Population Growth versus Food Supply

In *An Essay on the Principle of Population,* published in 1798, Malthus claimed that population was growing much more rapidly than Earth's food supply, because population increased geometrically, while food supply increased arithmetically. According to Malthus, these growth rates would produce the following relationships between people and food in the future:

Today:	1 person,	1 unit of food
25 years from now:	2 persons,	2 units of food
50 years from now:	4 persons,	3 units of food
75 years from now:	8 persons,	4 units of food
100 years from now:	16 persons,	5 units of food

Malthus wrote during the second era of global population increase, which had begun around 1750 in association with the industrial revolution. He concluded that population growth would press against available resources in every country, unless "moral restraint" produced lower crude birth rates or unless disease, famine, war, or other disasters produced higher crude death rates.

Malthus's Critics. Malthus's theory has been severely criticized from a variety of perspectives. The Marxist theorist Friedrich Engels dismissed Malthus's arithmetic as an artifact of capitalism. Engels argued that the world possessed sufficient resources to eliminate global hunger and poverty, if only those resources were shared equally. Under capitalism, workers may not have enough food because they did not control the production and distribution of food and were not paid sufficient wages to purchase it.

Contemporary analysts such as economist Julian Simon criticize Malthus's theory that population growth produces problems. To the contrary, a larger population could stimulate economic growth and as a result production of more food. Population growth could generate more customers and more good ideas for improving technology.

Conditions during the past half-century—when the human population has grown at its most rapid rate ever—have not supported Malthus's theory. According to geographer Vaclav Smil, since 1950, world food production has consistently grown faster than the natural increase rate (Figure 2-17). Better growing techniques, higher-yielding seeds, and cultivation of more land have all contributed to the rapid expansion in food supply (see Chapter 13). Many people in the world cannot afford to buy food or do not have access to sources of food, but these are problems of distribution of wealth, rather than insufficient global production of food as Malthus theorized.

Despite the widespread criticism, contemporary geographers and other analysts are taking another look at Malthus's theories, because of the unprecedented rate of natural increase in less developed countries. In Malthus's time, only a few wealthy

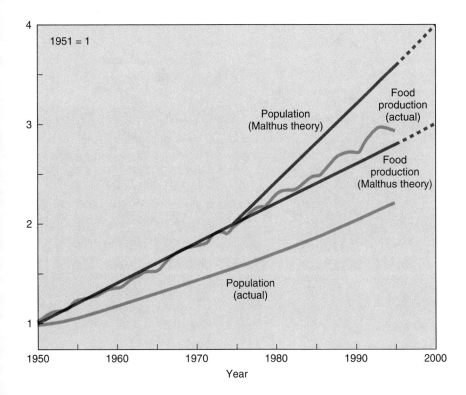

FIGURE 2-17 Malthus's theory compared to actual world food production and population 1951-1992. Malthus expected population to grow more rapidly than food production. In reality, during the second half of the twentieth century—when world population grew at its most rapid rate ever—food production actually expanded even more rapidly. (Source: United Nations Food and Agricultural Organization)

countries had entered stage 2 of the demographic transition, characterized by rapid population increase. Malthus did not foresee critical social, economic, and technological changes that would induce wealthy societies to move into stages 3 and 4 of the demographic transition. He also failed to anticipate that poorer countries would have the most rapid population growth, because of transfer of medical technology (but not wealth) from MDCs.

Neo-Malthusians. Contemporary analysts such as Robert Kaplan and Thomas Fraser Homer-Dixon have broadened Malthus's theory to encompass a wide variety of resources, rather than only food. They paint a frightening picture of a world in which billions of people are engaged in a desperate search for food and fuel. According to their "neo-Malthusian" argument, wars and civil violence will increase in the coming years because of scarcities of food, clean air, suitable farmland, and fuel.

Many LDCs have expanded food production significantly, but they also have more poor people than ever before. For example, income in East African countries rose during the past decade by approximately 2 percent per year above inflation, but the population grew by approximately 3 percent per year. Because population growth outpaced economic development, all the economic growth was absorbed simply in accommodating the additional population. Despite this economic growth, the average East African is worse off today than a decade ago.

Many geographers consider these pessimistic forecasts to be unrealistic, because they are based on a belief that the world's resources are fixed, rather than expanding. According to the principles of possibilism discussed in Chapter 1, our well-being is influenced by conditions in the physical environment, but humans have some ability to choose courses of action that can expand the supply of food and other resources.

Geographers also recognize the diversity of conditions among regions of the world. The world as a whole may not be in danger of "running out" of food, but some regions with rapid population growth do indeed face food shortages.

Debate Over How to Reduce Natural Increase

Only two approaches can reduce the current natural increase rate: increase the crude death rate or decrease the crude birth rate. Experts sharply disagree on the best solution to reduce the natural increase rate.

Increased Death Rate

Increasing the crude death rate is dismaying, but we must explore it. An increase in the crude death rate could halt the growth of the human population. For example, if the population increases faster than the expansion of the food supply, widespread famine could result. Some argue that sending food to starving Africans is well-intentioned but a mistake, because a higher death rate now may prevent even greater mass starvation in the future. Other causes could drastically cut the population; millions could die in wars—especially nuclear—or from a natural disaster, such as a major earthquake.

The crude death rate may also rise from the spread of disease. One-third of all deaths among children in LDCs (other than China) are from diarrhea that results from poor sanitation and resulting infections. Another one-third of child deaths result from six infectious diseases: polio, measles, diphtheria, tetanus, whooping cough, and tuberculosis. These diseases have been virtually eliminated in MDCs through immunization and improved nutrition and hygiene. But only a minority of children in less developed countries have been immunized against these diseases, and water supplies remain unsafe in many places. Even where programs have been implemented to fight these preventable diseases, they have not always been successful because of a lack of qualified medical staff.

The diffusion of AIDS (acquired immunodeficiency syndrome) in both MDCs and LDCs could produce a rise in the crude death rate. The distribution of AIDS within the United States was discussed in Chapter 1 (see Figure 1-14). Although information on the incidence of AIDS in Africa is not as easy to obtain, AIDS may be more extensive there than in MDCs, and its diffusion across that continent has not been stopped.

Birth Control

Few people wish to see population growth curbed through an increase in the death rate. The only demographic alternative is to reduce the birth rate. Analysts and public health officials debate over the best means to achieve lower birth rates.

One approach to lowering birth rates emphasizes improved education for women. According to this approach, if more women attend school, and remain

Overpopulation in Mali. A region can be sparsely inhabited yet overpopulated if it has rapid population growth and limited resources, as is the case in Mali. (Steve McCurry/Magnum Photos, Inc.)

in school longer, they are more likely to learn employment skills, as well as the advantages of alternative methods of birth control. Improved education for women is an important element of a long-term process by which a society develops (see Chapter 8).

The other approach to lowering birth rates emphasizes the importance of rapidly diffusing contraceptives. Bangladesh is an example of a country that has seen little improvement in the wealth and literacy of its people, but the percentage using contraceptives rose from 3 percent to 40 percent during the 1970s and 1980s. Similar increased use of contraceptives has occurred in other less developed countries, including Colombia, Morocco, and Thailand. Rapid acceptance of family planning is evidence of how rapidly ideas can diffuse in the modern world.

Regardless of which alternative is most successful, many people oppose birth control for religious and political reasons. Adherents of several religions, including Roman Catholics, fundamentalist Protestants, Muslims, and Hindus, have religious convictions that

A health center in Ethiopia distributes free birth control pills (Marta Sentis/Photo Researchers, Inc.)

prevent them from using some or all birth control devices. Opposition is strong within the United States to terminating pregnancy by abortion, and the U.S. government has at times withheld aid to countries and family-planning organizations that advise abortion, even when such advice is only a small part of the overall program.

The percentage of women using contraceptives is especially low in Africa. A United Nations report found that only 12 percent of African women were employing contraceptive devices in the late 1980s, compared with 55 percent in Latin America and over 70 percent in Asia. The reason is partly economic, religious, and educational. Very high birth rates in Africa and southwestern Asia reflect the relatively low status of women. In societies where women receive less formal education and hold fewer legal rights than men, women regard having a large number of children as a measure of status, and men regard it as a sign of virility.

The track toward overpopulation already may be irreversible in Africa. Rapid population growth has led to the overuse of land. As the land declines in quality, more effort is needed to yield the same amount of crops. This situation extends the working day of women, who have the primary responsibility for growing food for their families. Women then regard having another child as a means of securing additional help in growing food.

Summary

Overpopulation—too many people for the available resources—has already hit regions of Africa and threatens other countries in Asia and Central and South America. The world as a whole does not face overpopulation immediately, but current trends must be reversed to prevent a future crisis.

Geographers caution that the number of people living in a region is not by itself an indication of overpopulation. Some densely populated regions are not overpopulated; some sparsely inhabited areas are. Instead, overpopulation is a relationship between the size of the population and a region's level of resources. The capacity of the land to support life derives partly from characteristics of the natural environment and partly from human actions to modify the environment through agriculture, industry, and exploitation of raw materials.

We cannot completely explain the overpopulation problem until we see how people in different regions earn a living and modify the environment. But we can reach some conclusions by briefly reviewing the key issues discussed in this chapter.

1. How is the world's population distributed?

Global population is concentrated in a few places. Human beings tend to avoid those parts of Earth's surface that they consider to be too wet, too dry, too cold, or too mountainous. The capacity of Earth to support a much larger population depends heavily on people's ability to use sparsely settled lands more effectively.

2. **How has the world's population increased?**

The natural increase rate of the world's population rose dramatically during three periods in history: the agricultural revolution around 8000 B.C., the industrial revolution around A.D. 1750, and the medical revolution around 1950. On each occasion significant changes in technology enabled more people to survive. Today, virtually all the world's population increase is concentrated in the poorer countries of Africa, Asia, and Latin America. Many of these countries lack the resources to meet the needs of their rapidly growing populations. In contrast, most European and North American countries now have low population growth rates, and some are experiencing population declines.

3. **Why is population increasing at different rates in different countries?**

The demographic transition is a change in a country's population. A country moves through four stages—from a condition of high birth and death rates, with little population growth, to a condition of low birth and death rates, with low population growth. During this process, the total population increases enormously, because the death rate declines some years before the birth rate does. The MDCs of Europe and North America have reached or neared the end of the demographic transition. African, Asian, and Latin American countries are at the stages of the demographic transition characterized by rapid population growth, in which death rates have declined sharply, but birth rates remain relatively high.

4. **Does the world face an overpopulation problem?**

The rate at which global population has grown in the last three decades is unprecedented in history. A dramatic decline in the death rate has produced the increase. With death rates controlled, for the first time in history the most critical factor determining the size of the world's population is the birth rate. Scientists agree that the current rate of natural increase must be reduced, but they disagree on the appropriate methods for achieving that goal.

CASE STUDY REVISITED
India versus China

The world's two most populous countries, China and India, will heavily influence future prospects for global overpopulation. These two countries—together encompassing more than one-third of the world's population—have adopted different policies to control population growth. In the absence of strong family-planning programs, India adds about 2 million more people each year than China. At current rates of natural increase, India will surpass China as the world's most populous country by the middle of the twenty-first century.

India's Population Policies

India, like most countries in Africa, Asia, and Latin America, remained in stage 1 of the demographic transition until the late 1940s. During the first half of the twentieth century, population increased modestly—less than 1 percent per year—and even decreased in some years because of malaria, famines, plagues, and cholera epidemics. For example, more than 16 million Indians—approximately 5 percent of the population—died of influenza in 1918 and 1919, and the population at the 1921 census was lower than that ten years earlier.

Immediately following independence from England in 1947, India's death rate declined sharply, to 20 per 1,000 by 1951, while the crude birth rate remained about 40. Consequently, the natural increase rate jumped to 2 percent per year. The demographic pattern has not changed much in India during the past 40 years. Birth and death rates have both drifted a few points lower since the 1950s, but the natural increase has consistently remained around 2 percent per year. In the half-century since independence, India's population has grown by more than one-half billion.

The government of India has launched various programs to encourage family planning, but none have been very successful. In 1952, India became the first country to embark on a national family-planning program. The government has established clinics and distributes information about alternative methods of birth control. Birth control devices are distributed free or at subsidized prices. Abortions, legalized in 1972, have been performed at a rate of several million per year. Altogether, the government spends several hundred million dollars per year on various family-planning programs.

India's most controversial family-planning program was the establishment of camps in 1971 to perform sterilizations, surgical procedures by which people were made incapable of reproduction. A sterilized person was entitled to a payment, which has been adjusted several times but generally has been equivalent to the average monthly income in India. At the height of the program, in 1976, 8.3 million sterilizations were performed during a 6-month period, mostly on women.

The birth control drive has declined in India since 1976. Widespread opposition to the sterilization program grew in the country, because people feared that they would be forcibly sterilized. The prime minister, Indira Gandhi, was defeated in 1977, and the new government emphasized the voluntary nature of birth control programs. The term *family planning,* which the Indian people associated with the forced sterilization policy, was replaced by *family welfare* to indicate that compulsory birth control programs had been terminated. Although Gandhi served again as prime minister from 1980 until she was assassinated in 1984, she did not emphasize family planning because of the opposition during her previous administration.

A government-sponsored family-planning program continues, but it emphasizes education, including advertisements on national radio and television networks and information distributed through local health centers. Given the cultural diversity of the Indian people, the national campaign has had only limited success. The dominant form of birth control continues to be sterilization of women, many of whom have already borne several children, rather than vasectomies of men. Effective methods have not been devised to induce recently married couples to have fewer children.

China's Population Policies

In contrast with India, China has made substantial progress in reducing its rate of natural increase. Growth declined from approximately 2.0 percent per year in the 1950s to 1.2 percent during the mid-1980s.

The government of the People's Republic of China has acted forcefully to reduce the number of children. The core of the government's policy is to limit families to one child. Couples receive financial subsidies, a long maternity leave, better housing, and (in rural areas) more land if they agree to have just one child. The government prohibits marriage for men until they are 22 and women until they are 20. To discourage births further, the government provides free contraceptives, abortions, and sterilizations. A family with more

The government of China aggressively promotes a one-child policy on public billboards. (Mark Avery/AP/Wide World Photos)

than one child must pay a fine, amounting to 5 or 10 percent of its income for 10 years, and job promotions may be denied. Some officials in rural villages maintain records of women's menstrual cycles to assure that no unplanned babies are born.

But China's crude birth rate has increased somewhat since the mid-1980s. The increase has resulted partly from looser enforcement of the "one-child" rule, especially in rural villages, where families may receive permission to have a second child. Recent changes in China's government have reduced national control over remote rural areas, particularly those inhabited by restive ethnic minorities.

Another factor is female infanticide. If limited to one child, most Chinese families prefer to have a boy, in part because of cultural tradition and in part because a boy is regarded as stronger and better able to take care of aging parents. The one-child policy encouraged the killing of baby girls. In American culture, such a practice is abhorrent, but one of geography's great lessons is that societies have very different values. Because of international criticism, the Chinese government has relaxed enforcement of the one-child rule.

The crude birth rate is also rising in China because of greater wealth. The average Chinese family increasingly can afford the fine for the opportunity of having a second child. Although small changes in the crude birth rate may not be significant in other countries, in China an increase of 0.1 percent translates into 1 million additional babies per year. To bring the crude birth rate below 20 again, the Chinese government has enforced its strict rules more vigorously.

Despite recent increases, China is likely to maintain a much lower natural increase rate than India into the twenty-first century. After years of intensive educational programs, as well as coercion, the Chinese people have accepted to a greater degree than the Indian people the benefits of family planning. As China moves closer to a market economy, especially in rural areas, women increasingly recognize that having fewer children opens greater opportunities to obtain a job and earn more money.

Should the current world rate of natural increase continue for several decades, global population would far exceed even the most optimistic estimates of world food and energy capacities. In another thousand years, there would be less than 1 square foot of land per person in the world, including deserts, mountains, and ice caps.

These projections are not intended as *predictions*. They are offered to illustrate the significance of current growth rates and to demonstrate the need to modify current trends. The challenge is to lower the current rate of population growth before the negative consequences of a large population pose insoluble social and economic problems.

Key Terms

Agricultural density The ratio of the number of farmers to the total amount of land suitable for agriculture.

Agricultural revolution The time when humans first domesticated plants and animals and no longer relied entirely on hunting and gathering. See Chapter 9.

Arithmetic density The total number of people divided by the total land area. Also called *population density.*

Crude birth rate (CBR) The total number of live births in a year for every 1,000 people alive in the society.

Crude death rate (CDR) The total number of deaths in a year for every 1,000 people alive in the society.

Demographic transition The process of change in a society's population from a condition of high crude birth and death rates and low rate of natural increase to a condition of low crude birth and death rates, low rate of natural increase, and a higher total population.

Demography The scientific study of population characteristics.

Dependency ratio The number of people under the age of 15 and over age 64 compared with the number of people active in the labor force.

Doubling time The number of years needed to double a population, assuming a constant rate of natural increase.

Industrial revolution A series of improvements in industrial technology that transformed the process of manufacturing goods starting in the late eighteenth century. See Chapter 10.

Infant mortality rate (IMR) The total number of deaths in a year among infants under 1 year old for every 1,000 live births in a society.

Life expectancy The average number of years an individual can be expected to live, given current social, economic, and medical conditions. Life expectancy at birth is the average number of years a newborn infant can be expected to live.

Medical revolution Diffusion of medical technology invented in Europe and North America to the poorer countries of Latin America, Asia, and Africa. Improved medical practices have eliminated many of the traditional causes of death in poorer countries and enabled more people to live longer and healthier lives.

Natural increase The percentage growth of a population in a year, computed as the crude birth rate minus the crude death rate.

Overpopulation The number of people in an area exceeds the capacity of the environment to support life at a decent standard of living.

Physiological density The number of people per unit of area of arable land, which is land suitable for agriculture.

Population pyramid A bar graph representing the distribution of population by age and sex.

Sex ratio The number of males per 100 females in the population.

Total fertility rate (TFR) The average number of children a woman will have throughout her childbearing years.

Zero population growth (ZPG) The total fertility rate declines to the point where the natural increase rate equals 0.

Thinking Geographically

1. The current method of counting a country's population by requiring every household to complete a census form once every 10 years has been severely criticized as inaccurate. The census allegedly fails to count people who cannot read the form or who do not wish to be found. This undercounting produces a geographic bias, because people who are missed are likely to live in inner cities, remote rural areas, or communities that attract a relatively high number of recent immigrants. Given the availability of reliable statistical tests, should the current method of trying to count 100 percent of the population be replaced by a survey of a carefully drawn sample of the population, as is done with political polling and consumer preferences? Why or why not?

2. Scientists disagree about the effects of high density on human behavior. Some laboratory tests have shown that rats display evidence of increased aggressiveness, competition, and violence when very large numbers of them are placed in a box. Is there any evidence that very high density causes humans to behave especially aggressively or violently? Discuss.

3. Paul and Anne Ehrlich argued in *The Population Explosion* (1990) that a baby born in an MDC such as the United States poses a graver threat to global overpopulation than a baby born in an LDC. The reason is that people in MDCs place much higher demands on the world's supply of energy, food, and other limited resources. Do you agree with this view? Why?

4. The baby-boom generation—people born between 1946 and 1964—totals nearly one-third of the U.S. population. (They are the bulge in the U.S. population pyramid, Figure 2-11.) Baby boomers have received more education than their parents, and women are more likely to enter the labor force. They have delayed marriage and parenthood and have fewer children than their parents. They are more likely to divorce, to bear children while unmarried, and to cohabit. As they grow older, what impact will baby boomers have on the U.S. population in the twenty-first century?

5. What policies should governments in MDCs pursue to reduce global population growth? If an MDC provides funds and advice to promote family planning in LDCs, does it gain the right to tell the developing countries how to spend the funds and how to use the expertise? Explain your answer.

Further Readings

Ashford, Lori S. "New Perspectives on Population: Lessons from Cairo." *Population Bulletin* 50 (1). Washington, DC: Population Reference Bureau, 1995.

Beaujeu-Garnier, Jacqueline. *Geography of Population,* 2d ed. London: Longman, 1978.

Bennett, D. Gordon. *World Population Problems: An Introduction to Population Geography.* Champaign, IL: Park Press, 1984.

Bouvier, Leon F., and Carol J. DeVita. "The Baby Boom—Entering Midlife." *Population Bulletin* 46 (3). Washington, DC: Population Reference Bureau, 1991.

Brown, Lester R., and Jodi L. Jacobson. "Our Demographically Divided World." *Worldwatch Paper* 74. Washington, DC: Worldwatch Institute, December 1986.

Carr-Saunders, A. B. *World Population: Past Growth and Present Trends.* New York: Oxford University Press, 1936.

Clarke, John I. *Population Geography,* 2d ed. Oxford and New York: Pergamon Press, 1972.

_____. *Geography and Population: Approaches and Applications.* New York: Pergamon Press, 1984.

Coleman, David, and Roger Schofield, eds. *The State of Population Theory: Forward from Malthus.* New York: Basil Blackwell, 1986.

Demko, George, George Schnell, and Harold Rose. *Population Geography: A Reader.* New York: McGraw-Hill, 1970.

Donaldson, Peter J., and Amy Ong Tsui. "The International Family Planning Movement." *Population Bulletin* 45 (3). Washington, DC: Population Reference Bureau, 1990.

Ehrlich, Paul, and Anne Ehrlich. *The Population Explosion.* New York: Simon and Schuster, 1990.

Freedman, Ronald. "Family Planning Programs in the Third World." *Annals of the American Academy of Political and Social Science* 510 (July 1990): 33–43.

Goliber, Thomas J. "Africa's Expanding Population: Old Problems, New Policies." *Population Bulletin* 44 (3). Washington, DC: Population Reference Bureau, 1989.

Gould, W. T. S., and R. Lawton, eds. *Planning for Population Change*. Totowa, NJ: Barnes and Noble Books, 1986.

Homer-Dixon, Thomas F. *Environmental Scarcity and Global Security*. Ephrata, PA: Science Press, 1993.

Huab, Carl. "Population Change in the Former Soviet Republics:" *Population Bulletin* 49 (4). Washington, DC: Population Reference Bureau, 1994.

Jacobsen, Judith. "Promoting Population Stabilization: Incentives for Small Families." *Worldwatch Paper* 54. Washington, DC: Worldwatch Institute, June 1983.

Lutz, Wolfgang. "The Future of World Population." *Population Bulletin* 49 (1). Washington, D.C.: Population Reference Bureau, 1994.

Malthus, Thomas. *An Essay on the Principles of Population*. New York: Cambridge University Press, 1989.

McFalls, Joseph A., Jr. "Population: A Lively Introduction." *Population Bulletin* 46 (2). Washington, DC: Population Reference Bureau, 1991.

Menken, Jane, ed. *World Population and U.S. Policy*. New York: W. W. Norton, 1986.

Merrick, Thomas W. "World Population in Transition." *Population Bulletin* 41 (2). Washington, DC: Population Reference Bureau, 1986.

Mosley, W. Henry, and Peter Cowley. "The Challenge of World Health." *Population Bulletin* 46 (4). Washington, DC: Population Reference Bureau, 1991.

Peters, Gary L., and Robert P. Larkin. *Population Geography: Problems, Concepts, and Prospects,* 3d ed. Dubuque, IA: Kendall-Hunt, 1989.

Robert, Godfrey. *Population Policy, Contemporary Issues*. New York: Praeger, 1990.

Scientific American. *The Human Population*. San Francisco: W. H. Freeman, 1974.

Simon, Julian. *The Ultimate Resource*. Princeton, NJ: Princeton University Press, 1981.

Smil, Vaclav. "How Many People Can the Earth Feed?" *Population and Development Review* 20 (June 1994): 255–92.

Thompson, Warren S. *Population Problems,* 4th ed. New York: McGraw-Hill, 1953.

Tien, H. Yuan, with Zhang Tianlu, Ping Yu, Li Jingneng, and Liang Zhongtang. "China's Demographic Dilemmas." *Population Bulletin* 47 (1). Washington, DC: Population Reference Bureau, 1992.

Trewartha, Glenn T. *A Geography of Population*. New York: Wiley, 1969.

_____. *The Less Developed Realm: A Geography of Its Population*. New York: Wiley, 1972.

United Nations. *Demographic Yearbook*. New York: United Nations, published annually.

_____. *Statistical Yearbook*. New York: United Nations, published annually.

United States Department of Commerce, Bureau of the Census. *Statistical Abstract of the United States*. Washington, DC: Government Printing Office, published annually.

Van der Kaa, Dirk J. "Europe's Second Demographic Transition." *Population Bulletin* 42 (1). Washington, DC: Population Reference Bureau, 1987.

Visaria, Pravin, and Leela Visaria. "India's Population: Second and Growing." *Population Bulletin* 36. Washington, DC: Population Reference Bureau, 1981.

Weeks, John R. *Population: An Introduction to Concepts and Issues,* 4th ed. Belmont, CA: Wadsworth, 1989.

World Bank. *World Bank Development Report*. New York: Oxford University Press, published annually.

Wrigley, E. A. *Population and History*. New York: World University Library, 1969.

Zelinsky, Wilbur. "A Bibliographic Guide to Population Geography." Research Paper 80. Chicago: University of Chicago Department of Geography, 1962.

_____. *A Prologue to Population Geography*. Englewood Cliffs, NJ: Prentice Hall, 1966.

_____, Leszek A. Kosinski, and R. Mansell Prothero, eds. *Geography and a Crowding World*. New York: Oxford University Press, 1970.

Also consult the following journals: *American Demographics; Demography; Intercom; Population; Population Bulletin; Population and Development Review; Population Studies*. In addition, the Population Reference Bureau publishes a World Population Data Sheet every year.

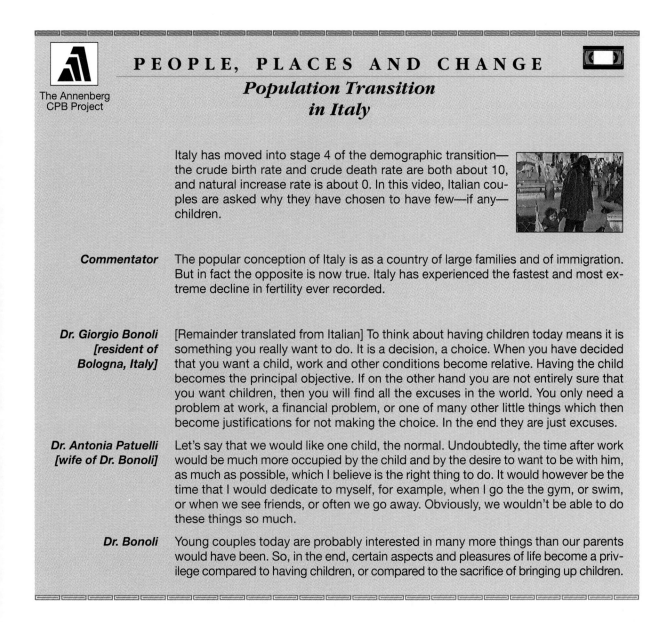

The Annenberg
CPB Project

PEOPLE, PLACES AND CHANGE
Population Transition in Italy

Italy has moved into stage 4 of the demographic transition—the crude birth rate and crude death rate are both about 10, and natural increase rate is about 0. In this video, Italian couples are asked why they have chosen to have few—if any—children.

Commentator	The popular conception of Italy is as a country of large families and of immigration. But in fact the opposite is now true. Italy has experienced the fastest and most extreme decline in fertility ever recorded.
Dr. Giorgio Bonoli [resident of Bologna, Italy]	[Remainder translated from Italian] To think about having children today means it is something you really want to do. It is a decision, a choice. When you have decided that you want a child, work and other conditions become relative. Having the child becomes the principal objective. If on the other hand you are not entirely sure that you want children, then you will find all the excuses in the world. You only need a problem at work, a financial problem, or one of many other little things which then become justifications for not making the choice. In the end they are just excuses.
Dr. Antonia Patuelli [wife of Dr. Bonoli]	Let's say that we would like one child, the normal. Undoubtedly, the time after work would be much more occupied by the child and by the desire to want to be with him, as much as possible, which I believe is the right thing to do. It would however be the time that I would dedicate to myself, for example, when I go the the gym, or swim, or when we see friends, or often we go away. Obviously, we wouldn't be able to do these things so much.
Dr. Bonoli	Young couples today are probably interested in many more things than our parents would have been. So, in the end, certain aspects and pleasures of life become a privilege compared to having children, or compared to the sacrifice of bringing up children.

3

MIGRATION

KEY ISSUES

- Why do people migrate?
- Why do people voluntarily emigrate from a country?
- Why do people migrate within a country?
- Why are people forced to emigrate from a country?

How many times has your family moved? In the United States, the average family moves once every 5 years. Was your last move traumatic or exciting? The loss of old friends and familiar settings can hurt, but the experiences awaiting you at a new location can be stimulating. Think about the multitude of Americans—maybe including yourself—who have migrated from other countries. Imagine the feelings of persons migrating from another country when they arrive in a new land without a job, friends, or—for many—the ability to speak the local language.

Why would people make a perilous journey across thousands of kilometers of ocean? Why did the pioneers cross the Great Plains, the Rocky Mountains, or the Mojave Desert to reach the American West? Why do people continue to migrate by the millions today? The hazards that many migrants have faced are a measure of the strong lure of new locations and the desperate conditions in their former homelands. Most people migrate in search of three things: economic opportunity, political freedom, and environmental comfort. This chapter studies the reasons why people migrate.

Migrating in Somalia

The Omer family lived for many generations in the village of Rahole in southern Somalia. Like most Somalis, the Omers were farmers who raised animals and traded animal products for grain or consumed the milk themselves. The Omers were prosperous by Somali standards, because they had fifty camels, forty goats, and thirty cattle.

In 1989, members of a rival clan stole all the Omers' livestock at gunpoint. With the collapse of organized government in Somalia, fighting spread among the country's six major clans, as well as dozens of subclans and sub-subclans.

For three years, the Omer family struggled to survive in their village. Stripped of their animals—their main source of wealth—the Omers planted millet (a cereal grain) and sorghum (a grain grown to make sugar), but the crops failed for lack of rain. During the summer of 1992, the family's three youngest children died. Desperate for food, the parents and three surviving teenage children walked 100 kilometers (60 miles) westward to a camp near Bardera (Baadheere), where international relief organizations were thought to be dispensing food.

Weak from hunger, the family carried only a handful of their most prized possessions—an aluminum pot, a kettle, and a metal mixing bowl—essential for preparing the food they hoped to receive. They left behind their beds, tools, and clothing and lived in the camp in a hut made of sticks and plastic.

For a few months, food reached the refugee camp. But in late 1992 and early 1993, rival clans captured most of the supplies intended for the camp. In 1992, an estimated 300,000 people, mostly women and children, died from famine and from warfare between clans. The United States sent several thousand troops in December 1992 to protect delivery of food to the starving Somali refugees.

Hungry Somalis were first fed a sugar-laden biscuit, which provided quick energy, followed by a mix of beans, oil, and wheat or maize (corn). Severely malnourished people ate as often as eight times a day, because they could not digest very much at one time. Stronger individuals received a mix of rice and beans.

Saved from starvation, the surviving Omer family members hope to migrate back to their home village and resume farming. To succeed, they will need a lot of help: seeds to plant, tools to work the fields, food to tide them over until the first harvest, an end to the warfare, and a stable government to provide security and basic services.

In Chapter 1, we defined *diffusion* as a process by which a characteristic spreads across the landscape, and *relocation diffusion* as the spread through bodily movement of people from one place to another. Human beings have a great ability to move from one place to another, which we define as **mobility**.

People display their mobility in a variety of ways—by journeying daily from their homes to places of work or education and weekly to shops, places of worship, or recreation areas. These are examples of *periodic* or *cyclical* movements—journeys that recur on a regular basis, such as daily, monthly, or annually. Many college students display another form of mobility—*seasonal* mobility—by moving to a dormitory each fall and returning home the following spring.

The subject of this chapter is a specific type of relocation diffusion called **migration,** which is a permanent move to a new location. Migrants permanently change their place of residence—where they sleep, store their possessions, and receive legal documents. Migration occurs much less frequently than other forms of mobility, but it produces far more profound changes for individuals and entire societies. A permanent move to a new location disrupts access to family, friends, and community activities, and it prevents commuting to the same place of work.

Migration has two forms, emigration and immigration. **Emigration** is migration *out from* a location; **immigration** is migration *into* a location. Given locations A and B, some people *emigrate* out from A to B, while at the same time others *immigrate* into A from B. The difference between the number of immigrants and the number of emigrants is the **net migration.** If the number of immigrants exceeds the number of emigrants, the net migration is positive, and the region has *net in-migration*. If the number of emigrants exceeds the immigrants, the region has *net out-migration*.

Historically, ideas diffused from one place to another primarily through *relocation diffusion*. When people migrated they took with them their language, religion, and other cultural traits and their methods of farming and other economic practices. Modern transportation systems, such as motor vehicles, airplanes, and railroads, make relocation diffusion more feasible than in the past, when people had to rely on walking, animal power, or slow ships.

At the same time, thanks to modern communications systems, relocation diffusion is no longer essential for transmission of ideas from one place to another. Culture and economy now diffuse rapidly around the world through forms of *expansion diffusion*. But, if people can participate in a global culture and economy regardless of place of residence, why do they still migrate in large numbers? The answer is that location is still important to an individual's cultural identity and economic prospects. Within a global economy, an individual's ability to earn a living varies widely by location. Even in a global culture, people still migrate to escape domination by other cultural groups or to reunite with others of similar culture.

Although migration is a form of relocation diffusion, reasons for migrating can be gained from expansion diffusion. Someone may migrate and communicate back information that gives others the idea of migrating. For example, many Europeans migrated to the United States in the 1800s because very favorable reports from early migrants led them to believe that the streets of American cities were paved with gold.

K E Y   I S S U E   1

Why Do People Migrate?

- Push Factors
- Pull Factors
- Intervening Obstacles
- International and Internal Migration

Refer to Figure 2-1 (world population distribution) for a moment. If a series of such maps were created for several points in time and shown one after the other like frames in a movie, the pattern would change constantly. Some regions would suddenly increase in population, and others would decline. In part, these changes result from regional differences in crude birth and death rates. Most of the changes, however, result from migration.

A decision to migrate stems from a perception that somewhere else is a more desirable place to live. People may hold very negative perceptions of their current place of residence or very positive perceptions about the attractiveness of somewhere else. Negative perceptions about their place of residence that induce people to move away are **push factors**, whereas **pull factors** attract people to a particular new location. As was the case in Somalia, most people migrate for a variety of reasons, influenced by a combination of push and pull factors. Frequently, though, a single push or pull factor emerges as the most important reason, if not the sole one, for migration.

Push Factors

We can identify three major kinds of push factors—political, economic, and environmental. Each involves a different type of decision on the part of the migrant.

Political Push Factors

Refugees are people forced to migrate from a particular country for political reasons. The United Nations defines political refugees as people who have fled their home country and cannot return for fear of persecution because of their race, religion, nationality, membership in a social group, or political opinion. Such people have no home until another country agrees to allow them in. In 1993, the U.S. Committee for Refugees estimated that more than 16 million refugees exist, an increase of about 50 percent in 5 years. Warfare in southeastern Europe and East Africa since then has probably pushed the total number of refugees to about 20 million.

The largest number of refugees are in southwestern Asia as a result of the former Soviet Union's invasion of Afghanistan in 1979. More than 5 million Afghans fled to refugee camps set up in neighboring countries (Figure 3-1). Because of a very high natural increase rate—an average of 2.6 percent since 1979—the population in the refugee camps has swelled to more than 6 million.

More than 3 million Afghan refugees now live in tents or mud huts set up in 250 camps in Pakistan. The largest number live near the town of Peshāwar, in northern Pakistan. Peshāwar is situated near the eastern end of the Khyber Pass, the major land route through the mountains between Afghanistan and Pakistan. Other Afghan refugees settled in camps in Pakistan's Baluchistan and Punjab provinces. More than 2 million Afghan refugees migrated westward to Iran, primarily to the border cities of Mashhad, Bīrjand, and Zāhedān, as well as the capital Tehrān.

The Soviet Union withdrew its troops from Afghanistan in 1989, and the Soviet-installed government collapsed in 1992. Since then, several thousand refugees have returned home, trading the

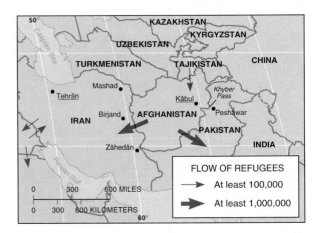

FIGURE 3-1 Refugees from Afghanistan. Nearly one-third of the population of Afghanistan was forced to migrate after the Soviet invasion in 1979, mostly to Pakistan and Iran. Afghan rebels, known as Mujahedeen, took advantage of the country's rugged terrain to offset the Soviet advantage in number of troops and sophisticated equipment. Even though the civil war has ended, most of the Afghan refugees have been reluctant to return home, because of fighting among the many ethnic groups that control different regions of the country.

security of the camps for the possibility of reclaiming their farms. The United Nations, which had issued ration books to the refugees so that they could obtain food while living in the camps, provided each returning family with about 300 kilograms (650 pounds) of wheat and the equivalent of $150 to pay for transportation. The majority of refugees have not yet returned to Afghanistan, however, because rival ethnic groups are fighting for control of the country.

Other than Afghanistan, the largest groups of refugees have been pushed from their homelands by wars in Africa (discussed under Key Issue 4 in this chapter), the Middle East (Chapter 5), and Southeast Europe (Chapter 7). Wars in these three regions, plus Afghanistan, are responsible for two-thirds of today's refugees (Figure 3-2).

Economic Push Factors

Economic reasons frequently push people from their homes. For example, several million Irish were pushed from their island in the 1840s because a blight (fungus) destroyed most of the potato crop, their major food source, and produced mass starvation.

Residents of Kabul, Afghanistan, walked past buildings devastated in the country's civil war. (Rainer Unkel/SABA Press Photos, Inc.)

English landlords, who owned most of the arable land, did little to alleviate the disastrous economic conditions in Ireland (see Chapter 5). Millions of Irish people died during the famine, and many of the survivors left in search of better economic conditions.

Economic factors are again pushing hundreds of thousands of Irish from their country. During the past decade, one-fourth of the labor force—10 percent of the total population—emigrated from Ireland. Most of the emigrants were young and well educated. In a country where one-third of the young people are unemployed, a high school or college diploma is a ticket out of Ireland.

Environmental Push Factors

People are also pushed from their homes by an adverse physical environment. Water—either too much or too little—poses the most common environmental threat.

According to a study by Ian Burton, Robert Kates, and Gilbert White, 40 percent of the world's natural disasters are flood-related and 20 percent are storm-related. Many people are forced to move by water-related disasters because they live in a vulnerable area, such as a floodplain. The **floodplain** of a river is the area subject to flooding during a specific number of years, on the basis of historical trends. People living in a "100-year floodplain," for example, can

expect flooding on average once every 100 years. Many people are unaware that they live in a floodplain, and even people who do know often choose to live there anyway. In the United States, families living in floodplains may not be eligible for government insurance to help rebuild after flood damage.

A lack of water pushes other people from their land. Hundreds of thousands have been forced to move from the Sahel region of northern Africa because of drought conditions. The people of the Sahel have traditionally been pastoral nomads, a form of agriculture adapted to dry lands but effective only at low population densities (see Chapter 9). The capacity of the Sahel to sustain human life—never very high—has declined recently because of population growth and several years of unusually low rainfall. Consequently, many of these nomads have been forced to move into cities and rural camps, where they survive on food donated by the government and international relief organizations.

In the United States, people were pushed from their land by severe drought as recently as the 1930s. Portions of Oklahoma and surrounding states became known as the Dust Bowl, after several years of limited rainfall. Strong, dry winds blew across the plains and buried farms under several feet of dust. Thousands of families abandoned their farms and migrated to California, where they were called Okies. The

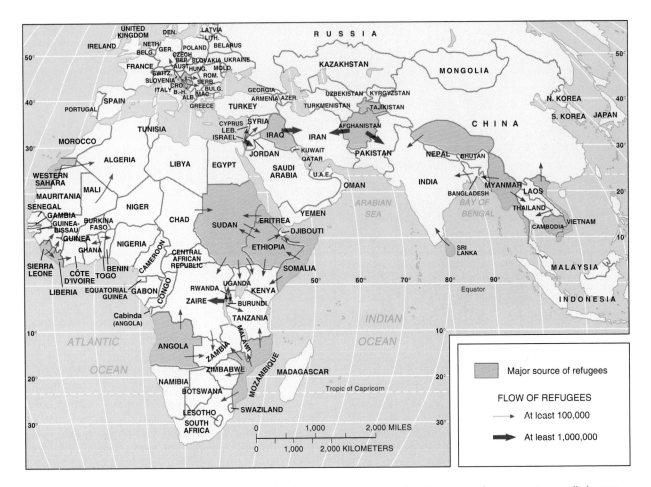

FIGURE 3-2 Major sources and destinations of refugees. A refugee is a person who is forced to migrate from a country, usually because of political reasons. The U.S. Committee for Refugees estimated that in 1993 there were 16 million refugees in the world, although the organization warns that the figure is difficult to determine because many refugees are not documented.

plight of the Okies was graphically portrayed by John Steinbeck in his novel *The Grapes of Wrath* (1939).

Pull Factors

Attractive features of a new location may lure migrants there. As with push factors, we can identify three types of pull factors: political, economic, and environmental.

Political Pull Factors

The major political pull factor is the lure of freedom. People are attracted to democratic countries that encourage individual choice in education, career, and place of residence. This pull factor is particularly difficult to distinguish from a political push factor because the pull of democracy is normally accompanied by the push from a totalitarian country.

Democracy was an important pull factor in Germany after World War II, when the defeated country was divided into four occupied zones, controlled by the United States, the United Kingdom, France, and the former Soviet Union. The Soviet portion became the German Democratic Republic (East Germany); the other three zones became the German Federal Republic (West Germany). People caught in the portion controlled by the Soviet Union, as well as those in other countries of Soviet-dominated Eastern Europe, fled to the West until this migration was forcibly ended.

Large-scale migration from Eastern Europe to Western Europe resumed in the late 1980s during the transition from Communist-dominated governments to multiparty political systems in several Eastern European countries (Figure 3-3). In 1989, Hungary became the first Communist-controlled country to permit unrestricted travel to a bordering democratic state, Austria. By opening its borders first, Hungary sparked a large-scale, circuitous migration pattern within Europe for several weeks. People in East Germany realized that the opening of the Hungary-Austria border gave them their first opportunity in 35 years to migrate to West Germany. Fearful that this "hole" in the Iron Curtain would be closed quickly, thousands of East Germans traveled across Czechoslovakia to Hungary, crossed the border from Hungary to Austria, and passed through Austria to reach West Germany, a 1,500-kilometer (900-mile) journey.

With the election of democratic governments in Eastern Europe, Western Europe's political pull has disappeared as a migration factor. Eastern Europeans now can visit where they wish, although few have

FIGURE 3-3 Iron Curtain. In Europe from the late 1940s until the late 1980s, an important intervening obstacle to migration was the Iron Curtain. The name was invented by British Prime Minister Winston Churchill to describe the division of Europe between a communist-dominated East and a democratic West. Communist-controlled countries prevented people from crossing the border to the West.

the money to pay for travel-related expenses beyond a round-trip bus ticket. But Western Europe continues to pull an increasing number of migrants from Eastern Europe for economic reasons.

Economic Pull Factors

People migrate to places where they think jobs are available. Because of economic restructuring, job prospects often vary from one country to another and within regions of the same country. A region that has valuable natural resources, such as petroleum or uranium, may attract miners and engineers. A new industry in a region may lure factory workers, technicians, and scientists. Construction workers, restaurant employees, and public service officials may move to regions where rapid population growth stimulates demand for additional services and facilities.

The most important pull of the United States and Canada is economic rather than political. As noted, many Europeans were pulled to North America in the nineteenth century because they actually thought the streets were paved with gold. Although not literally so gilded, the United States and Canada did offer prospects for economic advancement. This same perception of economic plenty now lures people from Latin America and Asia.

In West Africa, economic pull factors have historically been important reasons for migration. When most of the region was part of European colonial empires, groups migrated there to seek economic opportunity. Sierra Leoneans migrated to other regions to work as craftspeople, Dahomeyans and Beninese became assistants to the French administrators in the region, and Hausa and Yoruba people traded in the markets of a number of cities.

Since colonial West Africa was carved into a collection of independent states during the 1950s and 1960s, millions of people have migrated for economic reasons from one country in the region to another. Laborers from Burkina Faso, Niger, and Mali work in the Côte d'Ivoire and Ghana. Ghanaians, Nigerans, Togolese, Beninese, and Cameroonians migrated to Nigeria during the 1970s, lured by the rapid expansion of the Nigerian economy as a result of increasing revenues from the sale of petroleum.

In the case of Nigeria, an economic pull factor turned to a push factor in 1983, when the Nigerian government ordered a large number of foreign workers to leave the country. The Nigerian economy had been jolted by a drastic decline in the world price of petroleum, and unrest was widespread among Nigerians dissatisfied with cutbacks in government services. To reduce competition for jobs, the Nigerian government expelled more than 1 million foreigners, primarily Ghanaians.

The relative attractiveness of a region can shift with economic change. After experiencing decades of net out-migration, northeastern Scotland has attracted migrants in recent years. After petroleum was discovered in the North Sea off the coast of northeast Scotland, thousands of people have been lured to jobs in the drilling or refining of petroleum or in supporting businesses.

Environmental Pull Factors

Environmental conditions also attract migrants. In surveys, most Americans express a preference for living in a small town. In an age of improved communications and transportation systems, people can live in relatively remote locations of the United States and still not feel too isolated from employment, shopping, and entertainment opportunities.

Mountains also attract an increasing number of migrants. Proximity to the Rocky Mountains lures Americans to the state of Colorado, and the Alps pull French people to eastern France. Some migrants are shocked to find polluted air and congestion in these areas.

Regions with relatively temperate climates—such as the southern coast of England, the Mediterranean coast of France and Spain, and the Southwest of the United States—attract migrants from harsher climates. Retired people are especially pulled to climates with a mild winter; one-third of all elderly people who move from one state to another in the United States select Florida as their destination.

Persons with bronchitis, asthma, tuberculosis, and allergies have been pulled to Arizona by the dry desert climate. Ironically, the large number of migrants has modified Arizona's environmental conditions. The pollen count in Tucson has increased 3,500 percent since the 1940s, and the percentage of people with allergies there is now twice the national average.

Local experts attribute two-thirds of the pollen count in Tucson to three types of vegetation imported by migrants: the mulberry tree, the olive tree, and Bermuda grass. Some communities have banned these three species. The mulberry tree dies after 30 years, but the olive tree—an attractive species in Arizona because it is drought-resistant—can live for 500 years. Bermuda grass sinks deep roots and is difficult to eradicate. Arizona's recent experience shows that migration may no longer be the answer for people with allergies.

Intervening Obstacles

Migrants who are attracted to a new location do not always reach their desired destination. They may be blocked by an **intervening obstacle,** which is an environmental or cultural feature that hinders migration.

Historically, intervening obstacles have primarily been environmental. Before the invention of modern transportation such as railroads and motor vehicles, people migrated across land masses by horse or on foot. Such migration was frequently difficult because of hostile features in the physical environment such as mountains and deserts. For example, many migrants who were lured to California during the nineteenth century by the economic pull factor of the Gold Rush failed to reach their destination because they could not cross such intervening obstacles as the Great Plains, the Rocky Mountains, or desert country.

Bodies of water long have been important intervening obstacles (see Geography in Action box). The Atlantic Ocean proved a particularly significant intervening obstacle for most European migrants to North America. Tens of millions of Europeans spent their life savings for the right to cross the rough and dangerous Atlantic in the hold of a ship shared with hundreds of other immigrants.

Some Eastern Europeans who booked passage on ships to North America never made it. An unscrupulous ship owner would sail the boat through the Baltic Sea and North Sea and land at Liverpool or some other British port. Told that they had reached America, the passengers—none of whom could speak English—paid for a transatlantic journey of 7,000 kilometers (4,400 miles) but received a voyage of 1,300 kilometers (800 miles) to an undesired destination.

International and Internal Migration

We have seen that people migrate for a combination of political, economic, and environmental push and pull factors. These factors fall into two gen-

Vietnamese Emigrants and Intervening Obstacles—Water and Laws

Water has been a formidable intervening obstacle for 1.5 million people who have emigrated from Vietnam since the late 1970s. Fleeing overland to neighboring Cambodia, China, and Laos has been unattractive because of communist domination or political unrest in those countries. Given the country's situation along the South China Sea, most emigrants leave by sea (Figure 1). Consequently, they are called *boat people.*

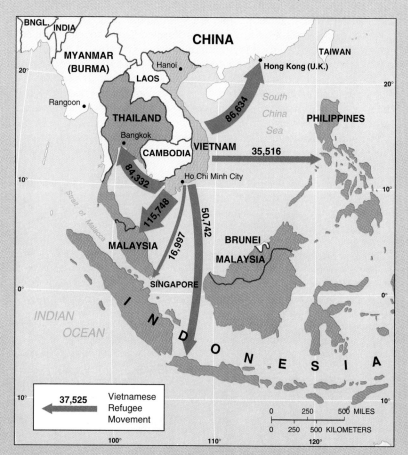

FIGURE 1 Destinations of Vietnamese boat people, late 1980s and early 1990s. During the 1970s, Vietnamese boat people were regarded as political refugees after the end of a long war. In recent years, neighboring countries have severely restricted the number of Vietnamese permitted to stay. Other countries have argued that the boat people can no longer make legitimate claims to be refugees from a war that ended back in 1975.

The first wave of boat people emigrated from Vietnam during the late 1970s, after the end of the Vietnam War (1954–1975). North Vietnam captured South Vietnam's capital city of Saigon (since renamed Ho Chi Minh City). The United States, which had supported the government of South Vietnam, evacuated several thousand people who had been closely identified with the American position during the war. Refugees who could not get space on an American evacuation helicopter were forced to emigrate by boat.

The Vietnamese boat people drifted into the open sea, hoping they would be saved by the U.S. Navy. U.S. naval officers wished to save the boat people, but hesitated because of U.S. law. Once taken on board, the boat people would technically be on U.S. territory and could apply for admission to the United States as refugees. This situation would be unfair to the large numbers of people elsewhere in the world, as well as those still in Vietnam, who had been waiting a long time for the U.S. government to consider their claims for admission as refugees. Consequently, some boat people were not allowed to board U.S. vessels.

A second surge of Vietnamese boat people began in the late 1980s. The most popular places where they first sought asylum were Malaysia, Hong Kong, and Thailand. Smaller numbers sought asylum in Indonesia, the Philippines, and Singapore. As memories of the Vietnam War faded, officials in these countries of first asylum were less sympathetic to the boat people. Thailand, in particular, pushed the Vietnamese boats back out to sea, even though some of them capsized and many refugees drowned. Other countries placed the Vietnamese in detention camps surrounded by barbed wire and patrolled by armed soldiers. More recent boat people have not been considered refugees, except for a handful who could prove they had been victims of specific incidents of political persecution.

According to an international agreement, most of the Vietnamese boat people who were judged to be refugees have been transferred from the Asian countries where they first sought asylum to other places. Since the 1970s, approximately half have come to the United States; another fifth have immigrated to Canada, Australia, and France. Those boat people who are not considered to be political refugees have languished in camps or have been sent back to Vietnam.

The small, crowded boats are not always seaworthy and make inviting targets for pirates. Many Vietnamese perish during the journey, when the boats capsize or become disabled in the open sea. The hardship willingly endured by the boat people reflects the intensity of continuing political problems in Vietnam that push them toward more hospitable lands simultaneously as these attractive countries pull them.

Transportation improvements, such as motor vehicles and airplanes, have diminished the importance of environmental features as intervening obstacles. Today's migrant, however, faces legal obstacles: a passport (which permits departure from their current home), a visa (which grants permission to enter the desired country), and other legal papers.

Haitian boat people. Vietnam is not the only source of boat people. Haitians attempted to migrate to the United States in the early 1980s and again in the early 1990s in overcrowded boats that were not seaworthy. U.S. officials claiming that Haitians are migrating for economic rather than political reasons, prevent the boats from reaching the United States, but they don't wish to see the boats capsize. Boat people have also emigrated from Cuba in recent years. (Randy Taylor/Sygma)

eral categories of migration: international and internal. **International migration** is permanent movement from one country to another, whereas **internal migration** is permanent movement within a country. Typically, people undertake international migration for economic or political reasons, rather than environmental reasons, whereas internal migration normally results from economic and environmental reasons, rather than political reasons.

International migration is further divided into two types: forced and voluntary. **Voluntary migration** implies that the migrant has *chosen* to move for economic improvement, whereas **forced migration** means that the migrant has been *compelled* to move by political factors. Economic push and pull factors usually induce voluntary migration, whereas political factors normally compel migration. In one sense, migrants may also feel compelled by pressure inside themselves to migrate for economic reasons, such as search for food or jobs, but they have not been explicitly compelled to migrate by the violent actions of other people.

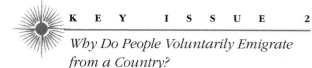

K E Y I S S U E 2

Why Do People Voluntarily Emigrate from a Country?

- European Emigration to the United States
- Changes in U.S. Immigration Policy
- Guest Workers

Most people choose to migrate from one country to another because they hope for economic advancement. In general, people emigrate from countries where they have limited prospects for earning a living, and they migrate to countries where they believe that economic opportunities await them.

European Emigration to the United States

Historically, the largest stream of voluntary migration for economic reasons has been from Europe. In the 500 years since Christopher Columbus sailed from Spain to the Western Hemisphere, approximately 60 million Europeans have migrated to other continents. The reasons so many Europeans have

chosen to migrate to other parts of the world include both push and pull economic factors.

Rapid population growth in Europe fueled the push factor, especially after 1800. Application of new technology spawned by the industrial revolution—in areas such as public health, medicine, and food—produced a rapid decline in the death rate and pushed much of Europe into stage 2 of the demographic transition (high growth rate).

As the population increased, many Europeans found limited opportunities for economic advancement. Family farms, for example, often had to be divided among a great number of relatives, and the average farm was becoming too small to be profitable. To promote more efficient agriculture, some European governments forced the consolidation of several small farms into larger units. In England, this consolidation policy was known as the *enclosure movement*. The enclosure movement forced millions of people to emigrate from rural areas. Displaced farmers could choose to work in factories in the large cities or to migrate to another part of the world where farmland was plentiful.

At the same time, many Europeans were pulled to other continents by the prospect of economic improvement. European migrants were most attracted to the temperate climates of North America, Australia, New Zealand, southern Africa, and southern South America, where farming methods used in Europe could be most easily transplanted.

In more tropical climates, especially in Latin America and Asia, European migrants established plantations that grew cotton, rice, sugar, and tobacco for sale back in Europe. Europeans owned most of the plantations, but relatively few worked on them. Instead, most of the workers were native Asians or Latin Americans or were slaves from Africa.

Waves of Emigration from Europe to the United States

The most popular destination for European emigrants has been the United States. Of the 60 million European migrants since 1500, 37 million have come to the United States. Germany has sent the largest number, 7.1 million; followed by Italy, 5.4 million; Great Britain, 5.1 million; Ireland, 4.7 million; Austria-Hungary, 4.3 million; and Russia/Soviet Union, 3.4 million. The frequent boundary changes in Europe make precise counts impossible. For example, most Poles migrated to the United States at a time when

Poland did not exist as an independent country. Therefore, they may have been counted as immigrants from Germany, Russia, or Austria-Hungary.

To most European migrants, the United States offered the greatest opportunity for economic success. Early migrants extolled the virtues of the United States to friends and relatives back in Europe, thereby encouraging still others to come. The lure of the United States was summarized in the following popular nineteenth-century song. Steel magnate-philanthropist Andrew Carnegie remarked that this song had inspired his father to come to America:

To the west, to the west, to the land of the free
Where mighty Missouri rolls down to the sea;
Where a man is a man if he's willing to toil,
And the humblest may gather the fruits of the soil.
Where children are blessings and he who hath most
Has aid for his fortune and riches to boast.
Where the young may exult and the aged may rest,
Away, far away, to the land of the west.
Away, far away, let us hope for the best
And build up a home in the land of the west.

The total flow of European migrants to the United States and the number from individual countries have varied from year to year. From the first permanent English settlers to arrive at the Virginia colony's Jamestown, in 1607, until 1840, a steady stream of Europeans migrated to the American colonies (and after 1776 to the newly independent United States of America). Although early migrants included some Dutch, Swedes, French, Germans, Swiss, Spanish, and Portuguese, 90 percent of U.S. immigrants before 1840 came from Great Britain. Perhaps 1 million Europeans migrated to the American colonies before independence, and another 1 million from the late 1700s until 1840.

First Peak of European Immigration. During the 1840s and 1850s, the level of immigration to the United States surged (Figure 3-4). More than 4 million people migrated to the United States during those two decades, more than twice as many as in the previous 250 years combined. Immigration jumped from approximately 20,000 people per year during the first 50 years of independence to over one-quarter million in the peak immigration years of the 1840s and 1850s.

More than 90 percent of all U.S. immigrants during the 1840s and 1850s came from northern and western Europe, including two-fifths from Ireland and another one-third from Germany. At first, desperate economic push factors compelled the Irish and Germans to cross the Atlantic. When the potato crop was devastated by blight, Ireland was thrown into a severe famine. The famine was made worse by the fact that most of the land was owned by people living in England rather than in Ireland. These absentee landowners did not encourage the Irish who were working the land to change their farming practices. By the end of the famine, Ireland's population was reduced by one-half through mortality and emigration. Germans migrated to escape from political unrest, as well as from poor economic conditions.

Second Peak of European Immigration. U.S. immigration declined somewhat during the 1860s as a result of the Civil War (1861–1865). But it began to climb again in the 1870s. A second peak was reached during the 1880s, when more than one-half million people per year immigrated to the United States.

Again, more than three-fourths of the immigrants during the late 1800s came from northern and western Europe. Germans accounted for one-third and the Irish still constituted a large percentage. However, other countries in northern and western Europe sent increasing numbers of migrants, especially the Scandinavian countries of Norway and Sweden.

The industrial revolution had diffused to these countries, and population was growing rapidly, as a result of entering stage 2 of the demographic transition (rapidly declining crude death rates). Most of the people who could not find land to farm at home—such as those whose older siblings had inherited their parents' farm—migrated to the cities. But some decided to migrate to other countries in search of farmland or jobs in foreign cities.

Third Peak of European Immigration. Economic problems in the United States discouraged immigration during the early 1890s, but by the end of the decade the level reached a third peak. Nearly 1 million people per year immigrated during the first 15 years of the twentieth century. The record year was 1907, with 1.3 million immigrants.

During the third peak, more than 90 percent of the immigrants were European. But, instead of coming from Great Britain, Ireland, and Germany, most came

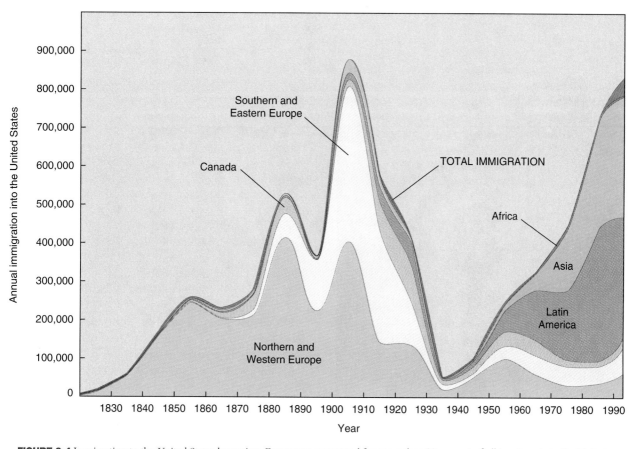

FIGURE 3-4 Immigration to the United States by region. Europeans accounted for more than 90 percent of all immigrants to the United States during the 1800s. Even as recently as the early 1960s, Europeans continued to account for more than 50 percent. Since the 1960s, Latin America and Asia have replaced Europe as the most important source of immigrants to the United States. The curves have been smoothed to reflect rolling five-year averages.

from countries that previously had sent few people. Nearly one-fourth each came from Italy, Russia, and Austria-Hungary. (Austria-Hungary encompassed portions of present-day Austria, Bosnia-Herzegovina, Croatia, Czech Republic, Hungary, Italy, Poland, Romania, Slovakia, Slovenia, and Ukraine.)

Immigrants came from southern and eastern Europe in the early twentieth century for the same reason that northern and western Europeans had migrated in the previous century. The shift in the primary source of immigrants coincided with the diffusion of the industrial revolution from northern and western Europe to southern and eastern Europe. The population of these countries grew rapidly as a result of improved technology and health care. For many, the option of migrating to the United States proved irresistible.

According to the 1910 U.S. census, taken at the peak of immigration, 12.9 million U.S. residents were either born in a foreign country or had at least one foreign-born parent. This amounted to 13.9 percent of the country's total population of 92.2 million. These recent immigrants constituted more than 20 percent of the population in the Northeast, across a northern tier between Michigan and Montana, and along the Pacific coast.

Impact of European Migration

The emigration of 60 million Europeans has profoundly changed the world's cultural landscape. As do all migrants, Europeans brought their cultural heritage to their new homes. Because of migration, Indo-European languages now are spoken by half of the world's people (as discussed in the next chap-

This Italian family immigrated through Ellis Island, in New York harbor, in 1905. (Lewis W. Hine)

ter), and Europe's most prevalent religion, Christianity, has the world's largest number of adherents. European art, music, literature, philosophy, and ethics have also diffused throughout the world.

Regions that were sparsely inhabited before European immigration, such as North America and Australia, have become closely integrated into Europe's cultural traditions. Distinctive European political structures and economic systems have diffused to these regions.

But, Europeans also planted the seeds of conflict by migrating to regions that have large indigenous populations, especially in Africa and Asia. Europeans frequently imposed political domination on existing populations and injected their cultural values with little regard for local traditions. Economies in Africa and Asia became based on extracting resources for export to Europe rather than on using those resources to build local industry. Many of today's conflicts in former European colonies result from past practices by European immigrants, such as drawing arbitrary boundary lines and discriminating among different local ethnic groups.

Changes in U.S. Immigration Policy

The era of massive European migration to the United States ended with the start of World War I in 1914, because the war involved the most important source countries, such as Austria-Hungary, Germany, and Russia (as well as the United States in 1917). The level of European emigration has steadily declined since. Europeans accounted for one-third of all U.S. immigrants in the 1960s and only 10 percent since 1980.

For several hundred years, the United States was Europe's safety valve. When Europe's population began to increase rapidly because of the Industrial revolution, migration to the United States drained off some of the growth. As a result, people remaining in Europe enjoyed more of the economic and social benefits from the industrial revolution.

Most European countries now have very low natural increase rates (stage 3 or 4 of the demographic transition) and economies capable of meeting the needs of their people. Countries such as Germany, Italy, and Ireland, which once sent several hundred thousand people per year to the United States, now send only a few thousand. The safety valve is no longer needed.

Changing Attitudes

The number of Europeans coming to the United States has also decreased because of changing attitudes toward immigrants. Americans have always regarded new arrivals with suspicion, but they tempered their dislike during the nineteenth century because immigrants helped to settle the frontier and extend U.S. control across the continent. European immigrants converted the forests and prairies of the vast North American interior into productive farms.

By the early twentieth century, though, most Americans believed that the frontier had closed. In 1912, New Mexico and Arizona were admitted as the forty-seventh and forty-eighth states. Thus, for the first time in its history, all the contiguous territory of this country was a "united" state (other than the District of Columbia). This symbolic closing of the frontier meant to many Americans that the country no longer had the space to accommodate an unlimited number of immigrants.

Opposition to immigration intensified when the majority of immigrants ceased to come from Northern and Western Europe. German and Irish immigrants in the nineteenth century suffered some prejudice from so-called native Americans, who had in reality arrived only a few years earlier from Britain. But Italians, Russians, Poles, and other Southern and Eastern Europeans who poured into the United States around 1900 faced much more hostility. A government study in 1911 reflected popular attitudes when it concluded that immigrants from Southern and Eastern Europe were racially inferior, "inclined toward violent crime," resisted assimilation, and "drove old-stock citizens out of some lines of work." (There is nothing new about racism, prejudice, fear of unknown groups, suspicion of different cultures, economic fears, and anti-immigration sentiment. Only the players on the stage change.)

At about the peak of immigration from southern and eastern Europe, a handful of Chinese and Japanese immigrants began to arrive. Although Asians never accounted for more than 5 percent of immigrants during the late nineteenth and early twentieth centuries, many Americans nevertheless were alarmed at the prospect of millions of Asians flooding into the country, especially to states along the Pacific coast.

Quota Laws

The era of unrestricted immigration to the United States ended when Congress passed the Quota Act in 1921 and the National Origins Act in 1924. These laws established **quotas,** or maximum limits on the number of people who could immigrate to the United States from each country during a 1-year period. The quota was simple: for each country that had native-born persons living in the United States, 2 percent of their number (based on the 1910 census) could immigrate each year. This restriction limited the number of immigrants from the Eastern Hemisphere to 150,000 per year, virtually all of whom had to be from Europe. The system continued with minor modifications until the 1960s.

The result of the quota laws was to perpetuate the nineteenth-century mixture of immigrants to the United States, but at a sharply reduced level. The Great Depression of the 1930s and World War II during the 1940s further reduced immigration to the lowest level since the early nineteenth century.

After the Immigration Act of 1965 was passed, quotas for individual countries were eliminated in 1968 and replaced with quotas for each hemisphere, western and eastern. The annual number of U.S. immigrants was restricted to 170,000 from the Eastern Hemisphere and 120,000 from the Western Hemisphere. In 1978, the hemisphere quotas were replaced by a global quota of 290,000, including a maximum of 20,000 per country. The Immigration Act of 1990 raised the total to 714,000 per year for fiscal years 1992, 1993, and 1994, and 675,000 beginning in fiscal year 1995. (The U.S. federal fiscal year runs from October 1 each year to the following September 30.)

Because the number of applicants for admission to the United States far exceeds the quotas, Congress has set a preference system. As of 1995, 480,000 of the 675,000 visas are issued to spouses, children, and other relatives of existing U.S. citizens. Skilled workers and exceptionally talented professionals receive 140,000 visas. The remaining 55,000 immigrants are admitted for other reasons. Under the 1980 Refugee Act, refugees are a special case: the quota does not apply to them, and they are admitted simply because they are refugees.

Impact of Quota Laws on National Origin. Since the abolition of individual country quotas in the late 1960s, the national origin of immigrants to the United States has changed sharply. Today, five-sixths of all immigrants come from Asia and Latin America. Demand from Latin America grew rapidly during the 1960s. Latin Americans constituted about 40 percent of all immigrants during the 1960s and 1970s and about 50 percent since the late 1980s. In recent years, 25 percent of all U.S. immigrants have come from Mexico. Other major countries of origin have become Jamaica, Haiti, the Dominican Republic, and several other Caribbean islands (Figure 3-5).

The recent surge from Mexico and other Latin American countries resulted in part from the 1986 Immigration Reform and Control Act, which issued visas to several hundred thousand who had entered the United States in previous years without legal documents. Counting those legalized under the 1986 act, the United States admitted 1.5 million immigrants in 1990 and 1.8 million in 1991, more than any year in history.

Asia has been the leading source of immigrants since the late 1970s, except during the late 1980s and early 1990s, when an unusually large number of Latin Americans were admitted under the 1986 act. The largest numbers of Asians have come from the Philippines and South Korea, followed by China, India, and Vietnam (Figure 3-6). Asians have made good

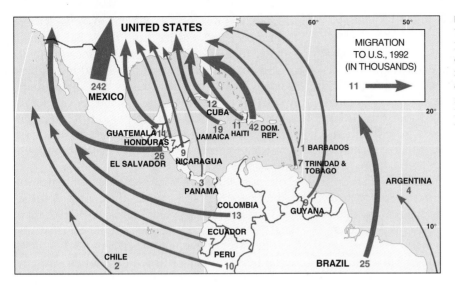

FIGURE 3-5 Immigration to the United States from Latin America. During the past decade, one-fourth of all U.S. immigrants have come from Mexico. Other major sources of U.S. immigrants from Latin America include Jamaica, Haiti, and the Dominican Republic. Figures are in thousands for 1993.

use of the priorities set by the U.S. quota laws. Many well-educated Asians enter the United States under the preference for skilled workers. Once admitted, they can bring in relatives under the family-reunification provisions of the quota. Eventually, these relatives can bring in a wider range of other relatives from Asia, a process known as **chain migration.**

Asians also constitute more than 40 percent of Canadian immigrants, but compared with the United States, Canada receives a much higher percentage of Europeans and a lower percentage of Latin Americans. Canada, however, takes in 50 percent more immigrants per capita than does the United States.

Many immigrants to the United States and Canada are poor people pushed from their homes by economic desperation, but others are young, well-educated people who are lured to economically growing countries. Scientists, researchers, doctors, and other professionals migrate to countries where they can make better use of their abilities. This migration causes a **brain drain,** meaning a large-scale emigration by talented people. Other countries fear that U.S. immigration policy now contributes to a brain drain by giving preference to skilled workers.

Why has the pattern of immigration to the United States changed? In part, the reason for immigration remains the same: people are pushed by poor conditions at home and lured by economic opportunity and social advancement in the United States. Europeans came in the nineteenth century because they saw the United States as a place to escape from

the pressures of land shortage and rapid population increase. Similar motives exist today for people in Asia and Latin America. Several Caribbean countries in stage 2 of the demographic transition are transferring the equivalent of all of their annual natural increase in population to the United States.

Although the motives for moving to the United States have not changed over time, the country has. Unfortunately for the people in less developed countries, the United States is no longer a sparsely settled, economically booming country with a large supply of unclaimed land. When the U.S. frontier closed, the gates to the country partially closed as well.

Undocumented Immigration into the United States

Legal immigration to the United States has reached the highest level since the early twentieth century. Yet, the number of people who wish to migrate to the United States is much higher than the quotas permit. Many people who cannot legally enter the United States are now immigrating illegally. Those who do so are entering without proper documents, and thus are called **undocumented immigrants.**

No one knows how many people immigrate to the United States without proper documents. The U.S. Immigration and Naturalization Service (INS), which apprehends more than 1 million persons per year trying to cross the southern U.S. border, estimates that for every person caught at least two enter successfully. More than half of the undocumented immigrants are thought to be Mexicans and another

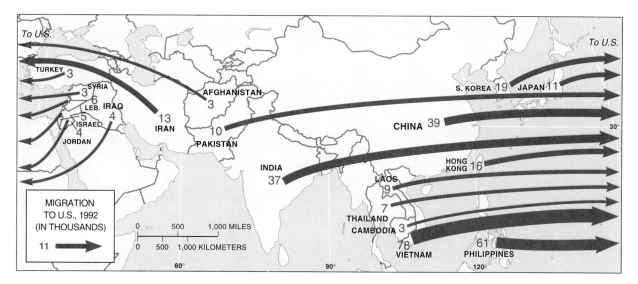

FIGURE 3-6 Immigration to the United States from Asia. The largest numbers of Asians have come from the Philippines and South Korea, followed by China, India, and Vietnam. Figures are in thousands for 1993.

one-fourth are thought to be from other Latin American countries.

Why do people enter or remain in the United States illegally? Many wish to immigrate for employment, but because of the quota only a handful receive a visa that permits them to work in the United States. Foreigners who fail to receive work visas have two choices if they still wish to work in the United States:

- Approximately half of the undocumented residents legally enter the country on a temporary student visa or tourist visa and then remain after it expires.
- The other half simply cross the border without a visa.

Once in the United States, undocumented immigrants can become "documented" by purchasing forged documents for as little as $25, including a birth certificate, alien registration card, and social security number.

Characteristics of Undocumented Immigrants. Although the number of undocumented residents living in the United States is only generally known, U.S. and Mexican government reports do contain information about them. More than three-fourths of Mexican immigrants are from rural areas, and over half come from the four Mexican states of Guanajuato, Jalisco, Chihuahua, and Zacatecas. The destination of choice within the United States is California for more than half, Texas for another fifth, and other southwestern states for most of the remainder.

The overwhelming majority of illegal immigrants from Mexico have been young males. People between ages 15 and 34 account for more than 70 percent of the undocumented Mexican immigrants, and females constitute 15 percent of the total. Most of the young men are married but leave their families in Mexico. The typical undocumented immigrant has attended school for 4 years, one year more than the average for all Mexicans.

Most illegal Mexican immigrants have jobs in their home village but migrate to the United States to earn more money. The largest number work in agriculture, picking fruits and vegetables, although some work in clothing factories. Even those who work long hours for a few dollars a day as farm laborers or factory workers prefer to earn relatively low wages by American standards than to live in poverty at home.

Most undocumented residents have no difficulty finding jobs in the United States. Some employers like to hire immigrants who do not have visas that permit them to work in the United States, because they can pay lower wages and don't have to provide health care, retirement plans, and other benefits. Unsatisfactory or troublesome workers can be fired and threatened with deportation.

Because farm work is seasonal, the flow of immigrants varies throughout the year. The greatest number of Mexicans head north to the United States in the autumn and return home in the spring. The money brought back by seasonal migrants is the primary source of income for many Mexican villages (and, of course, that money is removed from the U.S. economy). Shops give credit to the villagers through the winter until the men return in the spring with dollars. During the winter, these villages may be inhabited almost entirely by women and children.

Since the late 1980s, women have accounted for about half of the undocumented immigrants from Mexico, according to U.S. census and immigration figures. Some are joining male family members already in the United States, but most seek jobs. The increased female migration to the United States partly reflects the changing role of women in Mexican

society: in the past, rural Mexican women were obliged to marry at a young age and to remain in the village to care for children. At the same time, women also feel increased pressure to get a job in the United States because of poor economic conditions in Mexico.

What happens to the minority of illegal immigrants who are caught? Most of them are escorted by the U.S. back to Mexico; then they simply retrace their steps and recross the border.

Crossing the U.S.-Mexican Border. The U.S.-Mexican border itself is not difficult to cross illegally. Guards heavily patrol the official border crossings, most of which are located in urban areas such as El Paso, Texas, and San Diego, California, or along highways. But the border is 3,600 kilometers (2,000 miles) long. It runs through sparsely inhabited regions and is guarded by only a handful of agents. A barbed-wire fence runs along the border itself but is broken in many places.

The typical illegal immigrant from Mexico may have more difficulty reaching the U.S. border than

Mexicans reach the United States by climbing over the border fence separating Tijuana and San Diego. (AP/Wide World Photos)

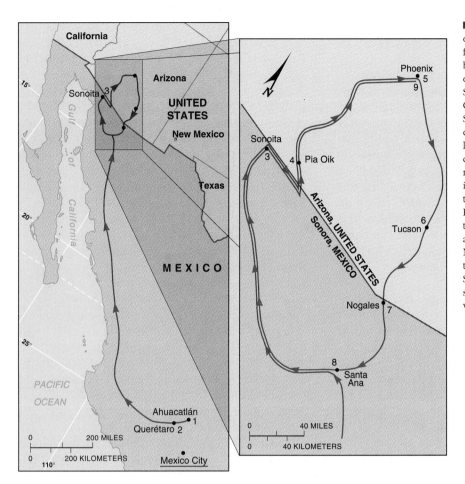

FIGURE 3-7 The documented route of one group of illegal immigrants from Mexico to the United States began in Ahuacatlán (1), a village of 1,000 inhabitants in Querétaro State. The immigrants took a bus to Querétaro (2) and another bus to Sonoita (3), where they hired a driver to take them to a remote location on the border. They crossed the U.S. border on foot near Pia Oik, Arizona (4, detail of inset) and paid a driver to take them to Phoenix (5). Arrested in Phoenix by the Border Patrol, they were driven to Tucson (6) and then to the Mexican border at Nogales (7), where they took buses to Santa Ana (8) and back to Sonoita. They then repeated the same route back to Phoenix (9), where they found work.

actually crossing it. One documented case is illustrated in Figure 3-7. A group of illegal immigrants started from Ahuacatlán, a village of 1,000 in the state of Querétaro. The group first took a bus from the village to the state capital of Querétaro City, followed by another bus for the 1,800-kilometer (1,100-mile) trip to Sonoita, a town near the U.S. border. At Sonoita, the Mexicans hired a driver to transport them to a deserted border location, where they crossed on foot to Pia Oik, Arizona.

Once inside the United States, the group contacted a smuggler, known as a *coyote,* or sometimes a *pollero* ("one who sells chickens for a living"). The smuggler took them by car to Phoenix, approximately 250 kilometers (150 miles) away. A U.S. Border Patrol agent arrested them in Phoenix and took them to Tucson for processing and then across the border to Nogales. From Nogales, they took a bus 110 kilometers (70 miles) to Santa Ana and a second one 260 kilometers (160 miles) back to Sonoita. Re-

peating their earlier moves to cross the border at Pia Oik, Arizona, they eventually reached Phoenix once more, where they remained. The entire journey cost several hundred dollars.

The United States faces a dilemma. Allowing illegals to stay would encourage more to come and raise the U.S. unemployment rate. On the other hand, most undocumented residents take very low-paying jobs that most U.S. nationals will not accept.

The 1986 Immigration Reform and Control Act tried to reduce the flow of illegal immigrants to the United States. Under the law, aliens who could prove that they had lived in the U.S. continuously between 1982 and 1987 could become permanent resident aliens and apply for U.S. citizenship after 5 years. Seasonal agricultural workers could also qualify for permanent residence and citizenship. However, only 1.3 million agricultural workers and 1.8 million others applied for permanent residence, far fewer than government officials had estimated would take advantage of the program. Other undocumented residents apparently feared that if their applications were rejected, they would be deported.

At the same time, the law discouraged further illegal immigration by making it harder for recent immigrants to get jobs without proper documentation. An employer must verify that a newly hired worker can legally work in the United States and may be fined or imprisoned for hiring an undocumented worker.

During the 1990s, hostile citizens in California and other states have voted to deny undocumented immigrants access to most public services, such as schools, day-care centers, and health clinics. The laws have been difficult to enforce and of dubious constitutionality, but their enactment reflects the unwillingness on the part of many Americans to help out needy immigrants.

Other countries experience illegal immigration as well. Estimates of illegal foreign workers in Taiwan range from 20,000 to 70,000. Most are Filipinos, Thais, and Malaysians who are attracted by employment in textile manufacturing, construction, and other industries. These immigrants accept half the pay demanded by Taiwanese, for the level is much higher than what they are likely to get at home, if they could even find employment.

Guest Workers

Millions of people also migrate to countries in Western Europe and the Middle East in search of economic advancement. Foreigners who work in these countries are known as **guest workers.**

Guest workers serve a useful role in Western European and Middle Eastern countries because they take low-status and low-skilled jobs that local residents won't accept. In cities such as Berlin, Brussels, Paris, and Zurich, guest workers provide essential services, such as driving buses, collecting garbage, repairing streets, and washing dishes. Although relatively low-paid by European standards, guest workers earn far more than they would at home. Unlike most undocumented workers in the United States, European guest workers are protected by minimum wage laws and labor union contracts.

The economy of the guest worker's native country also gains from the arrangement. By letting their people work elsewhere, poorer countries reduce their own unemployment problem. Guest workers also help their native country by sending a large percentage of their earnings back home to their families. The injection of foreign currency then stimulates the local economy.

Origin and Destination of Guest Workers

Guest workers exceed 10 percent of the population in Switzerland and Luxembourg and 5 percent in Germany, Belgium, and France. Two-thirds of the workers in Middle Eastern petroleum-exporting states such as Kuwait, Qatar, Saudi Arabia, and United Arab Emirates are foreign.

Most guest workers in Europe come from Southern and Eastern Europe, northern Africa, the Middle East, and Asia. Distinctive migration routes have emerged among the exporting and importing countries. Italy and Turkey send the largest number of guest workers to Northern Europe, especially to Germany as a result of government agreements. Many guest workers in France come from former French colonies in North Africa—Algeria, Morocco, and Tunisia. Switzerland attracts a large number of Italians; Luxembourg receives primarily Portuguese (Figure 3-8). Migration to Northern Europe from Eastern Europe has also increased since the fall of communism, as Eastern Europeans immigrate in search of jobs.

The petroleum-exporting countries of the Middle East attract guest workers primarily from poorer Middle Eastern countries and from Asia. One-fourth of the labor force in Jordan, Lebanon, Syria, and Yemen migrate to petroleum-exporting states to seek employment. India, Pakistan, Thailand, and South Korea also send several million guest workers to the Middle East.

Problems with Guest Workers

Many guest workers suffer from poor social conditions. The guest worker is typically a young man who arrives alone in a city. He has little money for food, housing, or entertainment, because his primary objective is to send home as much money as possible. He is likely to use any surplus money for a railway ticket home for the weekend.

Far from his family and friends, the guest worker can lead a lonely life. His isolation may be heightened by unfamiliarity with the host country's language and distinctive cultural activities. Many guest workers pass their leisure time at the local railway station. There they can buy native-language newspapers, mingle with other guest workers, and meet people who have just arrived by train from home.

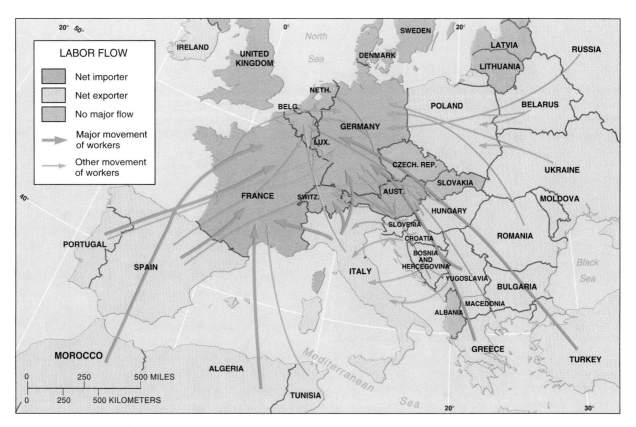

FIGURE 3-8 Guest workers in Europe. Guest workers emigrate primarily from Southern Europe and northern Africa to work in the more developed countries of Northern and Western Europe. Guest workers follow distinctive migration routes. The selected country may be a former colonial ruler, have a similar language, or have an agreement with the exporting country. (Countries shown in gray are neither major sources nor major destinations of guest workers.)

Both guest workers and their host countries regard the arrangement as temporary. In reality, however, many guest workers remain indefinitely, especially if they are joined by other family members. Some guest workers apply their savings to starting a grocery store, restaurant, or other small shop. These businesses can fill a need in European cities by remaining open on weekends and evenings when most locally owned establishments are closed.

Petroleum-exporting countries in the Middle East fear that the increasing numbers of guest workers will spark political unrest and abandonment of traditional Islamic customs. After the 1991 Gulf War, Kuwaiti officials expelled hundreds of thousands of Palestinian guest workers who had sympathized with Iraq's invasion of Kuwait in 1990. To minimize long-term stays, other host countries in the Middle East force migrants to return home if they wish to marry

and prevent them from returning once they have wives and children.

As a result of lower economic growth rates, Middle Eastern and Western European countries have reduced the number of guest workers in recent years. Several Western European governments pay guest workers to return home, but some of these countries have their own unemployment problems and sometimes refuse to take back their own nationals.

Many Western Europeans dislike the guest workers and oppose government programs to improve their living conditions. A recent incident in France illustrates the tension between guest workers and local citizens. The French government moved 300 black guest workers from Mali from condemned dwellings into a publicly owned building in the Paris suburb of Vitry-sur-Seine. On Christmas Eve, fifty townspeople vandalized the project, cut electrical

A guest worker works for an elevator repair company in Paris. Guest workers take low-status and low-skilled jobs in France and other Western European countries that local residents don't want. (Robert Harding Picture Library)

lines, sawed off water pipes, and ripped out telephones. Political parties that support restrictions on immigration have gained support in France, Germany, and other European countries, and attacks by local citizens on immigrants have increased.

British Policy. The United Kingdom severely restricts the ability of foreigners to obtain work permits. British policy, however, is complicated by the legacy of the country's former worldwide empire. When some of the United Kingdom's former colonies were granted independence, residents there could choose between remaining British citizens and becoming citizens of the new country. Millions of former colonials in India, Ireland, Pakistan, and the West Indies retained their British citizenship and eventually moved to the United Kingdom. But spouses and other family members who are citizens of the new countries do not have the right to come to Britain.

Migration in Asia

Voluntary international migration is not confined to the United States and Europe, of course. But lack of economic opportunity and immigration restric-

tions imposed by governments reduce the volume on other continents.

Millions of Asians have migrated to other countries for economic advancement. In the past, a large proportion of these voluntary migrants were time-contract laborers, recruited for a fixed period to work in mines or on plantations. When their contracts expired, many would settle permanently in the new country. Indians went as time-contract laborers to Burma (Myanmar), Malaysia, British Guiana (present-day Guyana in South America), eastern and southern Africa, and the islands of Fiji, Mauritius, and Trinidad. Japanese and Filipinos went to Hawaii, and Japanese also went to Brazil. Chinese worked on the U.S. West Coast and helped build the first railroad to span the United States, completed in 1869.

Today, more than 29 million ethnic Chinese live permanently in other countries, for the most part in Asia. Chinese constitute three-fourths of the population in Singapore, one-third in Malaysia, and one-tenth in Thailand. Most migrants were from southeastern China. Migration patterns vary among ethnic groups of Chinese. Chiu Chownese migrate to Cambodia, Laos, and Singapore; Hakka to Indonesia, Malaysia, and Thailand; and Hokkien to Indonesia and the Philippines (Figure 3-9).

Migration by Asians nearly a century ago is producing contemporary problems in several countries. For example, between 1879 and 1920, the British brought Indians as indentured laborers to the Fiji Islands in the South Pacific. Today, Fiji includes slightly more Indians than native Fijians. For many decades, Fiji was a model of how two culturally diverse groups could live together peacefully under a democratically elected government. Indians controlled most of the country's businesses, and Fijians dominated the government and army. After an Indian party won the elections in 1987, however, rioting broke out between the two groups, and Fijian army officers seized temporary control of the government. A new constitution in 1990 ensured that Fijians would hold a majority of seats in the parliament.

K E Y I S S U E 3

Why Do People Migrate Within a Country?

- Migration Between Regions of a Country
- Migration Within One Region

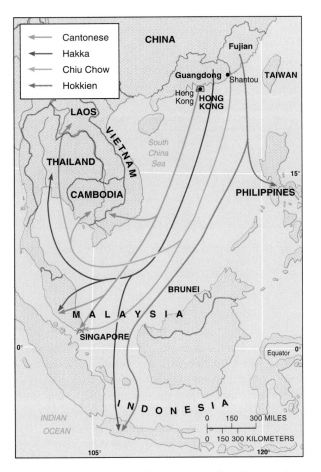

FIGURE 3-9 Migration from China. Various ethnic Chinese peoples have distinctive streams of migration to other Asian countries. Most migrate to communities where other members of the same ethnic group have already established businesses. Most emigrate from Guangdong and Hokkien (Fujian) provinces.

Internal migration is a permanent move to a new location within the same country. Most people find migration within a country less traumatic than international migration because they find familiar language, foods, broadcasts, literature, music, and other social customs after they move. Moves within a country also generally involve much shorter distances than those in international migration. However, internal migration can involve long-distance moves in large countries, such as the United States and Russia.

Internal migration can be divided into two types. **Interregional migration** is movement from one region of a country to another; **intraregional migra-** tion is movement within one region. Motives for the two types of moves may be different.

Migration between Regions of a Country

In the United States, interregional migration was more important in the past, when most people were farmers. Lack of farmland pushed many people from the more densely settled regions of the country and lured them to the frontier, where land was abundant. Today, most people still move to a new region for a better job, but an increasing percentage move for noneconomic reasons.

Migration between Regions in the United States

The most famous example of large-scale internal migration is the opening of the American West. Two hundred years ago, the United States consisted of a collection of settlements concentrated on the Atlantic coast. Through mass interregional migration, the interior of the continent was settled and developed.

Changing Center of Population. The U.S. Census Bureau computes the country's population center at the time of each census. The population center is the average location of everyone in the country, the "center of population gravity." If the United States were a flat plane placed on top of a pin, and all individuals weighed the same, the population center would be the point where the population distribution causes the flat plane to balance on the pin.

The changing location of the population center graphically demonstrates the march of the American people across the North American continent over the past 200 years. When the first U.S. census was taken in 1790, the population center was located in the Chesapeake Bay, east of Baltimore, Maryland. Throughout the colonial period, the population center remained roughly in the same place. This location reflects the fact that virtually all settlements were near the Atlantic coast (Figure 3-10).

Few colonists ventured far from coastal locations because they depended on shipping links with Europe to receive products and to export raw materials. Settlement in the interior was also hindered by an intervening obstacle, the Appalachian Mountains. The Appalachians blocked western development because of their steep slopes, thick forests, and few gaps that allowed easy passage through. Hostile in-

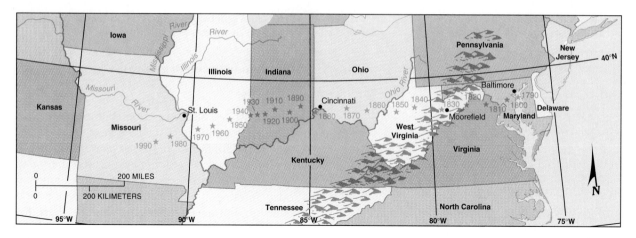

FIGURE 3-10 Changing center of population in the United States, calculated every decade by the Bureau of the Census. The center has consistently shifted westward, although the rate of movement has varied in different eras. In 1980, the center of population shifted west of the Mississippi River for the first time. In 1990, the center was the farthest south ever, as well as the farthest west.

digenous residents, commonly called Indians, also retarded western settlement.

Early Settlement in the Interior. Settlement of the interior began after 1790. By 1830 the center of population moved west of Moorefield, West Virginia. Encouraged by the opportunity to obtain a large amount of land at a low price, people moved into river valleys and fertile level lowlands as far west as the Mississippi River.

Transportation improvements, especially the building of canals, helped open the interior in the early 1800s. Most important was the 584-kilometer (363 mile) Erie Canal, which enabled people to travel inexpensively by boat between New York City and the Great Lakes. When the Erie Canal opened in 1825, the fare from New York to Detroit was $10 (not cheap in those days), yet traffic was so heavy on the canal that tolls paid for the $7 million construction cost within 9 years. Between 1816 and 1840, the network of new canals dug in the United States totaled 5,352 kilometers (3,326 miles). The diffusion of steam-powered boats further speeded water travel.

After 1830, the U.S. population center moved west more rapidly. By 1880, it was just west of Cincinnati, Ohio. The population center moved 11 kilometers (7 miles) per year during that period, compared with only 7 kilometers (4 miles) per year during the previous 40 years.

What accounts for the more rapid westward shift between 1830 and 1880? The primary reason was that

most western pioneers at the time passed through the interior of the country and headed for California. For nearly 40 years, the continuous westward advance of settlement stopped at the 98th meridian as migrants jumped directly to California. (The 98th meridian runs north-south through the eastern Dakota, Nebraska, Kansas, Oklahoma, and Texas.)

Large numbers of migrants passed through the interior without stopping, in part because they were pulled to California, especially by the Gold Rush beginning in the late 1840s. At the same time, the interior of the country confronted early settlers with a physical environment that was unsuited to familiar agricultural practices.

Early nineteenth-century Americans preferred to start farms in forested areas that receive 100 centimeters (40 inches) or more precipitation a year. They cut down the trees and used the wood to build homes, barns, and fences. But when they crossed west of the 98th meridian, pioneers found few trees. Instead, they saw vast rolling grasslands that average less than 50 centimeters (20 inches) of precipitation per year.

Without the technology to overcome this dry climate, lack of trees, and tough grassland sod, early explorers such as Zebulon Pike declared the region unfit for farming. Maps at the time labeled the region from the Dakotas through Nebraska, Kansas, and Oklahoma to Texas as "the Great American Desert." Ironically, with today's agricultural practices, the region west of the 98th meridian to the Rocky

Mountains, which we call the Great Plains, is one of the world's richest farming areas.

Settlement of the Great Plains. After 1880, the U.S. population center continued to migrate westward at a much slower pace. Between 1880 and 1950, the center moved approximately 5 kilometers (3 miles) per year, less than half the rate of the previous half century. The rate slowed in part because large-scale migration to the East Coast from Europe offset some of the migration from the East Coast to the U.S. West.

The westward movement of the U.S. population center also slowed after 1880 because people began to fill in the area between the 98th meridian and California that earlier generations had bypassed. The Dakota Territory, for example, grew from 14,000 inhabitants in 1870 to 135,000 in 1880 and 539,000 by 1890. Advances in agricultural technology in the late nineteenth century enabled people to cultivate the Great Plains. Farmers used barbed wire to reduce dependence on wood fencing, the steel plow to cut the thick sod, and windmills and well-drilling equipment to pump more water.

Beginning in the 1840s, the expansion of the railroads encouraged western settlement. By the 1880s, an extensive rail network permitted settlers on the Great Plains to transport their products to the large concentrations of customers in East Coast cities. The railroad companies also promoted western settlement by selling land to farmers. Companies that built

the railroad lines received large land grants from the federal government, not just narrow right-of-way strips to lay tracks. The railroad companies in turn financed construction of their lines by selling small parcels of the adjacent land to farmers. Rail companies established offices in major East Coast and European cities to sell land.

Recent Growth of the South. Since 1950, the population center has moved west faster, at 10 kilometers (6 miles) per year. In 1980, it was located near DeSoto, Missouri, southwest of St. Louis. The site was significant: for the first time in U.S. history, the population center had crossed the Mississippi River. By 1990, the center had migrated farther westward, 16 kilometers (10 miles) northwest of Stedville, Missouri.

The recent movement of the population center also shows a second trend, movement southward. In 1790, the center was at 39°16'30" north latitude. By 1920, it had moved only slightly southward to 39°10'21". Beginning in the 1920s, the center moved southward, at first slowly, but since 1950 at 4 kilometers (2 miles) per year. By 1990, the center had reached 37°52'20" north latitude.

The population center drifted southward because of net migration into the southern and western states. Between 1980 and 1988, for example, about 3 million people moved from the Midwest to the West, whereas about 2 million moved from the West to the Midwest (Figure 3-11). Net migration from the Midwest to the South and from the Northeast to the South

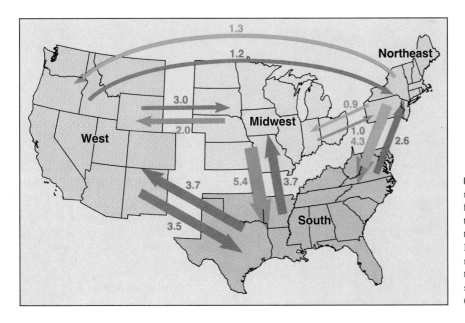

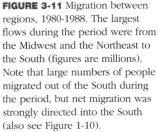

FIGURE 3-11 Migration between regions, 1980-1988. The largest flows during the period were from the Midwest and the Northeast to the South (figures are millions). Note that large numbers of people migrated out of the South during the period, but net migration was strongly directed into the South (also see Figure 1-10).

were both about 1.7 million during the period; in other words, 1.7 million more people moved to the South from each of the two northern areas than moved from the South to the Northeast and Midwest.

Interregional Migration to the South and West. Why are Americans emigrating from the North and East and immigrating to the South and West? More than half move primarily for job opportunities. New jobs created each year since 1960 have averaged about 3 percent in the United States as a whole, 5 percent in the South and West, but only 1 percent in the Northeast and Midwest.

People also migrate to the South and West for environmental reasons. Americans commonly refer to the South and West as the sunbelt, because of their more temperate climates. The Northeast and Midwest are labeled the rustbelt, because of the dependency on declining steel and other manufacturing industries (as well as the ability of the regions' climates to rust out cars relatively quickly). As people gain more leisure time, they are lured to the sunbelt for outdoor recreation throughout the year.

The growth in population and employment of the South and West and the decline of the Northeast and Midwest have aggravated interregional antagonism. Some people in the Northeast and Midwest believe that southern and western states have stolen industries from them. The fact is, however, that most industrial growth in the South and West comes from

newly established companies, although some industries have relocated from the Northeast and Midwest.

Overall, the regional difference in economic growth somewhat reduces a historical imbalance, because traditionally people in the Northeast have enjoyed higher incomes than residents of the South. If the average income of a U.S. family is arbitrarily designated as 100, then the average income in 1990 was 116 for people in the Northeast and 88 for people in the South. By comparison, as recently as 1929, average income was 138 in the Northeast and only 51 in the South. The gap between the Northeast and the South has widened since 1970, however, when the average was 107 in the Northeast and 90 in the South; the increase results from recent problems faced by southern industries (see Chapter 10).

Internal Migration of African–Americans. Net migration of African-Americans has followed a different pattern. A century ago, most African-Americans lived in the southern United States because their ancestors had been forced to migrate to the region from Africa (see the next Key Issue). During the twentieth century, large numbers of them migrated from the South to take jobs in the large cities of the Northeast, Midwest, and West.

African-Americans migrated from the South along several channels (Figure 3-12). Those in the Carolinas and other South Atlantic states generally moved to northeastern cities such as New York, Philadelphia,

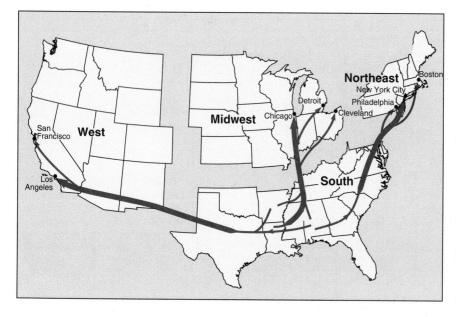

FIGURE 3-12 Net migration by African-Americans, 1950-1955. This time was a peak period for African-American migration from the South to other regions of the country. Migration followed distinctive channels, from the Carolinas to the Northeast, from Alabama and Mississippi to the Midwest, and from Texas to California. (From Report of the National Advisory Committee on Civil Disorders.)

and Boston. African-Americans in Alabama, Mississippi, and Tennessee migrated primarily to Chicago, Detroit, Cleveland, and other large Midwestern cities. Those in Texas and Oklahoma tended to migrate to Los Angeles and other California cities.

Migration between Regions in Other Countries

As in the United States, long-distance interregional migration has been an important means of opening new regions for economic development in other large countries. Incentives have been used to stimulate migration to other regions.

Russia. Interregional migration was important in developing the former Soviet Union. Soviet policy encouraged factory construction near raw materials rather than near existing population concentrations (see Chapter 10). Not enough workers lived nearby to fill all the jobs at the mines, factories, and construction sites established in these remote resource-rich regions. To build up an adequate labor force, the Soviet government had to stimulate interregional migration.

Soviet officials were especially eager to develop Russia's Far North, which included much of Siberia, because it is rich in natural resources—fossil fuels, minerals, and forests. The Far North encompassed 45 percent of the Soviet Union's land area but contained less than 2 percent of its people. Earlier in this century, the Soviet government had forced people to migrate to the Far North to construct and op-

erate steel mills, hydroelectric power stations, mines, and other enterprises. In later years, the Soviet government reduced the use of forced migration and instead provided incentives, including higher wages, more paid holidays, and earlier retirement, to induce voluntary migration to the Far North.

The incentives failed to pull as many migrants to the Far North as Soviet officials desired. People were reluctant because of the region's harsh climate and remoteness from population clusters. Each year, as many as half of the people in the Far North migrated back to other regions of the country and had to be replaced by other immigrants, especially young males willing to work in the region for a short period. One method the Soviet government used was to send a brigade of young volunteers, known as *Komsomol,* during school vacations to help construct projects. An example is the Baikal-Amur Railroad, which runs for 3,145 km (1,955 miles) from Taishet to Sovetskaia Gavan.

The collapse of the Soviet Union ended the policies to encourage interregional migration. In the transition to a market-based economy, Russian government officials no longer dictate "optimal" locations for factories.

Brazil. Another large country, Brazil, has encouraged interregional migration. Most Brazilians live in a string of large cities near the Atlantic coast, including Recife, Salvador, Rio de Janeiro, São Paulo, and Pôrto Alegre. São Paulo and Rio de Janeiro have become two of the world's largest cities. In contrast, Brazil's tropical interior is very sparsely inhabited.

This African-American family arrived in Chicago after migrating from the South, about 1910. (Stock Montage, Inc.)

To increase the attractiveness of the interior, in 1960 the government moved its capital from Rio to a newly built city called Brasília, situated 1,000 kilometers (600 miles) from the Atlantic coast. From above, Brasília's design resembles an airplane, with government buildings located at the center of the city and housing arranged along the "wings."

At first, Brasília's population grew slowly, because government workers and foreign embassy officials resented the forced move from Rio, one of the world's most animated cities. In recent years, thousands of people have migrated to Brasília in search of jobs. In a country with rapid population growth, many people will migrate where they think they can find jobs. Many of these workers could not afford housing in Brasília and were living instead in hastily erected shacks on the outskirts.

Indonesia. Since 1969, the Indonesian government has paid for the migration of more than 5 million people, primarily from the island of Java, where nearly two-thirds of its people live, to less-populated islands. Under the government program, families receive 2 hectares (5 acres) of land, materials to build

a house, seeds and pesticides, and food to tide them over until the crops are ready.

The number of participants has declined in recent years, primarily because of environmental concerns. Some families moved to land that could not support intensive agriculture; others disrupted the habitats of indigenous peoples. The program siphoned off only a very small percentage of Java's population growth during the past quarter-century.

Europe. The pattern of interregional migration throughout Western Europe is reflected in differences in per capita income and unemployment in different regions. The regions with net immigration are also the ones with the highest per capita incomes (Figures 3-13 and 3-14).

Even countries that occupy relatively small land areas have important interregional migration trends. People in Italy migrate from the south, known as the Mezzogiorno, to the north in search of job opportunities. Compared with the Mezzogiorno, Italy's north benefits from relatively rich agricultural land and a strong industrial base. The Mezzogiorno comprises 40 percent of Italy's land area and contains 35 per-

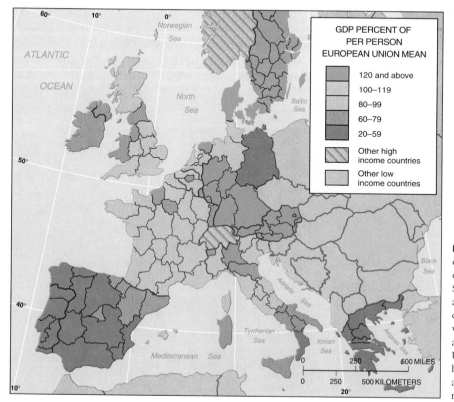

FIGURE 3-13 Per capita gross domestic product as a percentage of the European Union average. Sharp differences in wealth exist among regions of some European countries. Within Italy, for example, wealth is twice as high in the north as in the south. For the European Union as a whole, incomes are higher in regions near the center and lower in regions that are relatively remote from the center.

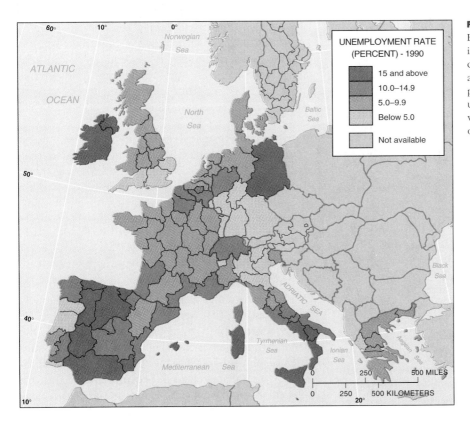

FIGURE 3-14 Unemployment in the European Union. The distribution is closely associated with the distribution of wealth. People are migrating from the poorer peripheral regions with high unemployment rates to the wealthier core where job opportunities are greater.

cent of the population but only 24 percent of the national income. Per capita income is nearly twice as high in the north as in the south, and unemployment rates are less than 5 percent in the north, compared with more than 20 percent in the south.

Similarly, people in the United Kingdom are migrating because of regional differences in job opportunities, although the pattern is the opposite of Italy's: economic growth is in the south, while the north is declining. The northern regions of the United Kingdom were the first in the world to enter the industrial revolution in the eighteenth century. Today, many of the region's industries are no longer competitive in the global economy. On the other hand, industries in the south and east—especially the region around London—are relatively healthy.

Regional differences in economic conditions within European countries may become greater with increased integration of the continent's economy. Regions closer to European markets, such as the south of Britain and the north of Italy, may hold a competitive advantage over more peripheral regions.

India. Some governments limit the ability of people to migrate from one region to another. For example, Indians need a permit to migrate—or even to visit—the state of Assam in the northeastern part of the country. The restrictions, which date from the British colonial era, are designed to protect the ethnic identity of Assamese by limiting the ability of outsiders to compete for jobs and purchase land. Because Assam is situated on the border with Bangladesh, the restrictions also limit international migration.

Migration within One Region

Although interregional migration attracts considerable attention, far more people move within the same region, which is *intraregional* migration. Since 1800, the most prominent type of intraregional migration in the world has been from rural to urban areas. Less than 5 percent of the world's people lived in urban areas in 1800, compared with nearly half today.

Migration from Rural to Urban Areas

Urbanization began in the 1800s in the countries of Europe and North America that were undergoing rapid industrial development. The percentage of people living in urban areas in the United States, for example, increased from 5 percent in 1800 to 50 percent in 1920. Today, approximately three-fourths of the people in the United States and other more developed countries live in urban areas (see Chapter 11).

Migration from rural to urban areas has skyrocketed in recent years in the developing countries of Africa, Asia, and Latin America. Studies conducted in several LDCs show that migration from rural areas accounts for nearly half of the population increase in urban areas, and the natural increase (excess of births over deaths) accounts for the remainder. Worldwide, more than 20 million people are estimated to migrate each year from rural to urban areas.

Migration to one of the world's largest cities, São Paulo, Brazil, has reached 300,000 people per year. Many of these migrants cannot find housing in the city and must live in squatter settlements, known in Brazil as *favelas*. The favelas may lack electricity, running water, and paved streets (see Chapter 12).

Like interregional migrants, most people who move from rural to urban areas seek economic advancement. They are pushed from rural areas by declining opportunities in agriculture and are pulled to the cities by the prospect of work in factories or services.

Migration from Urban to Suburban Areas

In more developed countries, most intraregional migration is from central cities out to the suburbs. Annual net migration from cities to suburbs exceeds 1 million people in the United States; comparable rates of suburbanization are found in Canada, the United Kingdom, and other Western European countries. The population of most central cities has declined in North America and Western Europe, while suburbs have grown rapidly.

The major reason for the large-scale migration to the suburbs is not related to employment, as was the case with other forms of migration. For most people, migration to suburbs does not coincide with changing jobs. Instead, people are pulled by a suburban lifestyle.

Suburbs offer the opportunity to live in a detached house rather than an apartment, surrounded by a private yard where children can play safely. A garage or driveway on the property guarantees space to park automobiles at no charge. Suburban schools tend to be more modern, better equipped, and safer than those in cities. Automobiles and trains enable people to live in suburbs, yet have access to jobs, shops, and recreation facilities throughout the urban area (see Chapter 12).

As a result of suburbanization, the territory occupied by urban areas has rapidly expanded (see Chapter 11). To accommodate suburban growth, builders convert farms on the periphery of urban areas to housing developments, where new roads, sewers, and other services must be built.

Migration from Metropolitan to Nonmetropolitan Areas

During the 1970s, the more developed countries of North America and Western Europe witnessed a new trend. For the first time in U.S. history, rural areas grew more rapidly than urban areas. Canada, the United Kingdom, and several other European countries displayed similar patterns. Net migration from urban to rural areas is called **counterurbanization.**

Counterurbanization results in part from very rapid expansion of suburbs. The boundary where suburbs end and the countryside begins cannot be precisely defined. Most counterurbanization, however, represents genuine migration from cities and suburbs to small towns and rural communities.

As they do in suburbanization, people move from urban to rural areas for lifestyle reasons. People are lured to rural areas by the prospect of swapping the rat race of urban life for the opportunity to live on a farm where they can own horses or grow vegetables. Most people who move to farms do not earn their living from agriculture. Instead, they work in nearby factories or small-town shops and services.

With modern communications and transportation systems, no location in a more developed country is truly isolated, either economically or socially. Computers enable us to work anywhere and still have access to an international network. We can obtain money at any time from a conveniently located electronic transfer machine rather than by going to a bank building. We can select clothing from a mail-order catalogue, place the order by telephone, pay by credit card, and have the desired items delivered within a few days. We can follow the fortunes of our favorite baseball teams on television anywhere in the country, thanks to satellite dishes.

Somalis were forced to migrate during the early 1990s as a result of civil war among rival clans and sub-clans. U.S. military intervention in 1992 and 1993 helped international organizations deliver food to Somalis living in refugee camps, but violence increased again after the United States withdrew its forces in 1994. (Wendy Stone/Gamma-Liaison, Inc.)

Many migrants from urban to rural areas are retired people who are attracted by access to leisure activities, such as fishing and hiking. Retirement communities—in reality, small towns restricted to older people, typically over age 50—appeal to retired people who like to participate in recreation activities. In France, some elderly people migrate from Paris to the rural village where they were born; others are attracted to the mild climate in the south of the country along the Mediterranean coast.

Counterurbanization has stopped in the United States since the early 1980s, because job opportunities have declined in rural areas. Many factories that located in rural areas during the 1970s are no longer competitive in a rapidly changing global economy. Industries that located in rural areas to take advantage of the lower costs of doing business are being undersold by Asian competitors who have even lower production costs. Surviving industries in rural parts of the United States and other more developed countries have had to become more efficient, often by eliminating jobs.

The rural economy has also been hurt by poor agricultural conditions. The price of farm products has declined, and many farmers have gone bankrupt. Although farmers constitute a small percentage of the labor force, they play an important role in the economy of rural areas. For example, the typical farmer borrows large sums of money from local banks and buys expensive equipment from local farm implements stores.

Future migration trends are unpredictable in more developed countries, because future economic conditions are difficult to forecast. Have these countries reached long-term equilibrium, in which approximately three-fourths of the people live in urban areas and one-fourth in rural areas? Will counterurbanization resume in the future, because people prefer to live in rural areas? Is the decline of the rural economy reversible?

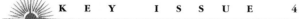

Why Are People Forced to Emigrate from a Country?

- Slavery
- Political Instability

People usually migrate because of a combination of push and pull factors. But some have no choice; they are forcibly moved by others from one country to another. Forced international migration has historically occurred for two main reasons. First, some people have been shipped to other countries as slaves or as prisoners. Second, people have been forced to migrate because of cultural diversity resulting from war, boundary change following independence of colonies, or government policy.

Slavery

Slavery is a system whereby one person owns another person like a piece of property and can force that slave to work for the owner's benefit. The practice was widespread during the time of the Roman Empire, about 2,000 years ago. During the Middle Ages, slavery was replaced in Europe by a feudal system, in which laborers (known as serfs) who worked the land were bound to the land and not free to migrate elsewhere. Serfs had to turn over a portion of their crops to the lord and provide other services as demanded by the lord.

African Slaves

Although slavery was rare in Europe, Europeans were responsible for diffusing the practice to the Western Hemisphere. At least 10 million Africans were uprooted from their homes and sent to the Western Hemisphere for sale in the slave market. This large-scale slave trade was a response to a shortage of labor in the sparsely inhabited Americas. Europeans who owned large plantations in the Americas turned to African slaves as a cheap and abundant source of labor.

The forced migration began when people living along the east and west coasts of Africa, taking advantage of their superior weapons, captured members of other groups living farther inland and sold the

captives to Europeans. Europeans in turn shipped the captured Africans to the Americas, selling them as slaves, either on consignment or through auctions. The Spanish and Portuguese first participated in the slave trade in the early sixteenth century, and the British, Dutch, and French joined the trade during the next century.

Two-thirds of the captured Africans were forced to migrate to the Western Hemisphere as slaves during a 100-year period that began in 1710. During the eighteenth century, the British sent 2 million slaves to the Western Hemisphere, including approximately 400,000 to the United States and most of the remainder to Caribbean islands. The Portuguese sent approximately 2 million slaves to Brazil during the same period.

Different European countries operated in various regions of Africa, each sending slaves to different destinations in the Americas. The Portuguese shipped slaves primarily from their principal African colonies—Angola and Mozambique—to their major American colony, Brazil (Figure 3-15, right). Other European countries took slaves primarily from a coastal strip of West Africa between what is now Liberia and Angola, 4,000 kilometers (2,500 miles) long and 160 kilometers (100 miles) wide. The majority of these slaves went to Caribbean islands, and most of the remainder to Central and South America. Fewer than 5 percent of the slaves ended up in the United States.

At the height of the eighteenth-century demand for slaves, several European countries adopted the **triangular slave trade,** an efficient triangular trading pattern (Figure 3-15, left). Ships left Europe for Africa with cloth and other trade goods, used to buy the slaves. They then transported slaves and gold from Africa to the Western Hemisphere, primarily to the Caribbean islands. To complete the triangle, the same ships then carried sugar and molasses from the Caribbean on their return trip to Europe. Some ships added another step, making a rectangular trading pattern, in which molasses was carried from the Caribbean to the North American colonies and rum from the colonies to Europe.

The large-scale forced migration of Africans obviously caused them considerable hardship, separating families and destroying villages. Traders generally seized the stronger and younger villagers, who could be sold as slaves for the highest price. The Africans were packed onto ships at extremely

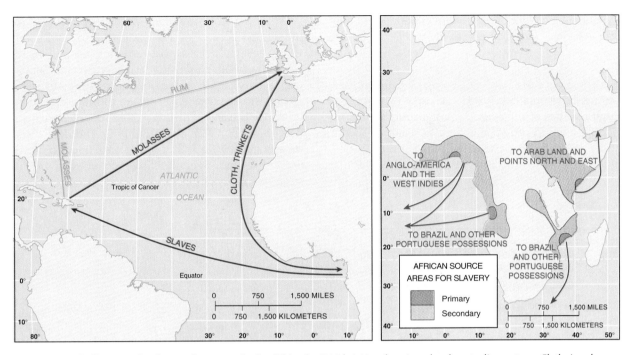

FIGURE 3-15 (Left) Triangular slave trade pattern. In the 1700s, the British initiated a triangular slave-trading pattern. Cloth, iron bars, and other goods were carried by ship from Britain to Africa to buy slaves. The same ships then transported slaves from Africa to the Caribbean islands. The ships then completed the triangle by returning to Britain with molasses to make rum. Sometimes the ships formed a rectangular pattern by carrying the molasses from the Caribbean islands to the North American colonies, where the rum was distilled and shipped to Britain. (Right) The British and other European powers obtained slaves primarily from a narrow strip along the west coast of Africa, from what is now Liberia to Angola. In the early days of colonization, Europeans secured territory along the Atlantic coast and rarely ventured more than 160 kilometers (100 miles) into the interior of the continent.

high density, kept in chains, and provided with minimal food and sanitary facilities. Approximately one-fourth died crossing the Atlantic.

Australian Convicts

The first Europeans to settle in Australia were primarily forced migrants, mostly convicts deported from England. During the late eighteenth and early nineteenth centuries, British judges sentenced many people convicted of serious crimes to deportation to Australia.

Australia's first penal colony was located in present-day New South Wales, in the southeastern part of the country. The colony began in 1786 and received its first shipload of convicts 2 years later. By the middle of the nineteenth century, 165,000 convicts had been transported there. Like the African slaves, the convicts endured poor conditions on the ships. In one documented case, more than 1,000 convicts were crammed into the hold of a vessel,

and more than 300 died, either during the passage or shortly after reaching Australia.

Many convicts chose to remain in Australia at the conclusion of their sentences. They were eventually joined by other English colonists who had voluntarily moved to Australia in response to economic push and pull factors. The last shipload of convicts arrived in Australia in 1849. By the middle of the nineteenth century, Australia had become an attractive destination for voluntary migrants looking for farmland and jobs.

Political Instability

No longer are large groups of people forced to migrate as slaves. However, forced international migration has increased in the contemporary world because of political instability resulting from cultural diversity. Three types of political instability force international migration: war, new independence of former colonies, and government ideology.

War

Global conflicts have twice engulfed the planet during the twentieth century, each time producing a large number of refugees. Approximately 6 million people were forced to migrate as a result of World War I (1914–1918). That figure, however, pales beside the upheaval caused by World War II (1939–1945).

Approximately 45 million people were forced to migrate because of events leading up to World War II, the war itself, and postwar adjustments. Forced migration resulted primarily from German and Japanese military expansions during the 1930s and early 1940s, and again when the allied forces of the United States, Britain, France, and others counterattacked, beginning in 1942. Between 1939 and 1947, approximately 27 million people were forced to move in Europe, and several million more died in the infamous concentration camps (Figure 3-16).

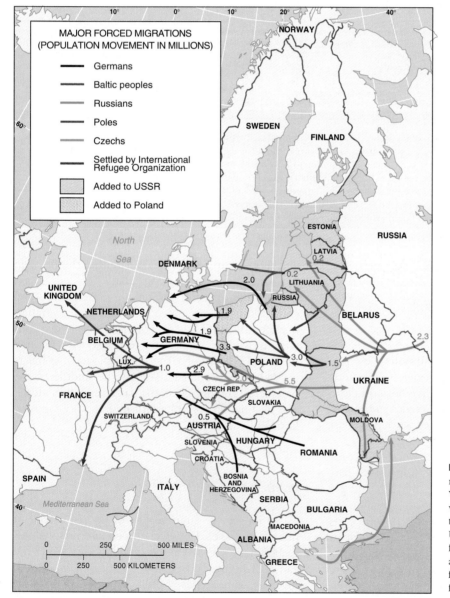

FIGURE 3-16 Forced migration as a result of territorial changes after World War II. The largest number were Poles forced to move from territory occupied by the Soviet Union, Germans forced to migrate from territory taken over by Poland and the Soviet Union, and Russians forced to return to the Soviet Union from Western Europe.

In recent years, people have been forced to migrate because of wars in other regions of the world. Particularly disruptive wars have been waged in three regions of eastern Africa—the Horn of Africa, Rwanda, and Mozambique—as well as in the Middle East.

African Wars Force Complex Migration. Wars in four states in the Horn of Africa—Eritrea, Ethiopia, Somalia, and Sudan—have forced several million people to migrate (Figure 3-17). Eritrea became an Italian colony in 1890. Ethiopia, an independent country for more than 2,000 years, was captured by Italy during the 1930s. After World War II, Ethiopia regained its independence, and the United Nations awarded Eritrea to Ethiopia.

Eritrea was to control its territory, despite ownership by Ethiopia. But Ethiopia dissolved the Eritrean legislature and banned the use of Eritrea's major local language, Tigrinya. The Eritreans rebelled, beginning a 30-year fight for independence (1961–1991). During this civil war, an estimated 665,000 Eritrean refugees fled to neighboring Sudan, especially north to the city of Būr Sūdān (Port Sudan) along the Red Sea and west to Khartoum, the capital, as well as Kassalā, a smaller border town.

Ethiopia further suffered from warfare in its eastern region of Ogaden, a desert area also claimed by Somalia. The Ethiopian army uprooted several million Somalis living in the Ogaden who preferred that the province be part of Somalia. According to international refugee organizations, approximately 365,000 Ethiopians fled to Somalia (Somali officials argue that more than 800,000 actually arrived). Half of these refugees lived in camps near the border, and the remainder wandered from village to village in Somalia.

In 1991, rebels defeated the Ethiopian army and took control of the national government. Eritrea became an independent state in 1993, and many Eritrean refugees returned home. But a reduction in the number of refugees in Eritrea has been offset by increases of refugees elsewhere in Ethiopia.

In Sudan, a civil war has raged since the late 1960s between largely Christian rebels in the southern provinces and the Muslim-dominated government forces in the north. More than 1 million Sudanese have been forced to migrate from the south to the north, and another 350,000 have fled to Ethiopia.

Meanwhile, a civil war in Somalia has generated refugees in the hundreds of thousands, as described in this chapter's introductory case study. With the collapse of a national government in Somalia, clans and subclans claimed control over other portions of the country. As the armies of the individual clans and subclans seized food, property, and weapons, members of less-powerful clans and subclans were forced to migrate for safety and food. The United States intervened in late 1992 to protect delivery of

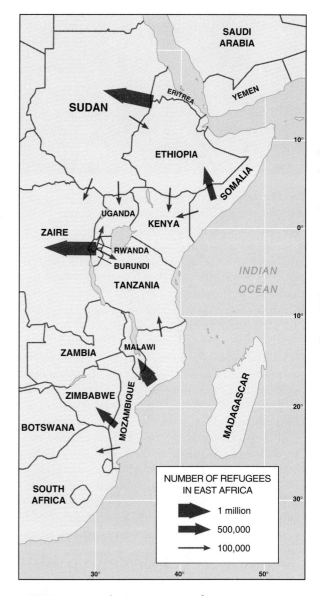

FIGURE 3-17 Forced migration in East Africa. Eritreans, Ethiopians, Somalis, and Sudanese have been forced to move because of civil wars. To escape civil wars, Hutus have been forced to migrate from Rwanda, and residents of Mozambique have fled to Malawi and other neighboring countries.

Hutus in Rwanda migrated to neighboring countries, such as Tanzania, after Tutsis won the civil war in 1994. (Steve Lehman/SABA Press Photos, Inc.)

food by international relief organizations and to reduce the number of weapons in the hands of the clan and subclan armies.

In Rwanda, 40 percent of the country's 8.5 million inhabitants were killed or forced to migrate in a civil war between ethnic groups that began in 1994. Early that year, the presidents of Rwanda and neighboring Burundi were killed in a plane crash. The death ended negotiation toward a peace accord between Rwanda's two ethnic groups, the Hutus and Tutsis. Hutus comprised 86 percent of the population, but when Rwanda was a Belgian colony, Tutsis enjoyed positions of power. After Rwanda gained independence in 1962, the Hutu majority gained control of the government and suppressed several Tutsi uprisings.

After the plane crash, the Hutu-dominated military killed many Tutsis, as well as moderate Hutu members of the government who favored reconciliation with the Tutsis. Tutsi rebels formed the Rwanda Patriotic Front to fight the Hutu-controlled army. Within a few months, the Tutsi rebels had won the civil war, and millions of Hutus had fled into neighboring Zaire and Tanzania.

Violence spread during the summer of 1994 to neighboring Burundi, where 85 percent of the population was Hutu and 15 percent Tutsi. As in Rwanda, Hutus controlled the government before the president died in the 1994 crash. Attempts failed to create a broad-based government with both Hutu and Tutsi representatives.

Farther south along the coast of East Africa, Mozambique has been the scene of a civil war that began in 1976, generating 1.4 million refugees. Nearly two-thirds have fled to neighboring Malawi, and the rest have gone to South Africa, Swaziland, Tanzania, Zambia, and Zimbabwe. In addition, several million people have been forced to migrate within Mozambique as a result of the civil war.

In Africa, drought, famine, and other environmental push factors have also forced international migration. In countries such as Ethiopia and Somalia, political refugees are not always clearly distinguished from forced migrants seeking food and water.

The physical condition of the refugees has often shocked Western observers. Many refugees are emaciated and deformed because of inadequate food and water. They have virtually no possessions, in many cases not even one set of clothes to wear. To reach another country, they may be forced to walk several hundred kilometers across the desert. Prospects for economic self-sufficiency are grim for most of these refugees. Even if they were given fertile land, they would not be healthy enough to farm it, nor could they obtain needed machinery and materials.

Middle East Conflicts. Nearly 5 million people were forced to migrate in the Persian Gulf region when Iraq invaded Kuwait in 1990 and the United States and others attacked Iraq in 1991 (the "Gulf

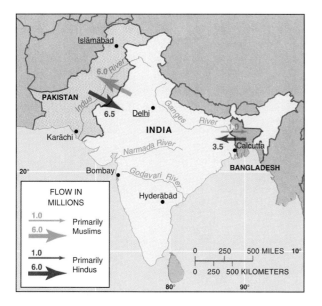

FIGURE 3-18 Forced migration in South Asia. In 1947, the partitioning of British India into two independent states, India and Pakistan, resulted in the forced migration of an estimated 17 million people. The train station in Amritsar, India, October 17, 1947, is crowded with Hindus who have been brought from Pakistan. (UPI/Bettmann)

War"). Forced migration came in two waves. During the first wave, approximately 1.5 million migrants left occupied Kuwait, including approximately 700,000 Egyptians, 380,000 Kuwaitis, 250,000 Palestinians or Jordanians, and 350,000 Asians (primarily from India, Sri Lanka, Pakistan, Bangladesh, and the Philippines). In addition, Saudi Arabia forced approximately 1 million Yemenis to emigrate in late 1990 after the government of Yemen criticized the Saudis for asking the Americans for military protection.

Only about 65,000 people were forced to migrate during the Gulf War itself, which lasted only 3 months. But in the weeks immediately following the war, more than 2 million Iraqis were forced to migrate, including more than 700,000 Iraqi Shiite Muslims, who crossed over into predominantly Shiite Iran, and nearly 1.5 million Kurds, who fled to Iran, to Turkey, or to other regions of Iraq.

Independence

Forced migration can also result when long-time colonies are carved up into several independent states. Boundaries of newly independent states often are drawn to coincide with important cultural bound-

aries of language, religion, or other characteristics. However, boundary lines rarely can segregate two cultural groups completely. Thus, members of a cultural group caught on the "wrong" side of a boundary may be forced to migrate to the other side.

Migration When the British Divided India and Pakistan. South Asia provides a vivid example of how independence can bring large-scale forced migration. When the British ended their colonial rule of the Indian subcontinent in 1947, they divided the colony into two irregularly shaped countries, India and Pakistan. Pakistan comprised two noncontiguous areas, West Pakistan and East Pakistan—1,600 kilometers (1,000 miles) apart, separated by India. East Pakistan became the independent state of Bangladesh in 1971. An eastern region of India was also practically cut off from the rest of the country, attached only by a narrow corridor north of Bangladesh that is less than 13 kilometers (8 miles) wide in some places (Figure 3-18).

The basis for this seemingly bizarre separation of West and East Pakistan from India was primarily religious. The people living in the two areas of Pakistan were predominantly Muslim; those in India were predominantly Hindu. Antagonism between the two re-

Muslims living in Bosnia-Herzegovina have been victims of ethnic cleansing by Serbs. Muslim men have been rounded up and placed in detention centers, such as this one at Manjaca. (Marleen Daniels/Gamma-Liaisons, Inc.)

ligious groups was so great that the British decided to place the Hindus and Muslims in separate states.

The partition of South Asia into two states resulted in massive forced migration, because the two boundaries did not correspond precisely to the territory inhabited by the two religious groups. In the late 1940s, approximately 17 million people caught on the wrong side of a boundary were forced to migrate. Some 6 million Muslims moved from India to West Pakistan, and about 1 million from India to East Pakistan. Hindus forced to migrate to India included approximately 6 million from West Pakistan and 3.5 million from East Pakistan.

Hindus in Pakistan and Muslims in India were killed attempting to reach the other side of the new border by people from the rival religion. Extremists attacked small groups of refugees traveling by road and halted trains to massacre the passengers.

Disputes concerning the correct location of the boundary between India and Pakistan have arisen periodically over the years since independence. The northernmost region of the former British colony—known as Jammu and Kashmir—contains a Muslim

majority, but two-thirds of it was given to India. Many of the Muslims living in India's portion of Jammu and Kashmir have long sought independence or a union with Pakistan. Pakistan has denied charges by India that it is helping to stir up unrest in Jammu and Kashmir (see Chapter 5).

Ethnic Cleansing in Former Yugoslavia. During the 1990s, the carving up of Yugoslavia along ethnic lines into a collection of independent states has forced about 2 million people to migrate. The largest number of forced migrants came from Bosnia and Herzegovina as a result of **ethnic cleansing,** in which a more powerful ethnic group forcibly relocates a less powerful one so that its members can be the sole inhabitants of a region. Ethnic cleansing in Bosnia and Herzegovina has been practiced primarily by Serbs against Bosnian Muslims (see Chapter 7).

The ethnic cleansing has involved several steps. First, Serbs take political and military control of villages inhabited by Muslims. Laws are enacted to draft the adult males into the Serb-dominated army and to remove both male and female Muslims from responsible jobs. Muslim men who refuse to join the army lose their health insurance and other social benefits. According to independent journalists, intoxicated Serb soldiers instigate individual acts of violence against Muslims in the villages. When Muslims retaliate, the Serb army restores peace in the villages by killing the professional and able-bodied male Muslims and deporting the others to camps.

Deported Muslims are divided into two groups: Potential troublemakers are held in detention camps, while Muslims not considered a threat (essentially women, children, and elderly people) are relocated to open centers. Refugees in the open centers can receive visits from international relief agencies and can leave the camps, but most have no place to go, because their homes and property have been seized by the Serbs and foreign countries accept only a small number of them. The breakup of Yugoslavia has produced more refugees in Europe than at any time since World War II.

Government Ideology

Many people have been forced to migrate because of disagreement with their country's government. In some countries, disagreement with the government may result in persecution and threats. Minority religious or ethnic groups may migrate from fear of persecution by the majority.

Ideology Forces Turks from Bulgaria. After World War II, the Communist government of Bulgaria repressed cultural differences by banning the Turkish language and the practice of some Islamic religious rites. The government took these steps to remove what it saw as obstacles to unifying national support for the ideology of communism. More than 1 million Bulgarian citizens of Turkish ancestry were forced to migrate to Turkey. The town of Bursa, about 100 kilometers (60 miles) south of Istanbul, became the largest settlement of Turkish refugees from Bulgaria.

With the fall of the Communist government in the early 1990s, Bulgaria's Turkish minority has pressed for more rights, including permission to teach the Turkish language as an optional subject in school. But many Bulgarians continue to oppose these efforts. Although communism has declined in importance in Bulgaria—as well as in other former communist countries in Eastern Europe—it has been replaced by an ideology that encourages traditional cultural features, such as language and religion.

Ideology Forces Haitians and Cubans from Their Homelands. Government ideology has forced both Haitians and Cubans to seek asylum in the United States. More than 700,000 Cubans emigrated after the 1959 revolution that brought the Communist government of Fidel Castro to power. Under Castro's leadership, the Cuban government took control of privately owned banks, factories, and farms, and political opponents of the government were jailed. More than 600,000 Cuban emigrants came to the United States, with the largest number settling in South Florida, where they have become prominent in the region's economy and politics.

A second flood of Cuban emigrants reached the United States in 1980, when Prime Minister Castro suddenly decided to permit political prisoners, criminals, and mental patients to leave the country. More than 125,000 Cubans left within a few weeks to seek political asylum in the United States, a migration stream that became known as the "Mariel boatlift," named for the port from which the Cubans were allowed to embark. To reach the United States, most crossed the 200-kilometer (125-mile) Straits of Florida in small boats, many of which were unseaworthy and capsized. When they learned about Castro's new policy, many Cubans already living in Florida sailed from the United States to Cuba, found their relatives, and returned to Florida with them.

U.S. officials were unprepared for the sudden influx of Cuban immigrants. Most Cubans were processed at Key West, Florida, and transferred to camps. Officials identified families or social service agencies willing to sponsor the refugees. Sponsors were expected to provide food and shelter and help the people secure jobs. Most refugees quickly found sponsors, but several thousand who did not lived in army camps and temporary settlements. Approximately 1,000 inhabited Miami's Orange Bowl stadium until the start of the football season, when they were transferred to tents pitched under Interstate 95 in downtown Miami.

Seven years later, in 1987, the United States agreed to permit 20,000 Cubans per year to migrate to the United States. Cuba also agreed to the return of 2,500 criminals or mental patients who had come in the 1980 Mariel boatlift.

Shortly after the Mariel boatlift from Cuba, several thousand Haitians sailed in small boats for the

United States. At first, U.S. officials were unwilling to let them remain, because they had migrated for economic advancement rather than political asylum. However, the Haitians brought a lawsuit against the U.S. government, arguing that if the Cubans were admitted, they should be, too. The government settled the case by agreeing to admit the Haitians.

After a 1991 coup that replaced elected president Jean-Bertrand Aristide with military leaders, thousands of Haitians fled their country. In boats that often were overcrowded and unseaworthy, they headed for the U.S. Guantánamo Bay naval base in southeastern Cuba, about 160 kilometers (100 miles) across the Windward Passage from Haiti. Although on Cuba, Guantánamo Bay naval base has been controlled by the United States for years.

Once safely ashore at Guantánamo, the Haitians could apply for asylum in the United States. Similarly, Haitians picked up by the U.S. Coast Guard from boats drifting in the Windward Passage were eligible to claim political asylum in the United States. The U.S. Immigration and Naturalization Service recognized the claim of political persecution made by many of the Haitians, but the State Department decided that most left Haiti for economic rather than political reasons. Although the United States invaded Haiti in 1994 and restored Aristide to power, many Haitians have continued to try to migrate to the United States, reinforcing the view that economic factors have been especially important in the Haitians' decisions.

The experience of the Haitians during the 1980s and again during the 1990s shows that economic and political push factors cannot always be easily distinguished. Although many people have been compelled to migrate for political reasons, most people move from one country to another at least in part because of economic push and pull factors.

Give Me Your Tired, Your Poor,…

Residents of the United States in the nineteenth and early twentieth centuries did not greet immigrants with open arms. But immigrants were given the opportunity to enter the country and make new lives. Some of them were successful. Even recently arrived undocumented immigrants stand a good chance of success, if given the chance.

The most famous symbol of migration in the world is surely the Statue of Liberty. Its inscription, written by Emma Lazarus, includes the famous words, "Give me your tired, your poor, your huddled masses yearning to breathe free." The statue stands at the mouth of New York Harbor, near Ellis Island, which was for many years the initial landing and processing point for tens of millions of immigrants.

For many people, however, the only way to enter the United States or Canada is illegally. In the latter part of the twentieth century, the tradition of universal ability to migrate to North America no longer exists. Paradoxically, in an era when human beings have invented easy means of long-distance transport, the right of free migration has been replaced by human barriers.

Summary Here again are the key issues we raised about migration.

1. Why do people migrate?

We can group the reasons into push and pull factors. People feel compelled (pushed) to emigrate from a location for political, economic, and environmental reasons. Similarly, people are induced (pulled) to immigrate because of the political, economic, or environmental attractiveness of a new location. We distinguish between international and internal migration, and within international migration, between forced and voluntary migration.

2. **Why do people voluntarily emigrate from a country?**

Most people voluntarily emigrate to another country for economic reasons, including limited job opportunities at home and brighter prospects for advancement elsewhere. For several hundred years, the largest stream of voluntary international migration came from Europe to North America. Today, Latin Americans and Asians constitute the largest group trying to migrate to the United States for economic opportunities, but immigration laws restrict the number who can legally enter the United States. As a result, millions of people immigrate to the United States without a valid visa, as undocumented or illegal immigrants.

3. **Why do people migrate within a country?**

We can distinguish between interregional and intraregional migration within the same country. Historically, interregional migration was especially important in settling the frontier of large countries such as the United States, Russia, and Brazil. Today, interregional migration persists because of differences among regions of a country in economic conditions, climate, and other environmental factors. The most important intraregional migration trends are from rural to urban areas within less developed countries and from cities to suburbs within more developed countries.

4. **Why are people forced to emigrate from a country?**

Forced international migration usually results from political push factors beyond the control of the migrants. In the past, people were forced to move to become slaves. The level of forced international migration in the world has risen sharply in recent years as a result of wars, creation of new countries, government ideology, and other political changes.

CASE STUDY REVISITED
The Migration Transition

Geographers know that migration results from a combination of political, economic, and environmental factors that push an individual to leave one location and pull the person to another place. The specific mixture of factors depends on whether the migration is international, interregional, or intraregional.

Push and pull factors explain why groups choose to migrate, but they do not explain the underlying social conditions. Some geographers have identified a **migration transition**, a series of changes in a society that is comparable to those in the demographic transition. The migration transition is a change in the migration pattern in a society that results from the social and economic changes that also produce the demographic transition.

A society in stage 1 of the demographic transition—characterized by high birth and death rates and a low natural increase rate—displays little migration. But a stage 1 society does have high mobility *daily* or *seasonally,* as the group searches for sources of food.

In stage 2 of the demographic transition—when the natural increase rate increases rapidly as a result of a sharp decline in the crude death rate—two forms of migration become important: migration from rural areas to cities and emigration to other countries. Like the sudden decline in the crude death rate, migration patterns in stage 2 societies are a consequence of technological change. Improvements in agricultural practices reduce the number of people needed in rural areas, while jobs in factories attract migrants to the cities, or to another country.

Crude birth rates begin to decline in stages 3 and 4 of the demographic transition as a result of a social change—people deciding to have fewer children. According to migration transition theory, societies in stages 3 and 4 are the destinations of the migrants leaving the stage 2 countries in search of economic opportunities. The principal form of intraregional migration within countries in stages 3 and 4 of the demographic transition is from cities to surrounding suburbs.

The migration transition applies to the current migration pattern in the Western Hemisphere, where countries in Latin America, which are in stage 2 of the demographic transition, export a large percentage of their population growth to the United States. For example, Jamaica, a country of approximately 2.6 million, has a crude birth rate of 25 (per 1,000), a crude death rate of 5, and a natural increase rate of 2.0 percent per year (calculated as crude birth rate minus crude death rate). Otherwise stated, in one year Jamaica has approximately 65,000 births, approximately 13,000 deaths, and therefore a natural increase of approximately 52,000. However, nearly 25,000 Jamaicans have migrated to the United States annually in recent years. As a result of this emigration, Jamaica's annual population increase is actually only about 1.1 percent, or half of the natural increase rate.

Jamaicans claim that the large-scale emigration subsidizes the U.S. economy, because most of the migrants are nurses, teachers, doctors, and other professionals who have been trained at the expense of the Jamaican government. But many of these migrants send their savings earned in the United States back to Jamaica to help out relatives who remain in the country. In addition, Jamaicans who have immigrated to the United States often return to Jamaica for visits, taking money and goods back with them. More important, they bring back to Jamaica the cultural values acquired through living in a more developed society.

In the Horn of Africa, a combination of wars, drought, and poverty forces people to migrate. Rapid rates of natural increase in these stage 2 countries add to the pressure on the limited resources. But in contrast to people emigrating from stage 2 countries in the Western Hemisphere, migrants in the Horn of Africa do not have a prosperous neighbor like the United States to serve as a destination.

Migration will play an increasing role in determining population growth of countries in stages 3 and 4 of the demographic transition. In the United States, the crude birth rate is approximately 16, the crude death rate is approximately 9, and the natural increase rate is approximately 0.7 percent per year. These rates translate into around 4 million births and 2 million deaths per year, and a natural increase of 2 million per year. However, the annual population increase in the United States is actually more than 2.5 million. The difference between actual growth and natural increase is due to net migration: annual immigration to the United States exceeds 1 million, whereas emigration from the United States is only around 300,000 per year.

In a couple of decades, the crude birth and crude death rates will be roughly equal in the United States. At that time, virtually all population growth will be attributable to net inmigration rather than to natural increase.

The migration transition does not fully explain the impact of migration on societies, because people migrate for multiple reasons. Parallels drawn between the demographic and migration transitions do not work, because the end of the demographic transition is a condition of equilibrium—low births and deaths and no growth—whereas the end of the migration transition appears to be high rates of immigration from poorer countries. Another problem with the migration transition model is that during the nineteenth century—the period of highest immigration rates—the United States was still in stage 2 of the demographic transition, which according to the migration transition should actually be a period of net out-migration. However, the concept of a migration transition does help to relate economic push and pull factors to social changes in a country.

Key Terms

Brain drain Large-scale emigration by talented people.

Chain migration Process by which people are given preference for being allowed into another country because a relative was previously admitted.

Counterurbanization Net migration from urban to rural areas in more developed countries.

Emigration Migration *out from* a location.

Ethnic cleansing The process by which a more powerful ethnic group forcibly relocates a less powerful one so that its members can be the sole inhabitants of a region.

Floodplain The area subject to flooding during a given number of years according to historical trends.

Forced migration Permanent movement compelled usually by political factors.

Guest workers Workers who migrate to the more developed countries of Northern and Western Europe, usually from Southern and Eastern Europe or from Northern Africa, in search of higher paying jobs.

Immigration Migration *into* a new location.

Internal migration Permanent movement within a particular country.

International migration Permanent movement from one country to another.

Interregional migration Permanent movement from one region of a country to another.

Intervening obstacle An environmental or cultural feature that hinders migration.

Intraregional migration Permanent movement within one region of a country.

Migration Form of relocation diffusion involving permanent move to a new location.

Migration transition Change in the migration pattern in a society that results from industrialization, population growth, and other social and economic changes that also produce the demographic transition.

Mobility The ability to move from one location to another.

Net migration The difference between the number of immigrants and the number of emigrants.

Pull factors Factors that induce people to move into a new location.

Push factors Factors that induce people to move out of their present location.

Quota In reference to migration, a law that places maximum limits on the number of people who can immigrate to a country.

Refugees People who are forced to migrate from a country for political reasons.

Triangular slave trade A practice, primarily during the eighteenth century, in which European ships transported slaves from Africa to Caribbean islands, molasses from the Caribbean to Europe, and trade goods from Europe to Africa.

Undocumented immigrants Citizens of less developed countries who migrate without proper documents to more developed countries, usually to find a job.

Voluntary migration Permanent movement undertaken by choice.

Thinking Geographically

1. Should preference for immigrating to the United States and Canada be given to individuals with special job skills, or should priority be given to reunification of family members? Should quotas be raised to meet increasing demand for both types of immigrants? Why or why not?

2. What is the impact of large-scale emigration on the places from which migrants depart? On balance, do these places suffer because of the loss of young, upwardly mobile workers, or do these places benefit from the draining away of surplus labor? In the communities from which migrants depart, is the quality of life improved overall through reduced pressures on local resources, or is it damaged overall through the deterioration of social structures and institutions? Explain.

3. According to the concept of chain migration, current migrants tend to follow the paths of relatives and friends who have moved earlier. Can you find evidence of chain migration in your community? Does chain migration apply primarily to the relocation of people from one community in a less developed country to one community in a more developed country, or is chain migration more applicable to movement within a more developed country? Explain.

4. What demographic characteristics (such as rates of natural increase, crude birth, and crude death) prevail in the four regions with the largest numbers of refugees—the Horn of Africa, Afghanistan, the Middle East, and Southeast Europe? Is large-scale forced migration alleviating or exacerbating population growth in these regions? Explain.

5. At the same time that some people are migrating from less developed countries to more developed countries in search of employment, transnational corporations have relocated some low-skilled jobs to LDCs to take advantage of low wage rates. Should less developed countries care whether their surplus workers emigrate or remain as employees of foreign companies? Why?

Further Readings

Appleyard, Reginald, ed. *International Migration Today. Vol. 1: Trends and Prospects.* Paris: UN-ESCO, 1988.

Bennett, D. Gordon, and Ole Gade. *Geographic Perspectives on Migration Behavior: A Bibliographic Survey.* University of North Carolina Studies in Geography, No. 12. Chapel Hill: University of North Carolina, 1979.

Berry, Brian J. L., and Lester Silverman, eds. *Population Redistribution and Public Policy.* Washington, DC: National Academy of Sciences, 1978.

Bigger, Jeanne C. "The Sunning of America: Migration to the Sunbelt." *Population Bulletin* 34 (3). Washington, DC: Population Reference Bureau, 1979.

Bouvier, Leon F. "Immigration and Its Impact on U.S. Population Size." *Population Bulletin* 36. Washington, DC: Population Reference Bureau, 1981.

_____, and Robert W. Gardner. "Immigration to the U.S.: The Unfinished Story." *Population Bulletin* 41 (4). Washington, DC: Population Reference Bureau, 1986.

Brown, Lawrence A., and Victoria A. Lawson. "Migration in Third World Settings, Uneven Development, and Conventional Modeling: A Case Study of Costa Rica." *Annals of the Association of American Geographers* 75 (March 1985): 29–47.

Brown, Lawrence A., and R. L. Sanders. "Toward a Development Paradigm of Migration: With Particular Reference to Third World Settings." In *Migration Decision Making: Multidisciplinary Approaches to Micro-level Studies in Developed and Developing Countries,* ed. G. F. DeJong and R. W. Gardner. New York: Pergamon Press, 1981.

Burton, Ian, Robert W. Kates, and Gilbert F. White. *The Environment as Hazard.* New York: Oxford University Press, 1978.

Cadwallader, M. *Migration and Residential Mobility: Macro and Micro Approaches.* Madison: University of Wisconsin Press, 1992.

Champion, A. G., ed. *Counterurbanization: The Changing Pace and Nature of Population Deconcentration.* London: Edward Arnold, 1989.

Chant, Sylvia, ed. *Gender and Migration in Developing Countries.* London: Belhaven Press, 1992.

Clark, Gordon L. *Interregional Migration, National Policy and Social Justice.* Totowa, NJ: Rowman and Allanheld, 1983.

Clark, W. A. V. *Human Migration.* Beverly Hills, CA: Sage Publications, 1986.

_____, and James E. Burt. "The Impact of Workplace on Residential Relocation." *Annals of the Association of American Geographers* 70 (March 1980): 59–67.

Clark, W. A. V., and Eric G. Moore, eds. *Residential Mobility and Public Policy.* Beverly Hills, CA: Sage Publications, 1980.

Davis, Cary, Carl Haub, and JoAnne Willette. "U.S. Hispanics: Changing the Face of America." *Population Bulletin* 38 (3). Washington, DC: Population Reference Bureau, 1983.

du Toit, Brian M., and Helen I. Safa, eds. *Migration and Development.* The Hague, Netherlands: Mouton, 1975.

Frey, William H. "Migration and Metropolitan Decline in Developed Countries: A Comparative Study." *Population and Development Review* 14 (December 1988): 599–628.

Gober, Patricia. "Americans on the Move." *Population Bulletin* 48. Washington, DC: Population Reference Bureau, 1993.

Jackson, J. D., ed. *Migration.* London: Cambridge University Press, 1969.

Jensen, Leif. *The New Immigration: Implications for Poverty.* Westport, CT: Greenwood Press, 1989.

Jones, Huw, Nicholas Ford, James Caird, and William Berry. "Counterurbanization in Societal Context: Long-Distance Migration to the Highlands and Islands of Scotland." *Professional Geographer* 36 (November 1984): 437–43.

Jones, Richard C. "Undocumented Migration from Mexico: Some Geographical Questions." *Annals of the Association of American Geographers* 72 (March 1982): 77–78.

Kidron, Michael, and Ronald Segal. *The New State of the World Atlas,* 4th ed. New York: Simon and Schuster, 1991.

Kontuly, Thomas, and Roland Vogelsang. "Explanations for the Intensification of Counterurbanization in the Federal Republic of Germany." *Professional Geographer* 40 (February 1988): 42–53.

Kosinski, Leszek A., and R. Mansell Prothero. *People on the Move.* London: Methuen, 1975.

Kritz, Mary M., Charles B. Keely, and Silvano M. Tomasi. *Global Trends in Migration: Theory and Research on International Population Movements.* New York: Center for Migration Studies, 1981.

Lee, Everett. "A Theory of Migration." *Demography* 3, no. 1 (1966): 47–57.

McNeill, William, and Ruth S. Adams. *Human Migration: Patterns and Policies.* Bloomington: Indiana University Press, 1978.

Morrison, Peter A. *Population Movements: Their Form and Functions in Urbanization and Development.* Liege, Belgium: Ordina Editions for International Union for the Scientific Study of Population, 1983.

Nam, Charles B., William J. Serow, and David F. Sly. *International Handbook on Internal Migration.* Westport, CT: Greenwood Press, 1990.

Newland, Kathleen. "International Migration: The Search for Work." *Worldwatch Paper* 33. Washington, DC: Worldwatch Institute, November 1979.

_____. "Refugees: The New International Politics of Displacement." *Worldwatch Paper* 43. Washington, DC: Worldwatch Institute, March 1981.

Organization for Economic Co-operation and Development. *Migration: The Demographic Aspects.* Paris: OECD, 1991.

Papademetrion, Demetrios G. "International Migration in a Changing World." *International Social Science Journal* 36, no. 3 (1984): 409–24.

Plane, David A. "Age-Composition Change and the Geographical Dynamics of Interregional Migration in the U.S." *Annals of the Association of American Geographers* 82 (March 1992): 64–85.

_____, and Peter A. Rogerson. "Tracking the Baby Boom, the Baby Bust, and the Echo Generations: How Age Composition Regulates U.S. Migration." *Professional Geographer* 43 (November 1991): 416–30.

Ravenstein, Ernest George. "The Laws of Migration." *Journal of the Royal Statistical Society* 48 (1885): 167–227.

Rogerson, Peter A. "Changes in U.S. National Mobility Levels." *Professional Geographer* 39 (August 1987): 344–50.

Rogge, John R., ed. *Refugees: A Third World Dilemma.* Totowa, NJ: Rowman and Littlefield, 1987.

Roseman, Curtis C. *Changing Migration Patterns within the United States.* Washington, DC: Association of American Geographers, 1977.

_____. "Migration as a Spatial and Temporal Process." *Annals of the Association of American Geographers* 61 (September 1971): 589–98.

Sanders, Alvin J., and Larry Long. "New Sunbelt Migration Patterns." *American Demographics* 9

(January 1987): 38–41.

Simon, Rita J., and Caroline B. Brettell, eds. *International Migration: The Female Experience*. Totowa, NJ: Rowman and Allanheld, 1986.

Stephenson, George M. *A History of American Immigration*. New York: Russell and Russell, 1964.

Svart, Larry M. "Environmental Preference Migration: A Review." *Geographical Review* 66 (1976): 314–30.

Tabbarah, Riad. "Prospects of International Migration." *International Social Science Journal* 36, no. 3 (1984): 425–40.

Waldorf, Brigitte. "Determinats of International Return Migration Intentions." *Professional Geographer* 47 (1995): 125-36.

White, Paul E., and Robert I. Woods, eds. *The Geographic Impact on Migration*. London and New York: Longman, 1980.

Williams, James D., and Andrew J. Sofranko. "Why People Move." *American Demographics* 3 (July–August 1981): 30–31.

Wolpert, Julian. "Behavioral Aspects of the Decision to Migrate." *Papers, Regional Science Association* 15 (1965): 159–69.

Zelinsky, Wilbur. "The Hypothesis of the Mobility Transition." *Geographical Review* 61 (July 1971): 219–49.

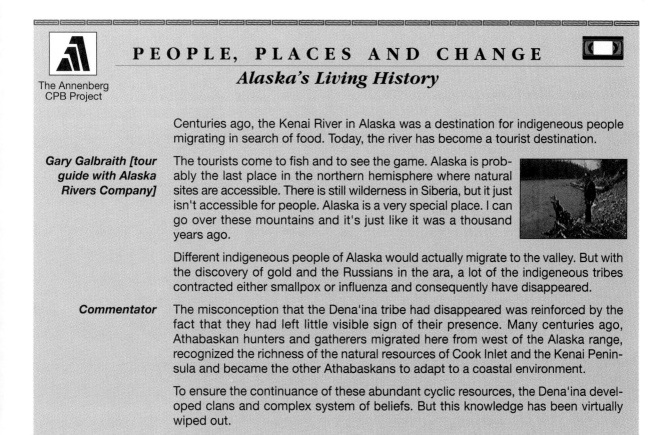

PEOPLE, PLACES AND CHANGE
Alaska's Living History

The Annenberg
CPB Project

Centuries ago, the Kenai River in Alaska was a destination for indigeneous people migrating in search of food. Today, the river has become a tourist destination.

Gary Galbraith [tour guide with Alaska Rivers Company]

The tourists come to fish and to see the game. Alaska is probably the last place in the northern hemisphere where natural sites are accessible. There is still wilderness in Siberia, but it just isn't accessible for people. Alaska is a very special place. I can go over these mountains and it's just like it was a thousand years ago.

Different indigeneous people of Alaska would actually migrate to the valley. But with the discovery of gold and the Russians in the ara, a lot of the indigeneous tribes contracted either smallpox or influenza and consequently have disappeared.

Commentator

The misconception that the Dena'ina tribe had disappeared was reinforced by the fact that they had left little visible sign of their presence. Many centuries ago, Athabaskan hunters and gatherers migrated here from west of the Alaska range, recognized the richness of the natural resources of Cook Inlet and the Kenai Peninsula and became the other Athabaskans to adapt to a coastal environment.

To ensure the continuance of these abundant cyclic resources, the Dena'ina developed clans and complex system of beliefs. But this knowledge has been virtually wiped out.

4

LANGUAGE

How many languages do you speak? If you are Dutch, you are likely to be able to speak at least four languages. All schoolchildren in the Netherlands are required to learn at least Dutch, English, German, and one other language, usually French or Russian.

For those of you who don't happen to be Dutch, the number is probably a bit lower. In fact, most people in the United States know only English. Less than 15 percent of U.S. high school students are currently studying a foreign language.

The study of language follows logically from migration, because the contemporary distribution of languages around the world re-

KEY ISSUES

- How did the English language originate and diffuse?
- How is English related to languages spoken elsewhere in the world?
- What is the spatial distribution of other language families?
- Why do people living in different locations speak English differently?

sults from decisions that people made in the past to migrate. Modern communications systems have increased our exposure to speakers of other languages. This exposure has two contradictory results: on the one hand, people around the world are learning English so that they can better participate in a global economy and culture. On the other hand, people seek to preserve their local language, because language is one of the basic elements of a society's culture. Differences in languages—like other cultural characteristics—can lead to disputes among cultural groups.

SOUK (MARKET) AREA OF EL KAIROUAN, TUNISIA. (D. WARREN/SUPERSTOCK)

French and Spanish in the United States and Canada

The Tremblay family lives in a suburb of Montréal, Québec. The parents and two young children speak French at home, work, school, and shops. The Lopez family—also two parents and two children—live in San Antonio, Texas, and speak Spanish in their household.

The Tremblay and Lopez families share a common condition: they live in countries with an English-speaking majority, but English is not their native language. The French-speaking inhabitants of Canada and the Spanish-speaking residents of the United States continue to speak their languages, although English dominates the political, econom-ic, and cultural life of their countries. The two families use languages other than Eng-lish because they feel that language is important to retaining and enhancing their cultural heritage. On the other hand, both families recognize that knowledge of Eng-lish is essential for career advancement and economic success.

These examples—French-speaking residents of Canada and Spanish-speaking res-idents of the United States—illustrate the two main functions of language that concern geographers. First, geographers look at the similarities and differences among lan-guages to understand the diffusion and interaction of people around the world. Lan-guage is like luggage: people carry it with them when they move from place to place. They incorporate new words into their own language when they reach new places, and they contribute words brought with them to the existing language at the new location.

Second, geographers study language because it is a major characteristic of a re-gion. Language is a source of pride to a people, a symbol of cultural unity. As a cul-ture develops, language is both a cause of that development, and a consequence. Studying language distribution helps geographers to identify regions occupied by var-ious cultural groups.

Why doesn't everyone speak the same language worldwide? The answer is, because of cultural diversity. Earth's heterogeneous collection of languages is one of its most obvious examples. Geographers use language to identify important regional differences on the cultural landscape and to understand the basis for political conflict.

Language is a system of communication through speech, a collection of sounds that a group of people understands to have the same meaning. Many languages also have a **literary tradition**, or a system of written communication. However, hundreds of spoken languages lack a literary tradition.

Although several thousand languages are spoken around the world, they are members of a small number of language families, language branches, and language groups. A **language family** includes individual languages related through a common ancestor that existed before recorded history.

Figure 4-1 shows the world's language families. About 50 percent of all people speak a language in the *Indo-European family;* and about 20 percent speak a language of the *Sino-Tibetan family.* Yet another 20 percent are accounted for by four smaller families—*Austronesian* (once known as Malay-Polynesian), *Afro-Asiatic* (once known as Semito-Hamitic), *Niger-Congo* (in Africa), and *Dravidian* (in India). The remaining 10 percent of the world's population speak a wide variety of other languages.

Within a language family, a **language branch** includes tongues that share a common origin but have further evolved into individual languages. For example, the Indo-European family has developed eight branches—Germanic, Romance, Balto-Slavic, Indo-Iranian, Greek, Albanian, Aremenian, and Celtic. Each has in turn evolved individual languages (Figure 4-2). Differences among individual languages are less than the differences among branches of a family.

Figure 4-2 shows further subdivisions of some language branches into language groups. A **language group** comprises individual languages within a branch that share a common origin in the relatively recent past and display relatively few differences in grammar and vocabulary. For example, the West Germanic group includes English and German. Although they sound very different, they are structurally similar and have many words in common.

Not shown in Figure 4-2 is the division of individual languages into dialects. A **dialect** is a form of a language spoken in a local area. Just as languages evolve from a common ancestor, so can several dialects derive from one language. In general, speakers of one dialect can understand speakers of another dialect of the same language. In a language with multiple dialects, one dialect normally is recognized as the **standard language,** the form used for government, business, education, and mass communication.

This chapter looks at the origin and spatial distribution of languages. We look first at English, not only because it is the language understood by readers of this book, but because English is becoming the world's most important language for business and culture.

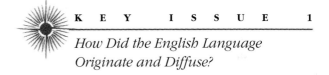

K E Y   I S S U E   1

How Did the English Language Originate and Diffuse?

- Development of English
- Other Germanic Languages

The location of English speakers serves as a case study for understanding the processes by which any language is distributed around the world. A language originates at a particular place and diffuses to other locations through the migration of its speakers.

Development of English

English is among the richest and most versatile languages on Earth. It is so for good reason: English has absorbed a broad vocabulary from several other languages.

Germanic Invaders

The British Isles had been inhabited for thousands of years, but we know nothing of these peoples' early languages. Tribes called the Celts arrived around 2000 B.C., speaking languages we call Celtic. Then, around A.D. 450, tribes from mainland Europe invaded, pushing the Celts into the remote northern and western parts of Britain, including Cornwall and the highlands of Scotland and Wales.

The invading tribes were the Angles, Jutes, and Saxons. All three were Germanic tribes, the Jutes

FIGURE 4-1 Language families. Most people's language can be classified into one of a handful of language families. The pie chart shows the percentage of people who speak a language from each major family. You can see that Indo-European and Sino-Tibetan languages dominate the world, with *Indo-European* spoken by about 50 percent of Earth's people, and *Sino-Tibetan* spoken by about 22 percent. The map colors show the distribution of each family. Note especially the worldwide span of Indo-European languages, but the relatively narrow diffusion of Sino-Tibetan tongues. Major languages —those that have more than 100 million speakers—are identified on the map.

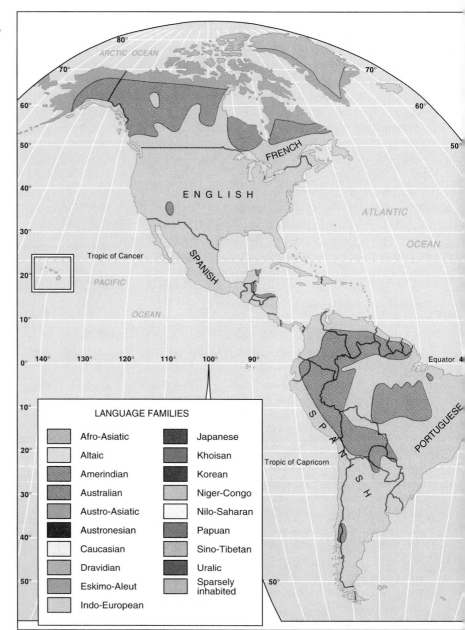

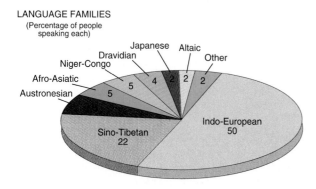

LANGUAGE FAMILIES
(Percentage of people speaking each)

from northern Denmark, the Angles from southern Denmark, and the Saxons from northwestern Germany (Figure 4-3). They brought their Germanic languages with them, and today's English has evolved primarily from dialects spoken by these three tribes. Thus, English is fundamentally a *Germanic* language and shares many structural similarities and common words with other Germanic languages. The name "England" comes from "Angles' land." In Old English, Angles were known as Engles, and their language was known as *englisc*. They came from a corner, or "angle," of Germany known as Schleswig-Holstein.

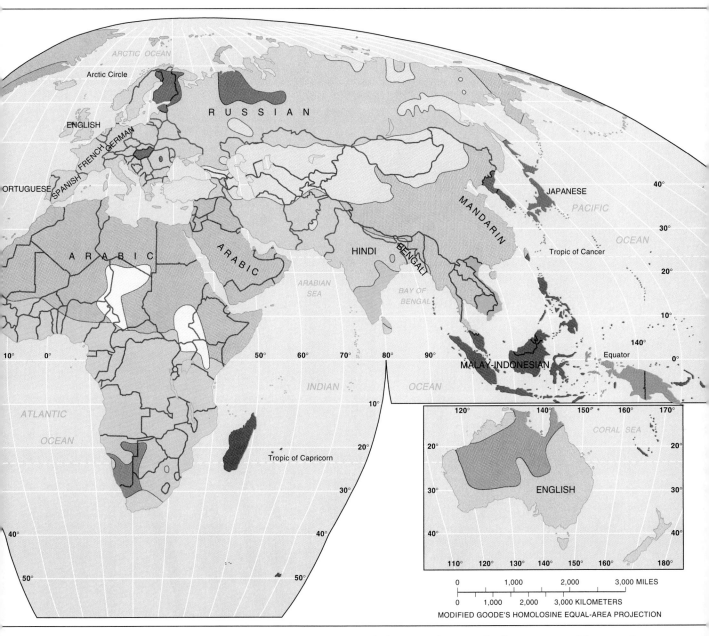

MODIFIED GOODE'S HOMOLOSINE EQUAL-AREA PROJECTION

Other peoples subsequently invaded England and added their languages to the basic English. Vikings from present-day Norway landed on the northeast coast of England in the ninth century. Although defeated in their effort to conquer the islands, the many Vikings who remained in the country enriched the language with new words.

The conquest of England by the Norman French in 1066 profoundly changed the language. The Normans spoke French, which they established as England's official language for the next 150 years. However, although the royal family, nobles, judges, and clergy spoke French, the majority of the people continued to speak English. By the thirteenth century, English again became the country's dominant language. In 1204, during the reign of King John, England lost control of Normandy and entered a long period of conflict with France. As a result, fewer people in England wished to speak French.

Given that nearly everyone in England spoke English anyway, Parliament enacted the Statute of Pleading in 1362 to change the official language of court business from French to English. English therefore regained its position as the official language for the in-

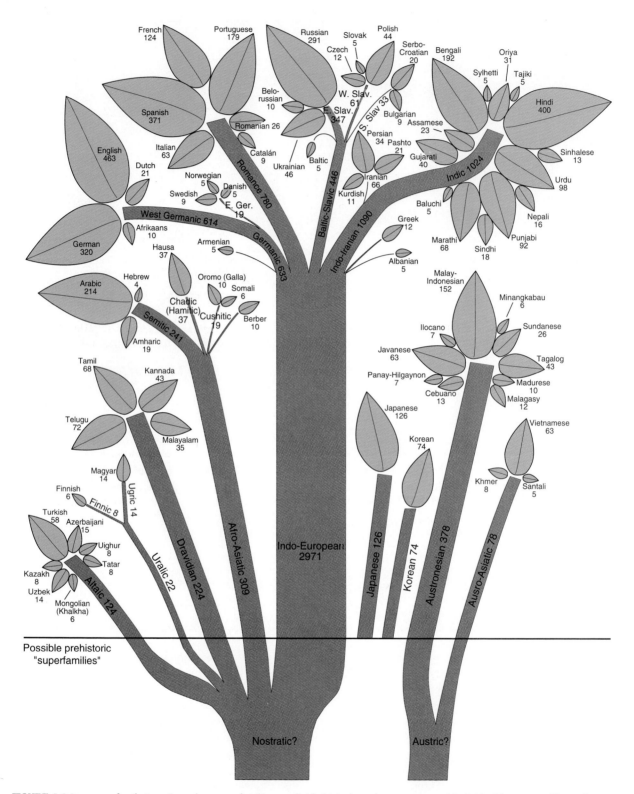

FIGURE 4-2 Language family tree. Some language families are divided into branches, groups, and individual languages. Shown here are language families and individual languages that have 5 million or more speakers. (Numbers are in millions of speakers.) Below ground level, the language tree's "roots" are shown. This theory, however, is a highly controversial speculation advocated by some linguists for a common origin of language families tens of thousands of years ago.

Mandarin
930

Hakka
(Kijia)
34

Cantonese
(Yue)
65

Wu
65

Sinitic
1144

Thai (& Lao)
53

Zhuang
15

Austro-Thai 86

Miao
6

Tibetan
5

Tibeto-
Burman
49

Burmese
31

Yi 7

Swahili
47

Nyanja 5

Xhosa 8

Luba-
Lulua
7

Lingala 7

Rundi 6

Ruanda
8

Zulu 8

Shona
8

Nyamwezi-Sokuma 5

Kikuyu
(Gekoyo)
5

Benue-Congo 184

Igbo
(Ibo)
17

Yoruba
19

Akan
7

Kwa 52

Malinke-Bambara-
Dyula
9

Fula
13

Mande
12

W. Atlantic 27

Wolof
7

Nilo-Saharan
13

Adamawa
Eastern
5

Gur
(More)
4

Nilo-Saharan 13

Niger-Congo 284

Quechua
8

Amerindian 14

Georgian
4

Caucasian 4

Sino-Tibetan 1279

Sino-
Caucasian

habitants of England, but with the enrichment of many French words.

Global Diffusion of English

The people of England then diffused their language around the world through the establishment of colonies. The first English colonies were built in North America, beginning with Jamestown, Virginia, in 1607, and Plymouth, Massachusetts, in 1620. The English proceeded to establish colonies worldwide, in South America, Africa, Asia, and many islands of the Atlantic, Indian, and Pacific oceans.

As recently as the 1950s, one-fourth of the world's people lived in a country where English was the **official language,** that is, the language adopted for use by the government. English was the official language even in colonies where only a small percentage of people actually spoke English. When independence was granted to most of these colonies during this century, their leaders selected an indigenous language as the official one but continued to use English for international communication. Thus has English become an important **lingua franca,** which is a language used in commerce by people who have different native languages.

A group that learns English or another lingua franca may learn a simplified form, called a **pidgin language**. In order to communicate with speakers of another language, two groups may construct a pidgin language by learning a few of the grammar rules and words of a lingua franca, while mixing in some elements of their own languages. A pidgin language has no native speakers—it is always spoken in addition to one's native language.

Other Germanic Languages

The Angles, Jutes, and Saxons who brought the beginnings of English to the British Isles came from present-day Denmark and Germany, where they shared a language similar to that of other peoples in the region. At some time in history, all Germanic people spoke a common language, but that time predates written records. The common origin of English with other Germanic languages can be reconstructed by analyzing language differences that emerged after Germanic groups migrated to separate territories and lived in isolation from each other, allowing their languages to continue evolving independently.

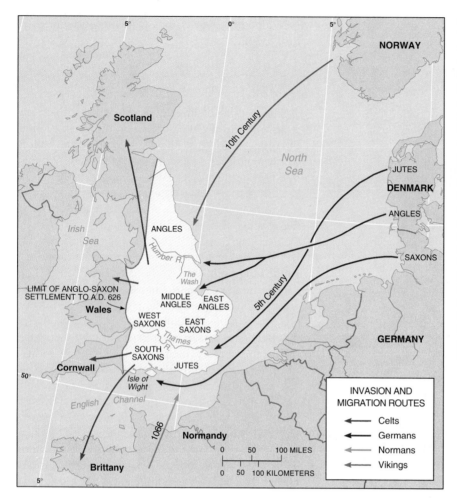

FIGURE 4-3 Invasions of England. The first speakers of the language that became known as English were tribes that lived in present-day Germany and Denmark. They invaded England in the fifth century A.D. The Jutes settled primarily in southeastern England, the Saxons in the south and west, and the Angles in the north, eventually giving the country its name: Angles' Land, or England. From this original spatial separation, the first major regional differences in English dialect developed, as Figure 4-13 shows. Invasions by Vikings in the tenth century and Normans in the eleventh century brought new words to the language spoken in the British Isles. The Normans were the last successful invaders of England. (From Albert C. Baugh and Thomas Cable, *A History of the English Language,* 3d ed., © 1978, p. 47. Reprinted by permission of Prentice Hall, Englewood Cliffs, NJ.)

Because English shares a common ancestry with other Germanic languages, it is classified as part of the Germanic language branch. This branch consists of two language groups: West Germanic and North Germanic. East Germanic, once a third group, is extinct (Figure 4-4).

West Germanic Group: English and German

West Germanic is of particular interest because it is the group to which English belongs. West Germanic is further divided into two subgroups: High and Low Germanic, literally based on altitude. High Germanic, spoken in the southern mountains of present-day Germany, became the basis for the modern standard German language. Low Germanic was spoken by people who lived in the northern lowlands, including the Angles, Jutes, and Saxons. Because the people who migrated to England came from the lowlands, English is classified as a Low Ger-

manic language, within the West Germanic group (Figure 4-4).

Other Low Germanic languages are Old Saxon, Old Low Franconian, and Old Frisian. Old Saxon, spoken by the Saxons who did not migrate to England, has become the major component of Low German, a modern German dialect spoken in the northern lowlands. Old Franconian is the basis for modern Dutch and Flemish, spoken in the Netherlands and northern Belgium. Old Frisian gave rise to modern Frisian, which is spoken by a few residents of the northeastern Netherlands.

North Germanic Group: Scandinavian Languages

The Germanic language branch also includes North Germanic languages, spoken in Scandinavia. All four Scandinavian languages—Swedish, Danish, Norwegian, and Icelandic—all derive from Old Norse, which was the principal language spoken

FIGURE 4-4 Germanic branch of Indo-European family. Germanic languages predominate in Northern and Western Europe. The main North Germanic languages include Swedish, Danish, Norwegian, and Icelandic. The main West Germanic languages are English and German, with Netherlandish (Dutch) spoken in the Netherlands and northern Belgium. Two rarely used Germanic languages are Faeroese, spoken by inhabitants of the Faeroe Islands (part of Denmark), and Frisian, used in the northeastern Netherlands.

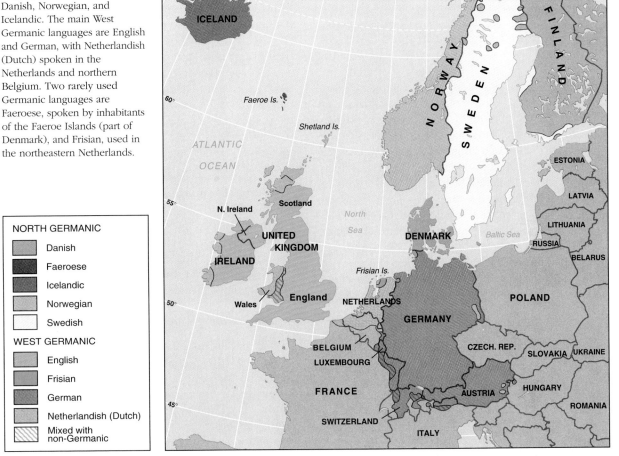

throughout Scandinavia before A.D. 1000. Four distinct languages emerged after that time because of migration and the political organization of the region into four independent and isolated countries.

For geographers, the most interesting Scandinavian language is Icelandic. The island of Iceland was colonized in A.D. 874 by Norwegian settlers, who soon developed a literary tradition. Because of the relative isolation of Iceland, its language has changed less than any other in the Germanic branch.

Icelandic helps geographers understand the diffusion of language across the landscape. When members of a group migrate to other locations, they take their language with them. After centuries of living in isolation from others of the same group, however, the migrants may speak an essentially different language. The language spoken by most migrants—such as the Germanic invaders of England—changes in part through interaction with speakers of other languages. Because the Germanic people who migrated to Iceland had less contact with speakers of other languages, they had less opportunity to learn new words.

Extinct East Germanic Group

East Germanic languages once existed, but they are now **extinct languages**—that is, they are no longer spoken or read in daily activities by anyone in the world. Thousands of languages once in use, even some in the recent past, no longer exist. The main East Germanic language was Gothic, spoken by people who lived in much of eastern and northern Europe in the third century A.D. The last speakers of Gothic lived in the Crimea in Russia in the sixteenth century. The language died because the descendants of the Goths were converted to other languages through processes of integration, such as political dominance and cultural preference. For example, many Gothic people switched to speaking the Latin language after their conversion to Christianity.

This review of the origin and diffusion of English and other Germanic languages demonstrates that the spatial distribution of a language is a measure of the fate of a distinctive cultural group. English has been diffused around the world from a small island in northwestern Europe because of England's cultural dominance over other territory on Earth's surface. On the other hand, Icelandic has remained a little-used language because of the isolation of the Icelandic people. Just as differences arise because of migration and geographic isolation among speakers of a particular language branch, so can differences arise between speakers of different branches within the same language family.

K E Y I S S U E 2

How Is English Related to Languages Spoken Elsewhere in the World?

- Romance Language Branch
- Other Indo-European Language Branches
- Search for the Indo-European Hearth

Take a moment to study the Indo-European trunk in Figure 4-2. Germanic languages, including English, constitute just one branch of this large language family, with its nearly 3 billion speakers worldwide. The Indo-European family includes languages with important artistic and literary traditions. It also encompasses four of the six official languages used by the United Nations (English, French, Russian, and Spanish). This section examines the spatial distribution of the Indo-European language family. It also presents evidence for the common origin of the Indo-European languages.

Indo-European languages are used on every continent of the world. Spoken since the dawn of recorded history in nearly all of Europe and much of Asia, the Indo-European language family has been diffused in modern times to Africa, Australia, and the Western Hemisphere through the migration of colonists, and even to Antarctica with research teams.

The Indo-European language family includes eight branches. More than 400 million people each speak languages in four of its branches: Germanic, Romance, Balto-Slavic, and Indo-Iranian. The four language branches within the Indo-European family less extensively used include Albanian, Armenian, Greek, and Celtic. Figure 4-5 shows the distribution of Indo-European languages in Europe and Asia today.

Romance Language Branch

The Romance branch of the Indo-European language family is the second-most familiar to most English-speaking people. The Romance languages evolved from the Latin language spoken by the ancient Romans, giving the branch its name.

Latin and the Roman Empire

The rise in importance of the city of Rome was paralleled by the diffusion of its Latin language. At its height in the second century A.D., the Roman Empire extended from the Atlantic Ocean on the west to the Black Sea on the east and encompassed all lands bordering the Mediterranean Sea (the Empire's boundary is shown in Figure 5-3). As the conquering Roman armies occupied the provinces of this vast empire, they brought the Latin language with them. In the process, the languages spoken by the natives of the provinces were either extinguished or suppressed in favor of the language of the conquerors.

After the collapse of the Roman Empire in the fifth century, however, Latin persisted only in parts of the former colonies. People in some areas reverted to former languages; others adopted the languages of conquering groups from the north and east, which spoke Germanic and Slavic.

Even during the period of the Roman Empire, however, Latin varied to some extent from one province to another. The empire grew over a period of several hundred years, so the Latin used in each province was based on that spoken by the Roman

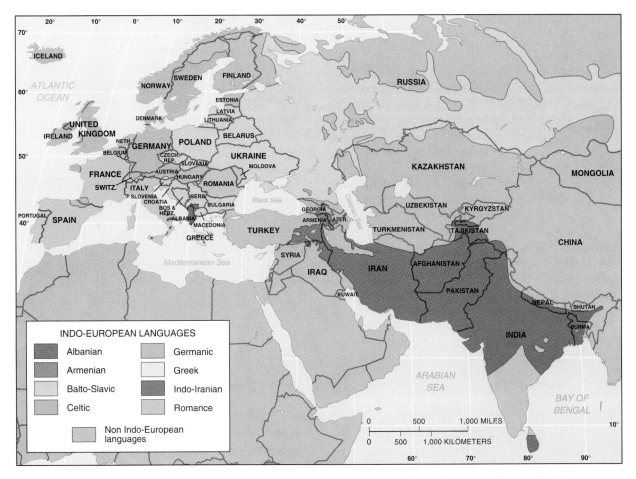

FIGURE 4-5 Branches of Indo-European family. Most Europeans speak languages from the Indo-European language family. In Europe, the three most important branches are Germanic (north and west), Romance (south and west), and Balto-Slavic (east). The fourth major branch, Indo-Iranian, clustered in southern and western Asia, has over 1 billion speakers, the greatest number of any Indo-European branch.

army at the time of occupation. The Latin spoken in each province also integrated words from the language formerly spoken in the area.

The Latin that people in the provinces learned was not the standard literary form but a spoken form, known as **Vulgar Latin,** from the Latin word referring to "the masses" of the populace. Vulgar Latin was introduced to the provinces by the soldiers stationed throughout the empire. For example, the literary term for "horse" was *equus,* from which English has derived such words as "equine" and "equestri-

an." The Vulgar term used by the common people was *caballus,* from which are derived the modern terms for horse in Italian (*cavallor*), Spanish (*caballo*), Portuguese (*cavalo*), French (*cheval*), and Romanian (*cal*).

After the collapse of the Roman Empire in the fifth century, communication among the former provinces declined, creating still greater regional variation in spoken Latin. By the eighth century, regions of the former empire had been isolated from each other long enough for distinct languages to evolve.

Modern Romance Languages

The four most widely used contemporary Romance languages are Spanish, Portuguese, French, and Italian. The European regions in which these four languages are spoken correspond somewhat to the boundaries of the modern states of Spain, Portugal, France, and Italy (Figure 4-6). Rugged mountains serve as boundaries among these four countries. France is separated from Italy by the Alps and from Spain by the Pyrenees, and a series of mountain ranges marks the border between Spain and Portugal. Physical boundaries such as mountains are strong "intervening obstacles" (Chapter 3), creating barriers to communication between people living on opposite sides.

The fifth most important Romance language, Romanian, is the principal language of Romania and Moldova. It is separated from the other Romance-speaking European countries by Slavic-speaking peoples.

Distinct Romance languages did not suddenly appear. As with other languages, they evolved over time. Numerous dialects existed within each province, many of which still are spoken today. The creation of standard national languages, such as French and Spanish, was relatively recent.

Dialects in France. The dialect of the Île-de-France region, known as *Francien,* became the standard form of French because the region included Paris, which became the capital and largest city of the country. Francien French became the country's official language in the sixteenth century, and local dialects tended to disappear as a result of the capital's long-time dominance over French political, economic, and social life.

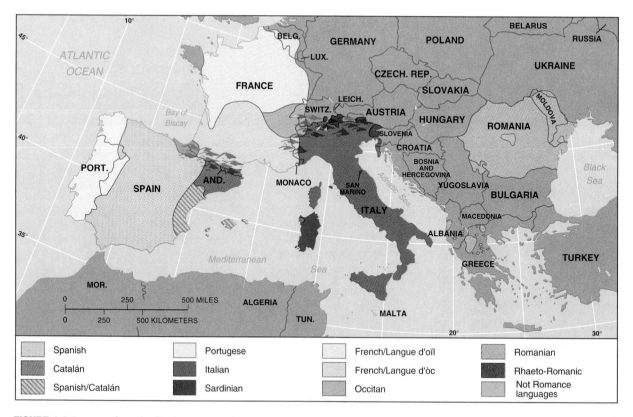

FIGURE 4-6 Romance branch of Indo-European family. Romance includes three of the world's most widely spoken languages (Spanish, Portuguese, and French) plus two other widely spoken tongues (Italian and Romanian). To varying degrees, these languages have spread worldwide. The map also shows boundaries among some dialects of Spanish and French. Catalán is a dialect of Spanish and the official language of Andorra. French dialects include Occitan, langue d'oïl, and langue d'òc. Rhaeto-Romanic languages include Romansh, Ladin, and Friulian.

The most important surviving linguistic difference within France is between the north and the south (Figure 4-6). The northern dialect is known as *langue d'oïl* and the southern as *langue d'òc*. It is worth exploring these names, for they provide insight into how languages evolve. These terms derive from different ways in which the word for "yes" was said.

One Roman term for "yes" was *hoc illud est,* meaning "that is so." In the south, the phrase was shortened to *hoc,* or *òc,* because the /h/ sound was generally dropped, just as we drop it on the word *honor* today. Northerners shortened the phrase to *o-il* after the first sound in the first two words of the phrase, again with the initial /h/ suppressed. If the two syllables of *o-il* are spoken very rapidly, they are combined into a sound like the English word "wheel." Eventually, the final consonant was eliminated, as in many French words, giving a sound for "yes" like the English "we," spelled in French *oui.*

A province where the southern dialect is spoken in southwestern France is known as Languedoc. The southern French dialect itself is now sometimes called Occitan, derived from the French region of Aquitaine, which in French has a similar pronunciation to Occitan. About 3 million people in southeastern France speak a form of Occitan known as Provençal.

Worldwide Diffusion of Spanish and Portuguese. Spain, like France, contained many dialects during the Middle Ages. One dialect, known as Castilian, arose during the ninth century in Old Castile, located in the north-central part of the country. The dialect spread southward over the next several hundred years as independent kingdoms were unified into one large country. Spain grew to its approximate present boundaries in the fifteenth century, when the Kingdom of Castile and Léon merged with the Kingdom of Aragón. At that time, Castilian became the official language for the entire country. Regional dialects, such as Aragón, Navarre, Léon, Asturias, and Santander, survived only in secluded rural areas. The official language of Spain is now called Spanish, although the term *Castilian* is still used in Latin America.

Spanish and Portuguese have achieved worldwide importance because of the colonial activities of their European speakers. Approximately 90 percent of the speakers of these two languages live outside Europe, mainly in Central and South America. Spanish is the official language of eighteen Latin American states, while Portuguese is spoken in Brazil, which has as many people as all the other South American countries combined and fifteen times as many as Portugal itself.

These two Romance languages were diffused to the Americas by Spanish and Portuguese explorers. The division of Central and South America into Portuguese- and Spanish-speaking regions is the result of a 1493 decision by Pope Alexander VI to give the western portion of the New World to Spain and the eastern part to Portugal. The Treaty of Tordesillas, signed one year later, carried out the papal decision.

The Portuguese and Spanish languages spoken in the Western Hemisphere differ somewhat from their European versions, as is the case with English. Brazil, Portugal, and several Portuguese-speaking countries in Africa have agreed to standardize the way their common language is written, effective in 1994. Many people in Portugal are upset that the new standard language more closely resembles the Brazilian version, which eliminates most of the accent marks—such as tildes (São Paulo), cedillas (Alcobaça), circumflexes (Estância), and hyphens—and the agreement recognizes as standard thousands of words that Brazilians have added to the language.

The standardization of Portuguese is a reflection of the level of interaction that is possible in the modern world between groups of people who live tens of thousands of kilometers apart. Books and television programs produced in one country diffuse rapidly to other countries where the same language is used.

How Many Romance Languages Exist? The spatial distribution of Romance branch languages shows the difficulty in trying to establish the number of distinct languages in the world. In addition to the five major languages—Spanish, Portuguese, French, Italian, and Romanian—several other Romance languages can be identified. If official languages are counted, we add two: Romansh and Catalán. *Romansh* is one of the four official languages of Switzerland, although it is spoken by only 25,000 people. *Catalán*, a Spanish dialect, is the official language of Andorra, a tiny country of approximately 50,000 inhabitants situated in the Pyrenees Mountains between Spain and France. Catalán is also spoken by another 9 million people, mostly around the city of Barcelona. A third Romance language, *Sardinian*—a mixture of Italian, Spanish, and Arabic—once was the official language of the Mediterranean island of Sardinia (Figure 4-6).

Language Conflicts in Europe

Conflict often arises in countries that have more than one widely spoken language. Two small European countries—Belgium and Switzerland—illustrate this point. Both countries are home to large numbers of Romance- and Germanic-language speakers. Belgium has had more difficulty than Switzerland in reconciling the interests of the different language speakers.

Belgium

Southern Belgians (known as Walloons) speak *French*, whereas northern Belgians (known as Flemings) speak a dialect of the Germanic language of Dutch, called *Flemish*. The language boundary sharply divides the country into two regions. Antagonism between the Flemings and Walloons is aggravated by economic and political differences. Historically, the Walloons dominated Belgium's economy and politics, and French was the official state language (Figure 1).

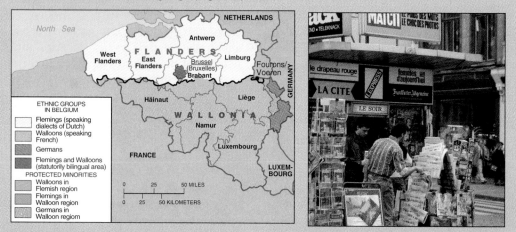

FIGURE 1 Languages in Belgium. Belgians are sharply divided by their language differences. Flemings in the north speak Flemish, a Dutch dialect. Walloons in the south speak French. Brussels, where this newsstand is located, is bilingual. The newsstand displays newspapers and magazines in both Flemish and French. (Craig Aurness/West Light)

In response to pressure from Flemish speakers, Belgium was divided into two independent regions, Flanders and Wallonia. Each elects an assembly that controls cultural affairs, public health, road construction, and urban development in its region. The national government turns over approximately 15 percent of its tax revenues to pay for the regional governments.

Motorists in Belgium clearly see the language boundary on expressways. Heading north, the highway signs suddenly change from French to Flemish at the boundary between Wallonia and Flanders. Brussels, the capital city, is an exception. Although located in Flanders, Brussels is officially bilingual and signs are in both French and Flemish. As an example, some stations on the subway map of Brussels are identified by two names, one French and one Flemish (for example, Porte de Hal and Halle Poort—see Figure 12-4).

Belgium had difficulty fixing a precise boundary between Flemish and French speakers, because people living near the boundary may actually use the language spoken on the other side. During the late 1980s, this problem jailed one town's mayor and collapsed the national government. The town is named *Voeren* in Flemish and *Fourons* in French. Jose Happart, its mayor, refused to speak Flemish, which is required by national law because the town is in Flanders. Happart had been elected on a platform of returning the town to French Wallonia, from which it had been transferred in 1963, when the national government tried to clear up the language boundary. After refusing to be tested on his knowledge of Dutch, Happart (who in fact knew Dutch) was jailed and removed from office. In protest, French-speaking members quit the coalition governing the country, forcing the Belgian prime minister to resign.

Switzerland

In contrast, Switzerland peacefully exists with multiple languages. The key is a very decentralized government, in which local authorities hold most of the power, and decisions are frequently made by voter referenda. Switzerland has four official languages: German (used by 65 percent of the population), French (18 percent), Italian (12 percent), and Romansh (1 percent). Swiss voters made Romansh an official language in a 1938 referendum, despite the small percentage who use the language (Figure 2).

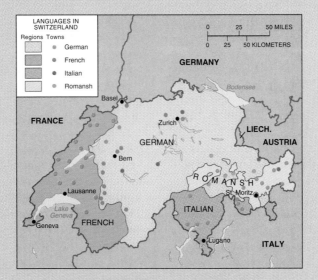

FIGURE 2 Languages in Switzerland. Unlike Belgium, Switzerland lives peacefully with four official languages, including Romansh, which is used by only 1 percent of the population. Although the country can be divided into four main linguistic regions as shown, people living in individual communities, especially in the mountains, may use a language other than the prevailing local one. The Swiss, relatively tolerant of speakers of other languages, have institutionalized cultural diversity by creating a form of government that places considerable power in small communities.

Brazil is the largest Portuguese-speaking country in the world. In Brazil, the words are written with fewer diacritical and accent marks than in Portugal, as can be seen in the banner advertising a sale across a pedestrian street in Manaus, Brazil.

In addition to these official languages, several unofficial Romance languages have individual literary traditions. In Italy, *Ladin* (not Latin) is spoken by 20,000 people living in the South Tyrol; *Friulian* is spoken by 500,000 in the northeast. Ladin and Friulian (along with the official Romansh) are dialects of *Rhaeto-Romanic*. A Romance tongue called *Ladino*—a mixture of Spanish, Greek, Turkish, and Hebrew—is spoken by 140,000 Sephardic Jews, most of whom now live in Israel. *Occitan* is a dialect of French. None of these languages has an official status in any country, although all are used in literature.

Difficulties arise in determining whether two languages are distinct or merely two dialects of the same language. *Galician,* spoken in northwestern Spain, is generally classified as a dialect of Portuguese, and *Flemish,* spoken in northern Belgium, is generally considered a dialect of Dutch. But many residents of these regions view their languages as distinct. The task of identifying individual languages and dialects is even more difficult in societies where the language is primarily spoken rather than written.

Creolized Languages. Romance languages spoken in some former colonies can also be classified as separate languages because they differ substantially from the original introduced by European colonizers. Examples include *French Creole* in Haiti, *Papiamento* (creolized Spanish) in Netherlands Antilles (West Indies), and *Portuguese Creole* in the Cape Verde Islands off the African coast. A **creole** or **creolized language** is one that results from the mixing of the colonizer's language with the indigenous language of the people being dominated.

A creolized language forms when the colonized group adopts the language of the dominant group but makes some changes, such as simplifying the grammar and adding words from their former language. The word *creole* itself derives from a word in several Romance languages for a slave who is born in the master's house. A creolized language evolves from a pidgin language to become the primary language of a cultural group. As it does so, the creole language needs to expand greatly its vocabulary.

Other Indo-European Language Branches

In addition to Germanic and Romance, two other Indo-European language families—Indo-Iranian and Balto-Slavic—are spoken by large numbers of people. Other Indo-European language families are less frequently used.

Indo-Iranian Language Branch of Indo-European

The branch of the Indo-European language family with the most speakers is Indo-Iranian. This branch includes more than 100 individual languages, spoken by more than 1 billion people. The branch can be divided into an eastern group (Indic) and a western group (Iranian).

Indic (Eastern) Group of Indo-Iranian Language Branch. Figure 4-7 shows that India has four important language families: Indo-European (the orange area dominating the north), Dravidian (south), Sino-Tibetan (northeast), and Southeast Asian (central and eastern highlands). The most widely used languages in India, as well as in the neighboring countries of Pakistan and Bangladesh belong to the Indo-European language family, and more specifically to the Indic group of the Indo-Iranian branch of Indo-European.

Approximately one-third of Indians, mostly in the north, use an Indic language called *Hindi*. Hindi is spoken many different ways—and therefore could be regarded as a collection of many individual languages—but there is only one official way to write the language, using a script called Devanagari, which has been used in India since the seventh century A.D. (For example, the word for "sun" is written in Hindi as ，pronounced surag.)

Local differences arose in the spoken forms of Hindi but not in the written form, because until recently few speakers of that language could read or write it.

Pakistan's principal language, *Urdu*, is spoken very much like Hindi but is written with the Arabic alphabet, a legacy of the fact that most Pakistanis are Muslims, and their holiest book (the Quran) is written in Arabic. The basis of both languages is *Hindustani*, a form of the language spoken as the lingua franca in much of India for many centuries. Hindi was originally a variety of Hindustani spoken in the area of New Delhi and grew into a national language in the nineteenth century when the British encouraged its use in government. Collectively, Indic languages constitute the second largest language group in the world.

Another Indic language, *Bengali,* is the most important language in Bangladesh. Other important Indic languages in South Asia include *Punjabi, Marathi,* and *Gujarati.*

One of the main cultural distinctions among the nearly 1 billion residents of India is language. After India became an independent state in 1947, Hindi was proposed as the official language, but Dravidian speakers from southern India strongly objected. Therefore, India's 1950 constitution recognized fourteen official languages, including ten Indo-European

(Assamese, Bengali, Gujarati, Hindi, Kashmiri, Marathi, Oriya, Punjabi, Sanskrit, and Urdu) and four Dravidian (Kannada, Malayalam, Tamil, and Telugu) languages. More than 90 percent of the population speak at least one of these fourteen languages, but as many as 10 million Indians use other languages.

As the language of India's former colonial ruler, English has an "associate" status, even though only 1 percent of the Indian population can speak it. Speakers of two different Indian languages who wish to communicate with each other sometimes are forced to turn to English as a common language.

Iranian (Western) Group of Indo-Iranian Language Branch. Indo-Iranian languages are also spoken in Iran and neighboring countries in southwestern Asia. These form a separate group from Indic within the Indo-Iranian branch of the Indo-European family.

The major Iranian group languages include *Persian* (sometimes called *Farsi*) in Iran, *Pashto* in eastern Afghanistan and western Pakistan, and *Kurdish,* used by the Kurds of western Iran, northern Iraq, and eastern Turkey. These languages are written in the Arabic alphabet.

Balto-Slavic Language Branch of Indo-European

The other Indo-European language branch with large numbers of speakers is Balto-Slavic. Slavic was once a single language, but differences developed in the seventh century A.D. when several groups of Slavs migrated from Asia to different areas of eastern Europe and thereafter lived in isolation from one another. As a result, this branch can be divided into East, West, and South Slavic groups as well as a Baltic group. Figure 7-15 shows the variety of Balto-Slavic languages in Southeast Europe.

East Slavic and Baltic Groups of Balto-Slavic Language Branch. The most widely used Slavic languages are the eastern ones, primarily *Russian,* which is spoken by more than 80 percent of Russian people. The importance of Russian increased with the Soviet Union's rise to power after World War II ended in 1945. Soviet officials forced native speakers of other languages to learn Russian as a way of fostering cultural unity among the country's diverse peoples. In Eastern European countries that were dominated politically and economically by the Soviet Union, Russian was taught as the second lan-

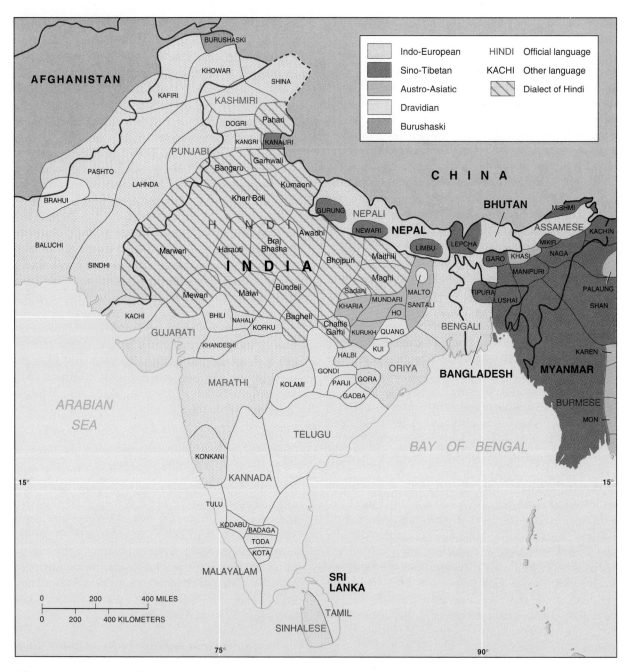

FIGURE 4-7 Languages and families in South Asia. The region has four main language families: Austro-Asiatic, Dravidian, Indo-European, and Sino-Tibetan. Individual languages and dialects number several hundred. More than 90 percent of the people of India speak at least one of the country's fourteen official languages. To draw a usable map, we show sharp language boundaries, but in reality they are very blurred, and speakers of some languages are dispersed, not clustered.

guage. Russian also was designated one of the six official languages of the United Nations. With the demise of the Soviet Union, the newly independent republics adopted official languages other than Russian, although Russian remains the lingua franca for communications among officials in the countries that were formerly part of the Soviet Union.

After Russian, *Ukrainian* and *Belorusian* are the two most important East Slavic languages, official languages in Ukraine and Belarus. *Ukraine* is a Slavic word meaning "border," and *Belo-* is translated "white." The presence of so many non-Russian speakers was a measure of cultural diversity in the Soviet Union, and the desire to use languages other than Russian was a major drive in the breakup of the country.

The two principal Baltic languages are *Latvian* and *Lithuanian,* official languages of Latvia and Lithuania. *Estonian,* the official language of Estonia, is a Uralic language unrelated to the Indo-European family.

West and South Slavic Groups of Balto-Slavic Language Branch. The most-spoken West Slavic language is *Polish,* followed by *Czech* and *Slovak.* The latter two are quite similar, and speakers of one can understand the other. The government of the former state of Czechoslovakia tried to balance the use of the two languages, even though the country contained twice as many Czechs as Slovaks. For example, the announcers on televised sports events would use one of the languages during the first half and switch to the other for the second half. These balancing measures were effective in promoting cultural unity during the Communist era, but in 1993, 4 years after the fall of communism, Slovakia split from the Czech Republic. Slovaks rekindled their long-suppressed resentment of perceived Czech dominance of the country's culture.

The two most important South Slavic languages are *Serbo-Croatian* and *Bulgarian.* Although Serbs and Croats speak the same language, they use different alphabets: Croatian is written in the Roman alphabet (what you are reading now), whereas Serbian is written in Cyrillic (for example, see how *Yugoslavia* is written in Serbian on the money in the photograph). *Slovene* is the official language of Slovenia, and *Macedonian* is used in the former Yugoslav republic of Macedonia.

In general, it is difficult to distinguish among Slavic languages and dialects of the same language, be-

Words on Yugoslav money, known as the dinar, are written in both Serbian (Cyrillic alphabet) and Croatian (Western alphabet). The extremely large denomination of the bill (500 billion dinars) reflects the very high rate of inflation in the country during the 1990s after Bosnia-Herzegovina, Croatia, Macedonia, and Slovenia broke away from Yugoslavia to form independent countries. (Art Zanur/Gamma-Liaison, Inc.)

cause differences among all Slavic languages are relatively small. Someone who understands one Slavic language can understand much of what is said or written in another. Because language is a major element in a people's cultural identity, however, relatively small differences among Slavic, as well as other, languages are being preserved and even accentuated in recent independence movements.

Celtic Branch of Indo-European

Relatively few people speak a language from the other Indo-European branches: Albanian, Armenian, Celtic, and Greek. *Celtic* is of particular interest to English speakers, because it was the major language in the British Isles before the Germanic Angles, Jutes, and Saxons invaded. Two thousand years ago, Celtic languages were spoken in much of present-day Germany, France, and northern Italy, as well as in the British Isles. Today, Celtic languages survive only in remoter parts of Scotland, Wales, and Ireland, and on the Brittany peninsula of France.

Celtic Groups. Celtic languages are divided into *Goidelic (Gaelic)* and *Brythonic.* Two Goidelic languages survive: Irish Gaelic and Scottish Gaelic. Irish Gaelic and English are the Republic of Ireland's two official languages, but only 75,000 people speak Irish Gaelic exclusively. In Scotland, fewer than 80,000 of the people (2 percent) speak Scottish Gaelic. An extensive body of literature exists in Gaelic languages, including the Robert Burns poem "Auld Lang Syne" ("old long since"), the basis for the popular New Year's Eve song. Gaelic was carried from Ireland to Scotland about 1,500 years ago.

Over time, speakers of Brythonic (also called *Cymric* or *Britannic*) fled westward to Wales, southwestward to Cornwall, or southward across the English Channel to the Brittany peninsula of France. Wales—the name derived from the Germanic invaders' word for "foreign"—was conquered by the English in 1283. But Welsh remained dominant in Wales until the nineteenth century, when many English speakers migrated there to work in coal mines and factories. An estimated one-fourth of the people in Wales still use Welsh as their primary language, although all but a handful know English as well. In some isolated communities in the northwest, especially in the county of Gwynedd, as many as 80 percent of the people speak Welsh.

Cornish became extinct in 1777, with the death of the language's last known native speaker, Dolly Pentreath, who lived in Mousehole (pronounced "muzzle"). Before Pentreath died, an English historian recorded as much of her speech as possible, so that future generations could study the Cornish language.

One of her last utterances was later translated as "I will not speak English…you ugly, black toad."

In Brittany—like Cornwall, an isolated peninsula which juts out into the Atlantic Ocean—50,000 people still speak *Breton*. Breton differs from the other Celtic languages in that it has more French words.

The survival of any language depends on the political and military strength of its speakers. The Celtic languages declined because the Celts lost most of the territory they once controlled to speakers of other languages. In the 1300s, the Irish were forbidden to speak their own language in the presence of their English masters. By the nineteenth century, Irish children were required to wear "tally sticks" around their necks at school. The teacher carved a notch in the stick every day the child used an Irish word, and at the end of the day meted out punishment based on the number of tallies. Parents encouraged their children to learn English so that they could compete for jobs. Most remaining Celtic speakers also know the language of their English or French conquerors.

Revival of Celtic Languages. Recent efforts have prevented the disappearance of Celtic languages. In

Road signs in Eire (Republic of Ireland) are written in both English and Goidelic (Gaelic). The English versions of the names are displayed in capital letters. This road sign, in Ballyvaughan, County Clare, shows the way to Galway, known in Goidelic as Gaillimh. (C. E. Nagele/FPG International)

Wales, the *Cymdeithas yr Iaith Gymraeg* (Welsh Language Society) has been instrumental in preserving the language. Britain's 1988 Education Act made Welsh language training a compulsory subject in all schools in Wales, and Welsh history and music have been added to the curriculum. All local governments and utility companies are now obliged to provide services in Welsh. Welsh-language road signs have been posted throughout Wales, and the British Broadcasting Corporation produces Welsh-language television and radio programs.

The number of people fluent in Irish Gaelic has grown in recent years, as well, especially among younger people. Irish singers, including many rock groups (although not U2), have begun to record and perform in Gaelic. An Irish-language television station begins broadcasting in 1996. The revival is being led by young Irish living in other countries who wish to distinguish themselves from the English (in much the same way that Canadians traveling abroad often make efforts to distinguish themselves from U.S. citizens).

A couple of hundred people have now become fluent in the formerly extinct Cornish language, which was revived in the 1920s. Cornish is taught in grade schools and adult evening courses and is used in some church services; some banks accept checks written in Cornish. However, a dispute has erupted over the proper way to spell Cornish words. Some prefer to revive the confusing, illogical medieval spellings; others, including the Cornish Language Board, advocate spelling words phonetically. When officials in Camborne erected a welcome sign with the name of the town spelled "Kammbronn," traditionalists were outraged, because the medieval spelling was "Cambron." They argued that "Kammbronn" looked too "German," a harsh insult because it recalled both the successful invasion by Germanic people 1,500 years ago and the failed attempt by the Nazis in 1940.

The European Union has established the European Bureau of Lesser Used Languages, based in Dublin, Ireland, to provide financial support for the preservation of about two dozen languages. However, the long-term decline of languages such as Celtic provides an excellent example of the precarious struggle for survival that many languages experience. Faced with the diffusion of alternatives used by people with greater political and economic strength, speakers of Celtic and other languages must make sacrifices to preserve their cultural identity.

Search for the Indo-European Hearth

Linguists have determined that all the Germanic, Romance, Balto-Slavic, and Indo-Iranian languages descended from a common ancestral language, known as Proto-Indo-European. The search for the Proto-Indo-European hearth is a fascinating study and exemplifies the geographic principles of area and spatial analysis, integrating cultural characteristics, region, diffusion, and distribution.

The evolution of French, Spanish, and other Romance languages from Latin can be clearly documented, because the process unfolded during historical time, within the past 2,000 years. Unfortunately, Proto-Indo-European, the ancestral language of all Indo-European speakers, predates the invention of writing or recorded history.

Evidence of Common Origin of Indo-European Languages

The evidence that Proto-Indo-European once existed is "internal," derived from the physical attributes of words themselves in various Indo-European languages. For example, the words for some animals and trees in modern Indo-European languages have common roots, including "beech," "oak," "bear," "deer," "pheasant," and "bee." Because all Indo-European languages share these similar words, linguists believe the words must represent things experienced in the daily lives of the original Proto-Indo-European speakers.

In contrast, words for other features, such as "elephant," "camel," "rice," and "bamboo," have different roots in the various Indo-European languages. Such words therefore cannot be traced back to a common Proto-Indo-European ancestor and must have been added later, after the root language split into many branches.

Interestingly, individual Indo-European languages share common root words for "winter" and "snow," but not for "ocean." Therefore, linguists conclude that original Proto-Indo-European speakers probably lived in a cold climate, or one that had a winter season, but did not come in contact with oceans.

Theory 1: Kurgan Origin. So, where did Indo-European originate? One influential hypothesis, espoused by Marija Gimbutas, is that the first Proto-Indo-European speakers were the Kurgan people, whose homeland was in the steppes near the border between present-day Russia and Kazakhstan.

The earliest archaeological evidence of the Kurgans dates to around 4300 B.C.

The Kurgans were nomadic herders. Among the first to domesticate horses and cattle, they migrated in search of grasslands for their animals. Their search took them westward through Europe, eastward to Siberia, and southeastward to Iran and South Asia. Between 3500 and 2500 B.C., Kurgan warriors, using their domesticated horses as weapons, conquered much of Europe and South Asia (Figure 4-8).

Theory 2: Origin in Anatolia. Not surprisingly, scholars disagree on where and when the first speakers of Proto-Indo-European lived. Archaeologist Colin Renfrew argues that they lived 2,000 years before the Kurgans, in eastern Anatolia, part of present-day Turkey (Figure 4-9). He believes they diffused from Anatolia westward to Greece (the origin of the Greek language branch) and from Greece westward toward Italy, Sicily, Corsica, the Mediterranean coast of France, Spain, and Portugal (the origin of the Romance language branch). From the Mediterranean coast, the speakers migrated northward toward central and northern France and on to the British Isles (perhaps the origin of the Celtic language branch).

Renfrew feels that Indo-European also diffused northward from Greece toward the Danube River (Romania) and westward to central Europe. From there, the language diffused northward toward the Baltic Sea (the origin of the Germanic language branch) and eastward toward the Dnestr River near Ukraine (the origin of the Slavic language branch). From the Dnestr River, speakers migrated eastward to the Dnepr River (the homeland of the Kurgans).

The Indo-Iranian branch of the Indo-European language family originated either directly through migration from Anatolia along the south shores of the Black and Caspian seas by way of Iran and Pakistan or indirectly by way of Russia north of the Black and Caspian seas.

Renfrew argues that Indo-European diffused into Europe and South Asia along with agricultural practices, rather than by military conquest. The language triumphed because its speakers became more numerous and prosperous through growing their own food instead of relying on hunting. Regardless of how Indo-European diffused, communication was poor among different peoples, whether warriors or farmers. After many generations of complete isolation, individual groups evolved increasingly distinct languages.

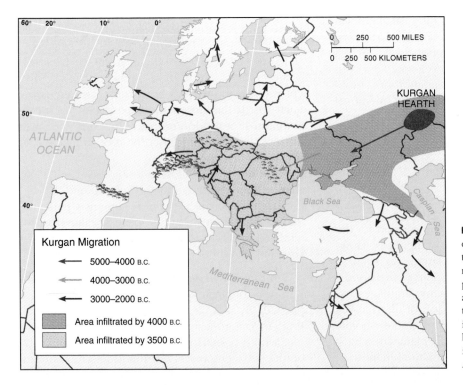

FIGURE 4-8 Origin and diffusion of Indo-European (Kurgan hearth theory). The Kurgan homeland was north of the Caspian Sea, near the present-day border between Russia and Kazakhstan. According to this theory, the Kurgans may have infiltrated into Eastern Europe beginning around 4000 B.C. and into central Europe and southwestern Asia beginning around 2500 B.C.

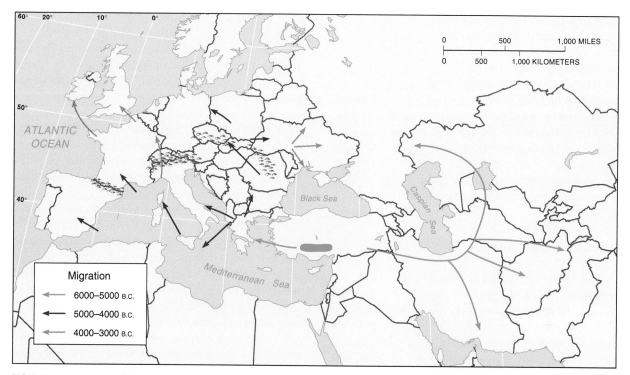

FIGURE 4-9 Origin and diffusion of Indo-European (Anatolian hearth theory). Indo-European may have originated in present-day Turkey 2,000 years before the Kurgans. According to this theory, the language diffused along with agricultural innovations west into Europe and east into Asia.

A Pre-Indo-European Survivor: Basque

Only one language currently spoken in Europe survives from the period before the arrival of Indo-European speakers. That language is Basque, spoken by approximately 1 million people in the Pyrenees Mountains of northern Spain and southwestern France. No attempt to link Basque to the common origin of the other European languages has been successful. Basque was probably once spoken over a wider area but was abandoned where its speakers came in contact with Indo-European.

The uniqueness of the Basque language reflects the isolation of the Basque people in their mountainous homeland. Similarities and differences between languages—our main form of communication—are a measure of the degree of interaction among groups of people. The diffusion of Indo-European languages demonstrates that a common ancestor dominated much of Europe before recorded history. Similarly, the diffusion of Indo-European languages to the Western Hemisphere is a result of conquests by Indo-European speakers in more recent times. On the other hand, the isolation of the Basques in their mountainous homeland has helped to preserve their language.

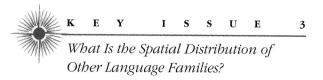

K E Y I S S U E 3

What Is the Spatial Distribution of Other Language Families?

- Asian Language Families
- African Language Families

With nearly 6 billion speakers diffused over Earth's seven continents during hundreds of thousands of years, and each group of speakers with its own unique heritage of innovation, contacts, and isolation, it is little wonder that experts widely disagree on the number of language families and individual languages. Estimates of distinct tongues range from 2,000 to 4,000 (Figure 4-2). You have already seen the difficulty in determining the exact number of Romance languages. The problem is more difficult with languages in other regions of the world, especially in Africa, because the precise distribution of these languages is inadequately documented.

Further, people around the world use an unknown number of **isolated languages,** such as Basque, which are unrelated to any other language and therefore not attached to any language family. Overall, however, we can group several thousand languages into a handful of language families. We have already studied the Indo-European family, so we now examine several other major language families, found primarily in Asia and Africa.

Asian Language Families

The principal language families of South Asia were discussed in the previous section, because the most widely spoken languages in the region belong to the Indo-European family. Other important language families in Asia include Sino-Tibetan, Japanese, Korean, and Austronesian (all in East and Southeast Asia), Afro-Asiatic (in Southwest Asia, as well as northern Africa), and Altaic (in Central Asia, as well as Turkey).

Sino-Tibetan Language Family

The Sino-Tibetan family encompasses languages spoken in the People's Republic of China—the world's most populous state at over 1 billion—as well as several smaller countries in Southeast Asia (Figure 4-1). The languages of China generally belong to the Sinitic branch of the Sino-Tibetan family. Austro-Thai and Tibetan-Burman are two smaller branches of the family.

Sinitic Branch. There is no single Chinese language. Rather, the most important is *Mandarin* (or, as the Chinese call it, *pu tong hua*—common speech). Spoken by approximately three-fourths of the Chinese people, Mandarin is by a wide margin the most used language in the world. Once the language of emperors in Beijing, Mandarin is now the official language of both the People's Republic of China and Taiwan, as well as one of the six official languages of the United Nations.

Four other Sinitic branch languages are spoken by tens of millions of people in China, mostly in the southern and eastern parts of the country—*Can-*

tonese (also known as *Yue*), *Wu, Min,* and *Hakka* (also known as *Kejia*). However, the Chinese government is imposing Mandarin countrywide. The relatively small number of languages in China (compared with India, for example) is a source of national strength and unity. Unity is also fostered by a consistent written form for all Chinese languages. Although the words are pronounced differently in each language, they are written in the same way.

You already know the general structure of Indo-European quite well, because you are a fluent speaker of at least one Indo-European language. But the structure of Chinese languages is quite different. They are based on 420 one-syllable words. This number far exceeds the possible one-syllable sounds that humans can make, so Chinese languages use each sound to denote more than one thing. The sound *shi,* for example, may mean "lion," "corpse," "house," "poetry," "ten," "swear," or "die." The sound *jian* has more than twenty meanings, including "to see." The listener must infer the meaning from the context in the sentence and the tone of voice the speaker uses.

In addition, two one-syllable words can be combined into two syllables, forming a new word. For example, the two-syllable word *Shanghai* is a combination of words that mean "above" and "sea." *Kan jian*—a combination of the words for "look" and "see," which would be redundant in English—clarifies that "to see" is the intended meaning for the multiple meanings of *jian.*

The other distinctive characteristic of the Chinese languages is the method of writing (Figure 4-10). The Chinese languages are written with a collection of thousands of *characters.* Some of the characters represent sounds pronounced in speaking, as in English. However, most are **ideograms,** which represent ideas or concepts, not specific pronunciations. The system is intricate and mature, having developed over 4,000 years.

The main language problem for the Chinese is the difficulty in learning to write because of the large number of characters. The Chinese government reports that 16 percent of the population over age 16 is unable to read or write more than a few characters.

Austro-Thai and Tibeto-Burman Branches of Sino-Tibetan Family. In addition to the Chinese languages included in the Sinitic branch, the Sino-Tibetan family includes two smaller branches,

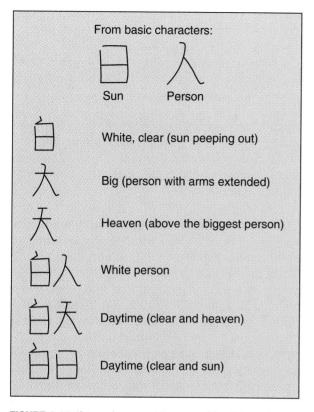

From basic characters:

Sun   Person

White, clear (sun peeping out)

Big (person with arms extended)

Heaven (above the biggest person)

White person

Daytime (clear and heaven)

Daytime (clear and sun)

FIGURE 4-10 Chinese language ideograms. The Chinese languages are written with ideograms, most of which represent ideas or concepts rather than sounds. About 240 key characters can be built into more complex words. These examples of words are built from two basic characters—"sun" and "person."

Austro-Thai and Tibeto-Burman. The major language of the Austro-Thai branch is *Thai,* used in Laos, Thailand, and parts of Vietnam. *Lao,* a dialect of Thai used in Laos, is classified by some linguists as a separate language. *Burmese,* the principal language of the Tibeto-Burman branch, is used in Myanmar (Burma).

Other East and Southeast Asian Language Families

To some Western observers, the written languages of the large East Asian population concentrations may be difficult to distinguish because they are written with such unfamiliar characters and their sound has a general similarity. *Japanese* and *Korean,* however, both form distinctive language families. If you look at their distribution in Figure 4-1, you can see a physical reason for their independent development: Japan is isolated because it is an island country, and Korea is isolated to some extent because it is a peninsular state.

Japanese. Chinese cultural traits have diffused into Japanese society, including the original form of writing the Japanese language. But the structures of the two languages differ. Japanese is written in part with Chinese ideograms, but it also uses two systems of phonetic symbols, as do Western languages, used either in place of the ideograms or alongside them. Foreign terms may be written with one of these sets of phonetic symbols.

Korean and Austro-Asiatic Language Families. Korean is usually classified as a separate language family, although it may be related to the Altaic languages of central Asia or to Japanese. In contrast to Sino-Tibetan languages and Japanese, however, Korean is written not with ideograms but in a system known as *hankul* (also called *hangul* and *onmun*). In this system, each letter represents a sound, as in Western languages. More than half of the Korean vocabulary derives from Chinese words. In fact, Chinese and Japanese words are the principal sources for creating new words to describe new technology and concepts.

Another important language family in Asia is Austro-Asiatic (Figure 4-1). *Vietnamese,* the most-spoken tongue of the Astro-Asiatic language family, is written with our familiar Latin alphabet, with the addition of a large number of diacritical marks above the vowels. The Vietnamese alphabet was devised in the seventh century by Roman Catholic missionaries.

Afro-Asiatic Language Family

The Afro-Asiatic—once referred to as the Semito-Hamitic—language family includes *Arabic* and *Hebrew,* as well as a number of languages spoken primarily in northern Africa and southwestern Asia (Figure 4-1). It is the world's fourth largest language family, but its international significance transcends the number of speakers because Afro-Asiatic languages were used to write the holiest books of three major religions, the Judeo-Christian Bible and the Islamic Quran.

Arabic. More than two-thirds of Afro-Asiatic speakers use Arabic, an official language in approximately two dozen countries of North Africa and

Southwest Asia, from Morocco to the Arabian Peninsula. Besides the 200 million native speakers of Arabic, a large percentage of the world's Muslims have at least some knowledge of Arabic because the Quran (Koran) was written in that language in the seventh century A.D. Although a number of dialects exist in Arabic, a standard Arabic has developed because of the influence of the Quran, newspapers, and radio. The United Nations added Arabic as its sixth official language in the General Assembly in 1973 and in the Security Council in 1982.

Hebrew. As a native language, Hebrew is spoken by only some 4 million people. Even so, it holds considerable interest for two reasons. First, most of the Bible's Old Testament was written in Hebrew (a small part of it was written in another Afro-Asiatic language, Aramaic). Second, Hebrew is one of the few "dead" languages ever to be revived. Once used in daily activity, Hebrew diminished in the fourth century B.C. and was thereafter retained only for Jewish religious services. In this way, Hebrew is comparable to Latin, which is kept alive in Roman Catholic services. At the time of Christ, people in present-day Israel generally spoke Aramaic, which in turn was replaced by Arabic.

When Israel was established in 1948, Hebrew became one of the new country's two official languages, along with Arabic, despite its dormancy for 2,000 years. Hebrew was chosen because the Jewish population of Israel consisted of refugees and migrants of many tongues from around the world, and no other language could so symbolically unify the disparate cultural groups in the new country.

The task of reviving Hebrew as a living language was formidable. Words had to be created for thousands of objects and inventions unknown in biblical times, such as telephones, cars, and electricity. The effort was initiated by Eliezer Ben-Yehuda, who lived in Palestine before the creation of the state of Israel and refused to speak any language other than Hebrew. Ben-Yehuda is credited with the invention of 4,000 new Hebrew words—related when possible to ancient ones—and the creation of the first modern Hebrew dictionary.

Altaic and Uralic Language Families

The Altaic and Uralic language families traditionally have been linked because the two display similar word formation, grammatical endings, and other structural elements. Recent studies, however, point to geographically separate origins of the two families. The Altaic languages are thought to have originated in the steppes bordering the Qilian Shan and Altai mountains between Tibet and China. Linguists do not know whether one group originally spoke a Proto-Altaic language, as with Proto-Indo-European and Proto-Uralic, or whether the language consisted of a mixture of several others that merged through interaction and acculturation of different peoples living in the steppes.

Altaic Languages. The Altaic languages are spoken across an 8,000-kilometer (5,000-mile) band of Asia between Turkey on the west and Mongolia and China on the east (Figure 4-1). Turkish, by far the most widely used Altaic language, was once written with Arabic letters. But in 1928, the Turkish government, led by Kemal Ataturk, ordered that the language be written with the Latin alphabet instead. Ataturk believed that switching to Latin letters would help modernize the economy and culture of Turkey through increased communications with European countries.

Other Altaic languages with at least 1 million speakers include *Azerbaijani, Bashkir, Chuvash, Kazakh, Kyrgyz, Mongolian, Tatar, Turkmen, Uighur,* and *Uzbek.* When the Soviet Union governed most of the Altaic-speaking region, use of Altaic languages was suppressed to create a homogeneous national culture. One element of Soviet policy was to force everyone to write with the Russian Cyrillic alphabet, although some Altaic languages traditionally employed Arabic letters. Most speakers of Altaic languages are Muslims and are familiar with Arabic letters because Islamic holy books are written in Arabic.

With the fall of the Soviet Union, Altaic languages became official in several newly independent countries, including Azerbaijan, Kazakhstan, Kyrgyzstan, Turkmenistan, and Uzbekistan. People in these countries may no longer be forced to learn Russian and write with Cyrillic letters. But unrest continues among speakers of Altaic languages, because enthusiasm for restoring languages long discouraged by the Soviet Union threatens the rights of minorities in those countries to speak other languages that are not officially recognized.

Problems also persist because the boundaries of the countries do not coincide with the regions in which the speakers of the various languages are clustered. The speakers of one Altaic language may find themselves divided among several countries, while the speakers of other Altaic languages—such as Bashkir, Chuvash, Tatar, and Uighur—do not control the governments of independent states.

Uralic Languages. Every European country is dominated by Indo-European speakers, except for three: Estonia, Finland, and Hungary (Figure 4-5). The Estonians, Finns, and Hungarians speak languages that belong to the Uralic family. Uralic languages are traceable back to a common language, *Proto-Uralic,* first used 7,000 years ago by people living in the Ural Mountains of present-day Russia, north of the Kurgan homeland.

Like Indo-European, the Uralic languages were carried to Europe by migrants. One branch moved north along the Volga River and then either turned westward toward Estonia and Finland or eastward into Siberia. The second branch moved southward and then westward to present-day Hungary. These Uralic-speaking migrants carved out homelands for themselves in the midst of Germanic- and Slavic-speaking peoples and retained their language as a major element of cultural identity.

African Language Families

No one knows the precise number of languages spoken in Africa, and scholars disagree on classifying the known ones into families. Nearly 1,000 distinct languages and several thousand named dialects have been documented. Figure 4-11 shows the broad view of African language families, and Figure 4-12 of Nigeria hints at the complex pattern of multiple tongues. This great number of languages results from at least 5,000 years of minimal interaction among the thousands of cultural groups inhabiting the continent. Each group developed its own language, religion, and other cultural traditions in isolation from other groups.

Documenting African languages is difficult, because most lack a written tradition, and only ten are spoken by more than 10 million people. In the 1800s, European missionaries and colonial officers began to record African languages using the Latin or Arabic alphabet. Twentieth-century researchers continue to add newly discovered languages to the African list. They have found no evidence that any have become extinct.

Principal Language Families in Sub-Saharan Africa

In northern Africa, the language pattern is relatively clear: *Arabic,* an Afro-Asiatic language dominates, although in a variety of dialects (Figure 4-11). Other Afro-Asiatic languages spoken by more than 5 million Africans include *Amharic, Oromo,* and *Somali* in the Horn of Africa and *Hausa* in northern Nigeria. In Sub-Saharan Africa, however, languages grow far more complex.

Niger-Congo Language Family. More than 95 percent of people in Sub-Saharan African speak languages of the *Niger-Congo* family, which includes six branches with many hard-to-classify languages. The remaining 5 percent speak languages of the *Khoisan* or *Nilo-Saharan* families. In addition, several million South Africans speak Indo-European languages, either English or *Afrikaans,* a Germanic Dutch-like language reflecting South Africa's Dutch colonial history (Figure 4-11).

The largest branch of the Niger-Congo family is Benue-Congo, and its most important language is *Swahili.* Although it is the official language only of Tanzania, Swahili has become the lingua franca among groups in much of eastern Africa. Swahili originally developed through interaction among African groups and Arab traders, so its vocabulary has strong Arabic influences. Also, Swahili is one of the few African languages with an extensive literature.

Nilo-Saharan and Khoisan Language Families. Nilo-Saharan languages are spoken by a few million people in north central Africa, immediately north of the Niger-Congo language region (Figure 4-11). Divisions within the Nilo-Saharan family exemplify the problem of classifying African languages. Despite fewer speakers, the Nilo-Saharan family is divided into six branches: *Chari-Nile, Fur, Koma, Maba, Saharan,* and *Songhai.* The Chari-Nile branch (East Africa from Egypt to Tanzania) can be subdivided into four groups: *Berta, Central Sudanic, East Sudanic,* and *Kunama.* The Central Sudanic group in turn comprises ten subgroups. Therefore, the total number of speakers of each individual Nilo-Saharan language is extremely small.

The third important language family of sub-Saharan Africa—Khoisan—is concentrated in the southwest. A distinctive characteristic of the Khoisan languages is the use of clicking sounds. Upon hear-

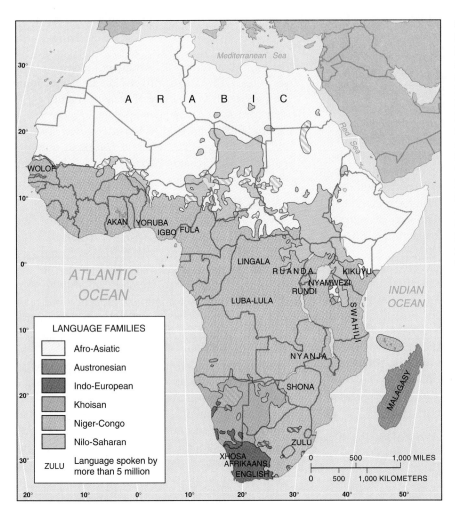

FIGURE 4-11 Africa's language families. Nearly 1,000 languages have been identified in Africa, and experts have not agreed on how to classify them into families, especially languages in central Africa. On the large island of Madagascar, the Malagasy language is unrelated to other African languages. Madagascar's Austronesian language is from a language family spoken across a wide area of the South Pacific (see Figure 4-1). This wide diffusion indicates that early speakers of Austronesian on the island of Madagascar must have migrated long distances. Languages with more than 5 million speakers are written on the map.

ing this sound, whites in southern Africa derisively and onomatopoeically named the most important Khoisan language *Hottentot.*

Austronesian Language Family. The map of world languages (Figure 4-1) shows a striking oddity: the people of Madagascar, the large island off the east coast, speak Malagasy, an Austronesian language, even though the island is separated by 3,000 kilometers (1,900 miles) from any other Austronesian-speaking country, such as Indonesia. This is certainly strong evidence of migration. Just as English is the predominant language of North America because of migration from England, so is Malagasy, the language of Madagascar, an Austronesian language because of migration from the South Pacific. Malayo-Polynesian people apparently sailed in small boats to reach Madagascar approximately 2,000 years ago.

Nigeria: Conflict among Speakers of Different Languages

Africa's most populous country, Nigeria, displays the problems that can arise from the presence of many speakers of many languages. More than 200 distinct languages are spoken in Nigeria. In the north, Hausa, an Afro-Asiatic language, is spoken by approximately one-fourth of the population, mostly Hausa and Fulani peoples. In the southeast, *Ibo* is the most common language, followed by *Efik* and *Ijaw.* In the southwest, *Yoruba* is the most important language, followed by Edo (Figure 4-12).

Nigeria's principal problem as a country is that none of its 200-plus indigenous languages has widespread use. Its colonial history is reflected in the fact that English is spoken by 2 percent of Nigerians. Indeed, English is the official language; it has the considerable advantage of being intelligible to governments of other countries.

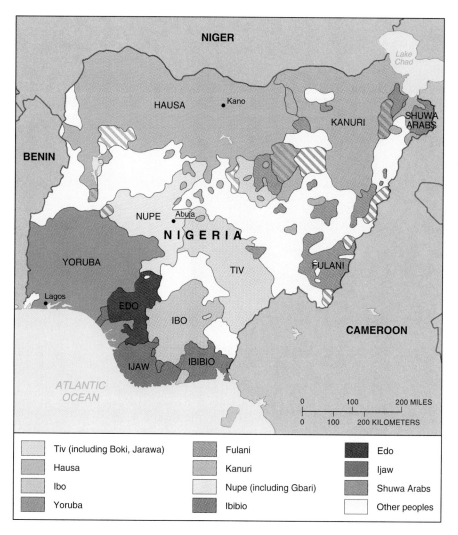

FIGURE 4-12 Nigeria's main groups of people and languages. These once-isolated groups speak over 200 languages. National unity is severely strained by the lack of a common language that a large percentage of the population can understand. To encourage unity among the disparate cultural groups, Nigeria has moved the national capital from Lagos, in the Yoruba southwest, to Abuja in the country's center.

Groups living in different regions of Nigeria have often battled. The southern Ibos attempted to secede from Nigeria during the 1960s, and northerners have repeatedly claimed that the Yorubas discriminate against them. To reduce these regional tensions, the government has moved the capital from Lagos in the Yoruba-dominated southwest to Abuja in the center of Nigeria.

Language Complexity: A Matter of Scale

From a global perspective, the distribution of Earth's language families is reasonably simple, because three-fourths of the people speak languages belonging to only two families—Indo-European and Sino-Tibetan.

But the view at this scale does not even hint at the extent of geographic differences in languages. Nigeria reflects the problems that can arise when great cultural diversity—and therefore, language diversity—is packed into a relatively small region. Nigeria also illustrates the importance of language in identifying distinct cultural groups at a local scale. Speakers of one language are unlikely to understand any of the others in the same family, let alone languages from other families. The picture of the spatial distribution of language cannot be based solely on the distribution of individual languages, though, because considerable diversity also exists among different speakers of the same language.

Construction of Abuja, Nigeria's
new capital. To foster unity in a
culturally diverse country, Nigeria
has relocated its capital from Lagos,
on the south coast, to Abuja, in an
interior region not considered
territory of one of the country's
most numerous cultural groups.
(W. Campbell/Sygma)

✦ K E Y   I S S U E   4

*Why Do People Living in Different
Locations Speak English Differently?*

- Development of Dialects in English
- Global Dominance of English

"If you use proper English, you're regarded as a
freak; why can't the English learn to speak?" asked
Professor Henry Higgins in the Broadway musical
My Fair Lady. He was referring to the Cockney-
speaking Eliza Doolittle, who pronounced "rain" like
"rine" and dropped the /h/ sound from the beginning of words like "happy." Eliza Doolittle's speech
illustrates that English, like other languages, has a
wide variety of dialects that use different pronunciations, spellings, and meanings for particular words.

Geographers study dialects to understand the relationship between culture and the landscape. Dialects, like language families, acquire distinctive
distribution through various social processes, such
as migration, interaction, and isolation. At the same
time, a dialect reflects unique characteristics of the
physical environment in which a group lives, and
languages change partially in response to modifications of the landscape. This section examines the
spatial distribution of dialects of English, first in England and then in the United States.

Development of Dialects in English

One particular dialect of English, the one associated with upper-class Britons living in the London
area, is recognized around the world as the standard
form of British speech. This speech, known as
British Received Pronunciation (BRP), is well
known to people elsewhere in the world, because it
is commonly used by politicians, broadcasters, and
actors. Why don't Americans or, for that matter, other
British people speak that way?

Dialects in England

As you have seen, English originated with three
invading groups from northern Europe who settled
in different parts of Britain: the Angles in the north,
the Jutes in the southeast, and the Saxons in the
south and west. The language each spoke was the
basis of distinct regional dialects of Old English: *Kentish* in the southeast, *West Saxon* in the southwest,
Mercian in the center of the island, and *Northumbrian* in the north (Figure 4-13).

In the 1950s Broadway and Hollywood musical *My Fair Lady*, based on George Bernard Shaw's play Pygmalion, language expert Professor Henry Higgins (played by Rex Harrison) encounters Eliza Doolittle, a Cockney from the poor East End of London (played in the movie by Audrey Hepburn), selling flowers in front of London's Covent Garden Opera House. Higgins accepts a wager from a friend that he can transform Doolittle into an upper-class woman primarily by teaching her to speak with the accent used by upper-class Britons. (Warner Bros./Photofest)

After the Norman invasion of 1066, French replaced English as the language of the government and aristocracy. By the time English again became the country's dominant language, five major regional dialects had emerged: *Northern, East Midland, West Midland, Southwestern,* and *Southeastern* or *Kentish*. The boundaries of these five regional dialects roughly paralleled the pattern before the Norman invasion (compare Figures 4-13 and 4-14). However, after 150 years of living in isolation in rural settlements under the control of a French-speaking government, people spoke English differently in virtually every county of England.

From this large collection of local dialects, one eventually emerged as the standard language for writing and speech throughout England: the dialect used by upper-class residents in the capital city of London and the two important university cities of Cambridge and Oxford. The diffusion of the dialect spoken in London and the university cities was first encouraged by the introduction of the printing press to England in 1476. Grammar books and dictionaries printed in the eighteenth century established rules for spelling and grammar that were based on the London dialect. These frequently arbitrary rules were then taught in schools throughout the country.

In other countries, the dialect spoken by upper-class residents of the capital city also has emerged as the standard language. For example, the Parisian dialect became the standard form of French, and the Madridian dialect became the standard form of Spanish. As was the case with language families and individual languages, the dominance of one dialect over others within a country is a measure of the relative political strength of the speakers of the various dialects.

Current Dialect Differences in England. Despite the current dominance of British Received Pronunciation, strong regional differences persist in English dialects spoken in the United Kingdom, especially in rural areas. Although several dozen dialects are identifiable, they can be grouped into three main ones: Northern, Midland, and Southern. Southern Englanders pronounce words such as "grass" and "path" with an /ah/ sound, whereas people in the Midlands and North use a short /a/, as do most people in the United States. People in the Midlands and North pronounce "butter" and "Sunday" with the /oo/ sound of words like "boot." Northerners pronounce "ground" and "pound" like "grund" and "pund," with the /uh/ sound similar to the word "punt" in U.S. football.

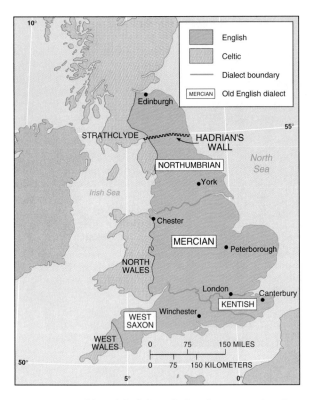

FIGURE 4-13 Old English dialects (before the Norman invasion of A.D. 1066). The Angles, Saxons, and Jutes retained their distinctive speech patterns after settling in England. Angles north of the Humber River spoke a German dialect that became known as *Northumbrian,* and those south of the Humber River spoke *Mercian.* Jutes in the southeast spoke a German dialect that became known as *Kentish.* The Saxons settled in the south and west. (From Albert C. Baugh and Thomas Cable, *A History of the English Language,* 3d ed., © 1978, p. 53. Reprinted by permission of Prentice Hall, Englewood Cliffs, NJ.)

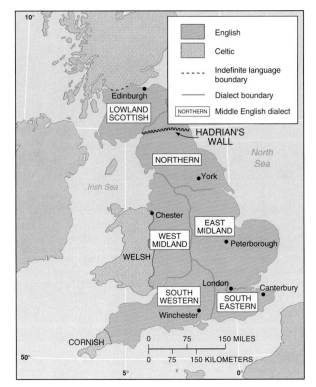

FIGURE 4-14 Middle English dialects (1150–1500). Comparing this map with Figure 4-13, you can see that important dialects of Middle English corresponded closely to those of Old English. The Old English Northumbrian dialect split into Scottish and Northern dialects. The Old English Mercian dialect divided into East Midland and West Midland. The Old English Kentish dialect extended considerably in area and became known as the Southeastern dialect. West Saxon became known as the Southwestern dialect. (From Albert C. Baugh and Thomas Cable, *A History of the English Language,* 3d ed., © 1978, p. 53. Reprinted by permission of Prentice Hall, Englewood Cliffs, NJ.)

Further, distinctive southwestern and southeastern accents occur within the Southern dialect. People in the southwest, for example, pronounce "thatch" and "thing" with the /th/ sound of "then," rather than "thin." "Fresh" and "eggs" have an /ai/ sound. Southeasterners pronounce the /a/ in "apple" and "cat" like the short /e/ in "bet." Local dialects can be further distinguished, and some words have distinctive pronunciations and meanings in each county of the United Kingdom.

Children's words particularly show strong regional differences. For example, words used by children in games vary in different regions of the country and in specific communities within particular regions (Figure 4-15).

English in North America

The English language was brought to the North American continent by colonists from England who settled along the Atlantic coast beginning in the seventeenth century. The early colonists naturally spoke the language used in England at the time and established seventeenth-century English as the dominant form of European speech in colonial America. Later immigrants from other countries found English already implanted here. Although they made significant contributions to American English, they became acculturated into a society that already spoke English. Therefore, the earliest colonists were most responsible for the dominant language patterns that exist

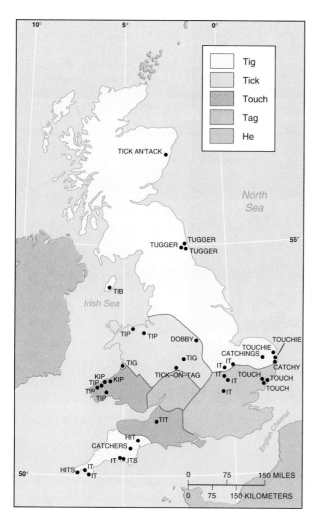

FIGURE 4-15 Contemporary dialects in Great Britain. Regional differences in vocabulary continue to exist in Great Britain, despite the small size of the country and the diffusion of standard language through television, radio, and print. One example is the word that children use in a game of tag to signal that they have touched another participant. The map also shows that distinctive words indicating "touch" can exist in individual communities as well. (From Iona Opie and Peter Opie, *Children's Games in Street and Playground* London: Clarendon Press, 1969.)

today in the English-speaking part of the Western Hemisphere.

Differences between British and American English. Why is the English language in the United States so different from that in England? As so often is the case with languages, the answer is isolation. Separated by the Atlantic Ocean, the United States and England evolved English independently during the eighteenth and nineteenth centuries, with little in-

fluence on one another. Few residents of one country could visit the other, and the means to transmit the human voice over long distances would not become available until the twentieth century.

U.S. English differs from that of England in three significant ways: *vocabulary, spelling,* and *pronunciation.* The vocabulary is different largely because settlers in America encountered many new objects and experiences. The new continent contained physical features, such as large forests and mountains, that had to be given new names. New animals were encountered, including the *moose, raccoon,* and *chipmunk,* all of which were given names borrowed from Native Americans. Indigenous American "Indians" also enriched American English with names for objects such as *canoe, moccasin,* and *squash.*

As new inventions appeared, they acquired different names on either side of the Atlantic. For example, the elevator is called a *lift* in England, and the flashlight is known as a *torch.* The British call the hood of a car the *bonnet* and the trunk the *boot.*

Spelling diverged from the British standard because of a strong national feeling in the United States for an independent identity. Noah Webster, the creator of the first comprehensive American dictionary and grammar books, was not just a documenter of usage; he had an agenda. Webster was determined to develop a uniquely American dialect of English. He either ignored or was unaware of recently created rules of grammar and spelling developed in England. Webster argued that spelling and grammar reforms would help establish a national language, reduce cultural dependence on England, and inspire national pride. The spelling differences between British and American English, such as the elimination of the *u* from the British spelling of words such as "honour" and "colour" and the substitution of *s* for *c* in "defence," are due primarily to the diffusion of Webster's ideas inside the United States.

Differences in pronunciation between British and U.S. speakers are immediately recognizable. Again, geographic concepts help explain the reason for the differences. From the time of their arrival in North America, colonists began to pronounce words differently than the British. Such divergence is normal, for interaction between the two groups was largely confined to exchange of letters and other printed matter rather than direct speech.

One prominent difference between British and U.S. English is the pronunciation of the letters *a* and *r.* Such words as "fast," "path," and "half" are pro-

When Americans board red double-decker buses in Piccadilly Circus, London, they can see differences between the two English-speaking countries. Because the British drive on the left side of the road, passengers board the bus on the left side, while the driver sits on the right side—the opposite of the arrangement in the United States. The sign for Panasonic is spelled colour, and the signs on the bus advertise sun-and-fun holidays in Spain. Cultural diffusion is also apparent—American companies are advertising Coca-Cola, McDonald's, and Kodak in the heart of London. (Ulf Sjostedt/FPG International)

nounced in England with the /ah/ in "father" rather than the /a/ in "man." The British also eliminate the letter *r* from pronunciation except before vowels. Thus, "lord" in British pronunciation sounds like "laud." Further, Americans pronounce unaccented syllables with more clarity. The words "secretary" and "necessary" have four syllables in American English but only three in British ("secret'ry" and "necess'ry").

Surprisingly, pronunciation has changed more in England than in the United States. The letters *a* and *r* are pronounced in the United States the way they used to be pronounced in Britain, specifically in the seventeenth century when the first colonists arrived.

A single dialect of Southern English did not emerge as the British national standard until the late eighteenth century, after the American colonies had declared independence and were politically as well as physically isolated from England. Thus, people in the United States do not speak "proper" English because when the colonists left England, "proper" English was not what it is today. Furthermore, few colonists were drawn from the English upper classes.

Dialects in the United States

Major differences in U.S. dialects originated because of differences in dialects among the original settlers. The English dialect spoken by the first colonists, who arrived in the seventeenth century, determined the future speech patterns for their communities, because later immigrants adopted the language used in their new homes when they arrived. The language may have been modified somewhat by the new arrivals, but the distinctive elements brought over by the original settlers continued to dominate.

Settlement in the East. The original American settlements stretched along the Atlantic Coast in thirteen separate colonies. The settlements can be grouped into three areas: New England, Middle Atlantic, and Southeastern. Massachusetts and the other New England colonies were established and inhabited almost entirely by settlers from England. Two-thirds of the New England colonists were Puritans from East Anglia in southeastern England, and only a few came from the north of England.

Spanish-language newspapers circulate widely in New York. This is not surprising, because one-fourth of New Yorkers identified themselves as Hispanic for the 1990 census. (Gerd Ludwig/Woodfin Camp & Associates)

The nucleus of the southeastern colonies was Virginia, where the first permanent settlement by the English in North America was established at Jamestown in 1607. About half of the southeastern settlers came from Southeast England, although they represented a diversity of social class backgrounds, including deported prisoners, indentured servants, and political and religious refugees. The English dialects now spoken in the U.S. Southeast and New England are easily recognizable. Current distinctions result from the establishment of independent and isolated colonies in the seventeenth century.

The immigrants to the Middle Atlantic colonies were more diverse. The early settlers of Pennsylvania were predominantly Quakers from the north of England. Scots and Irish also went to Pennsylvania, as well as to New Jersey and Delaware. In addition, the Middle Atlantic colonies attracted many German, Dutch, and Swedish immigrants who learned their English from the English-speaking settlers in the area. The dialect spoken in the Middle Atlantic colonies thus differed significantly from those spoken farther north and south, because most of the settlers came from the north rather than the south of England or from other countries.

Current Dialect Differences in the East. Today, major dialect differences within the United States continue to exist, primarily on the East Coast, although some distinctions can be found elsewhere in the country. The different dialects have been documented through the study of particular words. Every word that is not used nationally has some geographic extent within the country and therefore has boundaries. Such a word-usage boundary, known as an **isogloss,** can be constructed for each word. These isoglosses are determined by collecting data directly from people, particularly natives of rural areas. They are shown pictures to identify or are given sentences to complete with a particular word. Although every word has a unique isogloss, boundary lines of different words coalesce in some locations to form regions.

Two important isoglosses separate the eastern United States into three major dialect regions, known as Northern, Midland, and Southern. The northern boundary runs across Pennsylvania; the southern one runs along the Appalachian Mountains (Figure 4-16).

Some words are commonly used within one of the three major dialect areas, but rarely in the other two. In most instances, these words are related to rural life, food, and objects from daily activities. Language differences tend to be greater in rural areas than in cities, because farmers are relatively isolated from interaction with people from other dialect regions.

For example, a container commonly used on farms is known as a "pail" in the North and a "bucket" in the Midlands and South. A small stream is known as a "brook" in the North, a "run" in the Midlands, and a "branch" in the South. The term *run* was apparently used in the north of England and Scotland, which was the area of origin for many Middle Atlantic settlers but for few New England or Southern settlers.

Phrases for some farm activities, such as calling cows from pasture, show particularly sharp differences among the three regional dialects. New England farmers call cows with "Boss!" or "Bossie!", sometimes preceded by "Co" or "Come." In the Midlands, the preferred call is "Sook!" or sometimes "Sookie!" or "Sook cow!" The choice in the South is "Co-wench!" or its alternative forms, "Co-inch!" and "Co-ee!"

Many words that were once regionally distinctive are now national in distribution. Mass media, especially television and radio, influence the adoption of the same words throughout the country. For example, a "frying pan" was once commonly called a "spider" in New England and a "skillet" in the Middle Atlantic area.

Pronunciation Differences. Regional pronunciation differences are more familiar to us than word differences, although it is harder to draw precise isoglosses for them. Pronunciations that distinguish the southern dialect include making such words as "half" and "mine" into two syllables ("ha-af" and "mi-yen"), pronouncing "poor" as "po-ur," and pronouncing "Tuesday" and "due" with a /y/ sound ("Tyuesday" and "dyue").

The New England accent is well known for dropping the /r/ sound, so that "heart" and "lark" are pronounced "hot" and "lock." Also, "ear" and "care" are pronounced with /ah/ substituted for the /r/ endings. This characteristic dropping of the /r/ sound is shared with speakers from the south of England and reflects

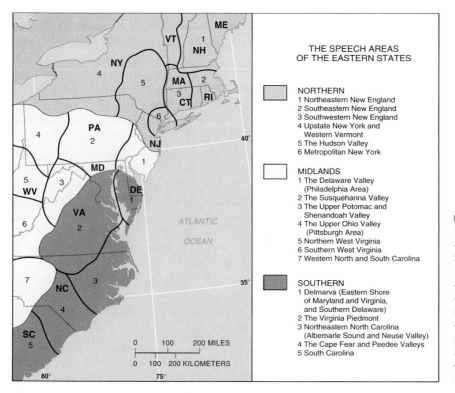

THE SPEECH AREAS
OF THE EASTERN STATES

NORTHERN
1 Northeastern New England
2 Southeastern New England
3 Southwestern New England
4 Upstate New York and
  Western Vermont
5 The Hudson Valley
6 Metropolitan New York

MIDLANDS
1 The Delaware Valley
  (Philadelphia Area)
2 The Susquehanna Valley
3 The Upper Potomac and
  Shenandoah Valley
4 The Upper Ohio Valley
  (Pittsburgh Area)
5 Northern West Virginia
6 Southern West Virginia
7 Western North and South Carolina

SOUTHERN
1 Delmarva (Eastern Shore
  of Maryland and Virginia,
  and Southern Delaware)
2 The Virginia Piedmont
3 Northeastern North Carolina
  (Albemarle Sound and Neuse Valley)
4 The Cape Fear and Peedee Valleys
5 South Carolina

FIGURE 4-16 Dialects in eastern United States. The most comprehensive classification of dialects in the United States was made by Hans Kurath in 1949. He found the greatest diversity of dialects in the eastern part of the country, especially in vocabulary used on farms. Kurath divided the eastern United States into three major dialect regions—Northern, Midlands, and Southern—each of which contained a number of important subareas.

the place of origin of most New England colonists. It also reflects the relatively high degree of contact between the two groups. Residents of Boston, New England's main port city, maintained especially close ties to the important ports of southern England such as London, Plymouth, and Bristol. Compared with other colonists, New Englanders received more exposure to changes in pronunciation that occurred in Britain during the eighteenth century.

The New England and southern accents sound odd to most Americans because the standard pronunciation throughout the American West comes from the Middle Atlantic states rather than the New England and southern regions. This pattern occurred because the Middle Atlantic states provided most of the western settlers.

The diffusion of particular English dialects into the middle and western parts of the United States is a result of the westward movement of colonists from the three dialect regions of the East. The area of the Midwest south of the Ohio River was settled first by colonists from Virginia and the other southern areas. The Middle Atlantic colonies sent most of the early settlers north of the Ohio River, although some New Englanders moved to the Great Lakes area.

As more of the West was opened to settlement during the nineteenth century, people migrated from all parts of the East Coast. The California gold rush attracted people from throughout the East, many of whom subsequently moved to other parts of the West. The mobility of Americans has been a major reason for the relatively uniform language that exists throughout much of the West.

African–American Dialects of English.

African–Americans speak a dialect of English heavily influenced by the group's distinctive heritage of forced migration from Africa during the eighteenth century to be slaves in the southern colonies. African–American slaves preserved a distinctive dialect in part to communicate in a code not understood by their white masters. Black dialect words such as "gumbo" and "jazz" have diffused into the standard English language.

In the twentieth century, many African–Americans migrated from the South to the large cities in the Northeast and Midwest (see Chapter 3). Living in racially segregated neighborhoods within northern cities, and attending segregated schools, many blacks preserved their distinctive dialect.

At one time, black English was generally regarded as "substandard" and a measure of poor education. This was the view of persons who failed to understand that black English was a dialect with a definite history. Today, African-Americans seek to preserve this dialect because of its central role in identifying a distinctive culture within white-dominated American society. An African-American trying to succeed in the modern economy may be regarded as bilingual: a black doctor or nurse, for example, may speak standard English to white patients and African–American dialect to black patients.

Global Dominance of English

In the twentieth century, English has become the world's most important lingua franca, or language of international communication. When well-educated speakers of two different languages wish to communicate with each other in countries such as India or Nigeria, they frequently use English. A Polish airline pilot who flies over France speaks to the traffic controller on the ground in English.

A recent survey conducted by *Reader's Digest* among young people in European Union countries found that 70 percent between ages 18 and 24 speak English. The number of people around the world who speak English as a second language is unknown, but their numbers at least match the number who use English as a primary language.

English words have become increasingly integrated into other languages. The Japanese, for example, refer to "beisboru" (baseball), "naifu" (knife), and "sutoroberi keki" (strawberry cake). "Cowboy," "hamburger," "jeans," and "T-shirt" have entered the French language.

The emergence of English as an international language has facilitated the diffusion of popular culture and science and the growth of international trade. However, people who forsake their native language must weigh the benefits of using English against the cost of losing a fundamental element of local cultural identity.

Traditionally, language has been a very important source of national pride and identity in France. The French are particularly upset with the increasing worldwide domination of English, especially the invasion of their language by English words and the substitution of English for French as the most important language of international communications.

Since 1635, the French Academy has been the supreme arbiter of the French language. In modern times, it has promoted the use of French terms in France, such as *stationnement* rather than *parking,* and *fin du semaine* rather than *le weekend.* The widespread use of English in the French language is called **franglais,** a combination of *français* and *anglais,* the French words for "French" and "English." In 1994, however, the highest court in France ruled that most of the country's laws banning franglais were illegal.

People in smaller countries need to learn English to participate more fully in a global economy and culture. All children learn English in the schools of countries such as the Netherlands and Sweden to facilitate international communication. This practice may seem culturally unfair, but, obviously, it is more likely that several million Dutch people will learn English than that several hundred million English speakers around the world will learn Dutch.

In view of the global dominance of English, many U.S. citizens do not recognize the importance of learning other languages. (Does your college require a foreign language for graduation?) But, one of the best ways to learn about the beliefs, traits, and other cultural characteristics of people in a particular region is to learn their language. The lack of effort by Americans to learn other languages is a source of resentment among people elsewhere in the world, especially when Americans visit or work in other countries.

The inability to speak other languages is also a handicap for Americans who try to conduct international business. Successful entry into new overseas markets requires knowledge of local cultural characteristics, and officials who can speak the local language are better able to obtain the needed knowledge. Japanese businesses that wish to expand in the United States send English-speaking officials, but American businesses that wish to sell products to the Japanese rarely are able to send a Japanese-speaking employee.

Summary

Here again are the key issues raised by the geography of languages.

1. **How did the English language originate and diffuse?**

   English is a Germanic language, related to other languages spoken in northwestern Europe. Germanic tribes invaded England and brought their language with them. From England, the language was diffused around the world through colonization.

2. **How is English related to languages spoken elsewhere in the world?**

   English is part of the Germanic branch of the Indo-European language family, a collection of languages used by half the world's population. All Indo-European languages can be traced to a common ancestor, Proto-Indo-European. Individual languages developed from this single root through migration, followed by the isolation of one group from others who formerly spoke the same language.

3. **What is the spatial distribution of other language families?**

   The precise number of languages in the world is unknown, but it is several thousand. These languages can be grouped into approximately two dozen language families. Other than Indo-European, the language family with the most speakers is Sino-Tibetan, used by 20 percent of the world's population.

4. **Why do people living in different locations speak English differently?**

Speakers of English as well as other languages use a wide variety of dialects. Differences in vocabulary, spelling, and pronunciation emerge primarily because speakers of one language, especially in rural areas, are isolated from other speakers of the same language. Geographers can document the boundaries (isoglosses) that separate different dialect regions within countries, such as those that exist in the United States and the United Kingdom. English has become the most important language for international communication in popular arts, science, and business.

CASE STUDY REVISITED

The Future of French and Spanish in Anglo-America

The French-speaking people of Canada and the Spanish-speaking people of the United States both live on a continent dominated by English speakers. But future prospects for these two languages in North America are different.

French Canada

In Canada, French is an official language, along with English. French speakers comprise one-fourth of the country's population, most of whom are clustered in Québec, where they comprise more than three-fourths of the province's speakers (Figure 4-17). Colonized by the French in the seventeenth century, Québec was captured by the British in 1763 and in 1867 became one of the provinces in the Confederation of Canada.

Until recently, Québec was one of Canada's poorest and least developed provinces. Its economic and political activities were dominated by an English-speaking minority, and the province suffered from cultural isolation and lack of French-speaking leaders. In recent years, Québec has strengthened its links to France. When French President Charles de Gaulle visited Québec in 1967, he encouraged the development of an independent Québec by shouting in his speech, *"Vive le Québec libre!"* ("Long live free Quebec!").

During the 1970s, the Québec government made the use of French mandatory in many daily activities. Alarmed at these pro-French policies, more than 100,000 English speakers and dozens of major corporations moved from Montréal, Québec's largest city, to English-speaking Toronto, Ontario. Many Québécois favored total separation of the province from Canada as the only way to preserve their cultural heritage. In a 1980 referendum, however, a majority of voters in Québec opposed separation.

In recent years, Québec has further restricted the use of languages other than French. Québec's Commission de Toponyme is renaming towns, rivers, and mountains that have names with English-language origins. The word "Stop" has been replaced by "Arrêt" on the red octagonal road signs, even though "Stop" is used throughout the world, even in other French-speaking countries. French must be the predominant language on all commercial signs, and the legislature passed a law that banned non-French outdoor signs altogether (ruled unconstitutional by the Canadian Supreme Court).

Québécois are committed to preserving their distinctive French-language culture. If necessary, they are willing to secede from Canada. Whether or not Québec remains part of Canada, people who wish to be integrated into the English-speaking culture and economy of North America are emigrating from Québec. Since 1969, around 500,000 people have immigrated to Québec—mostly from Italy, Greece, and Portugal—but more than 300,000 have simultaneously emigrated from Québec to English-speaking Canadian provinces.

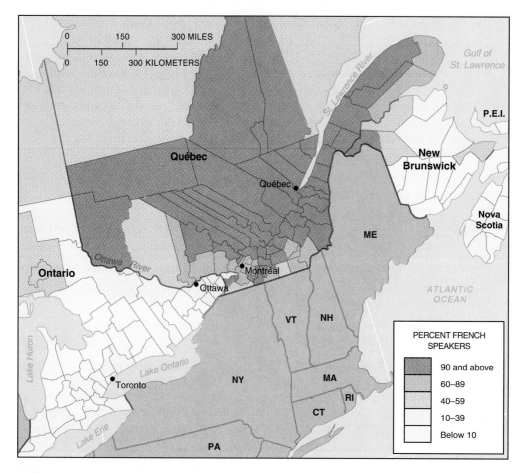

FIGURE 4-17 English/French language boundary in Canada. More than 80 percent of Québec's residents speak French, compared to approximately 6 percent for the rest of Canada. However, the boundary between the French- and English-speaking regions is not precise; mixed areas exist along the borders with New Brunswick, Newfoundland, Ontario, and the United States.

Hispanic America

Because of large-scale immigration from Latin America in recent years, Spanish has become an increasingly important language in the United States. In some communities, public notices, government documents, and advertisements are printed in Spanish. Several hundred Spanish-language newspapers and radio and television stations operate in the United States, especially in South Florida, the Southwest, and large northern cities, where most of the 17 million Spanish-speaking people live.

In reaction against the increasing use of Spanish in the United States, several states and localities have enacted legislation making English the official language. Some courts have objected, judging these laws to be unconstitutional restrictions on free speech. But such laws continue to be enacted as symbolic statements concerning the importance of English as the chief cultural bond in the United States in an otherwise heterogeneous society.

Americans have also debated whether schools should offer bilingual education. Some people want Spanish-speaking children to be educated in Spanish, because they think that children will learn more effectively if taught in their native language, as well as preserve their own cultural heritage. Other English and Spanish speakers argue that learning in Spanish creates a handicap for people in the United States when they look for jobs, virtually all

Linguistic diversity in Anglo-America. (Top) French dominates in Canada's Québec province, including the signs along this street, rue Saint-Louis, in the city of Québec, Canada. (Ron Watts/West Light)

(Bottom) Spanish dominates in Little Havana, a neighborhood of Miami, Florida. Many residents of the neighborhood, located west of downtown Miami, immigrated from Cuba, especially after Fidel Castro gained power in 1959. (Alon Reininger/Contact Press Images)

of which require knowledge of English. Bilingual education has also been hampered by the lack of teachers able to speak two languages and by the high cost of hiring additional personnel and purchasing additional teaching materials.

Despite efforts to promote the use of English, the number of U.S. residents speaking a language other than English at home increased by more than one-third during the 1980s, to 32 million people (over the age of 5). More spoke Spanish than all other foreign languages combined, but more than 1 million each speak French, German, Italian, or Chinese at home, and nearly 1 million speak Tagalog (a language found in the Philippines). In the face of the growing dominance of the English language in the global economy and culture, the increasing use of other languages in the United States itself is a reminder of the importance groups place on preserving cultural identity and the central role that language plays in maintaining that identity.

Key Terms

British Received Pronunciation (BRP) The dialect of English associated with upper-class Britons living in the London area and now considered standard in the United Kingdom.

Creole or **creolized language** A language that results from the mixing of a colonizer's language with the indigenous language of the people being dominated.

Dialect A form of a language spoken in a local area.

Extinct language A language that was once used by people in daily activities but is no longer used.

Franglais A term used by the French for English words that have entered the French language, a combination of *français* and *anglais,* the French words for "French" and "English," respectively.

Ideograms The system of writing used in China and other East Asian countries in which each symbol represents an idea or a concept rather than a specific sound, as is the case with letters in English.

Isogloss A boundary that separates regions in which different language usages predominate.

Isolated language A language that is unrelated to any other languages and therefore not attached to any language family.

Language A system of communication through the use of speech, a collection of sounds understood by a group of people to have the same meaning.

Language branch A group of languages that share a common origin but that have evolved into individual languages. The differences are not as extensive or as old as with language families, which may include several branches.

Language family A collection of individual languages related to each other by virtue of having a common ancestor before recorded history.

Language group Several individual languages within a language branch that share a common origin in the relatively recent past and display relatively few differences in grammar and vocabulary.

Lingua franca A language mutually understood and commonly used in trade by people who have different native languages.

Literary tradition A language that is written as well as spoken.

Official language The language adopted for use by the government for the conduct of business and publication of documents.

Pidgin language A form of speech that adopts a simplified grammar and limited vocabulary of a lingua franca, used for communications among speakers of two different languages.

Standard language The form of a language used for official government business, education, and mass communication.

Vulgar Latin A form of Latin used in daily conversation by ancient Romans, as opposed to the standard dialect, which was used for official documents.

Thinking Geographically

1. At least sixteen U.S. states have passed laws mandating English as the language of all government functions. In 1990 Arizona's law making English the official language was ruled an unconstitutional violation of free speech. Should the use of English be encouraged in the United States to foster cultural integration, or should bilingualism be encouraged to foster cultural diversity? Why?

2. Does the province of Québec possess the resources, economy, political institutions, and social structures to be a viable, healthy country? What would be the impact of Québec's independence on the remainder of Canada, on the United States, and on France?

3. How is American English different from British English as a result of contributions by African-Americans and immigrants who speak languages other than English?

4. The southern portion of Belgium (Wallonia) suffers from higher rates of unemployment, industrial decline, and other economic problems than Flanders in the north. How do differences in language exacerbate Belgium's regional economic differences?

5. Many countries now receive Cable News Network (CNN) broadcasts that originate in the United States, but even English-speaking viewers in other countries have difficulty understanding some American English. A recent business program on CNN created a stir outside the United States when it reported that McDonald's was a major IRA contributor. Viewers in the United Kingdom thought that the American hamburger chain was financing the purchase of weapons by the Irish Republican Army, which sometimes resorts to violence in its attempt to achieve the unification of Ireland. McDonald's in fact was contributing to Individual Retirement Accounts for its employees. Can you think of other examples where the use of a word could cause a British-American misunderstanding?

Further Readings

Aitchison, J. W., and H. Carter. "The Welsh Language in Cardiff: A Quiet Revolution." *Transactions of the Institute of British Geographers,* New Series 12, No. 4 (1987): 482–92.

Allen, Harold B. *The Linguistic Atlas of the Upper Midwest.* 3 vols. Minneapolis: University of Minnesota Press, 1973–1976.

Baugh, Albert C., and Thomas Cable. *A History of the English Language,* 3d ed. Englewood Cliffs, NJ: Prentice-Hall, 1978.

Bellwood, Peter. "The Austronesian Dispersal and the Origin of Languages." *Scientific American* 265 (July 1991): 88–93.

Cardona, George, Henry M. Hoeningswald, and Alfred Senn, eds. *Indo-European and Indo-Europeans.* Philadelphia: University of Pennsylvania Press, 1970.

Delgado de Carvalho, C. M. "The Geography of Languages." In *Readings in Cultural Geography,* ed. by Philip L. Wagner and Marvin W. Mikesell. Chicago: University of Chicago Press, 1962.

Dugdale, J. S. *The Linguistic Map of Europe.* London: Hutchinson University Library, 1969.

Gade, Daniel W. "Foreign Languages and American Geography." *Professional Geographer* 35 (August 1983): 261–65.

_____. *The Indo-European Language and the Indo-Europeans.* 2 vols. The Hague: Mouton, 1990.

Gamkrelidze, Thomas V., and V. V. Ivanov. "The Early History of Indo-European Languages." *Scientific American* 262 (March 1990): 110–116.

Greenberg, Joseph H. *Studies in African Language Classification.* Bloomington: Indiana University Press, 1963.

_____. *Language in the Americas.* Palo Alto, CA: Stanford University Press, 1987.

Hughes, Arthur, and Peter Trudgill. *English Accents and Dialects.* Birkenhead, England: Edward Arnold, 1979.

Kaplan, David H. "Differences in Migration Determinants for Linguistic Groups in Canada." *Professional Geographer* 47 (1995): 115-24.

Hymes, Dell H. *Language in Culture and Society.* New York: Harper and Row, 1964.

Katzner, Kenneth. *The Languages of the World.* New York: Funk and Wagnalls, 1975.

Kirk, John M., Stewart Sanderson, and J. D. A. Widdowson, eds. *Studies in Linguistic Geography: The Dialects of English in Britain and Ireland.* London: Croom Helm, 1985.

Krantz, Grover S. *Geographical Development of European Languages.* New York: Peter Lang, 1988.

Kurath, Hans. *Word Geography of the Eastern United States.* Ann Arbor: University of Michigan Press, 1949.

Laird, Charlton. *Language in America.* New York and Cleveland: World Publishing, 1970.

Lind, Ivan. "Geography and Place Names." In *Readings in Cultural Geography,* ed. by Philip L. Wagner and Marvin W. Mikesell. Chicago: University of Chicago Press, 1962.

Luckmann, Thomas. "Language in Society." *International Social Science Journal* 36, No. 1 (1984): 5–20.

McCrum, Robert, William Cran, and Robert McNeil. *The Story of English.* New York: Viking, 1986.

Meillet, Antoine, and Marcel Cohen. *Les langues du monde.* Paris: Centre National de la Recherche Scientifique, 1952.

Muller, Siegfried H. *The World's Living Languages.* New York: Frederick Ungar, 1964.

Opie, Iona, and Peter Opie. *Children's Games in Street and Playground.* London: Clarendon Press, 1969.

Ramanujan, A. K., and Colin Masica. "A Phonological Typology of the Indian Linguistic Area." In *Current Trends in Linguistics,* vol. 5, ed. by Thomas A. Sebeok. The Hague: Mouton, 1969.

Renfrew, Colin. *Archaeology and Language.* Cambridge: Cambridge University Press, 1988.

_____. "The Origins of Indo-European Languages." *Scientific American* 261 (October 1989): 106–14.

_____. "World Language Diversity." *Scientific American* 270 (January 1994): 116–123.

Ross, Philip E. "Hard Words." *Scientific American* 264 (April 1991): 138–47.

Sopher, David E., ed. *An Exploration of India: Geographical Perspectives on Society and Culture.* Ithaca, NY: Cornell University Press, 1980.

Thomas, Peter. "Belgium's North-South Divide and the Walloon Regional Problem." *Geography* 75, No. 1 (1990): 36–50.

Trudgill, Peter. "Linguistic Geography and Geographical Linguistics." *Progress in Geography* 7 (1975): 227–52.

Wagner, Philip L. "Remarks on the Geography of Language." *Geographical Review* 48 (January 1958): 86–97.

Wakelin, Martyn F. *English Dialects.* London: Athlone Press, 1972.

Williams, Colin H., ed. *Language in Geographic Context.* Clevedon, England: Multilingual Matters, 1988.

Wixman, Ronald. *Language Aspects of Ethnic Patterns and Processes in the North Caucasus.* Chicago: University of Chicago Department of Geography, 1980.

Zelinsky, Wilbur. "Generic Terms in the Place Names of the Northeastern United States." In *Readings in Cultural Geography,* ed. by Philip L. Wagner and Marvin W. Mikesell. Chicago: University of Chicago Press, 1962.

PEOPLE, PLACES AND CHANGE
Alaska's Living History

The Annenberg
CPB Project

Commentator	A language spoken by only a few people is hard to preserve. The practical advantages of communicating in English outweigh the emotional ties to a traditional local language. To preserve their languages, native Alaskans are teaching them in school.

Sally Ash The village was named by the Sukpik. This place was Nanwalek and then the Russians code-named us Alexandrovsk and then somehow there was a map mix-up and we became English Bay after awhile. Then we chose last year to go back to Nanwalek because we feel like we want to try to save our language.

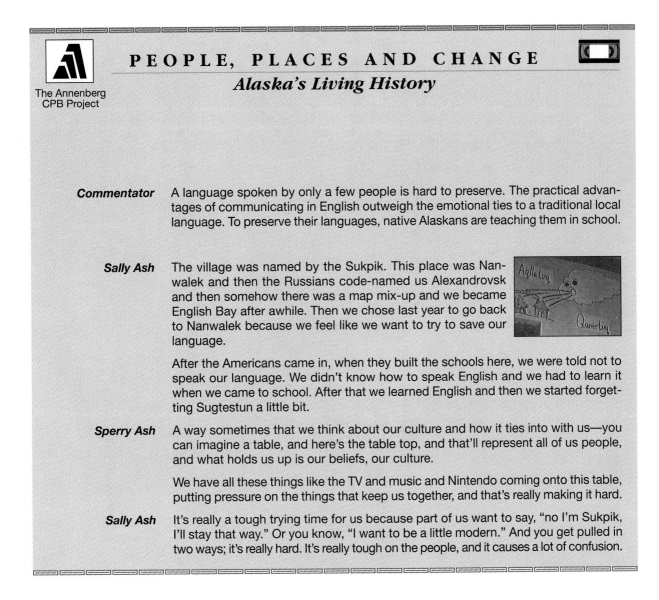

After the Americans came in, when they built the schools here, we were told not to speak our language. We didn't know how to speak English and we had to learn it when we came to school. After that we learned English and then we started forgetting Sugtestun a little bit.

Sperry Ash A way sometimes that we think about our culture and how it ties into with us—you can imagine a table, and here's the table top, and that'll represent all of us people, and what holds us up is our beliefs, our culture.

We have all these things like the TV and music and Nintendo coming onto this table, putting pressure on the things that keep us together, and that's really making it hard.

Sally Ash It's really a tough trying time for us because part of us want to say, "no I'm Sukpik, I'll stay that way." Or you know, "I want to be a little modern." And you get pulled in two ways; it's really hard. It's really tough on the people, and it causes a lot of confusion.

5

RELIGION

KEY ISSUES

- How are religions distributed?
- How do religions organize space?
- What is the impact of religion on the landscape?
- What territorial conflicts arise because of religion?

And He shall judge between the nations,

And shall decide for many peoples;

And they shall beat their swords into ploughshares,

And their spears into pruning-hooks:

Nation shall not lift up sword against nation,

Neither shall they learn war any more.

Isaiah 2:4

This passage from the holiest book of Christianity and Judaism, the Bible, is one of the most eloquent pleas for peace among the nations of the world.

Islam's holiest book, the Quran (sometimes spelled Koran), also evokes powerful images of a peaceful landscape:

He it is who sends down water from the sky, whence ye have drink, and whence the trees grow whereby ye feed your flocks.

He makes the corn to grow, and the olives, and the palms, and the grapes, and some of every fruit; verily, in that is a sign unto a people who reflect.

Sûrah (Chapter) of the Bee XVI.9

Most religious people pray for peace, but religious groups may not share the same vision of how peace will be achieved. Geographers see that the process by which one religion diffuses across the landscape may conflict with the distribution of others.

EASTER SERVICE, CHURCH OF THE HOLY SEPULCHRE, JERUSALEM. (DEMETRIO CARRASCO/TONY STONE IMAGES)

Conflict in the Middle East

Israeli citizen Yaakov Zimmerman was killed by terrorists after praying at the tomb of Abraham. Five other people, including two Americans, were killed, and sixteen, including two Americans, were wounded. The terrorists were members of the Palestine Liberation Organization (PLO), devoted to the cause of ridding the territory of all Israelis.

The tomb of Abraham is in Hebron, a town on the West Bank of the Jordan River. At the time of the attack, the town was controlled by the state of Israel. Until a war in 1967, however, the Hebron area belonged to Jordan. The Palestinians believe that the area should become part of a new state of Palestine. In fact, some argue that *all* Israeli territory should be included in a new state of Palestine. To support the cause, some PLO members resort to attacks on Israeli citizens, such as Zimmerman.

One of the alleged terrorists, Yasir Zeidat, came from the village of Bani Naim. He was not a hero in his home town; in fact, villagers said that he was not especially intelligent and had never helped his father.

To punish Zeidat for the act of terrorism, an Israeli demolition squad blew up the house in Bani Naim where his father lived. The act stemmed from a British colonial practice: a terrorist's house was blown up as punishment to the individual and as a warning to the entire village.

But Zeidat had left his father's house 5 years earlier. The Israeli retribution missed the mark, punishing the father and not the son. The punishment thus claimed another innocent victim in the fight between Israelis and Palestinians. It also generated sympathy for the terrorists in a village where few such feelings had previously existed.

Geographic concepts help us understand the religious landscape. Viewed geographically, each religion has a *hearth*, a pattern of *diffusion*, and a current *distribution* across Earth's surface. Geographers study how religion, like language and other cultural characteristics, diffuses from one location to another, creating distinctive spatial patterns. Regions where most residents adhere to a particular religion develop through interaction and immigration. The diffusion of a religion is important to geographers, because religion is a major spreader of cultural values.

As a major facet of culture, religion leaves a strong imprint on the physical environment. On the one hand, religious beliefs may be derived from processes in the physical environment, such as changes in seasons. On the other hand, religious ideas may underlie human changes to the physical environment, such as the development of burial grounds. In some societies, attempts to modify the environment according to religious principles may conflict with other political and economic values.

Religion, like other cultural characteristics, can be a source of pride and a means of identification with a distinct culture. Unfortunately, intense identification with one religion can lead adherents into conflict with followers of other religions. Unrest is especially severe in places like the Middle East, where three religions have strong historical roots. In this chapter, we will examine all of these factors.

K E Y   I S S U E   1

How Are Religions Distributed?

- Universalizing Religions
- Ethnic Religions

Only a few religions can claim the adherence of large numbers of people. Each of these faiths has a distinctive distribution across Earth's surface (Figure 5–1). Geographers distinguish two types of religions: universalizing and ethnic.

Universalizing Religions

Universalizing religions attempt to be universal, to appeal to all people, not just to those of one culture or location. In contrast, **ethnic religions** are likely to be based on the physical characteristics of a particular place. Consequently, an ethnic religion is limited in its appeal, suited to people either living in or attracted to a particular environment. Geographers study the distinctive spatial distributions and diffusion patterns of both universalizing and ethnic religions.

The world has three main universalizing religions: Christianity, Islam, and Buddhism. Each began with an individual (Jesus, Muhammad, Buddha) who preached a message that was accepted initially only by immediate followers. These three religions are all **monotheist**; that is, they believe that there is only one God. **Polytheist** religions worship more than one god.

We can identify hearths where each of the universalizing three religions originated, on the basis of the events in the lives of the three key individuals (Figure 5–2). All three hearths are in Asia (Christianity and Islam in the Southwest Asia (part of the Middle East), Buddhism in South Asia). Followers diffused the messages across Earth's surface along distinctive paths, as shown in Figure 5–2. Today, these three universalizing religions together have over 3 billion adherents distributed across wide areas of the world.

Each of the three large universalizing religions is divided into different branches, denominations, and sects. A **branch** is a large and fundamental division within a religion. A **denomination** is a division within a branch. A **sect** is a relatively small denominational group that has broken away from an established church.

Because the three main universalizing religions and some ethnic religions developed during recorded history, their origin, diffusion, and spatial distribution can be documented. We now use these geographic concepts to examine the three largest universalizing religions and some representative ethnic religions.

Christianity

Christianity has far more adherents (nearly 2 billion) than any other world religion and the most widespread distribution. It is the predominant religion in North America, South America, Europe, and Australia, and countries with a Christian majority exist in Africa and Asia as well.

Christianity was founded on the teachings of Jesus, who was born in Bethlehem between 8 and 4 B.C. and died in Jerusalem about A.D. 30. Raised as a Jew, Jesus gathered a small band of disciples and

FIGURE 5-1 World distribution of religions. About 70 percent of Earth's people adhere to one of four religions:

- *Christianity*—33 percent of the world population, especially in Europe, the former Soviet Union, Europe, and the Western Hemisphere
- *Islam*—18 percent of the population, especially in northern Africa and Southwestern and Southeast Asia
- *Hinduism*—13 percent of the population, virtually all living in India
- *Buddhism*—6 percent of the population, especially in East and Southeast Asia.

About 9 percent adhere to other religions. The remaining 21 percent of the population are nonreligions. The pie charts show the overall proportion of the world's religions in each world region.

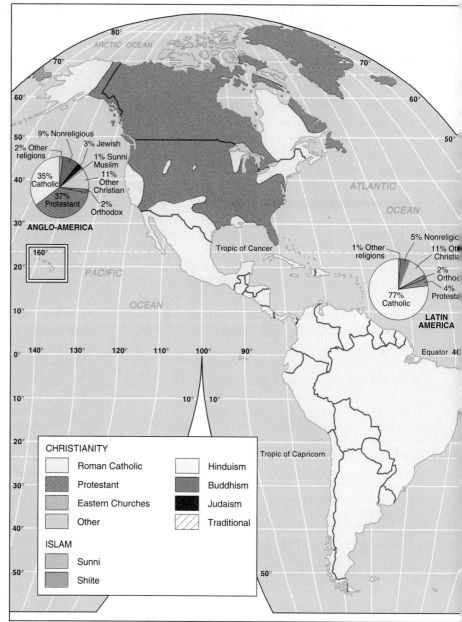

RELIGIONS
(Percentage of people
practicing each)

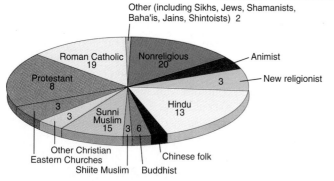

preached the coming of the Kingdom of God. The four Gospels (sections) of the Christian Bible—Matthew, Mark, Luke, and John—documented miracles and extraordinary deeds that Jesus performed. He was referred to as *Christ*, from the Greek word for the Hebrew word *messiah*, which means "anointed".

In the third year of his mission, he was betrayed to the authorities by one of his companions, Judas Iscariot. After sharing the Last Supper (the Jewish

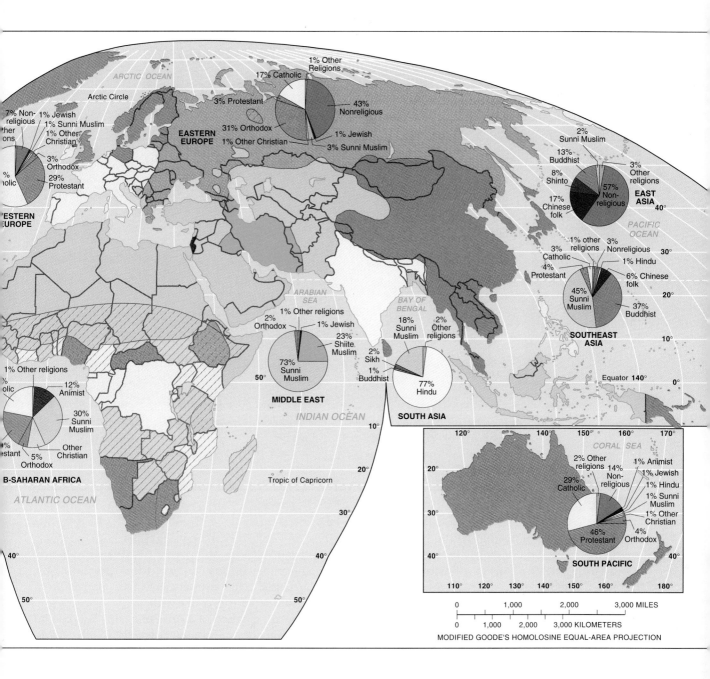

** EASTERN EUROPE**

1% Other Religions
17% Catholic
3% Protestant
43% Nonreligious
31% Orthodox
1% Other Christian
1% Jewish
3% Sunni Muslim

ESTERN EUROPE

7% Nonreligious her ons
1% Jewish
1% Sunni Muslim
1% Other Christian
3% Orthodox
29% Protestant
% olic

EAST ASIA

2% Sunni Muslim
13% Buddhist
8% Shinto
17% Chinese folk
57% Nonreligious
3% Other religions

SOUTHEAST ASIA

1% other religions
3% Catholic
4% Protestant
45% Sunni Muslim
3% Nonreligious
1% Hindu
6% Chinese folk
37% Buddhist

MIDDLE EAST

1% Other religions
2% Orthodox
1% Jewish
23% Shiite Muslim
73% Sunni Muslim

SOUTH ASIA

18% Sunni Muslim
2% Other religions
2% Sikh
1% Buddhist
77% Hindu

B-SAHARAN AFRICA

1% Other religions
12% Animist
30% Sunni Muslim
Other Christian
5% Orthodox
stant
olic

SOUTH PACIFIC

2% Other religions
14% Nonreligious
1% Animist
1% Jewish
1% Hindu
1% Sunni Muslim
1% Other Christian
29% Catholic
46% Protestant
4% Orthodox

ARCTIC OCEAN
Arctic Circle
ARABIAN SEA
BAY OF BENGAL
PACIFIC OCEAN
INDIAN OCEAN
ATLANTIC OCEAN
Tropic of Capricorn
CORAL SEA
Equator 140°

0   1,000   2,000   3,000 MILES
0   1,000   2,000   3,000 KILOMETERS
MODIFIED GOODE'S HOMOLOSINE EQUAL-AREA PROJECTION

Passover seder) with his disciples in Jerusalem, Jesus was arrested as an agitator and put to death by crucifixion. On the third day after his death, his tomb was found empty. Christians believe that Jesus died to atone for human sins, and his resurrection from the dead provides people with hope for salvation.

Origin and Diffusion. How did Christianity become the world's most practiced and most widely distributed religion? Christianity's diffusion has been rather clearly recorded since Jesus first set forth its tenets in the Roman province of Palestine. Consequently, geographers can examine its diffusion by reconstructing patterns of communications, decision making, and migration.

In Chapter 1, we identified two processes of diffusion—relocation (diffusion through migration) and expansion (diffusion through a snowballing effect).

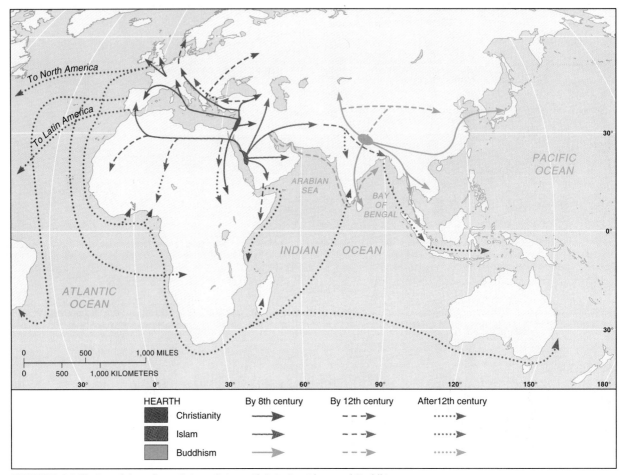

FIGURE 5–2 Diffusion of the universalizing religions: Christianity, Islam, and Buddhism.

Within expansion diffusion, we distinguished between hierarchical (through key leaders) and contagious (widespread) diffusion. Christianity diffused through a combination of those forms.

Christianity first diffused from its hearth in Palestine through *relocation diffusion*. **Missionaries**—individuals who help to transmit a universalizing religion through relocation diffusion—carried the teachings of Jesus along the Empire's protected sea routes and excellent road network to people in other locations. Paul of Tarsus, a disciple of Jesus, traveled especially extensively through the Roman Empire as a missionary. The outline of the Empire and the spread of Christianity are shown in Figure 5–3.

People in commercial towns and military settlements that were directly linked by the communications network received the message first from Paul and other missionaries. But Christianity spread widely within the Roman Empire through *contagious dif-fusion*—daily contact between believers in the towns and nonbelievers, or "pagans," in the surrounding countryside. ***Pagan***, the word for a follower of a polytheistic religion in ancient times, derives from the Latin word for "countryside".

The dominance of Christianity throughout the Roman Empire was assured during the fourth century through *hierarchical diffusion*—acceptance of the religion by the empire's key elite figure, the emperor. Emperor Constantine encouraged the spread of Christianity by embracing it in A.D. 313, and Emperor Theodosius proclaimed it the empire's official religion in 380. In subsequent centuries, Christianity further diffused into Eastern Europe through conversion of kings or other elite figures.

Migration and missionary activity by Europeans since the year 1500 have extended Christianity to other regions of the world, as shown in Figure 5–1. Through permanent resettlement of Europeans,

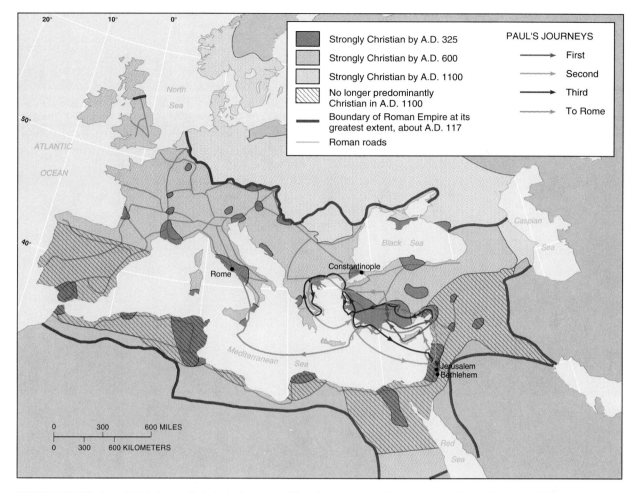

FIGURE 5–3 Diffusion of Christianity. Christianity began to diffuse from Palestine through Europe during the time of the Roman Empire and continued after the Empire's collapse. Muslims controlled portions of the Iberian peninsula (Spain) for more than 700 years, until 1492. Much of southwestern Asia was predominantly Christian at one time, but today it is predominantly Muslim.

Christianity became the dominant religion in North and South America, Australia, and New Zealand. Christianity's dominance was further achieved by conversion of indigenous populations and by intermarriage. In Africa, where Christianity had only small isolated clusters of adherents in the past, it is now the most widely practiced religion.

Branches. Christianity has three major branches—Roman Catholic, Protestant, and Eastern Orthodox—each with a distinctive spatial distribution (Figure 5–1). Roman Catholics account for approximately 56 percent of the world's Christians, Protestants 25 percent, and Eastern Orthodox 9 percent.

The remaining 10 percent include Catholics other than Roman and followers of isolated African, Asian, and Latin American Christian churches.

Roman Catholics accept the teachings of the Bible, as well as the interpretation of those teachings by the church hierarchy, headed by the Pope. According to Roman Catholic belief, God conveys grace directly to humanity through seven sacraments, including Baptism, Confirmation, Penance, Anointing the sick, Matrimony, Holy Orders, and the Eucharist (the partaking of bread and wine that repeats the actions of Jesus at the Last Supper). Roman Catholics believe that the Eucharist literally and miraculously becomes the body and blood of Jesus while keeping

FIGURE 5–4 Branches of Christianity in Europe. In the United Kingdom, Germany, and Scandinavia, the majority adhere to a Protestant denomination. In eastern and southeastern Europe, Eastern Orthodoxy dominates. Roman Catholicism is dominant in southern, central, and southwestern Europe.

CHRISTIANITY IN EUROPE

Protestant majority

☐ Lutheran

☐ Calvinist

☐ Church of England

☐ Roman Catholic majority

☐ Eastern Orthodox majority

☐ Not Christian majority

only the appearance of bread and wine, an act known as transubstantiation.

Eastern Orthodoxy comprises the faith and practices of a collection of churches that arose in the eastern part of the Roman Empire. The split between the Roman and Eastern churches dates to the fifth century, as a result of rivalry between the Pope of Rome and the Patriarch of Constantinople, which was especially intense after the collapse of the Roman Empire. The split between the two churches became final in 1054, when Pope Leo IX condemned the Patriarch of Constantinople. Eastern Orthodox Christians accepted the seven sacraments but rejected doctrines that the Roman Catholic church had added since the eighth century.

Protestantism originated with the principles of the Reformation in the sixteenth century. The Reformation movement is regarded as beginning when Martin Luther posted 95 theses on the door of the church at Wittenberg on October 31, 1517. According to Luther, individuals had primary responsibility for achieving personal salvation through direct communication with God. Grace is achieved through faith rather than through sacraments performed by the church.

Distribution of Branches in Europe. Within Europe, Roman Catholicism is the dominant Christian branch in the southwest and east, Protestantism in the northwest, and Eastern Orthodoxy in the east and southeast (Figure 5–4). The regions of Roman Catholic and Protestant majorities frequently have sharp boundaries, even when they run through the middle of countries. For example, the Netherlands and Switzerland have approximately equal percentages of Roman Catholics and Protestants, but the Roman Catholic populations are concentrated in the south of these countries and the Protestant populations in the north.

The Eastern Orthodox branch of Christianity is a collection of fourteen self-governing churches in Eastern Europe and the Middle East. Four of these churches—Constantinople, Alexandria, Antioch, and Jerusalem—trace their origins to the earliest days of Christianity. They have a combined membership of only 4 million today, or less than 3 percent of the total of the Eastern Orthodox branch.

Christianity came to Russia in the tenth century, and the Russian Orthodox Church was established in the sixteenth century. It includes over 40 percent of all Eastern Orthodox Christians. The other nine self-governing churches were established in the nineteenth or twentieth century. The largest of these, the Romanian church, includes 20 percent of all Eastern Orthodox Christians; the Bulgarian, Greek, and Serbian churches have approximately 10 percent each; and the churches in Albania, Cyprus, Georgia, Poland, and Sinai have a combined membership of fewer than 3 million, or a little more than 2 percent.

Religious Conflict in Ireland. As you might expect, religious boundaries are potential trouble

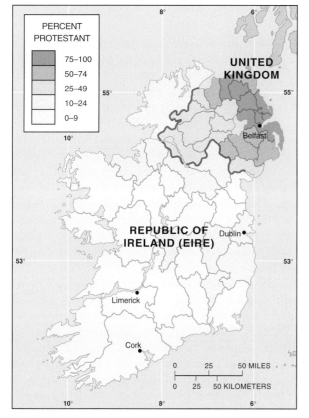

FIGURE 5–5 Distribution of Protestants in Ireland, 1911. Long a colony of England, Ireland became a self-governing dominion within the British Empire in 1921. In 1937, it became a completely independent country, but twenty-six districts in northern Ireland chose to remain part of the United Kingdom. The Republic of Ireland today is more than 95 percent Roman Catholic, whereas Northern Ireland has a Protestant majority. The boundary between Roman Catholics and Protestants does not coincide precisely with the international border, so Northern Ireland includes some communities that are predominantly Roman Catholic. This distribution is the root of a small-scale modern religious war that continues today.
British soldiers patrol Belfast, the capital of Northern Ireland, on the eve of a cease-fire that began in September, 1994. (Andrew Moore/Katz/SABA Press Photos, Inc.)

zones. The most troublesome in Western Europe lies in Ireland (Figure 5–5). The Republic of Ireland is approximately 95 percent Roman Catholic, but its six northern counties—part of the United Kingdom rather than Ireland—are divided between Roman Catholic and Protestant.

Ireland's religious problems have a long history. The entire island was an English colony for many centuries. In 1801, Ireland joined the United Kingdom, although agitation for independence was extremely strong. After bloody confrontations, Ireland became a self-governing dominion within the British Empire in 1921. Complete independence was declared in 1937, and a republic was created in 1949.

However, people in six counties of northern Ireland voted to remain in the United Kingdom rather than join the Republic of Ireland, because a majority were Protestant—as is the case elsewhere in the United Kingdom. Today, most Protestants in Northern Ireland wish to remain part of the United Kingdom, whereas many Roman Catholics there want the six counties to be unified with the Republic of Ireland.

Roman Catholics in Northern Ireland have been victimized by discriminatory practices, such as exclusion from higher-paying jobs and better schools. A small number of Irish Catholics in both Northern Ireland and the Republic have joined the Irish Republican Army (IRA), a militant organization dedicated to achieving Irish national unity. Similarly, a scattering of Protestants has created extremist organizations, including the Ulster Defense Force (UDF)

dedicated to keeping Northern Ireland part of the U.K. Although the overwhelming majority of Northern Ireland's citizens are peaceful, the Roman Catholic and Protestant extremists disrupt daily life. The British and Irish governments are currently negotiating to find a peaceful settlement, but as long as some Protestants are firmly committed to remaining in the United Kingdom and some Roman Catholics are equally committed to union with the Republic of Ireland, compromise is difficult.

Branches in the Western Hemisphere. A fairly sharp boundary between Roman Catholic and Protestant branches exists in the Western Hemisphere as well. Roman Catholics constitute 87 percent of the population in Latin America, compared with 35 percent in the United States and Canada. Latin Americans are predominantly Roman Catholic because their territory was colonized by the Spanish and Portuguese, who brought with them to the Western Hemisphere their religion as well as their languages. Canada (outside Québec) and the United States have Protestant majorities because their early colonists came primarily from Protestant England.

Different Protestant denominations have distinctive spatial distributions within the United States (Figure 5–6). The three largest Protestant denominations are Baptist, Methodist, and Lutheran. Baptists constitute over half the population in much of the southeastern United States, from Virginia to Texas. Lutherans are concentrated in the north central states, from Wisconsin to Montana, and Methodists are primarily in states between 35° and 40° north latitude, from Delaware to Colorado. Geographers trace the development of distinctive religious regions in the United States to the fact that migrants came from different parts of Europe, especially during the nineteenth century.

Although accounting for only 1 percent of the country's population, the Church of Jesus Christ of Latter-Day Saints, popularly known as the Mormons, plays a prominent role in the U.S. religious landscape, because they are highly clustered in Utah and several counties in adjacent states. The Mormons settled at Fayette, New York, but after the death of their founder, Joseph Smith, the group moved several times in search of religious freedom. Eventually, under the leadership of Brigham Young, they migrated to the sparsely inhabited Salt Lake Valley.

Some regions and localities within the United States and Canada are predominantly Roman Catholic because of immigration from Roman Catholic countries. New England and large midwestern cities such as Cleveland, Chicago, Detroit, and Milwaukee have concentrations of Roman Catholics because of immigration from Ireland, Italy, and Eastern Europe, especially in the late nineteenth and early twentieth centuries. Immigration from Mexico and other Latin American countries has concentrated Roman Catholics in the Southwest; French settlement from the seventeenth century, as well as recent immigration, has produced a predominantly Roman Catholic Québec.

Other Branches. Several other Christian churches developed independent of the three main branches. Many of these Christian communities were isolated from others at an early point in the development of Christianity, partly because of differences in doctrine and partly as a result of Islamic control of intervening territory in Southwest Asia and North Africa. Two small Christian churches survive in Northeast Africa: the Coptic Church of Egypt and the Ethiopian Church. The Ethiopian Church, with perhaps 10 million adherents, split from the Egyptian Coptic Church in 1948, although it traces its roots to the fourth century, when two shipwrecked Christians, who were taken as slaves, ultimately converted the king to Christianity.

The Armenian Church originated in Antioch, Syria, and was important in diffusing Christianity to South and East Asia between the seventh and thirteenth centuries. The church's few present-day adherents are concentrated in Lebanon and Armenia, as well as northeastern Turkey and western Azerbaijan. Despite the small number of adherents, the Armenian Church, like other small sects, plays a significant role in regional conflicts. For example, Armenian Christians have fought for the independence of Nagorno–Karabakh, a portion of Azerbaijan, because Nagorno-Karabakh is predominantly Armenian, whereas the remainder of Azerbaijan is overwhelmingly Shiite Muslim (see Chapter 7).

The Maronites are another example of a small Christian sect that plays a disproportionately prominent role in political unrest. They are clustered in Lebanon, which has suffered through a long civil war fought among religious groups (discussed at the end of the chapter).

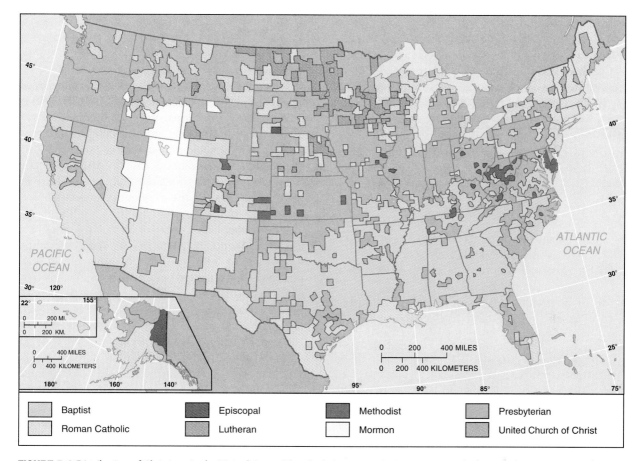

	Baptist		Episcopal		Methodist		Presbyterian
	Roman Catholic		Lutheran		Mormon		United Church of Christ

FIGURE 5–6 Distribution of Christians in the United States. The shaded areas are U.S. counties in which more than 50 percent of church membership is concentrated in either Roman Catholicism or one Protestant denomination. Baptists are concentrated in the Southeast, Lutherans in the upper Midwest, Mormons in Utah and contiguous states, and Roman Catholics in the Northeast and Southwest. The distinctive distribution of religious groups within the United States results from patterns of migration, especially from Europe in the nineteenth century and from Latin America in recent years.

Islam

Islam, the religion of approximately 1 billion people, dominates a region from North Africa to Central Asia, from Morocco to Pakistan (Figure 5–1). The two most important concentrations of Muslims outside this region are in Bangladesh and Indonesia. The word Islam in Arabic means "submission to the will of God," and it has a root similar to the Arabic word for "peace". An adherent of the religion of Islam is known as a Muslim, which in Arabic means "one who surrenders to God."

The Prophet of Islam, Muhammad was born in Makkah (spelled Mecca on many English-language maps) in present-day Saudi Arabia about A.D. 570.

At age 40, while engaged in a meditative retreat, Muhammad received his first revelation from God through the Angel Gabriel. The Quran, the holiest book in Islam, is a record of God's words, as revealed to the Prophet Muhammad through Gabriel. Arabic is used as the language of communication within the Muslim world, since it is the language in which the Quran is written.

As he began to preach the truth that God had revealed to him, Muhammad suffered persecution, and in 622 he was commanded by God to emigrate. His migration from Makkah to the city of Yathrib—an event known as the *Hijra* (from the Arabic word for "migration")—marks the beginning of the Muslim calendar. Yathrib was subsequently renamed Madina, Arabic for "the City of the Prophet." After several years, Muhammad and his followers returned to Makkah and established Islam as the city's religion. By Muhammad's death in 632 at about age 63, Islam had diffused to most of present-day Saudi Arabia.

Islam recognizes five essential pillars:

1. There is no god worthy of worship except the one God, the source of all creation, and Muhammad is the messenger of God.
2. Five times daily, a Muslim prays, facing the city of Makkah, as a direct link to God.
3. A Muslim gives generously to charity, as an act of purification and growth.
4. A Muslim fasts during the month of Ramadan, as an act of self-purification.
5. If physically and financially able, a Muslim makes a pilgrimage to Makkah.

Origin and Diffusion. Islam traces its origin to the same narrative as Judaism and Christianity. All three religions consider Adam to have been the first man and Abraham to have been one of his descendants. According to legend, Abraham married Sarah, who did not bear children. Polygamy being a custom of the culture, Abraham then married Hagar, who bore a son, Ishmael. Sarah's fortunes changed, however, and she bore a son, Isaac. Sarah then successfully prevailed upon Abraham to banish Hagar and Ishmael.

Jews and Christians trace their story through Abraham's first wife Sarah and their son Isaac. Muslims trace their story through his second wife Hagar and their son Ishmael. After their banishment, Ishmael and Hagar wandered through the Arabian desert, eventually reaching Makkah (Mecca). Centuries later, one of Ishmael's descendants, Muhammad, became the Prophet of Islam.

Muhammad's successors organized followers into armies that extended the region of Muslim control over an extensive area of Africa, Asia, and Europe. Within a century of Muhammad's death, Muslim armies conquered Palestine, the Persian Empire, and much of India, resulting in the conversion of many non-Arabs to Islam, often through intermarriage. To the west, Muslims captured North Africa, crossed the Strait of Gibraltar, and retained part of Western Europe, particularly much of present-day Spain, until 1492 (Figure 5–7). During the same century that the Christians regained all of western Europe, Muslims took control of much of southeastern Europe and Turkey.

As was the case with Christianity, Islam, as a universalizing religion, diffused well beyond its hearth in Southwest Asia through relocation diffusion of missionaries to portions of sub-Saharan Africa and Southeast Asia. Although it is spatially isolated from the Islamic core region in Southwest Asia, Indonesia, the world's fourth most populous country, is predominantly Muslim, because Arab traders brought the religion there in the thirteenth century.

Branches. Islam is divided into two important branches: *Sunni* and *Shiite*. Sunnis (from the Arabic word for "orthodox") constitute 83 percent of Muslims and are the largest branch in most Muslim countries (light green in Figure 5–1). Approximately 70 percent of all Shiites (from the Arabic word for "sectarian" and sometimes written *Shia* in English) live in Iran, where they constitute about 90 percent of the country's population. Another 15 percent of the world's Shiites are in Iraq, where they are twice as numerous as Sunnis. Shiites also outnumber Sunnis in Azerbaijan, Lebanon, and Bahrain. Most of the remaining Shiites live in Yemen and Afghanistan, where they constitute important minorities.

Differences between Shiites and Sunnis go back to the earliest days of Islam and basically reflect disagreement over the line of succession in Islamic leadership. Muhammad had no surviving son and no follower of comparable leadership ability. His successor was Abu Bakr (573–634), an early supporter from Makkah, who became known as *caliph* ("successor of the prophet"). The next two caliphs, Umar (634–644) and Uthman (644–656), expanded the territory under Muslim influence to Egypt and Persia.

Uthman was a member of a powerful Makkah clan that had initially opposed Muhammad before the clan's conversion to Islam. More zealous Muslims criticized Uthman for seeking compromises with other formerly pagan families in Makkah. Uthman's opponents found a leader in Ali (600?–661), a cousin and son-in-law of Muhammad, and thus Muhammad's nearest male heir. When Uthman was murdered in 656, Ali became caliph, although 5 years later he, too, was assassinated.

Ali's descendants claim leadership of Islam, and Shiites support this claim. But Shiites disagree among

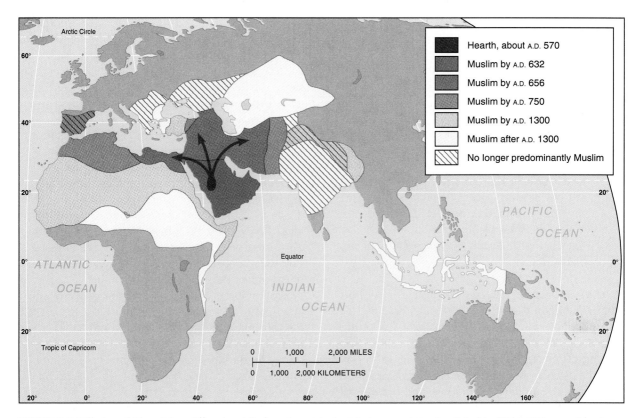

FIGURE 5–7 Diffusion of Islam. Islam diffused rapidly from its point of origin in present-day Saudi Arabia. Within 200 years, Islamic armies controlled much of North Africa, southwestern Europe, and southwestern Asia. Subsequently, Islam became the predominant religion as far east as Indonesia.

themselves about the precise line of succession from Ali to modern times. Although they acknowledge that the chain of leadership was broken, they dispute the date and events surrounding the disruption. During the 1970s, both the shah (king) of Iran and an ayatollah (religious scholar) named Khomeini claimed to be the divinely appointed interpreter of Islam for the Shiites. The allegiance of the Iranian Shiites switched from the shah to the ayatollah largely because the ayatollah made a more convincing case that he was more faithfully adhering to the rigid laws laid down by Muhammad in the Quran.

Nation of Islam in the United States. The Nation of Islam, also known as *Black Muslims,* was founded in Detroit in 1930 and led for more than 40 years by Elijah Muhammad, who called himself "the messenger of Allah." Black Muslims lived austerely and advocated a separate autonomous nation with-

in the United States for their adherents. During the 1960s, tension between Elijah Muhammad and Black Muslim minister Malcolm X divided the sect. After a pilgrimage to Makkah in 1963, Malcolm X converted to orthodox Islam and founded the Organization of Afro-American Unity. He was assassinated in 1965.

Since Muhammad's death in 1975, his son Wallace D. Muhammad led the Black Muslims closer to the principles of orthodox Islam, and the organization's name was changed to the American Muslim Mission. A splinter group adopted the original name, Nation of Islam, and continues to follow the separatist teachings of Elijah Muhammad.

Buddhism

Buddhism, the third of the world's major universalizing religions, has more than 300 million adherents, especially in China and Southeast Asia (Figure

5–1). The foundation of Buddhism is these concepts, known as the Four Noble Truths:

1. All living beings must endure suffering.
2. Suffering, which is caused by a desire to live, leads to reincarnation (repeated rebirth in new bodies or forms of life).
3. The goal of all existence is to escape from suffering and the endless cycle of reincarnation into Nirvana (a state of complete redemption), which is achieved through mental and moral self-purification.
4. Nirvana is attained through an Eightfold Path, which includes rightness of belief, resolve, speech, action, livelihood, effort, thought, and meditation.

Origin and Diffusion. The founder of Buddhism, Siddhartha Gautama, was born about 563 B.C. in Lumbinī, in present-day Nepal, near the border with India, about 160 kilometers (100 miles) from Váránasi (Benares). The son of a lord, he led a privileged existence sheltered from life's hardships. Gautama had a beautiful wife, palaces, and servants.

According to Buddhist legend, Gautama's life changed after a series of four trips. He encountered a decrepit old man on the first trip, a disease-ridden man on the second trip, and a corpse on the third trip. After witnessing these scenes of pain and suffering, Gautama began to feel he could no longer enjoy his life of comfort and security. Then, on a fourth trip, Gautama saw a monk, who taught him about withdrawal from the world.

At age 29, Gautama left his palace one night and lived in a forest for the next 6 years, thinking and experimenting with forms of meditation. Gautama emerged as the *Buddha,* the "awakened or enlightened one," and spent 45 years preaching his views across India. In the process, he trained monks, established orders, and preached to the public.

Buddhism did not diffuse rapidly from its point of origin in northeastern India. The individual most responsible for the spread of Buddhism was Asoka, emperor of the Magadhan Empire from about 273 to 232 B.C. The Magadhan Empire formed the nucleus of several powerful kingdoms in South Asia between the sixth century B.C. and the eighth century A.D. Around 257 B.C., at the height of the Magadhan Empire's power, Asoka became a Buddhist and thereafter attempted to put Buddhism's social principles into practice.

A council organized by Asoka at Pataliputra decided to send missionaries to territories neighboring the Magadhan Empire. Emperor Asoka's son, Mahinda, led a mission to the island of Ceylon (now Sri Lanka), where the king and his subjects were converted to Buddhism. As a result, Sri Lanka is the country that claims the longest continuous tradition of practicing Buddhism. Missions were also sent in the third century B.C. to the Kashmir, the Himalayas, Burma (Myanmar), and elsewhere in India.

In the first century A.D., merchants along the trading routes from northeastern India introduced Buddhism to China. Many Chinese were receptive to the ideas brought by Buddhist missionaries, and Buddhist texts were translated into Chinese languages. Chinese rulers allowed their people to become Buddhist monks during the fourth century A.D., and in the following centuries, Buddhism evolved into a genuinely Chinese religion. Buddhism further diffused from China to Korea in the fourth century and from Korea to Japan two centuries later. During the same era, Buddhism lost its original base of support in India (Figure 5–8).

Branches. Like the other two universalizing religions, Buddhism split into more than one branch as followers disagreed on interpretation of the founder's statements. The two main branches are Theravada and Mahayana.

Theravada means "the way of the elders," which indicates the Theravada Buddhists' belief that they are closer to Buddha's original approach. Theravadists believe that Buddhism is a full-time occupation, so to become a good Buddhist, one must renounce worldly goods and become a monk. Theravada Buddhism is most prevalent in Southeast Asia, especially Thailand, Myanmar, Cambodia, and Laos.

Mahayana is translated as "the bigger ferry," or "raft," and Mahayanists call Theravada Buddhism by the name "Hinayana," or "the little raft." Mahayanists claim that their approach to Buddhism can help more people because it is less demanding and all-encompassing. Whereas the Theravadists emphasize Buddha's life of self-help and years of solitary introspection, Mahayanists emphasize Buddha's later years of teaching and helping others. The Theravadists cite Buddha's wisdom, the Mahayanists his compassion.

Mahayana Buddhism predominates in central and eastern Asia, including Tibet, Mongolia, China, Japan, and Vietnam, as well as in Sri Lanka. Mahayana Bud-

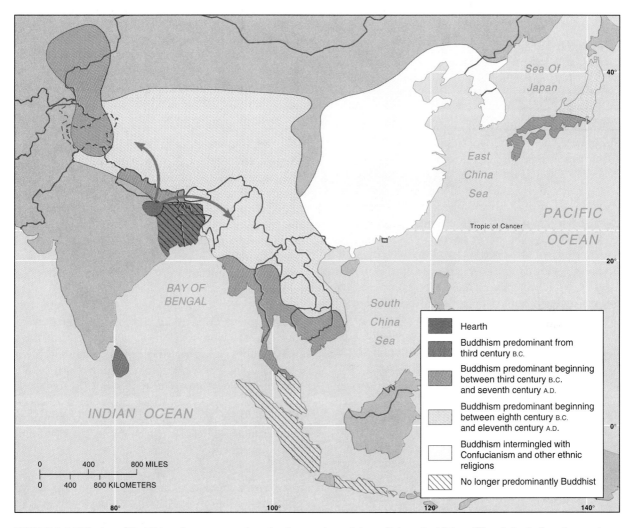

FIGURE 5–8 Diffusion of Buddhism. In contrast to the other large universalizing religions, Buddhism diffused slowly from its core in northeastern India. Buddhism was not well established in China until 800 years after Buddha's death.

dhism is divided into at least six distinct denominations. Because the different groups do not occupy distinct geographic areas, geographers cannot map the spatial distribution of Mahayana denominations, as they can U.S. Protestant denominations (Figure 5–6).

Buddhism currently has more than 300 million adherents, although an accurate count is impossible. Only a few people in Buddhist countries participate in Buddhist institutions, and religious functions are performed primarily by monks rather than by the general public. The number of Buddhists is also difficult to count, because Buddhism, although a universalizing religion, differs in significant respects from the Western concept of a formal religious system. Someone can be both a Buddhist and a believer in other Eastern religions, whereas Christianity and Islam both require exclusive adherence. Most Buddhists in China and Japan, in particular, believe in other religions simultaneously.

Ethnic Religions

Because its social forms are rooted in a specific location, an ethnic religion is harder to transmit to people elsewhere in the world. An ethnic religion may change as social, economic, and physical conditions in the homeland change, but the region of the religion's followers is unlikely to expand extensively.

Hinduism

The ethnic religion with the largest number of followers is Hinduism. Although Hinduism is the world's third largest religion, with over 700 million adherents, more than 99 percent of them are concentrated in one country, India.

Unlike the three universalizing religions, Hinduism did not originate with a specific founder. The word *Hinduism* is simply a term for the religious system of India. Whereas the origins of Christianity, Islam, and Buddhism are recorded in the relatively recent past, Hinduism existed before recorded history. The earliest surviving Hindu documents were written about 1500 B.C., although archaeological explorations have unearthed older objects relating to the religion. Aryan tribes from Central Asia invaded India around 1400 B.C. and brought with them Indo-European languages, as discussed in Chapter 4. In addition to their language, the Aryans brought their religion.

The Aryans first settled in the area now called the Punjab in northwestern India and later migrated east to the Ganges River valley, as far as Bengal. Centuries of intermingling with the Dravidians already living in the area modified their religious beliefs.

Hinduism adheres to the belief that there is more than one path to reach God. Because people start from different backgrounds and experiences, the appropriate form of worship for any two persons may not be the same. Hinduism does not have a central authority or a single holy book, so each individual selects suitable rituals. If one person practices Hinduism in a particular way, other Hindus will not think that the individual has made a mistake or strayed from orthodox doctrine.

The type of Hinduism practiced will depend in part on the individual's **caste,** which is the class or distinct hereditary order into which a Hindu is assigned according to religious law. A high-caste Brahman may practice a form of Hinduism based on knowledge of relatively obscure historical texts. At the other end of the caste system, a low-caste illiterate in a rural village may perform religious rituals without a highly developed set of written explanations for them.

Between these extremes, the average Hindu has allegiance to a particular god or concept within a broad range of possibilities. The three dieties that have the largest number of followers are probably Siva, Vishnu, and Shakti. Although a variety of deities and approaches are supported throughout India,

some geographic concentration exists: Siva and Shakti in the north, Shakti and Vishnu in the east, Vishnu in the west, and Siva, along with some Vishnu, in the south. However, holy places for Siva and Vishnu are dispersed throughout India.

Ethnic Asian Religions

Several hundred million people practice ethnic religions in East Asia, especially in China and Japan. The coexistence of Buddhism with these ethnic religions in East Asia differs from the Western concept of exclusive religious belief. Confucianism and Daoism (sometimes spelled Taoism) are often distinguished as separate ethnic religions in China, but many Chinese consider themselves both Buddhists and either Confucian, Daoist, or some other Chinese ethnic religion.

Buddhism does not compete for adherents with Confucianism, Daoism, and other ethnic religions in China, because many Chinese accept the teachings of both universalizing and ethnic religions. Such commingling of diverse philosophies is not totally foreign to Americans. The tenets of Christianity or Judaism, the wisdom of the ancient Greek philosophers, and the ideals of the Declaration of Independence can all be held dear without necessarily doing grave injustice to the others.

Confucianism. Confucius (551–479 B.C.) was a philosopher and teacher in the Chinese province of Lu. His sayings, which were recorded by his students, emphasized the importance of the ancient Chinese tradition of *li*, which can be translated roughly as *propriety*, or *correct behavior*. Confucianism is an ethnic religion because of its especially strong rooting in traditional values of special importance to Chinese people.

Confucianism prescribed a series of ethical principles for the orderly conduct of daily life in China, such as following traditions, fulfilling obligations, and treating others with sympathy and respect. These rules applied to China's rulers, as well as to their subjects.

Daoism (Taoism). Lao-Zi (604–531? B.C., also spelled Lao Tse), a contemporary of Confucius, organized Daoism. Although a government administrator by profession, Lao-Zi's writings emphasized the mystical and magical aspects of life rather than the importance of public service, as had Confucius.

Daoists seek *dao* (or *tao*), which means the "way" or "path." A virtuous person draws power (*de* or *te*) from being absorbed in *dao*. *Dao* cannot be comprehended by reason and knowledge, because not everything is knowable. Since the universe is not ultimately subject to rational analysis, myths and legends develop to explain events. Only by avoidance of daily activities and introspection can a person live in harmony with the principles that underlie and govern the universe.

Daoism split into many sects, some acting like secret societies, and followers embraced elements of magic. The religion was officially banned by the Communists after they took control of China in 1949, but it is still practiced in China, and it is legal in Taiwan.

Shintoism. Since ancient times, Shintoism has been the distinctive ethnic religion of Japan. Ancient Shintoists considered forces of nature to be divine, especially the sun and moon, as well as rivers, trees, rocks, mountains, and certain animals. The religion was transmitted from one generation to the next orally until the fifth century A.D., when the introduction of Chinese writing facilitated the recording of ancient rituals and prayers. Gradually, deceased emperors and other ancestors became more important deities for Shintoists than natural features.

Buddhism diffused to Japan from Korea in the ninth century A.D. After a period of resistance, Shintoists embraced Buddhism and amalgamated elements of the two religions. Buddhist priests took over most of the Shinto shrines, but Buddhist deities came to be regarded by the Japanese as Shintoist deities. Today, several million Japanese profess adherence to both Shintoism and Buddhism, especially in the rural central part of the country (Figure 5–9).

Under the reign of the Emperor Meiji (1868–1912), Shintoism became the official state religion, and the emperor was regarded as divine. Shintoism therefore was as much a political cult as a religion, and in a cultural sense all Japanese were Shintoists. After defeating Japan in World War II, the victorious Allies ordered Emperor Hirohito to renounce his divinity in a speech to the Japanese people, although he was allowed to retain ceremonial powers.

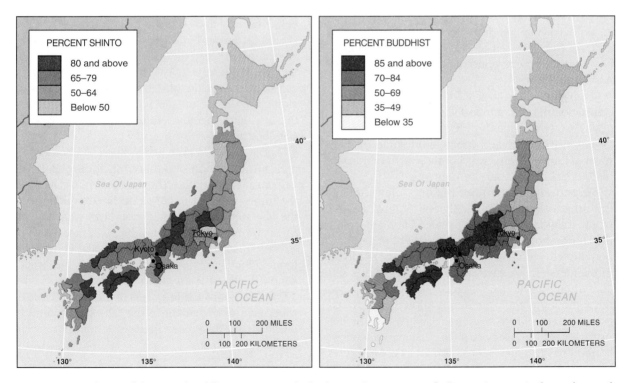

FIGURE 5–9 Distribution of Shintos and Buddhists in Japan. For both religions, the percentage of adherents is greater in the southern and central portions of Japan than in the north. In some areas, more than two-thirds of the people are Buddhists and more than two-thirds are Shintoists. This distribution is possible because many people adhere simultaneously to both religions.

Judaism

Judaism is an ethnic religion based in the lands bordering the eastern end of the Mediterranean Sea, called Canaan in the Bible, Palestine by the Romans, and the state of Israel since 1948. About 1500 years ago, Abraham, considered the patriarch or father of Judaism, migrated from present-day Iraq to Canaan, along a route known as the Fertile Crescent (see discussion of the Fertile Crescent in Chapter 7 and Figure 7–3). The Old Testament recounts the ancient history of the Jewish people.

Fundamental to Judaism was the belief in one all-powerful God. As the first recorded religion to espouse monotheism, Judaism offered a sharp contrast to the practice of neighboring people, who worshipped a collection of gods. Jews considered themselves the "chosen" people, because God had selected them to live according to His ethical and moral principles, such as the Ten Commandments.

The name *Judaism* derives from *Judah*, one of the patriarch Jacob's twelve sons; *Israel* is another biblical name for Jacob. Descendants of ten of Jacob's sons, plus two of his grandsons, constituted the twelve tribes of Hebrews who emigrated from Egypt in the Exodus narrative and were each given a portion of Canaan. Judah is one of the surviving tribes of Hebrews; ten of the tribes were considered lost after they were conquered and transported to Assyria in 721 B.C.

Judaism plays a more substantial role in Western civilization than its number of adherents would suggest. First, two of the three main universalizing religions—Christianity and Islam—find some of their roots in Judaism. Jesus was born a Jew, and Muhammad traced his ancestry to Abraham.

Second, the spatial distribution of Jews differs from that of other ethnic religions. Unique among ethnic religions, Judaism is practiced in many countries throughout the world, as a result of migrations, both forced and voluntary. Most Jews have not lived in their Eastern Mediterranean homeland since A.D. 70, when the Romans forced them to disperse throughout the world, an action known as the *diaspora,* from the Greek word for "dispersion". The Romans forced the diaspora after crushing an attempt by the Jews to rebel against Roman rule. Most Jews moved to Europe, although some went to North Africa and Asia. Only since the 1940s have a large percentage of the world's Jews lived in the Eastern Mediterranean.

Third, Jews have been subjected to unique problems in their attempt to occupy a portion of Earth's surface. Having been exiled from the home of their ethnic religion, Jews have lived among other nationalities, retaining separate religious practices but adopting other cultural characteristics of the host country, such as language.

Other nationalities have often persecuted the Jews living in their midst. Historically, the Jews of many European countries were forced to live in a **ghetto,** defined as a city neighborhood set up by law to be inhabited only by Jews. The term *ghetto* may have originated during the sixteenth century in Venice, Italy, as a reference to the city's foundry, or metal-casting, district, where Jews were forced to live. Ghettos were frequently surrounded by walls, and the gates were locked at night to prevent escape.

Beginning in the 1930s, but especially during World War II (1939–1945), the Nazis systematically rounded up a large percentage of European Jews, transported them to concentration camps, and exterminated them. About 4 million Jews died in the camps, and 2 million in other ways.

Today, fewer than 10 percent of the world's 18 million Jews live in Europe, compared with 90 percent a century ago. About 6 million Jews live in the United States, and another 4 million in Israel. Jews are integrated into the mainstream of U.S. life, although they are heavily concentrated in the large cities, including one-third in the New York City area alone. Jews constitute a majority in Israel, where for the first time since the biblical era an independent state has had a Jewish majority.

About 2 million Jews live in Russia and other former Soviet Union republics, including Belarus, Lithuania, and Ukraine. The number of Jews living in the former Soviet Union has declined rapidly since the late 1980s, when emigration laws were liberalized. For many years, their religious practices were strongly discouraged, but few were allowed to emigrate. The number of synagogues in the Soviet Union declined from about 400 in 1960 to 62 by 1975. Conditions for Jews remaining in Eastern Europe have worsened since the fall of communism, because they have been blamed by some for recent economic problems.

Ethnic African Religions

Many Africans follow traditional ethnic religions, sometimes called **animism.** Animists believe that such inanimate objects as plants and stones or such natural events as thunderstorms and earthquakes are "animated," or have discrete spirits and conscious life. Relatively little is known about African religions because few holy books or other written documents have come down from ancestors. Religious rituals are passed from one generation to the next by word of mouth.

African animist religions are apparently based on monotheistic concepts, although below the supreme god there is a hierarchy of divinities. These divinities may be assistants to god or personifications of natural phenomena, such as trees or rivers.

The universalizing religions, especially Christianity and Islam, have sent missionaries to regions of Africa where traditional ethnic religions once dominated. Nearly 50 percent of all Africans are now classified as Christians—split about evenly among Roman Catholic, Protestant, and other—and another 40 percent are Muslims. Followers of traditional African religions now constitute a majority in only a handful of small West African countries, including Benin, Côte d'Ivoire, Guinea-Bissau, Sierra Leone, and Togo. In addition, several East African countries contain important minorities of animists.

Some traditional African religious ideas and practices have been merged with Christianity. For example, African rituals may give relative prominence to the worship of ancestors. Anglican bishops have decided that an African man who has more than one wife can become a Christian, as long as he does not add to the number of wives by further marriages. Desire for a merger of traditional practices with Christianity has led to the formation of several thousand churches in Africa not affiliated with established ones elsewhere in the world.

Zoroastrianism: Diffusion in Reverse

Zoroastrianism is an ethnic religion that has almost completely disappeared. Its decline, therefore, serves as a good example of territorial contraction, the opposite process to spatial diffusion.

The religion's founder, Zoroaster (628?–551 B.C.), lived in the northeastern part of present-day Iran. The diffusion of Zoroastrianism began after the conversion of a prince, later called Cyrus the Great (600?–529 B.C.). Cyrus was the first ruler to unify the entire territory of present-day Iran into a monarchy, then known as the Persian Empire.

For over a thousand years, Zoroastrianism was the ethnic religion of the Persian Empire, and many of the religion's rituals and teachings were based on events in the Empire. In particular, Zoroastrianism helped settled farmers recognize the importance of changing some of the customs they practiced as nomads, such as the sacrifice of useful cattle and the glorification of drinking and robbing. Zoroaster argued that Earth and its inhabitants were created by the forces of good to help fight evil spirits. People control their own destiny and can choose between the forces of good and evil spirits, but at death, people's souls are judged on the basis of their performance on Earth.

Zoroastrianism completely disappeared from Persia after the Islamic army conquered the area in the seventh century A.D. A few Zoroastrians fled from Persia to China and India, and about a quarter million remain, for the most part living in Bombay, India. Many of the principles of Zoroastrianism became part of Judaism and Christianity.

KEY ISSUE 2

How Do Religions Organize Space?

- Incorporation of Natural Events
- Sacred Space
- Administration of Space

We have divided the world into a collection of religious regions, with a distinctive predominant religion in each region. We have also traced the process of diffusion of each religion from a hearth, for the most part in South and Southwest Asia. This section demonstrates that the distinctive spatial distribution of religions produces different approaches to organizing the environment.

Religions are influenced by events in the physical environment, from astronomical cycles to disasters. Certain features of the landscape become incorporated into the philosophy and rituals of every religion. Different religions incorporate environmental phenomena in different ways, depending on the distinctive physical conditions where the religion originated or diffused.

The physical environment influences the organization of religion in three basic ways. First, natural events are incorporated into the structure of the religion. Second, features of the physical environment are designated as holy. Third, religions organize portions of Earth's surface into administrative units to diffuse religious messages.

Incorporation of Natural Events

Events in the physical environment are incorporated into religious principles. These events range from the familiar and predictable to unexpected disasters.

Cosmogony

Individual religions have different concepts of the relationship between human beings and nature. These differences derive from distinctive concepts of **cosmogony,** which is a set of religious beliefs concerning the origin of the universe.

Chinese ethnic religions, such as Confucianism and Daoism, believe that the universe is made up of two forces, *yin* and *yang*, which exist in everything. The yin force is associated with earth, darkness, femaleness, cold, depth, passivity, and death. The yang force is associated with heaven, light, maleness, heat, height, activity, and life. Yin and yang forces interact with each other to achieve balance and harmony, but they are in a constant state of change. An imbalance results in disorder and chaos. The principle of yin and yang applies to the creation and transformation of all natural features.

The universalizing religions that originated in the Middle East, notably Christianity and Islam, consider that God created the universe, including Earth's physical environment and human beings. A religious person can serve God by cultivating the land, draining wetlands, clearing forests, building new settlements, and otherwise making productive use of natural features that God created. As the very creator of Earth itself, God is more powerful than any force of nature, and, if in conflict, the laws of God take precedence over laws of nature.

Christian and Islamic cosmogony do differ in some respects. For example, Christians believe that Earth was given by God to humanity to finish the task of creation. Obeying the all-supreme power of God meant independence from the tyranny of natural forces. Muslims regard humans as representatives of God on Earth, capable of reflecting the attributes of God in their deeds, such as growing food or other hard work to improve the land. But humans are not partners with God, who alone was responsible for Earth's creation.

In the name of God, some people have sought mastery over nature, not merely independence from it. Large-scale development of remaining wilderness is advocated by some religious people as a way to serve God. To those who follow this approach, failure to make full and complete use of Earth's natural resources is considered a violation of biblical teachings.

Christians are likely to consider floods, droughts, and other natural disasters to be preventable and may take steps to overcome the problem by modifying the environment. Some Christians, however, regard natural disasters as punishment for human sins.

Practitioners of animist religions do not attempt to transform the environment to the same extent. To animists, God's powers are mystical, and only a few people on Earth can harness these powers for medical or other purposes. God can be placated, however, through prayer and sacrifice. Environmental hazards may be accepted as normal and unavoidable.

Calendar—The Natural Cycles

The most significant regular event in the natural environment that becomes incorporated into many religions is the annual cycle of variation in climatic conditions—the calendar. Knowledge of the calendar is critical to successful agriculture, whether for sedentary crop farmers or nomadic animal herders. The seasonal variations of temperature and precipitation help farmers select the appropriate times for planting and harvesting and make the best choice of crops.

The Calendar in Ethnic Religions. A prominent feature of several religions is celebration of the seasons. Rituals are performed to pray for favorable environmental conditions or to give thanks for past success. The major religious events of the Bontok people of the Philippines, for example, revolve around the agricultural calendar. Sacred moments, known as *obaya*, include the times when the rice field is initially prepared, when the seeds are planted, when the seedlings are transplanted, when the harvest is begun, and when the harvest is complete.

Judaism is classified as an ethnic, rather than a universalizing, religion in part because its major holidays are based on events in the agricultural calendar of the religion's homeland in present-day Israel. In that Mediterranean agricultural region, grain crops generally are planted in autumn, which is a time of hope and worry over whether the winter's rainfall will be sufficient. The two holiest days in the Jewish calendar, Rosh Hashanah (New Year) and Yom Kippur (Day of Atonement), come in autumn.

Stonehenge is a collection of enormous stones (weighing 100 tons each), erected about 4,000 years ago, probably for religious ceremonies. The stones are arranged so that the sun rises between two of them on the summer solstice, and it is centered between other stones at other astronomically significant dates and times. (Robert Hallman/Tony Stone Images)

The other three most important holidays in Judaism originally were related even more closely to the agricultural cycle. *Sukkot* celebrates the final gathering of fruits for the year, and prayers, especially for rain, are offered to bring success in the upcoming agricultural year. *Pesach* (Passover) derives from traditional agricultural practices in which farmers offered God the first fruits of the new spring harvest and herders sacrificed a young animal at the time when cows began to calve. *Shavuot* (Feast of Weeks), comes at the end of the grain harvest.

These three agricultural holidays later gained importance, because they also commemorated events in the exodus of the Jews from Egypt, as recounted in the Old Testament. Pesach recalled the liberation of the Jews from slavery in Egypt and the miracle of their successful flight under the leadership of Moses. Sukkot derived from the Hebrew word for the booths or temporary shelters occupied by Jews during their wandering in the wilderness for 40 years after fleeing Egypt. Shavuot was considered the date during

the wandering when Moses received the Ten Commandments from God. The reinterpretation of natural holidays in the light of historical events has been especially important for Jews in the United States, Western Europe, and other regions who are unfamiliar with the agricultural calendar of the Middle East.

The Calendar in Universalizing Religions. Because universalizing religions are practiced in varied locations around the world, the role of the landscape in forming rituals is different from its role in ethnic religions. For example, the main holidays in the Buddhist and Christian are calendars related to events in their founders' lives. All Buddhists observe Buddha's birth, Enlightenment, and death, although not all Buddhists observe them on the same days. (Japanese Buddhists celebrate Buddha's birth on April 8, his Enlightenment on December 8, and his death on February 15; Theravadist Buddhists observe all three events on the same day, usually in April.)

To Christians, Easter commemorates the resurrection of Jesus Christ. Easter is observed on the first Sunday after the first full moon following the spring equinox in late March, calculated in Western churches on the Gregorian calendar and in Eastern Orthodox churches on the Julian calendar. Thus, not all Christians observe Easter on the same day.

Christians may relate Easter to the agricultural cycle, but that relationship differs with where they live. In southern Europe, Easter is a joyous time of harvest, whereas in northern Europe it is a time of anxiety over planting new crops, as well as a celebration of spring's arrival after a harsh winter. Christians outside the Mediterranean countries lack a specific harvest holiday—which would be placed in the fall—although Thanksgiving in the United States and Canada has been endowed with Christian prayers to play that role.

Holidays are even less related to events in the physical environment for Christians in the Southern Hemisphere. There, Easter comes in March or April, which in the Southern Hemisphere is autumn. Christmas comes in December, which in the Southern Hemisphere is summer.

Which Calendar? In daily business, we use the solar calendar of 12 months, each containing 30 or 31 days, taking up the astronomical slack with 28 or 29 days in February. But Judaism and Islam use a lunar rather than a solar calendar. The moon has a mystical quality because of its variation from one day to the next. From its fullest disk, the moon becomes smaller and disappears altogether ("new moon") before reappearing and expanding to a full moon again. The appearance of the new moon marks the new month in Judaism and Islam and is a holiday for both religions.

The lunar month is only about 29 days long, so a lunar year of about 350 days quickly becomes out-of-step with the agricultural seasons. As an ethnic religion with only 18 million adherents, Judaism wishes to celebrate its principal holidays in the same season every year; consequently, every few years the Jewish calendar inserts an additional month.

Islam, on the other hand, retains a strict lunar calendar of about 350 days. As a result, Muslim holidays arrive in different seasons from generation to generation. For example, during the holy month of Ramadan, Muslims fast during daylight every day and try to make a pilgrimage to the holy city of Makkah. Because Ramadan occurs at different times of the agricultural year in different generations, observances can interfere with critical agricultural activities. The number of hours of the daily fast could vary widely, because the amount of daylight varies by season and by location on Earth's surface.

As a universalizing religion with nearly 1 billion adherents all over the world, however, Islam is practiced in a wide variety of climates and latitudes. If Ramadan were fixed at the same time of the Middle East's agricultural year, Muslims in various places of the world would need to make different adjustments to observe Ramadan.

The *solstice* has special significance in some pagan religions. A major holiday in some pagan religions is the winter solstice, December 21 or 22 in the Northern Hemisphere and June 21 or 22 in the Southern Hemisphere. The winter solstice is the shortest day and longest night of the year, when the sun appears lowest in the sky and appears to stand still (*solstice* comes from the Latin, meaning "the sun stands still)." Stonehenge, a collection of rocks erected in southwestern England, probably by the Druids, is a prominent remnant of a pagan structure apparently aligned so the sun rises between two stones on the solstice.

If you stand at the western facade of the U.S. Capitol in Washington, at exactly noon on the summer solstice (June 21 or 22 in the Northern Hemisphere), and look down Pennsylvania Avenue, the sun is directly over the center of the avenue. Similarly, at the winter solstice the sun is directly aligned with the view from the Capitol down Maryland Avenue. Will archaeologists of the distant future think we erected the Capitol and aligned the streets as a religious ritual? Did the planner of Washington, Pierre L'Enfant, create the pattern accidentally or deliberately, and if deliberately, why?

Sacred Space

Religions may elevate particular elements in the landscape to a holy position. Two kinds of places may be endowed with holiness: distinctive physical environments, such as mountains, rivers, or rock formations, and objects on the landscape associated with the religion's origin or diffusion. Making pilgrimages to these holy places is important in some religions.

Hindus believe that the Ganges River springs from the hair of Siva, one of the main deities. The river attracts pilgrims from all over India, who achieve purification by bathing in it. Bodies of the dead are washed with water from the Ganges before being cremated. (Richard Vogel/Gamma--Liaison, Inc.)

Holy Places

Holy places are known as *shrines* and may be incorporated into the rituals of a particular religion. Among the most widely followed religions, holy places are especially important in Hinduism, Buddhism, and Islam.

Holy Places in Hinduism. As an ethnic religion of India, Hinduism is closely tied to the Indian landscape. According to a survey conducted by the geographer Surinder Bhardwaj, the natural features most likely to rank among the holiest shrines in India are riverbanks or coastlines.

Hindus believe that they achieve purification by bathing in holy rivers. The Ganges is the holiest river in India, because it is believed to spring forth from the hair of Siva, one of the main deities. Indians come from all over the country to Hardwar, the most popular location for bathing in the Ganges.

Hindu holy places are organized into a hierarchy. Some prominent shrines attract pilgrims from the entire country; others are important to a local community but are seldom visited by people from other regions (Figure 5–10). Because Hinduism has no central authority, the relative importance of shrines is established by tradition, not by doctrine. For example, many Hindus make long-distance pilgrimages to Mt. Kailās, located at the source of the Ganges in the Himalayas, which is holy because Siva lives there. At the same time, other mountains may attract only local pilgrims. Throughout India, local residents may consider a nearby mountain to be holy if Siva is thought to have visited it.

Buddhist Shrines. Several places are holy to Buddhists because they were the locations of important events in Buddha's life. The four most important places are concentrated in a small area of northeast-

FIGURE 5–10 Hierarchy of Hindu holy places. Some places are important to Hindus all over India and are visited frequently; others have importance only to nearby residents. The map also shows that holy places for particular deities are somewhat clustered in different regions of the country—Shakti in the east, Vishnu in the west, and Siva in the north and south.

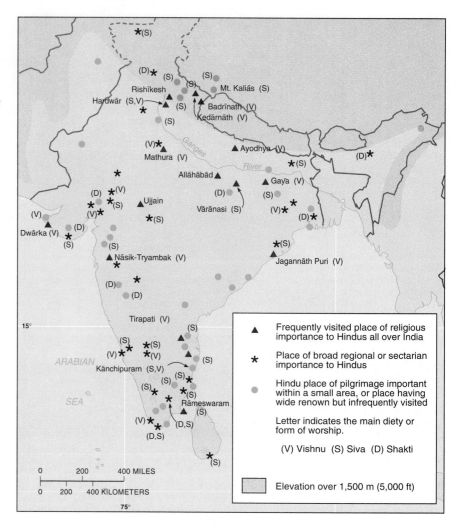

ern India and southern Nepal (Figure 5–11). Most important is Lumbinī, in southern Nepal, where Buddha was born, around 563 B.C. Many sanctuaries and monuments were built there, but all are in ruins today.

Since the third century B.C., a temple has stood near the site of the second great event in Buddha's life, and part of the surrounding railing, built in the first century A.D., still stands. At Bodh Gayā, 250 kilometers (150 miles) southeast of his birthplace, Buddha reached perfect wisdom. Because Buddha reached perfect enlightenment while sitting under a bo tree, trees of that species are considered holy objects as well. Bo trees have been diffused to other Buddhist countries, such as China and Japan, in honor of Buddha.

The third important location is Deer Park in Sarnath, where Buddha gave his first sermon. The

Dhamek pagoda at Sarnath, built in the third century B.C., is probably the oldest surviving structure in India. Nearby is an important library of Buddhist literature, including many works removed from Tibet when Tibet's Buddhist leader, the Dalai Lama, went into exile.

The fourth holy place is Kúsinagara, where Buddha died at age 80 and passed into Nirvana, a state of peaceful extinction. Temples built at the site are currently in ruins.

Four other sites in northeastern India are particularly sacred because they were the locations of Buddha's principal miracles. At Srāvastī, Buddha performed his greatest miracle. Before an assembled audience of competing religious leaders, Buddha created multiple images of himself and visited heaven. Srāvastī became an active center of Buddhism, and

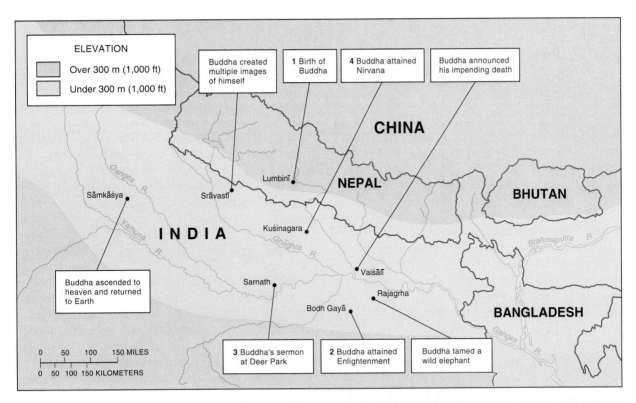

ELEVATION

☐ Over 300 m (1,000 ft)

☐ Under 300 m (1,000 ft)

Buddha created multiple images of himself

1 Birth of Buddha

4 Buddha attained Nirvana

Buddha announced his impending death

CHINA

NEPAL

BHUTAN

Lumbinī

Sāmkāśya

Srāvastī

INDIA

Kuśinagara

Buddha ascended to heaven and returned to Earth

Vaiśālī

Sarnath

Rajagrha

Bodh Gayā

BANGLADESH

0 50 100 150 MILES

0 50 100 150 KILOMETERS

3 Buddha's sermon at Deer Park

2 Buddha attained Enlightenment

Buddha tamed a wild elephant

FIGURE 5–11 Holy places in Buddhism. Most are clustered in northeastern India and southern Nepal, because they were the locations of important events in Buddha's life. Most of the sites are in ruins today. Shown at right is the Dhamek pagoda at Sarnath, built in the third century B.C. near where Buddha gave his first sermon two hundred years earlier. (Ric Ergenbright)

one of the most important monasteries was established there.

At the second miracle site, Sāmkāsya, Buddha is said to have ascended to heaven, preached to his mother, and returned to Earth. The third site, Rajagriha, is holy because Buddha tamed a wild elephant there, and shortly after Buddha's death it became the site of the first Buddhist Council. Vaisālī, the fourth location, is the site of Buddha's announcement of his impending death and the second Buddhist Council. All four miracle sites are in ruins today, although excavation activity is under way.

Holy Places in Islam. The holiest locations in Islam are cities rather than elements of the physical environment. The holiest city for Muslims is Makkah (Mecca), the birthplace of Muhammad. Now a city of more than a half million inhabitants, Makkah contains the holiest object in the Islamic landscape, the Ka'ba, a cubelike structure encased in silk, which stands at the center of the Great Mosque, al Haram al Sharīf (Figure 5–12). The Ka'ba, thought to have been built by Abraham and Ishmael, contains a black stone given to Abraham by Gabriel as a sign of the covenant with Ishmael and the Muslim people.

The Ka'ba had been a religious shrine in Makkah for centuries before the origin of Islam. After Muhammad defeated the local people, he captured the Ka'ba, cleared it of idols, and rededicated it to the all-powerful Allah (God). The al-Haram mosque also contains the well of Zamzam, considered to have the same water source as that used by Ishmael and Hagar when they were wandering in the desert after their exile from Canaan.

The second most holy geographic location in Islam is Madinah (Medina), approximately 350 kilometers (220 miles) north of Makkah. Muhammad received his first support from the people of Madinah and became the city's chief administrator. Muhammad's tomb is at Madinah, inside Islam's second mosque.

Pilgrimages

Religions that have a collection of important holy shrines may also have an organized procedure by which adherents from around the world visit them. Hindus and Muslims are especially encouraged to make **pilgrimages** to visit holy places in accordance with recommended itineraries, and Shintoists are encouraged to visit holy places in Japan. The concept is less important in Christianity and the other East Asian religions.

Every healthy Muslim who has adequate financial resources is expected to undertake a pilgrimage, called a *hajj,* to Makkah (Mecca). The word *mecca* now has a general meaning in the English language as a goal sought or a center of activity. Regardless of nationality and economic background, all pilgrims dress alike in plain white robes to emphasize common loyalty to Islam and the equality of people in the eyes of Allah. A precise set of rituals is practiced, culminating in a visit to the Ka'ba.

The *hajj* attracts 1 million Muslims a year to Makkah from countries other than Saudi Arabia. Roughly 40 percent each come from the Middle East and northern Africa, with the largest numbers from Nigeria, Turkey, and Yemen. Asian countries are responsible for most of the remaining 20 percent. Although Indonesia is the world's most populous Muslim country, it does not send the largest number of pilgrims to Makkah because of the relatively long travel distance.

Hindus consider a pilgrimage, known as a *tirtha,* to be an act of purification. Although not a substitute for meditation, the pilgrimage is an important act in achieving redemption. Particularly sacred places attract Hindus from all over India, despite the relatively remote locations of some; less important shrines attract primarily local pilgrims.

The remoteness of holy places from population clusters once meant that making a pilgrimage required major commitments of time and money as well as undergoing considerable physical hardship. But recent improvements in transportation have increased the accessibility of shrines. Hindus can now reach holy places in the Himalaya Mountains by bus or car, and Muslims from all over the world can reach Makkah by airplane.

Administration of Space

Followers of a religion must be connected, to assure communication and consistency of doctrine. The method of interaction varies among religions. Individual communities within some religions are highly **autonomous,** or self-sufficient, and interaction among communities is confined to little more than loose cooperation and shared ideas. At the other extreme, **hierarchical religions** have a well-

FIGURE 5–12 Makkah (Mecca) Saudi Arabia. Makkah is the holiest city for Muslims, because Muhammad was born there. Thousands of Muslims make a pilgrimage to Makkah each year and gather at al-Haram al-Sharīf, a mosque in the center of the city. The black, cubelike structure in the center of the mosque, called the Ka'ba, had been a shrine to tribal idols until Muhammad rededicated it to Allah. Muslims believe that Abraham and Ishmael originally built the Ka'ba. (Mohamed Lounes/Gamma-Liaison, Inc.)

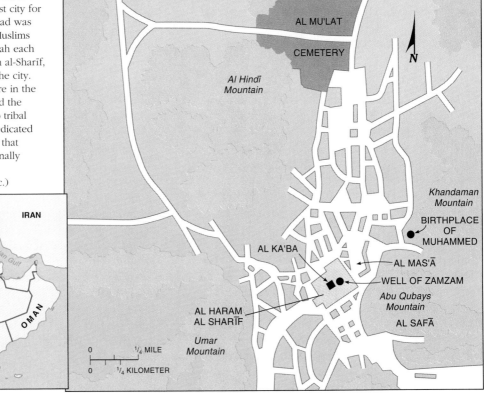

defined geographic structure and organize territory into local administrative units. Other religions may combine spatial elements of both self-sufficient and hierarchical administrative systems.

Hierarchical Religions

Roman Catholicism provides a good example of a hierarchical religion. The church has organized much of Earth's inhabited land into an administrative structure, ultimately accountable to the Pope in Rome. Here is the hierarchy of Roman Catholicism.

- The *Pope* is the highest authority. (He is also the bishop of the Diocese of Rome.)
- Reporting to the Pope are *archbishops.* Each heads a *province,* which is a group of several dioceses. The city containing the archbishop's headquarters is called the archdiocese.
- Reporting to each archbishop are *bishops.* Each administers a diocese, of which there are several thousand. The diocese is the basic unit of geographic organization in the Roman Catholic church. The bishop's headquarters, called a *see,* is typically the largest city in the diocese. (The archbishop also is bishop of one diocese within the province.)
- A diocese in turn is spatially divided into *parishes,* each headed by a *priest.*

The area and population of parishes and dioceses vary according to historical factors and the distribution of Roman Catholics across Earth's surface (for example, the United States is shown in Figure 5–13). In parts of southern and western Europe, the overwhelming majority of the dense population is Roman Catholic. Consequently, the density of parishes is high. A typical parish may encompass only a few square kilometers and fewer than a thousand people.

At the other extreme, Latin American parishes may encompass several hundred square kilometers and 5,000 people. The more dispersed Latin American distribution is attributable partly to a lower population density than in Europe. Because Roman Catholicism is a hierarchical religion, individual parishes must work closely with centrally located officials concerning rituals and procedures. If Latin America followed the European model of small parishes, many would be too remote for the priest to com-

municate with others in the hierarchy. The less intensive network of Roman Catholic institutions also results in part from colonial traditions because Portuguese and Spanish rulers discouraged parish development in Latin America.

The Roman Catholic population is growing rapidly in the U.S. Southwest and suburbs of some large North American and European cities. Some of these areas have a low density of parishes and dioceses compared with the population, so the church must adjust its territorial organization. They can create new local administrative units, although funds to provide the desired number of churches, schools, and other religious structures may be scarce. Conversely, the Roman Catholic population is declining in inner cities and rural areas. Maintaining services in these areas is expensive, but the process of combining parishes and closing schools is very difficult.

Among other Christian religions, Mormons exercise strong organization of the landscape. The territory occupied by Mormons, primarily Utah and portions of surrounding states, is organized into *wards,* with populations of approximately 750 each. Several wards are combined into a *stake* of approximately 5,000 people. The highest authority in the church—the board and president—frequently redraws ward and stake boundaries in rapidly growing areas to reflect the ideal population standards.

Locally Autonomous Religions

Among the three large universalizing religions, Islam provides the most local autonomy. Like other locally autonomous religions, Islam has neither a religious hierarchy nor a formal territorial organization. A mosque is a place for public ceremony, and a leader calls the faithful to prayer, but everyone is expected to participate equally in the rituals and is encouraged to pray privately. In the absence of a church hierarchy, the only formal organization of territory in Islam is through the coincidence of religious territory with secular states. Governments in some predominantly Islamic countries include in their bureaucracy people who administer Islamic institutions. These administrators interpret Islamic law and run welfare programs.

Strong unity within the Islamic world is maintained by a relatively high degree of communication and migration, such as the pilgrimage to Makkah. In addition, uniformity is fostered by Islamic doctrine, which offers more explicit commands than other religions.

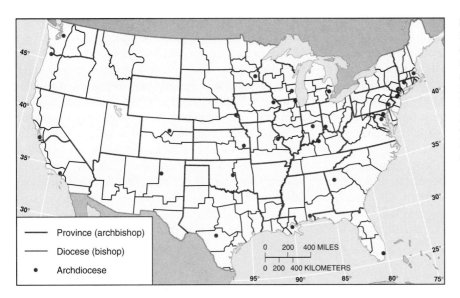

Province (archbishop)

Diocese (bishop)

• Archdiocese

FIGURE 5-13 The Roman Catholic hierarchy. The Roman Catholic church divides the United States into provinces, each headed by an archbishop. Provinces are subdivided into dioceses, each headed by a bishop. The archbishop of a province also serves as the bishop of a diocese. Dioceses that are headed by archbishops are called archdioceses.

Judaism and Hinduism also have no centralized structure of religious control. To conduct a full service, Judaism requires merely the presence of ten adult males. (Females count in some Jewish communities.) Hinduism is even more autonomous, because worship is usually done alone or with others in the household. Hindus share ideas primarily through undertaking pilgrimages and reading traditional writings.

Protestant Christian denominations vary in geographic structure from extremely autonomous to somewhat hierarchical. Extremely autonomous denominations such as Baptists and United Church of Christ are organized into self-governing congregations. Each congregation establishes the precise form of worship and selects the leadership.

The Episcopalian, Lutheran, and most Methodist churches have hierarchical structures, somewhat comparable to the Roman Catholic church. Presbyterian churches represent an intermediate degree of autonomy. Individual churches are united in a *presbytery,* several of which in turn are governed by a *synod,* with a *general assembly* as ultimate authority over all churches. Each Presbyterian church is governed by an elected board of directors with lay members.

Religions adapt to conditions in the physical environment in different ways, organizing space in a manner consistent with the particular doctrine. In turn, religions also modify the landscape, as we see in the next section.

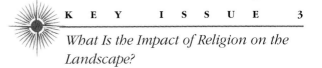

K E Y   I S S U E   3

What Is the Impact of Religion on the Landscape?

- Sacred Structures
- Use of the Land

All major religions have sacred structures, but the functions of the buildings influence the arrangement of the structures across the landscape. Some religions require a relatively large number of elaborate structures, while others have more modest needs.

Sacred Structures

Church, basilica, mosque, temple, pagoda, synagogue—these familiar names identify places of worship in various faiths. Sacred structures are physical "anchors" of religion. They may house shrines or be places where people can assemble for worship. In many cities and countries, the most prominent landmarks are sacred structures.

Christian Churches

The Christian landscape is dominated by a high density of churches. The word *church* derives from a Greek term meaning "lord", "master", and "power".

Church also refers to a gathering of believers, as well as the building where the gathering occurs.

The church building plays a more critical role in Christianity than in other religions, in part because the structure is an expression of religious principles, an environment in the image of God. The church is also more prominent in Christianity because attendance at a collective service of worship is considered extremely important.

The prominence of churches on the landscape also stems from their style of construction and location. Traditionally in some communities, the church was the largest and tallest building and was placed at an important square or other prominent location. Although such characteristics may no longer apply in large cities, they frequently remain true for small towns and neighborhoods within cities.

Underlying the large number and size of Christian churches is their considerable expense. Because of the importance of a place of worship, Christians have contributed much wealth to the construction and maintenance of churches. A wealthy congregation may build an elaborate structure designed by an architect to provide an environment compatible with the religious doctrine and ritual. Over the centuries, the most prominent architects have been commissioned to create religious structures, such as those designed by Christopher Wren in London during the late seventeenth century.

Church Architecture. Early churches were modeled after Roman buildings for public assembly, known as *basilicas.* The basilica was a rectangular building divided by two rows of columns that formed a central nave (hall) and two side aisles. At the western end of the church stood a semicircular apse, in front of which was the altar where the priest conducted the service. Later, the apse was placed on the eastern wall. The raised altar, symbolizing the hill of Calvary, facilitated the symbolic reenactment of Christ's sacrifice. Churches built during the Gothic period, between the twelfth and fourteenth centuries, had a floor plan in the form of the familiar Latin cross.

Because Christianity split into many denominations, no single style of church construction has dominated. Churches reflect both the cultural values of the denomination and the region's architectural heritage. Eastern Orthodox churches, for example, follow an architectural style that developed in the Byzantine Empire during the fifth century. Byzantine-style Eastern Orthodox churches tend to be highly ornate, topped by prominent domes. Many Protestant churches in North America, on the other hand, are simple, with little ornamentation. This austerity is a reflection of the Protestant conception of a church as an assembly hall for the congregation.

Availability of building materials also influences church appearance. In the United States, early churches were most frequently built of wood in the Northeast, brick in the Southeast, and adobe in the Southwest. Stucco and stone predominated in Latin America. This diversity reflected differences in the most common building materials found by early settlers.

Places of Worship in Other Religions

Religious buildings are highly visible and important features of the landscapes in regions dominated by religions other than Christianity. But unlike Christianity, other major religions do not consider their important buildings sanctified places of worship.

Muslim Mosques. Muslims consider the mosque as a space for community assembly. In contrast to a church, however, a *mosque* is not viewed as a sanctified place but rather as a location for the community to gather for worship. Mosques are found primarily in larger cities of the Muslim world, whereas simple structures may serve as places of prayer in rural villages.

The mosque is organized around a central courtyard—traditionally open air, although in harsher climates it may be enclosed. The pulpit is placed at the end of the courtyard facing Makkah, the direction toward which all Muslims pray. Surrounding the courtyard is a cloister used for schools and nonreligious activities. A distinctive feature of the mosque is the *minaret,* a tower where a man known as a *muzzan* summons people to worship (Figure 5–12 shows two minarets).

Hindu Temples. Sacred structures for collective worship are relatively unimportant in Asian religions. Instead, important religious functions are more likely to take place at home within the family. *Temples* are built to house shrines for particular gods rather than for congregational worship.

The Hindu temple serves as a home to one or more gods, although a particular god may have more than one temple. Wealthy individuals or groups usually maintain local temples. Size and frequency of temples are determined by local preferences and commitment of resources rather than standards imposed by religious doctrine.

The typical Hindu temple contains a small, dimly lit interior room where a symbolic artifact or some other image of the god rests. The remainder of the temple may be devoted to space for ritual processions. Because congregational worship is not part of Hinduism, the temple does not need a large closed interior space filled with seats. The site of the temple, usually demarcated by a wall, may also contain a structure for a caretaker and a pool for ritual baths.

Buddhist and Shintoist Pagodas. The *pagoda* is a prominent and visually attractive element of the Buddhist and Shintoist landscapes. Frequently elaborate and delicate in appearance, pagodas typically include tall, many-sided towers arranged in a series of tiers, balconies, and slanting roofs.

Pagodas contain relics that Buddhists believe to be a portion of Buddha's body or clothing. After Buddha's death, his followers scrambled to obtain these relics. As part of the process of diffusing the religion, Buddhists carried these relics to other countries and built pagodas for them. Pagodas are not designed for congregational worship. Individual prayer or meditation is likely to be undertaken at a nearby temple, a remote monastery, or home.

The Great Buddha, Kamakura, Japan. The 13-meter (42-foot) tall bronze statue was cast in 1252. (Raga/The Stock Market)

Use of the Land

The impact of religion is clearly seen in the arrangement of human activities on the landscape at several scales, from relatively small parcels of land to entire communities. How each religion distributes its elements on the landscape depends on its beliefs. The most significant religious land uses are for burial of the dead and religious settlements.

Disposition of the Dead

A prominent example of religiously inspired arrangement of land at a smaller scale is burial practices. Climate, topography, and religious doctrine combine to create differences in practices to shelter the dead.

Burial. Christians, Muslims, and Jews usually bury their dead in a specially designated area called a *cemetery.* The Christian burial practice can be traced to the early years of the religion. In ancient Rome, underground passages known as *catacombs* were used to bury early Christians (and to protect the faithful when the religion was still illegal).

After Christianity became legal, Christians buried their dead in the yard around the church. As these burial places became overcrowded, separate burial grounds had to be established outside the city walls. Public health and sanitation considerations in the nineteenth century led to public management of many cemeteries. However, some cemeteries are still operated by religious organizations.

Cremation is the most common form of disposal of bodies in India. In middle class families, bodies are more likely to be cremated in an electric oven at a crematorium. A poor person may be cremated in an open fire, such as this one within sight of the Taj Mahal. High-ranking officials and strong believers in traditional religious practices may also be cremated on an outdoor fire. (Raghu Rai/Magnum Photos, Inc.)

The remains of the dead are customarily aligned in some traditional direction. Some Christians bury the dead with the feet toward Jerusalem so that they may meet Christ there on the Day of Judgment. The Mandan Indians of the North American Plains placed the dead on scaffolds with the feet to the southeast, the direction the spirits were said to take to reach the Heart River, the place where the ancestors used to live. The face is often aligned toward the west, the direction where the sun "dies" in its daily setting.

Cemeteries may consume significant space in a community, increasing the competition for scarce space. In congested urban areas, Christians and Muslims have traditionally used cemeteries as public open space. Before the widespread development of public parks in the nineteenth century, cemeteries were frequently the only green space in rapidly growing cities. Cemeteries are still used as parks in Muslim countries, where the idea faces less opposition than in Christian societies.

Traditional burial practices in China have put pressure on agricultural land. By burying dead relatives, rural residents have removed as much as 10 percent of the land from productive agriculture. The government in China has ordered the practice discontinued, even encouraging farmers to plow over old burial mounds. Cremation is encouraged instead.

Other Methods of Disposing of Bodies. Not all faiths bury their dead. Hindus generally practice cremation rather than burial. Traditional Hindus may have their bodies washed with water from the Ganges River and then burned with a slow fire on a funeral pyre. Burial is reserved for children, ascetics, and people with certain diseases. Cremation is considered an act of purification, although it tends to strain India's wood supply. Most Hindus are now cremated in electric ovens.

Cremation was the principal form of disposing of bodies in Europe before Christianity. Outside of India, it is still practiced in parts of Southeast Asia, possibly because of Hindu influence.

Motivation for cremation may have originated from unwillingness on the part of nomads to leave their dead behind, possibly because of fear that the body could be attacked by wild beast or evil spirits, or even return to life. Cremation could also free the soul from the body for departure to the afterworld and provide warmth and comfort for the soul as it embarked on the journey to the afterworld.

To strip away unclean portions of the body, Parsis (Zoroastrians) expose the dead to scavenging birds and animals. The ancient Zoroastrians did not want the body to contaminate the sacred elements of fire, earth, or water. Tibetan Buddhists also practice exposure for some dead, with cremation reserved for the most exalted priests.

Disposal of bodies at sea is used in some parts of Micronesia, but the practice is much less common than in the past. The bodies of lower-class people would be flung into the sea, whereas elites could be set adrift on a raft or boat. Water burial was regarded as a safeguard against being contaminated by the dead.

Religious Settlements

Buildings for worship and burial places are smaller-scale manifestations of religion on the landscape, but there are larger-scale examples: entire settlements. Most human settlements serve an economic purpose (see Chapter 11), but some are established primarily for religious reasons.

A *utopian settlement* is an ideal community built around a religious way of life. By 1858, some 130 utopian settlements had begun in the United States in conformance with groups' distinctive religious beliefs. Examples include Oneida, New York; Ephrata, Pennsylvania; Nauvoo, Illinois; and New Harmony, Indiana. Buildings were sited and economic activities organized to integrate religious principles into all aspects of daily life.

An early utopian settlement in the United States was Bethlehem, Pennsylvania, founded in 1741 by Moravians, Christians who had emigrated from the present-day Czech Republic. The culmination of the utopian movement in the United States was the construction of Salt Lake City by the Mormons, begun in 1848. The layout of Salt Lake City is based on a plan of the city of Zion given to the church elders in 1833 by the Mormon prophet Joseph Smith. The city has a regular grid pattern, unusually broad boulevards, and church-related buildings situated at strategic points.

Most utopian communities declined in importance or disappeared altogether. Some utopian communities disappeared because the inhabitants were celibate and could not attract immigrants; in other cases residents moved away in search of better economic conditions. The utopian communities that have not been demolished are now inhabited by people who are not members of the original religious sect, although a few have been preserved as museums.

Although most colonial settlements were not planned primarily for religious purposes, religious principles affected many of the designs. Most early New England settlers were members of a Puritan Protestant denomination. The Puritans generally migrated together from England and preferred to live near each other in clustered settlements rather than on dispersed, isolated farms. Reflecting the importance of religion in their lives, New England settlers placed the church at the most prominent location in the center of the settlement, usually adjacent to a public open space, known as a *common* because it was for use by everyone.

Religious Toponyms

Roman Catholic immigrants frequently have given religious toponyms to their settlements in the New World, particularly in Québec and the U.S. Southwest. Québec's boundaries with Ontario and the United States clearly illustrate the difference between toponyms selected by Roman Catholic and Protestant settlers. Religious place names are common in Québec but rare in the two neighbors (Figure 5–14).

KEY ISSUE 4
What Territorial Conflicts Arise Because of Religion?

- Religion and Social Change
- Wars between Religious Groups

The distribution of religious elements on the landscape reflects the importance of religion in people's values. The impact of religion on the landscape is particularly profound, for many religious people believe that their life on Earth ought to be spent in service to God. As this section demonstrates, however, the attempt by adherents of one religion to organize Earth's surface can conflict with the spatial expression of other religious or nonreligious ideas.

FIGURE 5-14 A map of toponyms — near Québec's boundaries. Toponyms in Québec, Ontario and New York State show the impact of religion on the landscape. In Québec, a province with a predominantly Roman Catholic population, a large number of settlements are named for saints, whereas relatively few religious toponyms are found in predominantly Protestant Ontario and New York.

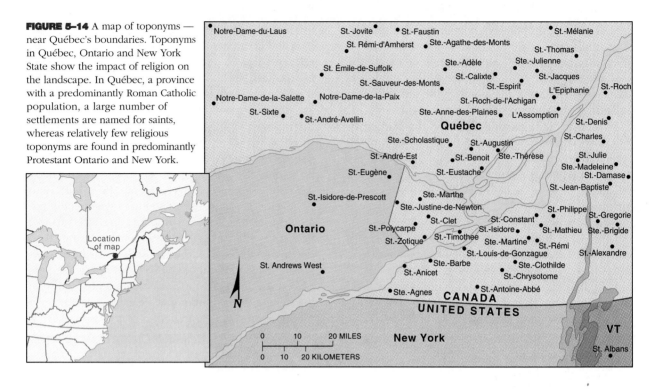

People of one faith frequently fight with people of other religions for control of Earth's surface. Such struggles reflect the power of religious belief. A group convinced that their religious view is the only correct one may spatially intrude upon the landscapes of other religions. In addition, the twentieth century has witnessed conflict between organized religion and *secularism* (nonreligion). We will look at examples of each type of conflict.

Religion and Social Change

The role of religion in organizing Earth's surface has diminished in some societies because of political and economic change. Islam has been particularly affected by a perceived conflict between religious values and modernization of the economy. Hinduism also has been forced to react to new nonreligious ideas from the West. Buddhism, Christianity, and Islam have all been challenged by communist governments that diminish the importance of religion in society. Yet, in recent years, religious principles have become increasingly important in the political organization of countries, especially where a branch of Christianity or Islam is the prevailing religion.

Hinduism and the West

Hinduism has been strongly challenged since the 1800s, when the British colonial administration brought unfamiliar social and moral concepts to India. The most vulnerable aspect of the Hindu religion was its rigid caste system. In Hinduism, because everyone is different, it is natural that each individual should belong to a particular position known as a *caste,* in the social order.

The caste system apparently originated around 1500 B.C. when Aryans invaded India from the west. The Aryans divided themselves into four castes, which developed strong differences in social and economic position: *Brahmans,* the priests and top administrators; *Kshatriyas,* or warriors; *Vaisyas,* or merchants; and *Shudras,* or agricultural workers and artisans. The Shudras occupied a distinctly lower status than the other three castes. Over the centuries, these original castes split into thousands of subcastes.

Below the four castes were the *outcasts,* or untouchables, who did the work considered too dirty for other castes. In theory, the untouchables were descended from the indigenous people who dwelt in India before the Aryan conquest. Until recently, social relations among the five groups were limited, and the rights of non-Brahmans, especially untouchables, were restricted.

British administrators and Christian missionaries pointed out the shortcomings of the caste system, such as neglect of the untouchables' health and economic problems. The rigid caste system has been considerably relaxed in recent years. The Indian government legally abolished the untouchable caste, and the people formerly in that caste now have equal rights with other Indians.

Although Hinduism has suffered attacks from British (Christian) values and Islamic fervor in the twentieth century, the religion came to be a great source of national unity in India. In modern India, with its hundreds of languages and ethnic groups, Hinduism has become the cultural trait shared by the largest percentage of the population.

Religion and Communism

Organized religion was challenged in the twentieth century by the rise of communism in Eastern Europe and Asia. The three religions most affected were Christianity (especially the Eastern Orthodox branch), Islam, and Buddhism.

Revival of Eastern Orthodoxy in Russia. The largest concentration of Eastern Orthodox Christians is in Russia. In 1721, Czar Peter the Great made the Russian Orthodox Church a part of the Russian government. The patriarch of the Russian Orthodox Church was replaced by a twelve-member committee, known as the Holy Synod, nominated by the czar.

In the years following the 1917 Bolshevik revolution, the government of the Soviet Union pursued antireligious programs. Socialist Karl Marx had called religion "the opium of the people," a view shared by V. I. Lenin and other early communist leaders. Marxism became the official doctrine of the Soviet Union, so religious doctrine was a potential threat to the success of the revolution. People's religious beliefs could not be destroyed overnight, but the role of organized religion in Soviet life could be reduced, and it was.

In 1918, the Soviet government eliminated the official church-state connection that Peter the Great had forged. All church buildings and property were nationalized and could be used only with local government permission. The Orthodox religion retained

adherents in the Soviet Union, especially among the elderly, but younger people generally had little contact with the church beyond attending a service perhaps once a year. With religious organizations prevented from conducting social and cultural work, religion dwindled in daily life.

The fall of communism in 1989 has brought a religious revival in Eastern Europe, especially where Roman Catholicism is the most prevalent branch of Christianity, including Croatia, the Czech Republic, Hungary, Lithuania, Poland, Slovakia, and Slovenia. Property confiscated by the Communist governments has reverted to church ownership, and attendance at church services has increased.

In Central Asian countries that were former parts of the Soviet Union—Kazakhstan, Kyrgyzstan, Tajikistan, Turkmenistan, and Uzbekistan—most people are Muslims. These newly independent countries are struggling to determine the extent to which laws should be rewritten to conform to Islamic custom rather than to the secular tradition inherited from the Soviet Union.

Suppression of Buddhism in Tibet. The assault on organized religion by Communist governments in Asia has crippled Buddhism in several countries, particularly in Tibet, which has been controlled by the People's Republic of China since 1950. The long war in Vietnam and neighboring countries also affected the practice of Buddhism.

Daily life in Tibet had long been dominated by Buddhist rites. By the 1950s, one-fourth of all males were monks, and polygamy was encouraged among other males to produce enough children for the long-term survival of the society. The spiritual and political leader of Tibetan Buddhists is the Dalai Lama. When the Dalai Lama dies, his spirit is believed to enter the body of a child. Priests identify the child who acquires the spirit of the Dalai Lama and train him to assume leadership at age 18. The fourteenth Dalai Lama was born in 1935 and identified as the future leader when he was only 2 years old.

After taking control of Tibet in 1950, the Chinese Communists sought to reduce the domination of Buddhist monks in the country's daily life by closing monasteries and temples and destroying religious artifacts and scriptures. The country became a Chinese province, and its Buddhist monk-dominated government was converted to a secular regime. After an

Lhasa, Tibet. On the hilltop is Potala Palace, part of which is 1,200 years old. The Dalai Lama, Tibet's traditional spiritual and political leader, lived in the Potala Palace until forced to emigrate after Tibet's unsuccessful rebellion against the Chinese in 1959. (Galen Rowell)

unsuccessful rebellion against the Chinese in 1959, Tibetans by the ten thousands were executed or imprisoned. More than 100,000 fled the country, including the Dalai Lama, who emigrated to India.

The Chinese have built new roads, power plants, hospitals, and schools to help raise the low standard of living in Tibet. Farmers were moved to agricultural communes and taught new techniques to increase productivity. Some monasteries have been rebuilt, but no new monks are being trained. When the current generation of priests dies, many Buddhist traditions may be lost forever in Tibet while being maintained by exiles living in other countries.

Vietnam War. In Southeast Asia, Buddhists were hurt by the long Vietnam War, waged between the French and later by Americans on one side and Communist groups on the other. Neither antagonist was particularly sympathetic to Buddhists. U.S. air bombing in Laos and Cambodia destroyed many Buddhist shrines, while others were vandalized by Vietnamese and by the Khmer Rouge Cambodian Communists. Many Buddhists immolated (burned) themselves to protest the South Vietnamese government.

The current Communist governments in Southeast Asia have discouraged religious activities and permitted monuments to decay, most notably the Angkor Wat complex in Cambodia, considered one of the world's most beautiful Buddhist structures. In any event, these countries do not have the funds necessary to restore the structures.

Wars Between Religious Groups

It is ironic that religions, which generally preach peace and cooperation, can be among the fiercest warring factions. The intensity reflects the level of emotional commitment that deeply religious people feel. Conflicts within and among all religions exist from time to time, and some persist for centuries.

Muslims versus Hindus in South Asia

Muslims have long fought with Hindus for control of territory, especially in South Asia. Around A.D. 1000, Mahmud, the Muslim king of Ghazni (modern-day Afghanistan), led raids on the Punjab area of northern India. His purpose originally was to acquire treasure from Hindu temples, but the raids turned into a Muslim-Hindu religious war. The Punjab became part of the Ghazni kingdom, with a governor at Lahore.

The fragmented Hindu kingdoms were unable to stop a second set of invasions by Muslims, who in the thirteenth century seized most of northern India as far east as Bengal. The population consisted primarily of Hindus and Buddhists, but the number of Muslims grew within a few generations as a result of intermarriage and further immigration from the west.

When the British took over India in the early 1800s, a three-way struggle began, with the Hindus and Muslims fighting each other as well as the British rulers. Muslims believed that the British discriminated more against them than against the Hindus.

When the British granted independence to the region after World War II, Hindus and Muslims fought over the organization of the newly independent region. The assassination in 1948 of Mahatma Gandhi, the leading Hindu advocate of nonviolence and reconciliation with Muslims, ended the possibility of creating a single state in which Muslims and Hindus could live together peacefully. The predominantly Muslim portions of South Asia became the state of Pakistan, and the Hindu portions were allocated to India. Millions of Muslims on the Indian side of the tentative boundary were forcibly uprooted and marched across the border into Pakistan, with similar movements of Hindus into India (see Figure 3–18).

Pakistan and India never agreed on the location of the boundary separating the two countries especially in the northern region of Kashmir. The original partition gave India two-thirds of Kashmir even though a majority of its people were Muslims. In recent years,

Muslims on the Indian side of Kashmir have begun a guerrilla war to secure independence. India blames Pakistan for the unrest and vows to retain its portion of Kashmir; Pakistan argues that Kashmiris on both sides of the border should choose their own future in a vote, confident that the majority Muslim population would break away from India (Figure 5–15).

India's religious unrest is further complicated by the presence of 17 million Sikhs, whose religion combines elements of Islam and Hinduism. Sikhs have long resented that they were not given their own independent country when India was partitioned. Although they constitute only 2 percent of India's total population, Sikhs are a majority in the Indian state of Punjab, situated south of Kashmir along the border with Pakistan (Figure 5–15). Sikh extremists have fought for more control over the Punjab, or even complete independence from India.

Hindus versus Buddhists in Sri Lanka

Sri Lanka, an island country off the Indian coast, has been torn by fighting between the Sinhalese (Buddhists who speak an Indo-European language) and the Tamils (Hindus who speak a Dravidian language). Violence has erupted periodically between the two groups for hundreds of years. The Tamils, who constitute about 20 percent of the island's population, have repeatedly felt that they have been dis-

FIGURE 5–15 The India-Pakistan border. India and Pakistan dispute the location of their border. India claims the northeastern part of Pakistan, known as the Kashmir. India also accuses Pakistan of encouraging unrest in the Indian state of Jammu and Kashmir, where a majority of the people are Muslims. At the same time, India and China disagree on the location of their border in the Himalaya Mountains.

criminated against by the Sinhalese majority, which controls the government, military, and most of the businesses (Figure 5–16).

India, separated from Sri Lanka only by the 80-kilometer-wide (50-mile) Palk Strait, supported the Tamils with troops during the late 1980s. Indians, like the Tamils, are predominantly Hindus, and the Tamil language is spoken by about 60 million Indians. Many of the Tamil-speaking Hindus living in Sri Lanka were born in India and do not enjoy full protection of civil rights in Sri Lanka. Some Indian-born Tamils, however, have been permitted to become citizens of Sri Lanka.

Religious Wars in the Middle East

Even casual viewers of newscasts cannot avoid the impression that the Middle East is a perpetual battleground. Christians and Muslims historically have fought for control of Europe and the Middle East, and Jews have been unable to live in the homeland of their religion for most of the past 2,000 years.

To some extent, the hostility among Christians, Muslims, and Jews stems from their similar heritage. All three groups trace their origins to Abraham in the Old Testament narrative, but the religions diverged in ways that have made it difficult for them to share the same space on Earth. All three religions make strong claims to live in the eastern Mediterranean region and, more important to control territory they regard as holy.

Thirteen centuries ago, the Muslim army captured most of North Africa and Southwest Asia and converted most of the people from Christianity to Islam (Figure 5–7). Invading Europe at Gibraltar in 710, Muslims conquered most of the Iberian Peninsula, crossed the Pyrenees Mountains a few years later, and, for a time, occupied much of present-day France. Their initial advance in Europe was halted by the Franks (a West Germanic people) who were led by Charles Martel, at Poitiers, France, in 732. Muslims made further gains in Europe in subsequent years and continued to control portions of present-day Spain until 1492, but Martel's victory ensured that Christianity would be Europe's dominant religion.

Muslims captured Eastern Orthodoxy's most important city, Constantinople (present-day Istanbul in Turkey) in 1453 and advanced a few years later into Southeast Europe, as far north as present-day Bosnia-Herzegovina. The current civil war in that country is a legacy of the fifteenth-century Muslim invasion (see Chapter 7).

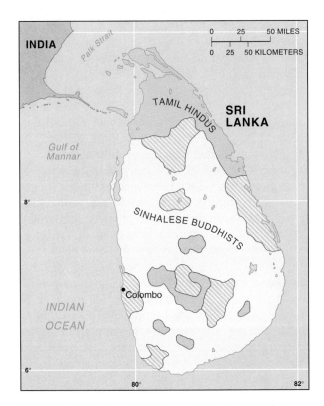

FIGURE 5–16 Tamils and Sinhalese in Sri Lanka. Sri Lanka is inhabited by two principal groups: Tamils and Sinhalese. The Tamils are Hindus who speak a Dravidian language, and the Sinhalese are Buddhists who speak an Indo-European language. Tamils feel that the Sinhalese, who are in the majority, discriminate against them. The stripes show areas where the two groups intermingle.

Battle for the Holy Land. Since the days of the Roman Empire, competing religious groups have battled to control Palestine, which is considered holy by Muslims, Christians, and Jews. To this day, you can count on frequent headlines of negotiations and terrorist activities from this region.

A special claim to Palestine is made by Judaism, as an ethnic religion. The major events in the Hebrew Bible took place there, and the religion's customs and rituals acquired meaning from the agricultural life of the ancient Hebrew tribe. As described earlier in the chapter, however, Jews were dispersed from Palestine by the Romans in A.D. 70, and only a handful were permitted to live in the region until the twentieth century. Most inhabitants of Palestine accepted Christianity, especially after the religion was officially adopted by the Roman Empire. But, Muslims captured Palestine and the holy city of Jerusalem in the seventh century and controlled the territory with only minor interruptions until 1917.

Muslims regard Jerusalem as their third holiest city, after Makkah and Madinah. The most important Muslim structure in Jerusalem is the mosque at the Dome of the Rock, built in 691. The rock is thought to be the place from which Muhammad ascended to heaven. Christians and Jews regard the rock as the altar on which Abraham prepared to sacrifice Isaac, although Muslims believe that Abraham prepared to sacrifice his other son Ishmael in Makkah.

Immediately to the south, the al-Aqsa mosque is built on the site of the two ancient Jewish temples. The only remaining portion of the Second Temple, which was destroyed by the Romans in A.D. 70, is the Western Wall. It is called the Wailing Wall by Christians and Muslims, because for many years Jews were allowed to visit the site only once a year to lament the destruction of their temple (Figure 5–17).

For their part, Christians consider Jerusalem and Palestine holy because the major events in Jesus's life were concentrated there. To recapture the Holy Land from its Muslim conquerors, European Christians launched a series of military campaigns, known as the Crusades, over a 150-year period. Crusaders captured Jerusalem from the Muslims in 1099 during the First Crusade, lost it in 1187 (which led to the Third Crusade), regained it in 1229 as part of a treaty ending the Sixth Crusade, and lost it again in 1244. Muslims then held Palestine continuously until 1917.

The Muslim Ottoman Empire controlled Palestine for most of the two centuries between 1516 and 1917. Upon the Empire's defeat in World War I, Great Britain took over Palestine under a mandate from the League of Nations and later from the United Nations. For a few years, the British allowed some Jews to return to Palestine, but immigration was restricted again during the 1930s in response to intense pressure by Arabs in the region (Figure 5–18a).

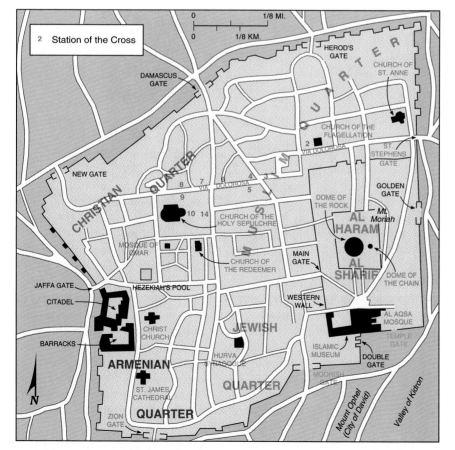

FIGURE 5–17 Shrines in Jerusalem. The Old City of Jerusalem contains holy shrines for three religions. The flattened hill on the eastern side of the Old City is the site of two structures holy to Muslims, the Dome of the Rock and the al-Aqsa Mosque, both of which were built on the site of ancient Jewish temples. The west side of the Old City contains the most important Christian shrines, including the Church of the Holy Sepulchre, where Jesus is thought to have been buried.

As violence initiated by both Jewish and Arab settlers escalated after World War II, the British announced their intention to withdraw from Palestine. The United Nations voted to partition Palestine into two independent states, one Jewish and one Arab Muslim. Jerusalem was to be an international city, open to all religions, and run by the United Nations (Figure 5–18b).

Recent Arab-Israeli Wars.

When the British withdrew in 1948, Jews declared an independent state of Israel within the boundaries prescribed by the U.N. resolution. The next day, neighboring Arab Muslim states declared war. Failing to defeat Israel, they signed an armistice in 1949. Israel won three more wars with its neighbors in 1956, 1967, and 1973.

After the 1949 armistice, Jerusalem became a divided city. The Old City of Jerusalem, which contained the famous religious shrines, became part of the Muslim country of Jordan. The newer, western portion of Jerusalem became part of Israel (Figure 5–18c).

During the Six-Day War in 1967, Israel captured the entire city and removed the barriers that had prevented Jews from visiting and living in the Old City of Jerusalem. Israel also captured four other territories in that war. From Jordan, it captured the West Bank (the territory west of the Jordan River taken by Jordan in the 1948–1949 war). From Syria, Israel acquired the Golan Heights. From Egypt came the Gaza Strip and Sinai Peninsula (Figure 5–18d).

Egypt's President Anwar Sadat and Israel's Prime Minister Menachem Begin signed a peace treaty in 1979 after a series of meetings with U.S. President Jimmy Carter at Camp David, Maryland. In accordance with the treaty, Israel returned the Sinai Peninsula, and, in return, Egypt recognized Israel's right to exist. Sadat was assassinated by Egyptian soldiers who were extremist Muslims opposed to compromising with Israel. But his successor, Hosni Mubarek, carried out the terms of the treaty.

More than a quarter-century after the Six-Day War, the status of the other territories occupied by Israel still has not been settled. In 1981, Israel formally annexed the Golan Heights, a sparsely inhabited, mountainous area from which Syria had launched attacks against Jewish settlements in the valley of the Sea of Galilee and the Jordan River. Israel is negotiating to return the Golan Heights to Syria in exchange for a peace treaty.

Palestinians.

The future of Gaza, the West Bank, and East Jerusalem has been especially difficult to resolve, because, in contrast to the Golan Heights and the Sinai Peninsula, it contains large populations. Israeli Jews are divided between those who wish to retain the occupied territories and those who wish to return most of them in exchange for peace treaties with neighboring states.

Most of the people living in the West Bank, Gaza, and East Jerusalem consider themselves Palestinians, and most are Muslims. The situation is further complicated by the fact that Palestinians include four groups other than those living in the occupied territories:

- Citizens of Israel who are Muslims rather than Jews
- People who fled from Israel to other countries after the 1948–1949 War
- People who fled from the West Bank or Gaza to other countries after the 1967 War
- Citizens of other countries, especially Jordan, Lebanon, Syria, Kuwait, and Saudi Arabia who identify themselves as Palestinians

The plight of the Palestinians who fled Israel or the occupied territories is especially acute. Many have lived for decades in "temporary" refugee camps in Lebanon, Syria, and Jordan, and they do not enjoy the protection of being citizens of any country.

Underlying the urgency for Israel to address the needs of the Palestinians are demographic patterns. Natural increase rates for Palestinians are 4 percent in the West Bank and 5 percent in Gaza, compared to about 1 percent for Jewish citizens of Israel. The difference is attributable to very high crude birth rates among the Palestinians—56 per 1,000 in Gaza and 46 per 1,000 in the West Bank. As a result of natural increase, the number of non-Jews in Israel and the occupied territories is expanding by 100,000 per year more than the number of Jews. If that difference continues, Jews will become a minority in Israel and the occupied territories in the first decade of the twenty-first century.

In recent years, growth in the number of Jews has kept pace with the non-Jewish population growth in Israel because of immigration of several hundred thousand Russians. Once the flow of immigrants from Russia slows, however, the different rates of natural increase between the Jewish and non-Jewish populations will increase pressure on Israel to relinquish control of the occupied territories.

FIGURE 5-18 Changing borders in the Middle East.

(a) Palestine under British control, 1922–1948.

(b) The 1947 U.N. plan to partition Palestine. The plan was to create two countries, with the boundaries drawn to separate the predominantly Jewish areas from the predominantly Arab Muslim areas. Jerusalem was intended to be an international city, run by the United Nations.

(c) Israel after the 1948–1949 War. The day after Israel declared its independence, several neighboring states began a war, which ended in an armistice. Israel's boundaries were extended beyond the U.N. partition to include the western suburbs of Jerusalem. Jordan gained control of the West Bank and East Jerusalem, including the Old City.

(d) The Middle East since the 1967 War. Israel captured the Golan Heights from Syria, the West Bank and East Jerusalem from Jordan, and the Sinai Peninsula and Gaza Strip from Egypt. Israel returned the Sinai to Egypt in 1979 and Gaza and a portion of the West Bank to the Palestinians in 1994. Israel still controls the Golan Heights, most of the West Bank, and East Jerusalem.

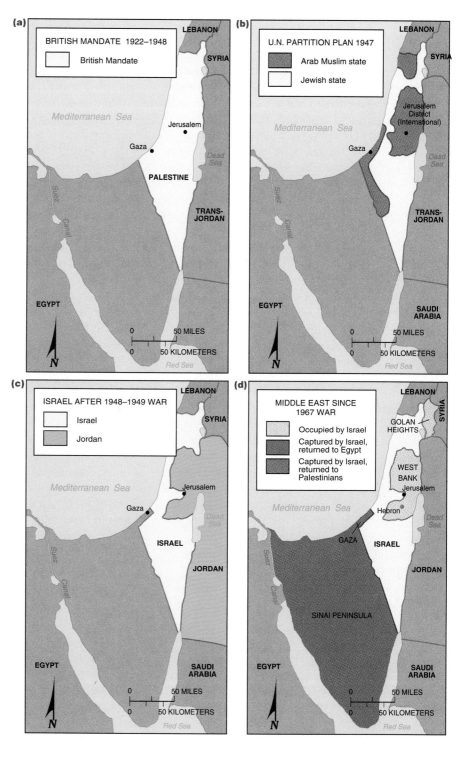

In 1994, Israel turned over Gaza and a portion of the West Bank surrounding the city of Hebron to the Palestinians. The Palestine Liberation Organization became the governing organization for Gaza and the Hebron area. Palestinians have achieved their ambition of controlling their own country, but they do not agree on how to regard their arrangement: settle for a country consisting of Gaza and a portion of the West Bank, or continue fighting Israel for the entire territory between the Jordan River and the Mediterranean Sea.

Iraq's Invasion of Kuwait. In recent years, wars have been fought in the Middle East among Muslim countries. Iraq and Iran fought during much of the 1980s over control of the Shatt-al-Arab waterway near the border between the countries. The war ended in a stalemate in 1988, after 8 years of war that resulted in several hundred thousand deaths.

In 1990, Iraq invaded Kuwait, claiming that the small oil-rich country belonged to it historically until taken away by the colonial powers earlier in the twentieth century. Iraq's case for invading Kuwait gained little support worldwide. Many small countries viewed Iraq's takeover of tiny Kuwait as a threat to their ability to remain independent from more powerful neighbors. Others supported military action to reduce Iraq's ability to attack Israel. But for many countries, protection of sources of petroleum in Kuwait and Saudi Arabia was the most important consideration in opposing Iraq's actions.

The United Nations, led by the United States, attacked in 1991 to expel Iraq from Kuwait. Iraq was defeated, but its leader Saddam Hussein remained in power.

The world maps of language (Figure 4–1) and religion (Figure 5–1) portray a large homogeneous region from northern Africa to southwestern Asia, where Arabic is the predominant language and Islam the predominant religion. The fragmentation of the Middle East into two dozen countries is a legacy of centuries of domination by the Ottomans (based in present-day Turkey), British, French, and other colonial powers. The British, in particular, made conflicting promises of land to Middle Eastern groups in exchange for their support in fighting the Ottomans during World War I (see Geography in Action box).

According to the Ba'ath party, which controls Iraq, this region of apparent cultural homogeneity comprises one unified nation of people. For the Ba'ath party, a major obstacle to Middle Eastern cultural unity is Israel with its Jewish majority. The Ba'ath party wants Israel eliminated as the single prominent exception to their perception of regional cultural unity.

The Ba'ath party also believes that political fragmentation of the Middle East has resulted in an unfair distribution of wealth because not every country possesses petroleum. Unifying the region would encourage sharing of the wealth generated from selling petroleum.

For geographers, the position of the Ba'ath party, as well as the reaction of the international community to Iraq's invasion of Kuwait, shows the global impact of cultural patterns and the interrelationship among cultural and economic factors. U.N. efforts to end wars in other regions of the world have been less forceful than in Iraq, in large measure because other regions do not have the economic assets of the Middle East, notably a large percentage of the world's petroleum reserves.

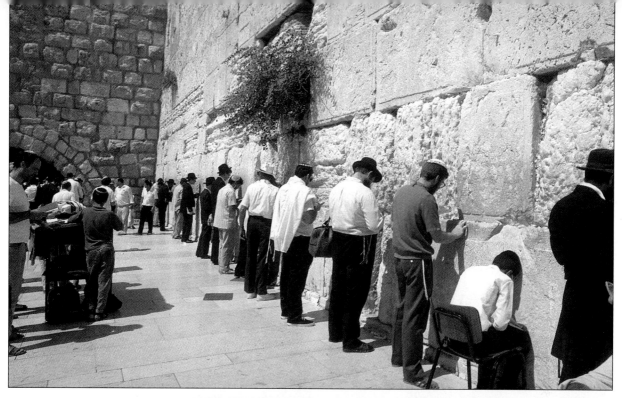

Jews pray in front of the Western Wall in Jerusalem (top). The wall is the only remaining portion of the Second Temple, which was destroyed in A.D. 70. For hundreds of years, Jews were allowed to visit the site only once a year. Jews are still restricted from visiting the rest of the temple site because it is occupied by structures holy to Muslims, including the Dome of the Rock (bottom), where Muhammad is thought to have ascended to heaven (Harold Glaser/Gamma-Liaison, Inc., top; Brent Petersen/The Stock Market, bottom.).

Civil War in Lebanon

Religious conflict in the Middle East is not confined to Israel. Lebanon, Israel's northern neighbor, exemplifies how complex religious differences and hostilities can become. Although it is smaller than Connecticut, Lebanon's 3.4 million people are members of seventeen officially recognized religious communities. Lebanon's religious groups coexisted fairly peacefully from the time of independence in 1943 until the mid-1970s. Since then, the country has been severely damaged by civil war among the religious factions.

The precise distribution of religions is unknown, because no census has been taken since 1932. Current estimate is about 60 percent Muslim, 33 percent Christian, and 7 percent Druze (Table 1).

TABLE 1
Religious groups in Lebanon

Group	Percentage of Population
Maronite	20
Greek Orthodox	5
Armenian Christian	4
Greek Catholic	4
Total Christian	33
Shiite	36
Sunni (Lebanese)	17
Sunni (Palestinian)	7
Total Muslim	60
Druze	7

Of the *Christian* minority, the largest Lebanese sect is *Maronite,* which split from the Roman Catholic church in the seventh century and was ruled by the patriarch of Antioch. Although some reconciliation has been made with the Roman Catholic church, the liturgy is still performed in the ancient Syrian language. Approximately one-fifth of Lebanon's total population and 60 percent of its Christians are Maronites.

The second largest Christian sect is *Greek Orthodox,* one of the Eastern Orthodox churches that split from Roman Catholicism in the eleventh century. Lebanon's Greek Orthodox Christians use a Byzantine liturgy, because Eastern Orthodox Christians were led by the patriarch of Constantinople from the time of the split with Roman Catholicism in 1054 until the city of Constantinople was captured by Muslims in 1453. Greek Orthodox Christians constitute approximately 5 percent of Lebanon's total population.

Other relatively small and little-known Christian sects in Lebanon include *Greek Catholic, Armenian, Syrian Orthodox (Jacobites),* and *Chaldeans (Assyrian).* Greek Catholics split from the Greek Orthodox church and migrated to Lebanon because of persecution elsewhere. Armenians separated from the Roman Catholic church in the fifth century and have a patriarch in Armenia.

Of the Muslim majority, about 36 percent of Lebanese belong to one of several *Shiite Muslim* sects. Largest is *Mitwali,* but in recent years, more militant sects have gained power, especially *Hezbollah,* the *Party of God,* which has taken American and European hostages. The *Sunni* branch, accepted by about 90 percent of the world's Muslims, is practiced by 24 percent of Lebanon's population, including Palestinian refugees.

Lebanon also has non-Christian and non-Muslim groups, most important of which is the *Druze* (about 7 percent of the population). The Druze religion combines elements of Islam and Christianity, but many of the rituals are kept secret from outsiders.

Lebanon's Constitution

In 1943, to preserve the identity of each religious group, Lebanon's constitution required that each religion be represented in the governing body according to its percentage in the 1932 census. Accordingly, the 99 members of the Chamber of Deputies comprised 54 Christians, including 30 Maronites, 11 Greek Orthodox, 6 Greek Catholics, 4 Armenian Christians, and 3 other Christians; 39 Muslims, including 20 Sunnis and 19 Shiites; and 6 Druzes. Thus, the 30 Maronite candidates with the largest vote totals were elected, as were the top vote getters for the other religions.

By unwritten convention, the president of Lebanon was a Maronite Christian, the premier a Sunni Muslim, the speaker of the Chamber of Deputies a Shiite Muslim, and the foreign minister a Greek Orthodox Christian. Other cabinet members and civil servants were similarly apportioned among the religions.

The system survived peacefully until 1975, when fighting among the different religious groups crippled the state. The delicate balance was upset by the arrival of a large number of Palestinian refugees after the 1967 Arab-Israeli War. The Palestine Liberation Organization (PLO) controlled much of southern Lebanon, where the refugee camps were clustered, and from which the PLO launched attacks against Israel. The United States sent marines to Lebanon in 1982 to supervise the PLO's evacuation, but they were removed in February 1984, 4 months after 241 of them died in their barracks from the explosion of a truck wired with a bomb.

Lebanon's Muslims were generally sympathetic to the PLO's cause, while most Lebanese Christians supported Israel. With the breakdown of the national government, each religious group formed a private army or militia to guard its territory.

Lebanon's deeper problem was how to deal with changing social and economic conditions. When the governmental system was created, Christians constituted a majority and controlled the country's main businesses, but as the Muslims became the majority, they demanded political and economic equality.

Lebanon is relatively peaceful now. A 1990 constitution divided Parliament seats and cabinet positions equally between Christians and Muslims. A Christian still is president, but most powers were transferred to the Muslim prime minister.

The real winner in the Lebanon civil war was Syria, which has a historical claim over the territory. The Syrian army controls much of Lebanon, once religious groups disbanded their private militias, and the government now is closely allied to Syria. The capital Beirut is being rebuilt, although it has a long way to go to reclaim its one-time reputation as a major banking and entertainment center in the Middle East. But after two decades of religious civil war in which 150,000 Lebanese have died, much of the country's economy and buildings lie in ruins.

Summary　The key issues of this chapter demonstrate the impact of religion on the cultural landscape. Here again are the key issues for Chapter 5.

1. How are religions distributed?

The world has three important universalizing religions: Christianity, Islam, and Buddhism. Each originated in a particular core area and diffused to other portions of Earth's surface. In addition, several ethnic religions can be identified that are closely rooted to the social customs and physical environment of particular places on Earth.

2. How do religions organize space?

Elements of the physical environment are organized by different religions in different ways. Some religions incorporate agricultural practices and environmental processes into their systems of belief and rituals. Religions may consider as holy certain areas of Earth's surface, either because of spiritual content or from their association with human events. Adherents are encouraged to make pilgrimages to these places. Some religions organize their territory into a rigid administrative structure to disseminate religious doctrine, while others are locally autonomous.

3. What is the impact of religion on the landscape?

Some religions establish sacred structures where adherents gather to pray. In Christianity, such structures are important as places for congregational worship. Other religions emphasize individual or family worship and reserve holy structures for infrequent visits. Religions affect the landscape in other ways: religious communities are built, religious toponyms mark the landscape, and extensive tracts are reserved for burying the dead.

4. What territorial conflicts arise because of religion?

With Earth's surface dominated by four large religions, expansion of the territory occupied by one religion may reduce the territory of another. In addition, religions must compete for control of territory with nonreligious ideas, notably communism and economic modernization.

CASE STUDY REVISITED
Conflict in the Middle East

Geographers look at the reciprocal relationships between patterns on the landscape and religious practices. Religions draw meaning from the environment and, in turn, modify the environment. This geographic perspective helps us understand the context for religious conflicts in the Middle East.

Israel sees itself as a very small country—20,000 square kilometers (8,000 square miles)—with a Jewish majority, surrounded by a region of hostile Muslim Arabs encompassing more than 25 million square kilometers (10 million square miles).

In dealing with its neighbors, Israel considers two elements of the local landscape especially meaningful. First, the country's major population centers are quite close to international borders, making them vulnerable to surprise attack. The country's two largest cities, Tel Aviv and Haifa, are only 20 and 60 kilometers (12 and 37 miles) from Jordan, and the third largest city, Jerusalem, is adjacent to the border.

The second geographic problem from Israel's perspective derives from local landforms. The northern half of Israel is a strip of land 80 kilometers (50 miles) wide between the Mediterranean Sea and the Jordan River. It is divided into three roughly parallel physical regions (Figure 5–19a):

- A coastal plain along the Mediterranean, extending inland as much as 25 kilometers (15 miles) and as little as a few meters
- A series of hills reaching elevations above 1,000 meters (3,300 feet)
- The Jordan River valley, much of which is below sea level

The United Nations plan for the partition of Palestine in 1947, as modified by the armistice ending the 1948–1949 War, allocated most of the coastal plain to Israel; Jordan took most of the hills between the coastal plain and the Jordan River valley, a region generally called the West Bank (of the Jordan River). Farther north, Israel's territory extended eastward to the Jordan River valley, but Syria controlled the highlands east of the valley, known as the Golan Heights.

Between 1948 and 1967, Jordan and Syria used the hills as staging areas to attack Israeli settlements on the adjacent coastal plain and in the Jordan River valley. During the 1967 war, Israel captured these highlands to stop attacks on the lowland population concentrations. A generation later, Israel still holds the Golan Heights and most of the West Bank, and the security concerns of the past have faded. In part, technological changes have made obsolete the strategic benefits of controlling the highlands. During the 1991 Gulf War, Iraq was able to attack Israel with SCUD missiles from 400 kilometers (250 miles) away.

To Palestinians, Middle Eastern geography looks very different. After capturing the West Bank from Jordan in 1967, Israel permitted Jewish settlers to construct more than 100 settlements in the territory (Figure 5–19b). Some Israelis built settlements in the West Bank because they regarded the territory as an integral part of the biblical Jewish homeland, known as Judea and Samaria. Others migrated to the settlements because of a severe shortage of affordable housing inside Israel's pre-1967 borders. Although Jewish settlers comprise only about 7 percent of the West Bank population, Palestinians see their presence as a reflection of Israel's reluctance to grant independence to the occupied territory.

Conflict among religious groups in the Middle East, as well as in other regions of the world, has been especially intense in recent years because of the rise of **fundamentalism**, which is a literal interpretation and strict adherence to basic principles of a religion (or a religious branch, denomination, or sect). In a world increasingly dominated by a global culture and economy, religious fundamentalism is one of the most important ways that a group maintains a distinctive cultural identity.

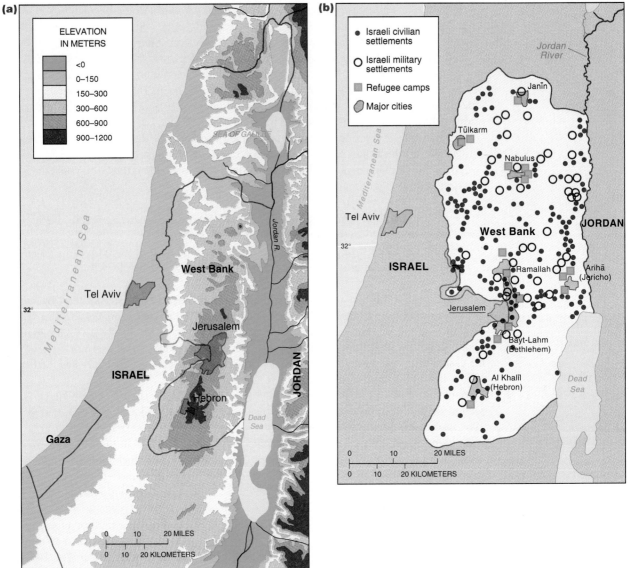

FIGURE 5–19 The West Bank. (a) Physical geography of Israel and West Bank. The land between the Mediterranean Sea and the Jordan River is divided into three roughly parallel physical regions: a narrow coastal plain along the Mediterranean, a series of hills reaching elevations above 1,000 meters (3,300 feet), and the Jordan River valley. Between 1948 and 1967, Israel's boundaries encompassed primarily the coastal lowlands, and Jordan and Syria controlled the highlands. During the 1967 War, Israel captured these highlands and retained them to stop attacks on population concentrations in the Jordan River valley and the coastal plain. (b) Since Israel captured the West Bank in 1967, Jewish settlers have constructed more than 100 settlements in the territory. More than 50,000 Jews now live in the West Bank, about 7 percent of the territory's total population.

Key Terms

Animism Belief that objects, such as plants and stones, or natural events, such as thunderstorms and earthquakes, have a discrete spirit and conscious life.

Autonomous religion A religion that does not have a central authority but shares ideas and cooperates informally.

Branch A large and fundamental division within a religion.

Caste The class or distinct hereditary order into which a Hindu is assigned according to religious law.

Cosmogony A set of religious beliefs concerning the origin of the universe.

Denomination A division within a branch of a religion.

Diocese The basic unit of geographic organization in the Roman Catholic church.

Ethnic religion A religion with a relatively concentrated spatial distribution whose principles are likely to be based on the physical characteristics of the particular location in which its adherents are concentrated.

Fundamentalism Literal interpretation and strict adherence to basic principles of a religion (or a religious branch, denomination, or sect).

Ghetto During the Middle Ages, a neighborhood in a city set up by law to be inhabited only by Jews; now used to denote a section of a city in which members of any minority group live because of social, legal, or economic pressure.

Hierarchical religion A religion in which a central authority exercises a high degree of control.

Missionary An individual who helps to diffuse a universalizing religion.

Monotheism The doctrine or belief of the existence of only one god.

Pilgrimage A journey to a place considered sacred for religious purposes.

Sect A relatively small denominational group that has broken away from an established church.

Solstice Time when the sun is farthest from the equator.

Universalizing religion A religion that attempts to appeal to all people, not just those living in a particular location.

Thinking Geographically

1. A widespread view outside of the Middle East is that peace between Israel and its neighbors can be achieved by trading land for peace. In other words, Israel would return the territories it occupies in exchange for enforceable peace treaties. What are some of the obstacles to acceptance of this formula?

2. Sharp differences in demographic characteristics, such as natural increase, crude birth, and migration rates, can be seen among Jews, Christians, and Muslims in the Middle East and between Roman Catholics and Protestants in Northern Ireland. How might demographic differences affect future relationships among the groups in these two regions?

3. People carry their religious beliefs with them when they migrate. Over time, change occurs in the regions from which most U.S. immigrants originate, and in the U.S. regions where they settle. How has the distribution of U.S. religious groups been affected by these changes?

4. To what extent have increased interest in religion and ability to practice religious rites served as forces for unification in Eastern Europe and the countries that formerly were part of the Soviet Union? Has the growing role of religion in the region fostered political instability? Explain.

5. Why does Islam seem strange and threatening to some people in predominantly Christian countries? To what extent is this attitude shaped by knowledge of the teachings of Muhammad and the Quran, and to what extent is it based on lack of knowledge of the religion?

Further Readings

Al Faruqi, Isma'il R., and Lois Lamaya' Al Faruqi. *The Cultural Atlas of Islam*. New York: Macmillan, 1986.

Al Faruqi, Isma'il R., and David E. Sopher. *Historical Atlas of the Religions of the World*. New York: Macmillan, 1974.

Archer, John Clark, and Carl E. Purinton. *Faiths Men Live By,* 2d ed. New York: Ronald Press, 1958.

Bapat, P. V., ed. *2500 Years of Buddhism*. Delhi: Government of India Ministry of Information and Broadcasting, 1959.

Barraclough, Geoffrey, ed. *The "Times" Concise Atlas of World History*. Maplewood, NJ: Hammond, 1982.

Barrett, David B., ed. *World Christian Encyclopedia*. Oxford: Oxford University Press, 1982.

Berger, Arthur, Paul Badham, Austin H. Kutscher, Joyce Berger, Michael Perry, and John Beloff, eds. *Perspectives on Death and Dying: Cross-Cultural and Multi-Disciplinary Views*. Philadelphia: The Charles Press, 1989.

Bhardwaj, Surinder M. *Hindu Places of Pilgrimage in India*. Berkeley: University of California Press, 1973.

Cooper, Adrian. "New Directions in the Geography of Religion." *Area* 24 (June 1992): 123–29.

Curry-Roper, Janet M. "Contemporary Christian Eschatologies and Their Relation to Environmental Stewardship." *Professional Geographer* 42 (May 1990): 157–69.

Fickeler, Paul. "Fundamental Questions in the Geography of Religions." In *Readings in Cultural Geography,* ed. by Philip L. Wagner and Marvin W. Mikesell. Chicago: University of Chicago Press, 1962.

Francaviglia, Richard V. *The Mormon Landscape*. New York: AMS Press, 1978.

Gaustad, E. S. *Historical Atlas of Religion in America*. New York: Harper and Row, 1962.

Hardon, John A. *Religions of the World,* 2 vols. Garden City, NY: Image Books, 1968.

Heatwole, Charles A. "Exploring the Geography of America's Religious Denominations: A Presbyterian Example." *Journal of Geography* 76 (March 1977): 99–104.

_____ "Sectarian Ideology and Church Architecture." *Geographical Review* 79 (January 1989): 63–78.

Hiller, Carl E. *Caves to Cathedrals: Architecture of the World's Great Religions*. Boston: Little, Brown, 1974.

Jackson, Richard H. "Mormon Perception and Settlement." *Annals of the Association of American Geographers* 68 (September 1978): 317–34.

_____, and Roger Henrie. "Perception of Sacred Space." *Journal of Cultural Geography* 3 (Spring/Summer 1983): 94–107.

Kay, Jeanne. "Human Dominion over Nature in the Hebrew Bible." *Annals of the Association of American Geographers* 79 (June 1989): 214–32.

Kong, L. "Geography and Religion: Trends and Prospects." *Progress in Human Geography* 14: 355–71.

Levine, Gregory J. "On the Geography of Religion." *Transactions of the Institute of British Geographers,* New Series 11, no. 4 (1987): 428–40.

Ling, Trevor. *A History of Religion East and West*. London: Macmillan, 1968.

Meinig, Donald W. "The Mormon Culture Region: Strategies and Patterns in the Geography of the American West, 1847–1964." *Annals of the Association of American Geographers* 55 (June 1965): 191–220.

Newman, David. *Population, Settlement and Conflict: Israel and the West Bank*. Cambridge: Cambridge University Press, 1991.

Nolan, Mary Lee, and Sidney Nolan. *Christian Pilgrimage in Modern Western Europe*. Chapel Hill: University of North Carolina Press, 1989.

Quinn, Bernard, Herman Anderson, Martin Bradley, Paul Geotting, and Peggy Shriver. *Churches and Church Membership in the U.S.* Atlanta: Glenmary Research Center, 1982.

Short, Ernest. *A History of Religious Architecture*. New York: W. W. Norton, 1951.

Shortridge, James R. "Patterns of Religion in the United States." *Geographical Review* 66 (October 1976): 420–34.

Smith, Huston. *The Religions of Man*. New York: Harper and Bros., 1958.

Sopher, David E. *The Geography of Religions*. Englewood Cliffs, NJ: Prentice Hall, 1967.

_____. "Geography and Religions." *Progress in Human Geography* 5 (1981): 510–24.

Stump, Roger W. "Regional Variations in Denominational Switching among White Protestants." *Professional Geographer* 39 (November 1987), pp. 438–49.

Thompson, Jan, and Mel Thompson. *The R. E. Atlas: World Religions in Maps and Notes*. London: Edward W. Arnold, 1986.

Topping, Gary. "Religion in the West." *Journal of American Culture* 3 (Summer 1980): 330–50.

Zelinsky, Wilbur. "An Approach to the Religious Geography of the United States: Patterns of Church Membership in 1952." *Annals of the Association of American Geographers* 51 (June 1961): 139–67.

PEOPLE, PLACES AND CHANGE

Population Transition in Italy

The Annenberg
CPB Project

The video's narrator points out that Italy is the physical center of the Roman Catholic church, which condemns contraception and abortion. How then, the narrator asks, can Italians equate a low birth rate with religious practice?

Dr. Giorgio Bonoli [resident of Bologna, Italy]	[Translated from Italian] I think that Catholic couples, and even young Italian Catholics, have for some time now made a distinction between their religious conscience and what might be considered as a dictate from the Church. Therefore they don't feel bound within their conscience to take notice of the rules which they probably don't agree with. But this doesn't mean that they feel any less Catholic.
Susanne Carella Sigra [resident of Rome]	I believe I'm a Catholic, but life has to be practical! You have to try and act according to your various needs. According to your personal problems, the type of family and the type of work you do.
Commentator	Religion is however still a strong traditional influence over Italians. One factor which helps explain the extreme decline in fertility is the Italian attitude to marriage and cohabitation.
Professor Antonio Golini [Institute for Population Research, Rome]	[Translated from Italian] In Italy we have low marriage rates, but we have very low cohabitation and very low share of births out of wedlock. So consider that in some countries of Northern Europe, births out of wedlock are between thrity and fifty percent. In Italy we are about six percent, so much much lower.
Varlerio Terra Abrami [National Institute of Statistics, Rome]	I think that as for the specific aspects of marriage, Italy's very different from other European countries, even different from some Southern European countries like Portugal, for example.

6

SOCIAL CUSTOMS ON THE LANDSCAPE

What did you do today? Presumably, your first activity was to get out of bed—for some of us the most difficult task of the day. Shortly thereafter, you got dressed. What did you wear? That depended on both the weather (shorts or sweater) and the day's activities (suit or T-shirt).

After work or school you ate dinner (pizza or salad). Later, you may have some free time for leisure activities (watching television, listening to music, or playing sports).

This narrative may not precisely describe you, but you can recognize the day of a "typical"

KEY ISSUES

- How do social customs originate and diffuse?
- What factors create unique folk regions?
- What factors influence the distribution of popular customs?
- What problems result from worldwide convergence of popular customs?

North American. The routine described and the choices mentioned in parentheses, however, do not accurately reflect the practices of many people elsewhere in the world. Imagine how people from other cultures would react if they were suddenly placed in the room. Despite striking differences in their social customs, your visitors would be familiar with some of your customs, as Earth becomes more of a "global village." Your visitors might even, within a short period of time, change their customs.

ABORIGINE, NEAR KIMBERLEY, AUSTRALIA, AWAITING CORROBOREE, A NOCTURNAL "CELEBRATION OF IMPORTANT EVENTS". (PAUL CHESLEY/TONEY STONE IMAGES)

The Aboriginal Artists of Australia at Lincoln Center

The Aboriginal Artists of Australia, a group of aborigines living in the isolated Australian interior, visited New York a few years ago and danced at the Lincoln Center for the Performing Arts. Their series of dances, handed down from their ancestors, reflected their customs and local landscape.

The aboriginal dancers challenged their New York audience to understand the meaning of their movements and music. Aborigines consider such dances an essential social custom, reflecting their daily experiences and activities, such as the need for rain or the behavior of particular animals. At best, the New York audience could recognize that the dances were meaningful to the aborigines. But understanding was inevitably limited by the lack of a comparable role for dance in Western customs.

The geographic contrast between the aboriginal dancers and the New York theater audience was heightened by differing attitudes toward the physical environment. The aboriginal dancers respond to specific landscape features and environmental conditions in their Australian homeland. In contrast, New York's Lincoln Center is not a product of an isolated and unique set of social customs. Nothing at Lincoln Center is indigenous to the unique conditions of the site—not the arrangement of structures, the building materials, the variety of performances, or the performers' places of origin. Lincoln Center reflects the diffusion of social customs across a large portion of Earth's surface. Lincoln Center exemplifies how, through interaction and integration, regional differences in social and physical characteristics become less important in the distribution of cultural activities.

Geographers focus on two aspects of social customs. First is spatial distribution. Each social custom, such as wearing jeans, has its own. Geographers study the custom's origin, diffusion, and integration with other social characteristics. The second is the relation between social customs and the physical environment. Geographers study how each social group takes particular elements from the environment in their culture and constructs landscapes ("built environments") that modify nature in distinctive ways.

Habit, custom, and culture: we must clearly distinguish among these three terms. A **habit** is a repetitive act that a particular *individual* performs, such as wearing jeans to class every day. A **custom** is a repetitive act of a *group,* performed to the extent that it becomes *characteristic* of the group—most American university students wear jeans to class every day. Unlike custom, habit does not imply that the act has been adopted by most of the society's population. A custom is therefore a habit that a group of people has widely adopted. *Culture* is one of the hardest words to define in English. In Chapter 1, we defined it as "the body of customary beliefs, social forms, and material traits of a group of people."

Social customs fall into two basic categories: folk and popular. **Folk customs** are traditionally practiced primarily by small, homogeneous groups living in isolated rural areas—such as wearing a sarong (a loose skirt made of a long strip of cloth wrapped around the body) in Malaysia or a sari (a long cloth draped so that one end forms a skirt and the other a head or shoulder covering) in India. **Popular customs** are found in large, heterogeneous societies that share certain habits despite differences in other personal characteristics—such as wearing jeans.

The most significant geographic process that distinguishes popular from folk customs is *interaction,* or lack of it. A group develops distinctive customs from experiencing local social and physical conditions in isolation from other groups. Even groups living in proximity may generate a variety of folk customs in a limited geographic area because of limited communication. Landscapes dominated by folk customs change relatively little over time.

In contrast, popular customs are based on rapid simultaneous global interaction through communications systems, transportation networks, and other modern technology. Rapid diffusion facilitates frequent changes in popular customs. Thus, folk customs are likely to vary from place to place at a given

time, whereas popular customs are likely to vary from time to time at a given place.

In Earth's "global village," popular customs are becoming more dominant, threatening the survival of unique folk customs. These folk customs—along with language and religion—provide a unique identity to each group of people who occupy a specific portion of Earth's surface. The disappearance of local folk customs—along with the diffusion of the English language and universalizing religions—reduces cultural diversity in the world and the intellectual stimulation that arises from differences in background.

The dominance of popular customs can also threaten the quality of the environment. Folk customs derived from local natural elements may be more sensitive to the protection and enhancement of their environment. Popular customs are less likely to reflect the diversity of local physical conditions and are more likely to modify the environment in accordance with global values.

As we study both folk customs and popular customs, we will examine two facets of each. The first are customs deriving from survival activities of everyone's daily life—food, clothing, and shelter. Each social group provides these in its own way. The second are customs involving leisure activities—the arts and recreation. Each social group has its own definition of meaningful art and stimulating recreation.

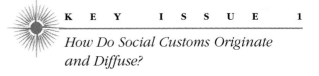

KEY ISSUE 1

How Do Social Customs Originate and Diffuse?

- Origin of Folk and Popular Customs
- Diffusion of Folk and Popular Customs

Each social custom has a unique spatial distribution, but, in general, distribution is more extensive for popular customs than for folk customs. Two basic factors help explain the spatial differences between popular and folk customs: the process of origin and the pattern of diffusion.

Origin of Folk and Popular Customs

Social customs originate at a hearth, a center of innovation. Folk customs often have anonymous hearths, originating from an anonymous source, at an unknown date, through an unidentified originator. They also often have multiple hearths, originating independently in isolated places.

In contrast to folk customs, popular customs are most often a product of economically developed countries, especially in North America, Western Europe, and Japan. Popular music and fast food are good examples. They arise from a combination of advances in industrial technology and increased leisure time. Industrial technology permits the uniform reproduction of objects in large quantities (CDs, stylish clothing, pizzas). Many of these objects help people enjoy leisure time, which has increased as a result of the widespread change in the labor force from predominantly agricultural to predominantly jobs in service and manufacturing.

Origin of Folk Music

Music exemplifies the differences in the origins of folk and popular customs. According to a Chinese legend, music was invented in 2697 B.C. when the Emperor Huang Ti sent Ling Lun to cut bamboo poles that would produce a sound matching the call of the phoenix bird. But, in reality, folk songs are usually composed anonymously and transmitted orally. A song may be modified from one generation to the next as conditions change, but the content is most often derived from events in daily life that are familiar to the majority of the people.

Folk songs tell a story or convey information about daily activities such as farming, life-cycle events (birth, death, and marriage), or mysterious events such as storms and earthquakes. In Vietnam, where most people are subsistence farmers, information about agricultural technology is conveyed through folk songs. For example, the following folk song provides advice about the difference between seeds planted in the summer and winter:

Ma chiêm ba tháng không già
Ma mùa tháng ru ôi ắt la ´không non.*

This song can be translated as follows:

While seedlings for the summer crop are not old when they are three months of age,
Seedlings for the winter crop are certainly not young when they are one-and-a-half months old.

The song hardly sounds lyrical to a Western ear. But when American folk songs appear in cold print, similar themes emerge, even if the specific information conveyed about the environment differs.

Folk customs may have multiple origins because of noncommunication among groups in different places. U.S. country music provides a recent example of the process by which folk customs originate independently at multiple hearths. Geographer George Carney identified four major hearths of country music in the southeastern United States during the late nineteenth and early twentieth centuries: southern Appalachia, central Tennessee and Kentucky, the Ozark plateau and Ouachita Mountains of western Arkansas and eastern Oklahoma, and north-central Texas (Figure 6-1). Carney documented these hearths on the basis of the birthplaces of performers and other individuals active in the field.

Origin of Popular Music

In contrast to folk music, popular music is written by specific individuals for the purpose of being sold to a large number of people. It displays a high degree of technical skill and is frequently capable of being performed only in a studio with electronic equipment.

Popular music as we know it today originated around 1900. At that time, the main popular musical entertainment in the United States and Western Europe was the variety show, called the *music hall* in the United Kingdom and *vaudeville* in the United States. To provide songs for music halls and vaudeville, a music industry developed in New York, along 28th Street between Fifth Avenue and Broadway, a district that became known as Tin Pan Alley (Figure 6-2). The name derived from the sound of pianos being furiously pounded by people called song pluggers, who were demonstrating tunes to publishers.

Tin Pan Alley was home to song writers, music publishers, orchestrators, and arrangers. Companies in Tin Pan Alley originally tried to sell as many printed song sheets as possible, although sales of recordings ultimately became the most important measure of success. Tin Pan Alley later moved uptown to Broadway and 32nd Street, and then along Broad-

---

*From John Blacking and Joann W. Kealiinohomoku, eds., *The Performing Arts: Music and Dance* (The Hague: Mouton, 1979), p. 144. Reprinted by permission of the publisher.

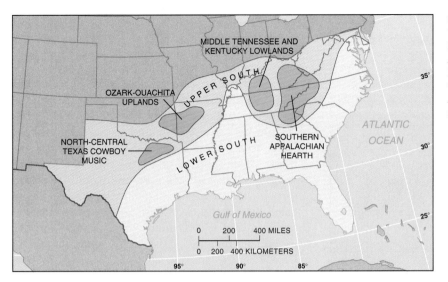

FIGURE 6-1 Origin of country music. U.S. country music has four major hearths, or regions of origin: southern Appalachia, central Tennessee and Kentucky, the Ozark Plateau and Ouachita Mountains of western Arkansas and eastern Oklahoma, and north-central Texas.

way between 42nd and 50th streets. After World War II, Tin Pan Alley disappeared as recorded music became more important.

The diffusion of American popular music worldwide began in earnest during World War II, when the Armed Forces Radio Network broadcast music to American soldiers and to citizens of countries where American forces were stationed or fighting. English became the international language for popular music. Today popular musicians in Japan, Poland, Russia, and other countries often write and perform in English, even though few people in their audiences understand the language.

Diffusion of Folk and Popular Customs

The broadcasting of American popular music on Armed Forces Radio illustrates the difference in diffusion of folk and popular customs. The spread of popular customs typically follows the process of hierarchical diffusion from hearths or nodes of innovation. In the United States, prominent nodes of innovation for popular customs include Hollywood, California, for the film industry and Madison Avenue in New York City for advertising agencies. Popular customs diffuse rapidly and extensively through the use of modern communications and transportation.

In contrast, folk customs are transmitted from one location to another more slowly and on a smaller scale, primarily through migration rather than electronic communication. The spread of folk customs is an example of relocation diffusion, the spread of a characteristic through migration. We will now look at several examples.

The Amish: Example of Relocation Diffusion

Amish customs illustrate how relocation diffusion influences the distribution of folk customs. The Amish have distinctive religious practices, clothing, farming, and other customs. They leave a unique pattern on landscapes where they settle. Shunning mechanical and electrical power, the Amish still travel by horse and buggy and continue to use hand tools for farming.

Although the Amish population in the United States numbers only about 70,000, a mere 0.03 percent of the total population, Amish folk customs remain visible on the landscape in at least seventeen states. The distribution of Amish folk customs across a major portion of the U.S. landscape is explained by examining the diffusion of their customs through migration.

In the 1600s, a Swiss Mennonite bishop named Jakob Ammann gathered a group of followers who became known as the Amish. The Amish originated in Bern, Switzerland; Alsace in northeastern France; and the Palatinate region of southwestern Germany. They migrated to other portions of northwestern Europe in the 1700s, primarily for religious freedom. In Europe, the Amish did not develop distinctive language, clothing, or farming customs and gradually merged with various Mennonite church groups.

Several hundred Amish families migrated to North America in two waves. The first group, primarily

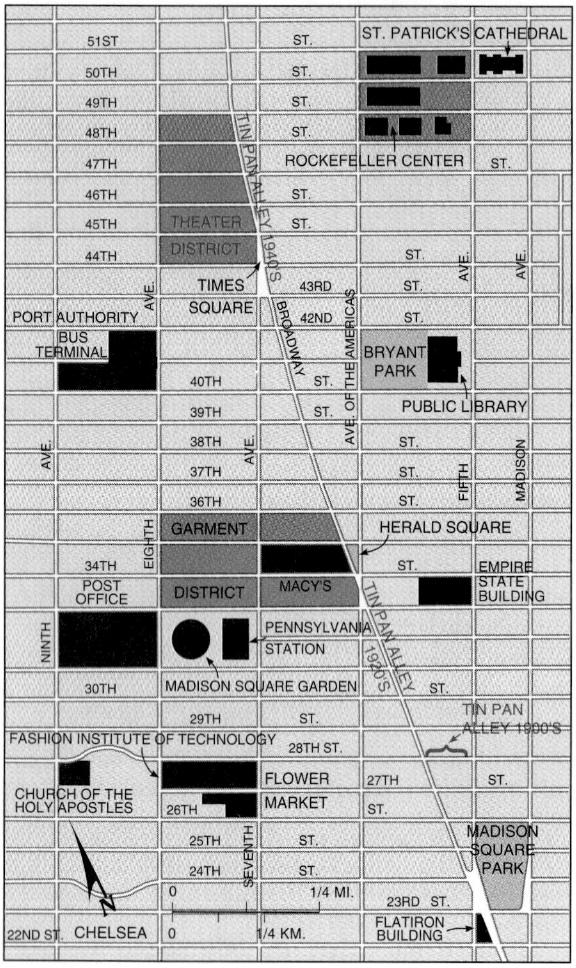

FIGURE 6-2 Tin Pan Alley. At the beginning of this century, most writers and publishers of popular music were clustered in New York City in a few buildings along 28th Street between Fifth Avenue and Broadway, which became known as Tin Pan Alley. Tin Pan Alley relocated north to 32nd Street and Broadway, and then along Broadway between 42nd and 50th streets. Tin Pan Alley is no longer a node of popular music, but performing arts are still clustered in New York City. The Theater District, near 45th Street and Broadway, contains the country's largest concentration of theaters featuring live plays and shows. Lincoln Center for the Performing Arts, a center for music and theater productions, is located near 63rd Street and Broadway.

from Bern and the Palatinate, settled in Pennsylvania in the early 1700s, enticed by William Penn's offer of low-priced land. Because of lower land prices, the second group, from Alsace, settled in Ohio, Illinois, Iowa, and Ontario in the early 1800s. From these core areas, groups of Amish migrated to other locations where inexpensive land was available.

Living in rural and frontier settlements relatively isolated from other groups, Amish communities retained their traditional customs, even as other European immigrants to the United States adopted new ones. We can observe Amish customs on the landscape in such diverse areas as southeastern Pennsylvania, northeastern Ohio, and east-central Iowa (Figure 6-3). These communities are relatively isolated from each other but share cultural traditions distinct from those of other Americans.

Amish folk customs continue to diffuse slowly through interregional migration within the United States. In recent years, Amish families have sold their farms in Lancaster County, Pennsylvania—the oldest and at one time largest Amish community in the United States—and migrated to Christian and Todd counties in southwestern Kentucky.

According to Amish tradition, every son is given a farm when he is an adult, but land suitable for farming is expensive and hard to find in Lancaster County because of its proximity to growing metropolitan areas. With the average price of farmland in southwestern Kentucky less than one-fifth that in Lancaster County, an Amish family can sell its farm in Pennsylvania and acquire enough land in Kentucky to provide adequate farmland for all their sons. Amish families are also migrating from Lancaster County to escape the influx of tourists from the nearby metropolitan areas who come to gawk at distinctive folk customs.

Sports: Example of Hierarchical Diffusion

In contrast with the Amish example of folk customs' diffusion by relocation, organized sport provides an example of popular customs' hierarchical diffusion. Many sports originated as isolated folk customs and were diffused like other folk customs, through the migration of individuals. The contemporary diffusion of organized sports, however, displays the characteristics of popular customs.

Folk Custom Origin of Soccer. Soccer is the world's most popular sport (it is called football outside North America). Its origin is obscure, although the earliest documented contest took place in England in the eleventh century. According to football historians, after the Danish invasion of England between 1018 and 1042, workers excavating a building

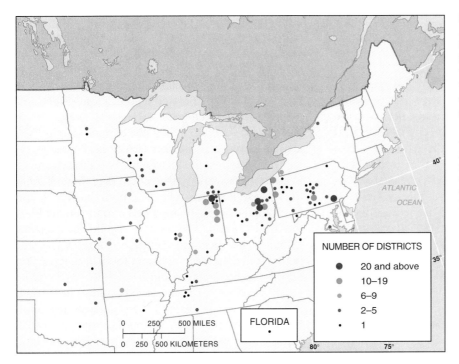

FIGURE 6-3 Amish distribution. Amish settlements are distributed throughout the northeastern United States. According to William Crowley, who documented this distribution, the number of church districts within a settlement indicates the relative number of Amish in the community.

In the photograph below, an Amish family in Pennsylvania drives past several Amish boys. Amish people avoid the use of motorized equipment, such as automobiles. (Sylvain Grandadam/Tony Stone Images)

site encountered a Danish soldier's head, which they began to kick. "Kick the Dane's head" was imitated by boys, one of whom got the idea of using an inflated cow bladder.

Early football games resembled mob scenes. A large number of people from two villages would gather to kick the ball. The winning side was the one that kicked the ball into the center of the rival village. In the twelfth century, the game—by then commonly called football—was confined to smaller vacant areas, and the rules became standardized. Because football disrupted village life, King Henry II banned the game from England in the late twelfth century. It was not legalized again until 1603 by King James I. At this point, football was an English folk custom, rather than a global popular custom.

Global Diffusion of Soccer. The transformation of football from an English folk custom to a global popular custom began in the 1800s. Football and other recreation clubs were founded in Britain, frequently by churches, to provide factory workers with organized recreation during leisure hours. Sport became a subject that was taught in school.

Increasing leisure time permitted people to view sporting events as well as to participate in them. With higher incomes, spectators paid to see first-class events. To meet public demand, football clubs began to hire professional players. Several British football clubs formed an association in 1863 to standardize the rules and to organize professional leagues. Organization of the sport into a formal structure in Great Britain marks the transition of football from folk custom to popular custom.

The word *soccer* originated after 1863 when supporters of the game formed the Football Association. "Association" was shortened to "assoc," which ultimately became twisted around into the word "soccer." The terms *soccer* and *association football* also helped to distinguish the game from rugby football, which permits both kicking and carrying of the ball. Rugby originated in 1823 when a football player at Rugby College picked up the ball and ran with it.

Beginning in the late 1800s, the British exported association football around the world, first to continental Europe and then to other countries. Football was first played in continental Europe in the late 1870s by Dutch students who had been in Britain. The game was diffused to other countries through contact with English players. For example, football went to Spain via English engineers working in Bilbao in 1893 and was quickly adopted by local miners. British citizens further diffused the game throughout the worldwide British Empire. In the twentieth century, soccer, like other sports, has been further diffused by new communication systems, especially radio and television.

Soccer diffused to Russia in a curious manner. The English manager of a textile factory near Moscow organized a team at the factory in 1887 and advertised in London for workers who could play football. After the Russian Revolution in 1917, both the factory and its football team were absorbed into the Soviet Electric Trade Union. The team, renamed the Moscow Dynamo, has become the country's most famous, but the official history of Soviet football does not acknowledge its English origin.

Although soccer was also exported to the United States, it has never gained the popularity it won in Europe and Latin America. The first college football game played in the United States, between Princeton and Rutgers in 1869, was really soccer, and officials of several colleges met 4 years later to adopt football rules consistent with those of British soccer. But Harvard's representatives successfully argued for adoption of rugby rules instead. Rugby was so thoroughly modified by U.S. colleges that an entirely new game—American football—emerged. Similar modifications of football were undertaken in other English-speaking countries, including Canada, Australia, and Ireland. This complex tale of diffusion is typical of many popular customs.

Other Sports. Each country has its own preferred sports (see Geography in Action box for a discussion of lacrosse, a sport played in Canada and a few eastern U.S. cities, especially Baltimore and New York). Cricket is popular primarily in Britain and former British colonies. Ice hockey prevails, logically, in colder climates, especially in Canada, northern Europe, and Russia. The most popular sports in China are martial arts, known as *wushu,* including archery, fencing, wrestling, and boxing. Baseball, once confined to North America, became popular in Japan after it was introduced by American soldiers who occupied the country after World War II.

Despite the diversity in distribution of sports across Earth's surface and the anonymous origin of some games, organized spectator sports today are a popular custom. The common element in profes-

GEOGRAPHY IN ACTION

Revival of Lacrosse, a Folk Custom

In the United States and Canada, Native Americans increasingly recognize the importance of retaining traditional folk customs. As one example, the sport of lacrosse has fostered cultural identity among the Iroquois Confederation of Six Nations (Cayugas, Mohawks, Oneidas, Onondagas, Senecas, and Tuscaroras), who live in the northeastern United States and southeastern Canada. As early as 1636, European explorers observed the Iroquois playing lacrosse, known in their language as *guhchigwaha,* which means "bump hips." European colonists in Canada picked up the game from the Iroquois and diffused it to a handful of U.S. communities, especially in Maryland, upstate New York, and Long Island. The name lacrosse derived from the French words *la crosse,* for a bishop's crosier or staff, which has a shape similar to that of the lacrosse stick.

In recent years, the International Lacrosse Federation has invited the Iroquois nation to participate in the Lacrosse World Championships, along with teams from Australia, Canada, England, and the United States. Although the Iroquois have not won, they have had the satisfaction of hearing their national anthem played and seeing their flag fly alongside those of the other participants.

An Iroquois defender (yellow shirt) tries to stop an Australian attacker in the 1992 Lacrosse World Championships. (Porter Gifford/Gamma-Liaison, Inc.)

sional sports is the willingness of people throughout the world to pay for the privilege of viewing, in person or on TV, events played by professional athletes. Competition for the World Cup in soccer is clear evidence of the global diffusion of sports. National soccer teams worldwide compete every 4 years, including in the United States in 1994 and France in 1998. Thanks to television, more spectators can view the final match than any other event in history.

KEY ISSUE 2

What Factors Create Unique Folk Regions?

- Isolation Promotes Cultural Diversity
- Influence of Physical Environment
- Folk Housing

Folk customs typically have unknown or multiple origins among groups living in relative isolation. Folk customs diffuse slowly to other locations through the process of migration. A combination of physical and cultural factors influences the distinctive distributions of folk customs.

Isolation Promotes Cultural Diversity

A group's unique folk customs develop through centuries of relative isolation from customs practiced by other cultural groups. As a result, folk customs observed at a point in time vary widely from one place to another, even among nearby places.

Himalayan Art

In a study of artistic customs in the Himalaya Mountains, geographers P.P. Karan and Cotton Mather demonstrated that distinctive views of the physical environment emerge among neighboring cultural groups that are isolated. The study area, a narrow corridor of 2,500 kilometers (1,500 miles) in the Himalaya Mountains of Bhutan, Nepal, and northern India, contains four religious groups: Tibetan Buddhists in the north, Hindus in the south, Muslims in the west, and Southeast Asian animists in the east (Figure 6-4). Despite their spatial proximity, limited interaction among these groups produces distinctive folk customs.

Subjects of paintings by each group reveal how their folk customs mirror their religions and individual views of their environment.

- Tibetan Buddhists in the northern region paint idealized divine figures, such as monks and saints. Some of these figures are depicted as bizarre or terrifying, perhaps reflecting the inhospitable environment.
- Hindus in the southern region create scenes from everyday life and familiar local scenes. Their paintings sometimes portray a deity in a domestic scene and frequently represent the region's violent and extreme climatic conditions.
- Paintings in the Islamic western portion show the region's beautiful plants and flowers, because the Muslim religion prohibits displaying animate objects in art. In contrast with the paintings from the Buddhist and Hindu re-

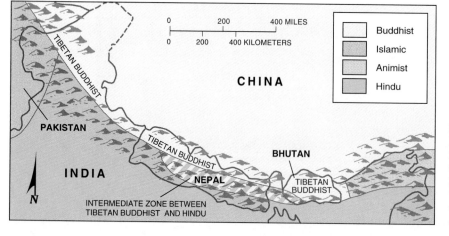

FIGURE 6-4 Cultural regions in the Himalaya Mountains. Karan and Mather found four cultural areas in the rugged Himalaya region of Bhutan, Nepal, and northern India. Variations among the four groups were found in painting, dance, and other folk customs.

gions, Muslim paintings do not depict harsh climatic conditions.

- Animist groups from Myanmar (Burma) and elsewhere in Southeast Asia, who have migrated to the eastern region of the study area, paint symbols and designs that derive from their religion rather than from the local environment.

The distribution of artistic subjects in the Himalayas shows how folk customs are influenced by cultural institutions such as religion and by environmental processes such as climate, land forms, and vegetation. Each of these groups displays uniqueness in its dance, music, architecture, and crafts.

Influence of the Physical Environment

Recall from Chapter 1 that environmental determinists theorized that processes in the environment cause social customs. This theory sounds reasonable on the surface, but most contemporary geographers reject the idea. Many examples exist of peoples who live in similar environments but adopt different social customs. Conversely, many examples exist of peoples who live under different environmental conditions but adopt similar social customs. Of course, people respond to their environment, but the point is that environment is only one of several influences over social customs.

Social customs such as provision of food, clothing, and shelter are clearly influenced by the prevailing climate, soil, and vegetation. For example, residents of arctic climates may wear fur-lined boots, which protect against the cold, and snowshoes to walk on soft, deep snow without sinking in. People living in warm and humid climates may not need any footwear if heavy rainfall and time spent in water discourage its use. The custom in the Netherlands of wearing wooden shoes may appear quaint, but it actually derives from environmental conditions. Dutch farmers wear the wooden shoes, which are waterproof, as they work in fields that often are extremely wet because much of the Netherlands is below sea level.

Environmental conditions can limit the variety of human actions anywhere, but folk societies are particularly responsive to the environment because of their low level of technology and the prevailing agricultural economy. People living in folk societies are likely to be farmers growing their own food, using hand tools and animal power.

Yet folk customs may ignore the environment. Not all arctic residents wear snowshoes, nor do all people in wet temperate climates wear wooden shoes. Geographers observe that broad differences in folk customs arise in part from physical conditions, and these conditions produce varied customs.

Two necessities of daily life—food and shelter—demonstrate the influence of cultural values and the environment on development of unique folk customs. Different folk societies prefer different foods and styles of house construction.

Distinctive Food Preferences

Folk food habits derive from the environment. According to nineteenth-century geographer Vidal de la Blache, "Among the connections that tie [people] to a certain environment, one of the most tenacious is food supply; clothing and weapons are more subject to modification than the dietary regime, which experience has shown to be best suited to human needs in a given climate."

Humans eat mostly plants and animals—living things that spring from the soil and water of a region. Inhabitants of a region must consider the soil, climate, terrain, vegetation, and other characteristics of the environment in deciding to produce particular foods. For example, rice demands a mild, moist climate, whereas wheat thrives in colder, drier regions.

People adapt their food preferences to conditions in the environment. A good example is soybeans, which are an excellent source of protein and are widely grown in Asia. In the raw state they are toxic and indigestible. Lengthy cooking renders them edible, but fuel is scarce in Asia. Asians have adapted to this environmental dilemma by deriving foods from soybeans that do not require extensive cooking. These include bean sprouts (germinated seeds), soy sauce (fermented soybeans), and bean curd (steamed soybeans).

In Europe, traditional preferences for quick-frying foods in Italy resulted in part from fuel shortages. In northern Europe, an abundant wood supply encouraged the slow stewing and roasting of foods over fires, which also provided home heat in the colder climate.

Food Diversity in Transylvania. Food customs are inevitably affected by the availability of prod-

Tokyo McDonald's. U.S. fast-food chains have diffused to other countries, including Japan. Corporate logos enable customers to instantly identify the establishment, such as this one in Tokyo, regardless of whether they know the language. (Greg Davis/The Stock Market)

ucts, but people do not simply eat what is available in their particular environment. Food habits are strongly influenced by cultural traditions. What is eaten establishes one's social, religious, and ethnic memberships. The surest way to identify a family's ethnic origins is to look in its kitchen.

In Transylvania, currently part of Romania, food preferences distinguish among groups who long have lived in close proximity. A century ago, before killings and emigrations during the World War II era, Transylvania contained about 4 million Hungarians, 4 million Romanians, 500,000–600,000 Saxons, 50,000–75,000 Jews, 20,000–25,000 Armenians, and several thousand Szeklers. The Saxons and Szeklers were German peoples who migrated to Transylvania in the ninth century. The Hungarians conquered Transylvania in 1003 and ruled it with few interruptions until losing it to Romania after World War I. Most Jews came to the region with the Hungarians. Most of the Armenians migrated to Transylvania in the 1600s to escape the Muslim-controlled Ottoman Empire to the southeast.

Soup, the food consumed by poorer people, shows the distinctive traditions of the neighboring cultural groups in Transylvania. Romanians made sour bran soups from cracked wheat, corn, brown bread, and cherry tree twigs. Saxons simmered fatty pork in water, added sauerkraut or vinegar, and often used fruits. Jews preferred soups made from beets and sorrel (a leafy vegetable), rather than from meat.

Armenians made soup based on churut (curdled milk) and ground vegetables. Hungarians added smoked bacon to the soup and thickened it with flour and onion fried in lard. Szeklers—who adopted many Jewish dietary practices, including avoidance of pork products—substituted smoked goose or other poultry for the bacon in the Hungarian recipes.

Distinctive food preferences among groups from Transylvania have continued, even after many migrated to the United States. Long after dress, manners, and speech have become indistinguishable from those of the majority, old food habits often continue as the last vestige of traditional folk customs.

Food Attractions and Taboos

According to many folk customs, everything in nature carries a *signature,* or distinctive characteristic, based on its appearance and natural properties. Consequently, people may desire or avoid certain foods in response to perceived beneficial or harmful natural traits.

Food Attractions. Certain foods are eaten because their natural properties are perceived to enhance qualities considered desirable by the society, such as strength, fierceness, or love-making ability. The Abipone Indians of Paraguay eat jaguars and bulls to make them strong, brave, and swift. The mandrake, a plant native to Mediterranean climates, was thought to enhance an individual's love-making abilities. The smell of the plant's orange berries is attractive, but the mandrake's association with sexual prowess comes primarily from the appearance of the root, which is thick, fleshy, and forked, suggesting a man's torso. In parts of Africa and the Middle East, the mandrake's root is administered as a drug, and several references to its powers are found in the Bible.

Food Taboos. People refuse to eat particular plants or animals that are thought to embody negative forces in the environment. Such a restriction on behavior imposed by social custom is a **taboo.** The Ainus in Japan avoid eating otters, because they are believed to be forgetful animals and consuming them could cause loss of memory. Europeans blamed the potato, the first edible plant they had encountered that grew from tubers rather than seeds, for a variety of problems during the seventeenth and eighteenth centuries, including typhoid, tuberculosis, and famine. Initially, Europeans also resisted eating the potato because it resembled human deformities caused by leprosy.

Before becoming pregnant, Mbum Kpau women of Chad do not eat chicken or goat. Abstaining from consumption of these animals is thought to help escape pain in childbirth and to prevent birth of an abnormal child. During pregnancy, Mbum Kpau women avoid meat from antelopes with twisted horns, which could cause them to bear deformed offspring. In the Trobriand Islands off the eastern tip of Papua New Guinea, couples are prohibited from eating meals together before marriage, but premarital sexual relations are an accepted feature of social life.

Some folk customs may establish food taboos because of concern for the natural environment. These taboos may help to protect endangered animals or to conserve scarce natural resources. For example, to preserve scarce animal species, only a few high-ranking people in some tropical regions are permitted to hunt, whereas the majority cultivate crops. But most food avoidance customs arise from cultural values.

Relatively well-known taboos against consumption of certain foods can be found in the Bible. The ancient Hebrews were prohibited from eating a wide variety of foods, including animals that don't chew their cud or that have cloven feet and fish lacking fins or scales. These taboos arose partially from concern for the environment by the Hebrews, who lived as pastoral nomads in lands bordering the eastern Mediterranean. The pig, for example, is prohibited in part because it is more suited to sedentary farming than pastoral nomadism and in part because its meat spoils relatively quickly in hot climates, such as the Mediterranean.

Similarly, Muslims embrace the taboo against pork, because pigs are unsuited for the dry lands of the Arabian Peninsula (Figure 6-5). Pigs would compete with humans for food and water, without offering compensating benefits, such as being able to pull a plow, carry loads, or provide milk and wool. Widespread raising of pigs would be an ecological disaster in Islam's hearth.

Hindu taboos against consuming cows can also be explained partly by environmental reasons. Cows are the source of oxen (castrated male bovine), the traditional choice for pulling plows as well as carts. A large supply of oxen must be maintained in India, because all fields have to be plowed at approximately the same time, when the monsoon rains arrive. Religious sanctions have kept India's cow population large as a form of insurance against the loss of oxen and an increasing population.

But the taboo against consumption of meat among many people, including Muslims, Hindus, and Jews, cannot be explained primarily by environmental factors. Social values must influence the choice of diet, because people in similar climates and with similar levels of income consume different foods. The biblical food taboos were established in part to set the Hebrew people apart from others. That Christians ignore the biblical food injunctions reflects their desire to distinguish themselves from Jews. Furthermore, as a universalizing religion, Christianity was less tied to taboos that originated in the Middle East than was Judaism.

Food taboos are significant even in countries dominated by popular customs, such as the United States. Americans avoid eating insects, despite their nutritional value. In Colombia, on the other hand, movie theaters sell roasted leaf-cutter abdomens rather than popcorn, and giant water bugs are a delicacy in Thailand and Myanmar (Burma). Mixing insects with rice provides lysine, an amino acid that is often deficient in the diet of people in less developed countries where rice is the staple food. The aversion of most Americans to eating insects is amusing, because many foods, such as canned mushrooms and tomato paste, contain insects even though that fact is not commonly recognized.

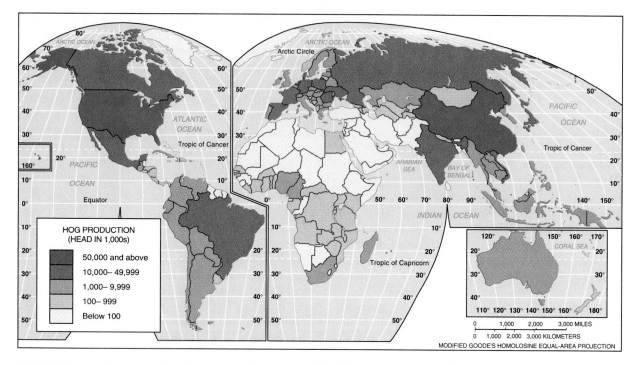

FIGURE 6-5 Annual hog production. The number of hogs produced in different parts of the world is influenced to a considerable extent by religious taboos against consuming pork. Hog production is virtually nonexistent in predominantly Muslim regions, such as northern Africa and southwestern Asia, but the level is high in predominantly Buddhist China and predominantly Christian countries.

Folk Housing

French geographer Jean Brunhes, a major contributor to human geography's cultural landscape tradition, views characteristics of the *house* as being among the essential facts of human geography. It is a product of both cultural tradition and natural conditions. American cultural geographer Fred Kniffen considered the house to be a good reflection of cultural heritage, current fashion, functional needs, and the impact of environment.

Distinctive Building Materials

The type of building materials used to construct folk houses is influenced partly by the resources available in the environment. The two most common building materials in the world are wood and brick, although stone, grass, sod, and skins are also used. If available, wood is generally preferred for house construction because it is easy to build with it. In the past, pioneers who settled in forested regions built log cabins for themselves. Today, people in more developed societies buy lumber that has

been cut by machine into the needed shapes. Cut lumber is used to erect a frame, and sheets or strips of wood are attached for the floors, ceilings, and roof. Shingles, stucco, vinyl, aluminum, or other materials may be placed on the exterior for insulation or decoration.

Some societies have limited access to forests and use alternative materials. In relatively hot, dry climates—such as the U.S. Southwest, Mexico, North China, and parts of the Middle East—bricks are made by baking wet mud in the sun. Stone is used to build houses in parts of Europe and South America and as decoration on the outside of brick or wood houses in other countries.

The choice of building materials may be influenced by social and economic factors as well as what is available from the environment. If the desired material is not locally available, then it must be imported. For example, migrants sometimes paved streets and built houses in their new location with the stone ballast placed in the hold of the ship that transported them. Even when building materials are available, they may be too expensive. For example, in the United States most new homes have interior walls made of drywall (filled with gypsum, a widely available cheap mineral) rather than wood because usig drywall saves money (as well as trees).

Distinctive House Form and Orientation

Social groups may share building materials, but the distinctive form of their houses may result from customary beliefs or environmental factors. In addition, the orientation of the houses on their plots of land can vary.

Social Factors in Housing Form. The form of houses in some societies may reflect religious values. For example, houses may have sacred walls or corners. The east wall of a house is considered sacred in Fiji, as is the northwest wall in parts of China. Sacred walls or corners are also noted in parts of the Middle East, India, and Africa.

In Madagascar, religious considerations influence the use of each part of the house, and even the furniture arrangement. The main door is on the west, considered the most important direction, while the northeast corner is the most sacred. The north wall is for honoring ancestors; in addition, important guests enter a room from the north and are seated against the north wall. The bed is placed against the east wall of the house, with the head facing north.

Beliefs govern the arrangement of household activities in a variety of Southeast Asian societies. In the south-central part of the island of Java, the front door always faces south, the direction of the South Sea Goddess, who holds the key to Earth.

Figure 6-6A shows an interesting housing custom in northern Laos, where the Lao people arrange beds perpendicular to the center ridgepole of the house. Because the head is considered high and noble and the feet low and vulgar, people sleep so that their heads will be opposite their neighbor's heads and their feet opposite their neighbor's feet. The principal exception to this arrangement: a child who builds a house next door to the parents sleeps with his or her head toward the parents' feet as a sign of obeying the customary hierarchy.

Although they speak similar Southeast Asian languages and adhere to Buddhism, the Lao do not orient their houses in the same manner as the Yuan and Shan peoples in nearby northern Thailand. The Yuan and Shan ignore the position of neighbors and all sleep with their heads toward the east, which Buddhists consider the most auspicious direction. Staircases must not face west, the least auspicious direction, the direction of death and evil spirits.

Housing and Environment. The form of housing is related in part to environmental as well as social conditions. The construction of a pitched roof is important in wet or snowy climates to facilitate runoff and to reduce the accumulation of heavy snow. Windows may face south in temperate climates to take advantage of the sun's heat and light. In hot climates, on the other hand, window openings may be smaller to protect the interior from the full heat of the sun.

Even in areas that share similar climates and available building materials, folk housing can vary because of minor differences in environmental features. For example, Robert W. McColl compared house types in four villages situated in the dry lands of northern and western China. All use similar building materials, including adobe and timber from the desert poplar tree, and they share a similar objective: protection from the extremes of temperatures, from very hot summer days to subfreezing winter nights.

Despite their similarities, the houses in these four Chinese villages have individual designs. Houses have second-floor open-air patios in Kashgar, small open courtyards in Turpan, sloped roofs in Dunhuang, and large private courtyards in Yinchuan. McColl attributed the differences to local cultural preferences (Figure 6-7).

U.S. Folk House Forms

In the United States, when families migrated westward in the 1700s and 1800s, they would cut trees to clear fields for planting and use the wood to build a house, barn, and fences. The style of pioneer homes reflected whatever upscale style was prevailing at the place on the East Coast from which they migrated.

Kniffen identified three major hearths, or nodes, of house forms in the United States: New England, Middle Atlantic, and Lower Chesapeake. Migrants carried house types from New England northward to upper New England and westward across the southern Great Lakes region; from the Middle Atlantic westward across the Ohio valley and southwestward along the Appalachian trails; and from the lower Chesapeake southward along the Atlantic coast (Figure 6-8).

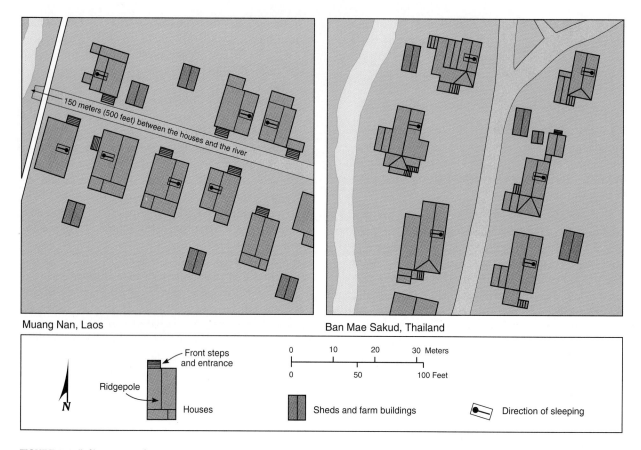

FIGURE 6-6 (left) Houses of Lao people in northern Laos. The fronts of Lao houses, such as those in the village of Muang Nan, Laos, face one another across a path, and the backs face each other at the rear. Their ridgepoles (the centerline of the roof) are set perpendicular to the path but parallel to a stream if one is nearby. Inside adjacent houses, people sleep in the orientation shown, so neighbors are head-to-head or feet-to-feet. (right) Houses of Yuan and Shan peoples in northern Thailand. In the village of Ban Mae Sakud, Thailand, the houses are not set in a straight line because of a belief that evil spirits move in straight lines. Ridgepoles parallel the path, and the heads of all sleeping persons point eastward.

New England Houses. Four major house types were popular in New England at various times during the eighteenth and early nineteenth centuries. They are described here and shown in Figure 6-9, along with a map of how they diffused.

- *Saltbox.* During the early 1700s, the house preferred by successful New Englanders typically consisted of two full stories plus an attic, with four rooms per story (two in the front and two in the rear), organized around a massive central chimney. In some cases, a one-story addition was placed on the rear of the house and the roof had a longer slope in the rear than in the front. This type of house became known as

the saltbox, because it resembled an old-fashioned salt container.
- *Two-Chimney.* After 1750, prosperous New Englanders slightly modified their idealized house type to give it a more formal, symmetrical appearance. A central hall was added, and the central chimney was replaced with two, set at opposite ends.
- *Cape Cod.* During the late 1700s and early 1800s, smaller houses became popular, especially among people who could not afford very large saltboxes. These smaller dwellings, later known as Cape Cod houses, had similar floor plans to the saltboxes, but had one full story rather than two.

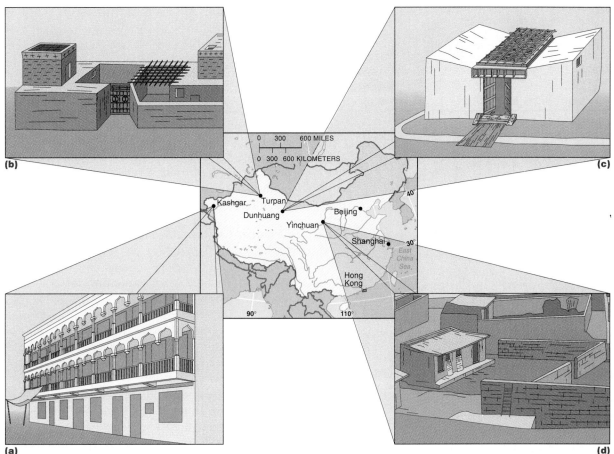

FIGURE 6-7 House types in four communities of western China. (a) Kashgar houses have second-floor open-air patios, where the residents can catch evening breezes. Poplar and fruit trees can be planted around the houses, because the village has a river that is constantly flowing rather than seasonal, as is the case in much of China's dry lands. These deciduous trees provide shade in the summer and openings for sunlight in the winter. (b) Turpan houses have small, open courtyards for social gatherings. Turpan is situated in a deep valley with relatively little open land, because much of the space is allocated to drying raisins. Second-story patios, which would use even less land, are avoided, because the village is subject to strong winds. (c) Dunhuang houses are characterized by walled central courtyards, covered by an open-lattice grape arbor. The cover allows for the free movement of air but provides shade from the especially intense direct summer heat and light. Rather than the flat roofs characteristic of dry lands, houses in Dunhuang have sloped roofs, typical of wetter climates, so that rainfall can run off. The practice is apparently influenced by Dunhuang's relative proximity to the population centers of eastern China, where sloped roofs predominate. (d) Yinchuan houses are built around large, open-air courtyards, which contain tall trees to provide shade. Most residents are Muslims, who regard courtyards as private spaces to be screened from outsiders. The adobe bricks are square rather than rectangular, as is the case in the other villages, though there is no apparent reason for this distinctive custom.

- *Front Gable and Wing.* During the 1800s, New Englanders began to build houses turned 90 degrees so that the ridge and gable (the triangular area of the wall near the roof) faced the front and rear rather than the sides. One or two side wings were sometimes added, with their gables at 90 degrees to the main struc-

ture. This arrangement gave the houses a more classical look.

When settlers from New England migrated westward, they took their house type with them. The New England house type can be found throughout the Great Lakes region as far west as Wisconsin, be-

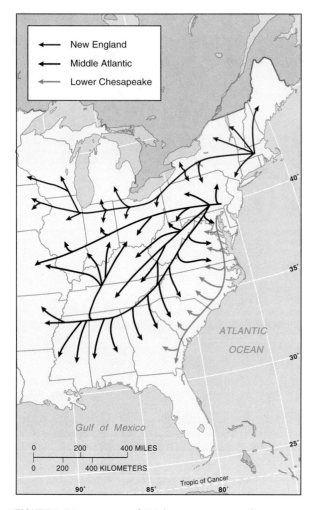

FIGURE 6-8 Source areas of U.S. house types. According to Kniffen, house types in the United States originated in three main source areas and diffused westward along different paths. These paths coincided with predominant routes taken by migrants from the East Coast toward the interior of the country.

cause that area was settled primarily by migrants from New England. As the house preferred by New Englanders changed over time, the predominant form found on the landscape varied, based on the date of initial settlement (Figure 6-9).

Middle Atlantic "I"-house. The major house type in the Middle Atlantic region was known as the "I"-house, typically two full stories in height, with gables to the sides. The I-house resembled the letter I—it was only one room deep and at least two rooms wide. The two rooms could be of equal or different size and connected by a central hall, a direct interi-

or door, or only outside doors. The house could contain one central staircase or two, one at either end, affording more privacy to the two second-floor bedrooms. One fireplace could be set at the center of the house or one at each end. I-houses could be built from brick, stones, timber, or logs, depending on local availability of materials.

The I-house became the most extensive style of construction in much of the eastern half of the United States, especially in the Ohio valley and Appalachia. Settlers built I-houses in much of the Midwest because most of them had migrated from the Middle Atlantic region.

Lower Chesapeake Houses. The Lower Chesapeake style of house typically had one story with a steep roof and chimneys at either end. These houses spread from the Chesapeake Bay–Tidewater Virginia area along the southeastern coast. As was the case with the Middle Atlantic I-house, the form of housing that evolved along the southeastern coast typically was only one room deep. In wet areas, houses in the coastal southeast were often raised on piers or a brick foundation.

Today, such distinctions are relatively difficult to observe in the United States. The style of housing does not display the same degree of regional distinctiveness because rapid communication and transportation systems provide people throughout the country with knowledge of alternative styles. Furthermore, most people do not build the houses in which they live. Instead, houses are usually mass-produced by construction companies.

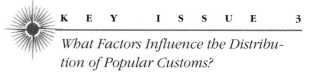

K E Y   I S S U E   3

What Factors Influence the Distribution of Popular Customs?

- Diffusion of Popular Housing, Clothing, and Food
- Importance of Television

Popular customs vary more in time than in place. Like folk customs, they may originate in one location, within the context of a particular social and environment. But, in contrast to folk customs, they diffuse rapidly across Earth to locations with a variety of physical conditions. Rapid diffusion depends on a group of people having a sufficiently high level of

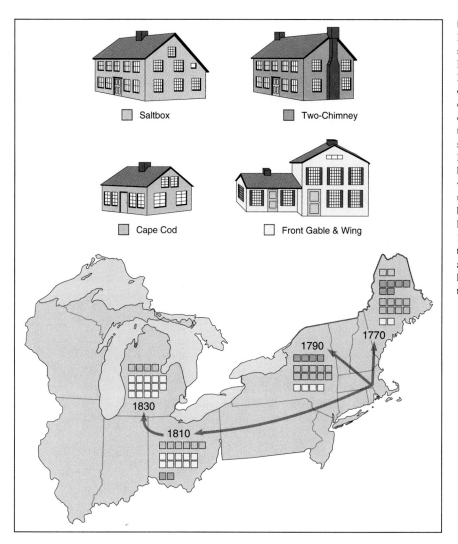

FIGURE 6-9 Diffusion of New England house types. Kniffen suggests that these four major house types were popular in New England at various times during the eighteenth and early nineteenth centuries. As settlers migrated, they carried memories of familiar house types with them and built similar structures on the frontier. Thus, New Englanders were most likely to build houses like the green one when they began to migrate to upstate New York in the 1790s, because that was the predominant house type they knew. During the 1800s, when New Englanders began to migrate farther westward to Ohio and Michigan, they built the type of house typical in New England at that time, shown here in yellow.

economic development to acquire the material possessions associated with the popular custom.

Diffusion of Popular Housing, Clothing, and Food

Some regional differences in food, clothing, and shelter persist in more developed countries, but differences are much less than in the past. Go to any recently built neighborhood on the outskirts of an American city from Portland, Maine, to Portland, Oregon: the houses look the same, the people wear jeans, and the same company delivers pizza.

Popular Housing Styles

Housing built in the United States since the 1940s demonstrates how popular customs vary more in time than in place. In contrast with folk housing characteristics of the early 1800s, newer housing in the United States has been built to reflect rapidly changing fashion concerning the most suitable house form.

Houses show the influence of shapes, materials, detailing, and other features of architectural style in vogue at any one point in time. In the years immediately after World War II, which ended in 1945, most U.S. houses were built in a *modern style*. Since the 1960s, styles that architects call *neo-eclectic* have predominated (Figure 6-10).

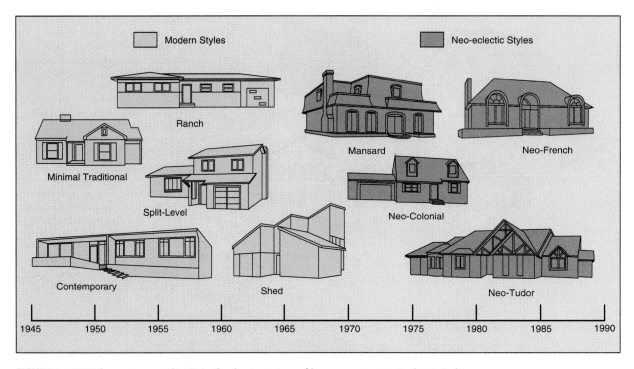

FIGURE 6-10 U.S. house types, 1945–1990. The dominant type of house construction in the United States was minimal traditional during the late 1940s and early 1950s, followed by ranch houses during the late 1950s and 1960s. The split-level was a popular variant of the ranch between the 1950s and 1970s, and the contemporary style was popular for architect-designed houses during the same period. The shed style was widely built in the late 1960s. Neo-eclectic styles, beginning with the mansard, were in vogue during the late 1960s. The neo-Tudor was popular in the 1970s and the neo-French in the 1980s. The neocolonial style has been widely built since the 1950s but never dominated popular architecture.

Modern House Styles (1945–1960). Specific types of modern-style houses were popular at different times. In the late 1940s and early 1950s, the dominant type was known as *minimal traditional,* reminiscent of Tudor-style houses popular in the 1920s and 1930s. Minimal traditional houses usually had one story, with a dominant front gable and few decorative details. They were small, modest houses designed to house young families and veterans returning from World War II.

The *ranch house* replaced minimal traditional as the dominant style of housing in the 1950s and into the 1960s. The ranch house had one story, with the long side parallel to the street. With all the rooms on one level rather than two or three, the ranch house took up a larger lot and contributed to the sprawl of urban areas (see Chapter 11).

The *split-level* house was a popular variant of the ranch house between the 1950s and 1970s. The lower level of the typical split-level house contained the garage and the newly invented "family" room, where the television set was placed. The kitchen and formal living and dining rooms were placed on the intermediate level, with the bedrooms on the top level above the family room and garage.

The *contemporary style* was an especially popular choice between the 1950s and 1970s for architect-designed houses. These houses frequently had flat or low-pitched roofs. The *shed style*, popular in the late 1960s, was characterized by high-pitched shed roofs, giving the house the appearance of a series of geometric forms.

Neo-Eclectic House Styles (1960–Present). In the late 1960s, *neo-eclectic styles* became popular, and by the 1970s they had surpassed modern styles in vogue. The first popular neo-eclectic style was the *mansard* in the late 1960s and early 1970s. The shingle-covered second-story walls sloped slightly inward and merged into the roof line.

The *neo-Tudor style*, popular in the 1970s, was characterized by dominant, steep-pitched front-facing gables and half-timbered detailing. The *neo-French style* also appeared in the early 1970s, and by the early 1980s it was the most fashionable style for new houses. It featured dormer windows, usually with rounded tops, and high-hipped roofs. The *neo-colonial style*, an adaptation of English colonial houses, has been continuously popular since the 1950s but never dominant. Inside many neo-eclectic houses, a large central "great room" has replaced separate family and living rooms, which were located in different wings or floors of ranch and split-level houses.

Regional differences in the predominant type of house do persist to some extent in the United States, as you can see in Figure 6-11. According to John Jakle, Robert Bastian, and Douglas Meyer, small towns in the southeastern United States were most likely to contain ranch houses. In northeastern small towns, the most numerous form was the so-called double pile, which was two rooms wide and two rooms deep. Northeastern houses were large, likely to be painted white, and had garages; southeastern houses were small, likely to be painted beige or brown, and had carports. Differences in roofs, porches, and building materials also distinguish northeastern and southeastern houses.

Differences in housing among U.S. communities derive largely from differences in the time period in which the houses were built. The ranch house was more common in the Southeast than in the Northeast primarily because the Southeast grew much more rapidly during the 1950s and 1960s, the period when the ranch house was especially popular. A housing development built in one region will resemble more closely developments built at the same time elsewhere in the country than developments built in the same region at other points in time.

Rapid Diffusion of Clothing Styles

Individual clothing habits reveal how popular customs can be distributed across the landscape with little regard for distinctive physical features. Such habits reflect availability of income as well as social forms such as job characteristics.

In the more developed countries of North America and Western Europe, clothing habits generally reflect occupations rather than particular environments. A lawyer or business executive, for example, tends to wear a dark suit, light shirt or blouse, and necktie or scarf, whereas a factory worker wears jeans and a work shirt. A lawyer in California is more likely to dress like a lawyer in New York than like a steelworker in California.

A second influence on clothing in more developed countries is higher income. Women's clothes, in particular, change in fashion from one year to the next. The color, shape, and design of dresses change to imitate pieces created by clothing designers. For social purposes, people with sufficient income may update their wardrobe frequently with the latest fashions.

Improved communications have permitted the rapid diffusion of clothing fashions from one region of Earth to another. Original designs for women's dresses, created in Paris, Milan, London, or New York, are reproduced in large quantities at factories in Asia and sold for relatively low prices at North American and European chain stores. Speed is essential in manufacturing copies of designer dresses because fashion tastes change quickly.

Until recently, a year could elapse from the time an original dress was displayed to the time when inexpensive reproductions were available in the stores. Now, the time lag is less than 6 weeks because of the diffusion of facsimile machines, computers, and satellites. Sketches, patterns, and specifications are sent instantly from European fashion centers to American corporate headquarters and then to Asian factories. Buyers from the major retail chains can view the fashions on large, high-definition televisions linked by satellite networks.

The internationalization of clothing styles has involved increasing awareness by North Americans and Europeans of the variety of folk costumes around the world. Increased travel and the diffusion of television have exposed people in more developed countries to other forms of dress, just as people in other parts of the world have come into contact with Western dress. The poncho from South America, the dashiki of the Yoruba people of Nigeria, and the Aleut parka have been adopted by people elsewhere in the world. The continued use of folk costumes in some parts of the world may persist not because of distinctive environmental conditions or traditional cultural values but to preserve past memories or to attract tourists.

Jeans. An important symbol of the diffusion of Western fashion customs is jeans, which became a

FIGURE 6-11 Regional differences in house types. Jakle, Bastian, and Meyer allocated the single-family housing in twenty small towns in the eastern United States into five groups: bungalow, double pile, irregular massed, ranch, and single pile. Ranch houses were more common in the southeastern towns, and double pile predominated in the northeast.

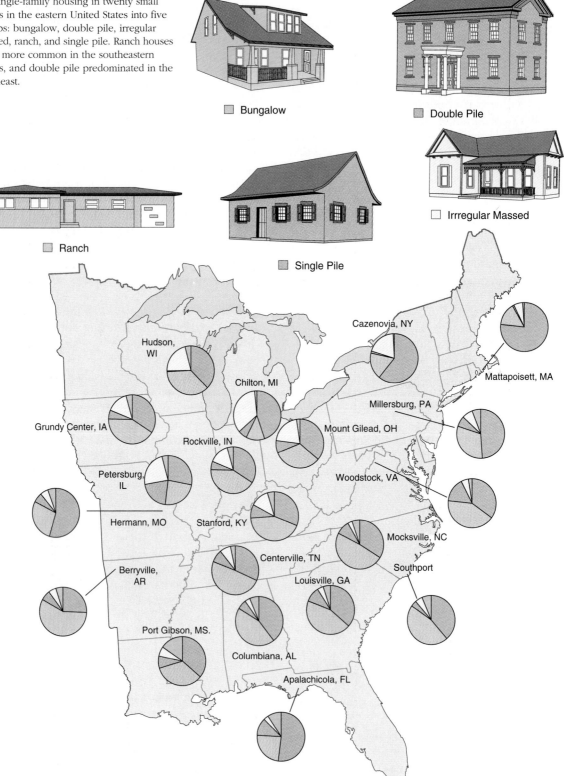

Exposure to modern technology does not necessarily change the traditional role of women in many societies. In Kyoto, Japan, a geisha girl, who is trained to provide entertainment for men, arranges appointments on her way to the restaurant where she entertains her male clients. (Paul Chesley/Paul Chesley)

prized possession for young people throughout the world. In the late 1960s, jeans acquired an image of youthful independence in the United States, as young people adopted a style of clothing previously associated with low-status manual laborers and farmers.

Jeans made by Levi Strauss have become one of the most highly sought objects throughout the world. Locally made jeans are available throughout Europe and Asia for under $10, but "genuine" Levis, priced at $50–$100, are preferred as a status symbol. Millions of second-hand Levis are sold each year in Asia, especially in Japan and Thailand, with most priced between $100 and $1,000.

Even in the face of globalization of popular customs such as wearing jeans, some local variation persists: according to sellers of used jeans, Asians especially prefer Levi's 501 model with a button fly rather than a zipper. And within the United States, the button fly is more common on the West Coast, whereas Easterners prefer the zipper fly because it doesn't let in cold air.

Jeans became an obsession and a status symbol among the young in the former Soviet Union, when the Communist government prevented their import. Gangs would attack people to steal their American-made jeans, and authentic jeans would sell for $400 on the black market. Ironically, jeans were brought into the Soviet Union by the elite, including diplomats, bureaucrats, and business executives—essentially, those who were permitted to travel to the West. These citizens obtained scarce products in the West and resold them inside the Soviet Union for a considerable profit.

The scarcity of high-quality jeans was just one of many consumer problems that were important motives in the dismantling of Communist governments in Eastern Europe during the late 1980s and early 1990s. Eastern Europeans, who were aware of Western fashions and products—thanks to television—could not obtain them, because government-controlled industries were inefficient and geared to producing tanks rather than consumer-oriented goods (see Chapter 10).

With the end of communism, jeans are now imported freely into Russia. Levi Strauss opened a store in the center of Moscow that sells jeans for about $50, about one week's wage for a typical Russian. In an integrated global economy, prominent symbols of popular culture have diffused around the world. Access to these products is now limited primarily by lack of money rather than government regulation.

Popular Food Customs

Popular customs flourish where people in a society have sufficient income to acquire the tangible elements of popular customs and the leisure time to make use of them. People in a country with a relatively developed economy are likely to have the income, time, and inclination to facilitate greater adoption of popular customs.

Alcohol and Fresh Produce. Consumption of large quantities of alcoholic beverages and fresh produce are characteristic of popular food customs. Nonetheless, the amounts of alcohol and produce consumed, as well as preferences for particular types, vary by region within relatively developed countries, such as the United States.

Americans choose particular beverages, fruits, or vegetables in part on the basis of preference for what is produced, grown, or imported locally. Bourbon consumption in the United States is concentrated in the Upper South, where most of it is produced. Rum consumption is heavily concentrated on the East Coast, where it arrives from the Caribbean; Canadian whiskey is preferred in communities contiguous to Canada (Figure 6-12).

Alcohol consumption is related partially to religious backgrounds and partially to income and advertising. Baptists and Mormons, for example, drink less than adherents of other denominations. Because Baptists are concentrated in the Southeast and Mormons in Utah, these regions have relatively low consumption rates. Nevada has a high rate because of the heavy concentration of gambling and other resort activities there.

Similarly, Figure 6-13 shows that Southerners prefer okra and other warm-weather fruits and vegetables grown in the region, but they consume relatively small quantities of oriental vegetables or oranges. Supermarkets in the Northeast and on the West Coast stock more varieties of fruits and vegetables, possibly because the clustering of larger percentages of foreign-born residents produces greater diversity in preferences.

Californians may consume more fresh produce than other Americans in part because the state grows nearly half of the total national output. However, cultural backgrounds also affect the amount of alcohol and fresh produce consumed. People in California may be more aware of the health benefits of consuming fresh produce, as evidenced by the relatively high concentration of health food stores in the state.

Geographers cannot explain all the regional variations in food preferences. Why do urban residents prefer Scotch, and easterners consume grapes and Temple oranges? Why is per capita consumption of fresh produce nearly four times higher in Columbia (South Carolina) and Boston, than in Washington, D.C., Baltimore, and Chicago? Why does consumption of gin, vodka, lemons, and cauliflower show little spatial variation within the United States?

In general, though, consumption of alcohol and fresh produce is a popular custom primarily dependent on two factors—high income and national advertising. Variations within the United States are much less significant than differences between the United States and less developed countries of Africa and Asia.

Wine Production. The spatial distribution of wine production demonstrates that the environment plays a role in the distribution of popular as well as folk food customs. The distinctive character of a wine derives from a unique combination of soil, climate, and other physical characteristics at the place where the grapes are grown.

Vineyards are best cultivated in temperate climates of moderately cold, rainy winters and fairly long, hot summers. Hot, sunny weather is necessary in the summer for the fruit to mature properly. Winter is the preferred season for rain because plant diseases that cause the fruit to rot are more active in hot, humid weather. Vineyards are planted on hillsides, if possible, to maximize exposure to sunlight and to facilitate drainage. A site near a lake or river is also desirable because water can temper extremes of temperature.

Grapes can be grown in a variety of soils, but the best wine tends to be produced from grapes grown in soil that is coarse-grained and well drained—a soil not necessarily very fertile for other crops. For example, the soil is generally sandy and gravelly in the Bordeaux wine region, chalky in Champagne country, and of a slate composition in the Moselle valley. The distinctive character of each region's wine is especially influenced by the unique combination of trace elements, such as boron, manganese, and zinc, in the rock or soil. In large quantities, these elements could destroy the plants, but in small quantities they lend a unique taste to the grapes.

Because of the unique product created by the distinctive soil and climate characteristics, the world's finest wines are most frequently identified by their place of origin. Wines may be labeled with the region, town, district, or specific estate. A wine expert can determine the precise origin of a wine just by tasting because of the unique taste imparted to the grapes by the specific soil composition of each estate. (Similarly, a coffee expert can tell precisely where the beans were grown.)

The year of the harvest is also indicated on finer wines because specific weather conditions each year affect the quality and quantity of the harvest. Wines may also be identified by the variety of grape used rather than the location of the vineyard. Less expensive wines may be composed of a blend of grapes from a variety of estates and years.

FIGURE 6-12 Per capita consumption of rum (a) and Canadian whiskey (b). Rum consumption is highest in East Coast states, where most of it is imported. States that have a high incidence of consumption of Canadian whiskey are located in the north, along the Canadian border. Preference for Canadian whiskey has apparently diffused southward from Canada into the United States.

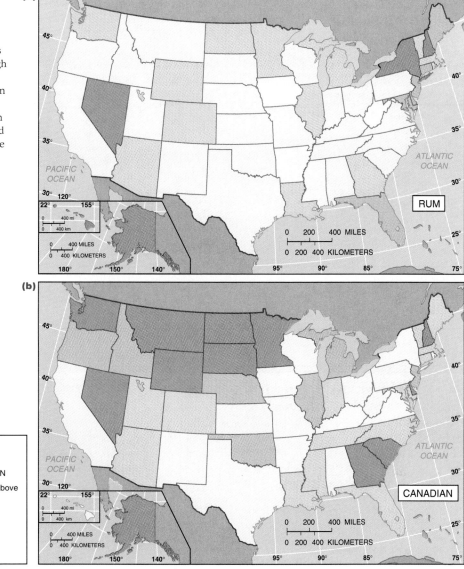

Although grapes can be grown in a wide variety of locations, wine distribution is based principally on cultural values, both historical and contemporary. Wine is made today primarily in locations where people like to drink it, have a tradition of excellence in making it, and have the money to purchase it.

The social custom of wine production in much of France and Italy extends back at least to the Roman Empire. Wine consumption declined after the fall of Rome, and many vineyards were destroyed. Monas-

teries preserved the wine-making tradition in medieval Europe, for both sustenance and ritual. Wine consumption has become extremely popular again in Europe in recent centuries, as well as in the Western Hemisphere, which was colonized by Europeans. Vineyards are now typically owned by private individuals and corporations rather than religious organizations.

Wine production is discouraged in regions of the world dominated by religions other than Christianity (Figure 6-14). Hindus and Muslims in particular

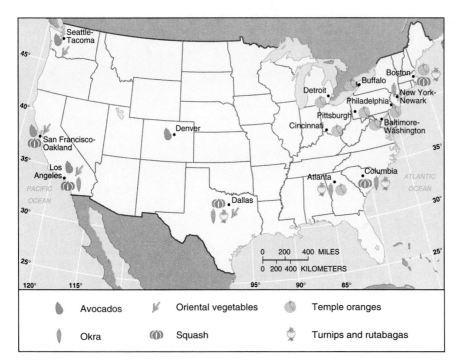

FIGURE 6-13 Preferences for fruits and vegetables. Preferences vary among U.S. regions. The items shown are consumed at a rate of at least twice the national average in the cities indicated. Variations derive at least somewhat from local growing conditions and from cultural characteristics of local residents.

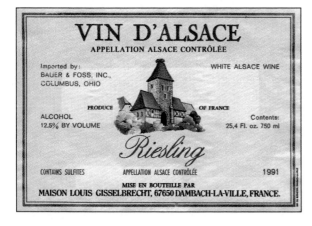

Alsace, in eastern France, is a major center for production of white wine. The major vineyards are strung out in a north-south linear arrangement, on the hillsides between the Vosges mountains to the west and the Rhine River on the east. (Nik Wheeler/West Light)

avoid alcoholic beverages. Thus, wine production is limited in the Middle East (other than Israel) and South Asia primarily because of cultural values, especially religion. The distribution of wine production shows that the diffusion of popular customs depends less on the distinctive environment of a location than on the presence of beliefs, institutions, and material traits conducive to accepting those customs.

Importance of Television

Watching television is an especially significant popular custom for two reasons. First, it is the most popular leisure activity in relatively developed countries throughout the world. Second, television is the most important mechanism by which knowledge of popular customs, such as professional sports, is rapidly diffused across Earth's surface.

Diffusion of Television

Inventors in a number of countries, including the United States, the United Kingdom, France, Germany, Japan, and the Soviet Union, simultaneously contributed to the development of television. The U.S. public first saw television in the 1930s, but its diffusion was blocked when broadcasting was curtailed or suspended entirely during World War II. In 1945, for example, there were only 10,000 television receivers in the United States. By 1949, the number rapidly increased to 1 million. It was 10 million in 1951, and 50 million in 1959. By the mid-1950s, three-fourths of all U.S. homes had television receivers.

During the early 1950s, television sets were being sold in only twenty countries, and more than 85 percent of the world's 37 million sets were in the United States. The United Kingdom had 9 percent of the world's television sets, the Soviet Union and Canada 2 percent each, and the rest of the world (primarily in Cuba, Mexico, France, and Brazil) the remaining 2 percent. The United States still possessed more than half of the world's 98 million television sets as late as the early 1960s, and the number of countries where sets were available increased to 62.

During the 1960s, the number of countries where people possessed television sets increased to 91, and the United States had one-third of the world's 229 million sets. By the early 1990s, more than 180 countries had 900 million television sets, with less than one-fourth in the United States (Figure 6-15).

Currently, the level of television service falls into four categories. The first category consists of countries where nearly every household owns a television set. This category includes the more developed countries of North America and Europe as well as Australia, New Zealand, and Japan. A second category consists

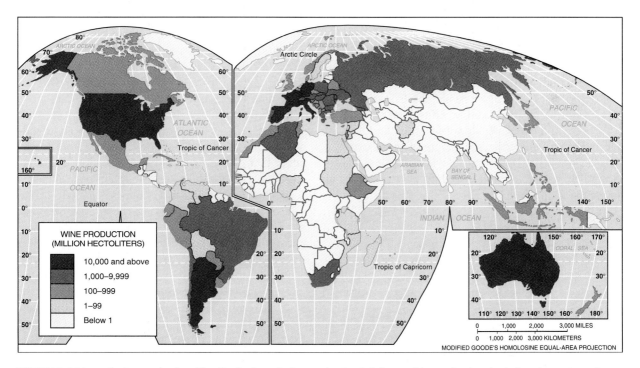

FIGURE 6-14 Annual wine production. The distribution of wine production is influenced in part by the physical environment and in part by social customs. Most grapes used for wine are grown near the Mediterranean Sea or in areas of similar climate. Income, preferences, and other social customs also influence the distribution of wine consumption, as seen in the lower production levels of predominantly Muslim countries south of the Mediterranean.

Watching television is an increasingly popular activity in less developed countries, although many people must share a television set. These Chinese viewers are watching the first live television broadcast from Mount Everest, the world's highest mountain peak, on the border of China and Nepal. A team of Chinese, Japanese, and Nepalese climbers carried a television camera to the top of Mount Everest in May 1988. (Reuters/Bettmann)

of countries in which ownership of a television is common but by no means universal. These are primarily Latin American countries and the poorer European states, such as Yugoslavia and Portugal.

The third category consists of countries in which television exists but has not yet been widely diffused to the population as a whole because of the high cost of receivers. This category includes some countries in Africa, Asia, and Latin America. Finally, about 30 countries, most of which are in Africa and Asia, have very few television sets. Some of these countries do not have operating television stations, although programs from neighboring countries may be received.

Government Control of Television

In the United States, most television stations are owned by private corporations, which receive licenses from the government to operate at specific frequencies (channels). The company makes a profit by selling air time for advertisements. Some stations, however, are owned by local governments or other nonprofit organizations and are devoted to educational or noncommercial programs.

The U.S. pattern of private commercial stations is found in other Western Hemisphere countries but is rare elsewhere in the world. In most countries, the government either directly operates the stations or appoints an autonomous board of directors to manage them. Most governments control television stations to minimize the likelihood that programs hostile to current policies will be broadcast—in other words, they are censored.

Operating costs are typically paid by the national government from tax revenues, although some government-controlled stations do sell air time to private advertisers. These advertisements are typically scheduled in extended blocks of time between programs, rather than in the midst of programs, as in the United States. The British Broadcasting Corporation (BBC) accepts no advertising and obtains revenue from the sale of licenses, required of all television receiver owners. Several Western European countries have transferred some government-controlled television stations to private companies.

Reduced Government Control. In the past, many governments viewed television as an important tool for fostering cultural integration; television could extol the exploits of the leaders or the accomplishments of the political system. People turned on their television sets and watched what the government wanted them to see. Because television signals weaken with distance, and are strong out to roughly 100

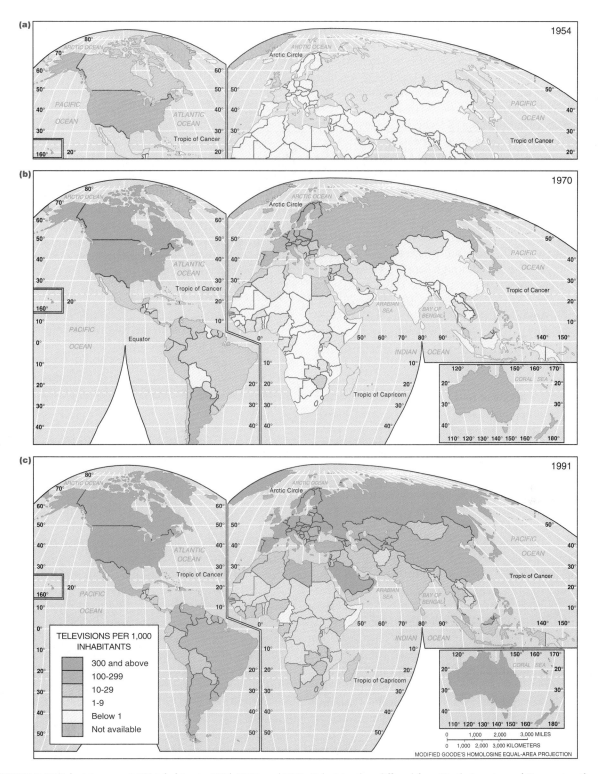

FIGURE 6-15 Televisions per 1,000 inhabitants, 1954, 1970, and 1991. Television has diffused from North America and Europe to other regions of the world, but the number of television sets per capita still varies considerably among countries. The number of television sets per capita is also an important indicator of a society's level of development, as shown in Chapter 8.

kilometers (60 miles), few people could receive television broadcasts from other countries. George Orwell's book *1984*, written in 1949, anticipated that television—then in its infancy—would play a major role in the ability of a totalitarian government to control people's daily lives.

In recent years, changing technology—especially the diffusion of small satellite dishes—has made television a force for political change rather than stability. Satellite dishes enable people to choose from a wide variety of programs produced in other countries and not just the local government-controlled station.

Governments in Asia have tried to prevent consumers from obtaining satellite dishes. The Chinese government banned private ownership of satellite dishes by its citizens, although foreigners and fancy hotels were allowed to keep them. The government of Singapore banned ownership of satellite dishes, yet it encourages satellite services, including MTV and HBO, to locate their Asian headquarters in the country. The government of Saudi Arabia ordered 150,000 satellite dishes dismantled, claiming that they were "un-Islamic."

Governments have had little success in shutting down satellite technology. Despite facing heavy fines, several hundred thousand Chinese still own satellite dishes. Consumers can outwit the government, because the small size of satellite dishes makes them easy to smuggle into the country and erect out of sight, perhaps behind a brick wall or under a canvas tarpaulin. A dish may be expensive by local standards—twice the annual salary of a typical Chinese—but several neighbors can share the cost and hook up all of their television sets to it.

The diffusion of small satellite dishes hastened the collapse of Communist governments in Eastern Europe during the late 1980s. For the first time, Eastern Europeans living beyond the signal range of Western broadcast stations could watch television broadcasts from Western Europe and North America. Eastern European countries have allocated some of their channels to such foreign broadcasters as CNN and MTV, because after many years under Communist control, citizens still do not trust the accuracy of locally produced television programs.

Satellite dishes represent only one assault on government control of the flow of information. Facsimile machines, portable video recorders, and cellular telephones have also put chinks in government censorship.

KEY ISSUE 4

What Problems Result from Worldwide Convergence of Popular Customs?

- Threat to Folk Customs
- Environmental Impact of Popular Customs

The international diffusion of popular customs has led to two problems, both of which can be understood from geographic perspectives. First, the diffusion of popular customs may threaten the survival of traditional folk customs in many countries. Second, popular customs may be less responsive to the diversity of local environments and consequently may generate adverse environmental impacts.

Threat to Folk Customs

Many countries fear the loss of folk customs for two reasons. First, the disappearance of folk customs may be symbolic of the loss of traditional values in society. Second, the diffusion of popular customs from relatively developed countries can lead to the dominance of Western perspectives.

Loss of Traditional Values

One example of the symbolic importance of folk customs is clothing. In African and Asian countries today, there is a contrast between the clothes of rural farm workers and those of urban business and government leaders. Adoption of a more developed society's types of clothing is part of a process of imitation and replication of foreign symbols of success. Leaders of African and Asian countries have traveled to developed countries and experienced the sense of social status attached to clothes, such as men's business suits. Adoption of clothing customs from developed countries has become a symbol of authority and leadership at home. The Western business suit has been accepted as the uniform for business executives and bureaucrats around the world.

Wearing clothes typical of developed countries is controversial in some Middle Eastern countries. Some political leaders in the region choose to wear Western business suits as a sign that they are trying to forge closer links with the United States and Western European countries. Fundamentalist Muslims oppose the widespread adoption of Western clothes, especially by women living in cities, as well as other so-

A diplomat from Niger, dressed in traditional clothing, meets two government officials in Senegal, dressed in Western-style business suits. (Owen Franken/Stock Boston)

cial customs and attitudes typical of more developed countries. Women are urged to abandon skirts and blouses in favor of the traditional black *chador,* a combination head covering and veil.

Change in the Traditional Role of Women. The global diffusion of popular customs affects the subservient role of women that is embedded in many folk customs. Women were traditionally relegated to performing household chores, such as cooking and cleaning, and to bearing and raising large numbers of children. Women who worked outside the home were likely to be obtaining food for the family, either through agricultural work or by trading handcrafts.

Advancement of women was limited by low levels of education and high rates of victimization from violence, often inflicted by husbands. The concepts of legal equality and availability of economic and social opportunities outside the home have become widely accepted in relatively developed countries, even where women in reality continue to suffer from discriminatory practices.

Contact with popular customs also has brought negative impacts for women in less developed societies, such as an increase in prostitution. Hundreds of thousands of men from relatively developed countries, such as Japan and northern Europe (especially Norway, Germany, and the Netherlands) purchase tours from travel agencies that include airfare, hotels, and the use of a predetermined number of women. The principal destinations of these "sex tours" include the Philippines, Thailand, South Korea, and to a lesser extent Indonesia and Sri Lanka. International prostitution is encouraged in these countries as a major source of foreign currency.

Through this form of global interaction, popular customs may regard women as essentially equal at home but as objects that money can buy in foreign folk societies.

Threat of Foreign Media Imperialism

Less developed countries fear the incursion of popular customs for other reasons. Leaders of some LDCs consider the dominance of popular customs by more developed countries as a threat to their independence. The threat is posed primarily by the media, especially news-gathering organizations and television.

Three countries—the United States, the United Kingdom, and Japan—dominate the television industry in LDCs. The Japanese operate primarily in South and East Asia, selling their electronic equipment. British companies have invested directly in management and programming for television in Africa. U.S. corporations own or provide technical advice to many Latin American stations. These three countries are also the major exporters of programs. For example, only 6 percent of all television programs in Japan are foreign-made, compared with 83 percent in Uganda and 66 percent in Ecuador.

Leaders of many LDCs view the spread of television as a new method of economic and cultural imperialism on the part of the more developed countries, especially the United States. American television, like other media, presents characteristically American beliefs and social forms, such as upward social mobility, relative freedom for women, glorification of youth, and stylized violence. These themes may conflict with and drive out traditional social customs.

For some Asian governments, MTV has become a metaphor for all that is bad about Western culture. To avoid offending Asian governments, the largest satellite broadcaster in Asia, Star TV (owned by Rupert Murdoch, who also owns the Fox television network), does not carry MTV in most markets. Star TV returned MTV to its programs in India only after it agreed to allow the government-owned channel to censor unacceptable videos.

Satellite broadcasters, which are owned by companies based in developed countries, try to be sensitive to local cultural preferences. The Turner Broadcasting System, which operates an all-cartoon channel in Indonesia, does not show cartoons featuring Porky Pig, because most Indonesians are Muslim and avoid pork products. Entertainment programs emphasize family values and avoid controversial cultural, economic, and political issues.

Western Control of News Media. Less developed countries fear the effects of the news-gathering capability of the media even more than their entertainment function. The diffusion of information to newspapers around the world is dominated by the Associated Press (AP) and Reuters, owned by American or British companies.

The process of gathering news worldwide is expensive, and most newspapers and broadcasters are unable to afford their own correspondents. Instead, they buy the right to use the dispatches of one or more of the main news organizations. AP transmits most news photographs as well and provides radio stations around the world with reports from their correspondents. Similarly, two joint British-American organizations, Visnews Ltd. and Worldwide Television News Corporation (WTN), supply most of the world's television news video.

The news media in most less developed countries are dominated by the government, which typically runs the radio and television service as well as the domestic news-gathering agency. Newspapers may be owned by the government, a political party, or a private individual, but in any event they are dependent on the government news-gathering organization for information. Sufficient funds are not available to establish a private news service.

Many African and Asian government officials criticize the Western concept of freedom of the press. They argue that the American news organizations reflect American values and do not provide a balanced, accurate view of other countries. U.S. news-gathering organizations are more interested in covering earthquakes, hurricanes, or other sensational disasters than more meaningful but less visual and dramatic domestic stories, such as birth control programs, health-care innovations, or construction of new roads.

Nevertheless, according to a study by the British International Institute of Communications, television newscasts throughout the world allocated the vast majority of time to domestic stories. On the same night, these were the first stories on the most widely watched nationwide newscasts:

- Brazil: traffic jam in Rio de Janeiro
- India: the birthday of the assassinated former prime minister, Indira Gandhi
- Japan: sumo wrestling results
- Kuwait: the day's activities of the ruling sheik
- Thailand: the increasing cost of eggs

Veteran travelers and journalists invariably pack a portable shortwave radio when they visit other countries. In many regions of the world, the only reliable and unbiased news accounts come from the British Broadcasting Corporation (BBC) World Service shortwave radio newscasts. During the civil war in Iran in 1979, the television news anchor, who was not allowed to report the government's deteriorating position, urged citizens to listen to the BBC World Service to learn the most accurate local news. During the 1990s, the BBC World Service again provided the most reliable information to local residents during the Persian Gulf War, the Somalian relief operation, and the Bosnian civil war.

Environmental Impact of Popular Customs

Popular customs are less likely than folk customs to be distributed with consideration for physical features. The spatial organization of popular customs reflects the distribution of social and economic characteristics. In a global economy and culture, popular customs appear increasingly uniform.

Modifying Nature

Popular customs can significantly modify or control the environment. They may be imposed on the environment, rather than springing forth from it, as with many folk customs. For many popular customs, the environment is something to be modified to enhance participation in a leisure activity or to promote the sale of a product. Even if the resulting built environment looks "natural," it is actually the deliberate creation of people in pursuit of popular social customs.

Diffusion of Golf. Golf courses, because of their large size (80 hectares, or 200 acres), provide a prominent example of imposing popular customs on the environment. A surge in U.S. golf popularity spawned construction of roughly 200 courses annually since the late 1980s. Geographer John Rooney attributes this burgeoning interest in golf to increased income and leisure time, especially among recently retired older people and younger people with flexible working hours.

According to Rooney, the provision of golf courses is not uniform across the United States. Although golf is perceived as a warm-weather sport, the number of golf holes per person is actually greatest in north-central states, from Kansas to North Dakota, as well as the northeastern states abutting the Great Lakes, from Wisconsin to upstate New York (Figure 6-16). People in these regions have a long tradition of playing golf, and social clubs with golf courses are important institutions in the fabric of the regions' popular customs.

In contrast, access to golf courses is more limited in the South, California, and in the heavily urbanized Middle Atlantic region between New York City and Washington, D.C. Rapid population growth in the South and West and lack of land on which to build in the Middle Atlantic region have reduced the number of courses per capita. However, selected southern and western areas, such as coastal South Carolina, southern Florida, and central Arizona, have high concentrations of golf courses as a result of the arrival of large numbers of golf-playing northerners, either as vacationers or permanent residents.

Golf courses are designed partially in response to local physical conditions. Grass species are selected to thrive in the local climate and still be suitable for the needs of greens, fairways, and roughs. Existing trees and native vegetation are retained if possible

Golf courses are large space-eaters in American cities. Houses in well-to-do suburban neighborhoods, such as this one along the Mississippi River near New Orleans, may be arranged around golf courses. Residents benefit by having views of open space, as well as proximity to a golf course. (Tom Carroll/FPG International)

(few fairways in Michigan are lined by palms). Yet, like other popular customs, golf courses remake the environment: creating or flattening hills, cutting grass or letting it grow tall, carting in or digging up sand for traps, and draining or expanding bodies of water to create hazards.

Cookie-Cutter Landscapes

The distribution of popular customs around the world tends to produce more uniform landscapes. The spatial expression of a popular custom in one location will be similar to that in another. In fact, promoters of popular customs *want* a uniform appearance, to generate "product recognition" and greater consumption.

Fast-Food Restaurants. The diffusion of fast-food restaurants is a fine example of such uniformi-

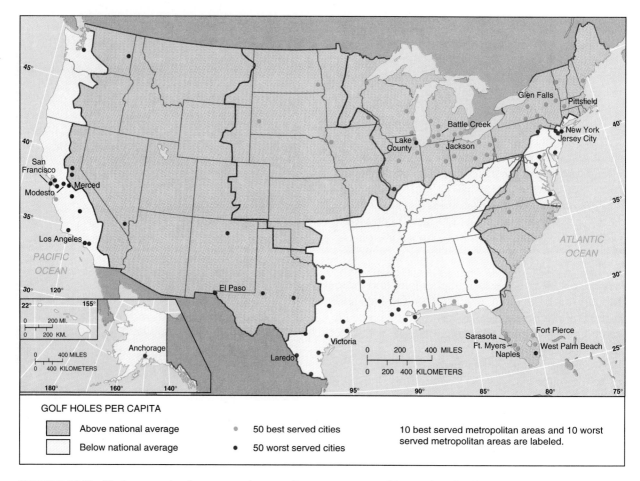

GOLF HOLES PER CAPITA

☐ Above national average   ● 50 best served cities   10 best served metropolitan areas and 10 worst
☐ Below national average   ● 50 worst served cities   served metropolitan areas are labeled.

FIGURE 6-16 The fifty best-served and worst-served metropolitan areas in terms of the number of golf holes per capita. In the North Central states, people have a long tradition of playing golf, even if it is confined to summer months. The ratio is less favorable for golfers in the large urban areas of the East Coast, as well as in the rapidly growing areas of the South and West.

ty. Such restaurants are usually organized as franchises. A franchise is a company's agreement with businesspeople in a local area to market that company's product. The franchise agreement lets the local outlet use the company's name, symbols, trademarks, methods, and architectural styles. The buildings are immediately recognizable to both local residents and travelers as part of a national or multinational company. A uniform sign is prominently displayed.

Much of the attraction of fast-food restaurants comes from the convenience of the product and the use of the building as a low-cost socializing location for teenagers or families with young children. At the same time, the success of fast-food restaurants depends on large-scale mobility: people who travel or move to another city immediately recognize a familiar place. Newcomers to a particular place know what to expect in the restaurant, because the establishment does not reflect strange and unfamiliar local customs that could be uncomfortable.

Fast-food restaurants originally developed to attract people who arrived by car. The buildings generally were brightly colored, even gaudy, to attract motorists. Recently built fast-food restaurants are more subdued, with brick facades, pseudo-antique fixtures, and other stylistic details. Reuse of the structure in case the restaurant fails is facilitated by using company signs that are freestanding rather than integrated into the building design.

Uniformity in the appearance of the landscape is promoted by a wide variety of other popular structures in North America, such as gas stations, supermarkets, and motels. These structures are designed so that both local residents and visitors immediately recognize the purpose of the building, even if not the name of the company.

Global Diffusion of Cookie-Cutter Landscapes.
Physical expression of uniformity in popular customs has diffused from North America to other parts of the world. American motels and fast-food chains have opened in other countries. These establishments appeal to North American travelers, yet most customers are local residents who wish to sample American customs they have seen on television.

Diffusion of popular customs across Earth's surface is not confined to products that originate in North America. With faster communications and transportation, customs from any place on Earth's surface can rapidly diffuse elsewhere. Japanese automobiles and electronics, for example, have diffused in recent years to the rest of the world, including North America. Until the 1970s, automobiles produced in North America, Europe, and Japan differed substantially in appearance and size, but in recent years styling has become more uniform, largely because of consumer preference around the world for Japanese cars. Auto makers such as General Motors, Ford, Toyota, and Honda now manufacture similar models in North and South America, Europe, and Asia, instead of separately designed models for each continent.

Negative Environmental Impact

The diffusion of some popular customs can adversely impact environmental quality in two ways: depletion of scarce natural resources and pollution of the landscape.

Increased Demand for Natural Resources.
Diffusion of some popular customs increases demand for raw materials, such as minerals and other substances found beneath Earth's surface. The depletion of resources used to produce energy, especially petroleum, is discussed in Chapter 13.

Popular habits may demand a large supply of certain animals, resulting in depletion, or even extinction, of some species. For example, some animals are killed for their skins, which can be shaped into fashionable clothing and sold to people living thousands of kilometers from the animals' habitat. The skins of the mink, lynx, jaguar, kangaroo, and whale, for example, have been heavily consumed for various articles of clothing, to the point that the survival of those species is endangered. Depletion of species unbalances the ecological systems of which the animals are members. Many folk customs may also encourage the use of animal skins, but the demand is usually smaller than for popular customs.

Increased demand for some products can strain the capacity of the environment. An important example is increased meat consumption. This increase has not caused extinction of cattle and poultry; we simply raise more. Although some meat is necessary in an ideal diet, animal consumption is an inefficient way for people to acquire calories—90 percent less efficient than if people simply ate grain directly. Production of 1 kilogram (2.2 pounds) of beef to be sold in the supermarket requires nearly 10 kilograms (22 pounds) of grain consumption by the animal. For every kilogram of chicken, nearly 3 kilograms (6.6 pounds) of grain are consumed by the fowl. This grain could be fed to people directly, bypassing the inefficient meat step. With a large percentage of the world's population undernourished, some people question this inefficient use of grain to feed animals for eventual human consumption.

Pollution.
Popular customs also can pollute the environment. Obviously, the environment can accept some level of waste from human activities. But popular customs generate a high volume of waste—solids, liquids, and gases—that must be absorbed into the environment. Although waste is discharged in all three forms, the most visible is solid waste—cans, bottles, old cars, paper, and plastics. These products are often discarded rather than recycled. With more people adopting popular customs worldwide, this problem grows.

Folk customs, like popular customs, can also cause environmental damage, especially when natural processes are ignored. A widespread belief exists that indigenous peoples of the Western

Route 66. The diffusion of popular customs can result in an ugly landscape, as well as an environmentally unsound one. Route 66 was once a well-known symbol of an especially prominent American popular custom—the freedom to drive a car across the country's wide open space. Route 66, which once connected Chicago and Los Angeles, has been largely replaced by interstate highways. Remaining stretches, such as this one, are often cluttered by unattractive strip development, dominated by large signs for national motel, gasoline, and restaurant chains. (Bryan F. Peterson/The Stock Market)

Hemisphere practiced more "natural," ecologically sensitive agriculture before the arrival of Columbus and other Europeans. Geographers increasingly question this assumption. In reality, pre-Columbian folk customs included burning grasslands for planting and hunting, cutting extensive forests, and over-hunting of some species. Very high rates of soil erosion have been documented in Central America from the practice of folk customs.

The developed societies that produce endless supplies for popular customs have created the technological capacity both to create large-scale environmental damage and to control it. However, a commitment of time and money must be made to control the damage. Adverse environmental impacts of popular customs are further examined in Chapter 13.

Summary

Social customs can be divided into two types, folk and popular. Folk customs most often exist among small, homogeneous groups living in relative isolation at a low level of economic development. Popular customs are characteristic of societies with good communications and transportation, which enable rapid diffusion of uniform concepts. Geographers are concerned with several aspects of folk and popular customs. Here again are the key issues for Chapter 6.

1. How do social customs originate and diffuse?

Because of distinctive processes of origin and diffusion, folk customs have different distribution patterns than popular customs. Folk customs are likely to have an anonymous origin and to diffuse slowly through migration, whereas popular customs are likely to be invented and diffused rapidly with the use of modern communications.

2. What factors create unique folk regions?

Unique regions of folk customs arise because of lack of interaction among groups, even those living nearby. Folk customs are likely to be influenced by the local environment.

3. What factors influence the distribution of popular customs?

Popular customs diffuse rapidly across Earth's surface, facilitated by modern communications, especially television. Differences in popular customs are more likely to be observed in one place at different points in time than among different places at one point in time.

4. What problems result from worldwide convergence of popular customs?

Geographers observe two kinds of problems from diffusion of popular customs across the landscape. First, popular customs—generally originating in Western economically developed countries—may cause elimination of some folk customs. Second, popular customs may adversely affect the environment.

CASE STUDY REVISITED
The Aboriginal Artists Return to Australia

The Aboriginal Australian Artists and their audience in New York's Lincoln Center highlight the contrast between folk customs—rooted in the uniqueness of an isolated landscape—and popular customs, which impose uniform standards on the landscape. Will the aboriginal dancers maintain their traditions? Or will they be enticed by the consumer goods characteristic of popular customs, such as televisions and cars? What did they take from the United States back with them to Australia?

Geographers study an array of thousands of social customs with distinctive spatial distributions. Groups display preferences in providing material needs such as food, clothing, and shelter, and in leisure activities such as performing arts and recreation. Examining where various social customs are practiced helps us to understand the extent of cultural diversity in the world.

Folk customs are especially interesting to geographers, because their distributions are relatively clustered, and their preservation can be seen as enhancing cultural diversity in the world. Popular customs are important too, because they derive from the high levels of material wealth characteristic of societies that are economically advanced. As societies seek to improve their economic level, they may abandon traditional folk customs and embrace popular customs associated with more developed economies.

Underlying the patterns of social customs are differences in the way people relate to their environment. Social customs contribute to the modification of the environment, and in turn nature influences the cultural values of an individual or a group.

Geographers, then, classify social customs into popular and folk customs, based on differences in the ways the environment is modified and meaning is derived from environmental conditions. Popular customs make relatively extensive modifications of the environment, given society's greater technological means and inclination to do so.

A critical consequence of cultural diversity is political unrest. A group practicing one set of social customs may aspire to govern the territory of Earth's surface that it inhabits. Conflicts arise when groups adopting other social customs seek to organize the same piece of territory. Cultural identity is a powerful force in forming the political landscape.

Key Terms

Custom The frequent repetition of an act, to the extent that it becomes characteristic of the group of people performing the act.

Folk custom A custom traditionally practiced by a small, homogeneous, rural group living in relative isolation from other groups; also known as a vernacular custom.

Habit A repetitive act performed by a particular individual.

Popular custom A custom found in a large, heterogeneous society that shares certain habits despite differences in other personal characteristics; also known as an international custom.

Taboo A restriction on behavior imposed by social custom.

Thinking Geographically

1. Should geographers regard culture and social customs as meaningful generalizations about a group of people, or should they concentrate instead on understanding how specific individuals interact with the physical environment? Why?

2. In what ways might gender affect the distribution of social customs in a community?

3. Are there examples of groups, either in more developed countries or in less developed countries, that have successfully resisted the diffusion of popular customs? Describe such a group, and tell how it has succeeded in preserving its culture.

4. What elements of the physical environment are emphasized in the portrayal of various places on television?

5. What images of social customs do countries depict in campaigns to promote tourism? To what extent do these images realistically reflect local social customs?

Further Readings

Bale, John. *Sport and Place: A Geography of Sport in England, Scotland, and Wales.* Lincoln: University of Nebraska Press, 1983.

———. *Sports Geography.* London: E. & F. N. Spon, 1989.

Ballas, Donald J., and Margaret J. King. "Cultural Geography and Popular Culture: Proposal for a Creative Merger." *Journal of Cultural Geography* 2 (1981): 154-63.

Bennett, Merril K. *The World's Foods.* New York: Harper and Bros., 1954.

Bigsby, C. W. E., ed. *Superculture: American Popular Culture and Europe.* Bowling Green, OH: Bowling Green Popular Press, 1975.

Blacking, John, and Joann W. Kealiinohomoku. *The Performing Arts: Music and Dance.* The Hague: Mouton, 1979.

Bourdier, Jean-Paul, and Nezar Alsayyad. *Dwellings, Settlements, and Tradition.* Lanham, MD: University Press of America, 1989.

Bull, Adrian. *The Economics of Travel and Tourism.* Melbourne, Australia: Pitman, 1991.

Carlson, Alvar W. "The Contributions of Cultural Geographers to the Study of Popular Culture." *Journal of Popular Culture* 11 (Spring 1978): 830–31.

Carney, George O. "Bluegrass Grows All Around: The Spatial Dimensions of a Country Music Style." *Journal of Geography* 73 (April 1974): 34-55.

_____. "From Down Home to Uptown: The Diffusion of Country-Music Radio Stations in the United States." *Journal of Geography* 76 (March 1977): 104–10.

Chakravarti, A. K. "Regional Preference for Foods: Some Aspects of Food Habit Patterns in India." *Canadian Geographer* 18 (Winter 1974): 395–410.

Chubb, Michael, and Holly R. Chubb. *One Third of Our Time?* New York: Wiley, 1981.

Crowley, William K. "Old Order Amish Settlement: Diffusion and Growth." *Annals of the Association of American Geographers* 68 (June 1978): 249–65.

DeBlij, Harm J. *A Geography of Viticulture.* Miami, FL: University of Miami Geographical Society, 1981.

Denevan, William E. "The Pristine Myth: The Landscape of the Americas in 1492." *Annals of the Association of American Geographers* 82 (1992): 367–85

Farb, Peter, and George Armelagos. *Consuming Passions: The Anthropology of Eating.* Boston: Houghton Mifflin, 1980.

Fusch, Richard, and Larry Ford. "Architecture and the Geography of the American City." *Geographical Review* 73 (July 1983): 324–39.

Jakle, John A. "Roadside Restaurants and Place-Product-Packaging." *Journal of Cultural Geography* 3 (1982): 76–93.

_____, Robert W. Bastian, and Douglas K. Meyer. *Common Houses in America's Small Towns.* Athens: The University of Georgia Press, 1989.

Jakle, John A., and Richard L. Mattson. "The Evolution of a Commercial Strip." *Journal of Cultural Geography* 1 (Spring/Summer 1981): 12–25.

Karan, Pradyumna P., and Cotton Mather. "Art and Geography: Patterns in the Himalayas." *Annals of the Association of American Geographers* 66 (December 1976): 487–515.

Knapp, Ronald G. *China's Traditional Rural Architecture: A Cultural Geography of the Common House.* Honolulu: University of Hawaii Press, 1986.

Kniffen, Fred B. "Folk-Housing: Key to Diffusion." *Annals of the Association of American Geographers* 55 (December 1965): 549–77.

Lamme, Ary J., III, ed. *North American Culture,* vol. 1. Stillwater, OK: Society for the North American Cultural Survey, 1984.

Lewis, Peirce F., Yi-Fu Tuan, and David Lowenthal. *Visual Blight in America.* Washington, DC: Association of American Geographers, 1973.

Lomax, Alan. *The Folk Songs of North America.* Garden City, NY: Doubleday, 1960.

Lornell, Christopher, and W. Theodore Mealor, Jr. "Traditions and Research Opportunities in Folk Geography." *Professional Geographer* 35 (February 1983): 51–56.

McAlester, Virginia, and Lee McAlester. *A Field Guide to American Houses.* New York: Alfred A. Knopf, 1984.

McColl, Robert W. "By Their Dwellings Shall We Know Them: Home and Setting among China's Inner Asian Ethnic Groups." *Focus* 39 (Winter 1989): 1–6.

Pounds, Norman J. G. *Hearth and Home: A History of Material Culture.* Bloomington: Indiana University Press, 1989.

Rapoport, Amos. *House Form and Culture.* Englewood Cliffs, NJ: Prentice Hall, 1969.

Rooney, John F., Jr. *A Geography of American Sport.* Reading, MA: Addison-Wesley, 1974.

_____, and Paul L. Butt. "Beer, Bourbon and Boone's Farm: A Geographical Examination of Alcoholic Drink in the United States." *Journal of Popular Culture* 11 (Spring 1978): 832–56.

Rooney, John F., Jr., Wilbur Zelinsky, and Dean R. Louder, eds. *This Remarkable Continent: An Atlas of United States and Canadian Society and Culture.* College Station, TX: Texas A & M University Press, for the Society for the North American Cultural Survey, 1982.

Rowe, Peter G. *Making a Middle Landscape.* Cambridge, MA: MIT Press, 1991.

Rubin, Barbara. "A Chronology of Architecture in Los Angeles." *Annals of the Association of American Geographers* 69 (September 1979): 339–61.

Shortridge, Barbara G., and James R. Shortridge. "Consumption of Fresh Produce in the Metropolitan United States." *Geographical Review* 79 (January 1989): 79–98.

Szalai, Alexander, ed. *The Use of Time.* The Hague: Mouton, 1972.

Tunstall, Jeremy. *The Media Are American.* New York: Columbia University Press, 1977.

Van Doren, Carlton S., George B. Priddle, and John E. Lewis. *Land and Leisure: Concepts and Methods in Outdoor Recreation,* 2d ed. Chicago: Maaroufa Press, 1979.

Zelinsky, Wilbur. "North America's Vernacular Regions." *Annals of the Association of American Geographers* 70 (March 1980): 1–16.

Also consult the following journals: *International Folk Music Council Journal, Journal of American Culture, Journal of American Folklore, Journal of American Studies, Journal of Cultural Geography, Journal of Leisure Research, Journal of Popular Culture, Journal of Sport History, Landscape, Leisure Science.*

The Annenberg
CPB Project

PEOPLE, PLACES AND CHANGE
Global Tourism

Leisure activities, such as golf, require large-scale transformations of the physical environment, even in regions of the world once considered too remote for tourists to reach.

Commentator Langkawi, near the northeast corner of Malaysia, close to Thailand, is the latest to be drawn into Southeast Asia's expanding network of paradise islands. Here they are targeting a much more selective market, far away from the world of mass tourism. It's called "niche marketing"—designing hotels to fit into a particular niche.

Exclusive golf courses are an increasingly essential part of these resort developments. The problem is that they are disastrous environmentally. Not only do they destroy the natural vegetation, but they use an enormous amount of water and pesticides.

The Datai, on the northwest coast of Langkawi, is aimed at the wealthy international traveller, with its tranquility, and its get-away-from-it-all amenities.

The Datai has been designed with environmental considerations taken seriously. Very few trees were cleared in the construction. They are targeting the lucrative Southeast Asian market, with people coming for short breaks from Japan, Singapore, and further afield.

Jamie Case [General Manager of the Datai resort] Hotels like this, which have saved the environment and have chosen an unusual location, such as within a rainforest, are the future of the hotel business. As the travelling public becomes more sophisticated, they will seek out different experiences, and properties such as this can satisfy the demand.

7

POLITICAL GEOGRAPHY

KEY ISSUES

1. What is the difference between a state and a nation?
2. How are boundaries drawn between states?
3. What problems result when nations and states do not have the same boundaries?
4. Why do states cooperate with each other?

How many countries can you name? Old-style geography sometimes required memorization of countries and their capitals. Today, human geography emphasizes a thematic approach. We are concerned with the *location* of activities in the world, the *reasons* for particular spatial distributions, and the *significance* of the arrangements. Despite this change in emphasis, you still need to know the locations of countries. Without such knowledge, you lack a basic frame of reference: knowing where things are. It is like trans-

lating an article in a foreign language by looking up each word in a dictionary.

In recent years, we have repeatedly experienced military conflicts and revolutionary changes in once-obscure places. Political geographers study how people have organized Earth's land surface into countries and alliances, reasons underlying the observed arrangements, and the conflicts that result from the organization. Political geography helps you understand the cultural and physical factors that underlie political unrest in the world.

BLACKS AND WHITES VOTE TOGETHER FOR THE FIRST TIME IN SOUTH AFRICA, APRIL 1994. (HAVIV/SABA PRESS PHOTOS, INC.)

Changing Borders in Europe

Daniel Lenig lives in the village of Rittershoffen and works at a Mercedes-Benz truck factory in the town of Worth, about 50 kilometers (30 miles) away. Lenig's journey to work takes him across an international border, because Rittershoffen is in France, whereas Worth is in Germany.

As a citizen of France, Lenig has no legal difficulty crossing the German-French border twice a day; no guards ask him to show his passport or require him to pay customs duties on goods he purchases on the other side. If he is delayed, the cause is heavy traffic on the bridge that spans the Rhine River, which serves as the border between the two countries.

The boundary between France and Germany has not always been so easy to cross peacefully. The French long have argued that the Rhine River forms the logical physical boundary between France and Germany. But the Germans once claimed that they should control the Rhine River, including the lowlands on the French side between the west bank of the river and the Vosges Mountains, an area known as Alsace. In fact, Alsace was initially inhabited by Germanic tribes but was annexed by France in 1670.

Two centuries later, in 1870, Alsace and its neighboring province of Lorraine were captured by Prussia (which one year later formed the core of the newly proclaimed German Empire). France regained Alsace and Lorraine after Germany was defeated in World War I and has possessed them ever since, except during 1940–1945 when Germany controlled them in World War II.

After Germany was defeated in World War II, the victorious allies carved the country, and its capital city of Berlin, into four zones. Each zone was controlled by one of the victors: the United States, France, the United Kingdom, and the former Soviet Union. When sharp political differences between the Soviet Union and the other three made reestablishment of a single Germany impossible, two new countries were created: East Germany (the German Democratic Republic) under the Soviets and West Germany (the Federal Republic of Germany) under the other three powers. The two Germanies existed from 1949 until 1990, when they were reunified as one country.

During the Cold War (between the late 1940s and early 1990s), West Germany (the Federal Republic) and France became allies. The two countries recognized that an alliance would strengthen both of their economies and reduce the threat of attack from the Soviet Union. Along with several other Western European countries and the United States, France and West Germany joined a military alliance called the North Atlantic Treaty Organization (NATO). They also joined an economic alliance, now known as the European Union (EU). With the end of the Cold War and the demise of communism in Eastern Europe, France and Germany now lie at the core of the world's wealthiest market area. Most French and German people consider the pursuit of higher standards of living to be more important than re-hashing centuries-old boundary disputes.

While old boundaries between France and Germany have been virtually eliminated, new ones have been erected elsewhere in Europe. Travelers between Ljubljana and Zagreb now must show their passports and convert their cash into a different currency. These two cities were once part of the same country—Yugoslavia—but now they are the capitals of two separate countries, Slovenia and Croatia. Similarly, travelers between Vilnius and Moscow—both once part of the Soviet Union—now must show their passports and change money when they cross the international boundary between Lithuania and Russia. Russians, who once made up a majority of the Soviet Union's population, now find themselves in the minority in such countries as Estonia, Turkmenistan, and Ukraine.

For several decades during the Cold War, many countries were polarized into two camps, one allied with the former Soviet Union and the other allied with the United States. But with the end of the Cold War in the 1990s, the global political landscape changed fundamentally. Geographic concepts help us to understand this changing political organization of Earth's surface. We can also use geographic methods to examine the causes of political change and instability and to anticipate potential trouble spots around the world.

When looking at satellite images of Earth, we easily distinguish land masses and water bodies, mountains and rivers, deserts and fertile agricultural land, urban areas and forests. What we cannot see are boundaries between countries. Boundary lines are not painted on Earth, but they might as well be, for these national divisions are very real to us. To many, national boundaries are more meaningful than natural features. One of Earth's most fundamental cultural characteristics—one that we take for granted—is the division of our planet's surface into a collection of states.

In the post–Cold War era, the familiar division of the world into states is crumbling. Geographers observe two principal reasons for this change: globalization and cultural diversity.

Globalization is an important political trend in which individual states have transferred military, economic, and political authority to regional and worldwide collections of states. This trend is quite a turnabout. Between the 1940s and the 1980s, two superpowers—the United States and the Soviet Union—essentially "ruled" the world. As superpowers, they were involved in events around the globe.

But the United States is less dominant in the political landscape of the 1990s, and the Soviet Union no longer exists. Today, power is increasingly exercised by collections of states that have organized—for both cooperation and competition—primarily around economic considerations.

Despite (or perhaps because of) this greater global political cooperation, local-scale *cultural diversity* has increased in political affairs as individual cultural groups demand more control over the territory they inhabit. States' transference of power to local governments does not placate cultural groups who seek complete independence. Wars have broken out in recent years—both between small neighboring states and among cultural groups within

countries—over political control of territory. Old countries have been broken up into collections of smaller ones, some barely visible on world maps.

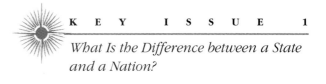

K E Y   I S S U E   1

What Is the Difference between a State and a Nation?

- What Makes a State (Country)?
- What Makes a Nation?

We often confuse two important political geography concepts: state (country) and nation. In fact, in everyday speech, news media, and books, those terms are used interchangeably. Before examining the distribution of political units across Earth's surface, we first must understand the difference between these two fundamental concepts:

- A **state** is an area organized into a *political unit* and ruled by a government with control over its internal and foreign affairs (Nigeria, Belgium, Japan).
- A **nation** or **nationality** is a strongly unified *group of people* in a place who share beliefs and cultural characteristics (the Yoruba, the Flemish, the Japanese).

In this section, we will examine these concepts in detail.

What Makes a State (Country)?

People have divided Earth's land surface into states. A state occupies a defined territory on Earth's surface and contains a permanent population. A state has **sovereignty,** which means independence from control of its internal affairs by other states. Because the entire area of a state is managed by its national government, laws, army, and leaders, it is a good example of a formal or uniform region. The term *country* is a synonym for state.

The term *state*, as used in political geography, does not refer to the fifty regional governments inside the United States. The fifty U.S. States are *subdivisions of a single state:* the United States of America.

People have allocated Earth's land surface to nearly 200 states (Figure 7-1). Included in the total are 185 sovereign states belonging to the United Nations as of 1995, plus 7 other states that are not U.N. members (Table 7-1). The number of sovereign states in the United Nations has increased dramatically since 1945, when there were only about 50.

States from Vast to Micro

The land area occupied by the states of the world varies considerably. The largest state is Russia, which encompasses 17.1 million square kilometers (6.6 million square miles), or 11 percent of the world's entire land area. The distance between the country's borders with Eastern European countries and the Pacific Ocean extends more than 7,000 kilometers (4,300 miles).

Other states with more than 5 million square kilometers (2 million square miles) include China (9.3 million square kilometers, or 3.6 million square miles), Canada (9.2 million square kilometers, or 3.6 million square miles), United States (9.2 million square kilometers, or 3.5 million square miles), Brazil (8.5 million square kilometers, or 3.3 million square miles), and Australia (7.6 million square kilometers, or 2.9 million square miles).

At the other extreme, the smallest state in the United Nations—Monaco—encompasses only 1.5 square kilometers (0.6 square miles), about the size of downtown Reno, Nevada. Other U.N. member states that are smaller than 1,000 square kilometers (600 miles) include Andorra, Antigua and Barbuda, Bahrain, Barbados, Dominica, Grenada, Liechtenstein, Maldives, Malta, Micronesia, Palau, St. Kitts and Nevis, St. Lucia, San Marino, St. Vincent and the Grenadines, São Tomé e Príncipe, the Seychelles, and Singapore. Many of these are islands, which explains both size and sovereignty.

Problems of Defining States

There is some disagreement about the actual number of sovereign states. Let us look at three interesting cases that test the definition of a state—Korea, China, and Antarctica.

Is Korea One Sovereign State or Two? A colony of Japan for many years, Korea was divided into two occupation zones by the United States and former Soviet Union after they defeated Japan in World War II. The country was divided into northern and southern sections along 38° north latitude.

The division of these zones became permanent in the late 1940s, when the two superpowers established separate governments and withdrew their armies. The new government of North Korea then invaded South Korea in 1950, touching off a 3-year war that ended with a cease-fire line near the 38th parallel. Both Korean governments are committed to reuniting the country into one sovereign state, but they do not agree on how this reunification can be accomplished. Meanwhile, in 1992, North Korea and South Korea were admitted to the United Nations as separate countries.

China and Taiwan: One State or Two? Is the island of Taiwan a sovereign state? According to its government officials, Taiwan is not a separate sovereign state but is a part of China. The government of China agrees. Yet, most other governments in the world consider China and Taiwan as two separate and sovereign states.

This confusing situation arose from a civil war between the Nationalists and the Communists in China during the late 1940s. After losing, Nationalist leaders in 1949 fled to the island of Taiwan, 200 kilometers (120 miles) off the Chinese coast. The Nationalists proclaimed that they were still the legitimate rulers of the entire country of China. Until some future occasion when they could defeat the Communists and recapture all of China, the Nationalists argued, at least they could continue to govern one island of the country.

The question of who constituted the legitimate government of China plagued U.S. officials during the 1950s and 1960s. The United States had supported the Nationalists during the civil war, so many Americans opposed acknowledging that China was firmly under the control of the Communists. Consequently, the United States continued to regard the Nationalists as the official government of China until 1971, when U.S. policy finally changed, and the United Nations voted to transfer China's seat from the Nationalists to the Communists.

Antarctica. Antarctica is the only large land mass on Earth's surface that is not part of a sovereign state.

TABLE 7-1
Sovereign states, 1995

Members of the United Nations (185)

Afghanistan	Chad	Guinea	Malaysia	Qatar	Togo
Albania	Chile	Guinea-Bissau	Maldives	Romania	Trinidad and
Algeria	China	Guyana	Mali	Russia	Tobago
Andorra	Colombia	Haiti	Malta	Rwanda	Tunisia
Angola	Comoros	Honduras	Marshall	Saint Kitts	Turkey
Antigua and	Congo	Hungary	Islands	and Nevis	Turkmenistan
Barbuda	Costa Rica	Iceland	Mauritania	Saint Lucia	Uganda
Argentina	Côte d'Ivoire	India	Mauritius	Saint Vincent	Ukraine
Armenia	Croatia	Indonesia	Mexico	and the	United Arab
Australia	Cuba	Iran	Micronesia	Grenadines	Emirates
Austria	Cyprus	Iraq	Moldova	Samoa	United Kingdom
Azerbaijan	Czech Republic	Ireland	Monaco	(Western)	United States
Bahamas	Denmark	Israel	Mongolia	San Marino	Uruguay
Bahrain	Djibouti	Italy	Morocco	São Tomé e	Uzbekistan
Bangladesh	Dominica	Jamaica	Mozambique	Príncipe	Vanuatu
Barbados	Dominican	Japan	Myanmar	Saudi Arabia	Venezuela
Belarus	Republic	Jordan	(Burma)	Senegal	Vietnam
Belgium	Ecuador	Kazakhstan	Namibia	Seychelles	Yemen
Belize	Egypt	Kenya	Nepal	Sierra Leone	Yugoslavia*
Benin	El Salvador	Korea, North	Netherlands	Singapore	Zaire
Bhutan	Equatorial	Korea, South	New Zealand	Slovakia	Zambia
Bolivia	Guinea	Kuwait	Nicaragua	Slovenia	Zimbabwe
Bosnia and	Eritrea	Kyrgyzstan	Niger	Solomon	
Herzegovina	Estonia	Laos	Nigeria	Islands	
Botswana	Ethiopia	Latvia	Norway	Somalia	
Brazil	Fiji	Lebanon	Oman	South Africa	
Brunei	Finland	Lesotho	Pakistan	Spain	**Not members**
Bulgaria	France	Liberia	Panama	Sri Lanka	**of the United**
Burkina Faso	Gabon	Libya	Papua New	Sudan	**Nations (7)**
Burundi	Gambia	Liechtenstien	Guinea	Suriname	
Cambodia	Germany	Lithuania	Paraguay	Swaziland	Kiribiti
Cameroon	Georgia	Luxembourg	Paulu	Sweden	Nauru
Canada	Ghana	Macedonia	Peru	Syria	Switzerland
Cape Verde	Greece	Madagascar	Philippines	Tajikistan	Taiwan
Central African	Grenada	Malawi	Poland	Tanzania	Tonga
Republic	Guatemala		Portugal	Thailand	Tuvalu
					Vatican

*The U.N. General Assembly voted to expel Yugoslavia from membership September 22, 1992.

FIGURE 7-1 United Nations members. When it was organized in 1945, the United Nations had only 51 members, including 49 sovereign states plus Byelorussia (now Belarus) and Ukraine, then part of the Soviet Union. In 1995, the number had increased to 185. The greatest increase in sovereign states has occurred in Africa. Only four African states were original members of the United Nations—Egypt, Ethiopia, Liberia, and South Africa—and only six more joined during the 1950s. Beginning in 1960, however, a collection of independent states was carved from most of the remainder of the region. In 1960 alone, sixteen newly independent African states became U.N. members. Creation of new sovereign states slowed during the 1980s. Among the states that joined the United Nations during the 1980s, only Zimbabwe had a population in excess of 200,000. The breakup of the Soviet Union and Yugoslavia stimulated the formation of more new states during the early 1990s.

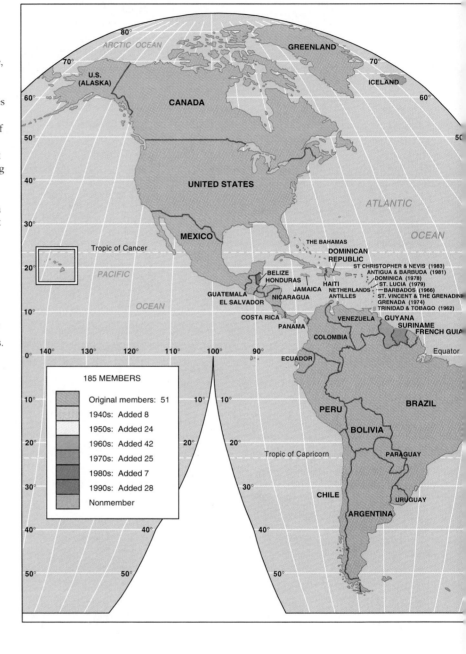

185 MEMBERS

Original members: 51
1940s: Added 8
1950s: Added 24
1960s: Added 42
1970s: Added 25
1980s: Added 7
1990s: Added 28
Nonmember

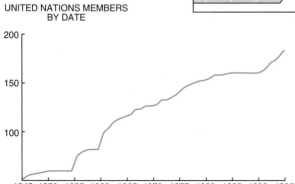

UNITED NATIONS MEMBERS
BY DATE

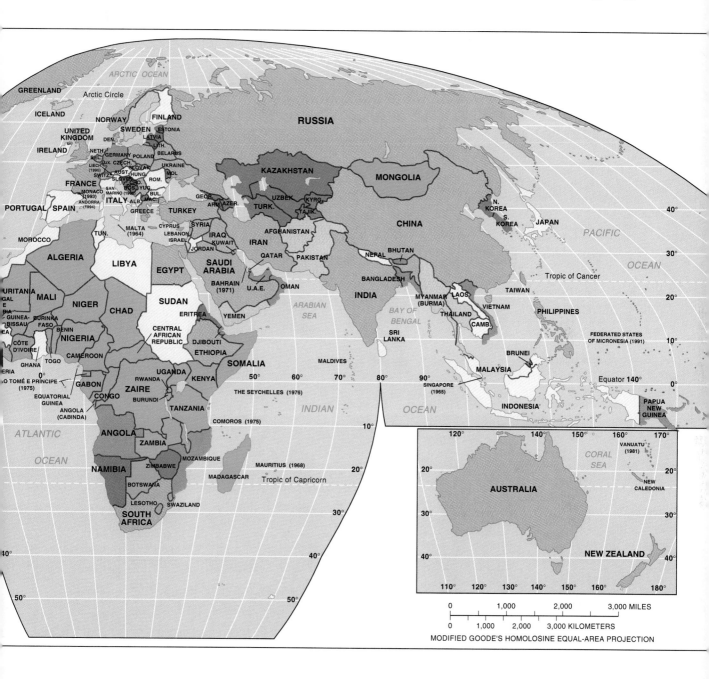

Several states, including Argentina, Australia, Chile, France, New Zealand, Norway, and the United Kingdom, claim portions of Antarctica (Figure 7-2). Argentina, Chile, and the United Kingdom make conflicting, overlapping claims. The United States, Russia, and a number of other states do not recognize the claims of any country to Antarctica. Several states have established research stations on Antarctica, but as yet no permanent settlement exists there.

How the State Concept Developed

The concept of dividing the world into a collection of independent states is recent. Before the 1800s, Earth's surface was organized in other ways, such as

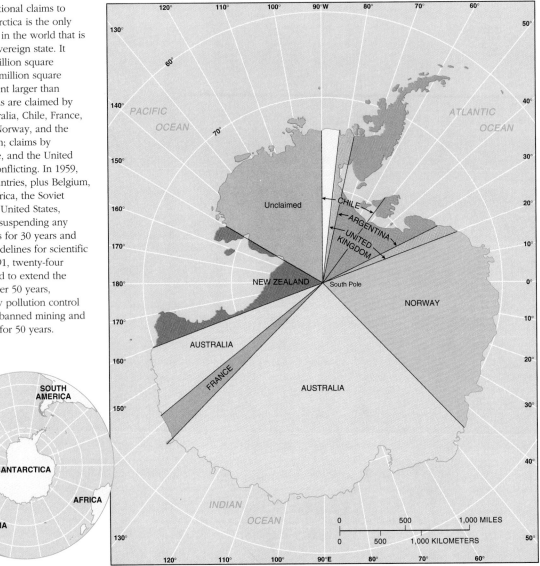

FIGURE 7-2 National claims to Antarctica. Antarctica is the only large land mass in the world that is not part of a sovereign state. It comprises 14 million square kilometers (5.4 million square miles), 50 percent larger than Canada. Portions are claimed by Argentina, Australia, Chile, France, New Zealand, Norway, and the United Kingdom; claims by Argentina, Chile, and the United Kingdom are conflicting. In 1959, these seven countries, plus Belgium, Japan, South Africa, the Soviet Union, and the United States, signed a treaty suspending any territorial claims for 30 years and establishing guidelines for scientific research. In 1991, twenty-four countries agreed to extend the treaty for another 50 years, established new pollution control standards, and banned mining and oil exploration for 50 years.

city-states, empires, and tribes. Much of Earth's surface consisted of unorganized territory. The modern movement to divide the world into states originated in Europe. The development of states can be traced to the ancient Middle East, in an area known as the Fertile Crescent.

Ancient States. The ancient Fertile Crescent formed an arc between the Persian Gulf and the Mediterranean Sea. The eastern end, Mesopotamia, was centered in the valley formed by the Tigris and Euphrates rivers, in present-day Iraq. The Fertile Crescent then curved westward over the desert, turning southward to encompass the Mediterranean coast through present-day Syria, Lebanon, and Israel. The Nile River valley of Egypt is sometimes regarded as an extension of the Fertile Crescent. Situated at the crossroads of Europe, Asia, and Africa, the Fertile Crescent was a center for land and sea communications in ancient times (Figure 7-3).

The first states to evolve in Mesopotamia were known as city-states. A **city-state** is a sovereign state that comprises a town and the surrounding countryside. Walls clearly delineated the boundaries of

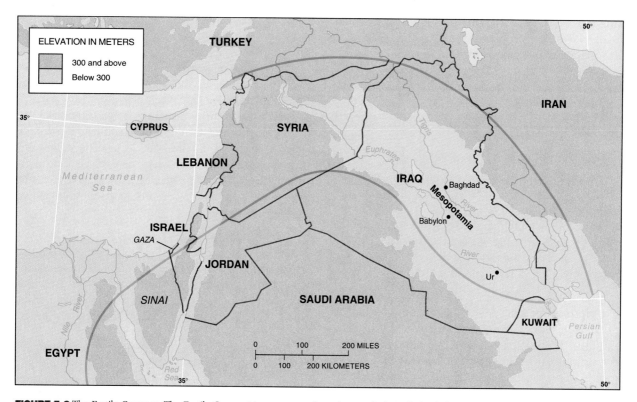

FIGURE 7-3 The Fertile Crescent. The Fertile Crescent is a crescent-shaped area of relatively fertile land situated between the Persian Gulf and the Mediterranean Sea. The Nile River valley of Egypt is sometimes included. Starting several thousand years ago, the territory has been organized into a succession of empires. As shown in Chapter 9, many important early developments in agriculture also originated in this region.

the city, and outside the walls the city controlled agricultural land to produce food for urban residents. The countryside also provided the city with an outer line of defense against attack by other city-states. Periodically, one city or tribe in Mesopotamia would gain military dominance over the others and form an empire. Mesopotamia was organized into a succession of empires by the Sumerians, Assyrians, Babylonians, and Persians.

Meanwhile, the state of Egypt emerged as a separate empire at the western end of the Fertile Crescent. Egypt controlled a long, narrow region along the banks of the Nile River, extending from the Nile Delta at the Mediterranean Sea southward for several hundred kilometers. Egypt's empire lasted from approximately 3000 B.C. until the fourth century B.C.

European States. Political unity in the ancient world reached its height with the establishment of the Roman Empire, which controlled most of Europe, North Africa, and Southwest Asia, from modern-day Spain to Iran and from Egypt to England. At its largest, the empire comprised thirty-eight provinces, all using the same set of laws that were created in Rome. Massive walls helped the Roman army defend many of the empire's frontiers. The Roman Empire collapsed in the fifth century A.D. after a series of attacks by people living on its frontiers, as well as internal disputes.

The European portion of the Roman Empire was fragmented into many estates owned by competing kings, dukes, barons, and other nobles. A victorious noble would seize control of a defeated rival's estate, but after a noble died, others fought to take possession of the land. Meanwhile, most people were forced to live on an estate, working and fighting for the benefit of the noble.

Beginning about the year 1100, a handful of powerful kings emerged as rulers. The consolidation of neighboring estates under the unified control of a king formed the basis for the development of such modern Western European states as England, France, and Spain. But much of central Europe—notably present-day Germany and Italy—remained as fragmented estates and were not consolidated into states until the nineteenth century.

Colonies

A **colony** is a territory that is legally tied to a sovereign state rather than being completely independent. In some cases, a sovereign state runs only the colony's military and foreign policy. In others, it controls the colony's internal affairs as well. At one time, colonies were widespread over Earth's surface—the United States and Canada began as colonies—but today only a handful remain (Table 7-2).

Colonialism. European states came to control much of the world through **colonialism**, which is the effort by one country to establish settlements in previously uninhabited or sparsely inhabited land and to impose its political, economic, and cultural principles on such territory. European states established colonies elsewhere in the world for three basic reasons.

1. European missionaries established colonies to promote Christianity.
2. Colonies provided resources that helped the economy of European states.
3. European states considered the number of colonies to be an indicator of relative power.

The three motives can be summarized as God, gold, and glory.

The colonial era began in the 1400s, when European explorers sailed westward for Asia but encountered and settled in the Western Hemisphere instead. The European states eventually lost most of their Western Hemisphere colonies: independence was declared by the United States in 1776 and by most Latin American states between 1800 and 1824. European states then turned their attention to Africa and Asia (Figure 7-4).

The United Kingdom assembled by far the largest colonial empire. Britain planted colonies on every continent, including much of eastern and southern Africa, South Asia, the Middle East, Australia, and Canada. The British proclaimed that the "sun never set" on their empire. France had the second largest overseas territory, although its colonies were concentrated in West Africa and Southeast Asia. Both the British and the French took control of strategic islands in the Atlantic, Pacific, and Indian oceans as well.

Portugal, Spain, Germany, Italy, Denmark, the Netherlands, and Belgium all established colonies outside Europe but controlled less territory than the British and French. Germany tried to compete with Britain and France by obtaining African colonies that would interfere with communications in the rival European holdings.

Colonial Practices. The colonial practices of European states varied. France attempted to assimilate its colonies into French culture and educate an elite group to provide local administrative leadership. After independence, most of these leaders retained close ties with France.

The British created different government structures and policies for various territories of their empire. This decentralized approach helped to protect the diverse cultures, local customs, and educational systems in their extensive empire. British colonies generally made peaceful transitions to independence, although exceptions can be found in the Middle East, Southern Africa, and Ireland.

Most African and Asian colonies became independent after World War II. Only 15 African and Asian states were members of the United Nations when it was established in 1945, compared with 101 in 1995 (see Figure 7-1). The boundaries of the new states frequently coincide with former colonial provinces, but not always.

The Few Remaining Colonies. The most populous remaining colony is Hong Kong, with nearly 6 million inhabitants. Hong Kong is a British colony encompassing several islands and a small portion of the Chinese mainland. Britain gained control of portions of Hong Kong in several ways. China surrendered Hong Kong Island in 1841 during the First Opium War (so-named because China fought to prevent the British from selling opium to the Chinese; opium was illegal but in high demand in China). It surrendered Stonecutters Island and the Kowloon Peninsula in 1860 at the end of the Second Opium

TABLE 7-2
Inhabited colonies of the world

Colony	Population	Area (sq. km.)	Status
American Samoa	53,139	199	U.S. territory
Anguilla	8,800	91	British dependency
Aruba	65,117	193	Dutch self-governing territory
Bermuda	60,686	52	British self-governing dependency
Cayman Islands	29,700	259	British Crown dependency
Channel Islands (Guernsey & Jersey)	142,975	311	British Crown dependencies
Christmas Island (Kiritimati)	929	135	Australian External Territory
Cocos (Keeling) Islands	597	6	Australian External Territory
Cook Islands	17,977	241	New Zealand self-governing territory
Falkland Islands	1,900	12,173	British dependency
French Polynesia	200,000	4,000	French Overseas Territory
Gibraltar	28,848	6	British self-governing dependency
Guam	133,152	541	U.S. territory
Hong Kong	5,800,000	1,077	British Crown dependency
Isle of Man	69,788	572	British self-governing Crown dependency
Macao	400,000	16	Portuguese Overseas Territory
Mayotte	89,983	378	French Territorial Collectivity
Montserrat	12,617	98	British dependency
Netherlands Antilles	200,000	800	Dutch self-governing territory
New Caledonia	200,000	19,103	French Overseas Territory
Niue	1,751	259	New Zealand self-governing territory
Norfolk Island	2,620	36	Australian External Territory
Northern Mariana Islands	48,581	477	U.S. self-governing Commonwealth
Pitcairn Island	65	5	British dependency
Puerto Rico	3,522,037	8,959	U.S. self-governing Commonwealth
St. Helena (including Ascension and Tristan da Cunha)	6,698	310	British dependency
Svalbard	3,181	62,700	Norwegian dependency
Tokelau	1,600	10	New Zealand territory
Turks and Caicos Islands	12,697	500	British dependency
Virgin Islands (British)	16,108	153	British dependency
Virgin Islands (U.S.)	98,130	342	U.S. territory
Wallis and Futuna Islands	14,175	274	French Overseas Territory

War between Great Britain and China (Figure 7-5). In 1898, China leased the New Territories, which are mainly agricultural lands, to Britain for 99 years.

Anticipating the end of the lease in 1997, China and Britain reached an agreement in 1985 whereby the entire Hong Kong colony returns to Chinese sov-

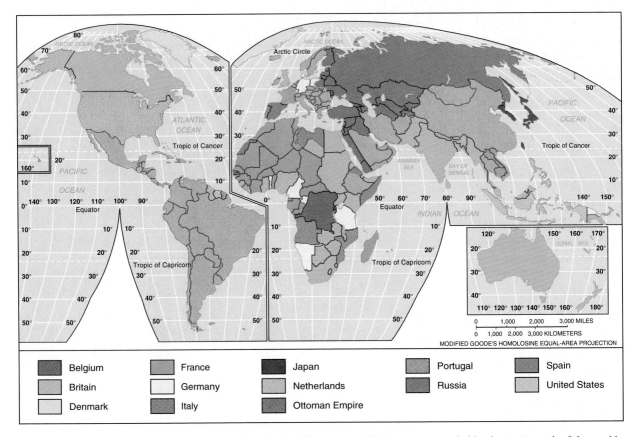

Belgium

Britain

Denmark

France

Germany

Italy

Japan

Netherlands

Ottoman Empire

Portugal

Russia

Spain

United States

FIGURE 7-4 Colonial possessions, 1914. At the outbreak of World War I in 1914, European states held colonies in much of the world, especially in Africa and Asia. Most of the countries in the Western Hemisphere at one time had been colonized by Europeans but gained their independence in the eighteenth and nineteenth centuries.

ereignty on July 1, 1997. In return, China has agreed that Hong Kong will continue its status as a free port and maintain its separate social, economic, and legal systems for another 50 years. China has also guaranteed that the people of Hong Kong can retain their freedoms of speech, religion, and unrestricted travel.

China's takeover, however, has provoked concern in Hong Kong that the former colony will not continue to enjoy its political liberties and unrestricted international trade. Many Hong Kong residents have migrated to Britain, Canada, and the United States. The British have restricted the number of people from Hong Kong who can emigrate.

The world's smallest colony is also British. Pitcairn Island in the South Pacific has about 65 people on less than 5 square kilometers (2 square miles) of land. The island was settled in 1790 by British mutineers from the ship *Bounty,* commanded by Cap-

tain William Bligh. Today, the islanders survive by selling fish and postage stamps to collectors.

What Makes a Nation?

A nation, or nationality, is a collection of people occupying a particular portion of Earth who have a strong sense of unity based on a set of shared beliefs and cultural characteristics. The concept of a nation differs from that of a state: *nation* refers to people, whereas *state* refers to a political structure.

There is no precise method of distinguishing among nationalities. In general, two elements are defining: common cultural characteristics and shared attitudes and emotions.

Common cultural characteristics can include language and religion. For example, in Europe, a strong

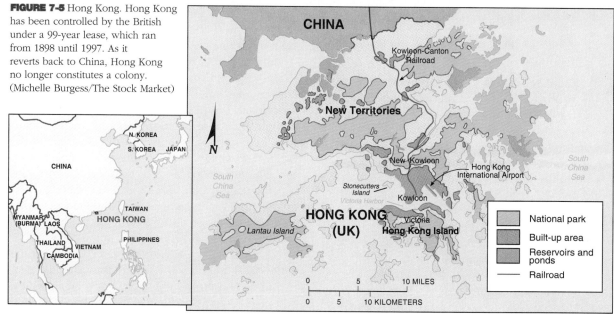

FIGURE 7-5 Hong Kong. Hong Kong has been controlled by the British under a 99-year lease, which ran from 1898 until 1997. As it reverts back to China, Hong Kong no longer constitutes a colony. (Michelle Burgess/The Stock Market)

sense of national unity exists among speakers of Italian, most of whom also are Roman Catholic. A national culture also encompasses distinctive forms of food, architecture, and creative arts—music, theater, painting, sculpture, and literature.

The other element, shared attitudes and emotions, defines a nationality because people of that nation-

ality share a common ancestry and take pride in their own history. For example, in Latin America, the people of each country have their own cultural identity, despite the fact that most are Roman Catholic and speak Spanish. Their nationality results in large measure from a unique history, beginning with the events leading to national independence. Being a

European countries carved up much of Africa into colonies during the late nineteenth century. The United Kingdom assembled the largest collection. This 1891 photograph shows the British commanders and governors asserting control of people of West Africa. (Mary Evans Picture Library/Photo Researchers Inc.)

nation involves being different, and being proud of one's differences.

Nation-States

Desire for self-rule is a very important shared attitude for many nations. To preserve and enhance distinctive cultural characteristics, nationalities seek the ability to govern themselves without interference. The concept that nationalities have the right to govern themselves is known as **self-determination.**

During the nineteenth and twentieth centuries, world political leaders have generally supported the right of self-determination for many nationalities and have attempted to organize Earth's surface into a collection of nation-states. A **nation-state** is a state whose territory corresponds to that occupied by a particular nation. Yet, despite continuing attempts to create nation-states, boundaries of states rarely correspond precisely to the boundaries of a nation.

Nation-States in Europe. By around 1900, most of Western Europe was made up of nation-states. They disagreed over their boundaries and competed to control territory in Africa and Asia. Eastern Europe included a mixture of empires and states that did not match the distribution of nationalities. After they were defeated in World War I, the Austro-Hun-

garian and Ottoman empires were dismantled, and many European boundaries were redrawn according to the principle of nation-states.

During the 1930s, German *Nazionalsozialists* (Nazis) claimed that all German-speaking parts of Europe constituted one nationality and should be unified into one state. They pursued this goal forcefully, and other European powers did not attempt to stop the Germans from taking over Austria and the German-speaking portion of Czechoslovakia, known as the Sudetenland. But in 1939, when Germany invaded Poland (clearly not a German-speaking country), World War II began. England and France, fearing Germany's invasion into Western Europe, rose to defend themselves.

From the end of World War II in 1945 until the early 1990s, attitudes toward communism and economic cooperation were more important political factors in Europe than the nation-state principle. During the 1990s, though, the nation-state concept revived, especially in southern and eastern Europe, where it had been suppressed for 40 years by the Communists.

Denmark: There Are No Perfect Nation-States. Denmark is a fairly good example of a European nation-state, because the territory occupied by the Danish nation closely corresponds to the state of Denmark. The Danes have a strong sense of unity that derives from shared cultural characteristics and attitudes and a recorded history that extends back more than 1,000 years. Nearly all Danes speak the same language, Danish, and nearly all the world's speakers of Danish live in Denmark.

But even Denmark is not a perfect example of a nation-state. The country's 80-kilometer (50-mile) southern boundary with Germany does not divide Danish and German nationalities precisely. The border region, known as Schleswig-Holstein, historically was part of Denmark. Denmark lost the region to Germany during the nineteenth century, but after the German defeat in World War I, the people in North Schleswig voted to rejoin Denmark (Figure 7-6). As a result, some German speakers live in Denmark, and some Danish speakers live in Germany.

The concept of a nation-state is diluted further by the fact that Denmark controls two territories in the Atlantic Ocean that do not share Danish cultural characteristics. One is the Faeroe Islands, a group of twenty-one islands ruled by Denmark for more than 600 years. The nearly 50,000 inhabitants of the Faeroe Islands speak Faeroese (see red area in Figure 4-4).

Denmark also controls Greenland, the world's largest island, which is fifty times larger than Denmark proper. Only 14 percent of the residents of Greenland are considered Danish; the remainder are native-born Greenlanders, primarily Inuit. In 1979, the nearly 60,000 Greenlanders received more authority from Denmark to control their own domestic affairs. One decision was to change all place names in Greenland from Danish to the local Inuit language. Greenland is now officially known as Kalaallit Nunaat, and the name of the capital city was changed from Godthaab to Nuuk.

Centripetal Forces Draw Nation-States Together

A state, once established, must hold the loyalty of its citizens to survive. Most states find that the best way to achieve citizen support is to emphasize *shared attitudes that unify the people*. Attitudes that tend to unify the people and enhance support for the state are known as **centripetal forces.** (The word centripetal means "directed toward the center"; it is the opposite of *centrifugal*, which means "to spread out from the center.")

FIGURE 7-6 Denmark. Denmark is a fairly good example of a nation-state. The Danes have a long-established shared sense of national unity and share distinctive cultural characteristics, such as the Danish language. Yet the boundary between the Danish and German nationalities is not precise, and the two groups intermingle in the region known as Schleswig-Holstein. Also, Denmark controls Greenland and the Faeroe Islands, although the majority of people in these two places are not Danish.

Nationalism. One of the most significant centripetal forces shared by citizens of a state is nationalism. **Nationalism** is loyalty and devotion to a state that represents a particular nation's distinctive cultural characteristics. People display nationalism by supporting a state that preserves and enhances the culture and attitudes of their nationality.

For many states, mass media are the most effective means of fostering nationalism. Americans regard independent news media as a strength and a watchdog over government. But most countries regard an independent source of news as more of a risk than a benefit to the stability of their government. Consequently, only a few states permit mass media to operate without government interference. Nearly all countries control, or at least regulate, most forms of communications, including mail, telephone, telegraph, television, radio, and satellite transmissions. The government either owns or controls newspapers in many countries.

States foster nationalism by promoting symbols of the nation-state, such as flags and songs. The symbol of the hammer and sickle on a field of red was long synonymous with the beliefs of communism. After the fall of communism, one of the first acts in a number of Eastern European countries was to redesign flags without the hammer and sickle. Legal holidays were changed from dates associated with Communist victories to those associated with historical events that preceded Communist takeovers. One of the strongest forms of political protest is to burn a state's flag, and there is wide support in the United States for laws to make burning the Stars and Stripes illegal.

Nationalism is also instilled through the creation of songs extolling the country's virtues. Nearly every state has a national anthem, which usually combines respect for the state with references to the nation's historic events or symbols of unity:

> Oh, say does that star-spangled banner yet wave
> O'er the land of the free and the home of the brave?

The centripetal force of such a song is very powerful, especially to older people and to those who have served in a country's armed forces.

Nationalism can have a negative impact. The sense of unity within a nation-state is sometimes achieved through the creation of negative images of other nation-states. Travelers in southeastern Europe during the 1970s and 1980s found that jokes directed by one nationality against another recurred in the same form throughout the region, with only the name of the target changed. For example, "How many [fill in the name of a nationality] are needed to change a light bulb?" Such jokes seemed harmless, but in hindsight reflected the intense dislike for other nationalities that led to conflict in the 1990s.

Rebirth of Nationalism in Eastern Europe.

Nationalism was effectively suppressed by Communists when they controlled the Soviet Union and other Eastern European countries. But during the 1990s, nationalism has become resurgent and once again is important in forming peoples' cultural identities in the region.

Until they lost power in the late 1980s and early 1990s, Communist leaders in Eastern Europe and the former Soviet Union used centripetal forces to discourage nationalities from expressing their cultural

uniqueness. Writers and artists were pressured to conform to a style known as "socialist realism," which emphasized communist economic and political values. Use of the Russian language was promoted as a centripetal device throughout the former Soviet Union. It was taught as the second language in other Eastern European countries. The role of organized religion was minimized, suppressing a cultural force that competed with the government.

The Communists did not completely suppress nationalities in Eastern Europe: the administrative structures of the former Soviet Union and two other multinational Eastern European countries—Czechoslovakia and Yugoslavia—recognized the existence of nationalities. In the Soviet Union, fifteen republics were created as principal units of local government. Six local units were created in Yugoslavia, and two in Czechoslovakia. All were designed to coincide as closely as possible with the territory occupied by the most numerous nationalities. Ten of the Soviet Union's fifteen republics and one in Yugoslavia were further divided into local government units to grant some autonomy to nationalities that were too few to merit designation as a republic.

The Soviet Union, Yugoslavia, and Czechoslovakia were dismantled in the early 1990s largely because minority nationalities opposed the long-standing dominance of the most numerous nationality in each country—Russians in the Soviet Union, Serbs in Yugoslavia, and Czechs in Czechoslovakia. The dominance was pervasive, including economic, political, and cultural institutions.

No longer content to be a majority within a local government unit in a country, cultural groups sought to be the majority in a completely independent nation-state. Republics that once constituted local government units within the Soviet Union, Yugoslavia, and Czechoslovakia have generally made peaceful transitions into independent countries—as long as their boundaries have corresponded reasonably well with the territory occupied by a clearly defined cultural group.

Slovenia is a good example of a nation-state that was carved from the former Yugoslavia in the 1990s. More than 90 percent of the residents of Slovenia are Slovenes, and nearly all the world's 2 million Slovenes live in Slovenia. The relatively close coincidence between the boundaries of the Slovene people and the country of Slovenia has promoted the country's relative peace and stability, compared with other former Yugoslavian republics.

For new nation-states in Eastern Europe such as Slovenia, sovereignty has brought difficulties in converting from communist economic systems and fitting into the global economy (see Chapters 8 and 10). But their problems of economic reform are minor compared with the conflicts that have erupted in portions of Eastern Europe and the former Soviet Union where nation-states could not be created. The two most severe areas of conflict, where the former local government units under the Communists do not come close to matching distributions of nationalities, are in the Balkans and Caucasus mountains, as discussed later in this chapter.

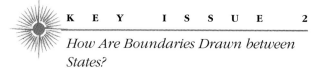

KEY ISSUE 2

How Are Boundaries Drawn between States?

- Shapes of States
- Types of Boundaries

A state is separated from its neighbors by a **boundary,** an invisible line marking the extent of a state's territory. Boundaries result from a combination of natural physical features (such as rivers, deserts, mountains) and cultural features (such as language and religion). Boundaries completely surround an individual state to mark the outer limits of its territorial control and give it a distinctive shape.

Boundaries interest us because the process of selecting their location is frequently difficult. Boundary locations also commonly generate conflict, both within a country and with its neighbors. The boundary line, which must be shared by more than one state, is the only location where direct physical contact must take place between two neighboring states. Therefore, the boundary has the potential to become the focal point of conflict between them.

Shapes of States

The shape of a state controls the length of its boundaries with other states. The shape therefore affects the potential for communications and conflict with neighbors. The shape of a state, such as the outline of the United States or Canada, is part of its unique identity. Beyond its value as a centripetal force, the shape of a state can influence the ease or difficulty of internal administration and affect social unity.

Five Basic Shapes

Countries fall into one of five basic shapes: compact, prorupted, elongated, fragmented, and perforated (Figure 7-7). Each shape displays distinctive characteristics and problems.

Compact States: Efficient. In a **compact state,** the distance from the center to any boundary does not vary significantly. The ideal theoretical compact

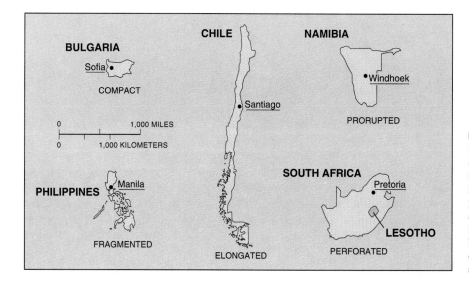

FIGURE 7-7 Shapes of states. Examples are shown of states that are compact (Bulgaria), prorupted (Namibia), elongated (Chile), fragmented (Philippines), and perforated (South Africa). The five states are drawn to the same scale. In general, compactness is an asset, because it fosters good communications and integration among all regions of a country.

state would be circular, with the capital at the center and the shortest possible boundaries to defend.

Compactness is a beneficial characteristic for most smaller states, because good communications can be easily established to all regions, especially if the capital is located near the center. Examples of compact states include Bulgaria, Hungary, and Poland.

Prorupted States: Access or Disruption.

An otherwise compact state with a large projecting extension is a **prorupted state.** Proruptions are created for two principal reasons. First, a proruption can provide a state with access to a resource, such as water. When the Belgians gained control of the Congo (now Zaire), they carved out a westward proruption about 500 kilometers (300 miles) long. The proruption, which followed the Zaire (Congo) River, gave the colony access to the Atlantic Ocean (Figure 7-8). The proruption also divided the Portuguese colony of Angola (now an independent state) into two discontinuous fragments, 50 kilometers (30 miles) apart. The northern fragment, called Cabinda, constitutes less than 1 percent of Angola's total land area.

Proruptions can also separate two states that otherwise would share a boundary. When the British ruled the otherwise compact state of Afghanistan, they created a long, narrow proruption to the east, approximately 300 kilometers (200 miles) long and as narrow as 20 kilometers (12 miles) wide. The proruption prevented Russia from sharing a border with Pakistan (you can see this proruption in Figures 3-1 and 7-1).

In their former colony of South West Africa (now Namibia), the Germans carved out a 500-kilometer (300-mile) proruption to the east in 1890. This proruption, known as the Caprivi Strip, provided the Germans with access to one of Africa's most important rivers, the Zambezi (Figure 7-9). The Caprivi Strip also disrupted communications among the British colonies of southern Africa. In recent years, South Africa, which controlled Namibia until its independence in 1990, stationed troops in the Caprivi Strip to fight enemies in Angola, Zambia, and Botswana.

Elongated States: Potential Isolation.

There are a few **elongated states,** or states with a long, narrow shape. The best example is Chile (Figure 7-7). Chile stretches north-south for more than 4,000 kilometers (2,500 miles) but rarely exceeds an east-

west distance of 150 kilometers (90 miles). Chile is wedged between the Pacific coast of South America and the rugged Andes Mountains, which rise more than 6,700 meters (20,000 feet).

A less extreme example of an elongated state is Italy, which extends more than 1,100 kilometers (700 miles) from northwest to southeast but is only approximately 200 kilometers (120 miles) wide in most places. In Africa, Malawi measures about 850 kilometers (530 miles) north-south but only 100 kilometers (60 miles) east-west.

In West Africa, Gambia is a small elongated state extending along the banks of the Gambia River about 300 kilometers (200 miles) east-west but only between 20 and 50 kilometers north-south (see Figure 7-1). Except for its short coastline along the Atlantic Ocean, Gambia is otherwise completely surrounded by Senegal. The shape of the two countries is a legacy of competition among European countries to establish colonies during the nineteenth century: Gambia became a British colony, whereas Senegal was French.

FIGURE 7-8 Zaire. Zaire is an example of a prorupted state. When the Belgians gained control of the territory, formerly known as the Congo, they created the proruption to assure direct access from the interior of the country to the Atlantic Ocean along the Congo (Zaire) River. The proruption also had the effect of making Angola a fragmented state.

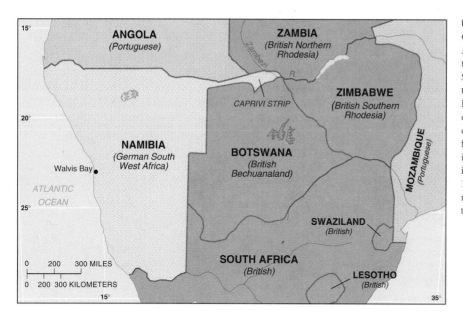

FIGURE 7-9 Namibia. Formerly the German colony of South West Africa, Namibia includes a proruption to the east known as the Caprivi Strip. The Caprivi Strip provided the Germans access to the Zambezi River, and it disrupted communications within the British colonies of southern Africa (their former colonial names are shown in brackets). Namibia became independent of South Africa in 1990, although South Africa did not turn over the port of Walvis Bay to Namibia until 1994.

Elongated states may suffer from poor internal communications. A region located at an extreme end of the elongation may be isolated from the capital, which is usually placed near the center.

Fragmented States: Problematic. A **fragmented state** includes several discontinuous pieces of territory. Technically, all states that have offshore islands as part of their territory are fragmented. Fragmentation is particularly significant for some states. There are two kinds of fragmented states: those with areas separated by water and those separated by an intervening state.

The Philippines are a good example of discontinuous areas separated by water (Figure 7-7). But the most extreme example is Indonesia, which comprises 13,677 islands that extend more than 5,000 kilometers (3,000 miles) across the Indian Ocean. Although more than 80 percent of the country's population live on two of the islands—Java and Sumatra—the fragmentation hinders communications and makes integration of people living on remote islands nearly impossible. To foster national integration, the Indonesian government has encouraged migration from the more densely populated islands to some of the sparsely inhabited ones. Other fragmented states that include more than one island are Japan and New Zealand.

A more difficult type of fragmentation occurs if the two pieces of territory are separated by another state. Picture how difficult communicating between Alaska and the lower forty-eight states would be if Canada were not a friendly neighbor. All land connections between Alaska and the rest of the United States must pass through a long expanse of Canada. The division of Angola into two pieces by Zaire's proruption creates a fragmented state.

Panama—otherwise an example of an elongated state, 700 kilometers (450 miles) long and 80 kilometers (50 miles) wide—is fragmented by the Panama Canal, built in 1914 and owned by the United States. U.S. ownership of the canal and the surrounding Canal Zone was a source of tension for many years, but the United States and Panama signed a treaty in the late 1970s that transfers the canal to Panama on December 31, 1999. The treaty guarantees the neutrality of the canal and permits the United States to use force if necessary to keep the canal operating (Figure 7-10).

Even Russia, the world's largest state, is fragmented by other independent states. Konigsberg (Kaliningrad), an area measuring 16,000 square kilometers (6,000 square miles), is along the Baltic Sea. It is west of the rest of Russia by 400 kilometers (250 miles), separated by the states of Lithuania and Belarus (see Figure 7-18). Until the end of World War

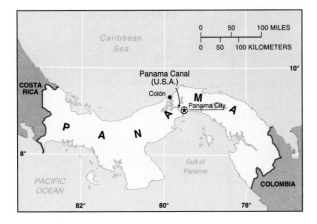

FIGURE 7-10 Panama. Panama currently is an example of a fragmented state, because the United States controls the canal. After the United States completes the process of turning over control of the canal to Panama in 1999, the country will become a good example of an elongated state.

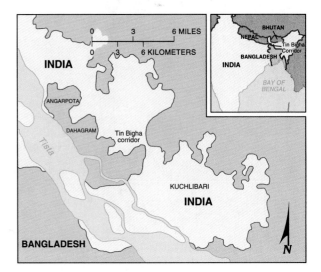

FIGURE 7-11 The Tin Bigha corridor. An area smaller than three football fields, the Tin Bigha corridor is a part of India that fragments Dahagram and Angarpota from the rest of Bangladesh. India agreed to lease the corridor to Bangladesh in perpetuity so that Dahagram and Angarpota could be connected to the rest of Bangladesh. But by eliminating one fragmentation, India created another: Kuchlibari is now fragmented from the rest of India.

II, the area was part of Germany, but the Soviet Union took it over after the German defeat. Virtually all of the area's 1 million residents are Russians; the German population fled westward after World War II. Russia wants Konigsberg because it has the country's largest naval base on the Baltic Sea.

Perhaps the most intractable fragmentation results from a tiny strip of land in India called Tin Bigha. The Tin Bigha corridor measures only 178 meters (about 600 feet) by 85 meters (about 300 feet). It fragments Dahagram and Angarpota from the rest of Bangladesh (Figure 7-11). The problem is a legacy of the late 1940s, when the British divided the region according to religion, allocating predominantly Hindu enclaves to India and predominantly Muslim ones to Bangladesh (formerly East Pakistan).

India agreed to lease the Tin Bigha corridor to Bangladesh in perpetuity so that Dahagram and Angarpota could be connected to the rest of Bangladesh. But by eliminating one fragmentation, India created its own: Kuchlibari is now fragmented from the rest of India. The agreement between the two countries gives Indians the right to move between Kuchlibari and the rest of India at certain times without submitting to passport inspection, customs

declarations, or other international border controls. But given the long history of unrest between Hindus and Muslims, maintaining peace in the Tin Bigha corridor is difficult.

Perforated States: South Africa. A state that completely surrounds another one is a **perforated state.** The one good example of a perforated state is South Africa, which completely surrounds the state of Lesotho (Figure 7-12). Lesotho must depend almost entirely on South Africa for the import and export of goods. Dependency on South Africa was especially difficult for Lesotho when South Africa had a government controlled by whites who discriminated against the black majority population.

Landlocked States

Lesotho is unique in being completely surrounded by only one other state. But it has another important feature that is more common in southern Africa as well as in other regions: it is landlocked. A **landlocked state** lacks a direct outlet to the sea because it is completely surrounded by other countries (only one country in the case of Lesotho). Land-

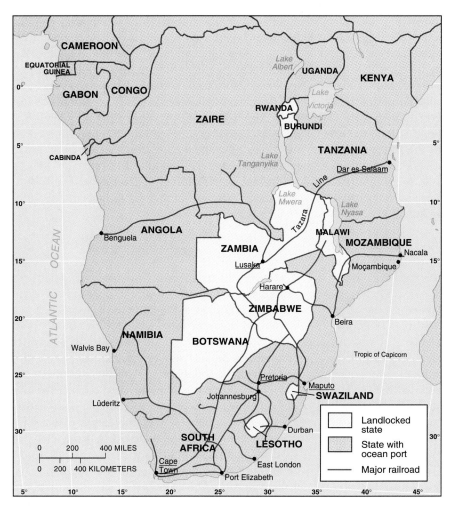

FIGURE 7-12 Water boundaries and landlocked states in southern Africa. Landlocked African states must import and export goods by land-based transportation, primarily rail lines, to reach ocean ports in cooperating neighbor states.

locked states are most common in Africa, where fourteen of the continent's fifty-four states have no direct ocean access. The prevalence of landlocked states in Africa is a remnant of the colonial era, when Britain and France controlled extensive regions.

The European powers built railroads, mostly in the early twentieth century, to connect the interior of Africa with seaports. Railroads moved minerals from interior mines to seaports and mining equipment and supplies from seaports to the interior. Now that the British and French empires are gone, and former colonies have become independent states, some important colonial railroad lines pass through several independent countries. The newly created landlocked states must cooperate with neighboring states that have seaports.

Direct access to an ocean is critical to states because it facilitates international trade. Bulky goods, such as petroleum, grain, ore, and vehicles, are nor-

mally transported long distances by ship. This means that a country needs a seaport where goods can be transferred between land and sea. To send and receive goods by sea, a landlocked state must arrange to use another country's seaport.

Landlocked States in Southern Africa. Cooperation among landlocked states in southern Africa has been complicated by racial patterns. Botswana, Lesotho, and Swaziland are landlocked states that ship 90 percent of their exports by rail through neighboring South Africa (Figure 7-12). Zaire, Zambia, and Zimbabwe must also transport most of their imports and exports through South Africa.

In the past, the states of southern Africa have had to balance their economic dependency on South Africa with their dislike of the country's racial policies. Although they constitute more than 80 percent of South Africa's population, blacks suffered from discrimination (see discussion later in chapter). But if neighboring states had severed ties with South Africa because of its racial discrimination, they could have faced economic disaster.

Zimbabwe's particularly delicate problem can be understood by looking back about three decades, when it was a British colony called Southern Rhodesia. When the white minority in this landlocked colony unilaterally declared itself the independent country of Rhodesia in 1965, most other countries reduced or terminated trade with it. But the impact of trade sanctions on Rhodesia was limited because its major seaports were in South Africa, also ruled by a white minority government. As you can see in Figure 7-12, however, one of Rhodesia's main rail lines ran through black-ruled Botswana to reach South Africa. Botswana was not cooperative, so the Rhodesian government completed a new rail line directly to South Africa in 1974, bypassing Botswana.

In 1979, the white-minority government of Rhodesia agreed to give blacks the right to vote, and blacks were elected to lead the government. The following year, Britain formally recognized the independence of the country, which was renamed Zimbabwe. The Zimbabwe government, now controlled by the black majority, faced a new set of relationships in southern Africa. Instead of working closely with South Africa, Zimbabwe tried to reduce its dependency on the neighboring white-minority government. The key element in Zimbabwe's strategy was to use railroads that connected to seaports outside South Africa. Doing so turned into a very complex problem. Reference to Figure 7-12 will make this explanation easier to follow.

The closest seaport to Zimbabwe is Beira, in Mozambique. A railroad known as the Beira corridor runs west from the seaport to the Zimbabwean capital of Harare. Since the mid-1970s, however, Mozambique has been caught in a devastating civil war between its Marxist-oriented government and rebels backed by South Africa. Zimbabwe has sent soldiers to Mozambique to keep the 500-kilometer (300-mile) Beira corridor repaired and protected from rebel attack, but the seaport of Beira itself has not been well maintained.

More distant seaports are not reliable either. Mozambique's other two major deep-water ports—Nacala in the north and Maputo in the south—have suffered even more than Beira from the civil war. The Benguela railway, which runs from the Atlantic coast eastward across Angola to Zaire and Zambia, has also been disrupted by a civil war in Angola. This conflict has continued since 1975 between the Marxist-oriented government and rebels supported by South Africa and the United States.

The Tazara line, which runs from Zambia to Dar es Salaam in Tanzania, remains open, but service is unreliable. The equipment, much of it supplied by the Chinese in the 1970s, frequently breaks down, and landslides have periodically closed the line. As a result of these obstacles, Zimbabwe has had to ship more than half of its freight through the South African seaport of Durban.

Types of Boundaries

Historically, frontiers rather than boundaries separated states. A **frontier** is a zone where no state exercises complete political control. A frontier is a tangible geographic area, whereas a boundary is an infinitely thin, invisible, imaginary line. A frontier provides an area of separation, often kilometers in width, but a boundary brings two neighboring states into direct contact, increasing the potential for violent face-to-face meetings. A frontier area is either uninhabited or sparsely settled by a few isolated pioneers seeking to live outside organized society.

Almost universally, frontiers between states have been replaced by boundaries. Modern communications systems permit countries to monitor and guard boundaries effectively, even in previously inaccessible locations. Once-remote frontier regions have become more attractive for agriculture and mining.

The only regions of the world that still have frontiers rather than boundaries are Antarctica and the Arabian Peninsula. Frontiers separate Saudi Arabia from Qatar, the United Arab Emirates, Oman, and Yemen. These frontier areas are inhabited by nomads who cross freely with their herds from one country to another. Until recently, part of Saudi Arabia's border with Iraq included an 8,000-square-kilometer (3,000-square-mile) frontier marked on maps as "Neutral Zone" (Figure 7-13). But, by stationing troops on either side of an east-west line across the Neutral Zone, Saudi Arabia and Iraq in 1990 transformed the frontier into a boundary, although not one officially ratified by the governments of the two countries.

Boundaries are of two types: physical and cultural. Physical boundaries coincide with significant features of the natural landscape (mountains, deserts, water),

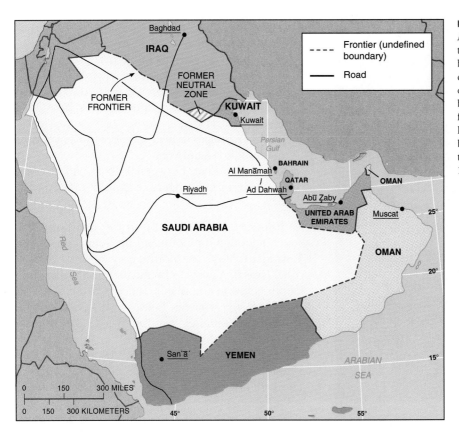

FIGURE 7-13 Frontiers in the Arabian peninsula. Several states in the Arabian peninsula are separated by frontiers rather than by precisely drawn boundaries. The principal occupants of this desert area have been nomads, who have wandered freely through the frontier. A frontier known as the Neutral Zone existed between Saudi Arabia and Iraq until the two countries split it during the 1991 Gulf War.

whereas cultural boundaries follow the distribution of cultural characteristics. Neither type of boundary is better or more "natural," and many boundaries are a combination of the two types. The best boundaries are those to which all affected states agree, regardless of the rationale used to draw the line.

Physical Boundaries

Important physical features on Earth's surface can make good boundaries because they are easily seen, both on a map and on the ground. Three types of physical elements serve as boundaries between states: mountains, deserts, and water.

Mountains. Mountains can be effective boundaries if they are difficult to cross. Contact between nationalities living on opposite sides may be limited, or completely impossible, if passes are closed by winter storms. Mountains are also useful boundaries because they are rather permanent and usually are sparsely inhabited.

Mountains do not always provide for the amicable separation of neighbors. Argentina and Chile agreed to be divided by the crest of the Andes Mountains but could not decide on the precise location of the crest. Was the crest a jagged line, connecting mountain peak to mountain peak? Or was it a curving line following the continental divide (the continuous ridge that divides rainfall and snowmelt between flow toward the Atlantic and Pacific)? The two countries almost fought a war over the boundary line. But with the help of U.S. mediators, they finally decided on the line connecting adjacent mountain peaks.

Desert. A boundary drawn in a desert can also effectively divide two states. Like mountains, deserts are hard to cross and sparsely inhabited. Desert boundaries are common in Africa and Asia. In North Africa, the Sahara has generally proved to be a stable boundary separating Algeria, Libya, and Egypt on the north form Mauritania, Mali, Niger, Chad, and the Sudan on the south. (For an illustration, look

The Great Wall of China historically served as one of the world's most visible boundaries. Originally built in the third century B.C. during the Qin (Ch'in) dynasty, the wall was extended the following century during the Han dynasty to keep out nomadic horsemen. The wall was partially reconstructed between the fourteenth and sixteenth centuries A.D. during the Ming dynasty. (R. Ian Lloyd/The Stock Market)

back to Figure 1-19, the world climate map.) In the early 1980s, the Libyan army moved south across the desert to invade Chad but retreated in 1987 when the French intervened.

Water. Rivers, lakes, and oceans are the physical features most commonly used as boundaries. Water boundaries are readily visible on a map and are relatively unchanging.

Water boundaries are especially common in East Africa (refer to Figure 7-12). For example:

- The boundary between Uganda and Zaire runs through Lake Albert.
- The boundary separating Kenya, Tanzania, and Uganda runs through Lake Victoria.
- The boundary separating Burundi, Tanzania, Zaire, and Zambia runs through Lake Tanganyika.
- The boundary between Zaire and Zambia runs through Lake Mwera.
- The boundary between Malawi and Mozambique runs through Lake Malawi (Lake Nyasa).

Boundaries are typically in the middle of the water, although the boundary between Malawi and Tanzania follows the north shore of Lake Malawi (Lake Nyasa). Again, the boundaries result from nineteenth-century colonial practices: Malawi was a British colony, whereas Tanzania was German.

Water boundaries can offer good protection against attack from another state, because an invading state must transport its troops by air or ship and secure a landing spot in the country being attacked. The state being invaded can concentrate its defense at the landing point.

The use of water as boundaries between states can cause difficulties, though. One problem is that the precise position of the water may change over time. Rivers, in particular, can slowly change their course. The Rio Grande, the river separating the United States and Mexico, has frequently meandered from its previous course since it became part of the boundary in 1848. Land that had once been on the U.S. side of the boundary came to be on the Mexican side, and vice versa. The United States and Mexico have concluded treaties that restore land affected by the shifting course of the river to the country in control at the time of the original nineteenth-century delineation.

Ocean boundaries also cause problems because states generally claim that the boundary lies not at the coastline but out at sea. The reasons are for defense and for control of valuable fishing industries. Beginning in the late eighteenth century, some states recognized a boundary, known as the territorial limit, that extended 3 nautical miles (about 5.5 kilometers, or 3.5 land miles) from the shore into the ocean. Some states claimed more extensive territorial limits, and others identified a contiguous zone of influence that extended beyond the territorial limits.

The Law of the Sea, signed by 117 countries in 1983, standardized the territorial limits for most countries at 12 nautical miles (about 22 kilometers, or 14 land miles). Under the Law of the Sea, states also have exclusive rights to the fish and other marine life within 200 miles (320 kilometers). Countries separated by less than 400 miles of sea must negotiate the location of the boundary for exclusive fishing rights. Disputes can be taken to a Tribunal for the Law of the Sea or to the International Court of Justice.

Cultural Boundaries

The boundaries between some states are drawn according to geometry: they simply are straight lines drawn on a map, although good reasons always exist for where the lines are located. Other cultural boundaries coincide with differences in cultural characteristics, especially religion and language.

Geometric Boundaries. Part of the northern U.S. boundary with Canada is a 2,100-kilometer (1,300-mile) straight line (more precisely, an arc) along 49° north latitude, running from Lake of the Woods between Minnesota and Manitoba to the Strait of Georgia between Washington State and British Columbia. This boundary was established in 1846 by treaty between the United States and Great Britain, which still controlled Canada at the time.

At the time, some people in the United States wanted the boundary to be fixed 600 kilometers (400 miles) farther north, at 54°40′ north latitude. Before a compromise was reached, U.S. militants proclaimed "fifty-four forty or fight." The United States and Canada share an additional 1,100-kilometer (700-mile) geometric boundary between Alaska and the Yukon Territory along the north-south arc of 141° west longitude.

The 1,000-kilometer (600-mile) boundary between Chad and Libya is a straight line drawn across the desert in 1899 by the French and British to set the northern limit of French colonies in Africa (Figure 7-14). But subsequent actions by European countries created confusion over the boundary. In 1912, Italy seized Libya from the Turks and demanded that the boundary with French-controlled Chad be moved southward. In 1935, France agreed to move the boundary 100 kilometers (60 miles) to the south, but the Italian government was not satisfied and never ratified the treaty. The land that the French would have ceded is known as the Aozou Strip, named for

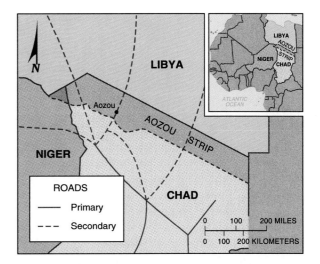

FIGURE 7-14 The Aozou Strip. The boundary between Libya and Chad is a straight line, drawn by European countries early in 1899 when the area comprised a series of colonies. Libya, however, claims that the boundary should be located 100 kilometers to the south and that it should have sovereignty over the Aozou Strip.

the only settlement in this 100,000-square-kilometer (36,000-square-mile) area (Figure 7-14).

When Libya and Chad both became independent countries, the boundary was set at the original northern location. Claiming that it had been secretly sold by the president of Chad, Libya seized the territory in 1973, as well as a tiny bit of northeastern Niger that may contain uranium ore. In 1987, Chad expelled the Libyan army with the help of French forces and regained control of the strip.

Religious Boundaries. Religious differences often coincide with boundaries between states, but in only a few cases has religion been used to select the actual boundary line. The most notable example was in South Asia, when the British partitioned India into two states on the basis of religion. The predominantly Muslim portions were allocated to Pakistan, while the predominantly Hindu portions became the independent state of India (see Figure 3-18).

Religion was also used to some extent to draw the boundary between two states on the island of Eire (Ireland). Most of the island became an independent country, but the northeast—now known as Northern Ireland—remained part of the United Kingdom. Roman Catholics constitute approximately 95 percent of the population in the twenty-six counties that joined the Republic of Ireland, and Protestants constitute the majority in the six counties of Northern Ireland (see Figure 5-5).

Language Boundaries. Language is an important cultural characteristic for drawing boundaries, especially in Europe. By global standards, European languages have substantial literary traditions and formal rules of grammar and spelling. Language has long been a significant means of distinguishing distinctive nationalities in Europe.

The French language was a major element in the development of France as a unified state in the seventeenth century. The states of England, Spain, and Portugal coalesced around distinctive languages. In the nineteenth century, Italy and Germany also emerged as states that unified the speakers of particular languages.

The movement to identify nation-states on the basis of language spread throughout Europe in the twentieth century. After World War I, leaders of the victorious countries met at the Versailles Peace Conference to redraw the map of Europe. One of the chief advisers to President Woodrow Wilson, the geographer Isaiah Bowman, played a major role in the decisions. Language was the most important criterion the allied leaders used to create new states in Europe and to adjust the boundaries of existing ones.

The conference was particularly concerned with eastern and southern Europe, regions long troubled by political instability and conflict. Boundaries were drawn around the states of Bulgaria, Hungary, Poland, and Romania to conform closely to the distribution of Bulgarian, Hungarian (Magyar), Polish, and Romanian speakers. Speakers of several similar South Slavic languages were placed together in the new country of Yugoslavia. Czechoslovakia was created by combining the speakers of Czech and Slovak, mutually intelligible West Slavic languages (Figure 7-15).

Although the boundaries imposed by the Versailles conference on the basis of language were adjusted somewhat after World War II, they proved to be relatively stable, and peace ensued for several decades. During the 1990s, however, the map of Europe drawn at Versailles in 1919 has collapsed. Despite speaking similar languages, Czechs and Slovaks

found that they could no longer live together peacefully in the same state. Neither could Croats, Macedonians, Serbs, and Slovenes.

K E Y   I S S U E   3

What Problems Result When Nations and States Do Not Have the Same Boundaries?

- One State with More Than One Nationality
- One Nationality in More Than One State
- Internal Organization of States

Despite the desirability of correlating the "natural" boundaries of nationalities with state boundaries to form nation-states, few true nation-states exist. Many of the world's problems derive from this fact. States are trying to meet the desire of nationalities for more self-determination by transferring authority from national to local units of government. But the lack of correspondence is provoking wars among nationalities and causing states to break apart.

In general, problems concerning the boundaries of nations and states develop for two reasons. In some cases, a state's boundaries encompass more than one nationality. In other cases, the population of a nation is split among more than one state. In this section, we look at both situations, and the often tumultuous results.

One State with More Than One Nationality

A state that contains more than one nationality is a **multinational state.** Relationships vary among nationalities within multinational states. In some states, one nationality tries to dominate another, especially if one has many more people. In other states, nationalities coexist peacefully. The people of one nation may be assimilated into the cultural characteristics of another nation, but in other cases, the two nationalities remain culturally distinct.

In some multinational states, nationalities coexist only by occupying geographically distinct regions. Cyprus is a multinational country that maintains

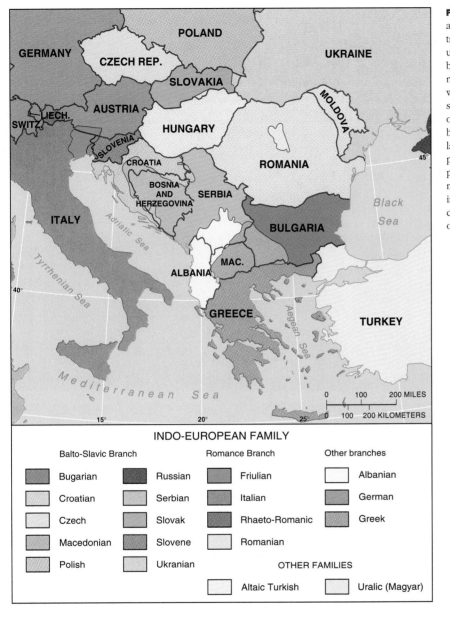

FIGURE 7-15 Languages in southern and Eastern Europe. The region traditionally has been politically unstable, partly because boundaries between states and nationalities do not correspond. After World War I, world leaders created several new states and realigned the boundaries of existing ones so that the boundaries of states matched language boundaries as closely as possible. These state boundaries proved to be relatively stable for much of the twentieth century. But in the 1990s, the region became a center of conflict among speakers of different languages.

INDO-EUROPEAN FAMILY

Balto-Slavic Branch

Bugarian
Croatian
Czech
Macedonian
Polish
Russian
Serbian
Slovak
Slovene
Ukranian

Romance Branch

Friulian
Italian
Rhaeto-Romanic
Romanian

Other branches

Albanian
German
Greek

OTHER FAMILIES

Altaic Turkish
Uralic (Magyar)

peace by allocating territory to two different nations that formerly mingled. South Africa is a multinational state where one nationality preserved its dominance over others by allocating a distinct geographic area to each nationality. The Soviet Union is an example of a multinational state that no longer exists. This section examines how each of these three countries has dealt with its various nationalities.

Cyprus: Unfriendly Division of an Island

Cyprus, the third largest island in the Mediterranean Sea, is a state that contains two nationalities: Greek and Turkish (Figure 7-16). Although the island is physically closer to Turkey, Greeks constitute 78 percent of the country's population, whereas Turks account for 18 percent. When Cyprus gained

FIGURE 7-16 Cyprus. Since 1974, Cyprus has been divided into Greek and Turkish portions, with little mingling between the two groups. The Turkish sector has declared itself to be the Turkish Republic of Northern Cyprus, but only Turkey recognizes it as an independent country. The boundary between the two sections, known as the Green Line, runs through the heart of the capital, Nicoria. In the photograph, Greek Cypriot troops patrol the Greek sector in the background, the Turkish portion is in the foreground. (Ricki Rosen/SABA Press Photos, Inc.)

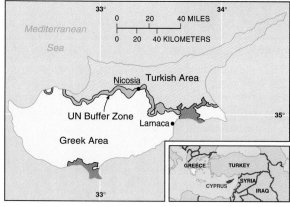

independence from Britain in 1960, its constitution guaranteed the Turkish minority a substantial share of elected offices and control over its own education, religion, and culture.

Cyprus has never peacefully integrated the Greek and Turkish nationalities. In 1974, several Greek Cypriot military officers who favored unification of Cyprus with Greece seized control of the government. Shortly after the coup, Turkey invaded Cyprus to protect the Turkish Cypriot minority, occupying 37 percent of the island. The Greek coup leaders were removed within a few months, and an elected government was restored, but the Turkish army remained on Cyprus.

Traditionally, the Greek and Turkish Cypriots mingled, but after the coup and invasion, the two nationalities became geographically isolated. The northeastern part of the island is now overwhelmingly Turkish, while the southern part is overwhelmingly Greek. Approximately one-third of the island's Greeks were forced to move from the region controlled by the Turkish army, and nearly one-fourth of the Turks moved from the region now considered to be the Greek side. The percentage of one nationality living in the region dominated by the other nationality is now very low. The Turkish sector declared itself the independent Turkish Republic of Northern Cyprus in 1983, but only Turkey recognizes it as a separate state.

A buffer zone patrolled by U.N. soldiers stretches across the entire island to prevent Greeks and Turks from crossing. The barrier even runs through the center of the capital, Nicosia. Only one official crossing point has been erected, and crossing is difficult except for top diplomats and U.N. personnel.

Nevertheless, some cooperation continues between sectors: the Turks supply the Greek side with water and in return receive electricity.

South Africa: Division by Race

South Africa is a multinational state where the government for many years divided the population into nationalities according to race. Although South Africa's government changed during the 1990s, it will take many years for it to erase the impact of past policies.

European Colonies in South Africa. The first whites arrived in South Africa from Holland in 1652 and settled Cape Town at the southern tip of the territory. They were known either as *Boers,* from the Dutch word for farmer, or *Afrikaners,* from the word *Afrikaans,* the name of their language, which is a dialect of Dutch.

In 1795, the British seized the Dutch colony at Cape Town for military reasons. To escape British administration and the freeing of slaves in 1833, about 12,000 Boers trekked northeast into the interior of South Africa and settled in the regions known as the Transvaal and the Orange Free State (Figure 7-17). After diamonds and gold were discovered in the Transvaal during the 1860s and 1870s, the British followed the Boers into South Africa's interior. A series of wars between the British and the Boers culminated in a British victory in 1902, and all of South Africa became part of the British Empire.

British descendants continued to control South Africa's government until 1948, when the Afrikaner-dominated Nationalist party won elections. The Afrikaners gained power at a time when colonial rule was being replaced in the rest of Africa by a collection of independent states run by the local black population. The Afrikaners vowed to resist pressures to turn over South Africa's government to blacks.

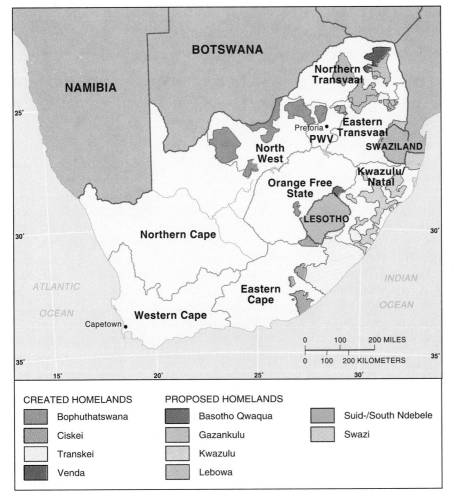

FIGURE 7-17 South Africa. As part of its apartheid system, the government of South Africa designated ten so-called homelands, expecting that ultimately every black would become a citizen of one of them. South Africa declared four of these homelands to be independent states, but no other country recognized the action. With the end of apartheid and the election of a black majority government, the homelands have been abolished, and South Africa has been reorganized into nine provinces.

CREATED HOMELANDS

Bophuthatswana
Ciskei
Transkei
Venda

PROPOSED HOMELANDS

Basotho Qwaqua
Gazankulu
Kwazulu
Lebowa

Suid-/South Ndebele
Swazi

South Africa's apartheid laws were designed to spatially segregate races as much as possible. Blacks and whites reached the platform at this train station in Johannesburg by walking up separate stairs. Whites waited at the front of the platform to get into cars at the head of the train, while blacks waited at the rear. (William Campbell/Sygma)

South Africa's Apartheid Policy. The cornerstone of the Afrikaners' policy was the creation of a legal system called apartheid. **Apartheid** was the physical separation of different races into different geographic areas. In South Africa, a newborn baby was classified as being of one of four races: black, white, colored (mixed white and black), or Asian. According to the most recent census, blacks constitute about 76 percent of South Africa's population, whites 13 percent, colored 9 percent, and Asians 3 percent.

Under apartheid, each of the four races had a different legal status in South Africa. The apartheid laws determined where different races could live, attend school, work, shop, and own land. Blacks were restricted to certain occupations and were paid far lower wages than whites for similar work. Blacks could not vote or run for office in national elections.

To assure further geographic isolation of different races, the South African government designated ten so-called *homelands* for blacks. The white minority government expected every black to become

a citizen of one of the homelands and to move there. More than 99 percent of the population in the ten homelands was black.

The first four homelands designated by the government were called Bophuthatswana, Ciskei, Transkei, and Venda (Figure 7-17). Bophuthatswana included six discontinuous areas, Transkei three discontinuous areas, and Venda two discontinuous areas. During the late 1970s, South Africa declared Bophuthatswana, Ciskei, Transkei, and Venda to be independent countries, but no other government in the world recognized the claim.

The first four homelands comprised about 9 percent of South Africa's land area and 19 percent of the population; if the government policy had been fully implemented, the ten black homelands together would have contained approximately 44 percent of South Africa's population on only 13 percent of the land.

Because they opposed apartheid, other countries cut off most relations with South Africa. Foreign companies such as Ford and General Motors stopped operating factories in South Africa, and foreign athletes and teams refused to play in the country. However, as discussed earlier in the chapter, neighboring land-locked countries felt compelled to maintain economic ties with South Africa, because they needed to ship their goods through South African ports. South Africa also played an important economic role; it provided jobs for unemployed people from the much poorer neighboring countries, and it supplied more developed countries with mineral resources—including chromium, platinum, and manganese—critical for manufacturing and chemical processes.

Dismantling of Apartheid. In 1991, the white-dominated government of South Africa repealed the apartheid laws, including restrictions on property ownership and classification of people at birth by race. The principal anti-apartheid organization, the African National Congress, was legalized, and its leader Nelson Mandela was released from jail after 27 1/2 years. When all South Africans were permitted to vote in national elections for the first time, in April 1994, Mandela was overwhelmingly elected the country's first black president. Whites were guaranteed representation in the government during a 5-year transition period, until 1999. As of 1994, South Africa no longer considered the four homelands to be independent countries.

Now that South Africa's apartheid laws have been dismantled and the country is governed by its black majority, other countries have reestablished economic and cultural ties. But the legacy of apartheid will linger for many years: South Africa's blacks have achieved political equality but they are much poorer than white South Africans. Average income among white South Africans is about ten times higher than for blacks.

Former Soviet Union: The Largest Multinational State

The Soviet Union had been an especially prominent example of a multinational state until its collapse in the early 1990s. The fifteen republics that once constituted the Soviet Union are now independent countries (Figure 7-18). Reasonably good examples of nation-states have been carved out of the former Soviet Union, including the Baltic states (Estonia, Latvia, and Lithuania), Belarus, and Ukraine. On the other hand, Russia—once the largest repub-lic in the Soviet Union—has quickly become an especially prominent example of a multinational state with major difficulties in keeping all of its nationalities contented.

New Nation-States in the Baltics. Estonia, Latvia, and Lithuania are known as the Baltic states for their location on the Baltic Sea. They had been independent countries between the end of World War I in 1918 and 1940, when the former Soviet Union annexed them under an agreement with Nazi Germany.

Of the three Baltic states, Lithuania most closely fits the definition of a nation-state, because 80 percent of its population are ethnic Lithuanians. In Estonia, ethnic Estonians constitute only 62 percent of the population; in Latvia, only 53 percent are ethnic Latvians. In 1990, Russians constituted 9 percent of the population in Lithuania, 30 percent in Estonia, and 34 percent in Latvia.

These three small neighboring Baltic countries have clear cultural differences and distinct historical traditions. Most Estonians are Protestant (Lutherans), most Lithuanians are Roman Catholics, and Latvians are predominantly Lutheran with a substantial Roman Catholic minority. Estonians speak a Uralic language related to Finnish, whereas Latvians and Lithuanians speak languages of the Baltic group within the Balto-Slavic branch of the Indo-European language family.

New Nation-States of Belarus and Ukraine. To some extent, the former Soviet republics of Belarus and Ukraine now qualify as nation-states. Belarusians constitute 79 percent of the population of Belarus, and Ukrainians constitute 73 percent of the population of Ukraine. But the cultural distinctions among Belarusians, Ukrainians, and Russians are somewhat blurred. The three groups speak similar East Slavic languages, and all are predominantly Eastern Orthodox Christians (some western Ukrainians are Roman Catholics).

Belarusians and Ukrainians became distinct nationalities because they were isolated from the main body of Eastern Slavs—the Russians—during the 1200s and 1300s. Their isolation was the consequence of Mongolian invasions and conquests by Poles and Lithuanians. Russians conquered the Belarusian and Ukrainian homelands in the late 1700s, but after five centuries of exposure to non-Slavic influences, the three Eastern Slavic groups displayed sufficient cultural diversity to be considered as three distinct nationalities.

FIGURE 7-18 Soviet Union. The former Soviet Union included fifteen republics, named for the country's largest nationalities. Russians constituted about half of the Soviet Union's population, followed by Ukrainians, Uzbeks, and Kazaks. With the breakup of the Soviet Union, the fifteen republics became independent states, but in many cases the new countries contain large percentages of minorities.

Russians actually constitute two-thirds of the population in the Crimean Peninsula of Ukraine. The Crimean Peninsula had been part of Russia until 1954, when the Soviet government turned over its administration to Ukraine, as a gift in honor of the 300th anniversary of Russian-Ukrainian friendship.

As long as both Russia and Ukraine were part of the Soviet Union, the Russians living in the Crimea were not concerned about the republic to which they were attached. After Russia and Ukraine became separate countries, a majority of the Crimeans voted to become independent of Ukraine. Control of the Crimean Peninsula was also important to both Russia and Ukraine because one of the Soviet Union's largest fleets was stationed there. The two countries agreed to divide the ships and to maintain jointly the naval base at Sevastopol.

Compounding the problem in the Crimea, 166,000 Tatars have migrated there from Central Asia in recent years. The Tatars once lived in the Crimea, but the Soviet leadership, suspecting them of sympathizing with the Germans during World War II, deported them to Central Asia. The Tatars prefer to be governed by Ukraine because of long-standing suspicion of the Russians, who dominated the government of the Soviet Union.

Russia's Nationalities. Russia officially recognizes the existence of thirty-nine nationalities, many of which are eager for independence. Russia's minorities are clustered in two principal locations (Figure 7-19). Some are located along borders with neighboring states, including Buryats and Tuvinians near Mongolia, and Chechens, Dagestani, Kabardins,

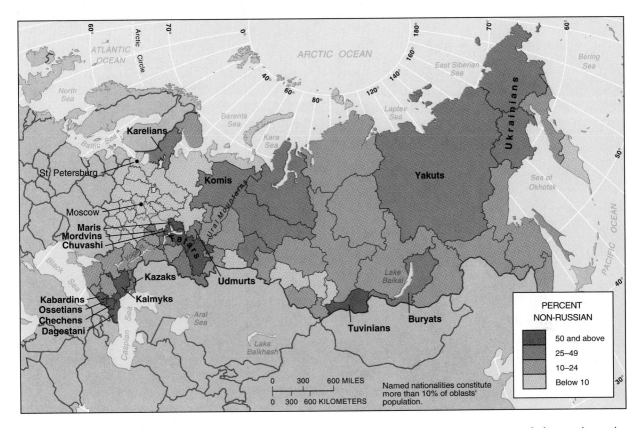

FIGURE 7-19 Nationalities in Russia. Russians are clustered in the western portion of Russia, and the percentage declines to the south and east. The largest numbers of non-Russians are found in the center of the country between the Volga River and the Ural Mountains and near the southern boundaries.

and Ossetians near the two former Soviet republics of Azerbaijan and Georgia.

Other minorities are clustered in the center of Russia, especially between the Volga River basin and the Ural Mountains. Among the more numerous in this region are Bashkirs, Chuvashi, and Tatars, who speak Altaic languages similar to Turkish, and Mordvins and Udmurts, who speak Uralic languages similar to Finnish. Most of these groups were conquered by the Russians in the sixteenth century under the leadership of Ivan IV (Ivan the Terrible).

Independence movements are flourishing because Russia is less willing to suppress these movements forcibly than the Soviet Union had once been. Particularly troublesome for the Russians are the Chechens, a group of Sunni Muslims who speak a Caucasian language and practice distinctive social customs.

Chechnya was brought under Russian control in the nineteenth century only after a 50-year fight.

When the Soviet Union broke up into fifteen independent states in 1991, the Chechens declared their independence and refused to join the newly created country of Russia. Russian leaders ignored the declaration of independence for 3 years, but late in 1994 they sent in the Russian army to regain control of the territory.

Russia fought hard to prevent Chechnya from gaining independence because it feared that other nationalities would follow suit. Chechnya was also important to Russia because the region contained deposits of petroleum. Russia viewed political stability in the area as essential for promoting economic development and investment by foreign petroleum companies.

Russians in Other Multinational States.
Decades of Russian domination have left a deep reservoir of bitterness among other nationalities once part of the Soviet Union. Because Russians were the dom-

Latvians celebrate independence from the Soviet Union with a massive demonstration in the streets of the capital, Riga, in 1991. (Ints Kalnins/Woodfin Camp & Associates)

inant nationality in the Soviet Union, they were blamed for confiscating property and prohibiting the use of local languages in schools, hospitals, and factories.

Years after the demise of the Soviet Union, Russian soldiers have remained stationed in other countries, in part because Russia cannot afford to rehouse them. Other nationalities fear that the slow withdrawal of Russian troops indicates that the Russians are trying to reassert the dominance over the economies and governments of other countries that they once exercised as the most numerous nationality in the Soviet Union.

For their part, Russians claim that they are now subject to discrimination as minorities in countries that were once part of the Soviet Union. Some of the countries once part of the Soviet Union have passed laws making it difficult for Russians to vote or to qualify as citizens with full civil rights. Russians are being passed over for hiring and promotion unless they learn the local languages. Yet, despite local hostility, Russians living in other countries of the former Soviet Union feel that they cannot migrate to Russia, because they have no jobs, homes, or land awaiting them there.

One Nationality in More Than One State

Conflicts may develop when one nation of people finds itself divided across more than one state. Some nationalities consider that they have been excluded from the goal of dividing Earth into a collection of nation-states. A nationality split among more than one state—unable to control the government of any state—may seek to carve out a new nation-state from portions of existing ones.

Unrest caused by the lack of correspondence between nationalities and states is especially severe in two regions of the world—Sub-Saharan Africa and Eastern Europe. In Sub-Saharan Africa, boundaries between states ignore the distribution of nationalities, because most were drawn by European colonial rulers for their military and economic benefit rather than the needs of local cultural groups.

In Eastern Europe, the breakup of the Soviet Union and Yugoslavia during the 1990s has given more numerous nationalities the opportunity to organize nation-states. But the less numerous nationalities still find themselves existing as minorities in

The Russian army attacked Chechnya to suppress the independence movement. When Chechens offered stiff resistance, the Russians destroyed much of the capital Grozny, including the presidential palace (in the background) and the main public square in front of it. A refugee carrying her possessions rushes across the square to get out of harm's way, while a Chechen soldier watches for snipers. (David Brauchli/AP/Wide World Photos)

multinational states or divided among more than one of the new states. Especially severe problems have occurred in the Caucasus and Balkans, two rugged, mountainous regions where nation-states could not be delineated peacefully.

Cultural Diversity in Africa

Conflict is widespread in Africa largely because the present-day boundaries of states were drawn by European colonial powers about a hundred years ago without regard for the traditional distribution of cultural groups (Figure 7-20). Africa contains several thousand ethnic groups (often referred to as tribes) with a common sense of language, religion, social customs (refer to Figure 4-11 for a map of African languages). Some tribes are divided among more than one modern state; others have been grouped with dissimilar tribes.

The precise number of tribes is impossible to determine because boundaries separating them are not usually defined clearly. Further, it is hard to determine whether a particular group forms a distinct tribe or is part of a larger collection of very similar groups.

Pre-European States in Africa. The traditional unit of African society was the tribe rather than independent states with political and economic self-determination. Nonetheless, Africa has some tradition of state control, especially in West Africa. Important

states in West Africa, based in present-day Mali and Mauritania, included Ghana (800 kilometers, or 500 miles, northwest of the present-day state of Ghana) between the 700s and 1100s, Mali between the 1100s and 1400s, and Songhai during the 1400s and 1500s. Songhai was destroyed by Morocco in 1591.

Other kingdoms were located closer to the coast of West Africa. The Kongo kingdom, based near the mouth of the Congo (Zaire) River in present-day Angola and Zaire, flourished from the fourteenth to the seventeenth century. A group of Ewe-speaking people called the Aja established the Great Ardra kingdom in present-day Benin, which reached its height in the sixteenth and early seventeenth centuries. The Aja mixed with other local groups to form the Fon, or Dahomey, ethnic group. Four hundred kilometers (250 miles) west, the Ashanti ethnic group established a confederation in the seventeenth century in the central part of present-day Ghana, which survived until the late nineteenth century.

Impact of European Colonialization. European exploration of the African coast began in the 1400s, but until the late nineteenth century Africa was largely free of foreign control. Between the 1880s and the outbreak of World War I in 1914, European countries carved up the continent into a collection of colonies. The shapes of these colonies were dictated primarily by competition among the European colonial powers to control resources in

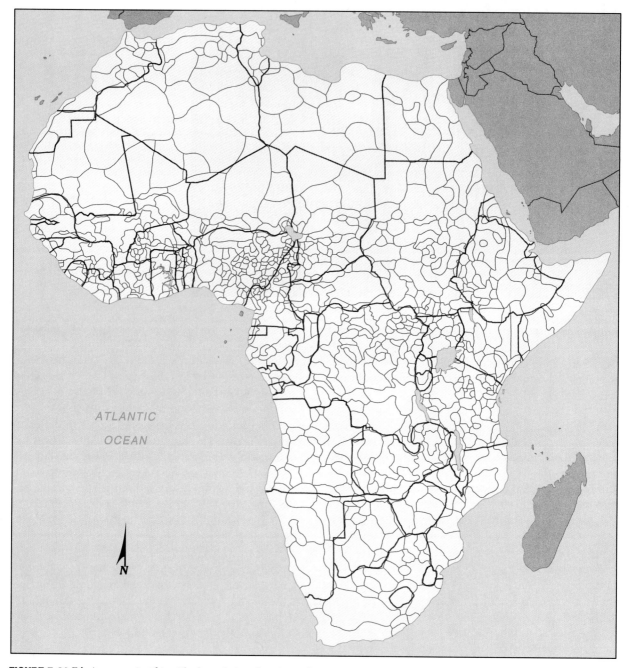

FIGURE 7-20 Ethnic groups in Africa. The boundaries of modern African states do not match the territories long occupied by thousands of ethnic groups. State boundaries derive from the administrative units imposed by European colonial powers a century ago.

the interior rather than the distribution of the thousands of tribes.

When the European colonies became independent states, especially during the 1950s and 1960s, the boundaries of the new states typically matched the colonial administrative units imposed by the Europeans. As a result, most African states contained large numbers of ethnic groups. For example, the British colony of the Gold Coast became the independent state of Ghana in 1956. Ghana's territory includes the historic homelands of the Ashanti, Fanti, Mole-Dagbani, Ewe, and Ga-Adangme tribes.

Turmoil in the Caucasus

The Caucasus region, an area about the size of Colorado situated between the Black and Caspian seas, gets its name from the mountains that separate Russia from Azerbaijan and Georgia (Figure 7-21). The region is home to several nationalities, with Azeris, Armenians, and Georgians the most numerous (Table 7-3). Other important nationalities include Abkhazians, Chechens, Ingushi, and Ossetians. Kurds and Russians—two nationalities that are more numerous in other regions—are also represented in the Caucasus.

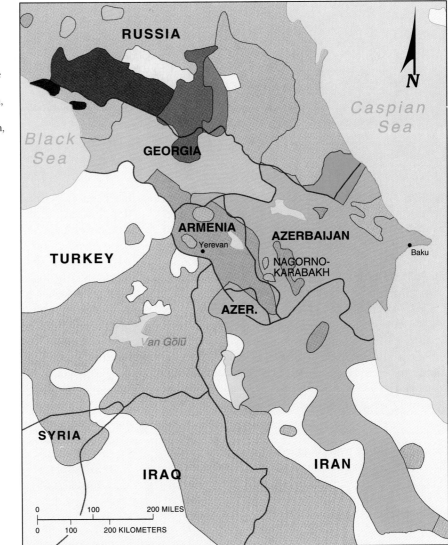

FIGURE 7-21 Nationalities in the Caucasus. Armenians, Azeris, and Georgians are examples of nationalities that have been able to dominate nation-states during the 1990s, following the breakup of the Soviet Union. But the boundaries of the states of Armenia, Azerbaijan, and Georgia do not match the territories occupied by the Armenian, Azeri, and Georgian peoples. The Abkhazians, Chechens, Kurds, and Ossetians are examples of nationalities that have not been able to organize nation-states.

TABLE 7-3
Principal nationalities in the Caucasus

Nationality	Population	Religion	Language Family
	(in millions)		
Abkhazians	0.1	Sunni Muslim	Caucasian
Armenians	3.7	Eastern Orthodox Christian	Indo-European
Azerbaijanis	5.3	Shiite Muslims	Altaic
Chechens	0.7	Sunni Muslim	Caucasian
Georgians	3.5	Eastern Orthodox Christian	Caucasian
Ingushi	0.2	Sunni Muslim	Caucasian
Kabardo-Cherkessians	0.4	Sunni Muslim	Caucasian
Karachay-Balkars	0.2	Sunni Muslim	Caucasian
Kurds	0.2[a]	Sunni Muslim	Indo-European
Lezghians	0.1	Sunni Muslim	Caucasian
Ossetians	0.3	Eastern Orthodox Christian	Indo-European
Russians	0.6[b]	Eastern Orthodox Christian	Indo-European

[a]Includes only Kurds in the former Soviet Union.
[b]Includes only Russians in Armenia, Azerbaijan, and Georgia.

When the entire Caucasus region was part of the Soviet Union, the Soviet government promoted allegiance to communism and the Soviet state and quelled disputes among nationalities, by force if necessary. But with the breakup of the region into several independent countries, long-simmering conflicts among nationalities have erupted into armed conflicts.

Each nationality has a long-standing and complex set of grievances against others in the region. But from a political geography perspective, every nationality in the Caucasus has the same aspiration: to carve out a sovereign nation-state. The region's nationalities have had varying success in achieving this objective, but none has achieved it fully.

Azeris. Azeris (or Azerbaijanis) trace their roots to Turkish invaders who migrated from central Asia in the eighth and ninth centuries and merged with the existing Persian population. An 1828 treaty allocated northern Azeri territory to Russia and southern Azeri territory to Persia (now Iran). In 1923, the Russ-

ian portion became the Azerbaijan Soviet Socialist Republic within the Soviet Union. With the Soviet Union's breakup in 1991, Azerbaijan became an independent country again.

Approximately 6 million Azeris now live in Azerbaijan, nearly 80 percent of the country's total population. Another 6 million Azeris are clustered in northwestern Iran, where they constitute 10 percent of that country's population. Azeris hold positions of responsibility in Iran's government and economy, but Iran restricts teaching of the Azeri language.

Azerbaijan is a good example of a fragmented state: the western part of the country, Nakhichevan (named for the area's largest city), is separated from the rest of Azerbaijan by a 40-kilometer (25-mile) corridor belonging to Armenia.

Armenians. More than 3,000 years ago, Armenians controlled an independent kingdom in the Caucasus. Converted to Christianity in A.D. 303, they lived for many centuries as an isolated Christian enclave under the rule of Turkish Muslims. During the late nineteenth and early twentieth centuries, hundreds of thousands of Armenians were killed in a series of massacres organized by the Turks. Others were forced to migrate to Russia, which had gained possession of eastern Armenia in 1828.

After World War I, the allies created an independent state of Armenia, but it was soon swallowed by its neighbors: in 1921, Turkey and the Soviet Union agreed to divide Armenia between them. The Soviet portion became the Armenian Soviet Socialist Republic and then an independent country in 1991. More than 90 percent of the population in Armenia are Armenians, making it the most ethnically homogeneous country in the region.

Armenians and Azeris both have achieved long-held aspirations of forming nation-states. But the two have been at war with each other since 1988 over the boundaries between them. The conflict concerns possession of Nagorno-Karabakh, a 5,000-square-kilometer (2,000-square mile) enclave within Azerbaijan that is inhabited primarily by Armenians but placed under Azerbaijan's control by the Soviet Union during the 1920s.

Georgians. The population of Georgia is more diverse than that in Armenia and Azerbaijan. Only 69 percent of the people living in Georgia are ethnic Georgians. The country includes about 9 percent each Armenian and Russian and 5 percent Azeri, 3 percent Ossetian, 2 percent Abkhazian, and 1 percent Ajar.

Georgia's cultural diversity has been a source of unrest, especially among the Ossetians and Abkhazians. The Abkhazians have fought for control of the northwestern portion of Georgia and would like to form an independent nation-state. The Ossetians want South Ossetia to be transferred from Georgia to Russia and united with North Ossetia, already part of Russia, rather than made a sovereign nation-state.

Kurds. The Kurds, who live south of the Armenians and Azeris, constitute another nationality that is divided among more than one state. The Kurds are a non-Arab group of Sunni Muslims who speak a language similar to Farsi and have distinctive literature, dress, and other cultural traditions. The Kurdish population is split among six countries,

including 10 million in eastern Turkey, 5 million in western Iran, 4 million in northern Iraq, and smaller numbers in Armenia, Azerbaijan, and northeastern Syria (Figure 7-21). Kurds constitute a fifth of the population in Iraq, a sixth in Turkey, and nearly a tenth in Iran.

When the victorious European allies carved up the Ottoman Empire after World War I, they created an independent state of Kurdistan to the south and west of Van Gölü (Lake Van) under the 1920 Treaty of Sèvres. Before the treaty was ratified, however, the Turks, under the leadership of Mustafa Kemal (later known as Kemal Ataturk), fought successfully to expand the territory under their control beyond the small area the allies had allocated to them. The Treaty of Lausanne in 1923 established the modern state of Turkey, with boundaries nearly identical to the current ones. Kurdistan became part of Turkey and disappeared as an independent state.

To foster the development of Turkish nationalism, the Turks have tried repeatedly to suppress Kurdish culture. Use of the Kurdish language was illegal in Turkey until 1991, and laws banning its use in broadcasts and classrooms remain in force. Kurdish nationalists, for their part, have waged a guerrilla war since 1984 against the Turkish army.

Kurds in other countries have fared just as poorly as those in Turkey. Iran's Kurds secured an independent republic in 1946, but it lasted less than a year. Iraq's Kurds have made several unsuccessful attempts to gain independence, including in the 1930s, 1940s, and 1970s. A few days after Iraq was defeated in the 1991 Gulf War, the country's Kurds launched another unsuccessful rebellion. The United States and its allies decided not to resume their recently concluded fight against Iraq on behalf of the Kurdish rebels, but after the revolt was crushed, they did send troops to protect the Kurds from further attacks by the Iraqi army.

Thus, despite their numbers, the Kurds are a nationality with no corresponding Kurdish state today. Instead, they are forced to live under the control of the region's more powerful nationalities.

The Balkans: Making and Breaking Yugoslavia

The Balkan Peninsula includes the states from Romania southward through Greece (Figure 7-22). The region, about the size of Texas, is named for the

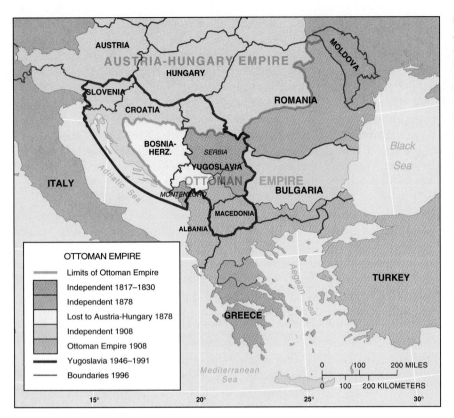

FIGURE 7-22 The Balkans in 1914. At the outbreak of World War I, Austria-Hungary controlled the northern part of the region, including all or part of Croatia, Slovenia, and Romania. The Ottoman Empire controlled some of the south, although during the nineteenth century it had lost control of Albania, Bosnia-Herzegovina, Greece, Romania, and Serbia.

Balkan Mountains (known in Slavic languages as Stara Planina), which extend east-west across central Bulgaria between Yugoslavia and the Black Sea.

Creation of Yugoslavia. The Balkan Peninsula has long been a hotbed of unrest, a complex assemblage of nationalities (refer to Figure 7-15 for a language map of the region). Northern portions were incorporated into the Austro-Hungarian Empire, whereas southern portions were ruled by the Ottomans. Austria-Hungary extended its rule farther south in 1878 to include Bosnia-Herzegovina, where the majority of the people had been converted to Islam by the Ottomans. In June 1914, the heir to the throne of Austria-Hungary was assassinated in Sarajevo by a Serb who sought independence for Bosnia. The incident sparked World War I.

After World War I, the allies created a new country, Yugoslavia, to unite several Balkan groups that spoke similar South Slavic languages. The most numerous cultural groups brought into Yugoslavia were Serbs and Croats; others included Slovenes, Macedonians, and Montenegrens. The prefix *Yugo* in the country's name derives from the Slavic word for "south."

Creation of Yugoslavia brought stability that lasted for most of the twentieth century. Old animosities among nationalities were submerged, and younger people began to identify themselves as Yugoslavs, rather than as Serbs, Croats, or Montenegrens (See Geography in Action box).

Destruction of Yugoslavia. As long as Yugoslavia was one country, nationalities were not especially troubled by the name of the republic they inhabited. But when Yugoslavia's six republics were transformed from local government units into independent countries, nationalities fought to redefine the boundaries (Figure 7-23).

Serbia attacked Croatia to gain control of the Krajina region of eastern Croatia, where Serbs outnumbered Croats. Albanians, who constituted 77 percent of the population in the Kosovo region of southern

Cultural Diversity in the Former Yugoslavia

Under the long leadership of Josip Broz Tito, who governed Yugoslavia from 1953 until his death in 1980, Yugoslavs liked to repeat a refrain that roughly translates as follows: "Yugoslavia has seven neighbors, six republics, five nationalities, four languages, three religions, two alphabets, and one dinar." Specifically:

- Yugoslavia's *seven* neighbors included three long-time democracies (Austria, Greece, and Italy) and four states then governed by Communists (Albania, Bulgaria, Hungary, and Romania). The diversity of neighbors reflected Yugoslavia's strategic location between the Western democracies and Communist Eastern Europe. Although a socialist country, Yugoslavia was militarily neutral after it had been expelled in 1948 from the Soviet-dominated military alliance for being too independent-minded. Yugoslavia's Communists permitted more communication and interaction with Western democracies than did other Eastern European countries.
- The *six* republics—Bosnia-Herzegovina, Croatia, Macedonia, Montenegro, Serbia, and Slovenia—had more autonomy from the national government to run their own affairs than was the case in other Eastern European countries.
- *Five* of the republics were named for the country's five recognized nationalities—Croats, Macedonians, Montenegrens, Serbs, and Slovenes. Bosnia-Herzegovina contained a mix of Serbs, Croats, and Muslims.
- The *four official languages* were Croatian, Macedonian, Serbian, and Slovene (the Montenegrens spoke Serbian).
- The *three major religions* included Roman Catholic in the north, Eastern Orthodox in the east, and Islam in the south. Croats and Slovenes were predominantly Roman Catholic, Serbs and Macedonians predominantly Eastern Orthodox, and Bosnians and Montenegrens predominantly Muslim.
- The *two alphabets* were Latin and Cyrillic. Two of the four official languages—Croatian and Slovene—were written in the Latin alphabet; Macedonian and Serbian were written in Cyrillic. Most linguists outside Yugoslavia considered Serbian and Croatian to be the same language except for different alphabets.
- The *dinar* was the national unit of currency. Despite cultural diversity, common economic interests kept Yugoslavia's nationalities unified. The photograph on page 165 shows the variety of languages written on the dinar.

Resurfacing rivalries among nationalities during the 1980s after Tito's death lead to the breakup of the country in the early 1990s. Not only did the boundaries of Yugoslavia's six republics fail to match the territory occupied by nationalities, but the country contained other important nationalities that had not received official recognition.

FIGURE 7-23 Yugoslavia, until its breakup in 1992. Yugoslavia comprised six republics (plus Kosovo and Vojvodina, autonomous regions within the Republic of Serbia). According to the country's last census, taken in 1981, the territory occupied by the various nationalities did not match the boundaries of the republics or autonomous regions.

Serbia, fought to free themselves from cultural and political domination of Serbs, who retained control of Kosovo because it was their historic homeland.

The creation of a viable country proved especially difficult in the case of Bosnia-Herzegovina because "Bosnian" was never clearly defined as a nationality in the old Yugoslavia. Yugoslavia's five officially recognized nationalities—Croats, Macedonians, Montenegrens, Serbs, and Slovenes—were able to constitute majorities in the other independent states carved out of Yugoslavia. In contrast, at the time of Yugoslavia's breakup, the largest group in Bosnia-Herzegovina, 40 percent, were classified not by nationality but as Muslims, while the remainder included 32 percent Serbs and 18 percent Croats.

Rather than live in an independent multinational country with a Muslim plurality, Bosnia-Herzegovina's Serbs and Croats fought to unite the portions of the republic that they inhabited with Serbia and Croatia (see Chapter 3 for description of *ethnic cleansing*, the process by which Serbs have captured Muslim territory and forced Muslims to migrate).

A century ago, the term **Balkanized** was widely used to describe a small geographic area that could not successfully be organized into one or more stable states because it was inhabited by many nationalities with complex, long-standing antagonisms toward each other. World leaders at the time regarded **Balkanization**—the process by which a state breaks down through conflicts among its nationalities—as a threat to peace throughout the world, not just in a small area. They were right: Balkanization directly led to World War I, because the various nationalities in the Balkans dragged the larger powers with whom they had alliances into the war.

At the end of the twentieth century—after two world wars and the rise and fall of communism—the Balkans have once again become Balkanized. Will the United States, Western Europe, and Russia once again be drawn reluctantly into conflict through entangled alliances in the Balkans?

Distinguishing between the Two Types of Boundary Problems

In this section, we have examined two situations: a state's boundaries may encompass more than one nationality, or the population of a nation may be spread over more than one state. Conflicts can result in either case. Further, disputes can even stem from disagreement over which type of boundary problem applies to a situation. One faction may argue that the issue derives from one nation's being divided among states, while the opposing faction may claim that the problem is one of accommodating more than one nationality in one state.

As an example, Romanians constitute two-thirds of the population of Moldova (Figure 7-24). The Soviet Union seized Moldova (then called Moldavia) from Romania in 1940. When Moldova changed from a Soviet republic back to an independent country in 1992, many Moldovans pushed for reunification with Romania, which has greater economic development.

But it was not to be that simple. When Moldova became a Soviet republic in 1940, its eastern boundary was the Dniester River. The Soviet government increased the size of Moldova by about 10 percent, transferring from Ukraine a 3,000-square-kilometer (1,200-square-mile) sliver of land on the east bank of the Dniester. The majority of the inhabitants of this area, known as Trans-Dniestria, are Ukrainian and Russian. They, of course, oppose Moldova's reunification with Romania.

Franz Ferdinand, Archduke of Austria, and his wife, were assassinated in Sarajevo by Gavrilo Princip, a Serbian nationalist, June 28, 1914. The event triggered World War I. (Culver Pictures, Inc.)

Internal Organization of States

In the face of increasing demands by nationalities for more self-determination, states have restructured their governments to transfer some authority from the national government to local government units. A nationality that is not numerous enough to gain control of the national government may be content with control of a regional or local unit of government.

Unitary and Federal States

The governments of states are organized according to one of two approaches: the unitary system or the federal system. The **unitary state** places most power in the hands of central government officials, whereas the **federal state** allocates strong power to units of local government within the country. A country's cultural and physical characteristics influence the evolution of its governmental system.

In principle, the unitary government system works best in nation-states characterized by few internal cultural differences and a strong sense of national unity. Because the unitary system requires effective communications with all regions of the country, smaller states are more likely to adopt it. Unitary states are especially common in Europe.

In reality, multinational states often have adopted unitary systems so that the values of one nationality can be imposed on others. In some African countries, such as Ghana, Kenya, and Rwanda, for instance, the mechanisms of a unitary state have

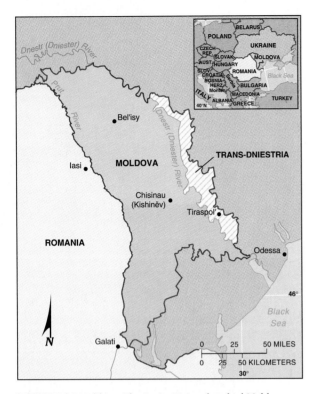

FIGURE 7-24 Moldova. The Soviet Union detached Moldova (then known as Moldavia) from Romania in 1940 and made it a republic of the Soviet Union. At the time, Moldova's boundary was extended eastward from the Dniester River to encompass a narrow strip known as Trans-Dniestria. Most Moldovans are ethnic Romanians, but the majority of the people living in the Trans-Dniestria region are Ukrainians and Russians.

enabled one ethnic group to extend dominance over weaker groups. When Communist parties controlled the governments, most Eastern European countries had unitary systems, to promote diffusion of communist values.

In a federal state, such as the United States, local governments possess more authority to adopt their own laws. Multinational states may adopt a federal system of government to empower different nationalities, especially if they live in separate regions of the country. Under a federal system, local government boundaries can be drawn to correspond with regions inhabited by different nations.

The federal system is also more suitable for very large states because the national capital may be too remote to provide effective control over isolated regions. Most of the world's largest states are federal, including Russia (as well as the former Soviet Union), Canada, the United States, Brazil, and India. The size of the state, however, is not always an accurate predictor of the form of government: tiny Belgium is a federal state (to accommodate the two main cultural groups, the Flemish and Walloons, as discussed in Chapter 4), whereas China is a unitary state (to promote communist values).

Trend toward Federal Government

In recent years, there has been a strong trend worldwide toward federal government. Unitary systems have been sharply curtailed in some countries and scrapped altogether in others.

France: Curbing a Unitary Government. A good example of a nation-state, France has a long tradition of unitary government in which a very strong national government dominates local government decisions. Their basic local government unit is the *département* (department). Each of the 100 departments has an elected general council, but its administrative head is a powerful *préfet* appointed by the national government rather than directly elected by the people. Engineers, architects, planners, and other technical experts working in the department are actually employed by national government ministries.

A second tier of local government in France is the *commune*. Each of the 36,000 communes has a locally elected mayor and council, but the mayor can be a member of the national parliament at the same time. Further, the average commune has only 1,500 inhabitants, too small to govern effectively, with the possible exception of the largest ones, such as in Paris, Lyon, Lille, and Marseille.

During the 1980s, the French government granted additional legal powers to the departments and communes. Local governments could borrow money freely to finance new projects without explicit national government approval, formerly required. The national government agreed to give a block of funds to localities with no strings attached. In addition, twenty-two regional councils that previously held minimal authority were converted into full-fledged local government units, with elected councils and the power to levy taxes.

Poland: A New Federal Government. Poland switched from a unitary to a federal system after control of the national government was wrested from the Communists. The federal system was adopted to dismantle legal structures by which Communists had maintained unchallenged power for more than 40 years.

Under the Communists' unitary system, local governments held no legal authority. The national government appointed local officials and owned public property. This system led to deteriorated buildings, roads, and water systems, because the national government did not allocate sufficient funds to maintain property, and no one had clear responsibility for keeping property in good condition.

Poland's 1989 constitution called for a peaceful revolution: creation of 2,400 municipalities, to be headed by directly elected officials. To these new municipalities, the national government turned over ownership of housing, water supplies, transportation systems, and other publicly owned structures. For existing schools, each local authority decided case by case whether to operate the school, let the national government continue to run it, or turn it over to a private group, such as a church. Similarly, businesses owned by the national government, such as travel agencies, were either turned over to the municipalities or turned into private enterprises. Local authorities were allowed for the first time to levy income and property taxes; as in France, the national government also allocated blocks of funds for localities to use as they see fit.

The transition to a federal system of government proved difficult in Poland and other Eastern European countries. In May 1990, Poles elected 52,000 municipal councillors; given the absence of local government for a half-century, not one of these officials had experience in governing a community. The first task for many newly elected councillors was to attend a training course in how to govern.

The problem of adopting a federal system was compounded by the fact that Poland's locally elected officials had to find thousands of qualified people to fill appointed positions, such as directors of education, public works, and planning. Municipalities had the option of hiring some of the 95,000 national government administrators who previously looked after local affairs under the unitary system. But many of these former officials were rejected by the new local governments because of their close

ties to the discredited Communist party. The national government was not allowed to intervene in local decisions on whether to retain or replace the former administrators.

KEY ISSUE 4

Why Do States Cooperate with Each Other?

- Political and Military Cooperation
- Economic Cooperation

The previous section illustrated examples of threats from within to the survival of states. The principal internal threat has been the desire of nationalities for the right of self-determination as an expression of unique cultural identity. In a number of cases, the inability to accommodate the diverse aspirations of nationalities has led to the break up of states into smaller ones.

The future of the world's current collection of sovereign states is also threatened by the trend toward globalization. All but a few states have joined the United Nations, although it has limited authority. But states are willingly transferring authority to regional organizations, established primarily for economic cooperation.

Political and Military Cooperation

During the Cold War era (late 1940s until early 1990s) most states joined the United Nations, as well as regional organizations. These international and regional organizations were established primarily to prevent a third world war in the twentieth century and to protect countries from a foreign attack.

The United Nations

The most important international organization is the United Nations, created at the end of World War II by the victorious Allies. When established in 1945, the United Nations comprised 49 states, but by the early 1990s, membership had grown to 185, making it a truly global institution.

Switzerland and Taiwan are the most populous territories on Earth that are not in the United Nations. Fearing loss of sovereignty, Switzerland has traditionally avoided membership in most international organizations. Taiwan resigned when the United Nations voted to admit the People's Republic of China in 1971, because the government of Taiwan still considered itself the proper ruler of the Chinese mainland.

The number of countries in the United Nations has increased rapidly on three occasions: 1955, 1960, and the early 1990s. Sixteen countries joined in 1955, mostly European countries that had been liberated from Nazi Germany during World War II. Seventeen new members were added in 1960, all but one a former African colony of Britain or France. Twenty-six countries were added between 1990 and 1993, primarily as a result of the breakup of the Soviet Union and Yugoslavia. U.N. membership has also increased in recent years because of the admission of numerous microstates.

The United Nations was not the world's first attempt at rational peacemaking. It replaced an earlier organization known as the League of Nations, which was established after World War I. The League was never an effective peace-keeping organization. The United States did not join, despite the fact that President Woodrow Wilson initiated the idea, because the U.S. Senate refused to ratify the membership treaty. By the 1930s, Germany, Italy, Japan, and the Soviet Union all withdrew, and the League could not stop aggression by these states against neighboring countries.

U.N. members can vote to establish a peace-keeping force and request states to contribute soldiers. During the Cold War era, U.N. peace-keeping efforts were often stymied because any one of the five permanent members of the Security Council—China, France, Russia (formerly the Soviet Union), the United Kingdom, and the United States—could veto the operation. In the past, the United States and Soviet Union often used the veto to prevent undesired U.N. intervention. The major exception came in 1950, when the United Nations voted to send troops to support South Korea after the Soviet Union's delegate walked out of a Security Council meeting.

During the 1990s, the United Nations has played an increasingly important role in trying to separate warring groups in various regions, especially in Eastern Europe, the Middle East, and sub-Saharan Africa. The number of U.N. peacekeepers worldwide increased from 11,500 in 1992 to 80,000 in 1994. About one-third of these troops were in Bosnia-Herzegovina and another one-third in Somalia (Figure 7-25).

The United Nations has had difficulty playing its enhanced role. Because it must rely on individual countries to supply soldiers, the United Nations often lacks enough of them to keep peace effectively. It tries to maintain strict neutrality in separating warring factions, but neutrality has proved difficult in places such as Bosnia-Herzegovina, where most of the world sees one nationality (Bosnian Serbs) as a stronger aggressor and another (Bosnian Muslims) as a weaker victim. Despite its shortcomings, though, the United Nations represents a forum where, for the first time in history, virtually all states of the world can meet and vote on issues without resorting to war.

Regional Military Alliances

In addition to joining the United Nations, many states joined regional military alliances after World War II. The division of the world into military alliances resulted from the emergence of two states as superpowers—the United States and the Soviet Union.

Era of Two Superpowers. During the Cold War era, the United States and the Soviet Union were the world's two superpowers. Before then, the world typically contained more than two superpowers. For example, during the Napoleonic Wars in the early 1800s, Europe boasted eight major powers: Austria, France, Great Britain, Poland, Prussia, Russia, Spain, and Sweden.

By the outbreak of World War I, eight great powers again existed. Germany, Italy, Japan, and the United States replaced Poland, Prussia, Spain, and Sweden on the list. By the late 1940s, most of the former great powers were beaten or battered by the two world wars, and only the United States and the Soviet Union remained as superpowers.

When a large number of states ranked as great powers of approximately equal strength, no single state could dominate. Instead, major powers joined together to form temporary alliances. A condition of roughly equal strength between opposing alliances is known as a **balance of power.**

Historically, the addition of one or two states to an alliance could tip the balance of power. The British in particular entered alliances to restore the balance of power and prevent any other state from becoming too strong. In contrast, the post–World War II balance of power was bipolar between the United States and the Soviet Union. Because the power of these two states was so much greater than

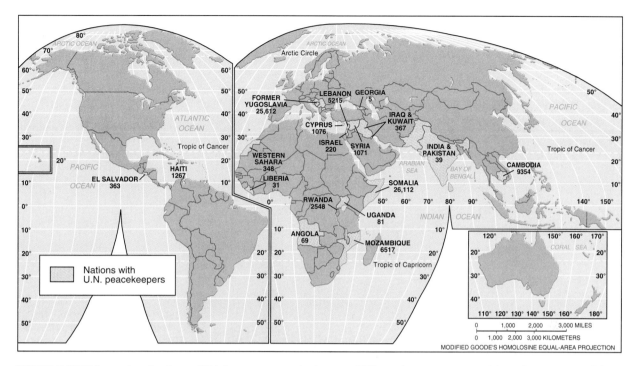

FIGURE 7-25 U.N. peacekeeping forces, 1994. In attempts to maintain peace, U.N. members sent troops to eighteen locations around the world. The largest number was in the former Yugoslavia. In the photo, U.N. soldiers overlook Sarajevo, the capital of Bosnia-Herzegovina. When the photo was taken in September 1994, Sarajevo had been without running water for 14 days, and residents had to carry water from a collection point. (Rikard Larma/AP/Wide World Photos)

A major confrontation during the Cold War between the United States and Soviet Union came in 1962 when the Soviet Union secretly began to construct missile launching sites in Cuba, less than 150 kilometers (90 miles) from U.S. territory. President Kennedy demanded that the missiles be removed and ordered a naval blockade to prevent further Soviet material from reaching Cuba. The crisis ended when the Soviet Union agreed to dismantle the sites. The U.S. Department of Defense took aerial photographs to show the Soviet buildup in Cuba. (top) Three Soviet ships are being loaded with missile equipment at Mariel naval port in Cuba. Within the outlined box (enlarged below and rotated 90° to the right) are Soviet missile transporters, fuel trailers, and oxidizer trailers (used to support the combustion of missile fuel). (UPI/Bettman)

that of all others, the world comprised two camps, each under the influence of one of the superpowers.

Other states lost the ability to tip the scales significantly in favor of one or the other superpower. They were relegated to a new role, that of ally or satellite. The two superpowers collected allies as if they were works of art. The acquisition of one state not only added to the value of one superpower's collection but also prevented the other superpower from acquiring it.

An ally could cause trouble for a superpower. States could remain in an alliance, either as willing and effective partners in pursuing the objectives of the superpower or as balky and unreliable members with limited usefulness. When the United States attacked Libya by air in 1986, the planes took off from England. The most direct route was over France, but the French refused to give the U.S. planes permission to fly through their airspace. Rather than risk a confrontation with an ally, the U.S. planes flew a more circuitous route over the Atlantic Ocean and the Mediterranean Sea, a route that added 1,200 kilometers (800 miles) to the total round-trip mission.

Both superpowers repeatedly demonstrated that they would use military force if necessary to prevent an ally from becoming too independent. The Soviet Union sent its armies into Hungary in 1956, Czechoslovakia in 1968, and Afghanistan in 1979 to install more sympathetic governments. Because these states were clearly within the orbit of the Soviet Union, the United States chose not to intervene militarily. Similarly, the United States sent troops to the Dominican Republic in 1965, Grenada in 1983, and Panama in 1989 to assure that they would remain allies.

As very large states, both superpowers could quickly deploy armed forces in different regions of the world. To maintain strength in regions that were not contiguous to their own territory, the United States and the Soviet Union established military bases in other countries. From these bases, ground and air support gained proximity to local areas of conflict. Naval fleets patrolled the major bodies of water.

Military Cooperation in Europe. After World War II, most European states joined one of two military alliances dominated by the superpowers: NATO (North Atlantic Treaty Organization) or the Warsaw Pact (Figure 7-26). NATO was a military alliance among sixteen democratic states, including the United States and Canada, plus fourteen European states.

Twelve of the fourteen European NATO members participated fully—Belgium, Denmark, West Germany, Greece, Iceland, Italy, Luxembourg, the Netherlands, Norway, Portugal, Turkey, and the United Kingdom. France and Spain were members but did not contribute troops. NATO headquarters, originally in France, were moved to Belgium when France reduced its involvement.

The Warsaw Pact was a military agreement among Communist Eastern European countries to defend each other in case of attack. Seven members joined the Warsaw Pact when it was founded in 1955: the Soviet Union, Bulgaria, Czechoslovakia, East Germany, Hungary, Poland, and Romania. In 1956, some of Hungary's leaders asked for the help of Warsaw Pact troops to crush an uprising that threatened Communist control of the government. Warsaw Pact troops also invaded Czechoslovakia in 1968 to depose a government committed to reforms.

NATO and the Warsaw Pact were designed to maintain a bipolar balance of power in Europe. For NATO allies, the principal objective was to prevent the Soviet Union from overrunning West Germany and nearby smaller countries. The Warsaw Pact provided the Soviet Union with a buffer of allied states between it and Germany to discourage a third German invasion of the Soviet Union in the twentieth century.

In a Europe no longer dominated by military confrontation between two blocs, the Warsaw Pact and NATO became obsolete. The number of troops under NATO command was sharply reduced, and the Warsaw Pact was disbanded.

The Conference on Security and Cooperation in Europe (CSCE), founded in 1975 by Western European countries, was expanded to more than fifty countries, including the United States, Canada, and former republics of the Soviet Union. The CSCE had played a limited role during the Cold War era, but during the 1990s it became a forum for all countries concerned with ending conflicts in Europe, especially in the Balkans and Caucasus. Although the CSCE does not directly command armed forces, it can call upon member states to supply troops if necessary.

Other Regional Organizations. The Organization of American States (OAS) includes thirty-two of the thirty-three states in the Western Hemisphere (except Canada). Cuba is a member but was suspended from most OAS activities in 1962. The organization's headquarters, including the permanent council and general assembly, are located in Washington, D.C. The OAS promotes social, cultural, political, and economic links among member states.

A similar organization in Africa is the Organization for African Unity (OAU). Founded in 1963, OAU includes every African state except South Africa. The organization's major effort has been to eliminate minority white-ruled governments in southern Africa.

The Commonwealth of Nations includes the United Kingdom and forty-eight other states that were once British colonies, including Australia, Bangladesh, Canada, India, Nigeria, and Pakistan. Most other members are African states or island countries in the Caribbean or Pacific. Commonwealth members seek economic and cultural cooperation.

The Nonaligned Movement, founded in 1961, has approximately 100 members, including nearly every country in Africa and the Middle East. The organization was established as a haven for countries that

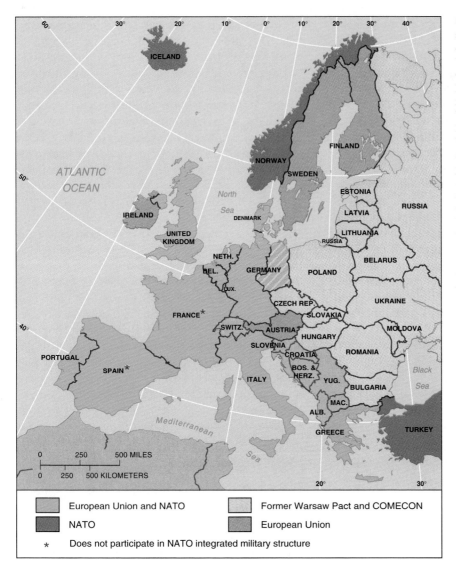

FIGURE 7-26 Economic and military alliances in Europe. Eleven European countries joined both the European Union and the North Atlantic Treaty Organization (NATO). Austria, Finland, Ireland, and Sweden are members of the European Union but not NATO, whereas Iceland, Norway, and Turkey are in NATO but not the European Union. Seven Eastern European countries joined an economic alliance, known as COMECON, and a military alliance, known as the Warsaw Pact. Once East Germany, the Soviet Union, and Czechoslovakia ceased to exist and the other Eastern European states adopted non-Communist governments, the Warsaw Pact and COMECON were disbanded.

did not wish to be forced into an alliance with one of the superpowers. With the end of the Cold War, the initial purpose of the organization has disappeared. The principal focus now has become to represent the interests of less developed countries. Such a change reflects the growing importance of economic competition among blocs of countries rather than military conflict. The Nonaligned Movement may merge with the Group of 77, another organization of developing countries established in the 1960s.

Economic Cooperation

The era of a bipolar balance of power formally ended when the Soviet Union was disbanded in 1992. Instead, the world has returned to the pattern of more than two superpowers that predominated before World War II.

But the contemporary pattern of global power displays two key differences:

1. The most important elements of state power are increasingly economic rather than military; Japan has joined the ranks of superpowers entirely on its economic success, whereas Russia has slipped in strength because of economic problems.
2. The leading superpower in the 1990s is not a single state, such as the United States or Russia, but an economic union of European states led by Germany.

European Union

With the decline in the military-oriented alliances, European states increasingly have turned to economic cooperation. Western Europe's most important economic organization is the European Union. It was formerly known as the European Economic Community, the Common Market, and the European Community.

When it was established in 1958, the European Union included six countries: Belgium, France, West Germany, Italy, Luxembourg, and the Netherlands. Membership was widened to include Denmark, Ireland, and the United Kingdom in 1973, Greece in 1981, Portugal and Spain in 1986, and Austria, Finland, and Sweden in 1995 (Figure 7-26). A European Parliament is elected by the people in each of the member states simultaneously.

The main task of the European Union is to promote development within the member states through economic cooperation. At first, the European Union played a limited role, such as providing subsidies to farmers and to depressed regions like southern Italy. Most of the European Union's budget still goes to those purposes.

The European Union has taken on more importance, however, as member states seek greater economic and political cooperation. It has removed most barriers to free trade: with a few exceptions, goods, services, capital, and people can move freely through Europe. Trucks can carry goods across borders without stopping, and a bank can open branches in any member country with supervision only by the bank's home country. The effect of these actions has been to turn Western Europe into the world's wealthiest market.

German Domination in Western Europe. Although economic and political unity may have reduced the importance of nation-states in Western Europe, many Europeans, especially those old enough to remember World War II, fear that Germany has become more powerful than the region's other nation-states. Because Germany is so dominant, a brief review of its history is important.

Germany is a newer nation-state than the others of Western Europe, for a state known as Germany was not created until 1871. Before that time, the map of the central European area now called Germany was just a patchwork of small states—more than 300 during the seventeenth century, for example.

Under Frederick the Great (1740–1786), the previously obscure state of Prussia gained control of a continuous stretch of territory abutting the Baltic Sea from Memel on the east to beyond the Elbe River on the west. Other consolidations reduced the number of states in the area to approximately two dozen by 1815. In 1871, Prussia's prime minister Otto von Bismarck was instrumental in forcing most of the remaining states in the area to join a Prussian-dominated German Empire, which extended westward beyond the Rhine River (Figure 7-27a). Bismarck failed to consolidate all German speakers into the empire, as Austria, Switzerland, and Bohemia were excluded. The German Empire lasted less than fifty years.

Germany lost much of its territory after World War I (Figure 7-27b). The boundaries of states in southern and eastern Europe were fixed to conform when possible to those of nationalities, but Germany's new boundaries were arbitrary. Germany became a fragmented state, with East Prussia separated from the rest of the country by the Danzig Corridor, created to give Poland a port on the Baltic Sea. Nazi takeovers of Austria, Poland, and portions of Czechoslovakia during the 1930s were justified by the Germans as attempts to reconstruct a true German nation-state.

After its defeat in World War II and in the Cold War that soon followed, Germany was divided into the Democratic (East) and Federal (West) republics (Figure 7-27c). Unification of Germany in 1990 brought together two groups of people who both spoke German and referred to their country as "Germany" (Figure 7-27d).

As the most populous and economically strongest member of the European Union, Germany has taken the lead in setting the political agenda for a united Europe. When the European Union was founded in 1958, Germany was a quiet member, content to subsidize inefficient French farmers and impoverished southern Italians in exchange for acceptance as a respectable ally and reliable trading partner. In the 1990s, Germany has succeeded through economic competition in achieving what previous generations failed to obtain through military means: it has become the most powerful state in the world's largest market.

Former Communist Countries and the European Union. While achieving a high degree of economic integration among its members, the European Union faces a challenge of working with neighboring states, especially in Eastern Europe. In 1949, the

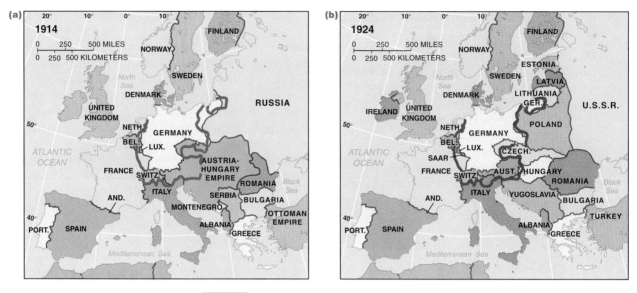

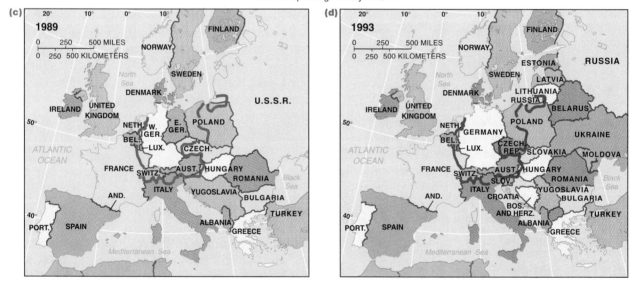

FIGURE 7-27 Europe's twentieth-century boundary changes. (a) In 1914, at the outbreak of World War I, Germany extended 1,300 kilometers (800 miles) from east to west. Germany's boundaries at the time coincided fairly closely to the German-speaking area of Europe, although German was also spoken in portions of Switzerland and the Austria-Hungary Empire. (b) After losing World War I, Germany was divided into two discontinuous areas, separated by the Danzig Corridor, part of the newly created state of Poland. (c) Germany's boundaries changed again after World War II, as eastern portions of the country were taken by Poland and the Soviet Union. (d) With the collapse of communism in Eastern Europe, East Germany and West Germany were united. Because of forced migration of Germans (as well as other peoples) after World War II, the territory occupied by German-speakers today is much farther west than the location a century ago.

seven Eastern European Communist states in the Warsaw Pact formed the Council for Mutual Economic Assistance (COMECON). Cuba, Mongolia, and Vietnam were also members of the alliance, which was designed to promote trade and sharing of natural resources. Like the Warsaw Pact, COMECON disbanded in the early 1990s after the fall of communism in Eastern Europe.

The former Communist Eastern European countries that have made the most progress in converting to market economies—Poland, Hungary, the Czech Republic, and the Baltic states—want to join the European Union. But current European Union members are wary of admitting a large number of relatively poor southern and eastern European countries. Admission would create administrative nightmares—such as expanding the number of official languages—and dilute the economic benefits that current members enjoy.

East Berliners cross the Berlin Wall at the Invalidenstrasse check point, following a shopping trip to West Berlin, November 12, 1989, one day after the Berlin Wall was opened for unrestricted travel between East and West Berlin. Within a year, the two parts of Berlin were united, and the German Democratic Republic ceased to exist. (Reuters/Bettmann)

Summary

Here is a review of issues raised in this chapter.

1. What is the difference between a state and a nation?

A state is a political unit, with an organized government and sovereignty, whereas a nation is a group of people with a strong sense of cultural unity. Most of Earth's surface is allocated to states, and only a handful of colonies and tracts of unorganized territory remain. In the modern world, states have been created to match the distribution of nations whenever possible.

2. How are boundaries drawn between states?

Boundaries between states, where possible, are drawn to coincide either with physical features, such as mountains, deserts, and bodies of water, or with such cultural characteristics as geometry, religion, and language. Boundaries affect the shape of countries and affect the ability of a country to live peacefully with its neighbors.

3. What problems result when nations and states do not have the same boundaries?

Problems arise when the boundaries of states do not coincide with the boundaries of nations. In some cases, one state contains more than one nation; in other cases, one nation is split among two or more states.

4. Why do states cooperate with each other?

After World War II, the United States and the Soviet Union, as the world's two superpowers, formed military alliances with other countries. With the end of the Cold War, nations now are cooperating with each other, especially in Western Europe, primarily to promote economic growth rather than to provide military protection.

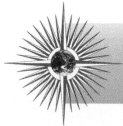

CASE STUDY REVISITED
The Future of the Nation-State in Europe

Two political trends dominate the 1990s. First, after a half-century dominated by the Cold War between two superpowers—the United States and the former Soviet Union—the world has entered a period characterized by an unprecedented increase in the number of new states created to satisfy the desire of nationalities for self-determination as an expression of cultural distinctiveness. Turmoil has resulted because in many cases the boundaries of the new states do not precisely match the territories occupied by distinct nationalities.

At the same time, with the end of the Cold War, military alliances have become less important than patterns of global and regional economic cooperation and competition among states. Economic cooperation has increased among neighboring states in Western Europe and North America, while competition between these two blocs, as well as with Japan, has increased.

The impact of both global political trends can be seen in Europe. The importance of the nation-state has diminished in Western Europe, the world region most closely associated with development of the concept during the past two hundred years. European nation-states have put aside their centuries-old rivalries to forge the world's most powerful economic union. In the future, Western Europeans will carry European Union passports and calculate costs in European currency units (ECUs) rather than in pounds, francs, and marks.

Travelers crossing international borders in Western Europe can still observe cultural differences in the organization of the landscape. For example, highways in the Netherlands are more likely than those in neighboring Belgium to be flanked by well-manicured vegetation and paths reserved for bicycles. From economic and political perspectives, though, boundaries between Western European countries, where hundreds of thousands of soldiers once stood guard, now have little more significance than boundaries between states inside the United States.

Problems persist in the economic integration of Western Europe. Because prices are much higher in Germany than in France, French workers apply for jobs in Germany, while Germans buy property in France. A more fundamental obstacle to Western European integration is the multiplicity of languages. The European Union must spend a very high percentage of its annual budget translating documents and speeches into all eleven of the community's official languages: Danish, Dutch, English, Finnish, French, German, Greek, Italian, Portuguese, Spanish and Swedish. English, understood by 70 percent of college-age Western Europeans, may in the future become the principal language of business—the lingua franca—within the European Union.

At the same time that residents of Western European countries are displaying increased tolerance for cultural values of neighboring nationalities, opposition has increased to the immigration of people from the south and east, especially those who have darker skins and adhere to Islam. Immigrants from poorer regions of Europe, Africa, and Asia fill low-paying jobs, such as cleaning streets and operating buses, that Western Europeans are not willing to perform. Nonetheless, many Western Europeans fear that large-scale immigration will transform their nation-states into multinational societies.

Underlying this fear of immigration is recognition that natural increase rates are higher in most African and Asian countries than in Western Europe as a result of higher crude birth rates. Many Western Europeans believe that Africans and Asians who immigrate to their countries will continue to maintain relatively high crude birth rates and consequently will constitute even higher percentages of the population in Western Europe in the future.

Even more troubling to Western Europeans is the prolonged war in the Balkans. Bosnia-Herzegovina lies only 250 kilometers (150 miles) from the borders of the European Union states of Austria and Italy. The barbaric practices of the combatants, such as ethnic cleansing, and the primitive conditions under which survivors must live, stand in stark contrast to the prosperity of European Union members.

For Europeans, Bosnia represents an uncomfortably nearby reminder that nationalities are still willing to throw away the prospect of economic prosperity through regional and global economic cooperation in order to preserve their individual cultural identities.

Key Terms

Apartheid Laws (no longer in effect) in South Africa that physically separated races into different geographic areas.

Balance of power Condition of roughly equal strength between opposing countries or alliances of countries.

Balkanization Process by which a state breaks down through conflicts among its nationalities.

Balkanized Small geographic area that can not successfully be organized into one or more stable states because it is inhabited by many nationalities with complex, long-standing antagonisms toward each other.

Boundary Invisible line that marks the extent of a state's territory.

Centripetal forces Attitudes that tend to unify a people and enhance support for the state.

City-state A sovereign state that comprises a town and surrounding countryside.

Colonialism Attempt by one country to establish settlements and to impose its political, economic, and cultural principles in another territory.

Colony A territory that is legally tied to a sovereign state rather than completely independent.

Compact state A state in which the distance from the center to any boundary does not vary significantly.

Elongated state A state with a long, narrow shape.

Federal state An internal organization of a state that allocates most powers to units of local government.

Fragmented state A state that includes several discontinuous pieces of territory.

Frontier A zone separating two states in which neither state exercises political control.

Landlocked state A state that does not have a direct outlet to the sea.

Multinational state A state that contains more than one nationality.

Nationalism Attitude of the people in a nation in support of the existence and growth of a particular state.

Nationality (or **nation**) A group of people who occupy a particular area and have a strong sense of unity based on a set of shared beliefs and attitudes.

Nation-state A state whose territory corresponds to that occupied by a particular nation.

Perforated state A state that completely surrounds another one.

Prorupted state An otherwise compact state with a large projecting extension.

Self-determination Concept that nationalities have the right to govern themselves.

Sovereignty Ability of a state to govern its territory free from control of its internal affairs by other states.

State An area organized into a political unit and ruled by an established government with control over its internal and foreign affairs.

Unitary state An internal organization of a state that places most power in the hands of central government officials.

Thinking Geographically

1. In his book *1984,* George Orwell envisioned the division of the world into three large unified states held together through technological controls. To what extent has Orwell's vision of a global political arrangement been realized?

2. In the winter 1992—1993 issue of *Foreign Policy,* Gerald Helman and Steven Ratner identified countries that they called failed nation-states, including Cambodia, Liberia, Somalia, and Sudan, and others that they predicted would fail. Helman and Ratner argue that the governments of these countries were maintained in power during the Cold War era through massive military and economic aid from the United States or the Soviet Union. With the end of the Cold War, these failed nation-states have sunk into civil wars, fought among groups who share language, religion, and other cultural characteristics. What obligations do other countries have to restore order in failed nation-states?

3. Given the movement toward increased local government autonomy on the one hand and increased authority for international organizations on the other hand, what is the future of the nation-state? Have political and economic trends in the 1990s strengthened the concept of nation-state or weakened it?

4. The world has been divided into a collection of countries on the basis of the principle that nationalities have the right of self-determination. National identity, however, derives from economic interests as well as from such cultural characteristics as language and religion. To what extent should a country's ability to provide its citizens with food, jobs, economic security, and material wealth, rather than the principle of self-determination, become the basis for dividing the world into independent countries?

5. A century ago, the British geographer Halford J. Mackinder identified a heartland in the interior of Eurasia (Europe and Asia) that was isolated by mountain ranges and the Arctic Ocean. Surrounding the heartland was a series of fringe areas, which the geographer Nicholas Spykman later called the rimland, oriented toward the oceans. Mackinder argued that whoever controlled the heartland would control Eurasia and hence the entire world. To what extent has Mackinder's theory been validated during the twentieth century by the creation and then the dismantling of the Soviet Union?

Further Readings

Arlinghaus, Sandra L., and John D. Nystuen. "Geometry of Boundary Exchanges." *Geographical Review* 80 (January 1990): 21–31.

Bennett, D. Gordon, ed. *Tension Areas of the World: A Problem Oriented World Regional Geography*. Champaign, IL: Park Press, 1982.

Boal, Frederick W., and J. Neville H. Douglas, eds. *Integration and Division: Geographical Perspectives on the Northern Ireland Problem*. London and New York: Academic Press, 1982.

Bradshaw, Michael J., and Nicholas J. Lynn. "After the Soviet Union: The Post-Soviet States in the World." *The Professional Geographer* 46 (November 1994): 439–48.

Brown, Curtis M., Walter G. Robillard, and Donald A. Wilson. *Boundary Control and Legal Principles*. New York: John Wiley and Sons, 1986.

Burghart, A. F. "The Bases of Territorial Claims." *Geographical Review* 63 (April 1973): 225–45.

Burnett, Alan D., and Peter J. Taylor, eds. *Political Studies from Spatial Perspectives*. Chichester: John Wiley and Sons, 1981.

Busteed, M. A., ed. *Developments in Political Geography*. London: Academic Press, 1983.

Christopher, A. J. *The British Empire at Its Zenith*. London: Croom Helm, 1988.

Cohen, Saul B. "Global Political Change in the Post–Cold War Era." *Annals of the Association of American Geographers* 81 (December 1991): 551–80.

Cox, Kevin R. *Location and Public Problems: A Political Geography of the Contemporary World*. Chicago: Maaroufa Press, 1979.

Dale, E. H. "Some Geographical Aspects of African Land-Locked States." *Annals of the Association of American Geographers* 58 (September 1968): 485–505.

Dikshit, R. D. "Geography and Federalism." *Annals of the Association of American Geographers* 61 (March 1971): 97–130.

Gottmann, Jean, ed. *Centre and Periphery: Spatial Variation in Politics*. Beverly Hills: Sage, 1980.

Johnston, R. J. *Geography and the State*. New York: St. Martin's Press, 1982.

Kidron, Michael, and Ronald Segal. *The New State of the World Atlas*, 4th ed. New York: Simon and Schuster, 1991.

Kliot, Nurit, and Stanley Waterman, eds. *Pluralism and Political Geography—People, Territory and State*. New York: St. Martin's Press, 1983.

Mathieson, R. S. "Nuclear Power in the Soviet Bloc." *Annals of the Association of American Geographers* 70 (June 1980): 271–79.

Mellor, Roy E. H. *Nation, State and Territory: A Political Geography*. London and New York: Routledge, 1989.

Morgenthau, Hans J. *Politics Among Nations,* 4th ed. New York: Knopf, 1967.

Murphy, Alexander B. "Historical Justifications for Territorial Claims." *Annals of the Association of American Geographers* 80 (December 1990): 531–48.

———. "Territorial Policies in Multiethnic States." *Geographical Review* 79 (October 1989): 410–21.

Nijman, Jan. "The Limits of Superpower: The United States and the Soviet Union since World War II." *Annals of the Association of American Geographers* 82 (December 1992): 681–95.

_____, et al. "The Political Geography of the Post Cold War World." *Professional Geographer* 44 (February 1992): 1–29.

O'Tuathail, Gearóid, and Timothy W. Luke. "Present at the (Dis)integration: Deterritorialization and Reterritorialization in the New Wor(l)d Order." *Annals of the Association of American Geographers* 84 (September 1994): 381–98.

O'Loughlin, John, and Herman van der Wusten. "Political Geography of Panregions." *Geographical Review* 80 (January 1990): 1–20.

O'Sullivan, Patrick. *Geopolitics.* New York: St. Martin's Press, 1986.

_____, and Jesse W. Miller. *The Geography of Warfare.* London: Croom Helm, 1983.

Pacione, Michael, ed. *Progress in Political Geography.* London: Croom Helm, 1985.

Parker, W. H. *Mackinder: Geography as an Aid to Statecraft.* Oxford: The Clarendon Press, 1982.

Pickles, John, and Jeff Woods. "South Africa's Homelands in the Age of Reform: The Case of QwaQwa." *Annals of the Association of American Geographers* 82 (December 1992): 629–52.

Prescott, J. R. V. *Boundaries and Frontiers.* London: Croom Helm, 1978.

_____. *The Geography of State Politics.* Chicago: Aldine Publishing, 1968.

_____. *Political Geography.* London: Methuen, 1972.

_____. *The Political Geography of the Oceans.* Newton Abbot, England: David and Charles, 1975.

Richmond, Anthony H. "Ethnic Nationalism: Social Science Paradigm." *International Social Science Journal* 39 (February 1987): 3–18.

Rose, Richard. "National Pride in Cross-National Perspective." *International Social Science Journal* 37 (February 1985): 85–96.

Slowe, Peter. *Geography and Political Power: The Geography of Nations and States.* London: Routledge, 1990.

Soffer, Arnon, and Julian V. Minghi. "Israel's Security Landscapes: The Impact of Military Considerations on Land Uses." *Professional Geographer* 38 (February 1986): 28–41.

Taylor, Peter J. *Political Geography of the Twentieth Century: A Global Analysis.* London: Belhaven, 1993.

_____, and John W. House, eds. Political Geography: *Recent Advances and Future Directions.* London: Croom Helm, 1984.

Williams, Allan M. *The European Community: The Contradictions of Integration.* Cambridge, MA: Blackwell, 1991.

Zelinsky, Wilbur. *Nation into State.* Chapel Hill: University of North Carolina Press, 1988.

Also consult the following journals: *American Journal of Political Science; American Political Science Review; Foreign Affairs; Foreign Policy; International Affairs; International Journal; International Journal of Middle East Studies; Political Geography; Post-Soviet Geography.*

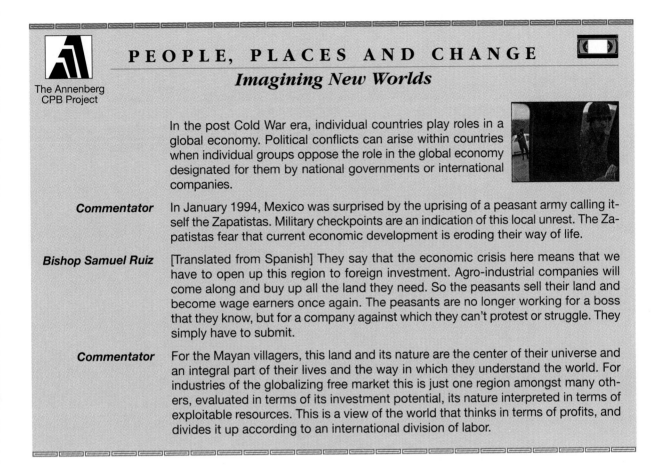

PEOPLE, PLACES AND CHANGE

Imagining New Worlds

The Annenberg
CPB Project

In the post Cold War era, individual countries play roles in a global economy. Political conflicts can arise within countries when individual groups oppose the role in the global economy designated for them by national governments or international companies.

Commentator In January 1994, Mexico was surprised by the uprising of a peasant army calling itself the Zapatistas. Military checkpoints are an indication of this local unrest. The Zapatistas fear that current economic development is eroding their way of life.

Bishop Samuel Ruiz [Translated from Spanish] They say that the economic crisis here means that we have to open up this region to foreign investment. Agro-industrial companies will come along and buy up all the land they need. So the peasants sell their land and become wage earners once again. The peasants are no longer working for a boss that they know, but for a company against which they can't protest or struggle. They simply have to submit.

Commentator For the Mayan villagers, this land and its nature are the center of their universe and an integral part of their lives and the way in which they understand the world. For industries of the globalizing free market this is just one region amongst many others, evaluated in terms of its investment potential, its nature interpreted in terms of exploitable resources. This is a view of the world that thinks in terms of profits, and divides it up according to an international division of labor.

8

DEVELOPMENT

Have you ever traveled to a Caribbean island? Even if you haven't, you have probably seen advertisements for resorts featuring a bronzed couple sipping exotic drinks, lying on a deserted beach surrounded by palm trees.

Beyond this paradise is another world, fleetingly glimpsed by tourists traveling between the resort and the airport. The permanent residents of the islands may live in poverty, earning less money in one year than a week's hotel bill. They are ill-fed, ill-clothed, and underemployed.

This depressing view of conditions on the islands is shielded from tourists, of course. They do not travel hundreds of kilometers to encounter misery on their vacation or honeymoon. Tourists bring money to the islands and

KEY ISSUES

1. How is development measured?
2. How does the level of development vary among regions?
3. How can countries promote development?

in the process help pay for whatever improvements can be made to the squalid living conditions.

But can you imagine the feelings of the local residents? What would you think if a very expensive and exclusive resort were built in your neighborhood, and you and your family, who were economically disadvantaged, were expected to work there (for good wages, perhaps) to serve the needs of the vacationers? You might welcome the money, but would you resent the wealthy tourists?

The world is divided between relatively rich and relatively poor countries. Geographers try to understand the reasons for this division and learn what can be done about it.

WORKERS UNLOADING SACKS FROM DHOW SHIP, ZANZIBAR HARBOR, TANZANIA. (JAMES STRACHAN/TONY STONE IMAGES)

Bangladesh's Development Problems

Rabea Rahman lives in the village of Bathoimuri, Bangladesh, with her three children—a son, 18, and two daughters, ages 10 and 7. Rahman's two other children died in infancy. Her husband died of tuberculosis.

Rahman's husband was a tenant farmer, or sharecropper. Under this arrangement, he shared a portion of his crops with the landowner instead of paying rent. After he died, Rahman went to work as a domestic servant and water carrier, working from 7 a.m. to 4 p.m. and from 6 p.m. to 11 p.m., seven days a week. Her son sells bread and prepares a midday meal for his two sisters. Total household income is $16 per month. (By comparison, average monthly household is more than $3,000 in the United States).

Their house has a dirt floor and leaky roof, but the rent is only $2 a month, plus $3 a month for fuel. The remaining $11 a month goes for food. The sum is sufficient to provide each member of the household with 100 grams (about a quarter-pound) of rice per day but little else. The diet is supplemented by leftover food Rahman receives from her employer. After paying for rent, fuel, and food, the family has no money left for other necessities. Because they can't afford shoes, the family members often go barefoot. Rahman suffers from a gastric ulcer but can't afford treatment.

Underlying the impoverished condition of the Rahman household is the role of women in a predominantly Muslim country such as Bangladesh. In rural villages, less than 10 percent of the women can read and write. The average woman is married as a teenager and bears six babies in her lifetime, although typically one of the six does not survive infancy. A woman like Rahman who is forced to find a job is limited to working as a servant or farm laborer. The condition of women—poor, illiterate, overburdened with children—is one of the most important factors holding back economic development in South Asian countries like Bangladesh.

In previous chapters, we examined global demographic and cultural patterns. We saw that birth, death, and natural increase rates vary from one state to another. People in different countries also have different languages, religions, and other social customs. We saw how political problems arise when the distribution of social customs does not match the boundaries between states.

The countries of the world fall into nine major regions according to these demographic and cultural characteristics (Figure 8-1). In the Western Hemisphere, Anglo-America (Canada and the United States) and Latin America can be distinguished on the basis of dominant languages, religions, and natural increase rates. Despite the considerable diversity within these regions, at a global scale the individual countries within these regions display cultural similarities.

Europe can be divided into two regions, Western and Eastern. Although they share cultural characteristics, distinctive political experiences have produced different levels of economic development.

Asia comprises four major demographic-cultural regions: East, South, Southeast, and Southwest. Major cultural, demographic, and political differences distinguish these four regions. Southwest Asia can be combined with Northern Africa to form a region known as the Middle East because of similarities in language, religion, and population growth. Africa south of the Sahara constitutes the ninth major region.

In addition to those nine major regions, three other important areas can be identified: Japan, South Africa, and the South Pacific. Japan and South Africa are populous countries with cultural and demographic characteristics that contrast sharply with their neighboring states. The South Pacific, primarily Australia and New Zealand, covers an extensive area of Earth's surface, but is much less populous than the nine major regions.

The nine major regions also differ from each other in their economic enterprises: how people earn their living, how the societies use their wealth, and other economic characteristics. As we move toward a global economy, geographers increasingly study the similarities and differences in the economic patterns of the various regions.

The most fundamental economic distinction among world regions is their level of development.

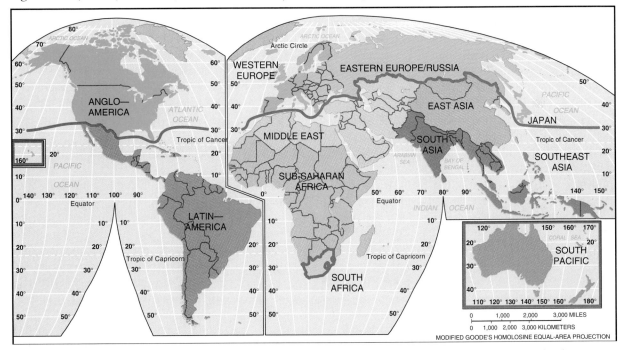

FIGURE 8-1 More and less developed regions. Earth's six less developed regions are the Middle East, Latin America, Sub-Saharan Africa, East Asia, Southeast Asia, and South Asia. The world's more developed regions include Anglo-America, Western Europe, and Eastern Europe/Russia. Three other more developed areas—Japan, the South Pacific, and South Africa—are surrounded by less developed regions.

Development is the process of improving the material conditions of people through diffusion of knowledge and technology. Economic development is a continuous process involving never-ending actions to constantly improve the health and prosperity of the people.

All of Earth's nearly 200 countries fall at some point along a continuum of economic development. However, countries tend to cluster at one end of the continuum or the other. A **more developed country** (abbreviated **MDC**, also known as a **relatively developed country** or simply a **developed country**) has progressed further along the development continuum. A country in an earlier stage of development is frequently called a **less developed country** (**LDC**), although many analysts prefer the term **developing country**. *Developing* implies that the country has already made some progress and expects to continue.

Countries that have achieved higher levels of development cluster in certain regions of the world, whereas LDCs are mostly in other regions. The question geographers ask, of course, is *why?* The prevailing levels of development correspond closely to the nine regions distinguished according to demographic, cultural, and political characteristics. Three of the nine major cultural regions—Anglo-America, Western Europe, and Eastern Europe—rank relatively high on a development continuum; the other six are less developed. Japan, South Africa, and the South Pacific are also relatively developed areas.

The distribution of these more developed and less developed regions reflects a clear global pattern. If we draw a line at about 30° north latitude, we find that the three major relatively developed regions, plus Japan, are all situated to the north, while every less developed region lies predominantly, if not entirely, south of the circle. This division of the world between more developed and less developed regions is known as the *north-south split*.

The distribution of these more and less developed regions appears somewhat different on a north polar projection (Figure 8-2). Most of the MDCs form a core region, while the LDCs occupy peripheral locations. Countries located in the periphery have less access to the world centers of consumption, communications, and economic and political power, which are clustered in the core region. This perspective demonstrates the development of an increasingly unified world economy in which the more developed regions clustered in the core play dominant roles in forming the economies of the less developed regions on the periphery.

For geographers, the task of distinguishing between more and less developed regions is becoming easier because the spread is increasing between the high and low ends of the development continuum. Less developed regions face considerable difficulty in achieving a level of development comparable to the level of countries that currently have more developed economies.

K E Y   I S S U E   1

How Is Development Measured?

- Indicators of Development
- Correlation of Development Indicators

Three types of characteristics distinguish a country's level of development: *economic*, *social*, and *demographic*. In this key issue, we will focus on eleven development indicators and how they interrelate: five economic factors (per capita income, economic structure, worker productivity, access to raw materials, and availability of consumer goods), two social factors (education/literacy and health/welfare), and four demographic factors (infant mortality rate, natural increase rate, crude birth rate, and age structure).

Indicators of Development

People in MDCs generally have higher *per capita incomes* than those in LDCs. The typical worker receives $5 to $10 per hour in developed countries, compared to less than $0.50 per hour in most developing countries. MDCs generally mandate a minimum wage of at least several dollars per hour.

Average per capita income is higher in MDCs because people typically earn their living by different means. Geographers classify jobs in three sectors: primary (including agriculture), secondary (including manufacturing), and tertiary (including retailing and services). To compare the *economic structure* (types of economic activities) found in more and less developed countries, we can compute the percentage of people working in each of these three sectors.

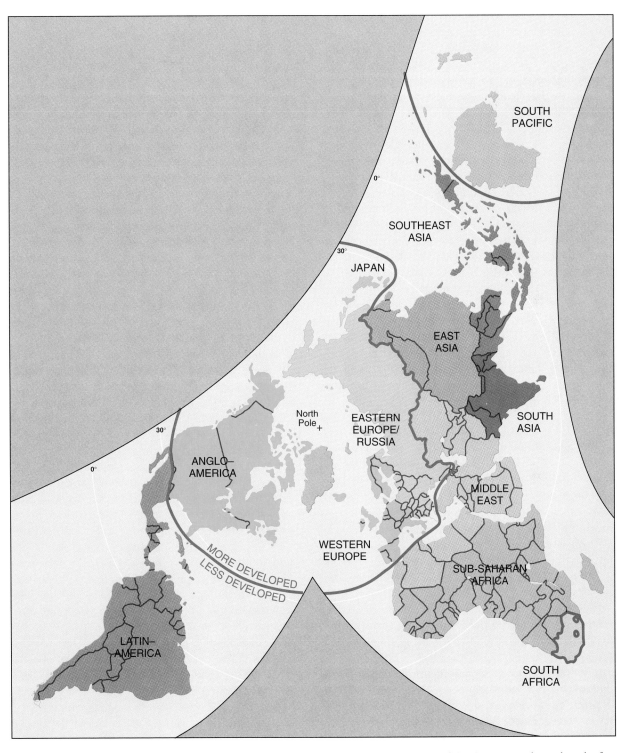

FIGURE 8-2 Core and periphery. Most of the countries that have achieved relatively high levels of development are located north of 30° north latitude. Viewed from this north polar projection, most of the developed countries appear clustered in an inner core; less developed countries are generally relegated to a peripheral or outer ring location.

Worker *productivity* is greater in MDCs, that is, each worker produces more for a given input of labor. Higher productivity results from taking advantage of modern technology to earn a living by working in a factory, office, or shop, rather than struggling every day to grow food.

Part of the wealth generated by productive industries pays for expensive modern technology required to operate efficient economic enterprises. Factories, offices, and shops also depend on expensive networks of communications and transportation. They depend on *access to raw materials:* large supplies of energy and mineral resources.

People in MDCs use part of the wealth generated by economic activities to buy *consumer goods* and services. Demand for these products in turn increases the need for factories, offices, and shops, so the overall economy of an MDC tends to keep expanding.

In general, the higher the level of development, the greater are both the quantity and the quality of a country's *education*. A measure of the quantity of education is the average number of school years attended. The assumption is that, no matter how poor the school, the longer pupils attend, the more likely they are to learn something. The quality of education is measured in two ways—student-teacher ratio and literacy rate. The fewer pupils a teacher has, the more likely that each will receive instruction.

Relatively developed countries publish more books, newspapers, and magazines per person because more of their citizens read and write. MDCs dominate scientific and nonfiction publishing worldwide; this textbook is an example. Students in developing countries must learn technical information from books that usually are not in their native language, but in English, German, Russian, or French.

More developed countries use part of their greater wealth to provide *health and welfare* services. As a result, their people are better educated, healthier, and better protected from hardships. In turn, this well-educated, healthy, and secure population can be more economically productive.

In more developed countries, infants are more likely to survive and adults are more likely to live longer. These *demographic characteristics* strongly affect the economic development of a country. More developed countries display many demographic differences compared to less developed countries. We described several demographic characteristics in Chapter 2. The four major ones that distinguish more

and less developed countries are infant mortality, natural increase, crude birth rates, and age structure.

We will now look at each of these eleven indicators in detail.

Economic Indicators of Development

1. Per Capita Income. Because per capita income is a difficult figure to obtain in many countries, geographers frequently substitute per capita gross domestic product, a more readily available indicator. The **gross domestic product (GDP)** is the value of the total output of goods and services produced in a country, normally during one year. Dividing the GDP by total population measures the contribution the average individual makes to generating a country's wealth in a year. For example, GDP in the United States is currently about $7 billion, and its population is about 260 million, so the GDP per capita is about $27,000. The gross national product (GNP) is similar to the GDP, except that it includes income people earn abroad, such as a Canadian working in the United States.

Annual per capita GDP exceeds $15,000 in most relatively developed countries, compared to less than $1,000 per year in most developing countries (Figure 8-3). Switzerland has the world's highest per capita GDP, more than $30,000, and the figure exceeds $20,000 in several other Western European countries, Anglo-America, and Japan.

As recently as the late 1980s, several oil-rich states bordering the Persian Gulf had the world's highest per capita GDPs, but the level is lower now because of declining petroleum prices and the lingering effects of conflict in the region. The lowest per capita GDPs are found in Sub-Saharan Africa, South Asia, and Southeast Asia. Nearly every country in these regions has a per capita GDP of less than $500 per year.

The gap in per capita GDP between more and less developed countries has been widening. Since the early 1980s, per capita GDP has increased by more than $10,000 in MDCs, compared with less than $200 in LDCs. Per capita GDP has actually declined over the past decade in many African and Latin American countries.

Per capita GDP—or, for that matter, any other single indicator—cannot measure perfectly the level of a country's development. Not everyone is starving in a less developed country that has a per capita GDP of a few hundred dollars. And not everyone is wealthy in a developed country like the United States,

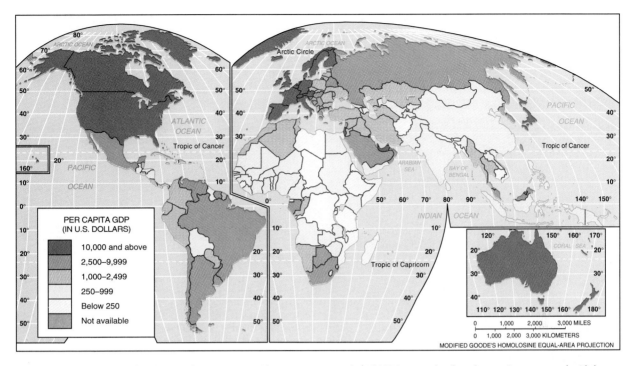

FIGURE 8-3 Annual gross domestic product per capita. This measure exceeds $15,000 in most developed countries, compared with less than $1,000 in most LDCs. Several petroleum-rich countries in the Middle East have relatively high figures, although by other measures they may rank among the LDCs. Since the early 1980s, the ratio in per capita GDP between more and less developed countries has grown.

with its per capita GDP of $27,000; one-sixth of U.S. citizens live in poverty. Per capita GDP measures *average (mean)* wealth, not its *distribution*. If only a few people receive much of the GDP, then the standard of living for the majority may be lower than the average figure implies. On the other hand, the higher the per capita GDP, the greater is the potential for ensuring that all citizens enjoy a comfortable life.

2. Economic Structure. Workers in the **primary sector** directly extract materials from Earth through *agriculture*, and sometimes by mining, fishing, and forestry. The **secondary sector** includes *manufacturers* that process, transform, and assemble raw materials into useful products. Other secondary-sector industries take manufactured goods and fabricate them into finished consumer goods. The **tertiary sector** involves the provision of goods and *services* to people and businesses in exchange for payment.

The tertiary sector can be split into five kinds of services:

- Transportation and communication (including trucking and television broadcasting)
- Producer services (including banking and law)
- Retail and wholesale services (including restaurants and shops)
- Personal and social services (including schools and hospitals)
- Public services (including federal and local governments).

The distribution of workers among the primary, secondary, and tertiary sectors varies sharply between more and less developed countries. The percentage of people working in agriculture exceeds 75 percent in many LDCs of Africa and Asia, compared with less than 5 percent in Anglo-America and many Western European countries (Figure 8-4).

The first priority for all people is to secure food for survival. A high percentage of agricultural workers in a country indicates that most of its people are spending their days producing food for their own survival. In contrast, a low percentage of primary

Workers in LDCs are less productive than those in MDCs, partly because they must rely on human and animal power to perform much of their work. This Indonesian farmer has placed rice in a tray and is allowing the lighter chaff to be blown away by the wind (see Chapter 9 for description of rice growing). In contrast, workers in developed countries make use of high-tech machinery, such as this computer-programmed steel welder. (Photo left: Harvey Lloyd/The Stock Market) (Photo below: Ted Horowitz/ The Stock Market)

sector workers indicates that a handful of farmers can produce enough food for the rest of society. Freed from the task of growing their own food, most people in a relatively developed country can contribute to an increase in the national wealth by working in the secondary and tertiary sectors.

Within developed countries, the number of jobs has decreased in the secondary sector and increased in the tertiary sector. The decline in manufacturing jobs reflects greater efficiency inside the factories as well as increased global competition in many industries. At the same time, employment in the service sector continues to expand as a result of increased demand by companies and individuals for many goods and services.

3. *Worker Productivity.* Workers in developed countries are more productive than those in LDCs. **Productivity** is the value of a particular product compared with the amount of labor needed to make it.

Workers in MDCs produce more with less effort because they have access to more machines, tools, and equipment to perform much of the work. On the other hand, production in less developed countries must rely more on human and animal power. The larger per capita GDP in developed countries in part pays for the manufacture and purchase of machinery, which in turn makes workers more productive and generates more wealth.

Productivity can be measured by the value added per worker. The **value added** in manufacturing is the gross value of the product minus the costs of raw materials and energy. The value added per worker is thirty times greater in relatively developed countries than in developing countries. The average production worker generates a value added of nearly $50,000 in the United States compared to only a few hundred dollars in developing countries.

4. *Access to Raw Materials.* Development requires access to raw materials, such as minerals and trees, that can be fashioned into useful products. It also requires energy to operate the factories, whether in the form of water power, coal, oil, natural gas, or uranium for nuclear power. Great Britain, the first country to be transformed into an economically de-

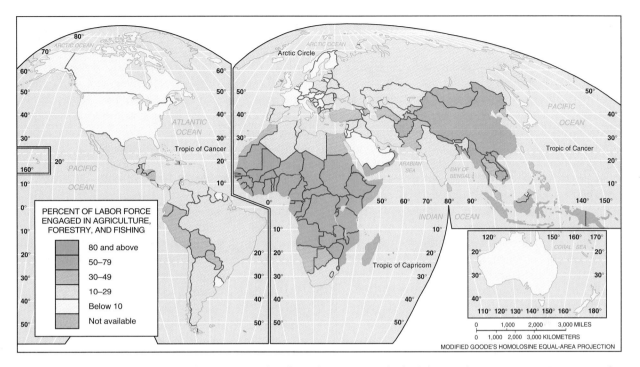

FIGURE 8-4 Percent primary-sector workers. A priority for all people is to secure the food they need to survive. In LDCs, most people work in agriculture to produce the food they and their families need. In MDCs, few people are farmers, and most people buy food with money earned by working in factories, offices, or other services.

veloped society late in the 1700s, had abundant supplies of coal and iron ore, the most important industrial raw materials at the time because they were used to make steel for tools. During the 1800s, other European countries took advantage of domestic coal and iron ore to promote industrial development.

European countries in the nineteenth century ran short of many raw materials essential for economic development and began to import them from other regions of the world. To ensure an adequate supply of these materials, European countries established colonies, especially in Africa and Asia. The international flow of raw materials helped to sustain economic development in Europe, but retarded it in Africa and Asia. Although most former colonies have become independent states, they still export raw materials to developed countries and import finished goods and services. In the twentieth century, both the United States and Russia (formerly the Soviet Union) became powerful industrial states, partly because both possessed most of the raw materials and energy resources essential to development.

As certain raw materials become more important, a country's level of development can advance. LDCs that possess energy resources, especially petroleum, have been able to use revenues from the sale of these resources to finance development. Prices for other raw materials, such as cotton and copper, have fallen because of excessive global supply and declining industrial demand. Developing countries that are dependent on the sale of these resources have been less successful in development.

In a global economy, availability of raw materials and energy resources measures a country's development *potential,* rather than its *actual* development. A country with abundant resources has a good chance of developing. Yet some countries that lack resources—such as Japan, Singapore, South Korea, and Switzerland—have developed economically through world trade.

5. Availability of Consumer Goods. Part of the wealth generated in developed countries goes for essential goods and services (food, clothing, and shelter). But the rest is available for *consumer* goods and services (cars, telephones, entertainment). The wealth used to buy "nonessentials" promotes expansion of manufacturing, which in turn generates additional wealth in the society.

The quantity and type of goods and services purchased in a society provide a good measure of the level of development. Among the thousands of things that consumers buy, three are particularly good indicators of a society's development: motor vehicles, telephones, and televisions.

These products are accessible to virtually all residents in relatively developed countries and are vital to the health of the economy. In developed countries, the ratio of people to motor vehicles, telephones, and televisions is approaching 1:1. In other words, there is nearly one motor vehicle, telephone, and television set for each person in developed countries.

The motor vehicle, telephone, and television all play important economic roles. Motor vehicles provide individuals with access to jobs and services and permit businesses to distribute their products. Telephones enhance communications with suppliers and customers of goods and services. Televisions pro-

vide exposure to activities in different locations.

In contrast, in less developed countries, these products do not play a central role in daily life for many people. Motor vehicles are not essential to people who live in a small village and work all day growing food in nearby fields. Telephones are not essential for those who live in the same village as their friends and relatives. Televisions are not essential to persons who have little leisure time.

The number of persons per telephone and motor vehicle—more than 100 in most LDCs—indicates that people are much less likely to have access to these products (Figure 8-5). The number of persons per television set varies widely among developing countries, from less than 10 in China and some Latin American countries to several hundred in Bangladesh and many African countries (see Figure 6-15). The variation reflects the rapid diffusion of television in recent years in developing countries: acquiring a television set is an important priority in the early stages of development.

Most people in developing countries are familiar with these consumer goods, even though they cannot afford them. These objects may be desired as

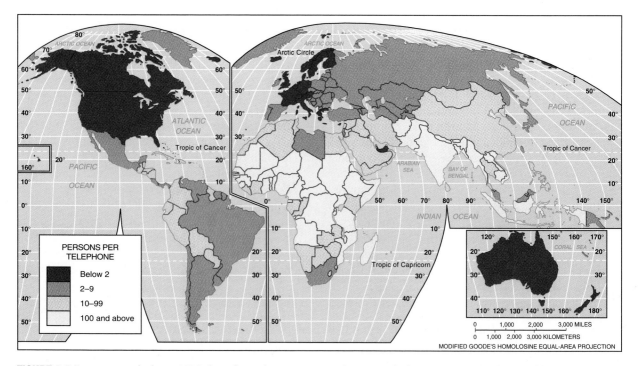

FIGURE 8-5 Persons per telephone. MDCs have fewer than two persons for every telephone, compared with several hundred in LDCs.

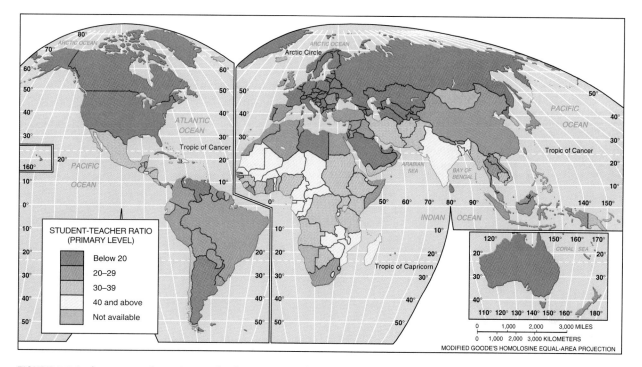

FIGURE 8-6 Students per teacher, primary school. Primary school teachers must deal with much larger average class sizes in LDCs than in MDCs.

symbols of development. Because possession of consumer goods is not universal in developing countries, a gap may emerge between the "Haves" and the "Have-nots." The minority who have these goods may include government officials, landowners, and other elites; the majority who are denied access to these goods may become resentful.

In many LDCs, the "Haves" are concentrated in urban areas, and the "Have-nots" live in the countryside. Technological innovations tend to diffuse from urban to rural areas. Access to consumer goods is more important in urban areas because of the dispersion of homes, factories, offices, and shops.

Motor vehicles, telephones, and televisions also contribute to social and cultural elements of development. These consumer goods provide people with access to leisure activities and exposure to new ideas. A person can explore new places in a motor vehicle, talk to people in distant locations by telephone, and see what life is like elsewhere by television. As a result of greater exposure to cultural diversity, people in developed countries display social characteristics different from those of people in LDCs.

Social Indicators of Development

6. Education and Literacy. The average pupil attends school for about 10 years in developed countries, compared with only a couple of years in LDCs. The *student-teacher ratio* is twice as high in developing countries as in developed ones (Figure 8-6).

Women are less likely to attend school in LDCs. Globally, 73 women attend secondary schools (high schools) for every 100 men. The ratio of women to men in high school is 99:100 in developed countries, but only 60:100 in developing countries. Stated another way, in LDCs, females are roughly half of the total population of high-school age but constitute less than 40 percent of the students. But the ratio in developing countries has improved over the past quarter-century: in 1970, it was 45:100.

The **literacy rate** is the percentage of a country's people who can read and write. It exceeds 95 percent in developed countries, compared with less than one-third in many LDCs (Figure 8-7a).

If we compare literacy rates for women rather than for both sexes, the gap between relatively de-

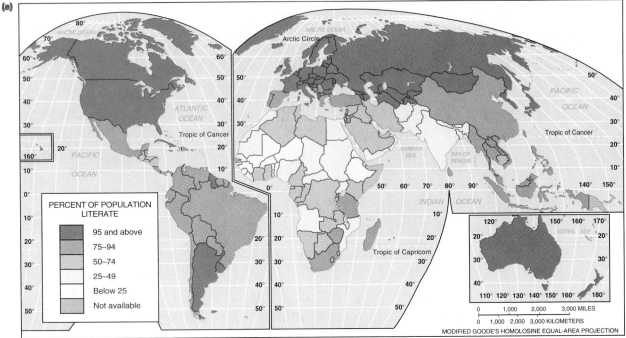

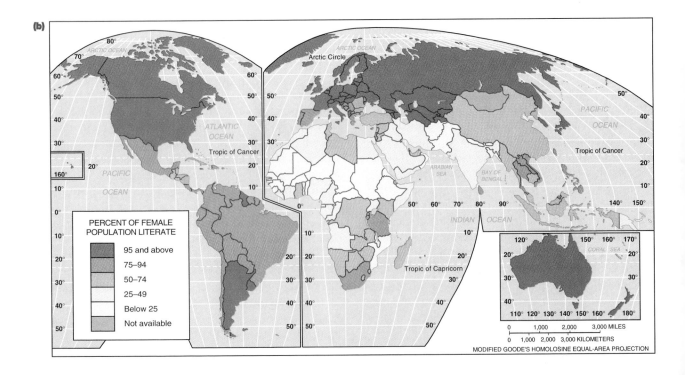

FIGURE 8-7 (a) Literacy rate. In most MDCs, at least 95 percent of adults are able to read and write. The percentage ranges from about 50 percent to only 10 percent in most LDCs, especially in Africa and Asia. (b) Female literacy rate. In some LDCs, the percentage of women who can read and write is much lower than that for men. Compare with total literacy; the gender gap is relatively high in South Asia and the Middle East.

Developed countries possess better equipped hospitals and more extensive medical technology to diagnose and treat people's illnesses, such as this CAT-scan, than is the case in less developed countries, such as this clinic in India. (Photo left: Gabe Palmer/The Stock Market) (Photo right: S. Nagendra/Photo Researchers, Inc.)

veloped and developing countries is greater (Figure 8-7b). In the Middle East and South Asia, literacy rates generally fall between 25 and 75 percent for both sexes combined but are less than 25 percent for women. Elsewhere in Asia and Latin America, gender differences are less. But, in nearly every developing country, the literacy rate is higher for men. In contrast, literacy rates for men and women are virtually the same in relatively developed countries. Low female literacy rates are an obstacle to development in some countries.

For many in LDCs, education is the ticket to better jobs and higher social status. Improved education is a major goal of many developing countries, but funds are scarce. Education may receive a higher percentage of the GDP in developing countries, but their GDP is far lower to begin with, so they spend far less per pupil than developed countries.

7. Health and Welfare. People are healthier in developed countries than in developing ones. The health of a population is influenced by diet. On average, people in MDCs receive more calories and proteins daily than they need. But in developing countries of Africa and Asia, most people receive less than the daily minimum allowance of calories and proteins recommended by the United Nations (Figure 8-8).

When people get sick, developed countries possess the resources to take care of them, and they have better ratios of people to hospitals, doctors, and nurses (Figure 8-9). In many wealthier countries, health care is a public service that is available at little or no cost. The United States is an exception and still considers health care to be an activity best performed by private, profit-making enterprises.

MDCs use part of their wealth to protect people who, for various reasons, are unable to work. In these states, some financial assistance is offered to people who are sick, elderly, poor, disabled, orphaned, veterans of wars, widows, unemployed, or single parents. This practice is generally called *public*

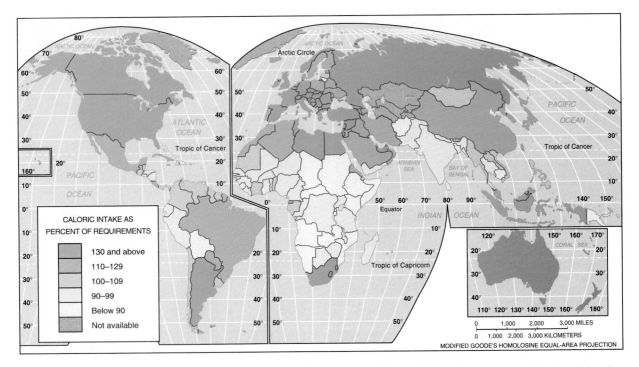

FIGURE 8-8 Daily available calories per capita as a percentage of requirements. Daily available calories per capita (food supply) is the domestic agricultural production plus imports, less exports and nonfood uses. To maintain a moderate level of physical activity, an average individual requires at least 2,360 calories per day, according to the United Nations Food and Agricultural Organization. The figure must be adjusted for age, sex, and region of the world. In developed countries, the average citizen consumes about one-third more calories than the minimum needed.

The typical resident of a less developed country receives almost precisely the minimum number of calories needed to maintain moderate physical activity—on average. At first glance, there seems to be no serious problem. Because these figures are *means,* however, a substantial proportion of the population must be receiving *less* than the necessary daily minimum. The problem is especially severe in Africa, where most people consume less than the needed minimum.

assistance. Countries in northwestern Europe, such as Denmark, Norway, and Sweden, typically provide the highest levels of public assistance payments.

Developed countries are hard-pressed to maintain their current levels of public assistance. In the past, rapid economic growth permitted these states to finance generous programs with little hardship. But in recent years, economic growth has slowed while the percentage of people who need public assistance has increased. Governments have faced a choice between reducing benefits or increasing taxes to pay for them. This dilemma is the origin of many U.S. political problems reported in the news.

Demographic Indicators of Development

8. Infant Mortality Rate. Better health and welfare in developed countries permit more babies to survive infancy. The number of babies that die before reaching 1 year of age is fewer than 10/1,000 per year in many developed countries compared with more than 100/1,000 in many LDCs (see Figure 2-6).

The infant mortality rate is greater in developing countries for several reasons. Lack of prenatal care is an important factor contributing to infant mortality. Babies die from malnutrition or lack of medicine needed to survive illness, such as dehydration from diarrhea. They also die from poor medical practices that arise from lack of education. For example, the use of a dirty knife to cut the umbilical cord is a major cause of fatal tetanus in India.

9. Natural Increase Rate. The natural increase rate averages more than 2 percent per year in developing countries and less than 1 percent in developed ones (see Figure 2-4). Greater natural increase strains a country's ability to provide hospitals, schools, jobs, and other services that can make its people healthier and more productive. Many LDCs must allocate

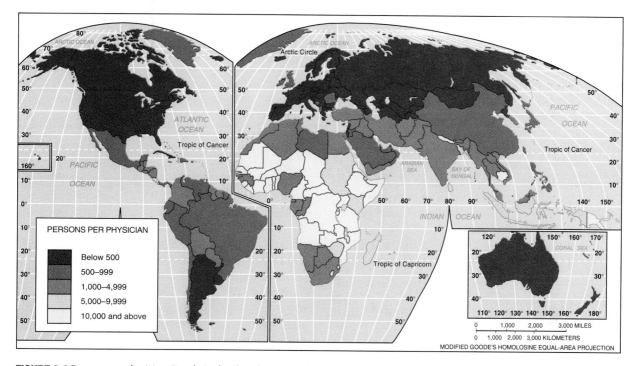

FIGURE 8-9 Persons per physician. People in developed countries have more access to health care, as shown in ratios of people to hospital beds, nurses, doctors, and other medical indicators. In MDCs, for example, each doctor is available to an average of 500 people, but in LDCs each doctor is shared by thousands.

increasing percentages of their GDPs just to care for the rapidly expanding population, rather than to improve care for the current population.

10. Crude Birth Rate. LDCs have higher natural increase rates because they have higher crude birth rates. The annual crude birth rate exceeds 40/1,000 in many developing countries, compared with less than 15/1,000 in developed countries (see Figure 2-5). Women in MDCs choose to have fewer babies for various economic and social reasons, and they have access to varied birth control devices to achieve this goal.

Crude death rate does not indicate a society's level of development. More and less developed countries both have crude death rates around 10/1,000 per year. There are two reasons for the lack of difference. First, diffusion of medical technology from developed countries has eliminated or sharply reduced the incidence of several diseases in developing countries. Second, MDCs have higher percentages of older people, who have high mortality rates, as well as lower percentages of children, who have low mortality rates once they survive infancy.

The mortality rate for women in childbirth is significantly higher in developing countries. For every 100,000 babies born, fewer than 10 mothers die giving birth in most developed countries, compared with several hundred in less developed countries.

11. Age Structure. The greater crude birth rates in LDCs result in age structures different from those of developed countries. Developing countries have a higher percentage of children under age 15, who are too young to work and must be supported by employed adults and government programs (see Figure 2-12). Developed countries have a higher percentage of older people who have retired and who also need to be supported. The overall percentage of young and old dependents is lower in relatively developed countries than in developing ones.

Correlation of Development Indicators

A country's development level is relative, and every state is at some position on a continuous development scale. However, many countries fall into one of two extreme positions on the scale. Geographers justify classifying countries into more and less developed because their economic, social, and demographic characteristics tend to coincide.

The correlation is clearly demonstrated by comparing the United States and India. By every measure of development, the United States ranks among the world's highest, whereas India falls among the world's lowest by most indicators (Figure 8-10).

Per capita GDP in India is less than 2 percent of the level in the United States, and the gap between the two countries has increased during the past two decades. The lower GDP per capita in India reflects the fact that three-fourths of the people are farmers, compared with less than 5 percent in the United States. The preponderance of non-primary-sector

workers in the United States produce a variety of goods and services that increase the country's wealth.

The United States has abundant raw materials needed for industrial production. It has the wealth to purchase resources with which it is less endowed, such as copper and petroleum, from other countries. India has many raw materials essential for manufacturing, but lacks a number of critical resources and the wealth to import them.

Consumer goods are scarcer in India. The number of people per motor vehicle, telephone, and television is several hundred times that in the United States. Because of its much higher GDP, the United States can afford to pay much more for education, social security, and other public assistance programs. Underlying the social and economic differences are demographic contrasts, discussed in more detail at the end of Chapter 2. The natural increase rate is much higher in India because of a higher crude birth rate. Women in India especially suffer from higher rates of illiteracy and mortality.

The same economic, social, and demographic indicators that distinguish the United States and India can be used at a global scale. Geographers divide the world into regions based on correlation of the various development measures, and we will look at these regions next.

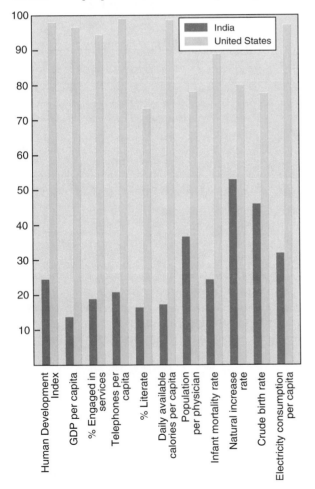

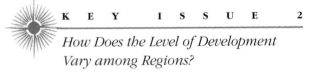

K E Y   I S S U E   2

How Does the Level of Development Vary among Regions?

- More Developed Regions
- Less Developed Regions

The United Nations measures the level of development for every country with more than 1 million inhabitants. The U.N. calls its measure the Human Development Index (HDI). The HDI combines several indicators of development, including economic (adjusted gross domestic product per capita), social (literacy rate and education), and demographic (life expectancy). The highest HDI possible is 1.0. Any measure of development is arbitrary, but the HDI is useful because it combines social, demographic, and economic indicators (Figure 8-11).

FIGURE 8-10 The percentage of all countries that rank below the United States or India according to the particular measure. As a developed country, the United States ranks among the highest percentages in a wide variety of development indicators.

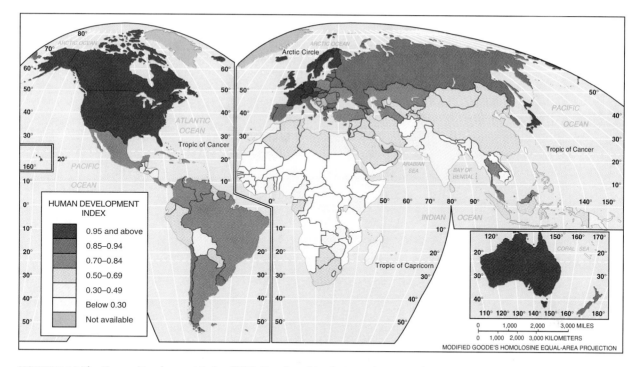

FIGURE 8-11 The Human Development Index (HDI). Developed by the United Nations, the HDI combines several measures of development: life expectancy at birth, adjusted GDP per capita, and knowledge (one-third mean years of schooling and two-thirds literacy). Each country received an index figure for the various measures, which range between minimum and desirable levels. The minimum for each index was set at the lowest level actually observed. The desirable levels were 100 percent for literacy and the maximum observed for life expectancy and mean years of schooling.

More Developed Regions

According to the 1993 HDI, Japan had the highest ranking. The United States ranked sixth among the 173 countries included in the study. If considered separately, U.S. whites would rank first in the world, ahead of Japan, while African–Americans would rank thirty-first and U.S. Hispanics thirty-fifth.

As mentioned, geographers group countries into nine major regions, plus three other areas, according to development (see Figure 8-1). Three of the nine regions are more developed, including Western Europe, Anglo-America, and Eastern Europe. The HDI exceeds .9 in two of these three regions, plus Japan and the South Pacific. Eastern Europe has a somewhat lower HDI (.87) because of restructuring after the fall of communism. Relatively developed South Africa has a lower HDI (.67) because of poorer conditions endured by its 75 percent nonwhite population (Table 8-1). The following sections briefly describe the more developed regions, in descending order of development level.

1. Anglo-America

With an HDI of .98, the United States and Canada, the two large countries in Anglo-America, rank among the world's most developed countries on the basis of various economic, social, and demographic characteristics. This region has the highest per capita GDP and is well endowed with most minerals needed for industry.

Although fewer than 5 percent of the region's workers are engaged in agriculture, Anglo-America is the world's most important food exporter and the only one with significant idle agricultural land. On the other hand, the region has the world's highest percentage of tertiary sector (service) employees. Anglo-America is the leading provider of word processing services, media, computer analysis, and information monitoring. The region also specializes in

TABLE 8-1
Human Development Index (HDI) by world regions

More Developed Regions and Areas	HDI	Less Developed Regions	HDI
Japan	0.98	Latin America	0.76
Anglo-America	0.98	East Asia	0.61
South Pacific	0.97	Southeast Asia	0.52
Western Europe	0.95	Middle East	0.51
Eastern Europe	0.87	South Asia	0.29
South Africa	0.67	Sub-Saharan Africa	0.23

The United States is the world's major producer of television programs and movies. The cast and production crew of Gilligan's Island gather on Malibu Beach, near Los Angeles, to film an update of the 1960s television series.

entertainment, mass media, sports, recreation equipment, and other industries that promote use of leisure time.

Compared with other regions, Anglo-America has relatively homogeneous language and religious patterns. More than 95 percent of the population speaks English, and 70 percent are Protestant. (Québec contains predominantly French-speaking Roman Catholics, and the United States has concentrations of Spanish-speaking Roman Catholics.) The relative cultural homogeneity of Anglo-America reduces the possibility that a large minority will be excluded from participating in the national economy, although protection of cultural diversity produces tension.

Economic growth in recent years has slowed in Anglo-America compared with other relatively developed areas, especially Japan and Western Europe. Global competition has increased for the region's industrial and agricultural products, and investment has lagged for the development of innovative products and techniques. Prospects for future U.S. economic growth are also clouded by a large budget deficit, a result of Americans' reluctance to raise taxes to cover spending for desired social welfare and military programs. To cover the budget deficit, the United States borrows large sums of money, and as a result owes by far more money to foreigners than does any other country.

2. Western Europe

The level of development is especially high in Western Europe's core area, which includes western Germany, northeastern France, northern Italy, Switzerland, southern Scandinavia, Belgium, the Netherlands, and Luxembourg. The region's peripheral areas—Ireland, southern Italy, Portugal, Spain, and Greece—rank somewhat lower in development.

To maintain a relatively high level of development, Western Europe must import food, energy, and minerals. In past centuries, Western Europeans explored and mapped the rest of the world and established colonies on every continent. These colonies supplied many resources needed to foster European economic development. Colonization also diffused Western European languages, religions, and social customs worldwide.

Now that most colonies have been granted independence, Western Europeans must buy raw materials from other countries. To pay for their imports, Western Europeans provide high-value goods and services, such as insurance, banking, and luxury motor vehicles, such as the Mercedes-Benz and Rolls-Royce.

On a global scale, Western Europe displays cultural unity, because most Western Europeans speak a language from the same family (Indo-European) and practice a branch of the same religion (Christianity). However, the large numbers of individual Christian denominations and sects and Indo-European languages have been consistent sources of conflict in Western Europe. Furthermore, with natural increase rates approaching zero or even negative numbers in most Western European countries, an increasingly important source of population growth in the region is migration of Muslims and Hindus from Africa and Asia. They add to the European stew the languages, religions, and customs from different cultures.

Competition among Western European states for control of territory has led to many wars, most notably the two world wars fought in this century. Since the end of World War II in 1945, however, most Western European states have joined multinational organizations that promote economic and military cooperation. The elimination of most economic barriers within the European Union has made Western Europe the world's largest and richest market.

3. Eastern Europe

Winston Churchill declared in a 1946 speech that an "Iron Curtain" had descended across Europe, from the Baltic Sea (near Germany) in the north to the Adriatic Sea (east of Italy) in the south. This became the dividing line between Western and Eastern Europe. Eastward of 15° east longitude, most European states came under Communist control in the late 1940s, while westward of this line, most were democratic. Between the late 1940s and late 1980s, Communist-dominated Eastern Europe comprised the Soviet Union, which occupied 15 percent of Earth's land area, plus eight small countries—Albania, Bulgaria, Czechoslovakia, East Germany (the German Democratic Republic), Hungary, Poland, Romania, and Yugoslavia.

Early communist theorists, such as Karl Marx and Friedrich Engels, believed that communism would triumph in relatively developed countries because exploited factory workers would lead a revolution and overthrow their governments. The social and economic programs of these theorists were based on conditions in advanced industrial societies. However, when Communist parties gained control of Russia in 1917 (the Bolshevik Revolution) and other Eastern European countries after World War II, few of these states were advanced industrial powers. Instead, the Communists had to promote socialism in poor, agricultural societies.

Under the Communists, the national governments exercised strong control over development (see Geography in Action box). The system promoted development of industries but neglected production of consumer goods. Although restricted from visiting Western countries, many Eastern Europeans could see on television the much higher level of comfort on the other side of the Iron Curtain.

During the 1990s, Eastern European countries dismantled the economic structure inherited from the

Centralized Planning for Development

As centrally planned societies, Eastern European countries typically had economies directed by government officials rather than private entrepreneurs. In the Soviet Union, for example, a national planning commission called *Gosplan* developed 5-year plans to guide economic development. The plans prescribed production goals for the whole country by economic sector and region. They specified the type and quantity of minerals, manufactured goods, and agricultural commodities to be produced and the factories, railways, roads, canals, and houses to be built in each part of the country.

The 5-year plans featured three main development policies. First, Soviet planners emphasized heavy industry—iron and steel, machine tools, petrochemicals, mining equipment, locomotives, and armaments. To allow industrial growth, the country also promoted development of mining, electric power, and transportation.

Second, the plans dispersed production facilities from the European to the Asian portion of the Soviet Union. Soviet decision makers considered the concentration of industry in the west to be a liability, with cause: the country had been invaded from the west by Napoleon Bonaparte (France) in the nineteenth century and Adolf Hitler (Germany) in the twentieth century, and they wanted to reduce the vulnerability of their vital industries to attack. Planners also wished to promote equal economic development throughout the country and believed that dispersal of industries would accomplish this goal.

Third, Soviet planners preferred to locate manufacturing facilities near sources of raw materials, rather than near markets. This policy reflected both the needs of industries emphasized in Soviet plans and the lack of effective consumer demand. By locating heavy industry near the raw materials, Soviet planners gave lower priority to producing consumer goods, such as telephones, washing machines, shoes, and dishes.

By centrally planning their economies, Eastern European states developed significantly by some measures, especially during the 1950s and 1960s. Annual per capita GDPs increased from a few hundred dollars to several thousand, and some social and demographic indicators became comparable to Western European countries.

During the late 1980s and early 1990s, central planning proved to be disastrous at running national economies:

- Scarce funds were used to meet annual production targets rather than to invest in long-term improvements in productivity, such as modernizing equipment and redeploying workers to other tasks.
- Despite an abundant supply of productive farmland, Eastern Europe had to import food from the West because of inefficient agricultural practices.
- Orders sent from national government offices hundreds of kilometers away were often not implemented in the factories.
- Some targets were impossible to achieve. Others were simply ignored: why work hard when your job is guaranteed and your supervisor can't fire you?
- Factories polluted the air and water, and citizens were unable to pressure their governments into investing in pollution control devices.

But for many Eastern Europeans, the most fundamental problem was that, by concentrating on basic industry, the Communists neglected consumer products such as automobiles, refrigerators, and clothing.

Under communism, factories such as this Russian auto parts manufacturer, were inefficient and unresponsive to market demands. Faced with the need to make a profit as well as compete against more modern plants in Western Europe, Japan, and North America, many Eastern European plants are closing. A large percentage of factory workers in Russia are women, in part because of the Communist tradition of encouraging female participation in the labor force. (Bill Swersey/Gamma-Liaison, Inc.)

Communists. Government-owned shops were sold to private individuals. Government factories were "privatized," in many cases to foreign corporations. Citizens have been able to buy shares in some privatized companies at low prices. Stock exchanges have been established to buy and sell the shares.

The level of development varies widely among Eastern European countries. The Czech Republic, Hungary, and Slovenia converted rapidly to market economies, taking advantage of their proximity to the relatively developed core region of Western Europe. Because workers in these countries are comparably skilled yet much lower-paid than their counterparts in Western Europe, some manufactured goods are being exported to wealthier countries in the West.

As memories of the Communist era fade, these countries will display social and economic characteristics similar to such Western European countries as Greece, Ireland, and Portugal. On the other hand, other former Communist countries in Eastern Europe—Albania, Belarus, Bulgaria, and Romania—have few factories that can compete in global markets.

Conversion to market economies has proved painful in some Eastern European countries. Closing inefficient businesses has increased unemployment, and prices for many goods have skyrocketed with the elimination of government subsidies.

In Czechoslovakia, the most important factor in its breakup into two countries was disagreement on the pace of economic reform. Czechs were willing to bear a short-term decline in their standard of living, because they believed that rapid conversion to a market economy would bring long-term benefits. Slovaks wanted to slow the pace of change: they feared high levels of unemployment in the large, inefficient factories that the Communists had clustered there to promote economic development during the 1950s.

Similarly, the Soviet Union and Yugoslavia fragmented in part because republics such as Russia and Slovenia preferred more rapid economic change than Belarus and Serbia. The end of communism in these countries, however, also unleashed long-suppressed friction among nationalities.

4. South Pacific, South Africa, and Japan

The South Pacific, South Africa, and Japan are also relatively developed areas. Japan and South Africa are surrounded by countries with much lower levels of development. The South Pacific is a relatively developed area with a much lower population than the regions already discussed.

South Pacific. More than 90 percent of the population in the South Pacific region is concentrated in two developed countries: Australia and New Zealand. The remaining people are scattered among sparsely inhabited islands that generally are less developed.

As former British colonies, Australia and New Zealand share many cultural characteristics with the United Kingdom. Over 90 percent of the residents are descendants of nineteenth-century British settlers, although indigenous populations remain.

Much of Australia is desert. But, because of the small total population, the ratio of people to resources is extremely favorable. Australia and New Zealand are net exporters of food and other resources and are closely tied economically to Western Europe, Japan, and Anglo-America.

South Africa. The level of development is much higher in South Africa than any other African country. But the benefits of a developed economy have been enjoyed primarily by the minority of the country's people who happen to be white, as a legacy of apartheid laws, as discussed in Chapter 7.

Japan. The developed regions and areas already examined share many cultural characteristics. They are dominated by the Indo-European language family and the Christian religion, and they share similar social customs and political traditions. All of these countries are in Europe or were colonized by European immigrants.

The level of development in Japan, the fifth most populous state in Asia, contrasts sharply with other large Asian countries. Japan ranks among the world's most productive states, while the GDP per capita is generally less than $1,000 per year in the rest of East, South, and Southeast Asia. The United Nations considers Japan to have a higher level of development than any other country.

Japan's development is especially remarkable because it has an extremely unfavorable ratio of population to resources. The country has some of the world's most intensively farmed land and one of the highest physiological densities (refer to Table 2-1).

The Japanese consume relatively little meat and grain other than rice but still must import these products. Japan also lacks many key raw materials for basic industry. For example, although Japan is the world's leading steel producer, it must import virtually all the coal and iron ore needed for steel production.

How has Japan become such a great industrial power? At first, the Japanese economy developed by taking advantage of the country's one asset, an abundant supply of people willing to work hard for low wages. The Japanese government encouraged manufacturers to sell their products in other countries at lower prices than domestic competitors. Having gained a foothold in the global economy by selling low-cost products, Japan then began to specialize in high-quality, high-value products, such as electronics, motor vehicles, and cameras.

Japan's dominance was achieved in part by concentrating resources in rigorous educational systems and training programs to create a skilled labor force. Japanese companies spend 8 percent of their revenues on research and development, twice as much as U.S. firms, and the government provides further assistance to develop new products and manufacturing processes.

Less Developed Regions

Six other regions are classified as less developed. The HDI is roughly .8 in Latin America, .6 in East Asia, .5 in the Middle East and Southeast Asia, .3 in South Asia, and .2 in Sub-Saharan Africa. This broad variation in HDI reflects different levels of progress, as well as future potential, in development.

The following sections briefly describe the less developed regions, in descending order of development level.

1. Latin America

The level of development varies within Latin America. Per capita GDP is relatively high along the South Atlantic coast from Curitiba, Brazil, to Buenos Aires, Argentina. This area enjoys high agricultural productivity and ranks among the world's leaders in production and export of wheat and corn (maize). Venezuela's per capita GNP is higher than the region's average, in part because it is the only South American country with extensive petroleum reserves. The region's lowest per capita GNPs are concentrat-

Brickmaking in China. Economic activities in China require a lot of labor, possible in a country with such a large workforce. (Paul Steel/The Stock Market)

ed in Central America, several Caribbean islands, and the interior of South America.

Most Latin Americans speak one of two Romance languages, Spanish or Portuguese, and adhere to Roman Catholicism. These cultural characteristics resulted from the fact that Brazil was a colony of Portugal and most of the remaining states once belonged to Spain. In reality, the region is culturally diverse. A large percentage of the population are descendants of inhabitants living in the region prior to the European conquest, while others trace their ancestors to African slaves.

Latin Americans are more likely to live in urban areas than people in other developing regions. Mexico City, São Paulo, Rio de Janeiro, and Buenos Aires rank among the world's ten largest, according to the U.S. Bureau of the Census. The region's population is highly concentrated along the Atlantic coast, but population density remains low in most of the region, especially the tropical interior of South America. Large areas of interior rainforest are being destroyed to sell the timber or to clear the land for settled agriculture.

Development in Latin America is hindered by inequitable income distribution. In many countries, a handful of wealthy families control much of the land and rent parcels to individual farmers. Many tenant farmers grow coffee, tea, and fruits for export to relatively developed countries rather than food for domestic consumption. Latin American governments encourage redistribution of land to peasants but do not wish to alienate the large property owners, who generate much of the national GDP.

During the 1970s, Latin America achieved the world's highest GDP growth rate for any region outside the petroleum-rich Middle East, but development has slowed since the 1980s. To finance development, the region's countries borrowed large sums from international organizations and banks in developed countries, but have been unable to repay some of them.

2. East Asia (China)

China, the largest country in East Asia, ranks among the world's poorest in per capita GDP. This ranking, however, does not accurately portray the region's potential for development.

Traditionally, most Chinese farmers were forced to pay high rents and turn over a percentage of their crops to a property owner. Farmers in a typical year produced enough food to survive but frequently suffered from famines, epidemics, floods, and other disasters. Exploitation of the country's resources by Europe and Japan further retarded China's development.

China had a watershed year in 1949. The Communist party won a civil war and created the People's Republic of China, and the old Nationalist government fled to the island of Taiwan, setting up a government in exile. Since then, dramatic changes have been made in the country's economy.

To ensure the production and distribution of enough food, the Communist government took control of most agricultural land. In some villages, officials assigned specific tasks to each farmer, distributed food to each family according to individual needs, and sold any remaining food to urban residents. In other cases, farmers rented land from the local government, received orders to grow specific amounts of particular crops, and sold for their own profit any crops above the minimum production targets.

In recent years, such strict control has been loosened. Individuals again are able to own land and control their own production. Farmers have an incentive to work hard, because the sale of surplus crops is their main source of revenue to buy household goods. However, agricultural land must be worked intensively to produce enough food for China's large population, and farmers in the country's less fertile areas may not be able to produce a large surplus.

The Chinese government controls its peoples' daily lives more than other countries, and they have difficulty obtaining some goods. Nonetheless, most Chinese recognize that they are better off now than before the 1949 revolution, because they have less fear of famine. Because government controls have given China a much lower natural increase rate than other developing regions, more of the country's growing GDP can contribute to increasing the standard of living of the existing population rather than meeting the needs of a rapidly expanding population.

3. Southeast Asia

The Southeast Asia region comprises eleven countries. Five are entirely on the Asian mainland—Cambodia, Laos, Myanmar (Burma), Thailand, and Vietnam. The six others are scattered across thousands of islands in the Indian and Pacific oceans. Most islands are part of Indonesia or the Philippines.

The region's tropical climate limits intensive cultivation of most grains. The heat is nearly continuous, the rainfall abundant, and the vegetation dense. Soils are generally poor, because the heat and humidity rapidly destroy nutrients when land is cleared for cultivation. Economic development is also limited in Southeast Asia by several mountain ranges, active volcanoes, and frequent typhoons.

This inhospitable environment kept population low in Southeast Asia. But the injection of Western medicine and technology has resulted in one of the most rapid rates of increase in the world, approximately 2.5 percent per year since the 1940s.

Southeast Asia's most populous country, Indonesia, includes 13,667 islands. Nearly two-thirds of the population live on the island of Java, which has one of the world's highest arithmetic densities. People have concentrated on Java partly because the island's soil, derived from volcanic ash, is more fertile than elsewhere in the region and partly because the Dutch established their colonial headquarters there.

Rice, the region's most important food, is exported in large quantities from some countries, such as Thailand and Vietnam, but must be imported to other countries in the region, such as Malaysia and the Philippines. Because of distinctive vegetation and climate, farmers in Southeast Asia concentrate on harvesting products that are used in manufacturing. The region produces a large percentage of the world's supply of palm oil and copra (coconut oil), natural rubber, kapok (fibers from the ceiba tree used for insulation and filling), and abaca (fibers from banana leaf stalks used in fabrics and ropes).

Southeast Asia contains a large percentage of the world's tin as well as some petroleum reserves. But development lags because of an unfavorable ratio of population to most resources essential for manufacturing.

The region has suffered from a half-century of nearly continuous warfare. Japan, the Netherlands, France, and the United Kingdom were all forced to withdraw from colonies they had established in the region. In addition, France and the United States both fought unsuccessfully to prevent Communists from controlling Vietnam during the Vietnam War, which ran from the 1950s to 1965. Wars have also devastated neighboring Laos and Cambodia.

4. The Middle East

Much of the Middle East is desert that can sustain only sparse concentrations of plant and animal life. Most products must be imported. The region does however, possess one major economic asset: it has a large percentage of the world's petroleum reserves.

Because of petroleum exports, the Middle East is the only one of the nine major world regions that enjoys a trade surplus. In every other major region, the value of imports exceeds exports. To a considerable extent, this is because countries in these other regions must purchase large quantities of petroleum from Middle Eastern states.

Government officials in Middle Eastern states, such as Saudi Arabia and the United Arab Emirates, have used the billions of dollars generated from petroleum sales to finance economic development. The Middle East is the only region in which development is not hindered by lack of capital for new construction. To the contrary, many governments in the region have access to more money than they can use to finance development.

Not every country in the region has abundant petroleum reserves. Most are concentrated in states that border the Persian Gulf. Development possibilities are limited in countries that lack significant petroleum reserves: Egypt, Jordan, Syria, and others (refer to Figure 13-4 for a map of petroleum production and reserves).

The large gap in per capita income between the petroleum-rich countries and those that lack resources causes great tension in the Middle East. People in poorer states held little sympathy for wealthy Kuwait when Iraq invaded it in 1990, triggering the Gulf War. Kuwait was accused of not sharing its petroleum-generated wealth and failing to provide good living conditions for guest workers from poorer Arab countries.

The challenge for many Middle Eastern states is to promote development without abandoning the traditional cultural values of Islam, the religion of more than 95 percent of the region's population. Many Middle Eastern countries sharply restrict the role of women in business. They also prevent diffusion of financial practices that are considered incompatible with Islamic principles. The low level of literacy among women is the main reason the United Nations considers the level of development among these petroleum-rich states to be lower than the per capita GDP would indicate.

Muslim women at a keyboard. Exposure to modern technology does not necessarily change all traditional social customs. Women in predominantly Muslim countries have been urged to wear the chador, a combination head covering and veil, as a sign of adherence to traditional religious principles. (Esaias Baitel/Gamma-Liaison, Inc.)

The region also suffers from serious internal cultural disputes, as discussed in Chapter 5. Iraq's long war with Iran and attempted annexation of Kuwait split the Arab world. Countries dominated by Shiite Muslims, especially Iran, have promoted revolutions elsewhere in the region to sweep away elements of development and social customs which they perceive to be influenced by Europe or Anglo-America.

Most Middle Eastern states have refused to recognize the existence of Israel, the region's only state controlled by Jews. Israel has successfully repelled several attacks by neighboring states and, since 1967, has occupied territory captured from its adversaries. Money that could be used to promote development is diverted to military funding and rebuilding war-damaged structures.

5. South Asia

The South Asia region has the world's second-highest population and second-lowest per capita GDP. The population density is very high throughout the region, and the natural increase rate is among the world's highest. The region includes India, Pakistan, Bangladesh, Sri Lanka, and the small Himalayan states of Nepal and Bhutan.

India, South Asia's largest country, is the world's leading producer of jute (used to make burlap and twine), peanuts, sugar cane, and tea. India has mineral reserves including uranium, bauxite (aluminum ore), coal, manganese, iron ore, and chromite (chromium ore). The overall population-resources ratio is unfavorable, however, because of the region's huge population.

India is one of the world's leading rice and wheat producers. The region was a principal beneficiary of the Green Revolution, a series of inventions beginning in the 1960s that dramatically increased agricultural productivity. As a result of the Green Revolution, "miracle" rice and wheat seeds were widely diffused through South Asia (see Chapter 13).

Agricultural productivity in South Asia also depends on climate. The region receives nearly all its precipitation from rain that falls during the monsoon season between May and August. Agricultural output declines sharply if the monsoon rains fail to arrive. In a typical year, farmers in South Asia produce a grain surplus that is stored for distribution during dry years. But several consecutive years without monsoon rains produce widespread hardship in South Asia.

Because few people can afford a car, walking and biking are more common in less developed countries, such as Kochi (Cochin), India, a city of nearly 1 million inhabitants. (Blain Harrington III/The Stock Market)

6. Sub-Saharan Africa

Africa has been allocated to three regions. Countries north of the Sahara share economic and cultural characteristics with the Middle East. At the southern end of the continent is white-dominated South Africa. The area in between is called Sub-Saharan Africa.

Per capita GDP in Sub-Saharan Africa is comparable to the level in South, East, and Southeast Asia. Population density is lower than in any other developing region. Sub-Saharan Africa contains many resources important for economic development, including bauxite in Guinea, cobalt and copper in Zaire and Zambia, iron ore in Liberia, manganese in Gabon, petroleum in Nigeria, and uranium in Niger (Figure 8-12).

Despite these assets, Sub-Saharan Africa has the least favorable prospect for development. Some of its economic problems are a legacy of the colonial era. Mining companies and other businesses were established to supply European industries with needed raw materials rather than to promote overall economic development in Sub-Saharan Africa. In recent years, African countries have suffered because world prices for their resources have fallen.

Poor leadership has also plagued Sub-Saharan Africa. After independence, leaders of many countries in the region pursued personal economic gain and local wars rather than policies to promote development of the national economy. Frequent wars within and between countries in Sub-Saharan Africa have retarded development.

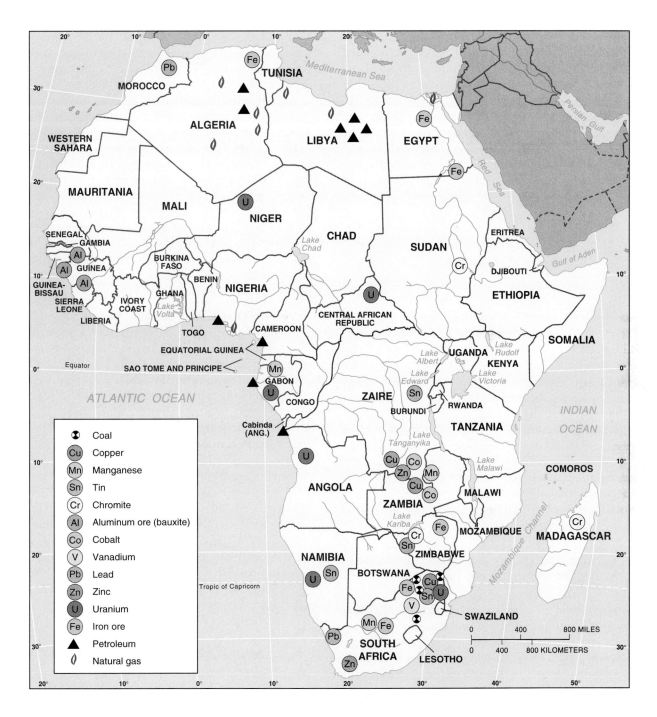

FIGURE 8-12 Minerals in Africa. Several African countries contain minerals important for industrial development. World prices for many of these minerals have declined or failed to rise at the same rate as the prices for industrial products, transportation, and energy.

The fundamental problem in many countries of Sub-Saharan Africa is a dramatic imbalance between the number of inhabitants and the capacity of the land to feed the population. Nearly all of the region consists of either tropical or dry climate. Both climate regions can support some people, but not large concentrations. Yet, because Sub-Saharan Africa has by far the world's highest rate of natural increase, the region's land is more and more overworked, and agricultural output has declined.

KEY ISSUE 3

How Can Countries Promote Development?

- Development through International Trade
- Development through Self-Sufficiency
- Financing Development

Clearly, the current level of development varies widely among regions. We next turn our attention to how countries can promote development in the future. LDCs in every region share the same priority: to increase their level of development. To do so, they must increase their per capita GDP and use the additional funds to improve the social and economic conditions of the people.

LDCs face two fundamental questions in trying to encourage development:

- What are the best policies to produce development?
- How can development be financed?

Less developed countries have chosen one of two models to promote development. One approach emphasizes international trade, while the other advocates self-sufficiency. Each has important advantages and serious problems. We will examine examples of countries that have tried each alternative, successfully and unsuccessfully.

Development through International Trade

The international trade model of development calls for a country to identify its distinctive or unique economic assets. What animal, vegetable, or miner-

al resources does the country have in abundance that other countries are willing to buy? What product can the country manufacture and distribute at a higher quality and a lower cost than other countries?

According to the international trade approach, a country can develop economically by concentrating scarce resources on expansion of its distinctive local industries. The sale of these products in the world market brings funds into the country that can be used to finance other development.

Rostow's Development Model

A leading advocate of this approach was W. W. Rostow, who in the 1950s proposed a five-stage model of development that several countries have adopted. According to Rostow, development should proceed in the following steps.

1. **The Traditional Society.** Rostow uses this term to define a country that has not yet started a process of development. A traditional society contains a very high percentage of people engaged in agriculture and a high percentage of national wealth allocated to what Rostow calls "nonproductive" activities, such as the military and religion.
2. **The Preconditions for Take-Off.** According to Rostow, the process of development begins when an elite group initiates innovative economic activities. Under the influence of these well-educated leaders, the country starts to invest in new technology and infrastructure, such as water supplies and transportation systems. These projects will ultimately stimulate an increase in productivity.
3. **The Take-Off.** Rapid growth is generated in a limited number of economic activities, such as textiles or food products. These few take-off industries achieve technical advances and become productive, while other sectors of the economy remain dominated by traditional practices.
4. **The Drive to Maturity.** Modern technology, previously confined to a few take-off industries, diffuses to a wide variety of industries, which then experience rapid growth comparable to the take-off industries. Workers become more skilled and specialized.
5. **The Age of Mass Consumption.** The economy shifts from production of heavy industry, such as steel and energy, to consumer goods, like motor vehicles and refrigerators.

According to Rostow's model, each country is in one of these five stages of development. More developed countries are in stage 4 or 5; less developed ones are in one of the three earlier stages. The model also asserts that today's developed countries have already passed through the early stages. The United States, for example, was in stage 1 before independence, stage 2 during the first half of the nineteenth century, stage 3 during the middle of the nineteenth century, and stage 4 during the late nineteenth century, before entering stage 5 during the early twentieth century.

A country that concentrates on international trade will benefit from exposure to consumers in other countries. To remain competitive, the take-off industries must constantly evaluate changes in international consumer preferences, marketing strategies, production engineering, and design technologies. This concern for international competitiveness in the exporting take-off industries will filter through less advanced economic sectors.

Rostow's optimistic projection for development was based on two factors. First, the developed countries of Western Europe and Anglo-America had been joined by others, notably Japan. If Japan could become more developed by following this model, why not other countries?

Second, many LDCs contain an abundant supply of raw materials sought by manufacturers and producers in developed countries. In the past, European colonial powers extracted many of these raw materials without paying compensation to the colonies. In a global economy, the sale of these raw materials could generate funds for LDCs to promote development.

States That Have Adopted the International Trade Approach

A few countries pioneered adoption of the international trade alternative over the past quarter-century. One such group is along the Arabian Peninsula near the Persian Gulf; the others are in East and Southeast Asia.

Petroleum-Rich Persian Gulf States. Saudi Arabia is the largest country in the Persian Gulf area; others include Kuwait, Bahrain, Oman, and the United Arab Emirates. Until the 1970s, this region was one of the world's least developed, but escalation of petroleum prices transformed these countries overnight into some of the wealthiest per capita.

These countries have used petroleum revenues to finance large-scale projects, such as housing, highways, airports, universities, and telecommunications networks. Recently built steel, aluminum, and petro-

Farmers in less developed countries who have produced a surplus may sell products in a market, such as this one at Xishuangbahna, in Yunnan Province, China. (Michele Burgess/The Stock Market)

chemical factories compete on world markets with the help of government subsidies.

The landscape has been further changed by the diffusion of consumer goods. Large motor vehicles, color televisions, audio equipment, and motorcycles are readily available and affordable. Supermarkets are stocked with food imported from Europe and Anglo-America.

Although the region's economy has changed dramatically in a short period of time, people's social customs have changed far more slowly. Daily life is dominated by Islamic religious principles, some of which conflict with Western business practices. Women are excluded from holding most jobs and visiting public places, such as restaurants and swimming pools. In some places they are expected to wear traditional black clothes, a shroud, and a veil. All business halts several times a day when Muslims are called to prayer. Shops close their checkout lines and permit people to unwrap their prayer rugs and prostrate themselves on the floor.

The Four Asian Dragons. Also following the international trade alternative are South Korea, Singapore, Taiwan, and the British colony of Hong Kong. These four areas have been given several nicknames, including the "four dragons," the "four little tigers," and "the gang of four."

Singapore (a British colony until 1965) and Hong Kong have virtually no natural resources. Both comprise large cities surrounded by very small amounts of rural land. South Korea and Taiwan have traditionally taken their lead from Japan, which occupied both of them until after World War II. Their adoption of the international trade approach was strongly influenced by Japan's success.

Lacking natural resources, the four dragons have promoted development by concentrating on producing a handful of manufactured goods, especially clothing and electronics. Low labor costs enable these countries to sell products inexpensively in developed countries.

Problems with the International Trade Alternative

Two problems have hindered countries outside the Persian Gulf and the four Asian dragons from developing through the international trade approach:

1. **Uneven Resource Distribution.** Resources are distributed unevenly among LDCs. Several Middle Eastern countries have successfully developed because petroleum prices skyrocketed during the 1970s. Other countries find that the prices of their commodities have not increased—and in some cases have actually decreased—in recent years. LDCs that depend on the sale of one product have suffered because the price of their leading commodity has not increased as rapidly as the cost of the products they need to buy. For example, Zambia's economy, which depends on the sale of copper, has suffered in recent years because of declining world prices for that commodity.
2. **Market Stagnation.** Countries such as the four dragons that depend on selling low-cost manufactured goods find that the world market for many products is expanding slower than in the past. Relatively developed countries have limited growth in population, consumer purchasing power, and market size. To increase sales, less developed countries may need to capture sales from established competitors rather than share in an expanding market.

Development through Self-Sufficiency

The second approach to promoting development is the *self-sufficiency*, or *balanced growth*, alternative. According to the self-sufficiency approach, a country should spread investment throughout all sectors of its economy rather than concentrate on one or two takeoff industries. This approach promotes balanced growth, because people and enterprises throughout the country receive a fair share of resources.

Countries that try to be self-sufficient encourage businesses to make goods for domestic consumption rather than for export. Economic growth may be modest, but in the long run the country benefits because it is not dependent on changing policies in other countries and fluctuations in the price of commodities.

States promote self-sufficiency by setting barriers that limit the import of goods from other places. These barriers may include setting high taxes on imported goods to make them more expensive than domestic goods, fixing quotas to limit the quantity of imported goods, and requiring licenses to restrict the number of legal importers.

Development is hindered in much of Africa by poor infrastructure, such as unpaved roads. Travel is slow and difficult even in a four-wheel-drive vehicle on roads such as this one near Kumasi, Ghana. (James Strachan/Robert Harding Picture Library)

India's Barriers to International Investment

For many years, the two most populous LDCs—China and India—strongly advocated self-sufficiency. Businesses were discouraged from exporting goods, and barriers prevented the importing of many goods.

India heavily used all three import barriers. To import goods into India, most foreign companies had to secure a license. The process was long and cumbersome, because several dozen government agencies had to approve the request. Once a company received an import license, the government severely restricted the quantity they could sell in India. The government also imposed heavy taxes on imported goods, which could double or triple the price to consumers.

At the same time, Indian businesses were discouraged from producing goods for export to more developed or other less developed countries. Instead, priority went to making goods for domestic consumption. If private companies were unable to make a profit selling goods only inside India, the government provided subsidies or took over direct operation of the company. As a result, India has produced more steel and motor vehicles per capita than generally found in LDCs, but the products have sold at twice the world market price.

In recent years, India's government has moved away from complete self-sufficiency. They lowered the tax on some imported goods and eliminated the license requirement for some importers. Indian companies are encouraged to become more competitive with foreign firms. India's GDP has increased by more than 4 percent per year over the past quarter-century, but population has increased by more than 2 percent per year. Therefore, more than half of India's economic growth goes to taking care of the additional people.

Problems with the Self-Sufficiency Alternative

India's experience illustrates some of the problems with self-sufficiency.

1. **Inefficiency.** Self-sufficiency policies may encourage inefficient industries. In a global economy, firms increasingly find the domestic market is too small to make a profit. Unable to make a profit through increased overseas sales, companies may need government subsidies to remain in operation. Companies protected from international competition may not feel pressure to keep abreast of rapid technological changes.

2. **Large Bureaucracy.** The second problem is that a large bureaucracy is needed to administer the controls. A complex administrative system encourages abuse and corruption. Potential entrepreneurs find that struggling to produce goods or services may be less rewarding financially than advising others on how to manipulate the controls. Other potential entrepreneurs may earn more money by illegally importing goods and selling them at inflated prices on the black market.

Financing Development

The most critical obstacle to development that most LDCs face is lack of money. Thus, less developed countries generally must obtain funds from more developed countries. They receive some funding as grants, but must borrow much of it from financial institutions in relatively developed countries. These institutions include commercial banks and international lending organizations, such as the World Bank and International Monetary Fund.

LDCs use much of the money to build new hydroelectric dams, electric transmission lines, flood protection systems, water supplies, roads, hotels, and other *infrastructure* projects. New infrastructure can improve people's living conditions and promote economic growth.

New projects do not always succeed. Tanzania, for example, built a new railroad line in the 1970s to transport copper from neighboring landlocked Zambia to the port of Dar es Salaam. More than a decade later, Tanzanians were still not trained to operate the system, little copper had been hauled out, and the trains ran only with foreign engineers. In Mali, a French-sponsored project to pump water from the Niger River using solar energy functioned for only one month. Even when it worked, the project, which cost over $1 million, produced no more water than could two diesel pumps that together cost $6,000.

In principle, new economic activities attracted to an area should provide additional revenue to repay the loans. But, in recent years, many developing countries have been unable to repay the interest on their loans, let alone the principal. Brazil, Mexico, Argentina, and several other Latin American countries have accumulated the largest debts, although several African countries have very high ratios of debt to GDP (Figure 8-13).

When these countries cannot repay their debts, financial institutions in relatively developed countries refuse to make further loans, so development of needed infrastructure stops. The inability of many developing countries to repay loans also hurts the relatively developed countries, whose financial institutions suffer losses.

Increasingly, more and less developed countries run the risk of confrontation. Although economically dominant, developed countries represent a minority of Earth's population. They have been pressed by LDCs to share the world's wealth more evenly. Less developed countries point out that prices have declined for many of their resources, but increased for most of the goods manufactured in developed countries. As a result, LDCs argue, they receive less for exporting their raw materials, and pay more to import manufactured goods.

LDCs also demand an increased role in loan-making decisions made by international agencies. A 1974 U.N. declaration called for creation of a "new international economic order," based on greater equality and economic interdependence between more and less developed countries.

For their part, developed countries are increasingly concerned about their own economic health. They have become more cautious in providing grants or loans to developing states. In exchange for canceling or refinancing the debts, the international lending agencies—which are dominated by the developed countries—require the governments of LDCs to impose economic austerity programs. LDCs must raise taxes, reduce government spending, and increase charges for using public services. These programs may be unpopular with the voters and encourage political unrest.

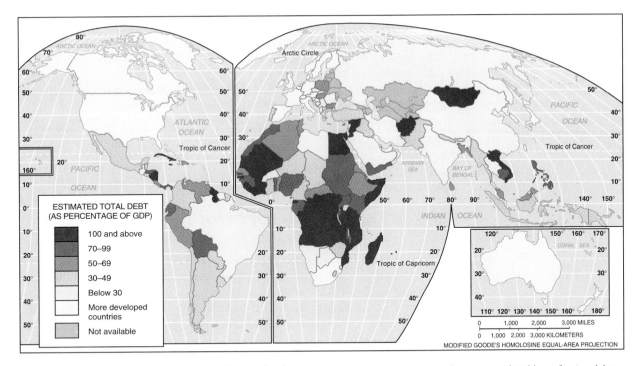

FIGURE 8-13 Debt as percentage of GDP. To finance development, many developing countries have accumulated large foreign debts relative to their annual GDPs. As a result, a large percentage of their national budgets must be used to repay loans. When LDCs cannot repay their debts, financial institutions in relatively developed countries suffer because they were a major source of the loans.

Summary In recent years, many countries have failed to make further progress in development and have suffered a declining standard of living. The world remains divided between more and less developed regions, and the gap between the two is widening. These again are the key issues for Chapter 8.

1. How is development measured?

Development is the process by which the material conditions of a country's people are improved. A more developed country has a higher level of per capita GDP, achieved through a transformation in the structure of the economy from a predominantly agricultural to an industrial and service-providing society. Developed countries use their wealth in part to provide better health, education, and welfare services. LDCs must use their additional wealth primarily to meet the needs of a rapidly growing population.

2. How does the level of development vary among regions?

We can identify three more developed regions—Anglo-America, Western Europe, and Eastern Europe—plus three other developed areas—South Pacific, Japan, and South Africa. Six less developed regions include Latin America, East Asia, Southeast Asia, the Middle East, South Asia, and sub-Saharan Africa. LDCs face different prospects for promoting development.

3. How can countries promote development?

Less developed countries choose between the international trade and the self-sufficiency paths toward development. In either alternative, LDCs may need to borrow considerable sums of money to promote development. The inability of many developing countries to pay back these loans is a source of considerable tension between them and more developed countries.

CASE STUDY REVISITED
Future Prospects for Development

Which approach has been more successful in promoting development, international trade or self-sufficiency? A few years ago, the World Bank attempted to answer the question by classifying forty-one developing countries into four groups: strongly oriented toward international trade, moderately oriented toward international trade, strongly oriented toward self-sufficiency, and moderately oriented toward self-sufficiency. The World Bank then compared the growth in per capita GDP achieved by the countries in the four groups for two periods, 1963–1973 and 1974–1985.

Between 1963 and 1973, the per capita GDP generally increased in all four groups. The countries strongly oriented toward international trade registered the largest increases (more than 7 percent per year), followed by those moderately oriented toward international trade (nearly 4 percent per year). Countries strongly oriented toward self-sufficiency had the lowest increases (less than 2 percent per year).

The rate of change in the GDP per capita was lower among all four groups of countries between 1974 and 1985, a period when higher petroleum prices triggered a worldwide economic slowdown. But the relative performance of the four groups compared to each other remained the same. The per capita GDP increased more than 6 percent per year in countries strongly oriented toward international trade, and it declined by more than 1 percent per year in countries strongly oriented toward self-sufficiency (Figure 8-14).

Evidence such as this World Bank study has convinced government officials in Eastern Europe, Latin America, Asia, and other regions that economic development can best be promoted through international trade. By trading with other countries, developing countries become more fully integrated into the world economy and gain some of the benefits produced by that system.

In geographic terms, less developed countries are on the periphery of the world economy, surrounding a core of the developed regions of Anglo-America, Western Europe, and Japan. To create conditions that encourage trade, LDCs adopt economic policies consistent with those in the relatively developed core regions, such as the sale of public utilities to private corporations and measures to control inflation. Industries in less developed regions may be producing primarily for sale in relatively developed countries, and LDCs may be more likely to buy products made in relatively developed countries. LDCs may need to reduce spending on social welfare programs and accept greater differentials between their wealthiest and poorest people.

To some geographers, the economies of developed core regions appear to be exploiting the people and resources of less developed peripheral regions. But from the perspective of people in developing regions, integration into a world economy through trade

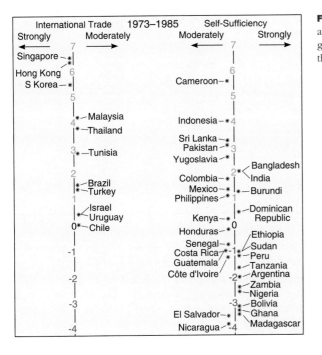

FIGURE 8-14 Approaches for development. Countries that have adopted the *international trade* approach to development have generally enjoyed greater levels of economic growth than those that have adopted the *self-sufficiency* approach.

with MDCs may be a small price to pay to receive material benefits of development, such as a steady job and a television.

Regardless of the alternative selected, LDCs still must finance development. The most effective means to promote development may be to provide small loans to a large number of individuals, rather than to concentrate funds in a handful of massive projects.

The Grameen Bank, based in Bangladesh, made over 300,000 loans to people in South Asia in the first decade after its founding in 1977. Three-fourths of the borrowers were women. Only 1 percent of the borrowers have failed to make their weekly loan repayments.

Rabea Rahman borrowed $90 from the Grameen Bank to buy a cow. Earnings from selling the cow's milk enabled her to buy her son an $85 rickshaw bicycle so that he could make a living. The smallest loan the bank has made was $1, to a woman who wanted to sell plastic bangles door to door. Other women have borrowed money to make perfume, bind books, and sell matches, mirrors, and bananas.

Key Terms

Developed country (MDC or relatively developed country or more developed country) A country that has progressed relatively far along a continuum of development.

Development A process of improvement in the material conditions of people through diffusion of knowledge and technology.

Gross domestic product (GDP) The value of the total output of goods and services produced in a country in a given time period (normally 1 year).

Less developed country (LDC or developing country) A country that is at a relatively early stage in the process of development.

Literacy rate The percentage of a country's people who can read and write.

Primary sector The portion of the economy concerned with the direct extraction of materials from Earth, generally through agriculture, although sometimes by mining, fishing, and forestry.

Productivity The value of a particular product compared with the amount of labor needed to make it.

Secondary sector The portion of the economy concerned with manufacturing products through processing, transforming, and assembling raw materials.

Tertiary sector The portion of the economy concerned with provision of all goods and services to people and businesses in exchange for payment.

Value added The gross value of the product minus the costs of raw materials and energy.

Thinking Geographically

1. Review the major economic, social, and demographic characteristics that contribute to a country's level of development. Which indicators can vary significantly by gender within countries and between countries at various levels of development? Why?

2. Some geographers have been attracted to the concepts of Immanuel Wallerstein, who argued that the modern world consists of a single entity, the capitalist world economy, that is divided into three regions: the core, semiperiphery, and periphery. How have the boundaries among these three regions changed?

3. China has relied on self-sufficiency to promote development, whereas Hong Kong has been a prominent practitioner of international trade. Can these two approaches be reconciled with Hong Kong becoming part of China as of 1997? Explain.

4. Some LDCs claim that the requirements placed on them by lending organizations such as the World Bank impede rather than promote development. Should LDCs be given a greater role in deciding how much the international organizations should spend and how such funds should be spent? Why or why not?

5. What obstacles do Eastern European countries face as they dismantle 40 years of socialism and convert to market economies?

Further Readings

Ballance, R., J. Ansari, and H. Singer. *The International Economy and Industrial Development: Trade and Investment in the Third World.* Totowa, NJ: Allanheld, Osmun, 1982.

Barker, Randolph, and Robert W. Herdt. *The Rice Economy of Asia.* Washington: Resources for the Future, 1985.

Bater, James H. *The Soviet Scene: A Geographical Perspective.* New York: Routledge, 1989.

Bebbington, Anthony J., Hernan Carrasco, Lourdes Peralbo, Galo Ramon, Jorge Trujillo, and Victor Torres. "Fragile Lands, Fragile Organizations: Indian Organizations and the Politics of Sustainability in Ecuador." *Transactions of the Institute of British Geographers,* New Series 18 (1993): 179–96.

Berry, Brian J. L., Edgar C. Conkling, and D. Michael Ray. *Economic Geography.* Englewood Cliffs, NJ: Prentice Hall, 1987.

Blakemore, Harold, and Clifford T. Smith, eds. *Latin America: Geographical Perspectives,* 2nd ed. London: Methuen, 1983.

Bobek, Hans. "The Main Stages in Socioeconomic Evolution from a Geographic Point of View." *Readings in Cultural Geography,* ed. by Philip L. Wagner and Marvin W. Mikesell. Chicago: The University of Chicago Press, 1962.

Chang, Sen-dou. "Modernization and China's Urban Development." *Annals of the Association of American Geographers* 71 (December 1981): 572–79.

Chisholm, Michael. *Modern World Development: A Geographical Perspective.* Totowa, NJ: Barnes and Noble Books, 1982.

_____. "The Wealth of Nations." *Transactions of the Institute of British Geographers*, New Series 5, no. 2 (1980): 255–76.

Cole, John P. *The Development Gap: A Spatial Analysis of World Poverty and Inequality*. New York: Wiley, 1980.

Crow, Ben, and Alan Thomas. *Third World Atlas*. Philadelphia: Open University Press, 1985.

Demko, George, ed. *Regional Development: Problems and Policies in Eastern and Western Europe*. New York: St. Martin's Press, 1984.

DeSouza, Anthony R., and Phillip Porter. *The Underdevelopment and Modernization of the Third World*. Washington, D.C.: Association of American Geographers, 1974.

DeSouza, Anthony R., and Frederick P. Stutz. *The World Economy: Resources, Location, Trade, and Development*, 2nd ed. New York: Macmillan, 1994.

Dickenson, J. P., C. G. Clarke, W. T. S. Gould, R. M. Prothero, D. J. Siddle, C. T. Smith, E. M. Thomas-Hope, and A. G. Hodgkiss. *A Geography of the Third World*. New York: Methuen, 1983.

Dott, Ashok K., ed. *Southeast Asia: Realm of Contrasts*. 3rd ed. Boulder, CO: Westview Press, 1985.

Dunford, Michael, and Dinae Perrons. "Regional Inequality, Regimes of Accumulation and Economic Developmentin Contemporary Europe." *Transactions of the Institute of British Geographers* New Series 19, no. 2 (1994): 163–82.

Flavin, Christopher. "Electricity for a Developing World: New Directions." *Worldwatch Paper* 70. Washington, D.C.: Worldwatch Institute, June 1986.

Forbes, D. K. *The Geography of Underdevelopment: A Critical Survey*. Baltimore: The Johns Hopkins University Press, 1984.

Fryer, Donald D. "The Political Geography of International Lending by Private Banks." *Transactions of the Institute of British Geographers*, New Series 12, no. 4 (1987): 413–32.

Ginsburg, Norton S. *Atlas of Economic Development*. Chicago: University of Chicago Press, 1961.

_____, ed. *Essays on Geography and Economic Development*. Chicago: University of Chicago Press, 1960.

Grossman, Larry. "The Cultural Ecology of Economic Development." *Annals of the Association of American Geographers* 71 (June 1981): 220–36.

Hoffman, George W., ed. *A Geography of Europe: Problems and Prospects*. 5th ed. New York: Wiley, 1983.

Holloway, Steve, R., and Kavita Pandit. "The Disparity Between the Level of Economic Development and Human Welfare." *Professional Geographer* 44 (February 1992): 57–71.

James, Preston E. *Latin America*. 4th ed. New York: Odyssey House, 1969.

Jones, D. B., ed. *Oxford Economic Atlas of the World*. 4th ed. London and New York: Oxford University Press, 1972.

Jumper, Sidney R., Thomas L. Bell, and Bruce A. Ralston. *Economic Growth and Disparities: A World View*. Englewood Cliffs, NJ: Prentice Hall, 1980.

Mabogunje, Akinlawon L. *The Development Process: A Spatial Perspective*. London: Hutchinson University Library, 1981.

Momsen, Janet Henshall. *Women and Development in the Third World*. London: Routledge, 1991.

_____, Janet Henshall, and Janet Townsend. *Geography of Gender in the Third World*. Albany: State University of New York Press, 1987.

Murphy, Alexander B. "Western Investment in East-Central Europe: Emerging Patterns and Implications for State Stability." *Professional Geographer* 44 (August 1992): 249–59.

Myrdal, Gunnar. *Rich Lands and Poor*. New York: Harper and Bros., 1957.

O'Connor, A. M. *The Geography of Tropical African Development*. 2nd ed. Oxford: Pergamon Press, 1978.

_____. *Poverty in Africa: A Geographical Approach*. London: Belhaven Press, 1991.

Ó'hUalláchain, Breandan, and Neil Reid. "Source Country Differences in the Spatial Distribution of Foreign Direct Investment in the United States." *Professional Geographer* 44 (August 1992): 272–85.

Porter, Doug, Bryant Allen, and Gaye Thompson. *Development in Practice: Paved with Good Intentions*. London and New York: Routledge, 1991.

Rostow, Walter W. *The Stages of Economic Growth*. Cambridge: Cambridge University Press, 1960.

Seager, Joni, and Ann Olson. *Women in the World: An International Atlas*. New York: Simon & Schuster, 1986.

Smith, David M. *Where the Grass is Greener: Living in an Unequal World*. London: Croom Helm, 1979.

Szentes, Tamas. *The Political Economy of Underdevelopment*. 4th ed. Budapest, Hungary: Akademiai Kiado, 1983.

Taylor, Peter J. "World-Systems Analysis and Regional Geography." *Professional Geographer* 40 (August 1988): 259–65.

Wallenstein, Immanuel. *The Capitalist World-Economy*. Cambridge: Cambridge University Press, 1979.

_____. *Geopolitics and Geoculture: Essays on the Changing World-System*. Cambridge: Cambridge University Press, 1991.

_____. *The Politics of the World-Economy*. Cambridge: Cambridge University Press, 1984.

Wheeler, James O., and Peter O. Muller. *Economic Geography*. New York: Wiley, 1981.

Wilbanks, Thomas J. "'Sustainable Development' in Geographic Perspective." *Annals of the Association of American Geographers* 84 (December 1994): 541–56.

World Commission on Environment and Development. *Our Common Future*. London: Oxford University Press, 1987.

Also consult the following journals: *Economic Development and Cultural Change, Economic Geography, International Development Review, International Economic Review, International Journal of Political Economy, Journal of Developing Areas, Netherlands Journal of Economic and Social Geography, Regional Studies.*

The Annenberg
CPB Project

PEOPLE, PLACES AND CHANGE
Global Tourism

Attracting tourists from more developed countries is an important tool of economic development for many less developed countries.

Commentator

Borneo is the third largest island in the world, straddling the Equator. The fabled home of headhunters is on the brink of becoming a mainstream tourist resort area.

This Cultural Center was built for the growing number of tourists who now visit Borneo each year. The post-tourist is searching increasingly for the extraordinary.

With this sort of development in an area so remote, the obvious impact will be on local traditional culture. How can it respond to the forces of modernization and tourism?

Chris Hamnett
[Professor of
Geography, Open
University]

Do you get the impression, Anthony, this is the real thing?

Anthony Long
[tourist]

I think it's pretty much the real thing as it currently exists. I'm not sure that you can say this is the way it was a hundred years ago, but this is the culture for Ibans as it currently exists and as far as this generation is concerned.

If there is not an effort made by the people themselves to preserve their culture or preserve their language, then it will tend to diminish as people move to the cities, or people stop speaking the language within their home and in their family. Then that bit of their culture is lost and it can be permanently lost and therefore hard to recapture. So tourism can assist in helping to preserve it through the rituals of the forms of dances. But also there should be a bit more too, because it just cannot survive if it's as a form of entertainment for tourists, if it doesn't exist still in some form of fashion within the homes of people. And that's the one way for it to preserve itself.

9

AGRICULTURE

KEY ISSUES

1. How did agriculture originate and diffuse?
2. What is agriculture like in less developed countries?
3. What is agriculture like in more developed countries?
4. What are the most important agriculture regions in more developed countries?

When you buy food in the supermarket, are you reminded of a farm? Not likely. The meat is carved into pieces that no longer resemble an animal and wrapped in paper or plastic film. The vegetables are often canned or frozen. The milk and eggs are in cartons.

Providing food in the United States and Canada is a vast industry. Only a few people are full-time farmers, and they may be more familiar with the operation of computers and advanced machinery than the typical factory or office worker.

The mechanized, highly productive U.S. or Canadian farm contrasts with the subsistence farm found in much of the world. The most "typical" human — if there is such a person — is an Asian farmer who grows enough food to survive, with little surplus. This sharp contrast in agricultural practices constitutes one of the most fundamental differences between the more developed and less developed countries of the world.

BERBER SHEPERD AND FLOCK, MOROCCO. (GERARD DEL VECCHIO/TONY STONE IMAGES)

Wheat Farmers in Kansas and Pakistan

The Iqbel family grows wheat on their 1-hectare (2.5-acre) plot of land in the Punjab province of Pakistan in a manner similar to that of their ancestors. They perform most tasks by hand or with the help of animals. To irrigate the land, for example, they lift water from a 20-meter (65-foot) well by pushing a water wheel. More prosperous farmers in Pakistan use bullocks to turn the wheel.

The farm produces about 1,500 kilograms (3,300 pounds) of wheat per year, enough to feed the Iqbel family. Most of the wheat from the Iqbel's farm is consumed in the village where it is grown. Some years, they produce a small surplus, which they can sell. They can then use that money to buy other types of food or household items. In drought years, however, the crop yield is lower, and the Iqbel family must receive food from government and international relief organizations.

A world away in Kansas, the McKinleys farm the prairie sod. Like the Iqbels, they grow wheat in a climate that receives little rain. Otherwise, the two farm families lead very different lives. The McKinley family's farm is 200 times as large—200 hectares (500 acres). The McKinleys derive several hundred times more income from the sale of wheat than do the Iqbels.

The McKinleys do not consume the wheat they grow. Instead, they sell it to a processing company. Ultimately, it is turned into bread wrapped in plastic and sold in a supermarket hundreds of kilometers away.

Approximately two-thirds of the people in the world are farmers. The overwhelming majority of them are like the Iqbels, growing enough food to feed themselves, but little more. In most African and Asian countries, more than 60 percent of the people are farmers. In contrast, fewer than 2 percent of the people in the United States and Canada are farmers. Yet, the advanced technology used by these farmers allows them to produce enough food for people in the United States and Canada at a very high standard, plus food for many people elsewhere in the world.

Geographers study agriculture across Earth and how its distribution is related to culture and the environment. Elements of the physical environment, such as climate, soil, and topography, set broad limits on agricultural practices, but farmers can also observe and modify the environment in a variety of ways.

How farmers deal with their physical environment varies according to customary beliefs, preferences, technology, and other cultural factors. In each society, farmers possess very specific knowledge of their environmental conditions and certain technology for modifying the landscape. Within the limits of their technology, farmers choose from a variety of agricultural practices, on the basis of their perception of the value of each alternative. These values are partly economic and partly cultural.

Farmers generally pursue the most profitable agriculture, although their economic calculations may be altered by government programs that subsidize the production of some products and discourage others. Farmers also select agricultural practices on the basis of cultural perceptions, because a society may hold some foods in high esteem while avoiding others (see Chapter 6).

This chapter examines the prevailing types of agriculture practiced around the world. Geographers observe a wide variety of agricultural practices on the landscape, but the most important distinction is what happens to the product of the farm. As discussed in Chapter 8, geographers divide the world into the less developed regions, where the output is frequently consumed on or near the farm where it is produced, and the more developed regions, where the farmer sells the crops and livestock off the farm.

After examining the origins and diffusion of agriculture, we will consider the agricultural practices used in less and more developed regions. We also will examine the problems farmers face in each type of region. Although each farm has a unique set of physical conditions and choice of crops, geographers group farms into several types by their distinctive environmental and cultural characteristics.

K E Y   I S S U E   1

How Did Agriculture Originate and Diffuse?

- How Did Agriculture Begin?
- Where Did Agriculture Start?
- Classifying Agricultural Regions

We cannot document the origins of agriculture with certainty, because it began before recorded history. Scholars try to reconstruct a logical sequence of events on the basis of fragments of information about ancient agricultural practices and historical environmental conditions. Improvements in cultivating plants and domesticating animals evolved over thousands of years.

How Did Agriculture Begin?

Determining the origin of agriculture first requires a definition of what it is. **Agriculture** is the deliberate modification of Earth's surface by cultivating or caring for plants and rearing animals to obtain sustenance or economic gain. Agriculture thus originated when humans domesticated plants and animals for their use. A **crop** is any plant cultivated by people.

Hunters and Gatherers

Before the invention of agriculture, all humans probably obtained the food they needed for survival through hunting for animals, fishing, or gathering plants (including berries, nuts, fruits, and roots). We call this activity *hunting and gathering*. Hunters and gatherers lived in small groups, usually fewer than fifty, because a larger number would quickly exhaust the available resources within walking distance. They survived by collecting food often, perhaps daily. The search for food might take only a short time or much of the day, depending on local conditions. The men hunted game or fished, and the women collected berries, nuts, and roots.

The group traveled frequently, establishing new home bases or camps. The direction and frequency of migration depended on the movement of game and the seasonal growth of plants at various locations. We can assume that groups communicated with each other concerning hunting rights, intermarriage, and other specific subjects. For the most part, they kept the peace by steering clear of each other's territory.

Contemporary Hunting and Gathering. Today, only about 250,000 people, or less than 0.005 percent of the world's population, still survive by hunting and gathering rather than by agriculture. These people live in isolated locations, including the Arctic and the interior of Africa, Australia, and South America. Examples include African Bushmen of Namibia and Botswana and Aborigines in Australia.

Contemporary hunting and gathering societies are isolated groups living on the periphery of world settlement. But they provide insight into human customs that prevailed in prehistoric times, before the invention of agriculture.

Invention of Agriculture

Why did nomadic groups convert from hunting, gathering, and fishing to agriculture? In gathering wild vegetation, people inevitably cut plants and dropped berries, fruits, and seeds. These hunters probably observed that, over time, damaged or discarded food produced new plants. They may have deliberately cut plants or dropped berries on the ground to see if they would produce new plants. Subsequent generations learned to pour water over the site and to introduce manure and other soil improvements. Over thousands of years, plant cultivation apparently evolved from a combination of accident and deliberate experiment.

Prehistoric people may have originally domesticated animals for noneconomic reasons, such as sacrifices and other religious ceremonies. Other animals probably were domesticated as pets, surviving on the group's food scraps.

Two Types of Cultivation. The earliest form of plant cultivation, according to prominent cultural geographer Carl Sauer, was **vegetative planting,** which is the reproduction of plants by direct cloning from existing plants, such as cutting stems and dividing roots. Plants found growing wild were deliberately divided and transplanted.

Coming later, according to Sauer, was **seed agriculture,** which is the reproduction of plants through annual planting of seeds that result from sexual fertilization. Seed agriculture is practiced by most farmers today.

Where Did Agriculture Start?

Agriculture probably did not originate in one location but began in multiple, independent hearths, or points of origin. From these hearths, agricultural practices diffused across Earth's surface.

Location of First Vegetative Planting

Sauer believed that vegetative planting probably originated in Southeast Asia (Figure 9-1). The region's diversity of climate and topography probably encouraged growth of a wide variety of plants suitable for dividing and transplanting. Also, the people obtained food primarily by fishing, rather than by hunting and gathering, so they may have been more sedentary and therefore able to devote more attention to growing plants.

The first plants domesticated in Southeast Asia through vegetative planting probably included roots such as the taro and yam and tree crops such as the banana and palm. Vegetative planting diffused from the Southeast Asian hearth northward and eastward to China and Japan and westward through India to Southwest Asia, tropical Africa, and the Mediterranean lands (Figure 9-1). The dog, pig, chicken, and other livestock probably were domesticated first in Southeast Asia.

Other early hearths of vegetative planting also may have emerged independently in West Africa and northwestern South America. It may have begun with the oil-palm tree and yam in West Africa and the manioc, sweet potato, and arrowroot in South America. The practice diffused from northwestern South America to Central America and eastern portions of South America.

Location of First Seed Agriculture

Seed agriculture also originated in more than one hearth. Sauer identified three hearths in the Eastern Hemisphere: western India, northern China, and Ethiopia (Figure 9-2). Seed agriculture diffused quickly from western India to Southwest Asia, where important early advances were made, including the cultivation of wheat and barley, two grains that became particularly important thousands of years later in European and American civilizations.

Apparently, inhabitants of Southwest Asia also were first to integrate seed agriculture with domestication of herd animals such as cattle, sheep, and

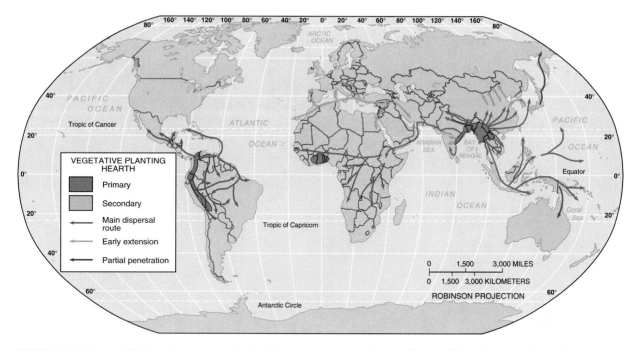

FIGURE 9-1 Origin and diffusion of vegetative planting. Vegetative planting is the reproduction of plants by direct cloning from existing plants. The practice originated primarily in Southeast Asia, according to Carl Sauer. Two other early centers of vegetative planting were in West Africa and northwestern South America. From these hearths, the practice diffused to other regions. (Adapted from Carl O. Sauer, *Agricultural Origins and Dispersals,* with the permission of the American Geographical Society.)

goats. These animals were used to plow the land before planting seeds and, in turn, were fed part of the harvested crop. Other animal products, such as milk, meat, and skins, were exploited at a later date, according to Sauer. This integration of plants and animals is a fundamental element of modern agriculture.

Diffusion of Seed Agriculture. Seed agriculture diffused from Southwest Asia across Europe and through North Africa (Figure 9-2). Greece, Crete, and Cyprus display the earliest evidence of seed agriculture in Europe. From these countries, agriculture may have diffused northwestward through the Danube River basin, eventually to the Baltic Sea and North Sea, and northeastward to Ukraine. Most of the plants and animals domesticated in Southwest Asia spread into Europe, although barley and cattle became more important farther north, perhaps because of cooler and moister climatic conditions.

Seed agriculture also diffused eastward from Southwest Asia to northwestern India and the Indus River plain. Again, a variety of domesticated plants and animals were brought from Southwest Asia, al-

though other plants, such as cotton and rice, arrived in India from different hearths.

From the northern China hearth, millet diffused to South and Southeast Asia. Rice, which ultimately became the most important crop in much of Asia, has an unknown hearth, although some geographers consider Southeast Asia to be its most likely location. Sauer identified a third independent hearth in Ethiopia, where millet and sorghum were domesticated early. He argued, however, that agricultural advances in Ethiopia did not diffuse widely to other locations. That Ethiopia is an ancient hearth for seed agriculture is ironic, because rapid population growth, devastating civil wars, and adverse environmental conditions have combined to make Ethiopia one of the modern world's centers for starvation.

Two independent seed agriculture hearths originated in the Western Hemisphere: southern Mexico and northern Peru. The hearth in southern Mexico, which extended into Guatemala and Honduras, was the point of origin for squash and maize (corn). Squash, beans, and cotton may have been domesticated in northern Peru. From these two hearths, agri-

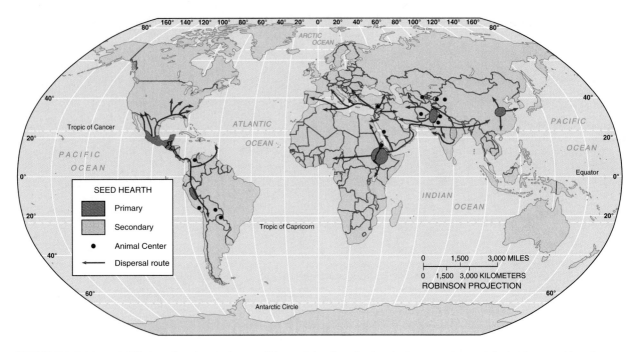

FIGURE 9-2 Origin and diffusion of seed agriculture and livestock herding. Seed agriculture may have originated in several hearths, including western India, northern China, and Ethiopia. Southern Mexico and northwestern South America may have been other early hearths. Early advances were made in Southwest Asia. (Adapted from Carl O. Sauer, *Agricultural Origins and Dispersals,* with the permission of the American Geographical Society.)

cultural practices diffused to other parts of the Western Hemisphere, although agriculture was not widely practiced until European colonists began to arrive some 500 years ago. The only domesticated animals were the llama, alpaca, and turkey; herd animals were unknown until European explorers brought them in the sixteenth century.

Classifying Agricultural Regions

That agriculture had multiple origins means that, from earliest times, people have produced food in distinctive ways in different regions. This diversity derives from a unique legacy of wild plants, climatic conditions, and cultural preferences in each region. Improved communications in recent centuries have encouraged the diffusion of some plants to other locations around the world. Many plants and animals thrive across a wide portion of Earth's surface, not just in their place of original domestication. Only after A.D. 1500, for example, were wheat, oats, and barley introduced to the Western Hemisphere, and maize to the Eastern Hemisphere.

Despite increased knowledge of alternatives, farmers still practice forms of agriculture unique to their area of the world. Characteristics of the physical environment continue to influence the type of agriculture, but areas with similar climates often show different agricultural practices because of their unique cultural traits. Several attempts have been made to classify the world's major types of agriculture into meaningful groups, but—significantly—few of these classifications include maps that distribute these groups into regions.

Many contemporary geographers accept Derwent Whittlesey's 1936 classification with some modification. Whittlesey identified eleven main agricultural regions, plus an area where agriculture was nonexistent (Figure 9-3). These eleven types of agriculture include five that are important in less developed countries and six that are important in more developed countries.

The next section considers four of the five types of subsistence agriculture types characteristic of LDCs: shifting cultivation, pastoral nomadism, and two types of intensive subsistence. The fifth type, plantation agriculture, physically occurs in LDCs, but is considered with agriculture in more developed countries because MDCs own and operate the plantations.

K E Y   I S S U E   2

What Is Agriculture Like in Less Developed Countries?

- Shifting Cultivation
- Pastoral Nomadism
- Intensive Subsistence Agriculture

The agriculture in LDCs is generally described as **subsistence agriculture,** which primarily provides food for consumption by the farmer's family. Regions where subsistence agriculture prevails have two distinguishing characteristics:

1. Most people work in agriculture rather than in industrial or service jobs.
2. Most people produce food for their own consumption. Some surplus may be sold to the government or to private firms, but the surplus product is not the farmer's primary purpose and may not exist in some years because of growing conditions.

Subsistence farmers employ a wide variety of agricultural practices. This section looks at four types: shifting cultivation, intensive subsistence with wet rice dominant, intensive subsistence with wet rice not dominant, and pastoral nomadism.

Shifting Cultivation

Shifting cultivation is practiced in much of the world's humid low latitude, or A, climate regions, which have relatively high temperatures and abundant rainfall (see Figure 1-19, the world climate map). It predominates in the Amazon area of South America, Central and West Africa, and Southeast Asia, including Indochina, Indonesia, and New Guinea.

We use the term *shifting cultivation* (as in "cultivate a garden") because *agriculture* implies greater use of tools and animals and more elaborate modification of the landscape. Shifting cultivation bears little relation to the agriculture practiced in developed regions of Western Europe and North America, or even in other developing countries such as China.

Characteristics of Shifting Cultivation

Shifting cultivation has two distinguishing hallmarks:

1. Farmers clear land for planting by slashing vegetation and burning the debris (**slash-and-burn agriculture**).
2. Farmers grow crops on a cleared field for only a few years until soil nutrients are depleted and then leave it fallow (plant nothing) for many years so that the soil can recover.

People who practice shifting cultivation generally live in small villages and grow food on the surrounding land, which the village controls. Well-recognized boundaries usually separate neighboring villages.

How Shifting Cultivation Works. Each year, villagers designate for planting an area surrounding the settlement. Before planting, they must remove the dense vegetation that typically covers tropical land. Using axes, they cut most of the trees, sparing only those that are economically useful. An efficient strategy they employ is to cut selected large trees, which bring down smaller trees that may have been weakened by notching.

The undergrowth is cleared away with a machete or other long knife. On a windless day, the debris is burned under carefully controlled conditions. The rains wash the fresh ashes into the soil, providing needed nutrients. The cleared area is known by different names in different regions, including **swidden,** *ladang, milpa, chena,* and *kaingin.*

Before they are planted, fields are prepared by hand, perhaps with the help of a simple implement such as a hoe; plows and animals are rarely used. The only fertilizer generally available is potash (potassium) from burning the debris when the site is cleared. Little weeding is done the first year that a cleared patch of land is farmed; weeds may be cleared with a hoe in subsequent years.

The cleared land can support crops only briefly, usually 3 years or less. In many regions, the most productive harvest comes in the second year after burning. Thereafter, soil nutrients are rapidly depleted, and the land becomes too infertile to nour-

FIGURE 9-3 The major agricultural practices of the world can be divided into subsistence and commercial regions.

Subsistence regions include: *shifting cultivation*—primarily the tropical regions of South America, Africa, and Southeast Asia; *intensive subsistence, wet rice dominant*—primarily the large population concentrations of East and South Asia; *intensive subsistence, crops other than rice dominant*—primarily the large population concentrations of East and South Asia, where growing rice is difficult; and *pastoral nomadism*—primarily the dry lands of North Africa and Asia.

Commercial regions include: *mixed crop and livestock*—primarily U.S. Midwest and central Europe; *dairying*—primarily near population clusters in northeastern United States, southeastern Canada, and northwestern Europe; *grain*—primarily north-central United States and eastern Europe; *ranching*—primarily the dry lands of western United States, southeastern South America, central Asia, southern Africa, and Australia; *Mediterranean*—primarily lands surrounding the Mediterranean Sea, western United States, and Chile; *Commercial gardening and fruit farming*—primarily southeastern United States and southeastern Australia; and *plantation*—primarily the tropical and subtropical regions of Latin America, Africa, and Asia.

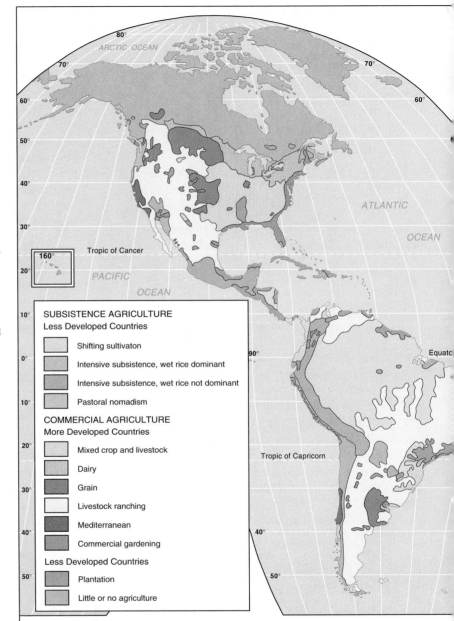

SUBSISTENCE AGRICULTURE
Less Developed Countries

- Shifting sultivaton
- Intensive subsistence, wet rice dominant
- Intensive subsistence, wet rice not dominant
- Pastoral nomadism

COMMERCIAL AGRICULTURE
More Developed Countries

- Mixed crop and livestock
- Dairy
- Grain
- Livestock ranching
- Mediterranean
- Commercial gardening

Less Developed Countries

- Plantation
- Little or no agriculture

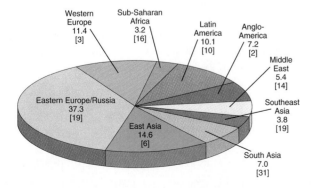

Western Europe 11.4 [3]
Sub-Saharan Africa 3.2 [16]
Latin America 10.1 [10]
Anglo-America 7.2 [2]
Middle East 5.4 [14]
Eastern Europe/Russia 37.3 [19]
East Asia 14.6 [6]
Southeast Asia 3.8 [19]
South Asia 7.0 [31]

ish crops. Rapid weed growth also contributes to the abandonment of a swidden after a few years.

When the swidden is no longer fertile, villagers identify a new site and begin clearing it. They leave the old site uncropped for many years, allowing it to become overrun again by natural vegetation. The field is not actually abandoned: the villagers will return to the site some day, perhaps as few as 6 years or as many as 20 years later, to begin the process of clearing the land again. In the meantime, they may still care for fruit-bearing trees on the site.

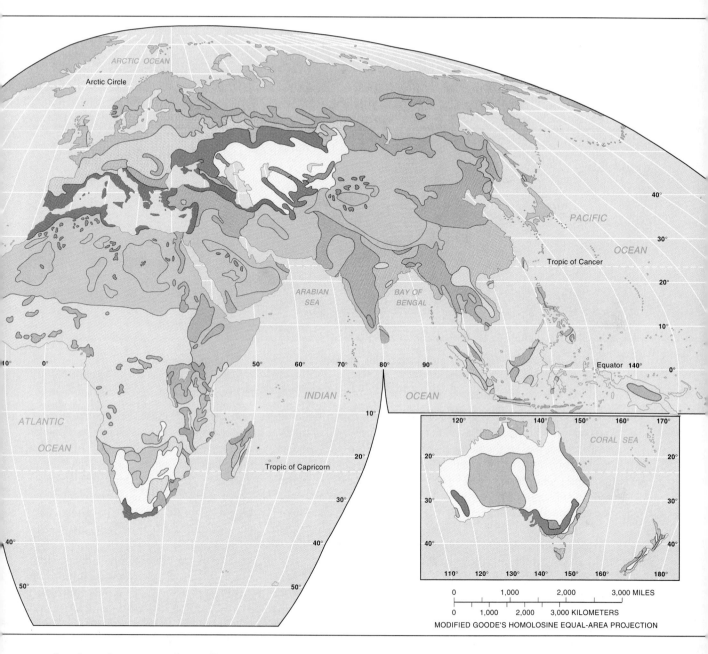

MODIFIED GOODE'S HOMOLOSINE EQUAL-AREA PROJECTION

If a cleared area outside a village is too small to provide food for the population, then some of the people may establish a new village and practice shifting cultivation there. Some farmers may move temporarily to another settlement if the field they are clearing that year is distant.

Crops of Shifting Cultivation. The precise crops grown by each village vary by local custom and taste. The predominant crops include upland rice in Southeast Asia, maize (corn) and manioc (cassava) in South America, and millet and sorghum in Africa. Yams, sugar cane, plantain, and vegetables also are grown in some regions. These crops may have begun in one region of shifting cultivation but then diffused to other areas.

The Kayapo people of Brazil's Amazon tropical rainforest do not arrange crops in the rectangular fields and rows that are familiar to us. They plant in concentric rings. At first, they plant sweet potatoes and yams in the inner area. In successive rings go corn and rice, manioc, and more yams. The outer-

These shifting cultivation farmers in Peru are preparing fields for planting by slashing and burning the vegetation. The dense vegetation is chopped down, and the debris is burned in order to provide the soil with needed nutrients. (Asa C. Thoresen/Photo Researchers, Inc.)

most ring contains papaya, banana, pineapple, mango, cotton, and beans. Plants that require more nutrients are located in the outer ring. It is here that the leafy crowns of cut trees fall when the field is cleared, and their rotting releases more nutrients into the soil. In subsequent years, the inner area of potatoes and yams expands to replace corn and rice.

Most families grow only for their own needs, so one swidden may contain a large variety of intermingled crops, which are harvested individually at the best time. In shifting cultivation, a "farm field" appears much more chaotic than fields in relatively developed regions, where a single crop such as corn or wheat may grow over an extensive area. In some cases, families may specialize in a few crops and trade with villagers who have a surplus of others.

Shifting Cultivation, Land Ownership, and Land Use. Traditionally, land is owned by the village as a whole rather than separately by each resident. The chief or ruling council allocates a patch of land to each family and allows it to retain the output. Individuals may also have the right to own or protect specific trees surrounding the village. Private individuals now own the land in some communities, especially in Latin America.

Shifting cultivation occupies approximately one-fourth of the world's land area, a higher percentage than any other type of agriculture. Only 5 percent of the world's population, however, engage in shifting cultivation. The gap between the percentage of people and land area is not surprising, because the practice of moving from one field to another every couple of years requires more land per person than other types of agriculture.

The percentage of land devoted to shifting cultivation is declining in the tropics, and its future role in world agriculture is not clear. Shifting cultivation is being replaced by logging, cattle ranching, and cultivation of cash crops. The reason is economic development (see Geography in Action box). Alternatives to shifting cultivation require cutting of vast expanses of forest.

Pastoral Nomadism

Pastoral nomadism is a form of subsistence agriculture based on the herding of domesticated animals. The word *pastoral* refers to sheep herding. It is adapted to dry climates where planting crops is im-

Shifting Cultivation and Deforestation

In recent years, tropical rainforests have been disappearing at the annual rate of 10 to 20 million hectares (25 to 50 million acres, or 40,000 to 80,000 square miles). This means that an area somewhere between the size of Virginia and Kansas is cleared each year, a very significant environmental problem. The amount of Earth's surface allocated to tropical rainforests has already been reduced to less than half of its original area, and unless drastic measures are taken, the area will be reduced by another 20 percent within a decade.

Governments in less developed countries have supported the destruction of rainforests. To them, selling timber to builders or raising beef cattle for fast-food restaurants is a more effective strategy for economic development than shifting cultivation. Until recent years, this view was supported by the World Bank, which provided loans to finance development schemes that required clearing forests. Less developed countries also see shifting cultivation as an inefficient way to grow food in a hungry world. Indeed, compared with other forms of agriculture, shifting cultivation can support only a small population in an area without causing environmental damage.

To its critics, shifting cultivation is at best a preliminary step in economic development. Pioneers use shifting cultivation to clear forests in the tropics and to open land for development where permanent agriculture never existed. People unable to find agricultural land elsewhere can migrate to the tropical forests and initially practice shifting cultivation. Critics say it then should be replaced by more sophisticated agriculture that yields more per land area.

But defenders of shifting cultivation consider it the most environmentally sound approach for the tropics. Practices used in other forms of agriculture, such as using fertilizers and pesticides and permanently clearing fields, may damage the soil, cause severe erosion, and upset balanced ecosystems. Large-scale destruction of the rainforests also may contribute to global warming. When large numbers of trees are cut, their burning and decay release large volumes of carbon dioxide. This gas can build up in the atmosphere, acting like the window glass in a greenhouse to trap solar energy in the atmosphere (the "greenhouse effect"). Deforestation is not only a local problem; it is a global problem.

Elimination of shifting cultivation could upset traditional cultures as well. The activities of shifting cultivation are intertwined with social, religious, political, and other folk customs. A drastic change in the agricultural economy could disrupt other activities of daily life.

As the importance of tropical rainforests to the global environment has become recognized, LDCs have been pressured to restrict further destruction of them. In one innovative strategy, Bolivia agreed to set aside 1.5 million hectares (3.7 million acres) in a forest reserve in exchange for cancellation of $650,000,000 of its debt to developed countries.

In Brazil's Amazon rainforest, deforestation is declining. From 2 million hectares (5.2 million acres) per year during the 1980s, including a peak of 2.9 million hectares (7.4 million acres) in 1985, deforestation has declined nearly half to 1.1 million hectares (2.8 million acres) per year during the 1990s.

Brazil's Amazon rainforest is being cleared for cattle ranching and other forms of agriculture. The timber is sold to builders. Mining activities have also provided stimulus for deforestation. (Antonio Ribeiro/Gamma-Liaison, Inc.)

possible. Pastoral nomads live primarily in the large belt of arid and semiarid land that includes North Africa, the Middle East, and parts of Central Asia (see Figure 9-3). The Bedouins of Saudi Arabia and North Africa and the Masai of East Africa are examples of nomadic groups. Only approximately 15 million people are pastoral nomads, but they sparsely occupy approximately 20 percent of Earth's land area.

Characteristics of Pastoral Nomadism

In contrast to other subsistence farmers, pastoral nomads depend primarily on animals rather than crops for survival. The animals provide milk, and their skins and hair are used for clothing and tents. Like other subsistence farmers, though, pastoral nomads consume mostly grain rather than meat. Their animals are commonly not slaughtered, although

dead ones may be consumed. To nomads, the size of their herd is both an important measure of power and prestige and their main security during adverse environmental conditions.

Some pastoral nomads obtain grain from sedentary subsistence farmers in exchange for animal products. More often, part of a nomadic group—perhaps the women and children—may plant crops at a fixed location while the rest of the group wanders with the herd. Nomads may hire workers to practice sedentary agriculture in return for grain and protection. Other nomads may sow grain in recently flooded areas and return later in the year to harvest the crop. Yet another strategy is to remain in one place and cultivate the land when rainfall is abundant; then, during periods that are too dry to grow crops, the group can increase the size of the herd and migrate in search of food and water.

Choice of Animals. Nomads select the type and number of animals for the herd according to local cultural and physical characteristics. The choice depends on the relative prestige of animals and the ability of species to adapt to a particular climate and vegetation. The camel is most frequently desired in North Africa and the Middle East, followed by sheep and goats. In Central Asia, the horse is particularly important.

The camel is well suited to arid climates, because it can go long periods without water, carry heavy baggage, and move rapidly. But the camel is particularly bothered by flies and sleeping sickness and has a relatively long period—12 months—from conception to birth. Goats need more water than camels but are tough and agile and can survive on virtually any vegetation, no matter how poor. Sheep are relatively slow-moving and are more affected by climatic changes than are camels and goats. They require more water and are more selective about the plants they will eat. The minimum number of animals necessary to support each family adequately varies according to the particular group and animal. The typical nomadic family needs twenty-five to sixty goats or sheep or ten to twenty-five camels.

Movements of Pastoral Nomads. Pastoral nomads do not wander randomly across the landscape but have a strong sense of territoriality. Every group controls a piece of territory and will invade another group's territory only in an emergency or if war is declared. The goal of each group is to control a territory large enough to contain the forage and water needed for survival. The actual amount of land a group controls depends on its wealth and power.

The precise migration patterns evolve from intimate knowledge of the area's physical and cultural characteristics. Groups frequently divide into herding units of five or six families and choose routes depending on experience concerning the most likely water sources during the various seasons of the year. The selection of routes varies in unusually wet or dry years and is influenced by the condition of their animals and the area's political stability.

Some pastoral nomads practice **transhumance,** which is seasonal migration of livestock between mountains and lowland pasture areas. **Pasture** is grass or other plants grown for feeding grazing animals, as well as land used for grazing. Sheep or other animals may pasture in alpine meadows in the summer and be herded back down into valleys for winter pasture.

Pastoral Nomadism, Past and Future

Agricultural experts once regarded pastoral nomadism as a stage in the evolution of agriculture, between the hunters and gatherers who migrated across Earth's surface in search of food and sedentary farmers who cultivate grain in one place. Because they had domesticated animals but not plants, pastoral nomads were considered more advanced than hunters and gatherers but less advanced than settled farmers.

Pastoral nomadism is now generally recognized as an offshoot of sedentary agriculture, not a primitive precursor of it. It is simply a practical way of surviving on land that receives too little rain for cultivation of crops. The domestication of animals—the basis for pastoral nomadism—probably was achieved originally by sedentary farmers, not by nomadic hunters. Pastoral nomads therefore had to be familiar with sedentary farming and in many cases practiced it.

Today, pastoral nomadism is a declining form of agriculture, a victim in part of modern technology. Before recent transportation and communications inventions, pastoral nomads played an important role as carriers of goods and information across the sparsely inhabited dry lands. Nomads used to be the most powerful inhabitants of the dry lands, but now their importance has diminished and national governments control their movement.

In the dry lands of less developed regions, pastoral nomads, such as these in Algeria, herd camels and other animals adapted to dry conditions. The size of a herd is a traditional measure of wealth among pastoral nomads. (Tom McHugh/Photo Researchers, Inc.)

Government efforts to resettle nomads have been particularly vigorous in China, Kazakhstan, and several Middle Eastern countries, including Egypt, Israel, Saudi Arabia, and Syria. Nomads are reluctant to cooperate, so these countries have experienced difficulty in trying to force settlement in collectives and cooperatives. Governments force groups to give up pastoral nomadism because they want the land for other uses. Land that can be irrigated is converted from nomadic to sedentary agriculture. In some instances, the mining and petroleum industries now operate in dry lands formerly occupied by pastoral nomads.

Some nomads are encouraged to try sedentary agriculture or to work for mining or petroleum companies. Others are still allowed to move about, but only within ranches of fixed boundaries. In the future, pastoral nomadism will be increasingly confined to areas that cannot be irrigated or that lack valuable raw materials.

Intensive Subsistence Agriculture

Shifting cultivation and pastoral nomadism are forms of subsistence agriculture found in regions of low density. But three-fourths of the world's people live in LDCs, and another form of subsistence agriculture is needed to feed most of them: **intensive subsistence agriculture**. The term *intensive* implies that farmers must work more intensively to subsist on a parcel of land.

In densely populated East, South, and Southeast Asia, the greatest number of farmers practice intensive subsistence agriculture. The typical farm in Asia's intensive subsistence agriculture regions is much smaller than elsewhere in the world. Many Asian farmers own several fragmented plots, frequently a result of dividing individual holdings among children over several centuries.

Because the agricultural density—the ratio of farmers to arable land—is so high in parts of East and South Asia, families must produce enough food for their survival from a very small area of land. They do this through careful agricultural practices, refined over thousands of years in response to local environmental and cultural patterns. Most of the work is done by hand or with animals rather than with machines, in part because of abundant labor, but largely from lack of funds to buy equipment.

To maximize food production, intensive subsistence farmers waste virtually no land. Corners of fields and irregularly shaped pieces of land are planted rather than left idle. Paths and roads are kept as narrow as possible to minimize the loss of arable land. Livestock are rarely permitted to graze on land that could be used to plant crops, and little grain is grown to feed the animals.

Intensive Subsistence—Wet Rice Dominant

The intensive agriculture region of Asia can be divided between areas where wet rice dominates and areas where it does not (see Figure 9-3). The term **wet rice** refers to the practice of planting rice on dry land in a nursery and then moving the seedlings to a flooded field to promote growth. Wet rice occupies a relatively small percentage of Asia's agricultural land, but it is the region's most important source of food. Intensive wet-rice farming is the dominant type of agriculture in Southeast China, East India, and much of Southeast Asia (Figure 9-4).

Successful production of large yields of rice is an elaborate time-consuming process and is done mostly by hand. The consumers of the rice also perform the work, and all family members, including children, contribute to the effort.

Growing rice involves several steps: first, a farmer prepares the field for planting, using a plow drawn by water buffalo or oxen. The use of a plow and animal power is one characteristic that distinguishes subsistence agriculture from shifting cultivation.

Then, the plowed land is flooded with water. The water is collected from rainfall, river overflow, or irrigation. Too much or too little can damage the crop—a particular problem for farmers in South Asia who depend on monsoon rains, which do not always arrive at the same time each summer. Before planting, dikes and canals are repaired to assure the right quantity of water in the field. The flooded field is called a **sawah** in the Austronesian language widely spoken in Indonesia, including Java. Europeans and North Americans frequently, but incorrectly, call it a **paddy,** the Malay word for wet rice.

The customary way to plant rice is by growing seedlings on dry land in a nursery and then transplanting the seedlings into the flooded field. Typically, one-tenth of a sawah is devoted to cultivation of seedlings. After about a month, they are transferred to the rest of the field. Rice plants grow submerged in water for approximately three-fourths of the growing period. Another method of planting rice is to broadcast dry seeds by scattering them through the field, a method used to some extent in South Asia.

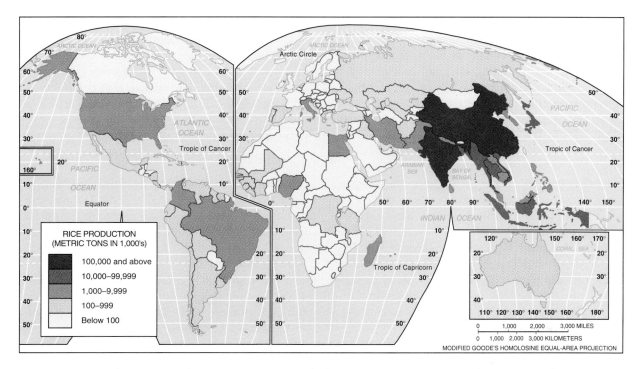

FIGURE 9-4 Rice production. Rice is the most important crop in the large population concentrations of East, South, and Southeast Asia. Asian farmers grow more than 90 percent of the world's rice, and two countries—China and India—account for more than half of world production. Growing rice is a labor-intensive operation, done mostly by hand. In Yunnan Province, China, rice seedlings grown in a nursery are transplanted to the field. (Ken Straiton/The Stock Market)

Rice plants are harvested by hand, usually with knives. To separate the husks, known as **chaff,** from the seeds, farmers **thresh** the heads by beating them on the ground or treading on them barefoot. The threshed rice is placed in a tray, and the lighter chaff is **winnowed,** that is, allowed to be blown away by the wind. If the rice is to be consumed directly by the farmer, the **hull,** or outer covering, is removed by mortar and pestle. Rice that is sold commercially is frequently whitened and polished, a process that removes some nutrients but leaves rice more pleasing in appearance and taste to many consumers.

Wet rice is most easily grown on flat land, because the plants are submerged in water much of the time. Thus most wet rice cultivation is located in river valleys and deltas. But the pressure of population growth in parts of East Asia has forced expansion of areas under rice cultivation. One method of developing additional land suitable for growing rice is to terrace the hillsides of river valleys.

Land is used even more intensively in parts of Asia by obtaining two harvests per year from one field, a process known as **double cropping.** Double cropping is common in places having warm winters, such as South China and Taiwan, but it is relatively rare in India, where most areas have dry winters. Normally, double cropping involves alternating between wet rice, grown in the summer when precipitation is higher, and wheat, barley, or another dry crop, grown in the drier winter season. Crops other than rice may be grown in the wet-rice region in the summer on nonirrigated land.

Intensive Subsistence—Wet Rice Not Dominant

Climate prevents farmers from growing wet rice in portions of Asia, especially where summer precipitation levels are too low and winters are too harsh (see Figure 9-3). Agriculture in much of interior India and northeast China is devoted to crops other than wet rice.

Aside from what is grown, this region shares most of the characteristics of intensive subsistence agriculture with the wet-rice region. Land is used intensively and worked primarily by human power with the assistance of some hand implements and animals. Wheat is the most important crop, followed by barley. A wide variety of other grains and legumes are grown for household consumption, including

Wet rice is the dominant crop in much of East, South, and Southeast Asia. Because wet rice should be grown on flat land, hillsides may be terraced in places such as the Philippines to increase the area of rice production. (William Waterfall/The Stock Market)

Canaris Indians plow a field north of Cuenca, Ecuador, a form of intensive agriculture where wet rice is not dominant. (Mireille Vautier/Woodfin Camp and Associates)

millet, oats, corn, kaoliang, sorghum, and soybeans. Also grown are some crops sold for cash, such as cotton, flax, hemp, and tobacco.

In milder parts of the region where wet rice does not dominate, more than one harvest can be obtained some years through skilled use of **crop rotation**, which is the practice of planting a different crop each year in a field to avoid exhausting the soil. In colder climates, wheat or another crop is planted in the spring and harvested in the fall, but no crops can be sown through the winter.

Since the Communist Revolution in 1949, private individuals have owned little agricultural land in China. Instead, the Communist government organized agricultural producer communes, which typically consisted of several villages of several hundred people. By combining several small fields into a single large unit, the government hoped to promote agricultural efficiency, because scarce equipment and animals could be shared, and larger improvement projects, such as flood control, water storage, and terracing, could be completed. In reality, productivity did not increase as much as the government had expected, because people worked less efficiently for the commune than when working for themselves.

China has dismantled the agricultural communes. They still hold legal title to agricultural land, but villagers sign contracts entitling them to farm portions of the land as private individuals. Chinese farmers may sell the right to use the land. By doing so they can no longer pass on the right to their children. Reorganization has been difficult because irrigation systems, equipment, and other infrastructure were developed to serve large communal farms rather than small individually managed ones, which cannot afford to operate and maintain the machinery. But production has increased greatly.

K E Y   I S S U E   3

What Is Agriculture Like in More Developed Countries?

- Characteristics of Commercial Agriculture
- How Do Commercial Farmers Choose Which Crops to Plant?

Farmers in developed regions, including the United States, Canada, Europe, South Africa, Australia, and New Zealand, practice commercial agriculture. **Commercial agriculture** is agriculture undertaken primarily to generate products for sale off the farm.

Characteristics of Commercial Agriculture

Five important characteristics distinguish commercial agriculture from subsistence agriculture, which predominates in the less developed countries:

1. Small percentage of farmers in the labor force
2. Heavy use of machinery
3. Large farm size
4. Output sold to processors
5. Integration with other businesses

We will now look at each characteristic.

Small Percentage of Farmers

The first distinctive characteristic of commercial agriculture is the small percentage of farmers in the labor force—fewer than 2 percent in the United States and Canada, compared with more than 60 percent in LDCs (see Figure 8-4). Yet the small percentage of farmers in the United States and Canada produces enough food, not only for themselves and the rest of the country, but a surplus to feed people elsewhere as well.

The number of farmers has declined dramatically in more developed societies during the twentieth century. Both push and pull migration factors have been responsible: people have been pushed away from farms by lack of opportunity to earn a decent income, and at the same time they have been pulled to higher-paying jobs in urban areas. The United States had approximately 5.6 million farms in 1950, 4 million in 1960, and 2 million in 1993.

Commercial agriculture is increasingly dominated by a handful of large farms. In the United States, the largest 5 percent of farms (those with cash receipts exceeding $250,000 per year) account for more than one-half of the country's total output (and the largest 2 percent of farms—those with annual cash receipts exceeding $500,000—account for more than one-third of total output).

Although there are fewer farms and farmers, the amount of land devoted to agriculture has remained fairly constant in Western Europe and Anglo-America since 1900. The annual loss of farmland in the United States is only 0.01 percent—primarily because of the growth of urban areas—but this loss has been offset by the creation of new agricultural land through irrigation and reclamation. A more serious problem in the United States is the loss of the most productive farmland, known as **prime agricultural land**, as urban areas sprawl into the surrounding countryside.

Heavy Use of Machinery

The second distinctive characteristic of commercial agriculture is reliance on technological and scientific improvements. A small number of farmers in relatively developed societies can feed many peo-

Commercial agriculture depends heavily on expensive machinery to manage large farms efficiently. These combine machines are reaping, threshing, and cleaning wheat in Sherman County, Kansas. (Cotton Coulson/Woodfin Camp & Associates)

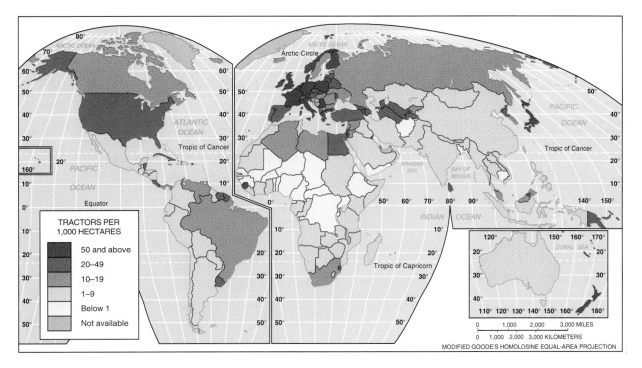

FIGURE 9-5 Tractors per 1,000 hectares of farmland. Farmers in more developed countries possess more machinery, such as tractors, than farmers in less developed ones. The machinery makes it possible for commercial farmers to farm extensive areas, a necessary practice to pay for the expensive machinery.

ple because they rely on machinery rather than people or animals to perform work (Figure 9-5).

Traditionally, the farmer or local craftspeople made equipment from wood, but beginning in the late 1700s, factories produced farm machinery. The first all-iron plow was produced in the 1770s and was followed in the nineteenth and twentieth centuries by a series of inventions that made farming less dependent on human or animal power. Tractors, combines, corn pickers, planters, and other factory-made farm machines have replaced or supplemented manual labor.

Transportation improvements also aid commercial farmers. The building of railroads in the nineteenth century and highways and trucks in the twentieth century have enabled farmers to transport crops and livestock farther and faster. Cattle arrive at market heavier and in better condition when transported by truck or train than when driven on hoof. Crops reach markets without spoiling.

Commercial farmers use scientific advances to increase productivity. Experiments conducted in uni-

versity laboratories, industry, and research organizations generate new fertilizers, herbicides, hybrid plants, animal breeds, and farming practices, which produce higher crop yields and healthier animals. Access to other scientific information has enabled farmers to make more intelligent decisions concerning proper agricultural practices. Some farmers conduct their own on-farm research.

Large Farm Size

The third distinctive characteristic of commercial agriculture is the relatively large average farm size, especially in the United States and Canada. U.S. farms average about 192 hectares (473 acres). Despite their size, most commercial farms in developed countries are family owned and operated—98 percent in the United States. Commercial farmers frequently expand their holdings by renting nearby fields.

Large size is partly a consequence of mechanization. Combines, pickers, and other machinery perform most efficiently at very large scales, and their considerable expense cannot be justified on a small farm. As a result of the large size and the high level of mechanization, commercial agriculture is an expensive business. Farmers spend hundreds of thousands of dollars to buy or rent land and machinery before beginning operations. This money is frequently borrowed from a bank and repaid after the output is sold.

Output Sold to Processors

The fourth distinctive characteristic of commercial farming is that farmers grow crops and raise animals primarily for sale off the farm rather than for their own consumption. Agricultural products are not sold directly to consumers but to food-processing companies. Large processors, such as General Mills and Ralston Purina, typically sign contracts with commercial farmers to buy their grain, chickens, cattle, and other output. Farmers may have contracts to sell sugar beets to sugar refineries, potatoes to distilleries, and oranges to manufacturers of concentrated juices.

Integration with Other Businesses

The fifth distinctive characteristic of commercial farming is its close ties to other businesses. The system of commercial farming found in the United States and other relatively developed countries has been called **agribusiness,** because the family farm is not an isolated activity but is integrated into a large food production industry.

Although farmers are less than 2 percent of the U.S. labor force, more than 20 percent of U.S. labor works in food production related to agribusiness: food processing, packaging, storing, distributing, and retailing. Agribusiness encompasses such diverse enterprises as tractor manufacturing, fertilizer production, and seed distribution. Although most farms are owned by individual families, many other aspects of agribusiness are controlled by large corporations.

How Do Commercial Farmers Choose Which Crops to Plant?

The type of agriculture practiced on a commercial farm depends on a combination of physical and human factors. Critical *physical* factors include *site* factors, such as climate, soil, and slope of the land, and *situation* factors (the farm's location in relation to the markets where its products are sold). Important *human* factors include the beliefs, traditions, and other *cultural* preferences of consumers and *government* policies.

von Thünen's Model

We will now look at an influential model that emphasized situation factors in deciding which crops to raise. The model was first proposed in 1826 by Johann Heinrich von Thünen, a farmer in northern Germany, in a book titled *The Isolated State.* According to von Thünen's model, which was later modified by geographers, a commercial farmer initially decides which crops to cultivate and animals to raise on the basis of market location.

Commercial farmers raise animals primarily for sale to large food processing companies and restaurant chains. Chickens are being processed at Holly Farms in North Wilksboro, North Carolina. (Charles Gupton/The Stock Market)

In choosing an enterprise, a commercial farmer compares two costs: the cost of the land versus the cost of transporting products to market. First, a farmer identifies a crop that can be sold for more than the cost of the land. Assume that a farmer's land costs $100 per hectare per year. The farmer would consider planting wheat if the output from 1 hectare could be marketed for more than $100 that year. Another crop, such as corn, will also be considered if the yield from 1 hectare can sell for more than $100.

A farmer will not necessarily plant the crop that sells for the highest price per hectare. The choice further depends on the distance of the farmer's land from the central market city. Distance to market is a critical factor because each crop has a unique transportation cost.

Example of von Thünen's Model. The following example illustrates the influence of transportation cost on the profitability of growing wheat.

1. Gross profit from sale of wheat grown on 1 hectare of land *not* including transportation costs:
   a. Wheat can be grown for $0.25 per kilogram
   b. Yield per hectare of wheat is 1,000 kilograms
   c. Gross profit is $250 per hectare ($0.25 per kilogram × 1,000 kilograms per hectare)
2. Net profit from sale of wheat grown on one hectare of land *including* transportation costs:
   a. Cost of transporting 1,000 kilograms of wheat to the market is $62.50 per kilometer
   b. Net profit from sale of 1,000 kilograms of wheat grown on a farm located 1 kilometer from the market is $187.50 ($250 gross profit – $62.50 per kilometer transport costs)
   c. Net profit from sale of 1,000 kilograms of wheat grown on a farm located 4 kilometers from the market is $0 ($250 gross profit – [$62.50 per kilometer × 4 kilometers])

The example shows that a farmer would make a profit growing wheat on land located less than 4 kilometers from the market. Beyond 4 kilometers, wheat is not profitable, because the cost of transporting it exceeds the gross profit.

The von Thünen model shows that a commercial farmer must combine two sets of monetary values to determine the most profitable crop:

- The value of the yield per hectare
- The cost of transporting the yield per hectare

These calculations demonstrate that farms located closer to the market tend to select crops with higher transportation costs per hectare of output, whereas more distant farms are more likely to select crops that can be transported less expensively.

Application of von Thünen's Model. Von Thünen based his general model of the spatial arrangement of different crops on his experiences as owner of a large estate in northern Germany during the early nineteenth century (Figure 9-6). He found that specific crops were grown in different rings around the cities in the area. Market-oriented gardens and milk producers were located in the first ring out from the cities. These products are expensive to deliver and must reach the market quickly because they are perishable.

The next ring out from the cities contained wooded lots, where timber was cut for construction and fuel; closeness to market is important for this commodity because of its weight. The next rings were used for various crops and for pasture; the specific commodity was rotated from one year to the next. The outermost ring was devoted exclusively to animal grazing, which requires lots of space.

Von Thünen did not consider site or human factors in his model. The model assumed that all land in a study area had similar site characteristics and was of uniform quality, although he recognized that the model could vary according to topography and other distinctive physical conditions. For example, a river might modify the shape of the rings because transportation costs change when products are shipped by water routes rather than over roads. The model also failed to understand that social customs and government policies influence the attractiveness of plants and animals for a commercial farmer.

Although von Thünen developed the model for a small region with a single market center, it also applies to a national or global scale. Farmers in relatively remote locations who wish to sell their output in the major markets of Western Europe and North America, for example, are less likely to grow highly perishable and bulky products.

Von Thünen's model helps explain the spatial distribution of various types of commercial agriculture. Farmers in one region tend to practice types of agriculture that are different from those of farmers in an-

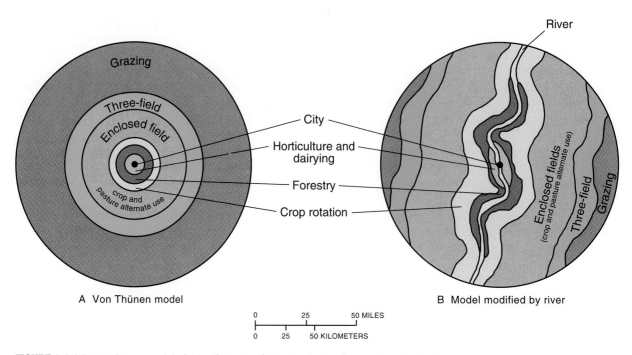

FIGURE 9-6 (A) Von Thünen model of role of situation factors in choice of crop. According to the von Thünen model, in the absence of topographic factors, different types of farming are conducted at different distances from a city, depending on the cost of transportation and the value of the product. (B) Von Thünen recognized that his model would be modified by site factors, such as a river in this sketch, which change the accessibility of different land parcels to the market center. Agricultural uses that seek highly accessible locations need to locate nearer the river.

other region, on the basis of a combination of environmental characteristics and access to markets. Some of the most important commercial agriculture regions are discussed in the next section.

☀ **K E Y   I S S U E   4**

What Are the Most Important Agriculture Regions in More Developed Countries?

- Mixed Crop and Livestock Farming
- Dairy Farming
- Grain Farming
- Livestock Ranching
- Mediterranean Agriculture
- Commercial Gardening and Fruit Farming
- Plantation Agriculture

Commercial agriculture in developed countries can be divided into six main types: mixed crops and livestock, dairying, grain farming, livestock ranch-

ing, Mediterranean agriculture, and gardening and fruit farming. Each type is predominant in distinctive regions within MDCs, depending on a combination of physical and human factors. The end of this section examines plantation farming, a form of commercial agriculture that occurs in LDCs but is owned and operated by companies in MDCs.

Mixed Crop and Livestock Farming

Mixed crop and livestock is the most common form of commercial agriculture in the United States west of the Appalachians and east of 98° west longitude and in much of Europe from France to Russia (see Figure 9-3).

Characteristics of Mixed Crop and Livestock Farming

The most distinctive characteristic of mixed crop and livestock farming is its integration of crops and livestock. Most of the crops are fed to animals rather than consumed directly by humans. In turn, the livestock supply manure to improve soil fertility to grow more crops. A typical mixed commercial farm devotes nearly all land area to growing crops but derives more than three-fourths of its income from the sale of animal products, such as beef, milk, and eggs. In the United States, pigs are often bred directly on the farms, while cattle may be brought in to be fattened on corn.

Mixed crop and livestock farming permits farmers to distribute the work load more evenly through the year. Fields require less attention in the winter than in the spring, when crops are planted, and in the fall, when they are harvested. Livestock, on the other hand, require attention throughout the year. A mix of crops and livestock also reduces seasonal variations in income; most income from crops comes during the harvest season, but livestock products can be sold throughout the year.

Crop Rotation Systems. Mixed crop and livestock farming typically involves crop rotation. The farm is divided into several fields, and each field is planted on a planned cycle, often of several years. The crop planted changes from one year to the next, typically going through a cycle of two or more crops and a year of fallow before the cycle is repeated. Crop rotation helps maintain the fertility of a field, because various crops deplete the soil of certain nutrients but restore others.

Crop rotation contrasts with shifting cultivation, in which nutrients depleted from a field are restored only by leaving the field fallow (uncropped) for many years. In any given year, crops cannot be planted in most of an area's fields, so overall production in shifting cultivation is much lower than in mixed commercial farming.

A two-field crop rotation system was developed in northern Europe as early as the fifth century A.D. A **cereal grain,** such as oats, wheat, rye, or barley, was planted in field A one year, while field B was left fallow. The following year, field B was planted, but A left fallow, and so forth. Beginning in the eighth century, a three-field system was introduced. The first field was planted with a winter cereal, the second with a spring cereal, and the third was left fallow. As a result, each field yielded four harvests every 6 years, compared with three every 6 years under the two-field system.

By the eighteenth century, a four-field system was used in Northwest Europe. The first year, the farmer could plant a root crop (such as turnips) in field A, a cereal in field B, a "rest" crop (such as clover, which helps restore the field) in field C, and a cereal in field D. The second year, the farmer might select a cereal for field A, a rest crop for field B, a cereal for field C, and a root for field D. The rotation would continue for two more years before the cycle would start again. Each field thus passed through a cycle of four crops: root, cereal, rest crop, and another cereal.

Cereals such as wheat and barley were sold for flour and beer production, and straw, which is the stalks that remain after the heads of wheat are threshed, was retained for animal bedding. Root crops such as turnips were fed to the animals during the winter. Clover and other rest crops were used for cattle grazing and restoration of nitrogen to the soil.

Choice of Crops

In the United States, mixed crop and livestock farmers select corn most frequently because of higher yields per area than other crops. Some of the corn is consumed by people either directly or as oil, margarine, and other food products, but most is fed to pigs and cattle (Figure 9-7). The most important mixed crop and livestock farming region in the United States—extending from Ohio to the Dakotas, with its center in Iowa—is frequently called the Corn Belt, because approximately half of the crop land is planted in corn (maize).

Soybeans have become the second most important crop in the U.S. mixed commercial farming region. Like corn, soybeans are sometimes used to make products consumed directly by people, but mostly to make animal feed. Tofu (made from soybean milk) is a major food source, especially for people in China and Japan. Soybean oil is widely used in U.S. foods, but as a hidden ingredient.

Dairy Farming

Dairy farming is the most important type of commercial agriculture practiced on farms near the large urban areas of the northeastern United States, southeastern Canada, and northwestern Europe (Figure 9-3). It accounts for approximately 20 percent of the total value of agricultural output throughout Western Europe and North America. Russia, Australia, and New Zealand also have extensive areas devoted to dairy farming. Nearly 90 percent of the world's sup-

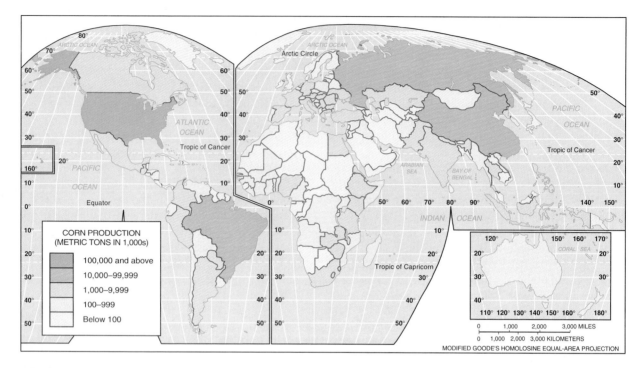

FIGURE 9-7 Corn (maize) production. The United States accounts for about 40 percent of the world's corn production. China is the second leading producer. Corn is called maize outside North America.

Soybeans (in the foreground of the photograph) are the second most important crop behind corn (in the background) in much of the eastern United States, including this farm in Michigan, adjacent to an oil refinery. (William Renwick)

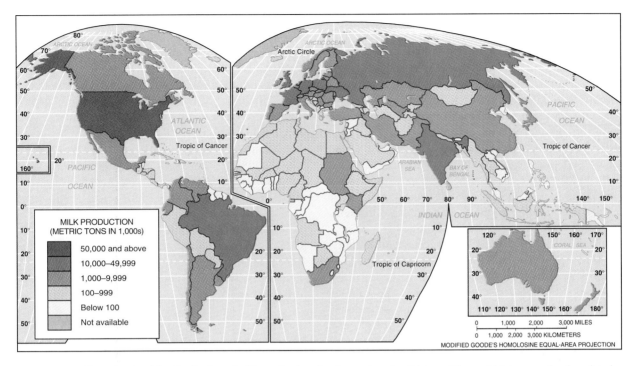

FIGURE 9-8 Milk production. The distribution of milk production closely matches the division of the world into more developed and less developed regions (see Figure 8-1). Consumers in more developed countries have the income to pay for milk products, and farmers in these countries can afford the high cost of establishing dairy farms. Two very populous countries—Brazil and India—rank among the world leaders in total milk production but not in production per capita.

ply of milk is produced and consumed in these developed regions (Figure 9-8).

Traditionally, fresh milk was rarely consumed except directly on the farm or in nearby villages. With the rapid growth of cities in relatively developed countries during the nineteenth century, demand for the sale of milk to urban residents increased. Rising incomes permitted urban residents to buy milk products, which were once considered luxuries. Average weekly consumption of milk per person in England, for example, rose from 0.8 liters (0.2 U.S. gallons) in the 1870s to 2.8 liters (0.7 U.S. gallons) by the 1950s.

Why Dairy Farms Locate Near Urban Areas

Dairying has become the most important type of commercial agriculture in the first ring outside large cities because of transportation factors. Dairy farms must be closer to their market than other products because milk is highly perishable. The ring surrounding a city from which milk can be supplied without spoiling is known as the **milkshed.**

Improvements in transportation have permitted dairying to be undertaken farther from the market.

Until the 1840s, when railroads were first used for transporting dairy products, milksheds rarely had a radius beyond 50 kilometers (30 miles). Today, refrigerated rail cars and trucks enable farmers to ship milk more than 500 kilometers (300 miles). As a result, nearly every farm in the U.S. Northeast and Western Europe is within the milkshed of at least one urban area.

Some dairy farms specialize in products other than milk. Originally, butter and cheese were made directly on the farm, primarily from the excess milk produced in the summer, before modern agricultural methods evened the flow of milk through the year. In the twentieth century, dairy farmers have generally chosen to specialize either in fresh milk production or other products such as butter and cheese.

Regional Differences

The choice of product varies within the U.S. dairy region, depending on whether the farms are within the milkshed of a large urban area. In general, the farther the farm is from large urban concentrations, the smaller is the percentage of output devoted to fresh milk. Farms located farther from consumers are more likely to sell their output to processors who make butter, cheese, or dried, evaporated, and condensed milk. The reason is that these products keep longer than milk and therefore can be safely shipped from remote farms.

In the East, virtually all milk is sold to consumers living in New York, Philadelphia, Boston, and the other large urban areas. Farther west, most milk is processed into cheese and butter. Virtually all of the milk in Wisconsin is processed, for example, compared with only 5 percent in Pennsylvania. The proximity of northeastern farmers to several large markets accounts for these regional differences.

Countries likewise tend to specialize in certain products. New Zealand, the world's largest producer of dairy products, devotes only 8 percent to liquid milk, compared with 68 percent in the United Kingdom. New Zealand farmers do not sell much liquid milk because the country is too far from North America and Western Europe, the two largest relatively wealthy population concentrations.

Dairy farmers, like other commercial farmers, usually do not sell their products directly to consumers.

Instead, they sell milk to wholesalers, who distribute it to retailers. Retailers then sell milk to consumers in shops or at home. Farmers also sell milk to butter and cheese manufacturers.

Distribution of milk to consumers differs between the United States and the United Kingdom. Home delivery of milk has become rare in the United States but is still common in the United Kingdom. Many British families have a small card that looks like a clock with one hand. Before they go to sleep, they set the hand to the number of pints of milk they want delivered the next morning and place the card outside the front door. Early the next morning the milk is delivered, in bottles rather than cartons. The cream usually rises to the top of the bottle and can be either poured off or mixed in. Empty bottles are then set outside and taken away the next morning by the milkman.

Problems for Dairy Farmers

Like other commercial farmers, dairy farmers face economic problems because of declining revenues and rising costs. Distinctive features of dairy farming have exacerbated the economic difficulties. First,

Milk and other dairy products are delivered to homes in Great Britain in small, silent, electric trucks. (Robert Harding Picture Library)

dairy farming is labor-intensive, because the cows must be milked twice a day, every day. Although the actual milking can be done by machines, dairy farming nonetheless requires constant attention throughout the year.

Dairy farmers also face the expense of feeding the cows in the winter, when they may be unable to graze on grass. In Northwest Europe and New England, farmers generally purchase hay or grain for winter feed. In the western part of the U.S. dairy region, crops are more likely to be grown in the summer and stored for winter feed on the same farm.

A recent survey by the Minnesota Department of Agriculture found that the state is losing 800 dairy farms a year, a decline of about 6 percent per year. Departing dairy farmers most often cite lack of profitability and excessive workload as reasons for leaving.

Grain Farming

Grain is the seed from various grasses, such as wheat, corn, oats, barley, rice, millet, and others. Some form of grain is the major crop on most farms. Commercial grain agriculture is distinguished from mixed crop and livestock farming because crops on a grain farm are grown primarily for consumption by humans rather than by livestock. Farms in less developed countries also grow crops for human consumption, but the output is consumed directly by the farmers. Commercial grain farms sell their output to manufacturers of food products, such as breakfast cereals and snack chip makers.

The most important crop grown is wheat, used to make bread flour. Wheat generally can be sold for a higher price than other grains, such as rye, oats, and barley, and it has more uses as human food. It can be stored relatively easily without spoiling and can be transported a long distance. Because wheat has a relatively high value per unit weight, it can be shipped profitably from remote farms to markets.

Grain-Farming Regions

Large-scale commercial grain production is found in only a few countries, including the United States, Canada, Argentina, Australia, France, and the United Kingdom. Commercial grain farms are generally located in regions that are too dry for mixed crop and livestock agriculture. China and India are major producers of grain through subsistence agriculture (Figure 9-9).

Within North America, large-scale grain production is concentrated in three areas (Figure 9-3). The first is the winter wheat belt that extends through Kansas, Colorado, and Oklahoma. In the **winter wheat** area, the crop is planted in the autumn and develops a strong root system before growth stops for the winter. The wheat survives the winter, especially if it is insulated beneath a snow blanket, and is ripe by the beginning of summer.

The second important grain-producing region in North America is the **spring wheat** belt of the Dakotas, Montana, and southern Saskatchewan in Canada. Because winters are usually too severe for winter wheat in this region, spring wheat is planted in the spring and harvested in the late summer. Approximately two-thirds of the wheat grown in the United States comes either from the winter or the spring wheat belt. A third important grain-growing region is the Palouse region of Washington State.

Large-scale grain production, like other commercial farming ventures in developed countries, is heavily mechanized, conducted on large farms, and oriented to consumer preferences. The McCormick **reaper** (a machine that cuts grain standing in the field), invented in the 1830s, first permitted large-scale wheat production. Today, the **combine** machine performs in one operation the three tasks of reaping, threshing, and cleaning.

Unlike work on a mixed crop and livestock farm, the effort required to grow wheat is not uniform throughout the year. Some individuals or firms may therefore have two sets of fields, one in the spring wheat belt and one in the winter wheat belt. Because the planting and harvesting in the two regions occur at different times of the year, the workload can be distributed throughout the year. In addition, the same machinery can be used in the two regions, thus spreading the cost of the expensive equipment. Combine companies start working in Oklahoma in early summer and work their way northward.

Importance of Wheat

Wheat's significance extends beyond the amount of land or number of people involved in growing it. Unlike other agricultural products, wheat is grown to a considerable extent for international trade and is the world's leading export crop. As the United States and Canada account for about half of the world's wheat exports, the North American prairies are accurately labeled the world's "breadbasket." The abil-

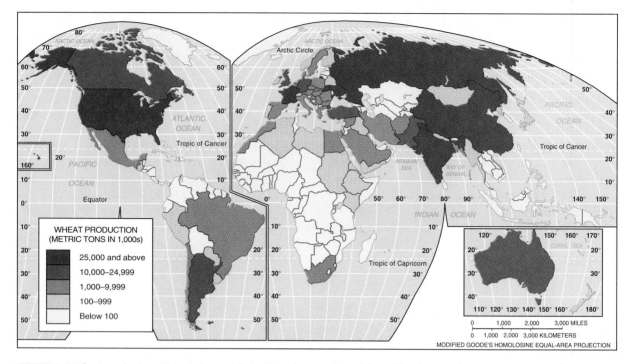

FIGURE 9-9 Wheat production. China is the world's leading wheat producer followed by the United States, Russia, and India. Wheat grown in the Asian countries is used principally to feed the local population, whereas a large percentage of the wheat grown in North America is exported to other countries.

ity to provide food for many people elsewhere in the world is a major source of economic and political strength for the United States and Canada (see Chapter 13, Figure 13-17).

Livestock Ranching

Ranching is the commercial grazing of livestock over an extensive area. This form of agriculture is adapted to semiarid or arid land. It is practiced in relatively developed countries where the vegetation is too sparse and the soil too poor to support crops.

Cattle Ranching in U.S. Popular Culture

The importance of ranching in the United States extends beyond the number of people who choose this form of commercial farming because of its prominence in popular culture, especially in Hollywood films and television. Cattle ranching in Texas, though, as glamorized in popular culture, actually dominated commercial agriculture for a short period—from 1867 to 1885.

Beginning of U.S. Cattle Ranching. Cattle were first brought to the Americas by Columbus on his second voyage, because they were sufficiently hardy to survive the ocean crossing. Living in the wild, the cattle multiplied and thrived on abundant grazing lands on the frontiers of North and South America. Immigrants from Spain and Portugal—the only European countries with a tradition of cattle ranching—began ranching in the Americas. They taught the practice to settlers from Northern Europe and the Eastern United States who moved to Texas and other frontier territories in the nineteenth century.

U.S. cattle ranching expanded because of demand for beef in the East Coast cities during the 1860s. The challenge for ranchers was to transport the cattle from Texas to eastern markets. Ranchers who could get their cattle to Chicago were paid $30 to $40 per head, compared to only $3 or $4 per head in Texas. Once in Chicago, the cattle could be slaughtered and processed by meat-packing companies and sold to consumers in the East.

Transporting Cattle to Market. To reach Chicago, cattle were driven on hoof by cowboys over trails from Texas to the nearest rail head. Distances were several hundred kilometers. There they were driven into cattle cars for the rest of their journey. In 1867, the western terminus of the rail line reached Abilene, Kansas. That year, a man named Joseph G. McCoy (on whom the expression "the real McCoy" was based) launched a massive construction effort to provide Abilene with homes, shops, and stockyards. As a result, the number of cattle brought into Abilene increased from 1,000 in 1867 to 35,000 in 1868 and 150,000 in 1869. McCoy became the first mayor of the city of Abilene.

Like other frontier towns, Abilene became a haven where cowboys let off steam. Gunfights, prostitution, gambling, and alcoholism were rampant until McCoy hired James B. "Wild Bill" Hickock as sheriff to clean up the town. After a few years, the terminus of the railroad moved farther west. Wichita, Caldwell, Dodge City, and other towns in Kansas took their turn as the main destination for cattle driven north on trails from Texas. Abilene became a ghost town for a while. Eventually, though, use of the surrounding land changed from cattle grazing to crop growing, and Abilene became a prosperous market center.

The most famous route from Texas northward to the rail line was the Chisholm Trail, which began near Brownsville at the Mexican border and extended northward through Texas, Indian Territory (now the state of Oklahoma), and Kansas. The trail had many branches, but the main line extended through Austin, Waco, Fort Worth, and Caldwell (Figure 9-10). The Western Trail became more important in the 1870s when the railroad terminus moved farther west. Today, U.S. Route 81 roughly follows the course of the Chisholm Trail.

Fixed-Location Ranching

Cattle ranching declined in importance during the 1880s, after it came in conflict with sedentary agriculture. Most early U.S. ranchers adhered to "The Code of the West," although the system had no official legal status. Under the code, ranchers had range rights—that is, their cattle could graze on any open land and had access to scarce water sources and grasslands. The early cattle ranchers in the West owned little land, only cattle.

Range Wars. The U.S. government, which owned most of the land used for open grazing, began to sell it to farmers to grow crops, leaving cattle ranch-

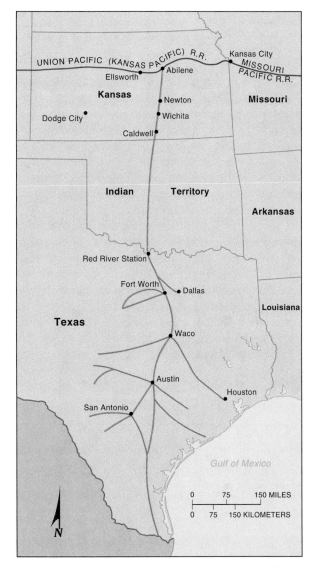

FIGURE 9-10 The Chisholm Trail. Although actively used for only a few years, the Chisholm Trail became famous in American folklore as the main route for cattle drives, from Texas ranches to Kansas rail heads.

ers with no legal claim to it. For a few years, the ranchers tried to drive out the farmers by cutting fences and then illegally erecting their own fences on public land, and "range wars" flared.

The farmers' most potent weapon proved to be barbed wire, first commercially produced in 1873. The farmers eventually won the battle, and ranchers were compelled to buy or lease land to accommodate their cattle. Large cattle ranches were established, primarily on land that was too dry to support crops. Ironically, 60 percent of cattle grazing today is on land leased from the U.S. government.

Changes in Cattle Breeding. Ranchers were also induced to switch from cattle drives to fixed-location ranching by a change in the predominant breed of cattle. Longhorns, the first cattle used by ranchers, were hardy animals, able to survive the long-distance drive along the trails with little weight loss. But longhorns were susceptible to cattle ticks, parasitic insects that carried a fever and were difficult to remove, and the meat of longhorns was of poor quality.

New cattle breeds introduced from Europe, such as the Hereford, offered superior meat but were not adapted to the old ranching system. The new breeds could not survive the winter by open grazing, as could the longhorns. Instead, crops had to be grown or feed purchased for them. The cattle could not be driven long distances, and they required more water. However, these breeds thrived once open grazing was replaced by fixed ranching, and long-distance trail drives and rail journeys to Chicago gave way to short rail or truck trips to nearby meat packers.

With the spread of irrigation techniques and hardier crops, land in the United States has been converted from ranching to crop growing. Ranching generates lower income per area of land, although it has lower operating costs. Cattle are still raised on ranches but are frequently sent for fattening to farms or to local feed lots along major railroad and highway routes rather than directly to meat processors. The average ranch is large, because the capacity of the land to support cattle is low in much of the semiarid West. Large ranches may be owned by meat-processing companies rather than individuals.

Cattle Ranching outside the United States

Commercial ranching is conducted in other relatively developed regions of the world (Figure 9-11). Ranching is rare in Europe, except in Spain and Portugal. In South America, a large portion of the pampas of Argentina, southern Brazil, and Uruguay are devoted to grazing cattle and sheep. The cattle industry grew rapidly in Argentina in part because the land devoted to ranching was relatively accessible to the ocean, and meat could be transported to overseas markets.

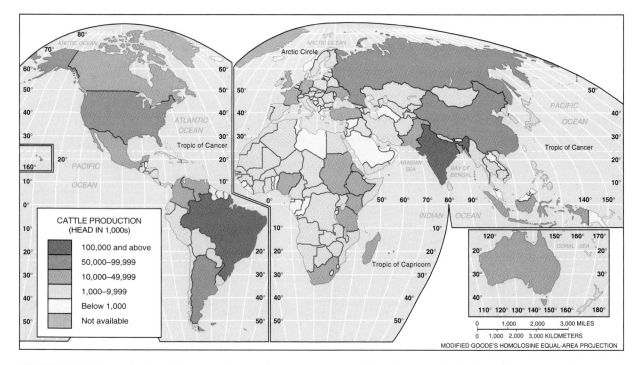

FIGURE 9-11 Cattle production. Cattle outnumber people in Argentina, Australia, and New Zealand, where commercial ranching is an important type of agriculture. Commercial ranching is not widely practiced in the developed countries of Western Europe, a region that lacks extensive dry lands.

Because the relatively humid climate on the pampas provides more browse for more cattle to graze on a given area of land than in the U.S. West, ranching grew quickly in South America. Land was divided into large holdings in the nineteenth century, in contrast to the U.S. practice of permitting common grazing on public land. Ranching has declined in Argentina, as in the United States, because growing crops is more profitable except on very dry lands.

The interior of Australia was opened for grazing in the nineteenth century, although sheep are more common than cattle. Ranches in the Middle East, New Zealand, and South Africa are also more likely to have sheep. Like the U.S. West, Australia's dry lands went through several land use changes. Until the 1860s, shepherding was practiced on the open range. Then large ranches with fixed boundaries were established, stock was improved, and water facilities were expanded. Eventually, ranching was confined to drier lands, and wheat—which yielded greater profits per hectare than ranching—was planted where precipitation levels permitted.

Thus, ranching has followed similar stages around the world. First was the herding of animals over open ranges, in a semi nomadic style. Then, ranching was transformed into fixed farming by dividing the open land into ranches. Many of the farms converted to growing crops, and ranching was confined to the drier lands. To survive, the remaining ranches experimented with new methods of breeding and sources of water and feed. Ranching became part of the meat-processing industry rather than an economic activity carried out on isolated farms. In this way, commercial ranching differs from pastoral nomadism, the form of animal herding practiced in developing regions.

Mediterranean Agriculture

Mediterranean agriculture exists primarily in the lands that border the Mediterranean Sea in southern Europe, northern Africa, and western Asia (Figure 9-3). Farmers in California, central Chile, the southwestern part of South Africa, and Southwest Australia practice Mediterranean agriculture as well.

These Mediterranean areas share a similar physical environment. Every Mediterranean area borders a sea. Mediterranean areas are on west coasts of continents (except for some lands surrounding the Mediterranean Sea). Prevailing sea winds provide

moisture and moderate the winter temperatures. Summers are hot and dry, but sea breezes provide some relief. The land is very hilly, and mountains frequently plunge directly to the sea, leaving very narrow strips of flat land along the coast.

Farmers derive a smaller percentage of income from animal products in the Mediterranean region than in the mixed crop and livestock region. Livestock production is hindered during the summer by the lack of water and good grazing land. Some farmers living along the Mediterranean Sea traditionally used transhumance to raise animals, although the practice is now less common. Under transhumance, animals—primarily sheep and goats—are kept on the coastal plains in the winter and transferred to the hills in the summer.

Mediterranean Crops

Most crops in Mediterranean lands are grown for human consumption rather than for animal feed. **Horticulture**—which is the growing of fruits, vegetables, and flowers—and tree crops form the commercial base of the Mediterranean farming. Most of the world's olives, grapes, fruits, and vegetables are grown in Mediterranean agriculture areas. A combination of local physical and cultural characteristics determines which crops are grown in each area. The hilly landscape encourages farmers to plant a variety of crops within one farming area.

In the lands bordering the Mediterranean Sea, the two most important cash crops are olives and grapes. Two-thirds of the world's wine is produced in countries that border the Mediterranean Sea, especially Italy, France, and Spain. Mediterranean agricultural regions elsewhere in the world produce most of the remaining one-third. The lands near the Mediterranean Sea are also responsible for a large percentage of the world's supply of olives, an important source of cooking oil.

Despite the importance of olives and grapes to commercial farms bordering the Mediterranean Sea, approximately half of the land is devoted to growing cereals, especially wheat for pasta and bread. As in the U.S. winter wheat belt, the seeds are sown in the fall and harvested in early summer. After cultivation, cash crops are planted on approximately 20 percent of the land, while the remainder is left fallow for a year or two to conserve moisture in the soil.

Cereals occupy a much lower percentage of the cultivated land in California than in other Mediterranean climates. Instead, 30 percent of California farmland is devoted to fruit and vegetable horticulture. California supplies much of the citrus fruits, tree nuts, and deciduous fruits consumed in the United States. Horticulture is practiced in other Mediterranean climates, but not to the extent found in California.

The rapid growth of urban areas in California, especially Los Angeles, has converted high-quality agricultural land into housing developments. Thus far, the loss of farmland has been offset by expansion of agriculture into arid lands. But farming in dry lands requires massive irrigation. In the future, agriculture may face stiffer competition to divert the Southwest's increasingly scarce water supply.

Commercial Gardening and Fruit Farming

Commercial gardening and fruit farming is the predominant type of agriculture in the U.S. Southeast. The region has a long growing season and humid climate and is accessible to the large markets of New York, Philadelphia, Washington, and the other eastern U.S. urban areas. The type of agriculture practiced in this region is frequently called **truck farming**, because *truck* was a Middle English word meaning "bartering," or "the exchange of commodities."

Truck farms grow many of the fruits and vegetables that consumers demand in relatively developed societies, such as apples, asparagus, cherries, lettuce, mushrooms, and tomatoes. Some of these fruits and vegetables are sold fresh to consumers, but most are sold to large processors for canning or freezing.

Truck farms are highly efficient, large-scale operations that take full advantage of machines at every stage of the growing process. Truck farmers are willing to experiment with new varieties, seeds, fertilizers, and other inputs to maximize efficiency. Labor costs are kept down by hiring migrant farm workers, some of whom are undocumented immigrants from Mexico who work for very low wages. Farms tend to specialize in a few crops, and a handful of farms may dominate national output of some fruits and vegetables.

A form of truck farming called *specialty farming* has spread to New England. Farmers are profitably growing crops that have limited but increasing demand among affluent consumers, such as asparagus, peppers, mushrooms, strawberries, and nursery plants. Specialty farming represents a profitable alternative for New England farmers, at a time when dairy farming is declining because of relatively high operating costs and low milk prices.

Plantation Agriculture

The plantation is a form of commercial agriculture found in the tropics and subtropics, especially in Latin America, Africa, and Asia. Although generally situated in less developed countries, plantations are often owned and operated by Europeans or North Americans and grow crops for sale primarily in relatively developed countries.

A **plantation** is a large farm that specializes in one or two crops. Among the most important crops grown on plantations are cotton, sugar cane, coffee, rubber, and tobacco. Also produced in large quantities are cocoa, jute, bananas, tea, coconuts, and palm oil. Latin American plantations are likely to grow coffee, sugar cane, and bananas, whereas Asian plantations provide rubber and palm oil.

Because plantations are usually situated in sparsely settled locations, they must import workers and provide them with food, housing, and social services. Plantation managers try to spread the work as evenly as possible throughout the year to make full use of the large labor force. Where the climate permits, more than one crop is planted and harvested during the year. Rubber tree plantations try to spread the task of tapping the trees throughout the year.

Crops such as tobacco, cotton, and sugar cane, which can be planted only once a year, are less likely to be grown on large plantations today than in the past. Crops normally are processed at the plantation before shipping, because processed goods are less bulky and therefore cheaper to ship long distances to the North American and European markets than are unprocessed goods.

Until the Civil War, plantations were important in the U.S. South, where the principal crop was cotton, followed by tobacco and sugar cane. Demand for cotton increased dramatically after the establishment of textile factories in England at the start of the industrial revolution in the late 1700s. Cotton production was stimulated by the improvement of the cotton gin by Eli Whitney in 1793 and the development of new varieties that were hardier and easier to pick. Slaves brought from Africa performed most of the labor until the abolition of slavery and the defeat of the South in the Civil War. Thereafter, plantations declined in the United States; they were subdivided and either sold to individual farmers or worked by tenant farmers.

Summary

Although most people in the world are farmers, significant differences exist among the types of farming practiced. A country's agricultural system is one of the best measures of its level of economic development and standard of material comfort. Here again are the key questions concerning agricultural geography.

1. How did agriculture originate and diffuse?

Before the development of agriculture, people survived by hunting animals, gathering wild vegetation, or fishing. Agriculture was not simply invented but was the product of thousands of years of experiments and accidents. Vegetative planting apparently originated primarily in Southeast Asia and diffused to the north and west. Significant advances in settled agriculture, including domestication of wheat and barley and integration of herd animals with crop grazing, originated in Southwest Asia. Agricultural practices probably originated independently in the Western Hemisphere.

2. What is agriculture like in less developed countries?

Most people in the world, especially those in less developed countries, are subsistence farmers, growing crops primarily to feed themselves. Several important kinds of subsistence agriculture exist, including shifting cultivation, intensive farming, and pastoral nomadism. Regions where subsistence agriculture is practiced are characterized by a large percentage of the labor force engaged in agriculture, with few mechanical aids.

3. What is agriculture like in more developed countries?

Few people in relatively developed regions are farmers, but through the use of expensive machinery and scientific techniques these few farmers produce abundant food. Farmers in more developed countries who grow crops and raise livestock for sale off the farm to processors are only one part of a large food-production industry.

4. What are the most important agriculture regions in more developed countries?

The most common type of farm found in more developed societies is mixed crop and livestock. Land is generally devoted to growing crops, but income is derived primarily from the sale of animal products, because most of the crops are used to feed animals rather than people. Where mixed crop and livestock farming is not suitable, commercial farmers practice a variety of other types of agriculture, including dairying, commercial grain, and ranching.

CASE STUDY REVISITED
Problems for Farmers

Ironically, subsistence and commercial farmers face a similar problem: neither type of farming produces sufficient income to support a desirable standard of living. However, the underlying cause of low incomes differs significantly between the two.

Problems for Subsistence Farmers

The fundamental problem in less developed countries, where most subsistence farming is practiced, is to assure an adequate supply of food for the people. Traditional subsistence farming can continue to produce enough food for people who live in rural villages to survive, assuming no drought, flood, or other natural disaster. But developing countries must provide enough food for a rapidly increasing population, as well as for the growing number of urban residents who cannot grow their own food.

Subsistence farmers lack the land and supplies needed to expand crop production: they need higher-yield seeds, fertilizer, pesticides, and tools. To some extent, farmers can secure needed supplies through the barter of food with urban dwellers. For many African and Asian countries, though, agricultural supplies must be obtained primarily by importation from other countries. Less developed countries lack the money to buy agricultural equipment and replacement parts from relatively developed countries.

To generate the funds they need to buy agricultural equipment, less developed countries must produce something they can sell to more developed countries. LDCs try to sell manufactured goods, but most raise funds through the sale of crops to MDCs. Consumers in developed countries are willing to pay high prices for fruits and vegetables that would otherwise be out of season or for crops such as coffee and tea that cannot be grown there because of the climate.

In developing countries such as Kenya, women practice most of the subsistence agriculture—that is, growing food for their families to consume—in addition to the tasks of cooking, cleaning, and carrying water from wells. Men may work for wages, either growing crops for export or in jobs in distant cities. Because men in Kenya frequently do not share the wages with their families, many women try to generate income for the household by making clothes, jewelry, baked goods, and other objects for sale in local markets.

Drug Crops. The export crops chosen in some developing countries, especially in Latin America and Asia, are those that can be converted to drugs (Figure 9-12). Various drugs, such as coca leaf, marijuana, opium, and hashish have distinctive geographic distributions.

Coca leaf is grown principally in four contiguous countries in northwestern South America. One-half of the supply comes from Peru, more than one-fourth from Bolivia, and most of the remainder from Colombia and Ecuador. Eighty percent of the processing of cocaine, as well as its distribution to the United States and other developed countries, is based in Colombia.

Mexico grows the overwhelming majority of the marijuana that reaches the United States, followed by Colombia, Jamaica, and Belize. Mexico is also responsible for some of the opium, but most originates in Asia. Southeast Asia is the center of opium produc-

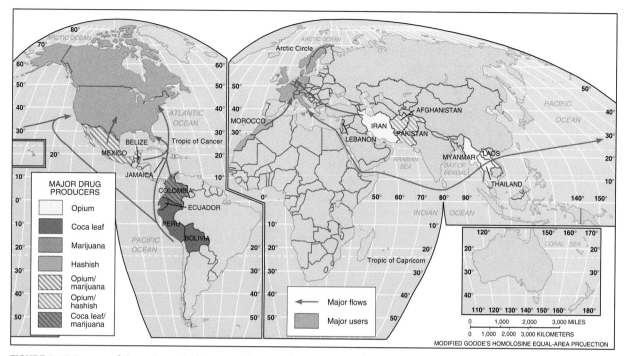

FIGURE 9-12 Sources of drugs. Instead of concentrating on subsistence agriculture, farmers in some LDCs make far more money growing crops that are converted to drugs sold in more developed countries.

tion, with more than half produced in Myanmar, followed by Laos. Thailand produces some opium, as well, but its main role is to serve as the transportation hub for distribution to more developed countries. Farther west in Asia, Afghanistan, Iran, and Pakistan are also major opium producers. Afghanistan and Pakistan are also major producers of hashish, as are Lebanon and Morocco.

The sale of export crops brings a developing country foreign currency, a portion of which can be used to buy agricultural supplies. But governments in developing countries face a dilemma: the more land that is devoted to growing export crops, the less that is available to grow crops for domestic consumption. Rather than helping to increase productivity, the funds generated through the sale of export crops may be needed to feed the people who switched from subsistence farming to growing export crops.

Problems for Commercial Farmers

Commercial farmers suffer from low incomes because they produce too much food, rather than too little. A surplus of food has been produced in part because of widespread adoption of efficient agricultural practices. New seeds, fertilizers, pesticides, mechanical equipment, and management practices have enabled farmers to obtain greatly increased yields per area of land.

Commercial farmers have dramatically increased the capacity of the land to produce food. For example, in 1960 about 20 million dairy cows produced 57 million metric tons (63 million tons) of milk in the United States. The number of dairy cows in the United States has declined to under 10 million during the 1990s, but they produce 68 million metric tons (75 million tons) of milk.

While the food supply has increased in developed countries, demand has remained constant, because the market for most products is already saturated. In MDCs, consumption of a particular commodity may not change significantly if the price changes.

Americans, for example, do not switch from wheat to corn products if the price of corn falls more rapidly than wheat. Demand is also stagnant for most agricultural products in developed countries because of low population growth.

U.S. Government Policies. Agricultural production is also increasing in the United States because of government programs. The U.S. government has three policies to attack the problem of excess productive capacity. First, farmers are encouraged to avoid producing crops that are in excess supply. Because soil erosion is a constant threat, the government encourages planting fallow crops, such as clover, to restore nutrients to the soil and to help hold the soil in place. These crops can be used for hay, forage for pigs, or producing seeds for sale.

Second, the government pays farmers when certain commodity prices are low. The government sets a target price for the commodity and pays farmers the difference between the price they receive in the market and a target price set by the government as a fair level for the commodity. The target prices are calculated to give the farmers the same price for the commodity today as in the past, when compared with other consumer goods and services.

Third, the government buys surplus production and sells or donates it to foreign governments. In addition, low-income Americans receive food stamps in part to stimulate their purchase of additional food.

The United States spends about $10 billion a year on farm subsidies, including an average of $6 billion for feed grains, such as corn and soybeans, $2 billion for wheat, and $2 billion for dairy products. Annual spending varies considerably from one year to the next: subsidy payments are lower in years when market prices rise and production is down, typically as a result of poor weather conditions in the United States or political problems in other countries.

U.S. policies point out a fundamental irony in worldwide agricultural patterns. In a relatively developed country such as the United States, farmers are encouraged to grow less food, while less developed countries struggle to increase food production to match the rate of the growth in population.

Key Terms

Agribusiness Commercial agriculture characterized by integration of different steps in the food-processing industry, usually through ownership by large corporations.

Agriculture The deliberate effort to modify a portion of Earth's surface through the cultivation of crops and the raising of livestock for sustenance or economic gain.

Cereal grain A grass yielding grain for food.

Chaff Husks of grain separated from the seed by threshing.

Combine A machine that reaps, threshes, and cleans grain while moving over a field.

Commercial agriculture Agriculture undertaken primarily to generate products for sale off the farm.

Crop Grain or fruit gathered from a field as a harvest during a particular season. Any plant cultivated by people.

Crop rotation The practice of rotating use of different fields from crop to crop each year to avoid exhausting the soil.

Double cropping Harvesting twice a year from the same field.

Grain Seed of a cereal grass.

Horticulture The growing of fruits, vegetables, and flowers.

Hull The outer covering of a seed.

Intensive subsistence agriculture A form of subsistence agriculture in which farmers must expend a relatively large amount of effort to produce the maximum feasible yield from a parcel of land.

Milkshed The area surrounding a city from which milk is supplied.

Paddy Malay word for wet rice, commonly but incorrectly used to describe a sawah.

Pastoral nomadism A form of subsistence agriculture based on herding domesticated animals.

Pasture Grass or other plants grown for feeding grazing animals, as well as land used for grazing.

Plantation A large farm in the tropical and subtropical climates of less developed countries that specializes in the production of one or two crops for sale, usually to a more developed country.

Prime agricultural land The most productive farmland.

Ranching A form of commercial agriculture in which livestock graze over an extensive area.

Reaper A machine that cuts grain standing in the field.

Sawah A flooded field for growing rice.

Seed agriculture Reproduction of plants through annual introduction of seeds, which result from sexual fertilization.

Slash-and-burn agriculture Another name for shifting cultivation, so named because fields are cleared by slashing the vegetation and burning the debris.

Shifting cultivation A form of subsistence agriculture in which people shift activity from one field to another; each field is used for crops for a relatively few years and left fallow for a relatively long period.

Spring wheat Wheat planted in the spring and harvested in the late summer.

Subsistence agriculture Agriculture designed primarily to provide food for direct consumption by the farmer and the farmer's family.

Swidden A patch of land cleared for planting through slashing and burning.

Thresh To beat out grain from stalks by trampling it.

Transhumance The seasonal migration of livestock between mountains and lowland pastures.

Truck farming Commercial gardening and fruit farming, so-named because *truck* was a Middle English word meaning "bartering" or "the exchange of commodities."

Vegetative planting Reproduction of plants by direct cloning from existing plants.

Wet rice Rice grown for much of the time in deliberately flooded fields.

Winnow To remove chaff by allowing it to be blown away by the wind.

Winter wheat Wheat planted in the fall and harvested in the early summer.

Thinking Geographically

1. Assume that the United States constitutes one agricultural market, centered around New York City, the largest metropolitan area. To what extent can the major agricultural regions of the United States be viewed as irregularly shaped rings around the market center, as von Thünen applied to southern Germany?

2. New Zealand once sold nearly all its dairy products to the British, but since the United Kingdom joined the European Union in 1973, New Zealand has been forced to find other markets. What are some other examples of countries that have restructured their agricultural production in the face of increased global interdependence and regional cooperation?

3. Review the concept of overpopulation (the number of people in an area exceeds the capacity of the environment to support life at a decent standard of living). What agricultural regions have relatively limited capacities to support intensive food production? Which of these regions face rapid population growth?

4. Compare world distributions of corn, wheat, and rice production. To what extent do differences derive from environmental conditions and to what extent from food preferences and other social customs?

5. How might the loss of farmland on the edge of rapidly growing cities alter the choice of crops that farmers make in a commercial agricultural society?

Further Readings

Babbington, Anthony, and Judith Carney. "Geography in the International Agricultural Research Centers: Theoretical and Practical Concerns." *Annals of the Association of American Geographers* 80 (March 1990): 34–48.

Bascom, Jonathan B. "Border Pastoralism in Eastern Sudan." *Geographical Review* 80 (October 1990): 416–30.

Cochran, Willard W., and Mary E. Ryan. *American Farm Policy 1948–73.* Minneapolis: University of Minnesota Press, 1976.

Cromley, Robert G. "The von Thünen Model and Environmental Uncertainty." *Annals of the Association of American Geographers* 72 (September 1982): 404–10.

Dahlberg, Kenneth A., ed. *New Directions for Agriculture and Agricultural Research: Neglected Dimensions and Emerging Alternatives.* Totowa, NJ: Rowman and Allanheld, 1986.

Dove, Michael R. *Swidden Agriculture in Indonesia: The Subsistence Strategies of the Kalimantan Kantu.* Amsterdam: Mouton, 1985.

Duckham, A. N., and G. B. Masefield. *Farming Systems of the World.* New York: Praeger, 1970.

Durand, Loyal, Jr. "The Major Milksheds of the Northeastern Quarter of the United States." *Economic Geography* 40 (January 1964): 9–33.

Ebeling, Walter. *The Fruited Plain: The Story of American Agriculture.* Berkeley: University of California Press, 1979.

Furuseth, Owen J., and John T. Pierce. *Agricultural Land in an Urban Society.* Washington, DC: Association of American Geographers, 1982.

Galaty, John G., and Douglas L. Johnson, eds. *The World of Pastoralism: Herding Systems in Comparative Perspective.* New York: Guilford Press, 1990.

Grigg, David B. *The Agricultural Systems of the World: An Evolutionary Approach.* London: Cambridge University Press, 1974.

_____. *English Agriculture: An Historical Perspective.* Oxford: Basil Blackwell, 1989.

_____. *An Introduction to Agricultural Geography.* London: Hutchinson Education, 1984.

_____. *The Transformation of Agriculture in the West.* Cambridge, MA: Blackwell, 1992.

Hart, John Fraser. "Change in the Corn Belt." *Geographical Review* 76 (January 1986): 51–73.

_____. *The Land That Feeds Us.* New York: W. W. Norton, 1991.

Heathcote, R. L. *The Arid Lands: Their Use and Abuse.* London: Longman, 1983.

Hewes, Leslie, and Christian I. Jung. "Early Fencing on the Middle Western Prairie." *Annals of the Association of American Geographers* 71 (June 1981): 177–201.

Ilbery, Brian W. *Agricultural Geography: A Social and Economic Analysis.* New York: Oxford University Press, 1985.

Lewthwaite, G. R. "Wisconsin and the Waikato: A Comparative Study of Dairy Farming in the United States and New Zealand." *Annals of the Association of American Geographers* 54 (March 1974): 59–87.

Pannell, Clifton. "Recent Chinese Agriculture." *Geographical Review* 75 (April 1985): 170–85.

Peters, William J., and Leon F. Neuenschwander. *Slash and Burn: Farming in the Third World Forest.* Moscow: University of Idaho Press, 1988.

Potter, Clive, Paul Burnham, Angela Edwards, Ruth Gasson, and Bryn Green. *The Diversion of Land: Conservation in a Period of Farming Contraction.* New York: Routledge, 1991.

Sauer, Carl O. *Agricultural Origins and Dispersals.* 2d ed. Cambridge, MA: MIT Press, 1969.

Sluyter, Andrew. "Intensive Wetland Agriculture in Meso-America: Space, Time, and Form." *Annals of the Association of American Geogrphers* 84 (December 1994): 557–84.

Smith, Everett G., Jr. "America's Richest Farms and Ranches." *Annals of the Association of American Geographers* 70 (December 1980): 528–41.

Symons, Leslie. *Agricultural Geography,* Rev. ed. London: G. Bell, 1979.

Tarrant, John R. *Agricultural Geography.* New York: Wiley, 1974.

Turner, B. L., II, and Stephen B. Brush, eds. *Comparative Farming Systems.* New York: Guilford, 1987.

von Thünen, Johann Heinrich. *Von Thünen's Isolated State: An English Edition of "Der Isolierte Staat."* Trans. Carla M. Wartenberg. Elmsford, NY: Pergamon Press, 1966.

Whittlesey, Derwent. "Major Agricultural Regions of the Earth." *Annals of the Association of American Geographers* 26 (September 1936): 199–240.

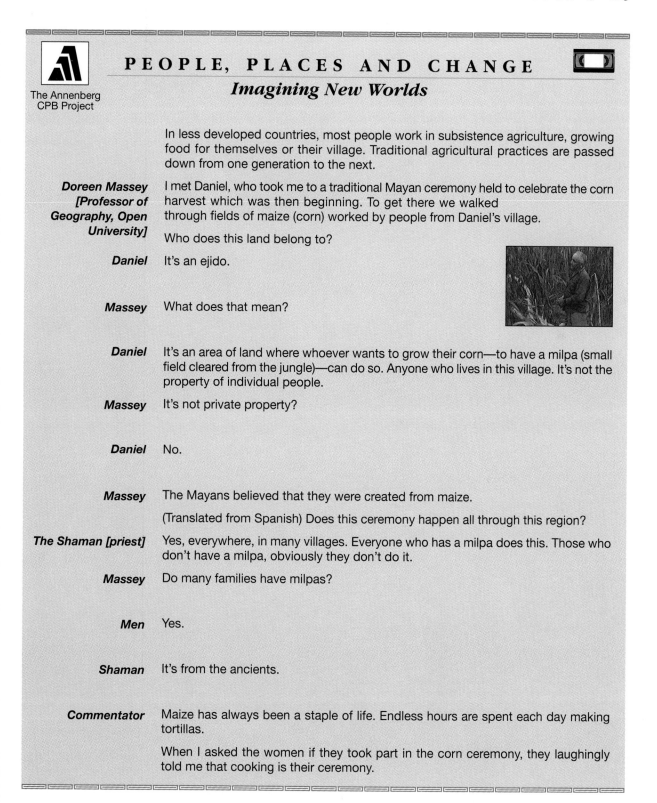

PEOPLE, PLACES AND CHANGE

Imagining New Worlds

The Annenberg
CPB Project

In less developed countries, most people work in subsistence agriculture, growing food for themselves or their village. Traditional agricultural practices are passed down from one generation to the next.

Doreen Massey [Professor of Geography, Open University]

I met Daniel, who took me to a traditional Mayan ceremony held to celebrate the corn harvest which was then beginning. To get there we walked through fields of maize (corn) worked by people from Daniel's village.

Who does this land belong to?

Daniel It's an ejido.

Massey What does that mean?

Daniel It's an area of land where whoever wants to grow their corn—to have a milpa (small field cleared from the jungle)—can do so. Anyone who lives in this village. It's not the property of individual people.

Massey It's not private property?

Daniel No.

Massey The Mayans believed that they were created from maize.

(Translated from Spanish) Does this ceremony happen all through this region?

The Shaman [priest] Yes, everywhere, in many villages. Everyone who has a milpa does this. Those who don't have a milpa, obviously they don't do it.

Massey Do many families have milpas?

Men Yes.

Shaman It's from the ancients.

Commentator Maize has always been a staple of life. Endless hours are spent each day making tortillas.

When I asked the women if they took part in the corn ceremony, they laughingly told me that cooking is their ceremony.

10

INDUSTRY

Japanese products, including televisions, cars, and cameras, have deluged the United States and Canada. Although manufactured thousands of kilometers away, these products often are less expensive than those of domestic competitors and, according to many people, are of better quality. This accomplishment of Japanese industry is even more remarkable when you recall that, only 50 years ago, Japan was a defeated and battered enemy from World War II.

The recent success of Japan, South Korea, Taiwan, and other Asian countries is a dramatic change from the historic dominance of world industry by Western countries. The industrial revolution originated in Great Britain in the 1700s and diffused to Europe and North America in the 1800s. The high standard of living enjoyed by most Western Europeans and North Americans is based on industrial power. Although the success of Asian countries is admirable, their profit may be North America's loss. For every new Toyota sold in the United States and Canada, one less U.S.- or Canadian-built Chevrolet may be manufactured.

But if we truly believe in international cooperation, then people should be encouraged to buy products regardless of national origin. The fact that Japanese or Koreans can build better cars at lower prices presents a challenge to North American companies.

KEY ISSUES

1. How did industrialization originate and diffuse?
2. How is industry distributed worldwide?
3. What factors influence the choice of location for a factory?
4. What industrial problems do countries face?

CHECKING QUALITY OF POTATO CHIPS. (DAVID JOEL/TONY STONE IMAGES)

Maquiladoras in Mexico

Edi Bencomo is a factory worker in Ciudad Juárez, Mexico. Her job is to clip together several color-coded wires for Alambrados y Circuitos Eléctricos, a factory that is owned by the Packard Electric Division of General Motors.

Bencomo migrated to Ciudad Juárez 4 years ago, at age 16, from Madera, a village in the Sierra Madre Occidental, a mountain range 300 kilometers (200 miles) southwest of Ciudad Juárez. One of seven children, Bencomo saw no future for herself on her parents' corn farm. Had she remained in Madera, Bencomo probably would have been unemployed, along with 25 percent of the villagers.

In Ciudad Juárez, Bencomo lives with her husband in a two-room shack more than an hour from the plant. They can afford to rent a somewhat better dwelling, but none are available in this rapidly growing city. She leaves home each weekday at 4 A.M. to battle hordes of workers who crowd onto buses that serve the factory area.

Bencomo earns Mexico's minimum wage, approximately 50¢ an hour. She also receives two important benefits by working for Alambrados: a bus pass so that she can reach the plant at no cost, and two meals in the cafeteria almost entirely paid for by the company. She considers her job to be superior to that of her husband, who makes piñatas; both are paid minimum wage, but he receives no benefits.

Packard's Ciudad Juárez plant is known as a **maquiladora**, from the Spanish verb *maquilar,* which means "to receive payment for grinding or processing corn." The term originally applied to a tax when Mexico was a Spanish colony. Under U.S. and Mexican laws, companies receive tax breaks if they ship materials from the United States, assemble components at a *maquiladora* plant in Mexico, and export the finished product back to the United States. More than 1,000 U.S. companies have *maquiladoras* in Mexico. General Motors alone has two dozen *maquiladoras* employing more than 25,000 people and is one of Mexico's largest employers.

In January 1985, General Motors revealed that it was designing an entirely new car called Saturn, and it would need a factory somewhere in the United States to build it. The announcement touched off a fierce competition among states and localities to become the home for the Saturn plant. All 1,700 school-children in New Hampton, Iowa, wrote letters to GM executives urging that their town be selected. Thousands of Cleveland residents sent GM "We Want Saturn" coupons clipped from their local newspapers. Seven governors appeared on Phil Donahue's popular daytime television show to explain why their state should be chosen.

Swamped with material from competing communities, GM took 7 months to select a factory site. The choice was Spring Hill, Tennessee, then a village of 1,000 inhabitants, 50 kilometers (30 miles) south of Nashville.

GM's process of selecting a location for its Saturn factory raises several issues that geographers address:

1. *What factors did GM consider in evaluating locations?* Geographers recognize two critical elements in locating factories: where the markets are (where the automobiles will be sold) and where the resources are that are needed to make the product.

2. *Why did communities nationwide compete for the Saturn factory?* Competition to attract new industries or, in many places, to retain existing ones is now global. Government officials worldwide recognize the powerful role of industry in the economic health of a community. Geographers identify a community's distinctive locational characteristics. They determine its assets that enable it to compete successfully for industries and its handicaps that must be overcome.

3. *Why did GM feel compelled to build a new plant at all?* As GM was building the new factory in Tennessee, the corporation closed more than a dozen others elsewhere in the country. Why didn't the corporation modernize one of its closed factories, or perhaps construct a new factory on land cleared by demolishing an older one? The answer is geographic: to succeed in an intensely competitive global market for products such as automobiles, corporations must find optimal factory locations.

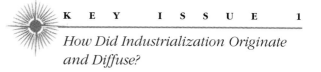

K E Y   I S S U E   1

How Did Industrialization Originate and Diffuse?

- The Industrial Revolution
- Diffusion of the Industrial Revolution

The modern concept of industry—meaning the manufacturing of goods in a factory—began in Great Britain in the late 1700s. This process of change is called the *industrial revolution,* discussed in Chapter 2 as a cause of population growth between 1750 and 1950. The industrial revolution transformed how goods are produced for society and the way people obtain food, clothing, and shelter. Today, the industrial revolution has penetrated virtually all economic, social, and political elements of society.

The Industrial Revolution

The root of the industrial revolution is technology, involving several inventions that transformed the way in which goods were manufactured. The revolution in industrial technology created an unprecedented expansion in productivity, resulting in substantially higher standards of living. The industrial revolution originated in the north of Great Britain around 1750. From there, it diffused to Europe and North America in the 1800s and to the rest of the world in the 1900s.

The industrial revolution actually was far more than industrial, and it didn't happen overnight. It also resulted in new social, economic, and political inventions and involved a gradual diffusion of new ideas and techniques over decades. Nonetheless, the term *industrial revolution* is commonly used to define the events of the late 1700s to early 1800s in Western Europe and North America.

Before the industrial revolution, industry was dispersed across the landscape. People made household tools and agricultural equipment in their own homes or obtained them in the local village. Home-based manufacturing was known as the **cottage industry** system. One important cottage industry was textile manufacturing. People known as putters-out were hired by merchants to drop off wool at homes, where women and children sorted, cleaned, and spun it. The putters-out then picked up the finished work and paid according to the number of pieces that were completed (a payment system known as piece-rate).

The industrial revolution was the collective invention of hundreds of mechanical devices. But the one invention most important to the development of factories was the *steam engine*, patented in 1769 by James Watt, a maker of mathematical instruments in Glasgow, Scotland.

When water is boiled into steam, its volume increases about 1,600 times, producing a force that can be used to move a piston back and forth inside a cylinder. If the piston is attached to a crankshaft, its back-and-forth motion can be converted into rotary motion suitable for driving machinery.

Inventors as far back as the ancient Greek scientist Hero of Alexandria had built engines operated by steam, but steam engines built by Watt's predecessors were not practical, because virtually all of the energy they generated was used in their own operation. Watt built the first useful steam engine that could pump water far more efficiently than the water wheels then in common use, let alone human or animal power. Watt's steam engine provided a separate chamber for condensing the steam and used the steam pressure to move the piston in both directions.

Diffusion of the Industrial Revolution

The iron industry was first to increase production through extensive use of Watt's steam engine and other inventions. The textile industry followed. From these two pioneering industries, new industrial techniques diffused during the nineteenth century.

Diffusion from the Iron Industry

The first step in the production of iron is mining *iron ore* from the ground. The ore is not in a useful form for making tools, so it has to be *smelted* (melted) in a *blast furnace* (blasted with air to make its fires burn hotly). The molten iron metal is poured into crude molds, where it hardens into *pigs,* fancifully named for their shape. This *pig iron* then can be transported and remelted to form useful tools and objects of *cast iron, wrought iron,* or *steel.*

The usefulness of iron and steel had been known for centuries, but the scale of production was small. The process demanded constant heating and cooling of the iron, a time-consuming and skilled operation

because energy could not be generated to keep the ovens hot for a sufficiently long period of time. The Watt steam engine provided a practical way to keep the ovens constantly heated.

Henry Cort, a navy agent, established an iron *forge* near Fareham, England, where iron was shaped into useful objects. He patented two processes, known as puddling and rolling, in 1783. *Puddling* involved reheating pig iron until it was pasty and then stirring it with iron rods until carbon and other impurities burned off. The *rolling* process involved passing pig iron between iron rollers to remove remaining *dross* (a scum of impurities that forms on the surface of melted metal). The combination of Watt's engine and Cort's iron purification process increased iron-manufacturing capability.

The needs of the iron industry in turn generated innovations in coal mining, engineering, transportation, and other industries. These inventions, in turn, permitted the modernization of other industrial activities.

Coal. Iron and steel manufacturing required energy to operate the blast furnaces and the steam engines. Wood, the main energy source before the industrial revolution, became increasingly scarce because it was needed for construction of ships, buildings, and furniture, as well as for heat. An obvious solution was to use high-energy coal, which was plentiful. Then Abraham Darby of Coalbrookdale in Shropshire, England, produced high-quality iron smelted not with ordinary coal, but with purified carbon made from coal, known as *coke*. This invention provided an abundant source of energy for the iron industry.

Because of the need for large quantities of bulky, heavy coal, the iron industry's geographic pattern changed from dispersed to clustered. Blast furnaces, forges, and mills, which had been scattered in separate small plants, were combined into large, integrated factories. These factories clustered at four locations: Staffordshire, South Yorkshire, Clydeside, and South Wales. Each site was near a productive coal field (Figure 10-1).

Engineering. In 1795, Watt decided to go into business for himself rather than serve as a consultant to industrialists. He and Matthew Boulton established the Soho Foundry at Birmingham, England, and produced hundreds of new machines to improve industrial processes still further. From this operation came our modern engineering and manufacture of

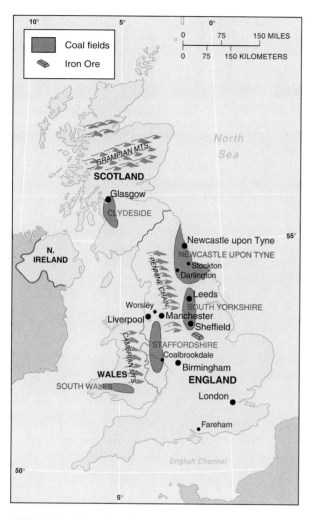

FIGURE 10-1 The industrial revolution originated in northern England and southern Scotland in the late 1700s. Factories clustered near productive coal fields.

machine parts. Their technical expertise was required to invent new machines, apply existing ones to new situations, and repair worn and broken equipment.

Transportation. The new engineering profession made its biggest impact on transportation, especially canals and railways. Transportation inventions played a critical role in diffusing the industrial revolution. New transportation systems enabled factories to attract large numbers of workers, bring in bulky raw materials such as iron ore and coal, and ship finished goods to consumers.

In 1759, Francis Egerton, the second Duke of Bridgewater, decided to build a canal between Wors-

ley and Manchester (center of map in Figure 10-1). He hired James Brindley to direct the project, which took 2 years to complete. This feat launched a generation of British canal construction that enabled industrial goods and workers to be moved long distances quickly and inexpensively. An extension of the duke's canal in 1767 permitted ships to travel between the sea and Manchester, which is 80 kilometers (50 miles) inland.

The canals soon were superseded by the invention of another transportation system, the railway, or "iron horse." More than any other invention, the railway symbolized the impact of the new engineering profession on the industrial revolution. The railway was not invented by one individual but through teamwork. Two separate but coordinated engineering improvements were required: the locomotive and iron rails for it to run on.

A locomotive using Watt's steam engine was invented by William Symington and William Murdoch in 1784. However, it was impractical to operate on bumpy, congested city streets made of dirt, brick, or stone. A few years earlier, Richard Reynolds had constructed an iron track for horse-drawn wagons to cross an uneven surface from the Coalbrookdale coal mines to the Severn River.

Many thought that running a steam locomotive on iron rails was impossible because the wheels would slip off the rails. But William Hedley demonstrated in 1812 that the steam locomotive could run on rails if the wheels had rims. The first public railway was opened between Stockton and Darlington in the north of England in 1825, using a locomotive, named *The Rocket*, designed by George Stephenson. It firmly established the benefits of steam locomotives when, in 1829, it won a race against a horse on the Liverpool and Manchester Railway, averaging 38 kilometers (24 miles) per hour.

Diffusion from the Textile Industry

As the engineering industries were developing, a revolution also was under way in the manufacturing of **textiles**, which are woven fabric. A series of inventions between 1760 and 1800 transformed textile production from a dispersed cottage industry to a concentrated factory system.

Richard Arkwright, a barber and wigmaker from the city of Preston, improved the process of *spinning* yarn. Spinning turns the short threads from cotton plants into the continuous yarn needed to weave cloth. First, he produced a *spinning frame* in 1768. It used rollers to untangle the twisted cotton fibers before it was spun around a spindle. Arkwright then patented a process for *carding* (untwisting the fibers before spinning). Because these two operations required more power than human beings could provide, the textile industry joined the iron industry early in adopting Watt's steam engine as a power source.

Like the iron industry, the textile industry was transformed from a large collection of dispersed home-based enterprises, each performing a separate task, to a small number of large, integrated firms clustered in a few locations. The large supply of steam power available from Watt's engines induced firms to concentrate all steps in one building attached to the same power source.

The changes in the textile industry just discussed are related to early stages in the process: spinning rough cotton fibers into usable thread, followed by *weaving*, or lacing together strands of yarn to form cloth. But cotton cloth also had to be bleached and dyed before it was cut into patterns to make into clothing. From the clothing industry's need for new bleaching techniques emerged another industry that is characteristic of the industrial revolution: chemicals.

Chemicals. The traditional method of *bleaching* cotton involved either exposing the fabric to the sun or boiling it. In the boiling technique, the cloth first was treated in a solution of ashes and then in sour milk. In 1746, John Roebuck and Samuel Garbett established a factory in which sulfuric acid, obtained from burning coal, was used instead of sour milk. Bleaching was further modernized in Glasgow by Charles Tennant, who in 1798 produced a bleaching powder made from chlorine gas and lime, a safer product than sulfuric acid.

Meanwhile, sulfuric acid was also used to dye clothing. When combined with various metals, sulfuric acid produced another acid, called vitriol, the color of which varied with the metal. Sulfuric acid produced a blue vitriol when combined with copper, green with iron, and white with zinc.

The chemical industry has greatly expanded and continues its role in textile manufacturing. Natural-fiber cloths, such as cotton and wool, are now combined with chemically produced *synthetic* fibers. They are made from petroleum or coal derivatives and include nylon, Dacron, and Orlon. Today, the largest textile factories are owned by chemical companies.

Food Processing. Another industry derived from the chemical industry: food processing. An increasing number of urban factory workers, who could not grow their own food or obtain fresh produce, required preserved food. Although some preserving techniques, such as drying, fermenting, and pickling, had been known since ancient times, they had limited application to the needs of nineteenth-century urban residents.

In 1810, a French confectioner, Nicholas Appert, developed *canning,* a method of preserving food in glass bottles that had been sterilized in boiling water. The process was made more practical by Peter Durand's 1839 invention of the tinned can, which was lighter, cheaper, and easier to handle than a glass bottle. The tinned can was 98.5 percent steel, with a thin coating of tin.

Canning works by killing the bacteria that cause food to spoil. It requires high temperature over time. The major obstacle to large-scale canning was the time that cans had to be kept in boiling water, some 4 to 5 hours, depending on the product. This is where chemical experiments contributed. In 1861, calcium chloride was added to the water, raising its boiling temperature from 100°C to 116°C (212°F to 240°F). This step reduced the time for proper sterilization to only 25 to 40 minutes. Consequently, production of canned foods increased tenfold that year.

Diffusion from Great Britain

Great Britain's Crystal Palace became the most visible symbol of the industrial revolution. A glass and iron building resembling a very large greenhouse, the Crystal Palace was built to house the 1851 World's Fair, more formally known as the "Great Exhibition of the Works of Industry of All Nations." The fair featured hundreds of exhibits of modern machinery, virtually all invented within the preceding 100 years.

When Queen Victoria opened the Crystal Palace, Great Britain was the world's dominant industrial power. The country produced more than half of the world's cotton fabric and iron, and mined two-thirds of its coal. As the first state to be transformed by the industrial revolution, Britain's production systems far outpaced the rest of the world.

From Britain, the industrial revolution diffused eastward through Europe and westward across the Atlantic Ocean to North America. From these places, industrial development continued diffusing to other parts of the world.

The Crystal Palace, designed by Sir Joseph Paxton, was erected in London's Hyde Park to house the Great Exhibition of 1851. The glass and iron building was longer than six football fields and enclosed two giant elm trees. After the fair closed, the structure was rebuilt in a South London park. It burned in 1936. (AP/Wide World Photos)

Diffusion to Europe. Europeans developed many early inventions of the industrial revolution in the late 1700s. The Belgians led the way in new coal-mining techniques, the French had the first coal-fired blast furnace for making iron, and the Germans made the first industrial cotton mill. But the industrial revolution did not make a significant impact elsewhere in Europe until the late 1800s.

Political instability delayed the diffusion of the industrial revolution in Europe. The French Revolution (1789–1799) and Napoleonic Wars (1796–1815) disrupted Europe, and Germany did not become a unified country until the 1870s. Other revolutions and wars plagued Europe throughout the 1800s.

Europe's political problems retarded development of modern transportation systems, especially the railway. Cooperation among small neighboring states was essential to build an efficient rail network and to raise money for constructing and operating the system. Because such cooperation could not be attained,

railways in some parts of Europe were delayed 50 years after their debut in Britain (Figure 10-2).

The industrial revolution reached Italy, the Netherlands, Russia, and Sweden in the late 1800s. But their industrial development did not match the levels in Belgium, France, and Germany until the twentieth century. Other southern and eastern European countries joined the industrial revolution during the twentieth century.

Diffusion to the United States. Industry arrived a bit later in the United States than in Western European countries such as France and Belgium, but it grew much faster. At the time of independence in 1776, the United States was a predominantly agricultural society, dependent on the import of manufactured goods from Great Britain. Manufacturing was more expensive in the United States than in Great Britain because labor and capital were scarce and shipping to European markets was expensive.

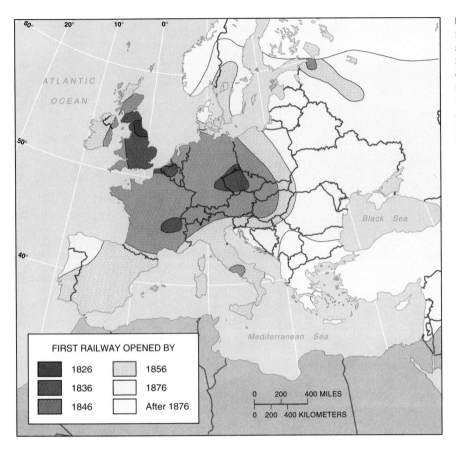

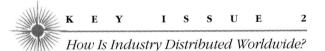

The first U.S. textile mill was built in Pawtucket, Rhode Island, in 1791, by Samuel Slater, a former worker at Arkwright's factory in England. The textile industry grew rapidly after 1808, when the U.S. government imposed an embargo on European trade to avoid entanglement in the Napoleonic Wars. The textile industry grew rapidly from 8,000 spindles per year in 1808 to 31,000 in 1809 and 80,000 in 1811.

By 1860, the United States had become a major industrial nation, second only to Great Britain. Except for textiles, however, leading U.S. industries did not widely use the new industrial processes. Instead, many engaged in processing North America's abundant food and lumber resources. Industries such as iron and steel did not apply new manufacturing techniques on a large scale in the United States until the final third of the nineteenth century.

In the twentieth century, industry has diffused to other parts of the world, including Japan, eastern Europe, and many former British colonies, such as Canada, Australia, New Zealand, South Africa, and India. Although industrial development has diffused across Earth's surface, much of the world's industry is concentrated in four regions. We will examine this concentration next.

KEY ISSUE 2

How Is Industry Distributed Worldwide?

- Eastern North America
- Western Europe
- Eastern Europe and Russia
- Japan

Approximately three-fourths of the world's industrial production is concentrated in four regions: eastern North America, Western Europe, eastern Europe and Russia, and Japan (Figure 10-3). Industrial distribution differs from agricultural distribution. Agriculture occupies one-fourth of Earth's land area and covers extensive areas throughout the inhabited world. In contrast, less than 1 percent of Earth's land

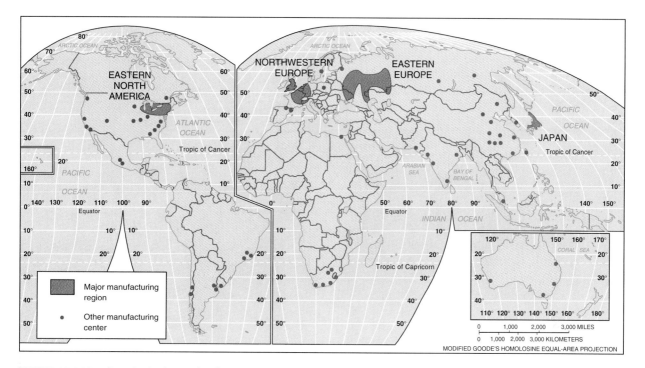

FIGURE 10-3 Manufacturing is clustered in four main regions:
Eastern North America: Primarily northeastern United States–southeastern Canada along the U.S. East Coast from Boston to Baltimore and along the Great Lakes from Toronto and Buffalo west to Chicago and Milwaukee.
Western Europe: Primarily near the Rhine and Ruhr rivers in Germany, France, Belgium, the Netherlands, and Luxembourg; also including southern Great Britain and northern Italy.
Eastern Europe: Primarily in western Russia and eastern Ukraine, although more recent industrial activities have been in Asian Russia, east of the Urals.
Japan: Primarily in the southern part; industrial growth has also occurred elsewhere in East Asia, especially South Korea, Taiwan, and China.

is devoted to industry. This section describes each of the four industrial regions, as well as important industrial subareas within each region.

Eastern North America

Manufacturing in North America is concentrated in the northeastern quadrant of the United States and in southeastern Canada. The region comprises only 5 percent of the land area of these countries but contains one-third of the population and nearly two-thirds of the manufacturing output.

This manufacturing belt has achieved its dominance through a combination of historical and environmental factors. As the first area of European settlement in the Western Hemisphere, the U.S. East Coast was tied to European markets and industries during the first half of the nineteenth century. The early date of settlement gave eastern cities an advantage in creating the infrastructure needed to become the country's dominant industrial center.

The northeast also had essential raw materials, including iron and coal. Good transportation moved raw materials to factories and manufactured goods to markets. The Great Lakes and major rivers (Mississippi, Ohio, St. Lawrence) were supplemented in the 1800s by canals, railways, and highways. All helped to connect the westward-migrating frontier with manufacturing centers.

Industrialized Areas within North America

Within the North American manufacturing belt, several heavily industrialized areas have developed (Figure 10-4).

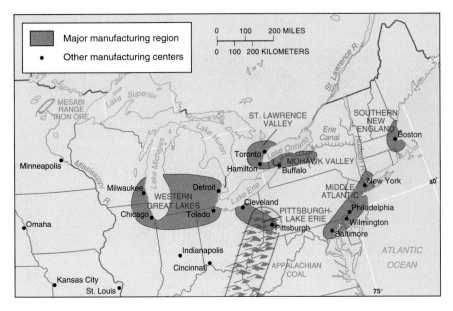

FIGURE 10-4 Major industrial regions of North America. Manufacturing in North America is highly clustered in several regions within the northeastern United States and southeastern Canada, although important manufacturing centers exist elsewhere in the two countries.

New England. The oldest industrial area in the northeastern United States is southern New England. It developed as an industrial center in the early 1800s, beginning with cotton textiles. Cotton was grown and imported from southern states, and finished cotton products were shipped to Europe. European immigrants provided abundant, inexpensive labor throughout the 1800s. Today, New England is known for relatively skilled but expensive labor.

Middle Atlantic. The Middle Atlantic area, between New York City and Washington, is the largest U.S. market. It has long attracted industries that need proximity to a large number of consumers. Many industries that depend on foreign markets or imported raw materials have located near one of this region's main ports: New York City (the nation's largest port), Baltimore, Philadelphia, and Wilmington, Delaware. Other firms seek locations near the financial, communications, and entertainment industries, which are highly concentrated in New York.

Mohawk Valley. A linear industrial belt developed in upper New York State along the Hudson River and Erie Canal, which connects New York City and the Great Lakes. Buffalo, near the confluence of the Erie Canal and Lake Erie, is the region's most important industrial center, especially for steel and food

processing. Inexpensive, abundant electricity, generated at nearby Niagara Falls, has attracted aluminum, paper, and electrochemical industries to the region.

Pittsburgh–Lake Erie. The area between Pittsburgh and Cleveland is the nation's most important steel-producing area. Steel manufacturing originally concentrated in the region because of its proximity to Appalachian coal and iron ore. When northern Minnesota became the main source of iron ore, the Pittsburgh–Lake Erie region could bring in ore via the Great Lakes.

Western Great Lakes. The western Great Lakes area extends from Detroit and Toledo, Ohio, on the east to Chicago and Milwaukee, Wisconsin, on the west. Chicago, the third-largest U.S. urban area, is the dominant market center between the Atlantic and Pacific coasts and the hub of the nation's transportation network. Because road, rail, air, and sea routes converge in Chicago, the city has become a transfer point among transportation systems (water, rail, truck, air) or between routes within the same type of transportation system.

Automobile manufacturers and other industries that have a national market locate in the western Great Lakes region to take advantage of this convergence of transportation routes. The region's industries are also the main suppliers of machine tools, transportation equipment, clothing, furniture, agricultural machinery, and food products to people living in the interior of the country.

St. Lawrence Valley–Ontario Peninsula. Canada's most important industrial area is the St. Lawrence Valley–Ontario Peninsula area, which stretches across southern Canada along the U.S. border. The region has several assets: centrality to the Canadian market, proximity to the Great Lakes, and access to inexpensive hydroelectric power from Niagara Falls. Most of Canada's steel production is concentrated in Hamilton, Ontario, while most automobiles are assembled in the Toronto area. Inexpensive electricity has attracted aluminum manufacturing, paper making, flour milling, textile manufacturing, and sugar refining.

Changing Distribution of U.S. Manufacturing

Industry has grown in areas outside the main U.S. manufacturing belt (Figure 10-5). Steel, textiles, tobacco products, and furniture industries have become dispersed throughout smaller communities in the South. The Gulf Coast is becoming an important industrial area because of access to oil and natural gas. Along the Gulf Coast are oil refining, petrochemical manufacturing, food processing, and aerospace product manufacturing.

The Southeast attracts manufacturers that seek a location where few workers have joined labor unions. Southeastern states are known as **right-to-work states**, because they have passed laws preventing a union and company from negotiating a contract that requires workers to join a union as a condition of employment.

Los Angeles is the largest industrial area on the West Coast for aircraft, electronics, oil refining, and sportswear. Other important West Coast industrial concentrations include the aerospace industry in Seattle, food processing in the San Francisco Bay area, and industries supporting the navy in San Diego.

Western Europe

Like the North American manufacturing belt, the Western European industrial region appears as one region on a world map (see Figure 10-3). But in reality, four distinct districts have emerged, primarily because European countries competed with each other to develop their own industrial areas: the Rhine-Ruhr Valley, the mid-Rhine, Great Britain, and northern Italy (Figure 10-6). Each of these areas is divided into subareas. These four became important for industry because of their proximity to raw materials (coal and iron ore) and markets (large concentrations of wealthy European consumers).

The Rhine-Ruhr Valley

Western Europe's most important industrial area is the Rhine-Ruhr Valley. The region lies mostly in northwestern Germany, but extends into nearby Belgium, France, and the Netherlands. Because of each country's political uniqueness, each country established its own industrial complex.

At the heart of the region lie two rivers: the Rhine, which flows northward through Germany and westward through the Netherlands, and the Ruhr, which flows westward across Germany into the Rhine. Within the region, industry is dispersed rather than concentrated in one or two cities. Although more than 20 million people live in the region, no individual city has more than 1 million inhabitants. Larger cities in the German portion include Dortmund, Düsseldorf, and Essen. The city of Duisburg is located near where the Ruhr flows into the Rhine.

The Rhine divides into multiple branches as it passes through the Netherlands. The city of Rotterdam is near to where several major branches flow into the North Sea. This location at the mouth of Europe's most important river has made Rotterdam the world's largest port.

Iron and steel manufacturing has concentrated in the Rhine-Ruhr Valley because of proximity to large coalfields. Access to iron and steel production stimulated the location of other heavy-metal industries, such as locomotives, machinery, and armaments.

The Mid-Rhine

The second most important industrial area in Western Europe includes southwestern Germany, northeastern France, and the small country of Luxembourg. In contrast to the Rhine-Ruhr Valley, the German portion of the mid-Rhine region lacks abundant raw materials, but it is at the center of Europe's most important consumer market. The mid-Rhine region became a major industrial center when Germany was split into two countries after World War II

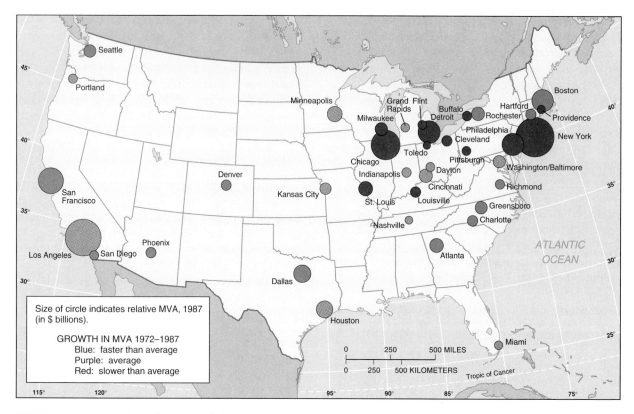

FIGURE 10-5 Amount of manufacturing and change in largest metropolitan areas, 1972–1987. Manufacturing is measured by the value added during the process. Manufacturing value added (MVA) is the gross value of manufactured products minus the cost of raw materials and energy. Manufacturing is still clustered in the northeast, but metropolitan areas in the south and west have had more rapid industrial growth.

because it was close to the population center of West Germany (Federal Republic of Germany). Although the mid-Rhine region is once again on the periphery of a reunified Germany, it remains the most central industrial area within the European union.

The three largest cities in the German portion are Frankfurt, Stuttgart, and Mannheim. Frankfurt became West Germany's most important financial and commercial center and the hub of its road, rail, and air networks. Consequently, Frankfurt attracted industries that produce goods for consumers countrywide, and the city is well situated to play a comparable role in the European union. Stuttgart's industries specialize in high-value goods and require skilled labor; Mercedes-Benz and Audi automobiles are among the city's best-known products. Mannheim, an inland port along the Rhine, has a large chemical industry that manufactures synthetic fibers, dyes, and pharmaceuticals.

The French portion of the mid-Rhine region—Alsace and Lorraine—contains Europe's largest iron ore field and is the production center for two-thirds

of France's steel. Tiny Luxembourg is also one of the world's leading steel producers, because the Lorraine iron ore field extends into the southern part of the country.

Great Britain

The industrial revolution originated in the Midlands and North of England and southern Scotland, as described earlier. Through the nineteenth century, this region dominated world production of iron and steel, textiles, and coal mining. Today, British industries are more likely to locate in southern England, near the country's largest concentrations of population and wealth.

In the twentieth century, the region lost its preeminent global position. International competition has hurt the British industrial region even more, because the world has an oversupply of steel and textiles, the industries traditionally associated with this area.

British industries have faced an especially difficult challenge in regaining global competitiveness. As the first country to enter the industrial revolution,

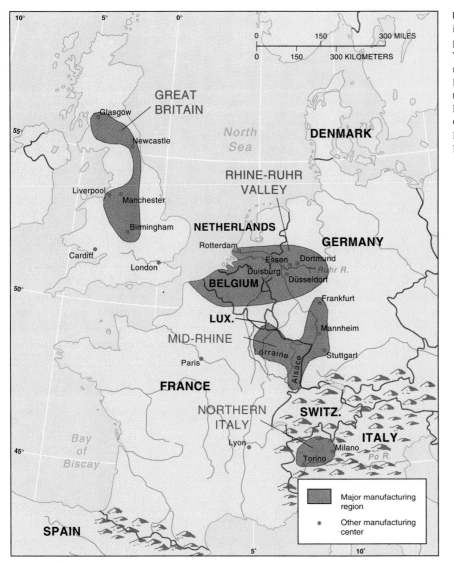

FIGURE 10-6 Manufacturing centers in Western Europe. A large percentage of manufacturing in Western Europe extends in a north-south belt, from the United Kingdom on the north to Italy on the south. At the core of the European manufacturing region lie Germany, France, and the so-called Benelux countries (Belgium, Netherlands, and Luxembourg).

Britain is saddled with what have become outmoded and deteriorating factories and support services. The British sometimes refer ironically to their "misfortune" of winning World War II. The losers, Germany and Japan, have become industrial powers in part because they received American financial assistance to build modern factories, replacing those destroyed during the war.

But the problems of British industries run deeper. The industrial revolution began in the northern regions of England and southern Scotland in part because those areas contained a remarkable concentration of innovative engineers and mechanics during the late eighteenth century. In the twentieth century, leadership in developing new products and industrial techniques has passed to Japanese, American, and German firms.

Northern Italy

A fourth European industrial region of some importance lies in the Po River basin of northern Italy. It contains about one-fifth of Italy's land area, but approximately half of the country's population and two-thirds of its industries.

Modern industrial development in the Po basin began with establishment of textile manufacturing during the nineteenth century. The Po basin has attracted textiles and other industries because it has two key assets that Europe's other industrial regions lack: numerous workers willing to accept lower wages, and inexpensive hydroelectricity from the nearby Alps. Industries concentrated in this region include raw-material processors and mechanical-parts assemblers.

Eastern Europe and Russia

Eastern Europe has six major industrial regions. Four are entirely in Russia, one is in Ukraine, and one is in southern Poland and northern Czech Republic (Figure 10-7). The Central industrial district, St. Petersburg, Eastern Ukraine, and Silesia became manufacturing centers in the 1800s. The Volga and Urals regions were established by the Communists in the twentieth century. In addition to these six industrial regions, Russia also contains another major industrial region, Kuznetsk, in the far eastern (Asian) portion of the country.

Central Industrial District

Russia's oldest industrial region is centered around Moscow, the country's capital and largest city. Although not well-endowed with natural resources, the central industrial district produces one-fourth of Russian industrial output, primarily because it is situated near the country's largest market. Products of the Central industrial district tend to be of high value relative to their bulk and require a large pool of skilled labor. Of Moscow's industrial work force, 30 percent is employed making linen, cotton, wool, and silk fabrics. Moscow factories also specialize in chemicals and light industrial goods.

St. Petersburg

St. Petersburg, Eastern Europe's second largest city, was one of Russia's early nodes of industrial innovation. Railways were built in the St. Petersburg area several decades earlier than in the rest of Russia. Given its proximity to the Baltic Sea, the St. Petersburg area specializes in shipbuilding and other industries

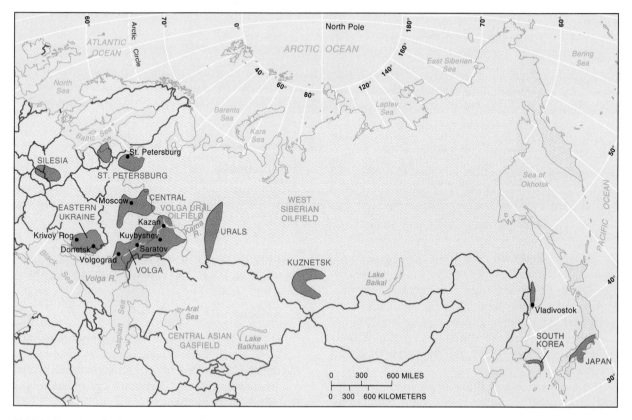

FIGURE 10-7 Manufacturing centers in Eastern Europe and Russia. In Eastern Europe, manufacturing is clustered in the western part of Russia and Ukraine. The former Soviet government encouraged development of manufacturing regions in the center of the country east of the Ural Mountains.

serving Russia's navy and ports. The area also produces goods that meet the needs of the local market, such as food processing, textiles, and chemicals.

Eastern Ukraine

The Donetsk coal field, in the far eastern portion of Ukraine, contains one of the world's largest coal reserves. Eastern Ukraine also possesses large deposits of iron ore, manganese, and natural gas. These assets make the region Eastern Europe's largest producer of pig iron and steel. Major plants are located at Krivoy Rog, near iron ore fields, and Donetsk, near coalfields.

Volga

Situated along the Volga and Kama rivers, the Volga industrial district grew rapidly during World War II, when many plants in the Central and Eastern Ukraine districts were occupied by the invading German army. The Volga district contains Russia's largest petroleum and natural gas fields. Within the district, the motor vehicle industry is concentrated in Togliatti, oil refining in Kuybyshev, chemicals in Saratov, metallurgy in Volgograd, and leather and fur in Kazan.

Urals

The Ural mountain range contains more than 1,000 types of minerals, the most varied collection found in any mining region in the world. Valuable deposits include iron, copper, potassium, manganese, bauxite (aluminum ore), salt, and tungsten. Proximity to these raw materials encouraged the Communists to locate in this region iron and steel manufacturing, chemicals, and machinery and metal fabricating.

Although the area is well endowed with metals, industrial development is hindered by a lack of nearby energy sources. Coal must be shipped nearly 1,500 kilometers (900 miles) from Kuznetsk, and oil and natural gas are piped in from the Volga-Ural, Bukhara, and central Siberian fields. Russia controls nearly all the Urals minerals, although the southern portion of the region extends into Kazakhstan.

Kuznetsk

Kuznetsk is Russia's most important manufacturing district east of the Ural Mountains. The region contains the country's largest reserves of coal and an abundant supply of iron ore. Soviet planners took advantage of these natural assets to invest considerable capital in constructing iron, steel, and other factories in the region.

Silesia

Outside the former Soviet Union, Eastern Europe's leading manufacturing area is in Silesia, which includes southern Poland and the northern Czech Republic. It is an important steel production center because it is near coalfields, although iron ore must be imported.

Japan

The most important industrial region outside Europe and North America, Japan, may appear to have few geographic assets. It lacks many natural resources and so must import nearly all its energy and raw materials. For example, Japan possesses only 0.2 percent of the world's iron ore; yet, it is one of the world's leading steel producers. The country is far from wealthy consumers in North America and Western Europe; yet it has become the world's leading exporter of consumer goods.

Faced with isolation from world markets and a shortage of nearly all essential resources, Japan has taken advantage of its one abundant resource: a large labor force. Although its industries were devastated during World War II, Japan became an industrial power in the 1950s and 1960s, initially by producing goods that could be sold in large quantity at cut-rate prices to consumers in other countries. (In those days, the label "Made in Japan" signified cheap, shoddy goods.) Prices were kept low, despite high shipping cost, because workers received much lower wages in Japan than in North America or Western Europe.

Japanese planners, aware that other countries were building industries based on even lower-cost labor, began to train workers for highly skilled jobs. At the same time, because wages remained lower than in other more developed countries, Japan could build high-quality products at a lower cost than those in North America or Western Europe. As a result, during the 1970s and 1980s, Japan earned a reputation for high-quality electronics, precision instruments, and other products that required well-trained workers. The country became the world's leading manufacturer of automobiles, ships, cameras, stereos, and televisions.

As in other countries, industry is not distributed uniformly within Japan. Manufacturing is concentrated in the central region between Tokyo and Nagoya, especially the two large urban areas of Tokyo-Yokohama and Osaka-Kobe-Kyoto (Figure 10-8). Kitakyushu is a major industrial center in the southwest.

Although industry is located elsewhere in the world, the four industrial regions of eastern North America, northwestern Europe, Eastern Europe and Russia, and Japan account for most of the world's industrial production. Having looked at the "where" question for industrial location, we can next consider the "why" question: Why are industries located where they are?

KEY ISSUE 3

What Factors Influence the Choice of Location for a Factory?

- Situation Factors
- Site Factors
- Obstacles to Optimal location

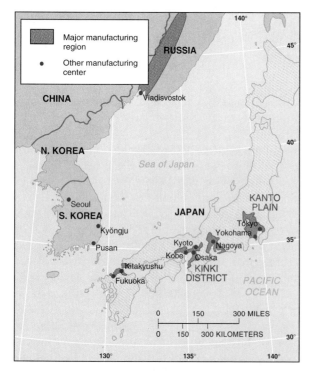

FIGURE 10-8 Manufacturing centers in Japan. Production is clustered along the southeast coast. The two largest centers are the Kanto Plain (including Tokyo and Yokohama) and the Kinki District (including Osaka, Kyoto, and Kobe).

Industry seeks to maximize profits by minimizing production costs. Geographers try to explain why one location may prove more profitable for a factory than others. A company ordinarily faces two geographic costs: situation and site.

Situation factors involve transporting materials to and from a factory. A firm seeks a location that minimizes the cost of transporting inputs to the factory and finished goods to the consumers.

Site factors result from the unique characteristics of a location. Land, labor, and capital are the three traditional production factors that may vary among locations.

Although a variety of situation and site costs explain the location of factories, the particular combination of critical factors varies among firms.

Situation Factors

All manufacturers buy and sell. They buy from companies and individuals who supply manufacturing inputs (materials, energy, machinery, services). They sell to companies and individuals who buy the product. One objective of every company is to minimize the aggregate cost of transporting inputs to its factory and transporting finished products from its plant to consumers. The farther something is transported, the higher the cost, so a manufacturer tries to locate its factory as close as possible to both buyers and sellers.

A company that obtains all inputs from one source and sells all products to one customer can easily compute the optimal location for its factory. If the cost of transporting the product exceeds the cost of transporting inputs, then optimal plant location is as close as possible to the customer. Conversely, if inputs are more expensive to transport, a factory should locate near the source of inputs.

Location Near Inputs

Every industry uses some inputs. These may be materials from the physical environment (minerals, wood, or animals), or they may be parts or materials made by other companies. If the weight and bulk of any one input is particularly great, the firm may locate near the source of that input to minimize transportation cost.

Copper Industry. The North American copper industry is a good example of locating near the source of heavy, bulky inputs to minimize transportation cost. In copper production, the first step is mining the copper ore. Much of the copper ore mined in North America is low-grade, less than 1 percent copper, whereas the rest is waste, known as *gangue*. Obviously, the weight and bulk of this low-grade ore are considerable.

The next step is to concentrate the copper. Concentration mills remove 98 percent of the waste from the ore. These mills are near the mines, because concentration transforms the heavy, bulky copper ore into a product of much higher value per weight. Copper concentration is a **bulk-reducing industry,** an economic activity in which the final product weighs less or has less volume than its inputs.

The concentrated copper then becomes the input for smelters, which separate the copper metal from the remaining impurities. Smelters further reduce the weight by about 60 percent. As a bulk-reducing industry, smelters also are built near their main inputs—the concentration mills—to minimize transportation cost.

The purified *blister copper* produced by smelters is further treated at *refineries*. No further weight loss occurs, but proximity to the mines, mills, and smelters still is a critical factor in locating a refinery.

A U.S. map demonstrates the location of copper-processing plants (Figure 10-9). The most important location for copper mining—Arizona—is also the center for concentration mills, smelters, and refineries. Note, however, that one of the largest refining centers is near Baltimore, 1,000 kilometers (600 miles) from the nearest copper mine. The Baltimore refinery imports most of its material from other countries.

Another important locational consideration is the source of energy to power these energy-demanding operations. In general, metal processors such as the copper industry also try to locate near economical electrical sources and to negotiate favorable rates from power companies.

Steel Industry. Steelmaking is another bulk-reducing industry that traditionally has been located to minimize the cost of transporting inputs. The U.S. steel industry also demonstrates how locations change when the source and cost of raw materials change.

The main inputs for steel production are iron ore and coal. These are heavy and bulky, contain a high percentage of impurities, and must be used in large quantities. These characteristics influence steel processors to minimize transportation cost through location.

In the mid-1800s, the U.S. steel industry concentrated in southwestern Pennsylvania around Pittsburgh, where iron ore and coal were both mined. Later in the 1800s, more steel mills were built around Lake Erie, in the Ohio cities of Cleveland, Youngstown, and Toledo, and around Detroit and in other communities (Figure 10-10). The locational

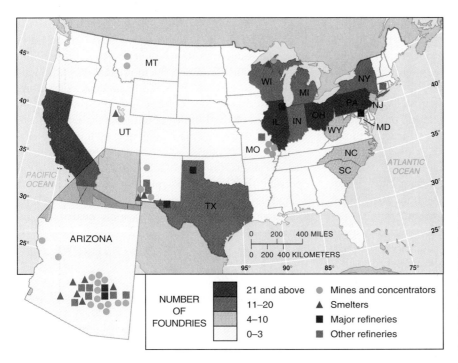

FIGURE 10-9 U.S. copper industry. Copper mining, concentrating, smelting, and refining are examples of bulk-reducing industries. In the United States, most plants that concentrate, smelt, and refine copper are in or near Arizona, where most copper mines are located. Copper-refining plants in coastal locations use imported material.

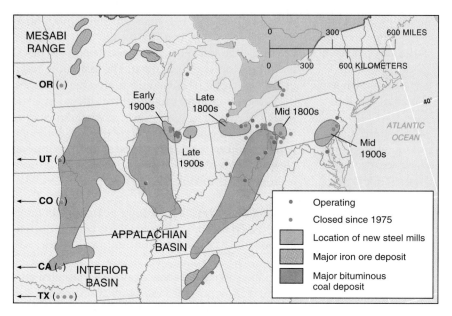

FIGURE 10-10 Integrated steel mills. These mills are highly clustered near the southern Great Lakes, especially Lake Erie and Lake Michigan. Historically, the most critical factor in siting a steel mill was to minimize transportation cost for raw materials, especially heavy, bulky iron ore and coal. In recent years, many integrated steel mills have closed. Most surviving mills are in the Midwest to maximize access to consumers.

shift was largely influenced by the discovery of rich iron ore in the Mesabi Range, a series of low mountains in northern Minnesota. This area soon became the source for virtually all iron ore used in the U.S. steel industry. The ore was transported by way of Lake Superior, Lake Huron, and Lake Erie. Coal was shipped from Appalachia by train.

Around 1900, new steel mills began to be located farther west, near the southern end of Lake Michigan—Gary in Indiana, Chicago, and other communities. The main raw materials continued to be iron ore and coal, but changes in steelmaking required more iron ore in proportion to coal. Thus, new steel mills were built closer to the Mesabi Range to minimize transportation cost. Coal was available from nearby southern Illinois as well as from Appalachia.

Most large U.S. steel mills built during the first half of the twentieth century were located in communities near the East and West coasts, such as Trenton in New Jersey, Baltimore, and Los Angeles. These coastal locations partly reflected further changes in transportation cost. Iron ore increasingly came from other countries, especially Canada and Venezuela, and locations near the Atlantic and Pacific oceans were more accessible to those foreign sources. Further, scrap iron and steel—widely available in the large metropolitan areas of the East Coast and West Coast—had become an important input in the steel-production process.

Recently, more steel plants have closed than have opened in the United States. Among the survivors,

plants around southern Lake Michigan and along the East Coast have significantly increased their share of national production. This success derives primarily from market access, rather than input access. In contrast with the main historical locational factor—transportation cost of raw materials—successful steel mills today are located increasingly near major markets. Coastal plants provide steel to large East Coast population centers, and southern Lake Michigan plants are centrally located to distribute their products countrywide.

The growth of steel *minimills* also demonstrates the increasing importance of access to markets rather than to inputs. Traditionally, most steel was produced at large, *integrated mills*. They processed iron ore, converted coal into coke, converted the iron into steel, and formed the steel into sheets, beams, rods, or other shapes. Minimills, generally limited to one step in the process—steel production—have captured one-fourth of the U.S. steel market. Less expensive than integrated mills to build and operate, minimills can locate near their markets because their main input—scrap metal—is widely available (Figure 10-11).

Location Near Markets

For many firms, the optimal location is close to markets, where the goods are sold. The cost of transporting goods to consumers is a critical locational factor for three types of industries: bulk-gaining, perishable, and single-market.

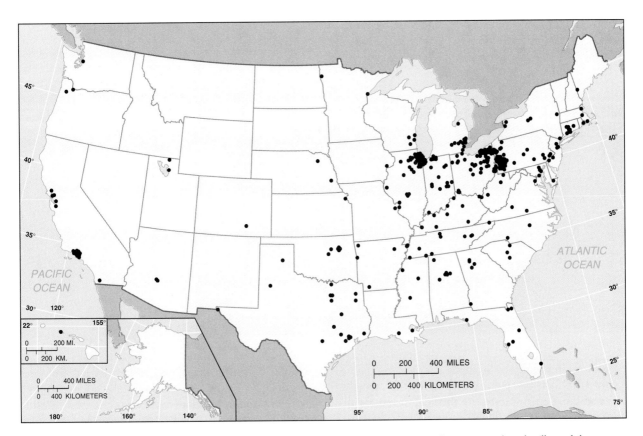

FIGURE 10-11 U.S. minimills. Minimills produce steel from scrap metal, are more numerous than integrated steel mills, and they are distributed around the country near local markets.

***Bulk-Gaining Industries.* Bulk-gaining industries** produce a product that gains *volume* or *weight* during production. Soft-drink bottling is a good example of an industry in which the product gains *weight.* Empty cans or bottles are brought to the bottler, filled with the soft drink, and shipped to consumers. A filled container has the same volume as an empty one, but it is much heavier—the container itself accounts for less than 5 percent of the weight of a filled can (355 milliliters, or 12 fluid ounces) or bottle (1 liter, or 33.8 fluid ounces). Because they are heavier, the filled containers are more expensive to ship than the empty ones, and bottlers locate near their customers rather than near the manufacturers of the containers.

Two main inputs are placed in the container: syrup (relatively concentrated and easy to transport) and water (relatively bulky, heavy, and expensive to transport). If water were available in only a few locations around the country, then bottlers might cluster near the source of such a scarce, bulky input. But because water is available everywhere people live,

bottlers minimize cost by producing soft-drinks near their consumers instead of shipping water (their heaviest input) long distances. Major soft-drink companies such as Coca-Cola and Pepsico manufacture syrups according to proprietary recipes and ship them to bottlers in hundreds of communities (Figure 10-12).

Major bottlers of beer, such as Anheuser-Busch and Miller, follow a similar pattern of locating facilities around the country, near major population centers, to minimize the cost of shipping to consumers. However, another major brewer, Coors, remains in one location—Golden, Colorado—because the company advertises that the community's water imparts a distinctive flavor to the beer.

Scotch whiskey is another bulk-gaining product that gains weight, but its spatial distribution differs from that of soft drinks. Although the product is mostly water, it does not have sufficient consumers to justify a bottling plant in many cities. One Scotch distiller must serve more than one market and charge higher prices to cover the delivery cost to dispersed consumers.

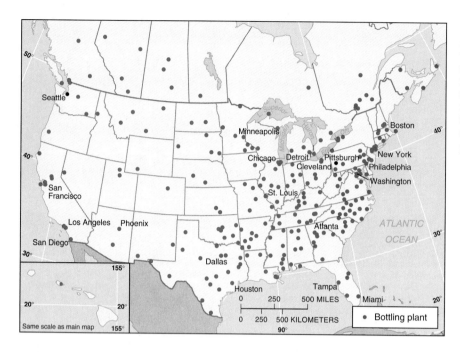

FIGURE 10-12 Coca-Cola bottling plants in the United States and Canada. A soft-drink bottling plant is a good example of a bulk-gaining industry, which needs to be located near consumers. Consequently, there are more than 200 soft-drink bottlers in the United States and Canada, situated near all major population concentrations.

More commonly, bulk-gaining industries manufacture products that gain *volume* rather than weight. A prominent example is the fabricated-metals industry. A fabricated-metals factory brings together previously manufactured parts as the main inputs and assembles them into a more complex product. Many common products are so fabricated, including television sets, refrigerators, and automobiles. If the fabricated product occupies a much larger volume than its individual parts, as does a car or freezer, then the cost of shipping the final product to consumers is likely to be a critical factor. A fabricated products industry locates to minimize the cost of shipping its bulky product to the market.

Perishable Products. To deliver their products to consumers as rapidly as possible, perishable-product industries must be located near their markets. For example, bakeries and dairies must locate near their customers to assure rapid delivery, because no one wants stale bread or sour milk.

Many food producers are located far from their customers, especially those engaged in processing fresh food into frozen, canned, or preserved products. Cheese and butter, for example, are manufactured in Wisconsin because rapid delivery to the urban markets is not critical for products with a long shelf-life and the area is well suited agriculturally for raising dairy cows. On the other hand, perishable milk and cream, which must be used within several days, are produced near the places where they are consumed.

The daily newspaper is an example of a product other than food that is highly perishable because it contains dated information. People demand their newspaper as soon after its printing as possible. Therefore, newspaper publishers must locate near markets to minimize transportation cost. Difficulty with timely delivery is one of the main factors in the demise of afternoon newspapers. Morning newspapers are printed between 9 P.M. and 6 A.M. and delivered during the night, when traffic is light. Afternoon newspapers, published between 9 A.M. and 5 P.M., must be delivered in heavy daytime traffic, so delivery is slower and total production cost is higher than for morning newspapers.

In European countries, national newspapers are printed in the largest city during the evening and delivered by train throughout the country overnight. This practice has been possible because of the comparatively compact size of most European states. In the past, publishers considered the United States to be too large to make a national newspaper feasible. With satellite technology, however, the *New York Times, Wall Street Journal,* and *USA Today* have moved in the direction of national delivery. These newspapers are composed in New York or Washington. Digitized page images are transmitted by satellite to other locations, such as Atlanta and Chicago, where the papers are printed. The papers are then delivered by air and surface transport to consumers nearest each city where printing is done.

Single-Market Manufacturers. Single-market manufacturers make products sold primarily in one location, so they also cluster near their markets. For example, several times a year, buyers from individual clothing stores and department-store chains come to New York City from all over the United States to select high-style clothing they will sell in the coming season. Manufacturers of fashion clothing then receive large orders for certain garments to be delivered in a short time. Consequently, manufacturers of high-style clothing concentrate around New York.

New York-based high-style clothing manufacturers in turn demand rapid delivery of specialized components, such as clasps, clips, pins, and zippers. The specialized-component manufacturers therefore also concentrate in New York.

Automobile Production

The location of U.S. and Canadian automobile production reflects the importance of situation fac-

tors. The industry also demonstrates how market changes can alter optimal plant locations.

The automotive industry comprises two types of factories—component and assembly. Several thousand components plants manufacture one or more parts that go into vehicles. These parts are then combined into finished vehicles at about 70 assembly plants across the United States and Canada.

For any fabricated product such as an automobile, the critical factor in factory location is minimizing transportation to customers throughout North America. Automotive component makers also minimize transportation cost, but most are specialized manufacturers that sell to only one or two customers—automobile producers such as General Motors and Ford.

Historically, GM and Ford divided North America into regions and located an assembly plant in or near a large metropolitan area within each region. For example, during the 1950s, GM operated eleven Chevrolet assembly plants, ten in the United States and one in Canada. All eleven assembled identical Chevrolets for distribution within a designated region (Figure 10-13). Ford had a similar geographic

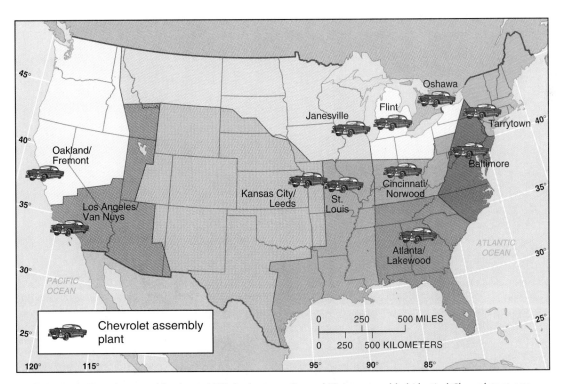

FIGURE 10-13 Chevrolet assembly plants, 1955. In that year, General Motors assembled identical Chevrolets at one Canadian and ten U.S. final assembly plants located near major population centers. This distribution enabled GM to minimize the cost of distributing its relatively bulky products to consumers.

arrangement for producing and distributing its corresponding models. Luxury cars, such as GM's Cadillac and Ford's Lincoln, each were assembled at only one plant, both in Detroit.

Since the 1970s, this long-standing distribution has changed. Assembly plants near East Coast and West Coast population centers have closed. New ones have opened in the country's interior, especially along interstate highways 65, 70, and 75 (see Geography in Action box for more about these changes).

Ship, Rail, Truck, or Air?

Inputs and products are transported in one of four ways: ship, rail, truck, or air. Firms seek the lowest-cost mode of transport, but the cheapest of the four alternatives changes with the distance that goods are being sent.

The farther something is transported, the lower is the cost per kilometer (or mile). Longer-distance transportation is cheaper per kilometer in part because firms must pay workers to on-load and off-load goods onto vehicles, whether the material travels 10 kilometers or 10,000. The cost per kilometer decreases at different rates for each of the four modes, because the loading and unloading expenses differ for each mode.

Trucks are most often used for short-distance delivery and trains for longer distances, because trucks can be loaded and unloaded more quickly and cheaply than trains. If a water route is available, ship transport is attractive for very long distances, because the cost per kilometer is even less.

Air is normally the most expensive alternative for all distances, but an increasing number of firms transport by air to ensure speedy delivery of small-bulk, high-value packages. Air transport companies such as Fedex, Airborne, and UPS promise overnight delivery for most packages. They pick up packages in the afternoon and transport them by truck to the nearest airport. Late at night, planes filled with packages are flown to a central hub airport in the interior of the country (Memphis and Dayton are used by two of these services). The packages are then transferred to other planes, flown to airports nearest their destination, transferred to trucks, and delivered the next morning.

Break-of-Bulk Points. Regardless of transportation mode, cost rises each time that inputs or prod-

Some firms locate production facilities at break-of-bulk points, such as Newark, New Jersey, where transfer among modes of transport is possible. Containers make it easier for firms to transfer products quickly between modes, especially between land- and sea-based transport. (Craig Hammell/The Stock Market)

ucts are transferred from one mode to another. For example, workers must unload goods from a truck and then reload them onto a plane. The company may need to build or rent a warehouse to temporarily store goods after unloading from one mode and before loading to another mode. Some companies may calculate that the cost of one mode is lower for some inputs and products, while another mode may be cheaper for other goods.

Many companies that use multiple transport modes locate at a break-of-bulk point. A **break-of-bulk point** is a location where transfer among transportation modes is possible. Important break-of-bulk points include seaports, railway stations, and airports. For example, a steel mill near the port of Baltimore receives iron ore by ship from South America and coal by train from Appalachia. The ore and coal are transferred at Baltimore to another transportation mode.

Situation factors remain important for many firms, but their relative importance has changed. Locations near markets or break-of-bulk points have become more important than locations near raw materials for firms in developed countries. Consumers concentrated in large urban areas have greater wealth with which to buy products. Communications improvements have increased demand for rapid access to products.

However, situation factors do not explain the growing importance of Japanese and other Asian manufacturers. Japan not only lacks key raw materials needed by industries but also is thousands of kilometers from the most important North American and European markets. Manufacturing has grown in Japan and other Asian countries primarily because *site factors* have become increasingly important in industrial location decisions.

Site Factors

The cost of conducting business varies among locations, depending on the cost of three production factors: land, labor, and capital.

Land

Modern factories are more likely to be located in suburban or rural areas than near the center city. Figure 10-14 shows the rural locations of Japanese-owned plants near cities in Ohio. Contemporary factories generally require large tracts of land, because they usually operate more efficiently when laid out

U.S. manufacturers increasingly build factories on low-cost rural sites, such as this fiberglass plant outside Amarillo, Texas. (Bob Daemmrich/Stock Boston)

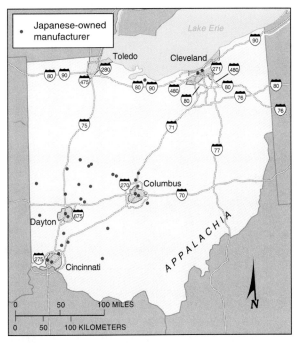

FIGURE 10-14 Japanese-owned plants in Ohio. To minimize situation costs, Japanese manufacturers have clustered in midwestern states such as Ohio. Within the Midwest, they have selected rural rather than urban locations because land costs are lower and rural workers are less likely to wish to join a union.

Shifting Geography of Automobile Production

Instead of producing the same model at several assembly plants for regional distribution, automakers now operate specialized assembly plants that build single models for distribution throughout the United States and Canada (Figure 1). In geographic terms, if a company has a product that is made at only one plant, and the critical locational factor is to minimize the cost of distributing it to U.S. and Canadian consumers, then the optimal factory location is in the U.S. interior. These interior locations were established because of an increase in the variety of models produced in North America. In the past, all models produced under one nameplate, such as Chevrolet, were substantially the same, differing only in minor details such as body trim and seat covers. Beginning in the 1960s, the models of a particular nameplate began to vary in size, ranging from subcompacts less than 150 inches long to full-sized vehicles exceeding 210 inches.

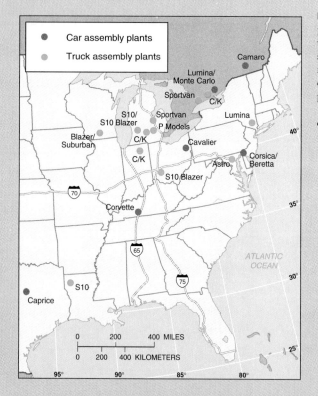

FIGURE 1 Chevrolet assembly plants, 1995. Since the 1970s, motor vehicle producers have located new assembly plants in the U.S. interior rather than near coastal population concentrations, which had been preferred in the past (see Figure 10-13). Most coastal plants have been closed during the 1980s and 1990s.

The diversity of motor vehicles produced in North America has also increased through construction of assembly plants owned by foreign companies, especially the Japanese. U.S. and Canadian customers were first attracted to Japanese vehicles during the 1970s because they were inexpensive to purchase and operate. Japanese companies offset the cost of overseas shipping by paying substantially less for parts and labor in Japan than manufacturers had to pay in North America.

The gap in wage rates between North American and Japanese autoworkers has disappeared. Many North Americans now worry about the sizable trade deficit with Japan. To protect their North American markets, Japanese automakers opened U.S. and Canadian assembly plants during the 1980s. Most cars sold in North America with Japanese nameplates are actually assembled in the United States or Canada rather than in Japan, although most of the parts are still made in Japan. The Japanese-built assembly plants in the United States have all been located in the interior of the country.

Auto assembly plants once were located around the country, but most component manufacturers clustered in Michigan and adjacent states. The parts industry typically sent its products to automakers' warehouses and distribution centers in Michigan. Parts producers also clustered near the southern Great Lakes because the region produced this industry's most important input, steel. Today, many parts are produced in factories near the assembly plant.

Proximity to the assembly plant is increasingly important for parts producers because of the diffusion of just-in-time delivery. Under just-in-time, parts are delivered to the assembly plant just in time to be used, often within minutes, rather than weeks or months in advance. The clustering of parts manufacturers around their customers—the new Japanese-operated U.S. assembly plants—clearly illustrates the adoption of just-in-time manufacturing (Figure 2).

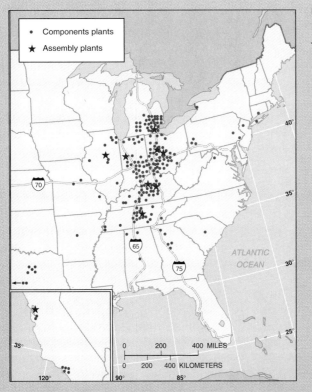

FIGURE 2 Japanese-owned auto plants in the United States. Japanese-owned auto parts makers have clustered in the U.S. interior, especially along interstates 65, 70, and 75. These locations facilitate rapid delivery of parts to final assembly plants, which are also clustered in the two corridors.

in one-story buildings. The land needed to build one-story factories is more likely to be available in suburban or rural locations.

Also, land is much cheaper in suburban or rural locations than near the center city. A hectare (or an acre) of land in the United States may cost only a few thousand dollars in a rural area, tens of thousands in a suburban location, and hundreds of thousands near a center city.

Industries may be attracted to specific parcels of land that are accessible to energy sources. Before the industrial revolution, many economic activities were located near rivers and close to forests, because running water and burning of wood were the two most important sources of energy. When coal became the dominant form of industrial energy in the late 1700s, location near coalfields became more important. Because coalfields were less ubiquitous than streams or forests, industry began to concentrate in fewer locations.

In the twentieth century, electricity became an important source of energy for industry. Electricity is generated using coal, oil, natural gas, running water (hydroelectricity), nuclear fuel, or solar and wind energy to a very limited degree. In the United States, electricity usually is purchased from a utility company, which is a publicly owned company or a privately owned monopoly regulated by the state government.

Industries are charged a certain rate per kilowatthour of electricity consumed, although they usually pay a lower rate than home consumers. Each utility company sets its own rate schedule, subject to approval by its state's regulatory agency. Industries with a particularly high demand for energy may select a location with lower electrical rates.

The aluminum industry, for example, requires a large amount of electricity to separate pure aluminum from bauxite ore. The first aluminum plant was located near Niagara Falls to take advantage of the large amount of cheap hydroelectric power generated there. Aluminum plants have been built near other sources of inexpensive hydroelectric power, including the Tennessee Valley and the Pacific Northwest.

Industry may also be attracted to a particular location because of amenities at the site. Not every location has the same climate, topography, recreational opportunities, cultural facilities, and cost of living. Some executives select locations in the U.S. South and West because they are attracted to the relative-ly mild climates and opportunities for year-round outdoor recreation activities. Others prefer locations that are accessible to cultural facilities or major-league sports franchises.

Labor

The cost of labor varies considerably, not only among countries but within regions of one country. A **labor-intensive industry** is one in which labor cost is a high percentage of expense. Some labor-intensive industries require highly skilled labor to maximize profit, whereas others need less-skilled, inexpensive labor.

Textile and Clothing Industries. Textile and clothing production are prominent examples of labor-intensive industries that generally require less-skilled, low-cost workers. Textile production involves three principal steps:

- *Spinning* fibers to make yarn
- *Weaving* or *knitting* yarn into fabric (as well as finishing fabric by bleaching or dyeing)
- *Cutting* and *sewing* fabric into clothing or other products (such as carpets and towels)

The global distributions of spinning, weaving, and sewing plants are not the same, because the three steps are not equally labor-intensive.

Fibers can be spun from natural or synthetic elements. The distribution of plants that spin natural fiber responds primarily to situation factors: manufacturing is concentrated in countries where the principal input—usually cotton—is grown. China, India, Pakistan, the United States, and Uzbekistan grow more than half of the world's cotton and produce more than half of the world's cotton fiber (Figure 10-15). The other major natural fiber—wool—is not typically produced near sheep farms.

Synthetic fibers—produced from petroleum and other chemical processes—account for an increasing share of textile production. Production was once dominated by a few developed countries, where the chemical industry was concentrated, but less developed countries now account for about half of global production of synthetic fibers. Synthetic production has expanded especially rapidly in China and Indonesia.

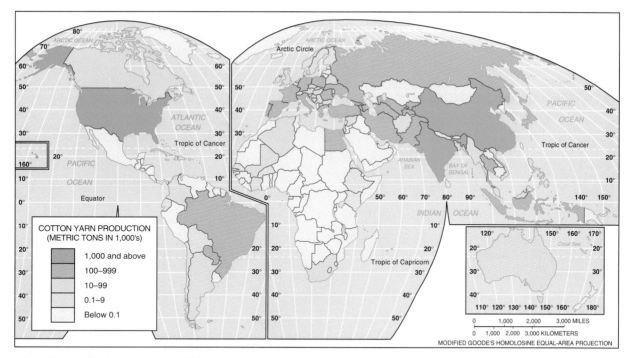

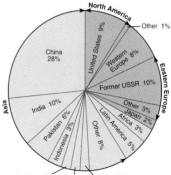

FIGURE 10-15 Cotton yarn production. Spinning of cotton fiber into yarn is clustered in countries where cotton is grown: the United States, Uzbekistan, China, India, and Pakistan. The spindles of spun cotton become inputs into the weaving of cotton fabric, which is done primarily in Asia. (Doug Handel/The Stock Market)

LDCs are responsible for three-fourths of the world's woven cotton fabric and two-thirds of its spun yarn (Figure 10-16). Weaving is more likely to locate in LDCs, because labor is a higher percentage of total production cost than in the other textile processes. Despite their remoteness from European and North American markets, Asian countries have become major fabric producers because lower labor cost offsets the expense of shipping inputs and products long distances.

Most of the world's cotton clothing, such as shirts, trousers, and underwear, still is produced in the MDCs of Europe and North America (Figure 10-17). During the 1980s, shirt production declined more

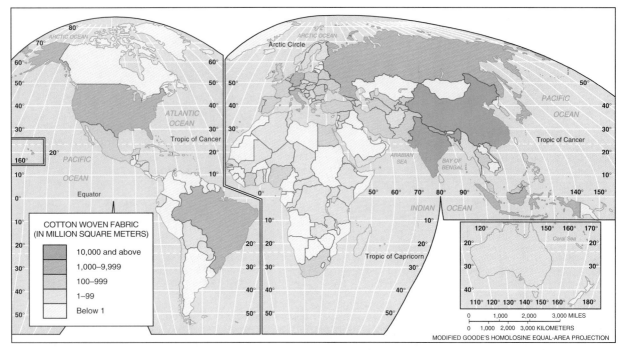

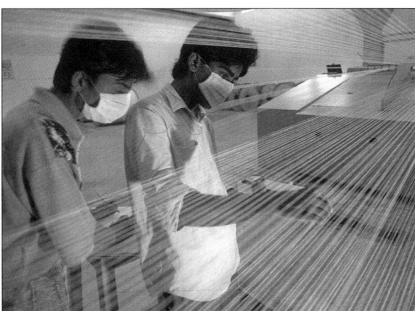

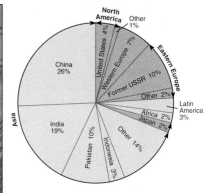

FIGURE 10-16 Woven cotton fabric. This material is likely to be produced in LDCs, because the process is more labor-intensive than the other major processes in textile and clothing manufacturing. (Contact Press Images)

than one-third in the United States and Europe while remaining about the same in the LDCs. As a result, the percentage of shirts produced in LDCs increased during the 1980s from about 45 percent to 55 percent.

U.S. Textile and Clothing Industries. U.S. textile weavers and clothing manufacturers have changed locations to be near sources of low-cost employees. During most of the 1800s, U.S. textile and clothing firms were concentrated in the Northeast. The region's major attraction was a large supply of European immigrants willing to sew long hours in sweatshops for low pay. In the late 1800s and early 1900s, textile and clothing workers began to demand

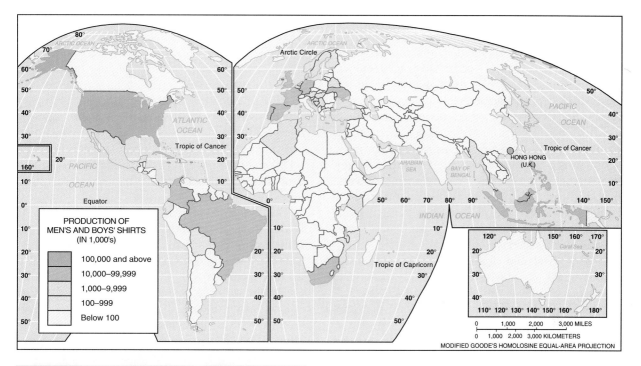

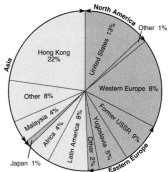

FIGURE 10-17 Production of men's and boys' shirts. Sewing of cotton fabric into men's and boys' shirts is more likely to take place in developed countries, although some production has moved to LDCs in recent years. Clothing producers must balance the need for low-wage workers with the need for proximity to customers. (Joseph Nettis/Photo Researchers, Inc.)

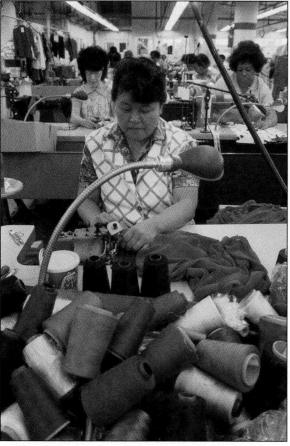

better working conditions and higher wages. They formed unions to represent their interests.

Their claim was bolstered by tragic events, such as the 1911 Triangle Shirtwaist Company fire in New York City. In the fire, 146 workers, mostly women, died because the owners locked the doors to the eighth-floor workroom, where the fire originated. The doors were locked to prevent workers from taking breaks and stealing company property.

Employers argued that they could not afford to pay high wages and still make a profit. Because so many workers were needed in the industry, the wages of each individual worker had to be kept low. Faced with union demands for higher wages in the Northeast, cotton textile and clothing manufacturers moved to the Southeast, where people were willing to work longer hours for lower wages. Although they earned less than their northeastern counterparts, southeastern workers cooperated because wages were higher than those paid for other types of work in the region. With better working conditions and higher wages than previously found in the region, workers were not likely to vote in the unions, thus keeping costs to industry low.

Cotton textile and clothing manufacturing in the United States is now located in the Appalachian Mountains and Piedmont of the Southeast, especially western North and South Carolina and northern Georgia and Alabama (Figure 10-18, left). Firms are dispersed among many communities rather than being concentrated in a few cities. They are in the same general region to take advantage of lower labor cost but do not need to be located in the same city.

The clothing industry has not completely abandoned the Northeast. The wool industry has remained there because its labor demands are different from those of the cotton textile industry. Wool clothing, such as knit outerwear, requires more skill to cut and assemble the material, and skilled textile workers are more plentiful in the Northeast (Figure 10-18, right).

Skilled-Labor Industries. More firms are requiring workers to perform highly skilled tasks, using complex equipment or performing precise cutting and drilling. Companies may become more successful by paying higher wages for skilled labor than by producing an inferior product made by lower-paid, less-skilled workers.

One industry that demands highly skilled workers is electronics. Computer manufacturers have concentrated in the highest-wage regions in the United States, especially New York, Massachusetts, and California (Figure 10-19). These regions have a large concentration of skilled workers because of proximity to major university centers.

Many industries are attracted to locations with relatively skilled labor to introduce new work rules. Traditionally, in large factories, each worker was assigned one specific task to perform repeatedly. Some geographers call this approach **Fordist,** because the Ford Motor Company was one of the first to organize its production this way early in the twentieth century. In recent years, companies have adopted more

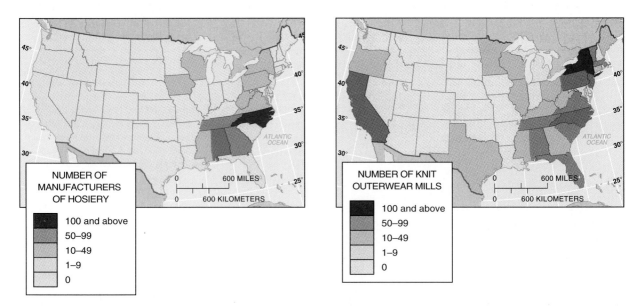

FIGURE 10-18 (Left) Hosiery manufacturers (SIC 2252). To support their labor-intensive industry, hosiery manufacturers locate where a low-cost workforce exists. In the United States, lowest-cost labor is concentrated in the Southeast.
(Right) Knit outerwear manufacturers (SIC 2253). Products, such as knit outerwear, that require more-skilled workers are still produced primarily in or near New York City.

The automobile industry innovated mass-production techniques during the 1910s, including the moving assembly line, shown here producing one of the first Chevrolet models in Flint, Michigan. Each worker repeatedly performed a specific task, such as attaching the spare tire to the back of the car. (Culver Pictures, Inc.)

flexible rules, such as the allocation of workers to teams that must perform a variety of tasks. Relatively skilled workers are needed to master the wider variety of assignments given them under more flexible **post-Fordist** work rules.

Capital

Manufacturers typically borrow funds to establish new factories or expand existing ones. The U.S. motor vehicle industry concentrated in Michigan early in the twentieth century partly because this region's financial institutions were more willing than Eastern banks to lend money to the industry's pioneers.

The ability to borrow money has become a critical factor in the distribution of industry in LDCs. Financial institutions in many LDCs are short of funds, so new industries must seek loans from banks in MDCs. But enterprises may not receive loans if they are located in a country that is perceived to have an unstable political system, a high debt level, or ill-advised economic policies.

Local and national governments increasingly attempt to influence the location of industry by providing financial incentives. These include grants, low-cost loans, and tax breaks. Communities compete to offer new factories the most attractive finan-

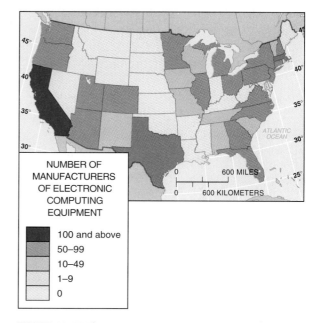

FIGURE 10-19 Electronic computing equipment manufacturers (SIC 3571). Manufacturers of computing equipment need access to highly skilled workers to perform precision tasks. They are willing to pay relatively high wages to attract the workers. The largest clusters of skilled workers are in the Northeast and on the West Coast.

U.S. industries feel a tension between increasing global cooperation and competition. (Top) A Japanese corporate executive is welcomed in the United States because his company plans to build a factory in the United States. (John Feingersh/The Stock Market)
(Bottom) Japanese cars are not welcomed at a U.S. auto parts manufacturer because their production is seen as taking jobs away from American workers. (Craig Hammell/The Stock Market)

cial package. In general, the cost of the financial package is less than the additional revenues the new firm will generate overall in taxes and employment.

Obstacles to Optimal Location

The location that a firm chooses cannot always be explained by situation and site factors. Many industries have become "footloose," meaning they can locate in a wide variety of places without a signifi-

cant change in their cost of transportation, land, labor, and capital.

The process by which corporate executives make decisions can explain the location of a firm's factories. An executive operating with high levels of knowledge and power may be able to identify precisely the location that maximizes the company's profits, whereas a less-skilled official might select an inferior location. An individual may choose a location on the basis of a corporate goal other than to maximize profits—for example, to promote growth or to assure survival of the firm. Personal preferences of the owner are especially important in influencing the location of a smaller firm. The location may be dictated by where the owner was born, went to school, participates in leisure activities, or visits friends.

The search for an optimal location may be time-consuming and costly. Consequently, the selected plant location may be the first acceptable alternative encountered, rather than the best possible one. The firm may select its location on the basis of inertia and history. Once a firm is located in a particular community, expansion in the same place is likely to be cheaper than moving operations to a new location. A large corporation may operate plants in inferior locations that were inherited through mergers and acquisitions.

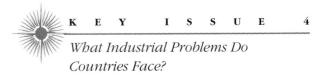

K E Y   I S S U E   4

What Industrial Problems Do Countries Face?

- A Global Perspective
- More Developed Countries
- Less Developed Countries

Leaders worldwide consider industrial growth to be a most fundamental concern. Each government defines problems of industrial development from its own perspective. But geographers point out that constraints on industrial growth faced by one country are related to conditions elsewhere in the world.

A Global Perspective

From a global perspective, the most basic industrial problem is a gap between the world *demand* for products and the world capacity to *supply* them. Global capacity to produce manufactured goods has increased more rapidly than demand for many products.

Stagnant Demand—A Recent Problem

During the past two centuries, industrial growth in developed countries was fueled by long-term increases in population and wealth. From the industrial revolution's beginnings in the late 1700s until the 1970s, the formula was simple: more people with more wealth demanded more goods. Demand was met by building more factories, which hired more people, who became wealthier and therefore demanded more goods. Times of major world conflict or economic depression were temporary exceptions to long-term growth in wealth, demand, and production.

Since the 1970s, however, demand for many manufactured goods has slowed in MDCs. Most developed countries now have little, if any, population growth. Because wages have not risen as fast as prices during the past two decades, individuals typically have not increased their level of spending, when adjusted for inflation.

Demand has also been flat for many consumer goods in MDCs because of market saturation. Nearly every household already has a color television, refrigerator, and automobile. Most contemporary purchasers of these products are replacing older models rather than buying for the first time.

Industrial output is also stagnant because of increased demand for high-quality goods. Consumers in MDCs increasingly select specific goods for quality and reliability rather than for low price, and then replace them less frequently.

During the 1980s, Japanese companies expanded their share of the North American automobile market to more than one-fourth by selling products that were comparably priced with American models but widely acknowledged to be better built. In recent years, the gap in quality between American and Japanese products has narrowed—if not disappeared altogether—although some American consumers still perceive that Japanese models are superior. Japanese automakers have retained their share of the North American market during the 1990s by selling larger, more luxurious models to customers who had positive experiences driving their smaller, inexpensive models.

Changing technology has resulted in declining demand for some industrial products. For example, the global steel demand is less than in the mid-1970s.

Today's typical automobile uses one-fourth less steel than cars built 20 years ago. Automakers now build smaller, lighter vehicles and have replaced steel with plastic and ceramic products in the body, chassis, passenger compartment, and trim.

Increased Capacity Worldwide

While demand for products such as steel has stagnated since the 1970s, global capacity to produce them has increased. Higher industrial capacity is primarily a result of two trends: the global diffusion of the industrial revolution and the desire by individual countries to maintain their production despite a global overcapacity.

Historically, manufacturing was concentrated in a few locations. From the beginning of the industrial revolution until recently, demand for products manufactured in MDCs increased in part through sales to new markets—countries that lacked competing industries. Such industrial growth through increased international sales was feasible when most of the world was organized into colonies and territories controlled by MDCs.

For much of the 1800s, the United Kingdom's output in some industrial sectors exceeded that of the rest of the world combined. From the late 1800s until recently, the British were joined in dominating global industrial production by the United States, Russia (and the former Soviet Union), Germany, and several other countries in Europe. Then, Asian countries such as Japan and South Korea blossomed into major industrial production. Few colonies remain in the world today, and nearly every independent country wants to establish its own industrial base.

The steel industry illustrates the changing distribution of the global economy. In 1973 the MDCs of North America, Western Europe, and Japan accounted for two-thirds of the world's steel production, compared with one-fourth in Eastern Europe and the Soviet Union, and less than 10 percent in LDCs (Figure 10-20).

The overall level of world steel production in the early 1990s remained virtually the same as in the mid-1970s, but the proportion changed significantly among various regions. Production declined by nearly one-fourth in MDCs and more than doubled in LDCs. In two decades, the share of the world's steel production concentrated in MDCs (other than Eastern Europe) has declined from nearly two-thirds to less than one-half, while the LDCs have increased

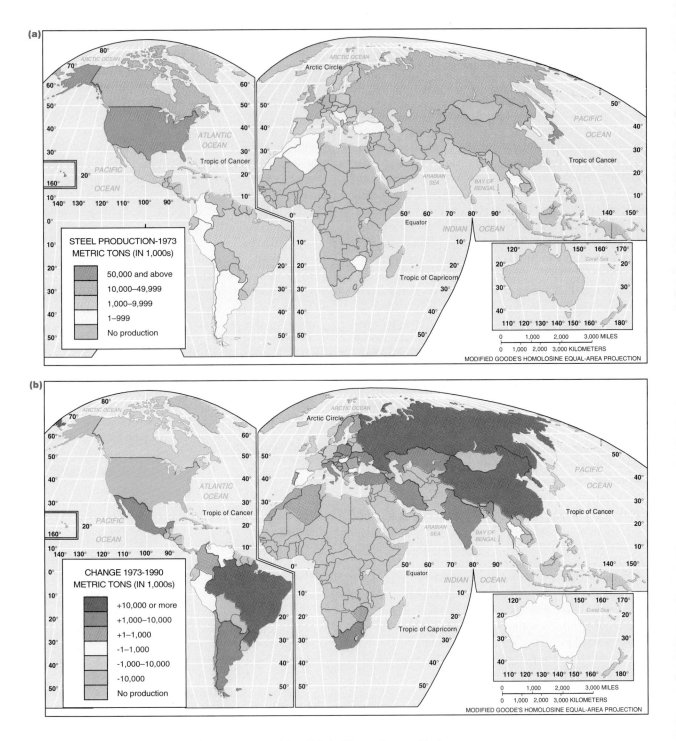

FIGURE 10-20 (a) World steel production, 1973. In 1973, MDCs in Western Europe, North America, and Japan accounted for 66 percent of global production (see 1973 pie chart). (b) Global steel production was about the same in 1993 as in 1973, but the distribution changed. Production declined in most MDCs and increased in LDCs, especially China and Brazil.

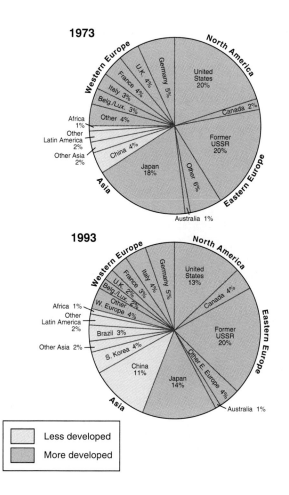

1973

Western Europe
- Germany 5%
- U.K. 4%
- France 4%
- Italy 3%
- Belg./Lux. 3%
- Other 4%

North America
- United States 20%
- Canada 2%

Eastern Europe
- Former USSR 20%
- Other 6%

Asia
- Japan 18%
- China 4%
- Other Asia 2%

Africa 1%
Other Latin America 2%

Australia 1%

1993

Western Europe
- Germany 5%
- Italy 3%
- France 4%
- U.K. 2%
- Belg./Lux. 2%
- Other W. Europe 4%

North America
- United States 13%
- Canada 4%

Eastern Europe
- Former USSR 20%
- Other E. Europe 4%

Asia
- Japan 14%
- China 11%
- S. Korea 4%
- Brazil 3%
- Other Asia 2%

Africa 1%
Other Latin America 2%

Australia 1%

Legend:
- Less developed
- More developed

from less than 10 percent to more than 20 percent of the world's output. LDCs such as Brazil, South Korea, Taiwan, India, and the People's Republic of China have substantially increased steel production, while MDCs—even Japan—have reduced production.

This global diffusion of steel mills has allowed capacity to exceed demand by a wide margin. Many companies have been unable to sell enough steel to make a profit and have closed. However, because the governments of many MDCs have been reluctant to let their steel mills close, the problem of excess capacity and unprofitable operations persists.

Steel mills in many countries receive substantial government financial support to remain open. Many European governments heavily subsidize the continued operation of their steel mills. The reason is economic: if the mills closed, governments would have to pay unemployment compensation to laid-off workers and deal with the social problems of increased

unemployment. Maintaining a steel industry also ensures a domestic steel source in times of crisis.

More Developed Countries

Countries at all levels of development face a similar challenge: to make their industries competitive in an increasingly integrated global economy. Although they share this same overall goal, each state faces distinctive geographic issues in ensuring that their industries compete effectively. Industries in more developed regions must protect their markets from new competitors, whereas less developed countries of Africa, Asia, and Latin America must identify new markets and sources of capital to generate industrial growth.

Impact of Trading Blocs

Industrial competition in the more developed world increasingly occurs not among individual countries, but within regional trading blocs. The three most important trading blocs are the Western Hemisphere, Western Europe, and East Asia. Within each bloc, countries cooperate in trade. Each bloc then competes against the other two.

Cooperation within Trading Blocs. In the Western Hemisphere, most trade barriers between the United States and Canada have been eliminated over the past several decades. The North American Free Trade Agreement (NAFTA), implemented in 1994, brought Mexico into the free trade zone with the United States and Canada. Since then, the three NAFTA partners have been negotiating with other Latin American countries to extend further the free trade provisions.

The European Union has eliminated most barriers to trade through Western Europe, as discussed in Chapter 7. European countries that are not members of the European Union, such as Switzerland and several former Communist Eastern European countries, depend heavily on trade with the European Union.

Japanese companies play leading roles in the economies of other East Asian countries. But cooperation among countries is less formal in East Asia, in part because Japan's neighbors have much lower levels of economic development and unpleasant memories of Japanese military aggression during the 1930s and 1940s.

The number of steel workers has declined by two-thirds in the United States since the 1970s. Since this photograph was taken in 1978, this steel mill in Youngstown, Ohio, has closed, and several thousand steelworkers have lost their jobs. (Roy Morsch/The Stock Market)

The free movement of most products across the borders has led to closer integration of industries within North America and within Western Europe. For example, most automobiles sold in Canada used to be manufactured in Canada, but today, most are assembled in the United States. Every Ford Taurus sold in Canada is actually assembled in the United States, but every Ford Crown Victoria sold in the United States is actually assembled in Canada. Canada exports twice as many automobiles to its southern neighbor as it imports. While admitting that they assemble a disproportionately large share of North American motor vehicles, Canadians complain that the United States has virtually all of the high-skilled engineering, design, and executive jobs. A similar integration of motor vehicle production and distribution exists within Europe. For example, Volkswagen manufactures cars in Germany, Spain, and the Czech Republic and sells them throughout the continent.

Competition among Trading Blocs. The three trading blocs have promoted internal cooperation, yet they have erected trade barriers to restrict other regions from competing effectively. European Union members slap a tax on goods produced in other countries. Japan has lengthy permit procedures that

effectively hinder foreign companies from selling there. The Japanese government maintains quotas on the number of automobiles that its companies can export to the United States to counter charges of unfair competition.

Faced with a decline in domestic steel production of about one-third during the late 1970s, the U.S. government negotiated a series of voluntary export restraint agreements with other major steel-producing countries. These quotas limited the sales of foreign-made steel to about 20 percent of the U.S. market.

When these quotas were in effect—from 1982 until 1992—U.S. steel companies spent $24 billion modernizing their plants and buying more-efficient equipment. This restructuring stabilized U.S. steel production levels, but the number of steelworkers fell by two-thirds. Because of declining employment, the number of hours of labor needed to produce a ton of steel—a widely used measure of industrial efficiency—is now lower in the United States than in Japan or Europe.

Steel towns have suffered severely from this decline. The country's largest steel mill at Gary, Indiana, operated by USX (formerly U.S. Steel), employed nearly 30,000 workers during the 1970s, but had fewer than 8,000 by the early 1990s. Youngstown,

Ohio, had more than 26,000 steel-industry jobs in the mid-1970s, but lost 80 percent of them. Some unemployed steelworkers have taken lower-paying jobs in other businesses, some have migrated elsewhere in search of jobs, and some have retired or remained unemployed. The steel industry's problems have affected the economy and morale of communities like Gary and Youngstown. Declines in other manufacturing sectors in MDCs have had similar impacts in their communities.

Transnational Corporations. Cooperation and competition within and among trading blocs take place primarily through the actions of large transnational corporations, sometimes called multinational corporations. A **transnational corporation** operates factories in countries other than the one in which its headquarters are located. Initially, transnational corporations were primarily American-owned, but in recent years corporations with headquarters in other developed countries (especially Japan, Germany, France, and the United Kingdom) have been active as well (Refer to figures 1-17 and 1-18 for patterns of foreign investment and an example of a transnational corporation, Nippondenso).

Some transnational corporations locate factories in other countries to expand their markets. Manufacturing the product where it is to be sold is done to overcome restrictions that many countries place on import. Further, given the lack of economic growth in many MDCs, a corporation may find that the only way it can increase sales is to move into another country. Transnational corporations also open factories in countries with lower site factors, to reduce their production cost. The site factor that varies most dramatically among countries is labor.

Japanese transnational corporations have been especially active in the United States in recent years. Several hundred Japanese-owned corporations have built U.S. factories, primarily to develop new markets for electronics, automotive components, and metal products. Most plants have been located in several interior states, including Ohio, Indiana, Kentucky, Michigan, Tennessee, and Illinois (see Figure 2 in the Geography in Action box, as well as Figure 10-14). German transnationals have clustered in the Carolinas.

Disparities within Trading Blocs

Within the major trading blocs, industries are concentrated in some regions and sparse elsewhere. One country or region within a country may have lower levels of income and amenities because it has less industry than other countries or regions within the trading bloc. The lack of a uniform internal distribution of industry has caused trouble for the trading blocs, as well as for individual countries.

Disparities within Western Europe. Within Western Europe, the relationship between wealth and industrialization can be seen by comparing the map of major industrial regions (Figure 10-6) with the maps of per capita gross domestic product and unemployment (Figures 3-13 and 3-14). Europe's most important industrial areas—western Germany and northern Italy—are relatively wealthy and have low unemployment rates.

Disparities exist at the scale of the individual country as well. For example, French industry and wealth are concentrated in the Paris region, while the south and west suffer. Per capita income is three times higher in the north of Italy than in the south. Within England, unemployment is 50 percent higher in the north and west, while average incomes are 25 percent higher in the south and east. Sweden's south is much more developed than its north. In each case, industry is concentrated in the regions most accessible to Western Europe's core of population, wealth, and industry, whereas more problems are found in peripheral regions.

Germany has had a particularly difficult problem with regional disparities. The eastern portion of the country has required massive financial assistance to modernize its industries. This is a legacy of the 40 years during which the region was Communist-run East Germany (German Democratic Republic).

The European Union, through its European Regional Development Fund, assists its three least industrialized member countries—Greece, Ireland, and Portugal—as well as regions in three other countries that lack industrial investment—Northern Ireland (part of the United Kingdom), southern Italy, and most of Spain (Figure 10-21). Funds also aid declining industrial areas, including the northern areas of Denmark, England, France, Italy, and Spain. Regions eligible for support must submit 5-year development plans explaining how the funds would be used.

A number of Western European countries use incentives to lure industry into poorer regions and discourage growth in the richer regions. In the United Kingdom, to aid development in the less prosper-

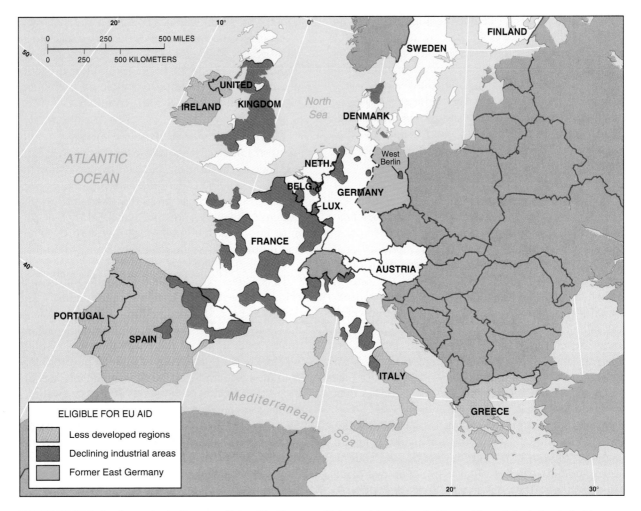

FIGURE 10-21 Assisted areas in the European Union. The European Union assists regions that have either relatively few industries or high concentrations of declining industries. Less industrialized regions are primarily in southern European countries; regions suffering from industrial decline are primarily in the north. Compare with distributions of wealth and unemployment (Figures 3-13 and 3-14).

ous north and west, the government has designated several Development Areas and Intermediate Areas (Figure 10-22). Industries that locate in one of these areas may be entitled to receive loans, grants, tax reductions, and other government aid. On the other hand, to discourage industries from locating in an Unassisted Area, they may be required to obtain government permission. Other European countries also use regional incentives and regulations to encourage industrial location in peripheral regions and to discourage it in the congested core.

Disparities within the United States. The problem of regional disparity is somewhat different in the United States. The South, historically the poorest U.S. region, has had the most rapid growth since the

1930s, stimulated partly by government policy and partly by changing site factors. The Northeast, traditionally the wealthiest and most industrialized region, claims that development in the South has been at the expense of old industrialized communities in New England and the Great Lakes states.

Regional development policies scored some successes as long as national economies were expanding overall, because the lagging regions shared in the national growth. But in the 1990s, an era of limited economic growth for MDCs, governments increasingly questioned policies that strongly encourage industrial location in poorer regions. Excessive control of industrial location could harm the overall national economy. MDCs have not completely abandoned policies that aid poorer regions,

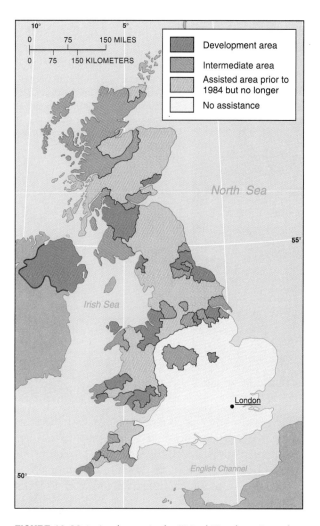

FIGURE 10-22 Assisted areas in the United Kingdom. Several European governments assist poorer regions within their countries. In the United Kingdom, for example, firms willing to locate in the north and west receive government subsidies.

but the level of financial commitment has been severely reduced.

Less Developed Countries

Poorer countries of Africa, Asia, and Latin America seek to reduce the disparity in wealth between themselves and European and North American countries. Knowing that their agrarian economies offer limited economic growth, the leaders of virtually every LDC encourage new industry. Industrial development not only can raise the value of exports, generating money these countries need to buy other products, but also can supply goods that are currently imported. If Western countries have built their wealth on industrial modernization, why can't the LDCs?

Old Problems for LDCs

In some respects, LDCs face obstacles similar to those once experienced by today's MDCs.

Distance from Markets. As in the past, today's newly industrializing countries are distant from wealthy consumers in MDCs. In the early 1800s, U.S. and central European factories were far from England, then the world's most important concentration of wealthy consumers. In the twentieth century, wealthy consumers in North America and Western Europe are distant from the LDCs of Africa, Asia, and Latin America. To minimize geographic isolation, industrializing countries invest scarce resources in constructing and subsidizing transportation facilities.

Inadequate Infrastructure. As in the past, today's LDCs lack support services critical to industrial development. These include transportation, communications, and domestic sources of equipment, tools, and machines needed to build and operate new factories. LDCs also lack universities capable of training factory managers, accountants, and other technical people needed for industrial development. LDCs obtain support services by importing advisers and materials from other countries or by borrowing money to develop domestic sources.

New Problems for LDCs

In addition, industrializing countries now face a new obstacle. New factories once could count on selling in countries that lacked competing industries. But few untapped foreign markets remain to be exploited. New industries must sell primarily to consumers inside their own country—often a market too small to support them—or compete with existing manufacturers in other countries.

Considering the obstacles to launching new industries for which market access is critical, what kind of factories can LDCs attract? According to principles of economic geography, there are two other critical locational factors: access to raw materials and site factors. In fact, new African factories generally are those for which these factors are important:

With one-fifth of the world's population and rising incomes, China has become attractive for market-oriented producers. If only one percent of the Chinese people traded in their bicycles for cars, for example, China would become the world's second-largest car market (behind only the United States). (Alain le Garsmeur/Tony Stone Worldwide)

1. Raw material access. Bauxite in Guinea, uranium in Niger, iron ore in Mauritania and Liberia, and copper in Zambia are processed for industrial uses elsewhere in the world. African countries also process food and agricultural products, such as palm and peanut oil, flour, and beer. Fertilizer is produced from phosphate or nitrate deposits in Côte d'Ivoire, Mozambique, Senegal, Uganda, Zambia, and Zimbabwe.

2. Site factors. Most critical usually is cheap, abundant labor. The textile and clothing industries still consider low-cost labor to be their most critical site-selection factor. Consequently, manufacturers that migrated from New England to the Southeast earlier this century have migrated again to Asia, Latin America, and Africa. Workers in LDCs receive a fraction of U.S. wages. For example, the Bata Company now has shoe factories in Sudan, Zambia, Nigeria, Côte d'Ivoire, and Cameroon.

Transnational corporations have been especially aggressive in using low-cost labor in LDCs. To remain competitive in the global economy, they carefully review their production processes to identify steps that can be performed by low-paid, low-skilled workers in LDCs. Given the substantial difference in wages between MDCs and LDCs, transnational corporations can profitably transfer some work to LDCs, despite greater transportation cost. At the same time, operations that require highly skilled workers remain in factories in MDCs. This selective transfer of some jobs to LDCs is known as the **new international division of labor.**

Many African countries possess iron ore. But steel, perhaps the most important industry for a less developed country, has had difficulty getting a foothold in Africa. The only large, integrated steel mill in Africa south of the Sahara and north of South Africa is in Zimbabwe. (Small plants have been established in Nigeria, Ghana, Uganda, Zaire, and Ethiopia, using scrap metal as the input.) Without cooperation among several small states, steel manufacturing is not likely to develop further in Africa.

Summary These again are the key issues in the geography of industry.

1. How did industrialization originate and diffuse?

The industrial revolution dates from the late 1700s in Great Britain, when a series of inventions transformed industrial production. By 1900, only four other countries could be classified as industrial: Belgium, France, Germany, and the United States. During the twentieth century, industrialization diffused to several dozen other countries in Europe, Asia, and the Western Hemisphere.

2. How is industry distributed worldwide?

In contrast to agriculture, which covers a large percentage of Earth's land area, industry is highly concentrated. Approximately three-fourths of the world's industrial output is concentrated in four regions: the North American manufacturing belt, Western Europe, Eastern Europe and Russia, and Japan.

3. What factors influence the choice of location for a factory?

Factories try to identify a location where production cost is minimized. Critical industrial location costs include situation factors for some firms and site factors for others. Situation factors involve the cost of transporting both inputs into the factory and products from the factory to consumers. Site factors—land, labor, and capital—control the cost of doing business at a location.

4. What industrial problems do countries face?

The whole world faces a problem with industry because global capacity to produce many goods now exceeds demand. MDCs in North America and Western Europe have a distinctive problem that results from an uneven internal distribution of industry and wealth. LDCs, located farther from markets, must attract industries for which access to inputs and low-cost labor are critical.

CASE STUDY REVISITED
Free Trade in North America

Three recent changes in the structure of manufacturing have geographic consequences.

1. Factories have become more productive through introduction of new machinery and processes. A factory may continue to operate at the same location but require fewer workers to produce the same output. Faced with meager prospects of getting another job in the same community, workers laid off at these factories migrate to other regions.

2. Companies are locating production in communities where workers are willing to adopt more-flexible work rules. Firms are especially attracted to smaller towns where low

levels of union membership and high visibility reduce vulnerability to work stoppages, even if wages are kept low and lay-offs become necessary.

3. By spreading production among many countries, or among many communities within one country, large corporations have increased their bargaining power with local governments and labor forces. Production can be allocated to locations where the local government is especially helpful and generous in subsidizing the costs of expansion and the local residents are especially eager to work in the plant.

Competition to attract new industries and to retain existing ones extends across international borders. The governments of Canada, Mexico, and the United States have agreed to eliminate barriers to free trade among the three countries. As competition increases among regional blocs of countries, U.S. and Canadian business and government leaders see substantial benefits to including Mexico in a free trade zone. With the addition of Mexico and other Latin American countries, the North American free trade area can rival the European Union as the world's most populous and wealthy market.

But creating an integrated North American economy is a formidable task, given the substantially lower standard of living in Mexico and Latin America than in the United States and Canada. U.S. and Canadian labor union leaders are concerned that with the removal of barriers, more manufacturers will relocate production to Mexico to take advantage of lower wage rates. Such labor-intensive industries as food processing and textile manufacturing may be especially attracted to a region where prevailing wage rates are lower.

Environmentalists fear that under a free trade agreement, firms will move production to Mexico, where laws governing air and water quality standards are less stringent than in the United States and Canada. Mexico has adopted regulations to reduce air pollution in Mexico City; catalytic converters were required on Mexican automobiles beginning in 1991. But enforcement of environmental protection laws is still lax in Mexico.

According to industrial location theory, firms select locations for various situation and site factors. Wage rates and environmental controls are two important factors, but such factors as access to markets and access to skilled workers are also critical. Geography's global perspective in analyzing industrial location reinforces the fact that the problems of an unemployed steelworker in Gary or Youngstown are not just local but are related to worldwide characteristics of the steel industry. The future health of industry in the United States depends on a national commitment to a combination of competition and cooperation in a global economy.

To recapture competitiveness with other nations' industries, North American business leaders must learn more about the culture, politics, and economy of other nations. The success enjoyed by Japanese and Korean businesses in North America derives to a considerable extent from the fact that executives in those countries know more about U.S. society than Americans know about Asia. Asian officials are likely to speak English and are familiar with the tastes and preferences of American consumers, whereas few American officials speak Japanese or Korean, and they have relatively little knowledge of the buying habits of Asians.

At the same time, global industrial development depends on increased cooperation among different nations. As a result of lower transportation cost, more people worldwide have access to more goods at lower prices than in the past. Given this trend, consumers in industrialized countries are increasingly challenged to choose between buying the highest-quality, lowest-cost goods regardless of where they were made and supporting local industries against foreign competitors at any price.

Key Terms

Break-of-bulk point A location where transfer is possible from one mode of transportation to another.

Bulk-gaining industry An industry in which the final product weighs more or has a greater volume than the inputs.

Bulk-reducing industry An industry in which the final product weighs less or has a lower volume than the inputs.

Cottage industry Manufacturing based in homes rather than in a factory, commonly found before the industrial revolution.

Fordist Form of mass production in which each worker is assigned one specific task to perform repeatedly.

Labor-intensive industry An industry for which labor costs constitute a high percentage of total expenses.

Maquiladora Factories built by U.S. companies in Mexico near the U.S. border, to take advantage of much lower labor costs in Mexico.

New international division of labor Transfer of some types of jobs, especially those requiring low-paid less-skilled workers, from more developed to less developed countries.

Post-fordist Form of production in which workers operate under flexible work rules and may be required to perform a variety of tasks as part of a team of workers.

Right-to-work state A U.S. state that has passed a law preventing a union and company from negotiating a contract that requires workers to join a union as a condition of employment.

Site factors Location factors related to the costs of factors of production inside the plant, such as land, labor, and capital.

Situation factors Location factors related to the transportation of materials into and from a factory.

Textile A fabric made by weaving, used in making clothing.

Transnational corporation A company that operates factories in countries other than the one in which its headquarters are located.

Thinking Geographically

1. What have been the benefits and costs to Canada of its free trade agreement with the United States? How are the benefits and costs to Canada likely to change with the implementation of NAFTA?

2. To induce Toyota to build its U.S. production facilities in Kentucky, the state spent $49 million to buy the 1,500-acre site ($32,667/acre), $40 million to construct roads and sewers, and $68 million to train new workers. Kentucky also agreed to spend up to $168 million to pay the interest on loans should Toyota decide to borrow money to finance the project. Did Kentucky overpay to win Toyota's business? Explain.

3. Foreign cars account for one-fourth of car sales in the midwestern United States, compared with half in California and other West Coast states. What factors might account for this regional difference?

4. Draw a large triangle on a map of Russia, with one point near Moscow, one point in the Ural Mountains, and one point in Central Asia. What are the principal economic assets of the three regions at each side of the triangle? How do the distributions of markets, resources, and surplus labor vary within Russia?

5. What are the principal manufacturers in your community or area? How have they been affected by increasing global competition?

Further Readings

Amin, Ash, and John Goddard, eds. *Technological Change, Industrial Restructuring, and Regional Development.* London: Allen and Unwin, 1986.

Ashton, Thomas S. *The Industrial Revolution.* New York: Oxford University Press, 1964.

Bagchi-Sen, Sharmistha, and Bruce Wm. Pigozzi. "Occupational and Industrial Diversification in the Metropolitan Space Economy in the United States, 1985–1990." *Professional Geographer* 45 (February 1993): 44–54.

Blackbourn, Anthony, and Robert G. Putnam. *The Industrial Geography of Canada.* New York: St. Martin's Press, 1984.

Bluestone, Barry, and Bennett Harrison. *The Deindustrialization of America: Plant Closings, Community Abandonment, and the Dismantling of Basic Industry.* New York: Basic Books, 1982.

Brotchie, John F., Peter Hall, and Peter W. Newton, eds. *The Spatial Impact of Technological Change.* London: Croom Helm, 1987.

Casetti, Emilio, and John Paul Jones III. "Spatial Aspects of the Productivity Slowdown: An Analysis of U.S. Manufacturing Data." *Annals of the Association of American Geographers* 77 (March 1987): 76–88.

Dicken, Peter. *Global Shift: Industrial Change in a Turbulent World.* 2nd ed. London: Harper & Row, 1991.

———, and Nigel Thrift. "The Organization of Production and the Production of Organization: Why Business Enterprises Matter in the Study of Geographical Industrialization." *Transactions of British Geographers,* New Series 17 (1992): 279–91.

Duncan, Simon. "The Geography of Gender Divisions of Labour in Britain." *Transactions of British Geographers,* New Series, no. 16 (1991): 420–29.

Earney, F. C. F. "The Geopolitics of Minerals." *Focus* 31 (May–June 1981): 1–16.

Erickson, Rodney A., and David J. Hayward. "The International Flows of Industrial Exports from U.S. Regions." *Annals of the Association of American Geographers* 81 (September 1991): 371–90.

Ettlinger, Nancy. "The Roots of Competitive Advantage in California and Japan." *Annals of the Association of American Geographers* 81 (September 1991): 391–407.

Gillespie, A. E., ed. *Technological Change and Regional Development.* London: Pion, 1983.

Glasmeier, Amy K. *The High-Tech Potential: Economic Development in Rural America.* New Brunswick, NJ: Center for Urban Policy Research, 1991.

———, Jeffery W. Thompson, and Amy J. Kays. "The Geography of Trade Policy: Trade Regimes and Location Decisions in the Textile and Apparel Complex." *Transactions of the Institute of British Geographers,* New Series 18 (1993): 19–35.

Gould, Peter. *Spatial Diffusion.* Washington, DC: Association of American Geographers, 1969.

Hamilton, F. E. Ian, ed. *Contemporary Industrialization.* London and New York: Longman, 1978.

———, and G. J. R. Linge, eds. *Spatial Analysis, Industry and the Industrial Environment: Progress in Research and Applications. Volume I: Industrial Systems* (1979); *Volume II: International Industrial Systems* (1981); *Volume 3: Regional Economies and Industrial Systems* (1983). Chichester, England: Wiley.

Harris, C. D. "The Market as a Factor in the Localization of Industry in the United States." *Annals of the Association of American Geographers* 44 (December 1954): 315–48.

Hoare, Anthony G. *The Location of Industry in Britain.* New York: Cambridge University Press, 1983.

———. "What Do They Make, Where, and Does It Matter Any More? Regional Industrial Structures in Britain Since the Great War." *Geography* 7 (October 1986): 289–304.

Hogan, William T. *Global Steel in the 1990s: Growth or Decline.* Lexington, MA: Lexington Books, 1991.

———. *Minimills and Integrated Mills: A Comparison of Steelmaking in the United States.* Lexington, MA: Lexington Books, 1987.

Langton, John. "The Industrial Revolution and the Regional Geography of England." *Transactions of the Institute of British Geographers,* New Series, 9, no. 2 (1984): 145–67.

———, and R. J. Morris, eds. *Atlas of Industrializing Britain, 1780–1914.* London: Methuen, 1986.

Law, Christopher M, ed. *Restructuring the Global Automobile Industry.* London: Routledge, 1991.

Massey, Doreen, and Richard Meegan, eds. *Politics and Method: Contrasting Studies in Industrial Geography.* New York: Methuen, 1986.

Oxford University Cartographic Department. *Oxford Economic Atlas: The United States and Canada.* London: Oxford University Press, 1975.

Pattie, Charles J., and R. J. Johnston. "One Nation or Two? The Changing Geography of Unemployment in Great Britain, 1983–1988." *Professional Geographer* 42 (August 1990): 288–98.

Peet, Richard, ed. *International Capitalism and Industrial Restructuring.* Boston: Allen & Unwin, 1987.

Rich, D. C., and G. J. R. Linge, eds. *The State and the Spatial Management of Industrial Change.* New York: Routledge, Chapman, and Hall, 1991.

Rubenstein, James M. *The Changing U.S. Auto Industry*. London: Routledge, 1992.

Sayer, Andrew, and Richard Walker. *The New Social Economy*. Cambridge, MA: Blackwell, 1991.

Schmenner, Roger W. *Making Business Location Decisions*. Englewood Cliffs, NJ: Prentice Hall, 1982.

Scott, Allen J., and Michael Storper, eds. *Production, Work, Territory*. Boston: Allen and Unwin, 1986.

Smith, David M. *Industrial Location: An Economic Geographical Analysis*. 2nd ed. New York: Wiley, 1981.

_____. "A Theoretical Framework for Geographical Studies of Industrial Location." *Economic Geography* 42 (April 1966): 95–113.

South, Robert B. "Transnational *Maquiladora* Location." *Annals of the Association of American Geographers* 80 (December 1990): 529–70.

Storper, Michael, and Richard Walker. *The Capitalist Imperative: Territory, Technology, and Industrial Growth*. New York: Basil Blackwell, 1989.

Toyne, Brian, Jeffrey S. Arpan, David A. Ricks, Terence A. Shimp, and Andy Barnett. *The Global Textile Industry*. London: Allen and Unwin, 1984.

Warren, Kenneth. "World Steel: Change and Crisis." *Geography* 70 (March 1985): 106–17.

Webber, Michael J. *Industrial Location*. Beverly Hills: Sage Publications, 1984.

ZumBrunnen, Craig, and Jeffrey Osleeb. *The Soviet Iron and Steel Industry*. Totowa, NJ: Rowmand and Allanheld, 1986.

Also consult these journals: *Journal of Industrial Economics, Journal of International Economics, Journal of Marketing, Journal of Transport Economics and Policy, Journal of Transport History, Journal of Urban Economics.*

The Annenberg
CPB Project

PEOPLE, PLACES AND CHANGE
Global Firms in the Industrializing East

In the global economy, large multinational corporations locate production facilities in a variety of countries. SGS Thomson, a large electronics firm, with headquarters in France, is a typical example.

Alan Dutheil [SGS Thomson official] — In the electronics industry, research and development are very important. About 90 percent of our R&D is done in Europe. R&D involves several levels. One is working on the silicon itself, on the physics. And most of the advance product development, such as working on a 16-megabyte flash memory, is done in Europe.

Commentator — While the bulk of the company's R&D is in Europe, Singapore is the site of its largest wafter fabrication plant, the front-end work that marks the beginning of life for electronic chips. That left the question as to where to locate the back-end assembly production. The company chose the town of Muar, a previously undeveloped area in Malaysia.

Eugenio Re [SGS Thomson official] — My first trip to Muar was in 1981. In 1981, around our factory was a jungle. Every morning to reach the factory you cross a bridge, and you could find then monkeys on the bridge. Now, no more.

Our workers are young, ranging from 17 to 25. Our workers have come immediately from school or from a plantation.

Commentator — The workers are attracted by wages higher than those elsewhere in the area, but still well below those of Singapore. Women work with state of the art technology to meet the demands of the expanding East Asia market for semiconductors.

11

SETTLEMENTS AND SERVICES

KEY ISSUES

1. Why are settlements established?
2. How did rural and urban settlements evolve?
3. Why do settlements grow?
4. Why are services concentrated in settlements?

Flying across the United States on a clear night, you look down on the lights of settlements, large and small. You see small clusters of lights from villages and towns, and large, brightly lit metropolitan areas. It may appear that the light clusters are random, but geographers discern a regular pattern in them. These regularities have been documented, and concepts from economic geography can be applied to understand why this pattern exists.

The regular distribution observed over North America and over other more developed countries, however, is not seen in less developed countries. Geographers explain this difference and why the absence of a regular pattern is significant.

The regular pattern of settlement in more developed countries reflects where services are provided. In more developed countries, the majority of the work force provides services. But worldwide, less than 10 percent of the labor force provides services.

SAN GIORGIO MAGGIORE CHURCH AND GRAND CANAL, VENICE, ITALY. (TELEGRAPH COLOUR LIBRARY/FPG INTERNATIONAL)

Obtaining Goods in Romania

The Preda family lives in Comena, a Romanian village of 800 inhabitants. The Predas are farmers, working the fields outside the village, earning just enough to survive without hardship. But some goods are hard to obtain. Because the village has only a few shops, Elena Preda must travel for an hour by bus to a larger town to buy everything she needs.

Romania lacks cities of certain sizes. The largest city, Bucharest, has 2 million inhabitants, and the second-largest, Braşov, has 350,000. In a country with a higher level of economic development, geographers expect to find at least four cities between 350,000 and 2 million inhabitants, but Romania has none. Geographers also expect to find more towns with population between 1,000 and 10,000 than Romania has.

The scarcity of cities with 350,000 to 2 million inhabitants and of towns with 1,000 to 10,000 inhabitants constitutes a hardship for people who must travel long distances to reach an urban settlement with shops and such services as hospitals. Because most Romanians do not have cars, the government must provide bus service for people to reach larger towns. A trip to a shop or a doctor that takes a few minutes in the United States could take several hours in Romania.

The state of Colorado is comparable in land area to Romania. Colorado's largest metropolitan area, Denver (including Boulder) has about the same number of inhabitants as Bucharest, and Colorado Springs, the state's second-largest metropolitan area, has about the same number of inhabitants as Braşov. But the absence of cities with 350,000 to 2 million inhabitants is not a hardship in Colorado; access to urban services is much greater in Colorado than in Romania, because virtually all Coloradans—including those living in rural areas—either own or have access to a car or truck. Life in rural Colorado would be much harder if most residents depended on public buses to transport them to shops and jobs.

Few people live in isolation. Most reside in some form of **settlement**, a permanent collection of buildings and inhabitants. Settlements occupy a very small percentage of Earth's surface, well under 1 percent, but they exert great influence on economy and culture. Settlements are places to work and to obtain goods and services. Settlements also are nodes of storage for the world's cultural and economic wealth. And settlements are hearths for the diffusion of innovative economic and cultural ideas.

Geographers distinguish between urban and rural settlements because each has distinctive characteristics. This chapter examines the origin and evolution of rural and urban settlements, as well as the recent rapid growth and economic restructuring of urban settlements. The next chapter looks at the internal structure of urban settlements.

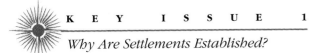

K E Y   I S S U E   1

Why Are Settlements Established?

- Cultural Reasons
- Economic Reasons

Contemporary settlements exist primarily to serve economic functions. But the earliest settlements were probably established for other reasons. To understand why, picture conditions at the time. People were nomadic, migrating in small groups across the landscape in search of food and water. They gathered wild berries and roots or killed wild animals for food. Why would these nomadic groups establish permanent settlements? No one knows the precise sequence of events through which settlements were established, because they occurred before recorded history, but analysts offer two explanations: cultural and economic.

Cultural Reasons

On the basis of archaeological research, we can deduce that most settlements probably originated for cultural rather than economic reasons. The earliest settlements may have been established for religious, nurturing, political, or military reasons.

A Religious Place

The first permanent settlements may have been places to bury the dead. Perhaps nomadic groups had rituals honoring the deceased, including memorial services on the anniversary of a death. Having established a permanent resting place for the dead, the group might then install priests at the site to perform ceremonies.

This practice would have encouraged the building of structures for ceremonies and dwellings for the priests. By the time recorded history began around 5,000 years ago, many settlements existed, and some featured a temple. In fact, until the invention of skyscrapers in the late nineteenth century, religious buildings were often the tallest structures in a community.

A Place to Nurture Families

Settlements also may have been places to house families, permitting unburdened males to travel farther and faster in their search for food. Women kept "home and hearth," making household objects, such as pots, tools, and clothing. Children were educated in settlements. Making pots and educating children may have originated for practical reasons, but over thousands of years these activities have provided the basis for creation and transmission of a group's values and heritage. Today, settlements contain society's schools, libraries, museums, and archives—permanent repositories for passing knowledge from one generation to the next.

In less developed countries, rural settlements often contain a high percentage of women and children. Men are more likely to migrate to large cities or to other countries in search of employment, leaving behind their wives and children in the villages.

A Protected Place

The group's political leaders also chose to live permanently in the settlement, which may have been located for strategic reasons, to protect the group's land claims. Everyone in a settlement was vulnerable to attack from other groups, so for protection, some members became soldiers, stationed in the settlement. The settlement likely was a good base from which the group could defend nearby food sources against competitors.

For defense, the group might surround the settlement with a wall. Defenders were stationed at

Medieval European cities were often surrounded by walls for protection. The walls have been demolished in most places, but they still stand around the old center of Carcassonne, in southwestern France. A small portion of the modern industrial city of 40,000 can be seen at far right. (Jonathan Blair/Woodfin Camp & Associates)

small openings or atop the wall, giving them a great advantage over attackers. Thus, settlements became citadels—centers of military power. Walls proved an extremely effective defense for thousands of years, until warfare was revolutionized by the introduction of gunpowder in Europe in the 1300s. Even though cannonballs could destroy walls, they continued to be built around cities. Paris, for example, surrounded itself with new fortifications as recently as the 1840s and did not completely remove them until 1932 (Figure 11-1).

Although modern settlements no longer have walls, their military and political functions continue to be important. The largest structure in our nation's capital—the Pentagon—houses the U.S. Department of Defense. Similarly, Russian military leaders work in the Kremlin, which is the medieval walled area of central Moscow.

Economic Reasons

Everyone in settlements needed food, which was supplied by the group through hunting or gathering. At some point, someone probably wondered: why not bring in extra food for hard times, such as drought or conflict? This is likely how the econom-

ic role of settlements began—as a *warehousing center* to store extra food.

Through centuries of experiments and accidents, people realized that some of the wild vegetation they had gathered could generate food if deliberately placed in the ground and nursed to maturity—in other words, agriculture. The settlement might then become an *agricultural center*, as explained in Chapter 9. Eventually, people were able to produce most of their food through deliberate agricultural practices. They no longer had to survive through hunting and gathering.

People also needed tools, clothing, shelter, containers, fuel, and other material goods. Settlements therefore became *manufacturing centers*. Men gathered the materials needed to make a variety of objects, including stones for tools and weapons, grass for containers and matting, animal hair for clothing, and wood for shelter and heat. Women used these materials to manufacture household objects and maintain their dwellings.

Not all groups had access to the same resources, because of the varied distribution of vegetation, animals, fuelwood, and mineral resources across the landscape. The settlement therefore was likely to take on yet another function and become a *trading*

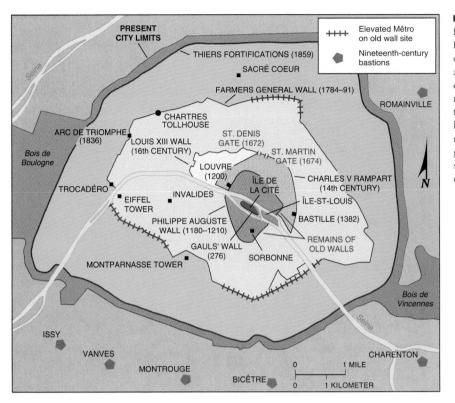

FIGURE 11-1 The growth of Paris from the third century to the present. Paris was surrounded by a wall, originally for protection. Periodically, a new wall (*barrière*) would be constructed to encompass new neighborhoods that had grown on the periphery. Highways and parks have been built on the sites of the nineteenth-century walls. The old gates of St. Denis and St. Martin still stand, although the walls have been demolished.

center. People brought objects and materials they collected or produced into the settlement and exchanged them for items brought by others. People could also trade services—one person could be skilled at repairing tools, another at training horses.

The settlement served as neutral ground where several groups could safely come together to trade goods and services. To facilitate this trade, officials in the settlement provided such services as regulating the terms of transactions, setting fair prices, keeping records, and creating a currency system.

K E Y   I S S U E   2

How Did Rural and Urban Settlements Evolve?

- Rural Settlements
- Urban Settlements

Settlements have evolved primarily to provide two types of economic activities: some have become centers for agriculture, and others have become centers for manufacturing, warehousing, and trading goods and services. Agriculture is the predominant economic activity in communities that we now call **rural settlements**. Manufacturing, warehousing, and trading goods and services are the main economic activities in **urban settlements**. We will now take a look at each type, and explore their differences.

Rural Settlements

Worldwide, most settlements are rural rather than urban, because most people survive by farming rather than by manufacturing or trading. Even in developed societies such as the United States, where most people work in manufacturing or services, rural settlements remain numerous, although their percentage of the total population living in them is small. Rural settlements are arranged in two patterns: clustered and dispersed.

Clustered Rural Settlements

Several families may live in a clustered rural settlement and work in the surrounding fields. Such a **clustered rural settlement** typically includes barns, tool sheds, and other farm structures, plus homes, re-

FIGURE 11-2 Satellite settlements. The rural landscape reflects the historical pattern of growth through establishment of satellite settlements. On the map, note the numerous places with "Offley" in their name. The parish of Offley is in Hestfordshire, England, north of London.

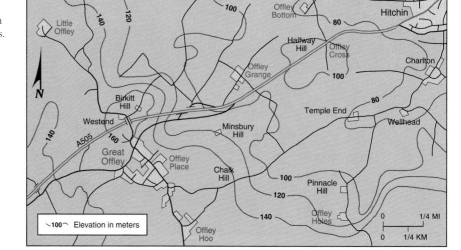

ligious structures, schools, and supporting services. In common language, such a settlement is called a *hamlet* or *village.*

Each person living in a clustered rural settlement is allocated strips of land in the surrounding fields. The fields must be accessible to the farmers and thus generally are limited to a radius of 1 or 2 kilometers (1/2 or 1 mile) from the buildings. The strips of land are allocated in different ways. In some places, individual farmers own or rent the land; in other places, the land is owned collectively by the settlement or by a lord, and farmers do not control the choice of crops or use of the output.

Parcels of land surrounding the settlement may be allocated to specific agricultural activities, either because of land characteristics or because of decisions by the inhabitants. Consequently, farmers typically own, or have responsibility for, a collection of scattered parcels in several fields. This pattern of controlling several fragmented parcels of land has encouraged living in a clustered rural settlement to minimize travel time to the various fields.

Traditionally, when the population of a settlement grew too large for the capacity of the surrounding fields, new settlements were established nearby. This was possible because not all land was under cultivation.

The establishment of satellite settlements often is reflected in place names. For example, the parish of Offley, in Hertfordshire, England, contains these rural settlements: Great Offley (the largest), Little Offley,

Most rural settlements in Africa, like this one in Côte d'Ivoire, are clustered. Houses and farm structures are built close to each other, and the fields and grazing land surround the settlement. (Marc & Evelyne Bernheim/Woodfin Camp & Associates)

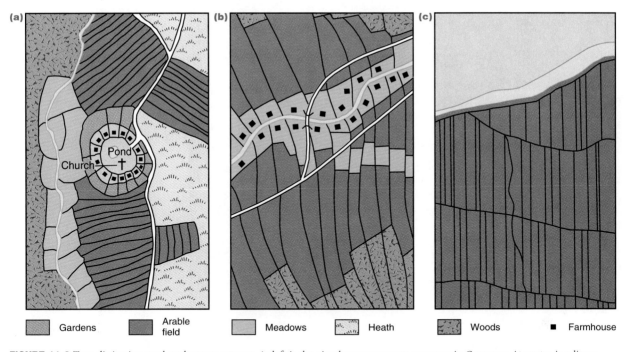

| | Gardens | | Arable field | | Meadows | | Heath | | Woods | ■ | Farmhouse |

FIGURE 11-3 Two distinctive rural settlement patterns. At left is the circular arrangement common in Germany. At center is a linear arrangement called "long-lot," used in France, which gives everyone access to the river. When French settlers came to America, the long-lot system came with them, as shown at right, in Québec.

Offley Grange (barn), Offley Cross, Offley Bottom, Offley Place, Offley Hoo (house), and Offley Holes (Figure 11-2). All are within a few kilometers of each other. The name "Offley" means the wooded clearing of Offa, who was a ruler of Mercia (see Figure 4-13) during the eighth century and is said to have died at the site of the settlement.

Homes, public buildings, and fields in a clustered rural settlement are arranged according to local cultural and physical characteristics. Clustered rural settlements are often arranged in one of two types of patterns: circular and linear.

Circular Rural Settlements. The circular form consists of a central open space surrounded by structures (Figure 11-3). The kraal villages in southern Africa have enclosures for livestock in the center, surrounded by a ring of houses (compare our English word *corral*). In East Africa, the Masai people, who are pastoral nomads, built kraal settlements as camps; women had principal responsibility for constructing them.

The German *Gewandorf* settlement consisted of a core of houses, barns, and churches, encircled by

different types of agricultural activities. Small garden plots were located in the first ring surrounding the village, with cultivated land, pastures, and woodlands in successive rings. Von Thünen observed this circular rural pattern in his landmark agricultural studies in the early nineteenth century (see Chapter 9).

Linear Rural Settlements. Linear rural settlements feature buildings clustered along a road, river, or dike, to facilitate communications. The fields extend behind the buildings in long, narrow strips. Today in North America, linear rural settlements exist in areas settled by the French. The French settlement pattern, called *long-lot* or *seigneurial*, was commonly used along the St. Lawrence River in Québec and the lower Mississippi River (Figure 11-3).

In the French long-lot system, houses were erected along a river, which was the principal water source and means of communication. Narrow lots from 5 to 100 kilometers deep (3 to 60 miles) were established perpendicular to the river, so that each original settler had access to the river. This arrangement created a linear settlement along the river.

New England rural settlements, such as Chelsea, Vermont, a village of 1,000 inhabitants, were originally organized around a common green and church. With population growth and modernization of agriculture, the village and surrounding land were turned over to individual private ownership. (John M. Roberts/Stock Montage, Inc.)

Eventually, these long, narrow lots were subdivided. French law required that all sons inherit an equal portion of an estate, so the heirs established separate farms in each division. Roads were constructed parallel to the river for access to inland farms. In this way, a new linear settlement emerged along each road, parallel to the original riverfront settlement.

Dispersed Rural Settlements

In the past 200 years, dispersed rural settlements have become more common, especially in Anglo-America and the United Kingdom, because in more developed societies they are generally considered more efficient than clustered settlements. **Dispersed rural settlement** patterns are characterized by farmers living on isolated farms rather than in villages.

To improve agricultural production, some European countries converted their rural landscapes from clustered settlements to dispersed patterns. A prominent example was the **enclosure movement** in Great Britain between 1750 and 1850. The British government transformed the rural landscape by consolidating individually owned strips of land surrounding a village into a single large farm owned by an individual. When necessary, the government forced people to give up their former holdings.

The benefit of enclosure was greater agricultural efficiency, because a farmer did not have to waste time scurrying among discontinuous fields. With the introduction of farm machinery, farms operated more efficiently at a larger scale. Because the enclosure movement coincided with the industrial revolution, villagers who were displaced from farming moved to urban settlements and became workers in factories and services.

The enclosure movement brought greater agricultural efficiency, but it destroyed the self-contained world of village life. Village populations declined drastically as displaced farmers moved to urban settlements. Some villages became the centers of the new, larger farms, but villages that were not centrally located to a new farm's extensive land holdings were abandoned and replaced with entirely new farmsteads at more strategic locations. As a result, the isolated, dispersed farmstead, unknown in medieval England, is now a common feature of that country's rural landscape.

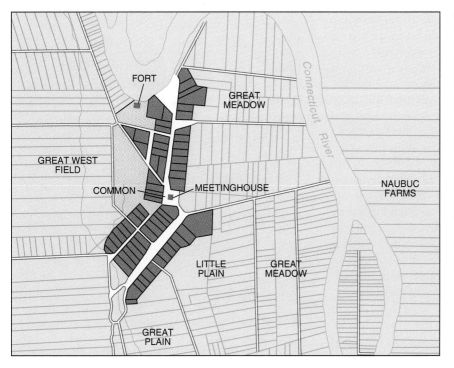

FIGURE 11-4 Traditional seventeenth-century New England village. The practical needs of early settlers were reflected in this typical layout of Wethersfield, Connecticut, in 1640. The layout also reflected the customs of the settlers' rural English heritage. Note the central common area, or "green," with its meetinghouse. Surrounded by close-packed homes, the common was a secure place to graze cattle. Outside the town was a fort (relations with Native Americans were at times unfriendly) and there were plains and meadows where crops were cultivated. This layout was typical of early New England villages, but it changed as population increased.

The first European colonists settled America's East Coast in three regions: New England, the Southeast, and the Middle Atlantic. The colonists in each of the three areas came from different places in Europe and for different reasons. Each brought their distinctive religion, language, political view, and individual farming experience. These backgrounds resulted in a variety of colonial rural settlement patterns, which we will now examine.

New England Rural Settlements. The rural landscape in New England reflects its settlement by groups who left England in the 1600s. They left primarily to gain religious freedom or for other cultural reasons. Typically, a group was granted land of 4 to 10 square miles (10 to 25 square kilometers) by the English government. They then traveled to America to settle the land. In each group, most came from the same English village and belonged to the same church. Once in the colony, members of the group stayed close to each other to reinforce their common cultural and religious values and for protection.

Such groups simulated the arrangement they knew in England: a clustered settlement, which they built near the center of the land grant. The village center usually had an open area called the *common*. Settlers grouped their homes and public buildings, such as the church and school, around the common. In addition to their houses, each settler had a home lot of 1 to 5 acres (1/2 to 2 hectares), which contained a barn, garden, and enclosures for feeding livestock (Figure 11-4).

This clustered pattern also was encouraged by the central role of the church in daily activities. The settlement's leader often was an official of the Puritan church. Land was not sold, but rather was *awarded* to an individual after the town's residents felt confident that the recipient would work hard. Outsiders could obtain land in the settlement only through permission of the town's residents. Colonists also favored clustered settlements for defense against Indian attacks.

The diversity of topography, soil, and drainage in the New England landscape led to a complex division of land ownership. Each villager owned several discontinuous parcels outside the village to provide the variety of land types needed for different crops. Beyond the fields, the town held pastures and woodland for the common use of all residents.

The clustered village system was appropriate for the original small, stable groups. But by the 1700s, a more dispersed distribution began to replace the clustered settlements in New England. There were two reasons: population increase and economic development. Population increased through the excess of births over deaths and through net in-migration. The problem was that villages had no spare land to offer newcomers. The solution was to establish a new village nearby. As in the older settlements, the new village contained a central common surrounded by houses and public buildings, home lots, and outer fields. However, the shortage of land eventually forced new arrivals to strike out alone and claim farmland on the frontier.

At the same time, demand for more efficient agricultural practices led to a redistribution of farmland. People bought, sold, and exchanged land to create large, continuous holdings instead of several isolated pieces. The old system of discontinuous fields had several disadvantages: farmers lost time moving between fields; villagers had to build more roads to connect the small lots; and farmers had been restricted in what they could plant.

Descendants of the original settlers grew less interested in the religious and cultural values that had unified the original immigrants. They permitted people to buy land regardless of their religious affiliation. The cultural bonds that had created clustered rural settlements had weakened.

The New England landscape today contains remnants of the old clustered rural settlement pattern. Many New England towns still have a central common surrounded by the church, school, and various houses. But the contemporary New England town is little more than a picturesque shell of a clustered rural settlement, because today's residents work in factories, shops, and offices, rather than on farms.

Southeastern Rural Settlements. The southeastern colonies were first settled in the 1600s with small, dispersed farms. Then a different style emerged, called a **plantation**, a large farm that used many workers to produce tobacco and cotton for sale in Europe and the northern colonies. Plantations grew more profitable in the 1700s when the tobacco and cotton markets expanded and two large sources of labor were identified. These were *indentured whites*, who were legally bound to work for the plantation for a period of time, and *black slaves* forcibly transported from Africa and sold to the plantation owner.

The plantation's wealthy owner lived in a large mansion, frequently facing a body of water. Surrounding the mansion were service buildings, in-

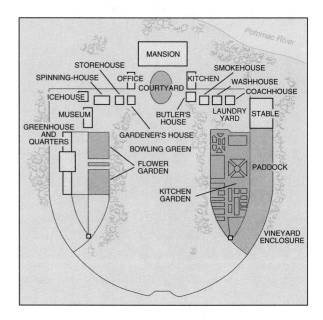

FIGURE 11-5 Southeastern plantation. George Washington's restored home at Mount Vernon, Virginia, illustrates the arrangement of buildings in a southern U.S. plantation. Flanking the main house are other structures, including kitchens, slave quarters, and storehouses.

cluding a laundry, kitchen, dairy, and bakery. Other buildings on the estate included a flour mill, carpenter shop, stables, coach house, and living quarters for the slaves (Figure 11-5).

Middle Atlantic Rural Settlements. The Middle Atlantic colonies were settled by a more heterogeneous group of people. In addition to English, they included immigrants from Germany, Holland, Ireland, Scotland, and Sweden. Further, most Middle Atlantic colonists came as individuals rather than as members of a cohesive religious or cultural group. Some bought tracts of land from speculators. Others acquired land directly from individuals who had been given large land grants by the British government, including William Penn (Pennsylvania), Lord Baltimore (Maryland), and Sir George Carteret (the Carolinas).

Inhabitants of the Middle Atlantic colonies were the main font for pioneers to the American West. They crossed the Appalachian Mountains and established dispersed farms on the frontier. Land was plentiful and cheap, and people bought as much as they could manage. As new agricultural practices favored larger farms, the settlement pattern in the American Midwest became more dispersed.

Urban Settlements

A majority of Earth's population still resides in rural settlements, but the percentage in urban settlements is rapidly increasing. At current rates, urbanites will constitute a majority within a few years. This transition from rural to urban settlements reflects a shift in the way people earn a living—a shift from agriculture to manufacturing and services.

Before modern times, virtually all settlements were rural, because the economy was based on the agriculture of the surrounding fields. Retailers and service providers met the needs of farmers living in the village. But urban settlements are nothing new and have existed for thousands of years, primarily as trading, administrative, and military centers.

Ancient Ur

Among the oldest well-documented urban settlements is Ur in Mesopotamia (present-day Iraq). Ur, which means "fire," was the settlement that Abraham inhabited before his journey to Canaan in approximately 1900 B.C. Archaeologists have unearthed ruins in Ur that date from approximately 3000 B.C. (Figure 11-6).

Archaeological expeditions have unearthed ruins in Ur from that period. The settlement was compact, perhaps covering 100 hectares (250 acres), and was

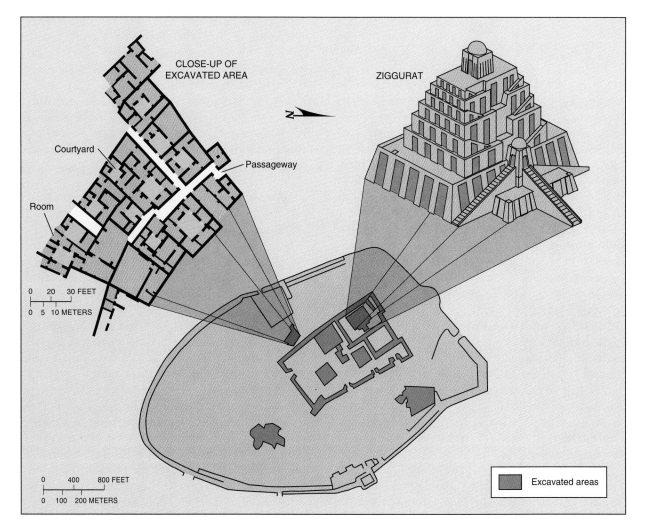

FIGURE 11-6 The remains of Ur in present-day Iraq. Excavation here has provided evidence of early urban civilization. The most prominent building was the stepped temple at right, called a ziggurat. Surrounding the ziggurat was a dense network of small residences built around courtyards and opening onto narrow passageways. The excavation site was damaged during the 1991 war in the Persian Gulf.

surrounded by a wall. The most prominent structure was a temple, known as a *ziggurat*, originally a three-story structure with a base of 64 by 46 meters (210 by 150 feet) and the upper stories stepped back. Four more stories were added in the sixth century B.C. Surrounding the ziggurat were residential areas containing a dense network of narrow winding streets and courtyards (Figure 11-6).

Settlements also date from the beginning of documented history elsewhere in Mesopotamia and in Egypt, the Indus Valley, and China. Settlements may have developed independently in each of these areas, or they may have diffused from Mesopotamia. In any case, from these four centers the concept of urban settlements diffused to the rest of the world.

Urban Settlements in Europe

Settlements were first established in the eastern Mediterranean around 2500 B.C. The oldest include Knossos on the island of Crete, Troy in Asia Minor (present-day Turkey), and Mycenae in Greece. These settlements were trading centers for the thousands of islands dotting the Aegean Sea and the eastern Mediterranean. They were organized into **city-states**—independent self-governing communities that included the settlement and nearby surrounding countryside.

The number of urban settlements grew rapidly during the eighth and seventh centuries B.C. Hundreds of new towns were founded throughout the Mediterranean lands. The residents of one settlement would establish a new settlement to fill a gap in trading routes and to open new markets for goods. The diffusion of urban settlements from the eastern Mediterranean westward is well documented. For example, the city-state of Syracuse (in the southeastern part of the island of Sicily) established new settlements in Italy and Sicily between 750 and 700 B.C. Farther west at Marseille, France (then known as Massilia), about 600 B.C., Massilians founded settlements along the coast of present-day Spain during the sixth century B.C.

Athens, the largest city-state in ancient Greece, was probably the first city to attain a population of 100,000. Athens made substantial contributions to the development of culture, philosophy, and other elements of Western civilization. The history of Athens demonstrates that urban settlements have been traditionally distinguished from rural ones not only by economic activities but by a concentration of cultural activities (Figure 11-7).

Rise and Fall of the Roman Empire. The rise of the Roman Empire encouraged urban settlement. With much of Europe, North Africa, and southwestern Asia under Roman rule, settlements were established as administrative, military, and trading centers. Trade was encouraged by new roads and the security the Roman army provided. The city of Rome—the empire's administrative, commercial, and cultural center—grew to at least a quarter-million inhabitants, although some claim that the population may have reached a million. The city's centrality in the empire's communications network was reflected in the old saying, "All roads lead to Rome" (see Figure 5-3).

The fall of the Roman Empire in the fifth century A.D. also saw the decline of urban settlements. Their prosperity had rested on trading in the secure environment of imperial Rome. With the empire fragmented under hundreds of rulers, trade diminished. Large urban settlements shrank or were abandoned. For several hundred years, Europe's cultural heritage was preserved largely in monasteries and isolated rural areas.

Medieval Settlements. Urban life began to revive in Europe in the eleventh century as feudal lords established new urban settlements. They gave residents *charters of rights* to establish independent cities, in exchange for fighting for the lord. Both the lord and urban residents benefited from this arrangement. The lord obtained people to defend his territory at less cost than maintaining a standing army. For their part, urban residents preferred periodic military service to the burden faced by rural serfs, who farmed the lord's land and could keep only a small portion of their own agricultural output.

With their newly won freedom from the relentless burden of rural serfdom, the urban dwellers set about expanding trade. Surplus from the countryside was brought into the city for sale or exchange, and markets were expanded through trade with other free cities. Trade among different urban settlements was enhanced by new roads and more use of rivers. By the 1300s, Europe was covered by a dense network of small market towns serving the needs of particular lords.

The typical medieval European urban settlement was a dense, compact town, frequently surrounded

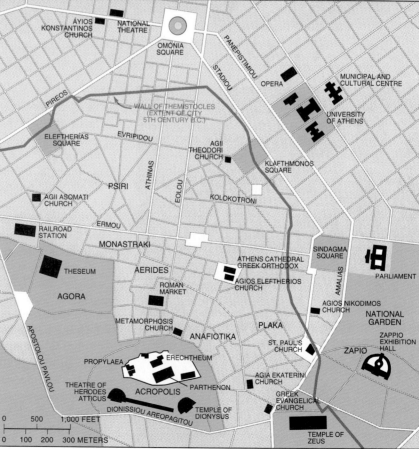

FIGURE 11-7 Athens. The Acropolis dominates the skyline of modern Athens. This is the original hilltop site of the city. Ancient Greeks selected this high place because it is defensible and to erect shrines to their gods. The most prominent structure on the Acropolis is the Parthenon, built in the fifth century B.C. to honor the goddess Athena. The structure to the left of the Parthenon, dating from the same time, is the Propylaea, the only opening in the wall surrounding the Acropolis. At the bottom of the hill is the Theater of Herodes Atticus, named for a wealthy Roman who built it as a memorial to his wife in A.D. 161. (David Pollack/The Stock Market)

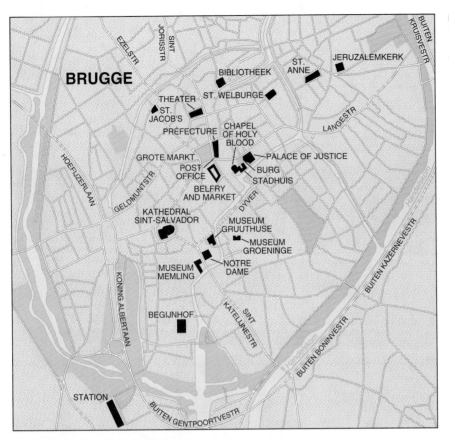

FIGURE 11-8 Modern Brugge, Belgium. Brugge (Bruges in French) is a town of more than 100,000 in western Belgium, near the North Sea coast. Beginning in the twelfth century, Brugge was the most important port in northwestern Europe and a major center for manufacturing wool. However, three events forced the city's decline during the fifteenth century: foreign competitors captured much of the wool industry; the Belgian city of Antwerpen developed a better port; and the river Zwin silted, stranding the town 13 kilometers (8 miles) inland from the North Sea. Typical of medieval towns, the center of Brugge is dominated by squares surrounded by public buildings, churches, and markets. The tower on the right contains the market. The building on the left is the post office and préfecture (government office). (Larry Lee/West Light)

by a wall. Important public buildings, palaces, and churches were arranged around a central market square (Figure 11-8). The tallest and most elaborate structure was usually the church, many of which still dominate the landscape of smaller European towns. Because space for construction within the settlement was lacking, ordinary shops and houses were nestled into the side of the church and surrounding walls.

In modern times, most of these modest medieval buildings have been demolished, and only the more substantial survive. Modern tourists can appreciate the architectural beauty of large medieval churches and palaces, but they do not receive an accurate image of a densely built medieval town.

From the collapse of the Roman Empire until the diffusion of the industrial revolution across Europe during the 1800s, most of the world's largest cities were in Asia, not Europe. Around A.D. 900, the five most populous cities are thought to have included Baghdad (in present-day Iraq), Constantinople (now called Istanbul, in Turkey), Kyoto (in Japan), and Changan and Hangchow (in China). Beijing (China) competed with Constantinople as the world's most populous city for several hundred years, until London claimed the distinction during the early 1800s. Agra (India), Cairo (Egypt), Canton (China), Isfahan (Iran), and Osaka (Japan) also ranked among the world's most populous cities before the industrial revolution.

KEY ISSUE 3

Why Do Settlements Grow?

- The Urbanization Explosion
- Social Differences between Urban and Rural Settlements
- Problems in Defining Urban Settlements

Some urban settlements have existed for thousands of years. But they attracted only a small percentage of a society's total population and rarely exceeded a few thousand inhabitants. Rome, the largest urban settlement of the ancient world, probably had no more people than modern Des Moines, Iowa. Most urban historians estimate that the first settlement to exceed 2 million inhabitants was London, in the early 1800s. Today, more than 100 cities exceed 2 million (Figure 11-9). Today's phenomenon of rapid urban growth on a global scale is a very recent development.

The Urban Explosion

In the past two centuries, the more developed countries have transformed themselves from predominantly rural societies to predominantly urban ones. The greater proportion of urbanites reflects the society's changing economic structure—most jobs are not in farm fields, but in factories, offices, and shops.

Urbanization

Urbanization is the increase in the *number* of urban dwellers combined with an increase in the *percentage* of urban dwellers.

- The increase in the *number* of urban residents results from an overall population increase in the society. As a country's population grows, some of the additional people inevitably live in urban settlements (refer to discussion of demographic transition in Chapter 2).

- Urbanization also means an increasing *percentage* of urban dwellers and a corresponding decrease in rural residents. The percentage of urban dwellers has grown because people have moved from the countryside to work in the factories and services that concentrate in cities.

Urbanization and the Industrial Revolution.

In 1800, only 3 percent of the world's population was urban, compared with more than 40 percent today (Table 11-1). The United Nations estimates that for the first time in human history, the population of urban settlements will exceed that of rural settlements in about the year 2005.

In 1800, as the industrial revolution began to diffuse from Great Britain to Western Europe, only three of the world's ten most populous cities were in Europe—London, Paris, and Naples—and the remainder were in Asia. By 1900, nine of the world's ten most populous cities were in countries that had rapidly industrialized during the 1800s. London, capital of the world's first industrial state, was by far the world's largest city.

The world's ten largest cities in 1900 included six in Europe (London, Paris, Berlin, Vienna, St. Petersburg, Manchester) and three in the United States (New York, Chicago, Philadelphia). Tokyo was the only top-ten city existing in a preindustrial country. As recently as 1950, seven of the ten largest cities in the world remained clustered in MDCs that had industrialized.

To some extent, the traditional relation between urbanization and economic development is still true, because the percentage of the population living in urban settlements is greater in more developed societies. Nearly three-fourths of the population in MDCs live in urban settlements, compared with only one-third in LDCs. This difference in urbanization level is due to economic conditions. The majority of people in LDCs are agricultural workers, who live in rural settlements. In MDCs, manufacturing and service jobs are concentrated in urban settlements.

Global Distribution of Large Cities

Developed countries have the greater percentage of urban residents, but less developed countries increasingly have very large urban settlements. In the 1990s, seven of the ten most populous cities are in LDCs rather than in MDCs (Table 11-2).

FIGURE 11-9 Cities having a population of 2 million or more. The proportion of urban dwellers is greater in more developed countries. The largest urban areas, however, now are mostly in less developed countries. Rapid city growth in LDCs reflects increasing overall population, plus migration from rural areas.

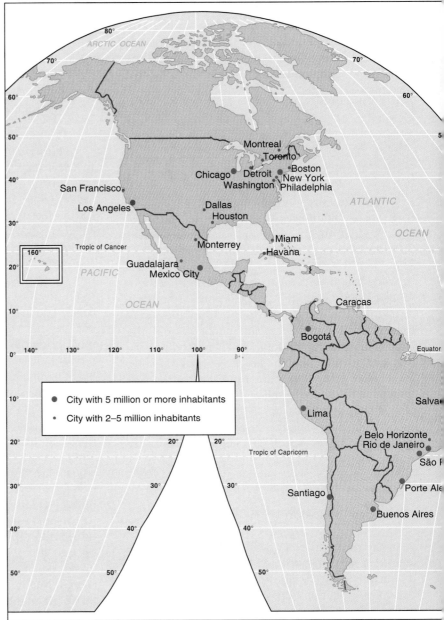

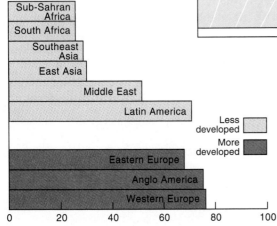

PERCENT URBAN

TABLE 11-1

Percentage of world's population living in urban areas

Year	Percent
1800	3
1850	6
1900	14
1950	30
1995	43

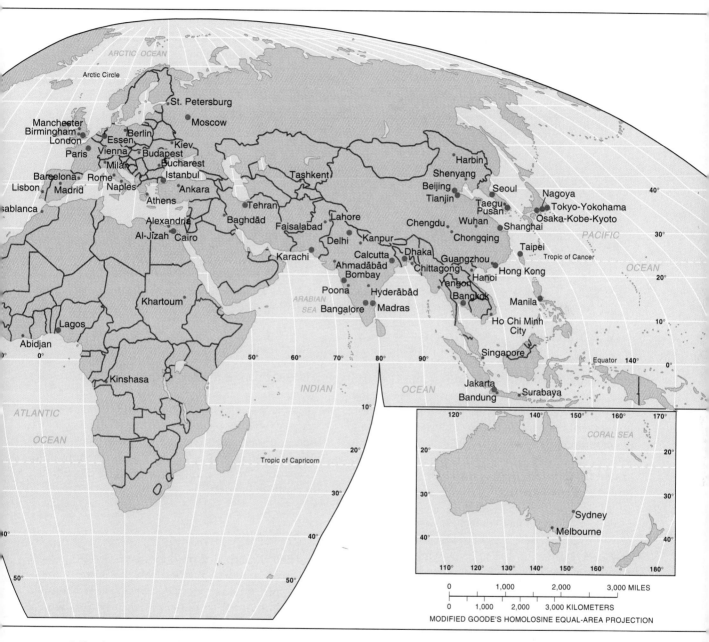

MODIFIED GOODE'S HOMOLOSINE EQUAL-AREA PROJECTION

It is difficult to rank the world's cities by population, because the definition of "urban area" differs among countries. Also, up-to-date figures are rarely available, even in MDCs. By using different methods to delineate their boundaries, London, New York, and Tokyo have all claimed in recent years to be the world's largest urban area. In 1992, the U.S. Bureau of the Census applied a consistent definition to estimate city populations worldwide: by that definition, the Tokyo-Yokohama region in Japan is the world's largest urban area, followed by Mexico City.

That places in LDCs dominate the list of largest urban areas is remarkable, because urban growth historically has resulted from diffusion of the industrial revolution. New jobs in factories, shops, and offices swelled cities with migrants from the countryside. In contrast, urban settlements in today's LDCs do not have rapidly expanding employment opportunities. People are migrating simply because economic conditions in rural settlements are even worse. The rapid urban growth in LDCs also partly reflects the overall population increase.

TABLE 11-2
World's most populous urban areas

1992 Rank	Urban Area	Country	1992 Population (in millions)	1950 Rank
1	Tokyo-Yokohama	Japan	27.5	4
2	Mexico City	Mexico	21.6	17
3	São Paulo	Brazil	19.4	23
4	Seoul	South Korea	17.3	50
5	New York	United States	14.6	1
6	Osaka-Kobe-Kyoto	Japan	13.9	12
7	Bombay	India	12.5	15
8	Calcutta	India	12.1	10
9	Rio de Janeiro	Brazil	12.0	16
10	Buenos Aires	Argentina	11.7	9

Source: 1950 ranks from Kingsley Davis, *World Urbanization 1950–1970,* vol. 1; 1992 population and ranks from U.S. Bureau of the Census, *International Data Base* (Washington, D.C.: Government Printing Office, 1993).

Thus, the rapid growth of cities in the LDCs is a reversal of the historical trend in western Europe and North America created by the industrial revolution; it is not a measure of an improved level of economic development.

Social Differences Between Urban and Rural Settlements

Early in the twentieth century, social scientists observed striking differences between urban and rural residents. During the 1930s, Louis Wirth argued that an urban dweller follows a way of life different from that of a rural dweller. Thus, Wirth defined a city as a permanent settlement that has three characteristics: large *size,* high population *density*, and socially *heterogeneous* people. These characteristics produced differences in the social behavior of urban and rural residents.

Large Size

If you live in a rural settlement, you know most of the other inhabitants and may even be related to many of them. The people with whom you relax are probably the same ones you see in local shops and at church.

In contrast, if you live in an urban settlement, you can know only a small percentage of the other res-

idents. You meet most of them in specific roles: your supervisor, your lawyer, your supermarket cashier, your electrician. Most of these relationships are contractual: you are paid wages according to a contract, and you pay others for goods and services. Consequently, the large size of an urban settlement influences social relationships different from those found in rural settlements.

High Density

High density also produces social consequences for urban residents. The only way that a large number of people can be supported in a small area is through specialization. Each person in an urban settlement plays a special role or performs a specific task to allow the complex urban system to function smoothly.

At the same time, high density also encourages people to compete for survival in limited space. Social groups compete to occupy the same territory, and the stronger group dominates. This competitive behavior distinguishes an urban settlement from a rural one.

Social Heterogeneity

The larger the settlement, the greater the variety of people. A person has greater freedom in an urban set-

The large size and high density of very large cities influences social relationships. People compete to occupy very little amounts of space in such places as the Tokyo subway. At the same time, to prevent a total chaotic situation the people of Tokyo cooperate by standing in line for their turn to be pushed into a crowded subway car. (Kim Newton/Woodfin Camp & Associates)

tlement than in a rural settlement to pursue an unusual profession, sexual orientation, or cultural interest. In a rural settlement, your actions might be noticed and scorned, but urban residents are more tolerant of diverse social behavior. No matter what your values and preferences, in a large urban settlement you usually can find people with similar interests.

Yet, though you may have freedom and independence in an urban settlement, you may also feel lonely and isolated. Residents of a crowded urban settlement often feel that they are surrounded by people who are indifferent and reserved.

Wirth's three-part distinction between urban and rural settlements may still apply in LDCs. But in more developed societies, social distinctions between urban and rural residents have blurred. According to Wirth's definition, nearly everyone in a developed society now is urban. More than 95 percent of workers in developed societies hold "urban" types of jobs. Nearly universal ownership of telephones, televisions, automobiles, and other modern communications and transportation devices and technologies also has reduced the differences between urban and rural lifestyles in more developed societies. Almost regardless of where you live in the United States, you have access to urban jobs, services, culture, and recreation.

Problems in Defining Urban Settlements

When you stand at the corner of Fifth Avenue and 34th Street in New York City, staring up at the Empire State Building, you know that you are in a city. When you are standing in an Iowa cornfield, you have no doubt that you are in the country. But defining where cities end and countryside begins is increasingly difficult, both in more developed and less developed societies.

Historically, physical differences between urban and rural settlements were easy to define, because cities were surrounded by walls. The removal of walls and the rapid territorial expansion of cities have blurred the traditional physical differences. Urban settlements today can be physically defined by these three approaches:

- Legal boundary
- Continuously built-up area
- Functional area

Legal Definition of a City

The term *city* formally defines an urban settlement that has been legally incorporated into an independent, self-governing unit. Virtually all countries have a local government system that recognizes cities as legal entities with fixed boundaries. A city has locally elected officials, the ability to raise taxes, and responsibility for providing essential services. The boundaries of the city define the geographic area within which the local government has legal authority.

Who's In Charge? The U.S. Constitution allocates specific powers to the federal government. All remaining powers are reserved for the states, except those rights reserved for the people, with which no government may interfere (freedom of speech, travel, religion, and so on). But nowhere in the U.S. Constitution are *cities* mentioned. Each state may establish any form of local government it chooses. Consequently, in the United States, cities are the legal creations of the states.

All U.S. states are divided into counties (parishes in Louisiana). Counties have considerable power in some states and little in others. A county, in turn, may encompass a variety of local governments, including independent cities and townships. The state decides the precise powers held by each government unit. Some states give local governments *home rule*, which means permission to perform a wide variety of activities and to raise tax revenue. Other states require local governments to apply to the state legislature each time they need something.

Annexation. Until recently in the United States, as cities grew, their legal boundaries were simply expanded to include the new territory. The process of legally adding land area to a city is known as **annexation**. Rules concerning annexation vary among states. Normally, land can be annexed into a city only if a majority of residents in the affected area vote in favor of doing so.

In the 1800s, peripheral residents generally desired annexation because the city offered better services, such as water supply, sewage disposal, trash pickup, paved streets, public transportation, and police and fire protection. Thus, while U.S. cities grew rapidly in the 1800s, the problem of defining a city seldom arose, because the legal boundaries frequently changed to accommodate newly developed areas.

Today, however, cities are less likely to annex peripheral land because the residents prefer to organize their own services rather than pay city taxes for them. As a result, today's cities are surrounded by a collection of suburban jurisdictions, whose residents prefer to remain legally independent of the large city. Originally, some of these peripheral jurisdictions were small, isolated towns that had a tradition of independent local government before being swallowed up by urban growth. Others are newly created communities whose residents wish to live close to the large city but not be legally a part of it.

20,000 Local Governments. The number of local governments exceeds 1,400 in the New York area, 1,100 in the Chicago area, and 20,000 throughout the United States. Approximately 40 percent of these 20,000 local governments are general units, such as cities and counties, and the remainder serve special purposes, such as schools, sanitation, transportation, water, and fire districts.

Long Island, which extends for 150 kilometers (90 miles) east of New York City and is approximately 25 kilometers (15 miles) wide, contains nearly 800 local governments. The island includes 2 counties, 2 cities, 13 towns, 95 villages, 127 school districts, and more than 500 special districts, such as for garbage collection.

The multiplicity of local governments on Long Island leads to problems. When police or fire fighters are summoned to the State University of New York at Old Westbury, two or three departments sometimes respond, because the campus is in five districts. The boundary between the communities of Mineola and Garden City runs down the center of Old Country Road, a busy, four-lane route. Mineola set a 40-mile-per-hour speed limit for the eastbound lanes, while Garden City set a 30-mile-per-hour speed limit for the westbound lanes.

Defining a City's Continuously Built-Up Area

The combination of rapid growth and political fragmentation demands new urban definitions. One now used in the United States is the **urbanized area**, which consists of the largest city in the area, or **central city**, plus its contiguous built-up suburbs where population density exceeds 1,000 persons per square mile (400 persons per square kilometer). Approximately 60 percent of the U.S. population live in urban areas, divided about equally between central cities and surrounding jurisdictions.

Unfortunately, few statistics are available about urbanized areas. Most data in the United States and other countries are published at the level of local government units. Urbanized areas do not correspond to local government boundaries, so the concept has been of limited usefulness in the United States.

Defining a City's Functional Area

The urbanized area also has limited applicability because it does not accurately reflect the full influence that an urban settlement has in contemporary society. The area of influence of a city extends beyond legal boundaries and adjacent built-up jurisdictions. For example, commuters may travel a long distance to work and shop in the city or built-up suburbs. People in a wide area watch the city's television stations, read the city's newspapers, and support the city's sports teams. Therefore, we need another definition of urban settlement to account for its more extensive zone of influence.

Metropolitan Statistical Area. The U.S. Bureau of the Census has created a method of measuring the functional area of a city, known as the **metropolitan statistical area (MSA)**. An MSA includes the following:

1. A central city with a population of at least 50,000
2. The county within which the city is located
3. Adjacent counties in which at least 15 percent of the residents work in the central city's county, and to which at least two of these tests apply:

   a. County has a residential density of at least 60 persons per square mile.

   b. County has at least 65 percent of its residents working in nonfarm jobs.

   c. County had a population growth rate during the 1970s of at least 20 percent.

   d. County has at least 10 percent of its population, or at least 5,000 persons, living in an urbanized area.

Studies of metropolitan areas in the United States are usually based on information about MSAs. MSAs are widely used because many statistics are published for counties, the basic MSA building block (Figure 11-10). Older studies may refer to SMSAs, or standard metropolitan statistical areas, which the census used before 1980 to designate metropolitan areas in a manner fairly similar to that used for MSAs.

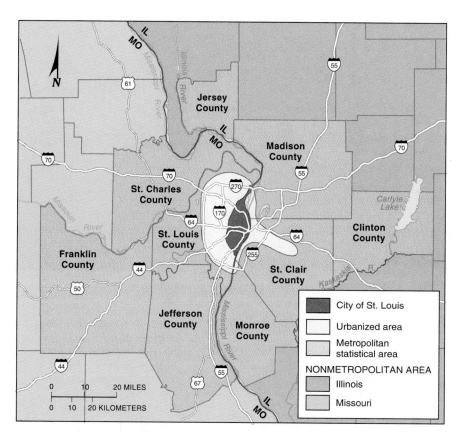

FIGURE 11-10 St. Louis city, urbanized area, and metropolitan statistical area. Surrounding the city of St. Louis is an urbanized area that spreads westward into St. Louis County and eastward across the Mississippi River into Illinois. The St. Louis metropolitan statistical area (MSA) includes four Missouri counties and five in Illinois, as well as the city of St. Louis. The map also shows St. Louis's *situation*, at the confluence of the Missouri and Mississippi Rivers and several federal highways.

Problems with MSAs. An MSA is not the perfect tool for measuring the functional area of a city, for it has two geographic problems: MSAs include considerable land that is not urban, and MSAs overlap.

The inclusion of nonurban land is illustrated by the Great Smokies National Park, which is partly in the MSA of Knoxville, Tennessee, and Sequoia National Park, which is in the MSA of Visalia-Tulare-Porterville, California. MSAs constitute some 20 percent of total U.S. land area, but urbanized areas constitute only 2 percent. The urbanized area typically occupies only 10 percent of an MSA land area, but contains over 75 percent of its population.

Megalopolis. Adjacent MSAs overlap. A county between two central cities may send a large number of commuters to jobs in each. In the northeastern United States, large metropolitan areas are so close together that they now form one continuous urban complex, extending from north of Boston to south of Washington, D.C. In 1961, the geographer Jean Gottmann named this region "Megalopolis," a

Greek word meaning "great city"; others have called it the "Boswash" corridor (Figure 11-11).

Within Megalopolis, the downtown areas of individual cities such as Baltimore, New York, and Philadelphia retain distinctive identities. Sharp physical and social differences are clearly visible among inner city, suburban, and peripheral neighborhoods within each metropolitan area, as will be discussed in Chapter 12. The cities are visibly separated from each other by open space used as parks, military bases, and dairy or truck farms.

But the boundaries among the metropolitan areas within Megalopolis overlap. Washingtonians attend major league baseball games in Baltimore, Baltimoreans attend major league football games in Washington, and both attend major league hockey and basketball games in an arena situated between the two cities. Once considered two separate areas, Washington and Baltimore were combined into a single metropolitan statistical area after the 1990 census.

Other continuous urban complexes exist in the United States: the southern Great Lakes between

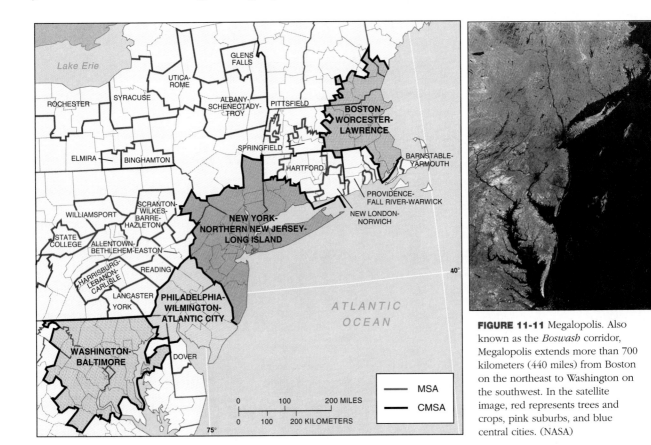

FIGURE 11-11 Megalopolis. Also known as the *Boswash* corridor, Megalopolis extends more than 700 kilometers (440 miles) from Boston on the northeast to Washington on the southwest. In the satellite image, red represents trees and crops, pink suburbs, and blue central cities. (NASA)

Chicago and Milwaukee on the west and Pittsburgh on the east, and southern California from Los Angeles to Tijuana. Among important examples in other MDCs are the German Ruhr (including the cities of Dortmund, Düsseldorf, and Essen), Randstad in the Netherlands (including the cities of Amsterdam, the Hague, and Rotterdam), and Japan's Tokaido (including the cities of Tokyo and Yokohama).

Consolidated Metropolitan Statistical Areas.

If two adjacent MSAs have overlapping commuting patterns, they may be combined into a **consolidated metropolitan statistical area (CMSA)**. Examples of CMSAs are New York-Northern New Jersey-Long Island, Los Angeles-Anaheim-Riverside, and Chicago-Gary-Lake County.

If part of a CMSA exceeds 1 million population, then it may be classified as a primary metropolitan statistical area, or PMSA. Again, the building block is the county. A PMSA consists of at least one county that has all of the following characteristics:

1. It has a population of more than 100,000.
2. At least 60 percent of the residents work in nonfarm jobs.
3. Less than 50 percent of the county's workers commute to jobs outside the county.

Importance of MSAs.

Difficulties involved in designating MSAs, CMSAs, and PMSAs can be seen in the southeastern corner of Wisconsin. Kenosha and Racine counties each have a city with more than 50,000 people and therefore qualify as separate MSAs. But these two metropolitan counties are sandwiched between the much larger Chicago and Milwaukee metropolitan areas. Northern Racine County is within a half hour of downtown Milwaukee, and southern Kenosha County is within an hour of downtown Chicago. The U.S. Bureau of the Census decided to call Kenosha County a separate MSA and to designate Racine County as a PMSA within the Milwaukee-Racine CMSA.

Why do officials in Kenosha and Racine counties care whether they are a separate MSA or merely part of Milwaukee or Chicago's CMSA? The reason is money: several types of federal assistance are allocated to MSAs. The separate designation of Kenosha County may bring more funds to be used at the dis-

cretion of the county, rather than to be shared with other counties in the Milwaukee or Chicago region.

Local officials also wish to preserve their separate MSA designation because it increases the county's visibility. The U.S. Bureau of the Census publishes considerable information at the MSA level. Many private companies also compile information and make initial investment decisions at the MSA level. Advertising agencies select MSAs as test markets, and developers choose MSAs for new shopping center sites. As a separate MSA, a county like Kenosha increases its likelihood of being selected by an investor.

Metropolitan Government

The fragmentation of local government in the United States makes it difficult to solve regional problems of traffic, solid-waste disposal, and building affordable housing. These difficulties have led to calls for *metropolitan government*, one which coordinates the numerous local governments in a metropolitan area.

Most U.S. metropolitan areas have a **council of government**, which is a cooperative agency consisting of representatives of the various local governments in the region. The council of government may be empowered to do some overall planning for the area that local governments cannot logically do.

Strong metropolitan-wide governments have been established in a few places in North America. Two kinds exist, federations and consolidations.

Federations.

Toronto, Ontario, has a federation system. Toronto's local government has two tiers. The region's six local governments, which range in size from 100,000 to 600,000 inhabitants, are responsible for police, fire, and tax collection services. A regional government, known as the Metropolitan Council, or Metro, sets the tax rate for the region as a whole, assesses the value of property, and borrows money for new projects. Metro shares responsibility with local governments for public services, such as transportation, planning, parks, water, sewage, and welfare.

Consolidations.

Several U.S. urban areas have consolidated metropolitan governments; Indianapolis and Miami are examples. Both have consolidated city and county governments. The boundaries of Indianapolis were changed to match those of Marion

County, Indiana. Government functions that were handled separately by city and county now are combined into a joint operation in the same office building. In Florida, Miami and surrounding Dade County have combined some services, but the city boundaries have not been changed to match the county's.

Metropolitan Governments in the United Kingdom. The creation of metropolitan governments has been somewhat easier in other countries in which the national government has more authority. In the United Kingdom, for example, the national government can change local government boundaries when it wishes. During the 1970s, the British government redrew the country's local government boundaries and created six new metropolitan governments, including Greater London, Greater Manchester, West Midlands around the city of Birmingham, West Yorkshire around Leeds, Merseyside around Liverpool, and Tyneside around Newcastle.

Then, in the 1980s, the British government decided to eliminate the Greater London Council, which had been created only a few years earlier to govern the London region. The national government decided that the 1,580-square-kilometer (610-square-mile) London metropolitan area would be better governed by 32 local boroughs than by one regional government.

Derek Senior, a geographer and a member of the royal commission that restructured local government, filed a minority report calling for a more radical local government restructuring in England. He identified the important cities in England and allocated the surrounding countryside to each, so that local government would truly be based on a series of urban regions. Senior's plan was rejected because the government wished to change the traditional counties as little as possible. In recent years, however, the idea has resurfaced.

K E Y I S S U E 4

Why Are Services Concentrated in Settlements?

- Factors in Locating a Service
- Central Place Theory
- Economic Base of Settlements
- Economic Restructuring and the Urban System

Regardless of why a settlement began or how it is organized, a settlement today exists as *a place to obtain services.* A **service** is any activity that fulfills a human want or need and returns money to those who provide it. In Chapter 8 we divided services into five sectors, according to the purpose of the activity:

- *Transportation and communication services,* such as trucking and television broadcasting, diffuse and distribute services.
- *Producer services,* such as banking and law, provide services primarily to manufacturers and other businesses.
- *Retail and wholesale services,* such as restaurants and shops, provide goods to consumers.
- *Personal and social services,* such as schools and hospitals, provide services for the well-being and personal improvement of individual consumers.
- *Public services,* such as federal and local governments, provide security and protection for citizens and businesses.

This brief list cannot show the wide variety of establishments in a settlement that offer services. Retail services include stores that sell hardware, groceries, clothing, or furniture, as well as bars, restaurants, and car dealers. Personal and social services include hospitals, dry cleaners, beauty salons, museums, and theaters. Nor can the list show the wide variety of specific occupations of service providers in a settlement. A bank includes tellers, investment consultants, loan officers, clerks, security guards, and custodians. A walk through the *Yellow Pages* reveals a community's variety of services.

In the United States, employment during the past quarter-century has declined in primary sector industries such as agriculture and the secondary sector (manufacturing), remained about the same in transportation services, and increased in the other service sectors (Figure 11-12). Professional and personal service have increased the most.

Urban settlements have always been both manufacturing and service centers, whereas rural settlements were centers for agriculture. But urban residents are now much more likely to work in services than in manufacturing—urban services have expanded, and urban factories have closed.

As in other economic and cultural features, geographers observe trends toward both globalization and local diversity in the distribution of services. On

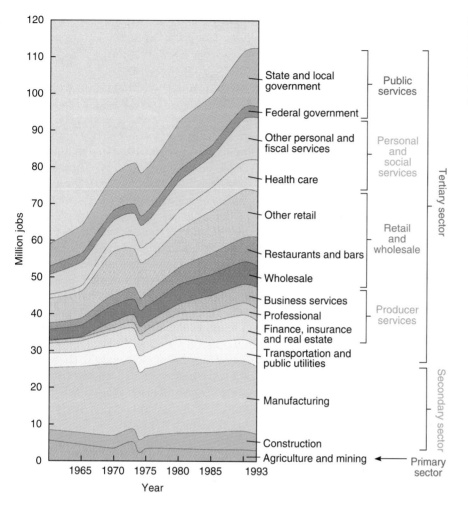

FIGURE 11-12 Employment change in the United States by sector. The number of employees has increased the most in the professional services and personal and social services sectors and decreased in the primary and secondary sectors.

the one hand, the provision of some services has become more uniform from one urban settlement to another, especially in developed countries. Every urban settlement in the United States above a certain size has a branch of a large retail chain, such as a McDonald's restaurant, and the larger cities have several. In England, every city above a certain size has at least one Sainsbury's supermarket. Every city above a certain size has at least one dry cleaner and law office, although national chains do not dominate the provision of these services. Geographers see a strong relation between the location of these types of services and the distribution of settlements. In a developed country, the demand for many types of services produces a regular distribution of settlements.

At the same time, the distribution of other services is becoming more diverse. Cities are specializing in particular types of services, such as financial, data processing, and medical. Some urban settlements are becoming more important than others, depending on the distinctive mix of services each one offers.

Factors in Locating a Service

A manufacturer or farm operator must balance several situation and site factors when choosing a location. But service providers generally consider only one geographic factor to be important: *access to markets*. Because a service seeks proximity to its consumers, the best location is likely to be in an urban settlement, because that is where consumers concentrate in a small area. The concentrations of population needed to support most services are found in urban settlements.

A prominent type of a retail service in a developed country such as the United States is the large supermarket. (Roy Morsch/The Stock Market)

Despite the apparent simplicity, the process of selecting the optimal location for a service can be more challenging than for a factory. The optimal location for a manufacturer may be an area of several hundred square kilometers. But for some retailers, locating on one side of a street may be profitable, whereas the other side of the street may not. It is notable that geographers are increasingly hired by large banks, department stores, supermarkets, and other service providers to calculate whether a site has the profit potential to justify corporate investment.

Market Area of a Service

The area surrounding a service from which customers are attracted is the **market area**, or **hinterland**. A market area is a good example of a *nodal region*—a region with a core where the characteristic is most intense. The market area is established by drawing a circle around the node of service on a map. The territory inside the circle is the service's market area.

Because most people prefer to get services from the nearest location, consumers near the center of the circle obtain services from local establishments. The closer to the periphery of the circle, the greater is the percentage of consumers who will choose to obtain services from other nodes. People on the circumference of the market area circle are equally likely to use the service or go elsewhere.

The market areas of services vary in size. To determine the extent of the market area, a firm needs

two vital pieces of geographic information about the good or service that will be provided at a new establishment: its *range* and *threshold*.

Range. How far are you willing to drive for a pizza? How far would you travel to see a doctor for a serious problem? How far would you travel for a major league ballgame or a concert? The **range** is the maximum distance people are willing to travel for a service. People are willing to go only a short distance for everyday services, such as groceries, laundromats, or video rentals. But they will travel a long distance for other services, such as a major league baseball game or concert. Thus, a convenience store has a small range, whereas a stadium or concert hall has a large range. The range is the radius of the circle drawn to delineate a service's market area.

If firms at other locations compete by providing the service, the range must be modified. As a rule, people tend to go to the nearest available service: someone in the mood for a McDonald's hamburger is likely to go to the nearest McDonald's. Therefore, the range of a service must be determined from the radius of a circle that is irregularly shaped rather than perfectly round. The irregularly shaped circle takes in the territory for which the proposed site is closer than competitors.

For example, on a map of Dayton, Ohio, we can indicate the location of all Kroger supermarkets and draw irregularly shaped circles around each of them (Figure 11-13). The radius of each circle shows the range for each store. The median radius for Kroger supermarkets in Dayton is approximately 2 kilometers (1.2 miles).

The range must be modified further because most people think of distance in terms of *time*, rather than a linear measure such as kilometers or miles. If you ask people how far they are willing to travel to a restaurant or a baseball game, they are more likely to answer in minutes or hours than in distance. If the range of a good or service is expressed in travel time, then the irregularly shaped circle must be drawn to acknowledge that travel time varies with road conditions. "One hour" may translate into 90 kilometers (55 miles) on an expressway but only 50 kilometers (30 miles) on congested city streets.

To determine the range of a service, geographers observe consumer behavior. We can ask people in a laundromat, supermarket, or stadium where they came

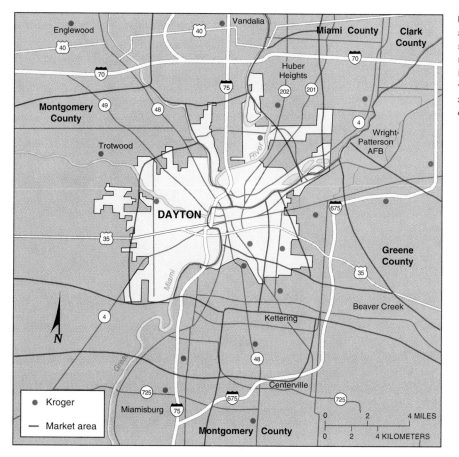

FIGURE 11-13 Market area, range, and threshold for Kroger supermarkets in the Dayton, Ohio metropolitan area. Fewer stores are in the southwest and northeast, which are predominantly industrial areas, and in the west, which contains lower-income residents.

from. We can ask people at home where they normally go to buy food, have their clothes cleaned, or attend a sporting event. The result shows how far the typical customer is willing to travel for various services.

Threshold. The second piece of geographic information needed is the **threshold**, which is the minimum number of people needed to support the service. Every enterprise has a minimum number of customers needed to generate enough sales to make a profit. Once the range has been determined, a service provider must determine whether a location is suitable by counting the potential customers inside the irregularly shaped circle. For example, the median threshold needed to support a Kroger supermarket in Dayton is about 30,000 people. Census data help us determine the population within the circle.

How potential consumers inside the range are counted depends on the product. Convenience stores and fast-food restaurants appeal to nearly everyone, whereas other goods and services appeal primarily to certain consumer groups. Movie theaters attract younger people, whereas chiropractors attract older people. Poorer people are drawn to thrift stores, whereas wealthier people may frequent upscale department stores. Amusement parks attract families with children, but nightclubs appeal to singles. If a good or service appeals to certain customers, then only those people should be counted inside the range.

Developers of shopping malls, department stores, and large supermarkets typically count only higher-income people, perhaps those whose annual incomes exceed $50,000. Even though the stores may attract people of all incomes, higher-income people are likely to spend more and purchase items that carry higher profit margins for the retailer. Hence, in the Dayton area, Kroger operates more supermarkets in the south, where higher-income people are clustered, and fewer in the west, a lower-income area.

Are Enough Customers Nearby? You can see that the range and threshold together determine whether a good or service can be profitable in a community. To illustrate, consider this: would a convenience store be profitable in your community? First, compute the range, the maximum distance people are willing to travel. You might survey local residents and determine that people are generally willing to travel up to 15 minutes to reach a convenience store.

Then, compute the threshold. Suppose a convenience store must sell at least $10,000 worth of goods per week to make a profit, and the average customer spends $2 a week. The store needs at least 5,000 customers per week, spending $2 each, to achieve the break-even sales level of $10,000. If the average customer goes to a convenience store once a week, the threshold in this example would be 5,000.

Finally, on a map, draw a circle around your community with a 15-minute travel radius, adjusting the boundaries to account for any competitors. Count the number of people within the irregularly shaped circle. If more than 5,000 people are within the radius, then the threshold may be high enough to justify locating the new convenience store in your community.

Small settlements are limited to services that have small thresholds and short ranges because too few people live in small settlements to support many services. A large department store or specialty store cannot survive in a small settlement because the minimum number of people needed exceeds the population within range of the settlement.

Larger settlements provide services having larger thresholds and ranges. But neighborhoods within large settlements also provide services having small thresholds and ranges. Services patronized by a small number of locals ("Mom & Pop stores") can coexist in a neighborhood along with services that attract many from throughout the settlement. This difference is vividly demonstrated by comparing the *Yellow Pages* for a small settlement with one for a major city. The major city's *Yellow Pages* are plump with more services, and diverse headings show widely varied services unavailable in small settlements.

We spend as little time and effort as possible in obtaining services, and thus go to the nearest place that fulfills our needs. There is no point in traveling to a distant department store if the same merchandise is available at a nearby one. We travel greater distances only if the price is much lower or if the item is unavailable locally.

World cities like London provide producer services, such as insurance, to companies around the world. Lloyd's of London, the world's most important insurer of high-risk ventures, has its headquarters in a new building in London's one-square-mile financial district known as the City. The bell in the foreground, salvaged from the company's old headquarters building, was traditionally rung when a ship insured by the company sunk. (Ed Pritchard/Tony Stone Images)

Selecting a Location for a Service

Having determined that the threshold and range justify providing a particular good or service, the next geographic question is: where should the service be located within the market area to maximize profit? According to geographers, the best location is the one that minimizes the distance to the service for the largest number of people. To compute this distance, geographers have adopted the gravity model from physics.

The **gravity model** predicts that potential use of a good or service at a location is related directly to the population and inversely to the distance people must travel to access it. According to the gravity model, consumers have two habits. First, the greater the number of people living in a particular place, the greater is the number of potential customers for a service. A community that contains 10,000 people will generate more customers than a community of only 1,000 people. Second, the farther people are from a particular service, the less likely they are to use it. People who live 1 kilometer from a store are more likely to patronize it than people who live 10 kilometers away.

Best Location in a Linear Settlement. Suppose that you want to establish your hot business idea, *Geographers Pizza*, in your community. Where is the best place to build it? Assume for a moment that you are seeking the optimal location for your business in an elongated community like Miami Beach, Florida, or Atlantic City, New Jersey, or Ocean City, Maryland. The community has only one major north-south street and several short east-west streets that are numbered consecutively.

The best location will be the one that minimizes the distance that your van must travel to deliver to all potential customers. That location can be determined precisely rather than through trial and error: it corresponds to the *median*, which mathematically is the middle point in any series of observations. In a linear community like Atlantic City, the service should be located where half of the customers are to the north and half to the south (see Geography in Action box).

Best Location in a Nonlinear Settlement. Most communities, however, are more complex than a single main street. For these, computing the best location is a bit more complicated, but the basic principle remains the same:

The best location can be calculated by combining population and distance. Geographers follow these steps:

1. Identify a possible location for a new service.
2. Determine the population for each community that contains people who might use the service.
3. Within the range, measure the distance from the possible location to each community.
4. Divide the population in each community by the distance from that community to the location being considered for the new service.
5. Sum all of the results (populations divided by distances).
6. Select a second possible location for the new service, and repeat steps 3, 4, and 5.

7. Compare the results (of the populations divided by distances computed in step 5) for each possible location. The location with the highest score has the highest potential number of users and is therefore the optimal location for the service.

Central Place Theory

A **central place** is a market center for the exchange of goods and services by people attracted from the surrounding area. The central place, is so called because it is centrally located to maximize accessibility from the surrounding region. Central places compete to serve as markets for goods and services. This competition creates a regular pattern of settlements, according to central place theory.

The geographic concept of **central place theory** explains not only the distribution of services but also why a regular pattern of settlements exists—at least in more developed countries like the United States. Central place theory was first proposed in the 1930s by German geographer Walter Christaller, on the basis of his studies of southern Germany. August Lösch in Germany and Brian Berry and others in the United States further developed the concept during the 1950s. The theory applies most clearly in regions such as the Great Plains which are neither heavily industrialized nor interrupted by major physical features such as rivers or mountain ranges.

Nesting of Market Areas

Circles can be drawn to designate market areas of entire urban settlements, not just individual services. But circles cause a geometric problem. When drawn to represent adjacent market areas, they either overlap or have gaps between them (Figure 11-14a). Neither pattern is consistent with the theory that people usually go to the nearest sources.

An arrangement of circles that leaves gaps indicates that people living in the gaps are outside the market area of any service, obviously not true. On the other hand, overlapping circles are unsatisfactory, for one service or another will be closer, and people will tend to patronize it. Therefore, market areas must be separated by a line that does not overlap territories.

Central place theory requires a geometric shape without gaps or overlaps, so circles are out. Squares fit without gaps, but they have a different problem.

Best Location for a Service

The best location for a service is the one that minimizes travel times for all of the potential users or customers.

Best Location in a Linear Community

To determine the optimal location for a good or service in a linear community, consider the case of Geographers Pizzas. First, find the *median*. Suppose Geo's has seven potential customers, families A through G, distributed in the community as shown in Figure 1. If the shop were at 5th Street, the delivery van would travel 4 blocks to deliver a pizza to family A (1st Street), 3 blocks to family B (2nd Street), 2 blocks to C (3rd Street), 0 blocks to D (5th Street), 2 to E (7th Street), 10 to F (15th Street), and 11 to G (16th Street). The van would have to travel a total of 4 + 3 + 2 + 0 + 2 + 10 + 11 blocks, or 32 blocks, to deliver a pizza to each of the seven customers.

Compare this location with any other possibility. For example, if Geo were at 7th Street, then the van would travel 6 blocks to reach family A, 5 blocks to B, 4 blocks to C, 2 blocks to D, 0 blocks to E, 8 to F, and 9 to G. The van would have to travel 6 + 5 + 4 + 2 + 0 + 8 + 9 blocks, or 34 blocks, to deliver pizza to all seven customers. This is a greater total distance than locating at 5th Street.

In fact, no other location results in a lower aggregate distance than 5th Street, so in this example, 5th Street is the *median* observation. At 5th Street, an equal number of potential customers are located on either side. Three are to the west (A, B, C), and three are to the east (E, F, G).

Suppose that the settlement has eleven potential customers, rather than seven (Figure 2). Note the distribution of families. Their *median location* is the middle observation among these eleven families, the place where five families live to the west and five families live to the east. Therefore, Geo's should be located at 7th Street, because five families live to the west (A, B, C, D, E) and five families live to the east (G, H, I, J, K).

Best Location in a Nonlinear Community

The best location of a service in a nonlinear community can be computed by using the gravity model. In this example (Figure 3), we use a census tract map of Hamilton, Ohio, divided into census tracts (equivalent to neighborhoods). Both Tract 7.01 and Tract 11 look like good locations, but which is really better?

1. Determine the potential population of users of the service in each tract (shown in italics).
2. Measure the distance from each neighborhood to one of the alternative locations. For example, the distance from Tract 1 to location B is about 2.8 miles (4.5 kilometers).
3. Divide the population in each neighborhood by the distance from that neighborhood to the proposed location of the service.
4. Sum all the populations divided by distances. This figure is the relative potential of a service at that location.
5. Repeat steps 2, 3, and 4 for alternative location A. The optimal location for a service is the tract with the highest number.

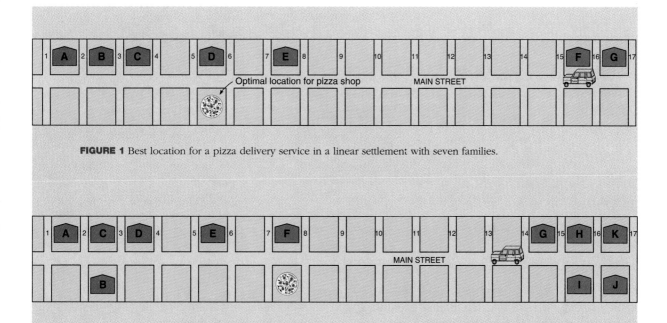

FIGURE 1 Best location for a pizza delivery service in a linear settlement with seven families.

FIGURE 2 Best location for a pizza delivery service in a linear settlement with eleven families.

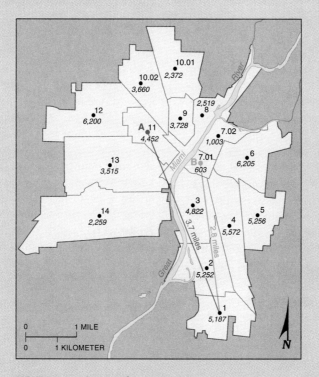

FIGURE 3 Best location for a pizza delivery service in a nonlinear settlement.

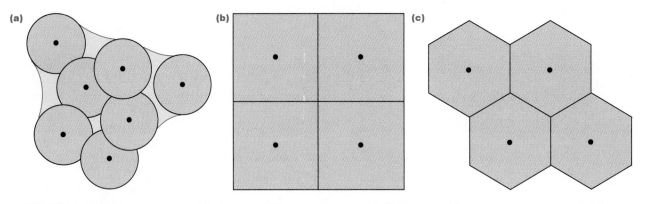

FIGURE 11-14 Why hexagons are used in theory to delineate market areas. (a) Circles are equidistant from center to edge, but they overlap or leave gaps. (b) Squares nest together without gaps, but their sides are not equidistant from the center. (c) Geographers use hexagons to depict the market area of a good or service, because hexagons offer a compromise between the geometric properties of circles and squares.

If the market area is a circle, the radius—the distance from the center to the edge—can be measured, because every point around a circle is the same distance from the center as any other point. But in a square, the distance from the center varies among points along a square (Figure 11-14b).

Therefore, to represent a market area, the hexagon is the best compromise between circles and squares (Figure 11-14c). Like squares, hexagons nest without gaps. Although all points along the hexagon are not the same distance from the center, the variation is less than with a square. Consequently, geographers draw hexagons around settlements to indicate market areas.

Hierarchy of Settlements

According to central place theory, market areas across a developed country would be a series of hexagons of various sizes, unless interrupted by physical features such as mountains and bodies of water. Developed countries have numerous small settlements with small thresholds and ranges and far fewer large settlements with large thresholds and ranges.

The hierarchical pattern can be illustrated with overlapping hexagons of different sizes (Figure 11-15). The figure shows four levels of market area, for hamlet, village, town, and city. Hamlets, with very small market areas, are represented by the smallest contiguous hexagons. Larger hexagons represent the market areas of larger settlements, and are overlaid on the smaller hexagons, because consumers from smaller settlements shop for some goods and services in larger settlements.

In his original study, Christaller showed that settlements in southern Germany were arranged according to a regular hierarchy. He identified seven sizes of settlements (market hamlet, township center, county seat, district city, small state capital, provincial head capital, and regional capital city). For example, the smallest (market hamlet) had an average population of 800 and a market area of 45 square kilometers (17 square miles). The average distance between market hamlets was 7 kilometers (4.4 miles). The figures were higher for the average settlement at each increasing level in the hierarchy. Brian Berry has documented a similar hierarchy of settlements in parts of the U.S. Midwest.

The principle of nesting market areas also works at the scale of services within cities. For example, compare the market areas within Dayton of Kroger (Figure 11-13) with those of United Dairy Farmers (UDF) and Elder-Beerman (Figure 11-16). The UDF convenience stores are more numerous than Kroger stores and have smaller thresholds, ranges, and market areas. The Elder-Beerman department stores are less numerous than Kroger stores and have larger thresholds, ranges, and market areas.

Rank-Size Distribution of Settlements. Geographers observe that ranking settlements in many MDCs, from largest to smallest (population) produces a regular pattern. This is the **rank-size rule**, in

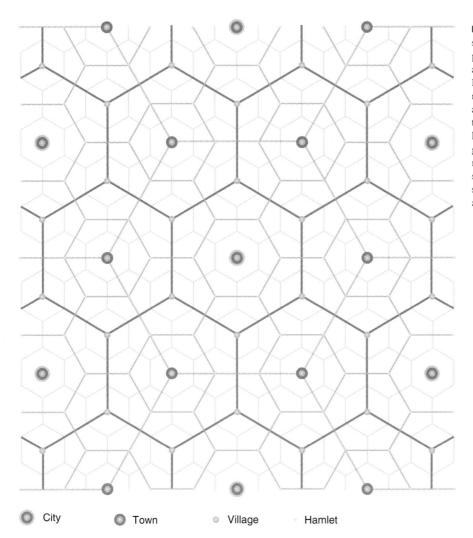

FIGURE 11-15 Arrangement of settlements. According to central place theory, settlements are arranged in a regular pattern. Larger settlements, with larger market areas, are fewer in number and farther apart from each other than smaller settlements. However, larger settlements also provide goods and services with smaller market areas; consequently, larger settlements have both larger and smaller market areas drawn around them.

◎ City ◉ Town ○ Village · Hamlet

which the country's nth largest settlement is $1/n$ the population of the largest settlement. In other words, the second-largest city is $1/2$ the population of the largest, the fourth-largest city is $1/4$ the population of the largest, and so on. When plotted on logarithmic paper, the rank-size distribution forms a fairly straight line. The distribution of settlements closely follows the rank-size rule in the United States (Figure 11-17) and some other countries.

If the settlement hierarchy does not graph as a straight line, then the society does not have a rank-size distribution of settlements. Several MDCs in Europe follow the rank-size distribution among smaller settlements, but not among the largest ones (Figure 11-17). Instead, the largest settlement in these countries follows the primate city rule. According to this

rule, the **primate city**, the largest settlement, has more than twice as many people as the second-ranking settlement.

In France, for example, Paris has around 9 million inhabitants, but the second-largest settlement, Marseille, has only around 2 million, instead of the 4.5 million that the rank-size rule predicts. The largest settlement in the United Kingdom—London—also has around 9 million, and Birmingham—the second-largest—has only around 2 million.

Many LDCs also follow the primate city rule. In these countries, however, the rank-size rule tends to fail at other levels in the hierarchy as well. As previously noted, Romania has no settlement between 350,000 and 2 million inhabitants and too few settlements of fewer than 10,000 inhabitants.

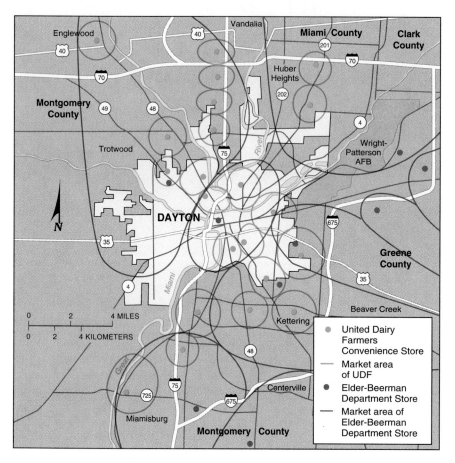

FIGURE 11-16 Market areas, ranges, and thresholds for United Dairy Farmers (UDF) convenience stores and Elder-Beerman department stores in the Dayton, Ohio metropolitan area. Compared with Kroger supermarkets (see Figure 11-13), UDF stores are more numerous and have smaller market areas, ranges, and thresholds, whereas Elder-Beerman stores are less numerous and have larger market areas, ranges, and thresholds.

The existence of a rank-size distribution of settlements is not merely a mathematical curiosity. It has a real impact on the quality of life for a country's inhabitants. A regular hierarchy—as in the United States—indicates that the society is sufficiently wealthy to justify provision of goods and services to consumers throughout the country. The absence of the rank-size distribution in a less developed country indicates that there is not enough wealth in the society to pay for a full variety of services.

Economic Base of Settlements

Each urban settlement in a more developed country such as the United States is a market center, serving people in the surrounding hinterlands. According to central place theory, the distribution of urban settlements across a developed country should be uniform, unless interrupted by physical features such as mountains and bodies of water. Yet, urban settlements are not distributed uniformly across the country. Why?

Basic and Nonbasic Industries

Part of the reason is that some settlements specialize in certain economic activities. Detroit specializes in motor vehicle production; Gary, Indiana, in steel manufacturing; Las Vegas in entertainment; Ann Arbor, Michigan, in university activities; and Washington, D.C., in government services.

Every settlement has the typical shops and offices, depending on its size, but not every city has a steel mill, university, auto factory, or casino. A community's distinctive economic structure derives from its **basic industries**, which sell their products or services primarily to consumers *outside* the settlement. **Nonbasic industries** are enterprises whose customers live *in* the same community.

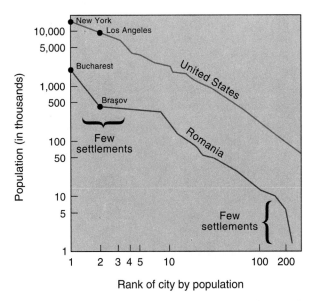

FIGURE 11-17 Rank-size distribution of settlements in the United States and Romania. U.S. settlements generally follow the rank-size distribution, as reflected by their nearly straight line on this logarithmic display. Romania has a shortage of settlements in two size groups: between 350,000 and 2,000,000 population, and fewer than 10,000 inhabitants. These gaps are reflected in the irregular shape of the line.

A community's unique collection of basic industries defines its **economic base**. The significance of an economic base cannot be overstated: it is the products exported from the settlement that bring money into the local economy, thus stimulating the provision of more nonbasic industries for consumers in the community. New basic industries attract new workers to a community, and they bring their families with them. Additional goods and services are established to meet the needs of the new workers and their families. Thus, a new basic industry, such as a factory, stimulates establishment of new drug stores, laundromats, restaurants, food stores, and other retailers. But a new nonbasic business, such as a supermarket, will not induce construction of new factories.

A community's basic industries can be identified by computing the percentage of the community's workers employed in different types of businesses. The percentage of workers employed in a particular industry in a settlement is then compared with the percentage of all workers in the country employed in that industry. If the percentage is much higher in the local community, then that type of business is a basic economic activity (Figure 11-18).

U.S. settlements can be classified by their type of basic activity. Compared with the national average, some communities have a very high percentage of workers employed in the production of durable manufactured goods, such as steel and automobiles. The economic base of other communities can be classified as nondurable manufactured goods (textiles and apparel, food products, chemicals, paper products), mining, construction, communications, public administration, finance, service, wholesale, or retail.

Each type of basic activity has a different spatial distribution in the United States:

- Most communities that have an economic base of durable goods manufacturing, such as cars, are clustered between northern Ohio and southeastern Wisconsin, near the southern Great Lakes.
- Nondurable manufacturing industries, such as textiles, are clustered in the Southeast, especially in the Carolinas.
- Public administration centers are dispersed around the country, because these communities typically have a state capital, large university, or military base.
- Service communities include entertainment and recreation centers such as Las Vegas and Reno in Nevada and Atlantic City in New Jersey, as well as medical centers such as Rochester, Minnesota.
- Mining communities are built where coal, petroleum, and other resources are located.
- Business and professional services are concentrated in large metropolitan areas, especially New York, Los Angeles, Chicago, and San Francisco.

Some settlements, especially larger ones, may specialize in more than one economic activity. New York and Chicago, for example, are both financial and wholesale centers.

Economic Restructuring and the Urban System

In the past, "basic industries" were assumed to be manufacturers. But in a postindustrial society such as the United States, increasingly a community's basic economic activity is provision of services. Steel was

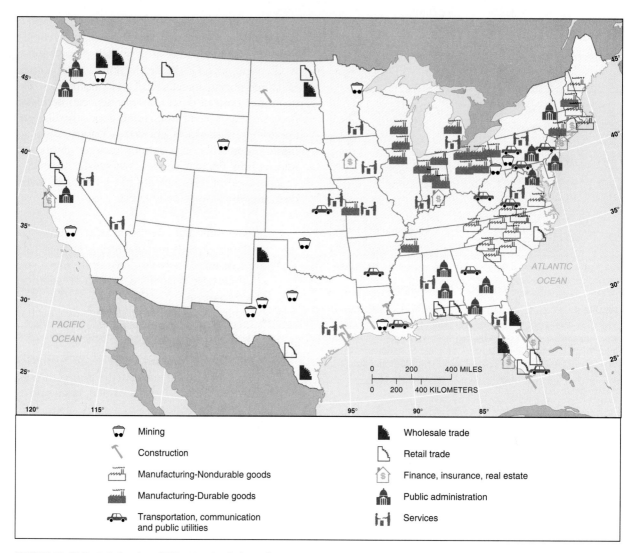

FIGURE 11-18 Basic industries of U.S. cities. Symbols on this map represent cities that have a significantly higher percentage of their labor force engaged in the type of economic activity shown. Other cities also engage in such activities but are not shown because they specialize in multiple activities or are near the national average for all sectors. (Mathematically, a city was included if the percentage of its labor force in one sector was more than two standard deviations above the mean for all U.S. cities.)

once the most important basic industry of Cleveland and Pittsburgh, but now medical services such as hospitals and clinics and medical high-technology research are more important.

Specialization of Cities in Different Services

The provision of services is an increasingly important role for all cities in developed countries, but cities offer varying mixes of services. Breandan Ó hUallacháin and Neil Reid documented some examples in the United States:

- Washington, D.C., specializes in providing management consulting services.
- Boston and San Jose specialize in providing computing and data-processing services.
- Austin, Orlando, and Raleigh-Durham specialize in providing services to high-technology industries.
- Albuquerque, Colorado Springs, Huntsville, Knoxville, and Norfolk specialize in providing military support services.

In recent years, cities in the south and west have grown relatively rapidly in population—but Ó hUallacháin and Reid found that services have expanded more rapidly in northern and eastern cities. Cities in the north and east that once were major manufacturing centers have been transformed into service-oriented centers. These cities have moved aggressively to restructure their economic bases to offset sharp declines in manufacturing jobs.

For example, Baltimore's economic base was built on manufacture of fabricated steel products by Bethlehem Steel, General Motors, and Westinghouse. The city's principal economic asset was its seaport, through which passed raw materials and fabricated products. As these manufacturers declined, the city's economic base turned to services, taking advantage of its clustering of research-oriented universities, especially in medicine. The city is trying to become a center for the provision of services in biotechnology.

Service-Based System of Cities

A global system of cities is emerging, based on the provision of services rather than simply on the number of inhabitants. The most important cities in the hierarchy are those where key decisions are being made about the movement of information and capital in the global economy.

Geographers distinguish four levels of cities, based on their roles in the global service economy:

- World cities
- Regional command and control centers
- Specialized producer-service centers
- Dependent centers

Differences also exist among cities within each level.

World Cities. A high percentage of the world's business is transacted in a few *world cities* (Figure 11-19). They are closely integrated into the global economic system because they are at the center of the flow of information and capital. The services that concentrate in disproportionately large numbers in world cities include law, banking, insurance, accounting, and advertising.

Three world cities stand out in a class of their own: London, New York, and Tokyo. Each is the largest city in one of the three main regions of the developed world (Western Europe, North America,

and East Asia), as discussed in Chapter 8. The world's most important stock exchanges operate in these three cities, and they contain large concentrations of financial and related business services.

A second tier of major world cities includes Chicago, Washington, and Los Angeles in North America; Brussels, Frankfurt, Paris, and Zurich in Europe; São Paulo in South America; and Singapore in Southeast Asia. A third tier of so-called secondary world cities includes Houston, Miami, and San Francisco, as well as cities in other countries. Major corporations and banks may have their headquarters in these world cities, rather than in London, New York, or Tokyo.

Regional Command and Control Centers. Cities in the second tier are called regional command and control centers. They contain the headquarters of many large corporations, well-developed banking facilities, and concentrations of such services as insurance, accounting, advertising, law, and public relations. Important educational, medical, and public institutions may be found in these command and control centers. Two levels of regional command and control centers can be identified: regional nodal centers and subregional nodal centers.

Specialized Producer-Service Centers. Cities in the third tier, specialized producer-service centers, offer narrower and highly specialized services. One group of these cities specializes in the management and R&D (research and development) activities related to specific industries, such as steel in Pittsburgh, office equipment in Rochester, and semiconductors in San Jose. A second group of these cities specializes as centers of government and education, notably state capitals that also have a major university, such as Albany, New York; Columbus, Ohio; Lansing, Michigan; Madison, Wisconsin; and Raleigh-Durham, North Carolina (Figure 11-20).

Dependent Centers. Cities at the fourth level, dependent centers, provide relatively unskilled jobs and depend for their economic health on decisions made in the world cities, regional command and control centers, and specialized producer-service centers. Four subtypes of dependent centers can be identified in the United States:

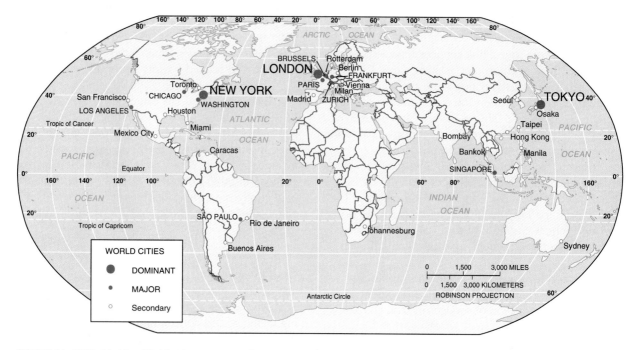

FIGURE 11-19 World cities. World cities are centers for provision of services in the global economy. London, New York, and Tokyo are the three dominant world cities. Major and secondary world cities play somewhat less central roles in the provision of services than the three dominant world cities.

- Resort, retirement, and residential centers, such as Albuquerque, Fort Lauderdale, Las Vegas, and Orlando, clustered in the south and west.
- Manufacturing centers, such as Buffalo, Chattanooga, Erie, and Rockford (Illinois), clustered mostly in the old Northeastern manufacturing belt.

- Industrial and military centers, such as Huntsville (Alabama), Newport News (Virginia), and San Diego, clustered mostly in the south and west.
- Mining and industrial centers, such as Duluth and Charleston (West Virginia), located in mining areas.

Summary

Here again are the key questions concerning settlements.

1. Why are settlements established?

Settlements were originally established for noneconomic reasons, including religious, cultural (nurturing), military, and political. Ultimately, settlements developed for economic reasons, as centers for warehousing surplus products, agriculture, manufacturing, and trading goods and services.

2. How did rural and urban settlements evolve?

Rural settlements evolved as places for farmers to live, whereas urban settlements were places for manufacturing, warehousing, and trading goods and services. Most rural residents clustered in small communities, but since the industrial revolution most farmers in MDCs operate dispersed, isolated farmsteads.

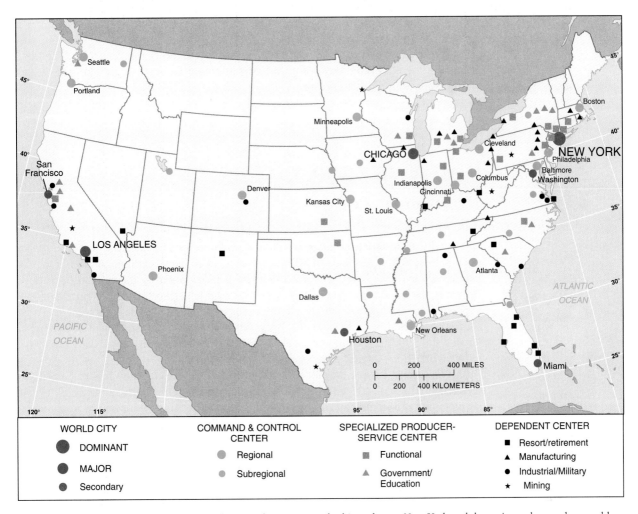

FIGURE 11-20 Economic system of cities in the United States. Atop the hierarchy are New York and the major and secondary world cities. Below the world cities in the hierarchy are regional and subregional command and control centers, specialized producer-service centers, and dependent centers. World cities and regional command and control centers are named on the map.

3. Why do settlements grow?

Since 1800, the percentage of the world's population living in urban settlements has increased from 3 percent to more than 40 percent. Until recently, urban growth was associated with economic development, but in the past quarter-century, the world's largest cities have increasingly been located in less developed countries. Rapid growth of urban settlements makes it difficult to delineate boundaries between urban and rural areas.

4. Why are services concentrated in settlements?

The concept of central place theory helps explain why urban settlements are distributed in a regular pattern in developed societies. Geographers observe a hierarchy of settlements, with larger settlements fewer and farther apart and smaller ones more numerous and closer together. The regular distribution of settlements is interrupted in MDCs because settlements have distinctive economic bases, built on basic industries that export most of their products outside the community. In developed countries, the economic base of an urban settlement is increasingly likely to be services rather than manufacturing.

CASE STUDY REVISITED
Romanian Policy

Virtually all residents of more developed countries are functionally tied to a metropolitan area. Not all residents of MDCs choose to work and shop in a metropolitan area, read a big-city newspaper, and watch television programs from the nearest metropolis. However, the opportunity to do so is available to virtually all residents in more developed societies. Recognizing that virtually all Americans have access to a major metropolitan area, studies conducted by C. A. Doxiadis, Brian Berry, and the U.S. Department of Commerce divided the forty-eight contiguous states into 171 *functional regions*, or "daily urban systems," which are centered around commuting hubs (Figure 11-21).

In LDCs, most people are not part of a daily urban system. They live in rural settlements that lack access to many goods and services. Recognizing the absence of a regular hierarchy of settlements by size, as found in MDCs, the government of Romania for years had a policy of improving the rank-size distribution of their settlements. Restrictions were placed on the growth of Bucharest, and people needed a permit to move there. The government built new apartments and shops in cities such as Brasov.

At the other end of the spectrum, rural Romanian settlements were designated for upgrading to small urban settlements. Government policy called for increasing the population of these small settlements from a few hundred to several thousand inhabitants. New apartments, schools, hospitals, and shops were planned, as well as electricity, paved roads, and sanitation. In this way, families living in rural areas would have greater access to the goods and services essential for achieving a higher standard of living.

Romanian government planners formulated the policy for what they saw as logical economic geography reasons. But Nicolae Ceaucescu, Romania's long-time leader, turned the policy into a nightmare for many people. Population was controlled in the center of Bucharest by razing entire historic neighborhoods. Eastern Orthodox churches and individual homes were demolished and replaced with apartment buildings, as well as massive squares and monuments honoring Ceaucescu and his family.

Believing that rural residents did not wholeheartedly support his programs for modernizing Romania, Ceaucescu ordered small villages to be destroyed, not expanded. Ironically, because of the isolation of many rural villages, Ceaucescu's policies could not be fully implemented. Typically, rural village leaders demolished only a small number of buildings, to show visiting government officials that they had done something to implement Ceaucescu's policy.

After Ceaucescu was overthrown in late 1989, the new Romanian government terminated the policy of indiscriminate demolition. But the challenge remained to bring electricity, paved roads, and other improvements to rural settlements, and to integrate them into a market-oriented economy.

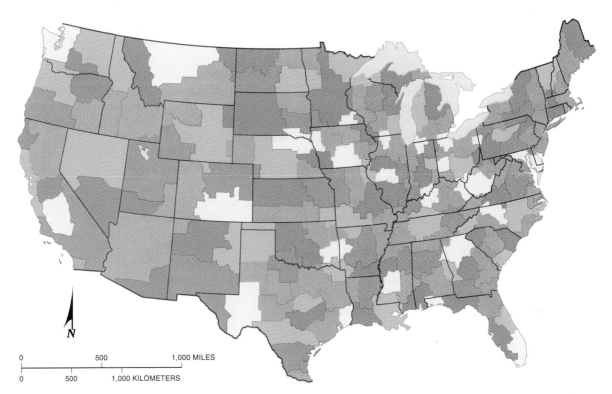

FIGURE 11-21 Daily urban systems. The U.S. Department of Commerce divided the forty-eight contiguous states into "daily urban systems." Regions are delineated by functional ties, especially commuting, to the nearest metropolitan area. Dividing the country into daily urban systems demonstrates that everyone in the United States has access to shops, jobs, and cultural activities in at least one metropolitan area.

Key Terms

Annexation Legally adding land area to a city in the United States.

Basic industries Industries that sell their products primarily to consumers outside the settlement.

Central city The largest city in the area.

Central place A market center for the exchange of goods and services by people attracted from the surrounding area.

Central place theory A theory that explains the distribution of settlements, based on the fact that settlements serve as market centers for people living in the surrounding area; larger settlements are fewer and farther apart than smaller settlements and serve a larger number of people who are willing to travel farther for goods and services.

City-state An independent state comprising a city and its immediate hinterland.

Clustered rural settlement A rural settlement in which the houses and farm buildings of all the families are situated close to each other and fields surround the settlement.

Consolidated metropolitan statistical area Two or more adjacent metropolitan statistical areas with overlapping commuting patterns.

Council of government A cooperative agency consisting of representatives of local governments in a metropolitan area in the United States.

Dispersed rural settlement A rural settlement pattern characterized by isolated farms rather than clustered villages.

Economic base A community's collection of basic industries.

Enclosure movement The process of consolidating small land holdings into a smaller number of larger farms in England beginning in the eighteenth century.

Gravity model A model that holds that the potential use of a good or service at a particular location is directly related to the number of people in a location and inversely related to the distance people must travel to reach the good or service.

Market area (or **hinterland**) The area surrounding a service location, from which people are attracted to use the services.

Metropolitan statistical area (MSA) In the United States, a central city of at least 50,000 population, the county within which the city is located, and adjacent counties meeting one of several tests indicating a functional connection to the central city.

Nonbasic industries Industries that sell their products primarily to consumers in the community.

Plantation A large farm that used many workers to produce tobacco and cotton for sale in Europe and the northern colonies.

Primate city The largest settlement in a country, if it has more than twice as many people as the second-ranking settlement.

Range The maximum distance people are willing to travel to use a service.

Rank-size rule A pattern of settlements in a country, such that the nth largest settlement is $1/n$ the population of the largest settlement.

Rural settlement A settlement in which the principal occupation of the residents is agriculture.

Service Any activity that fulfills a human want or need and returns money to those who provide it.

Settlement A permanent collection of buildings and inhabitants.

Threshold The minimum number of people needed to support the service.

Urbanization An increase in the percentage and in the number of people living in urban settlements.

Urbanized area In the United States, a central city plus its contiguous built-up suburbs.

Urban settlement A settlement in which the principal economic activities are manufacturing, warehousing, trading, and provision of services.

Thinking Geographically

1. Determine the economic base of your community. Consult the *U.S. Census of Manufacturing* or *County Business Patterns*. To make a rough approximation of your community's basic industries, compute the decimal fraction of the nation's population that lives in your community. It will be a small number, such as 0.0005. Then, find the total number of U.S. firms (or employees) in each economic sector that is present in your community. Multiply these national figures by your local population fraction. Subtract the result from your community's actual number of firms (or employees) for that type of industry. If the difference is positive, you have identified one of your community's basic industries.

2. Your community's economy is expanding or contracting as a result of the performance of its basic industries. Two factors can explain the performance of your community's basic industries. One is that the sector is expanding or contracting nationally. The second is that the industry is performing much better or worse in your community than in the nation as a whole. Which of the two factors better explains the performance of your community's basic industries?

3. Rural settlement patterns along the U.S. East Coast were influenced by migration during the colonial era. To what extent do distinctive rural settlement patterns elsewhere in the United States result from international or internal migration?

4. Nearly all residents of MDCs lead urban lifestyles even if they live in rural areas. In contrast, many residents in LDCs lead rural lifestyles even though they live in large cities. They practice subsistence agriculture, raising animals or growing crops. Lacking electrici-

ty, they gather wood for fuel. Lacking running water and sewers, they dig latrines. Why do so many urban dwellers in LDCs lead rural lifestyles?

5. What evidence can you find in your community of economic ties to world cities located elsewhere in North America, Western Europe, or Japan?

Further Readings

Archer, Clark J., and Ellen R. White. "A Service Classification of American Metropolitan Areas." *Urban Geography* 6 (1985): 122–51.

Bairoch, Paul. *Cities and Economic Development: From the Dawn of History to the Present.* Chicago: University of Chicago Press, 1988.

Benevolo, Leonardo. *The History of the City,* 2d ed. Cambridge, MA: MIT Press, 1991.

Berry, Brian J. L. *The Geography of Market Centers and Retail Distribution.* Englewood Cliffs, NJ: Prentice Hall, 1967.

_____. *The Human Consequences of Urbanization.* New York: St. Martin's Press, 1973.

Bourne, L. S., and J. W. Simmons. *Systems of Cities.* New York: Oxford University Press, 1978.

Bourne, L. S., R. Sinclair, and K. Dziewonski, eds. *Urbanization and Settlement Systems: International Perspectives.* New York: Oxford University Press, 1984.

Carter, Harold. *An Introduction to Urban Historical Geography.* London: Edward Arnold, 1983.

Chandler, Tertius, and Gerald Fox. *Three Thousand Years of Urban Growth.* New York: Academic Press, 1974.

Chisholm, Michael. *Rural Settlement and Land Use,* 3d ed. London: Hutchinson, 1979.

Christaller, Walter. *The Central Places of Southern Germany.* Englewood Cliffs, NJ: Prentice Hall, 1966.

Daniels, P. W. *Service Industries: A Geographical Appraisal.* London: Methuen, 1986.

Davis, Kingsley. *Cities: Their Origin, Growth, and Human Impact.* San Francisco: W. H. Freeman, 1973.

_____. *World Urbanization 1950–1970,* Vol. 1. Berkeley: University of California Institute of Environmental Studies, 1969.

Demangeon, Albert. "The Origins and Causes of Settlement Types." In *Readings in Cultural Geography,* ed. P. L. Wagner and M. W. Mikesell. Chicago: University of Chicago Press, 1962.

Detwyler, Thomas, and Melvin Marcus, eds. *Urbanization and Environment.* Belmont, CA: Duxbury Press, 1972.

Dickinson, Robert E. "Rural Settlements in the German Lands." *Annals of the Association of American Geographers* 39 (December 1949): 239–63.

Fuguitt, Glenn V., David L. Brown, and Calvin L. Beale. *Rural and Small Town America.* New York: Russel Sage Foundation, 1989.

Gottmann, Jean. *Megalopolis.* New York: Twentieth Century Fund, 1961.

Green, Milford B. "A Geography of Institutional Stock Ownership in the United States." *Annals of the Association of American Geographers* 83 (March 1993): 66–89.

Harris, Chauncey D. "A Functional Classification of Cities in the United States." *Geographical Review* 33 (January 1943): 86–99.

Hauser, Philip M., and Leo F. Schnore, eds. *The Study of Urbanization.* New York: Wiley, 1965.

Jacobs, Jane. *The Economy of Cities.* New York: Vintage Books, 1970.

King, Leslie J. *Central Place Theory.* Beverly Hills, CA: Sage Publications, 1984.

Kirn, Thomas J. "Growth and Change in the Service Sector of the U.S.: A Spatial Perspective." *Annals of the Association of American Geographers* 77 (September 1987): 353–72.

Longley, Paul A., Michael Batty, and John Shepherd. "The Size, Shape, and Dimensions of Urban Settlements." *Transactions of the Institute of British Geographers,* New Series 16, no. 1 (1991): 75–94.

Lösch, August. *The Economics of Location.* New Haven, CT: Yale University Press, 1954.

Marshall, J. N. "Services in a Postindustrial Economy." *Environment and Planning, A* 17 (1985): 1155–67.

Mitchelson, Ronald L., and James O. Wheeler. "The Flow of Information in a Global Economy: The Role of the American Urban System in 1990." *Annals of the Association of American Geographers* 84 (March 1994): 87–106.

Morrill, Richard. "The Structure of Shopping in a Metropolis." *Urban Geography* 8 (1987): 97–128.

Mumford, Lewis. *The City in History.* New York: Harcourt, Brace, and World, 1961.

Noyelle, T. J., and T. M. Stanback, Jr. *The Economic Transformation of American Cities*. Totowa, NJ: Rowman & Allanheld, 1984.

Ó hUallacháin, Breandan, and Neil Reid. "The Location and Growth of Business and Professional Services in American Metropolitan Areas, 1976–1986." *Annals of the Association of American Geographers* 81 (June 1991): 254–70.

O'Kelly, M. E. "Multipurpose Shopping Trips and the Size of Retail Facilities." *Annals of the Association of American Geographers* 73 (June 1983): 231–39.

Scofield, Edna. "The Origin of Settlement Patterns in Rural New England." *Geographical Review* 28 (October 1938): 652–63.

Scott, Peter. *Geography and Retailing*. London: Hutchinson University Press, 1970.

Trewartha, Glen T. "Types of Rural Settlements in North America." *Geographical Review* 36 (October 1946): 568–96.

United Nations. *World Urban Agglomerations*. New York: U.N. Population Division, 1992.

Wheeler. James O., and Ronald L. Mitchelson. "Information Flows among Major Metropolitan Areas in the United States." *Annals of the Association of American Geographers* 79 (December 1989): 523–43.

Wirth, Louis. *On Cities and Social Life*. Chicago: University of Chicago Press, 1964.

Also consult these journals: *Journal of Historical Geography, Journal of Regional Science, Journal of Rural Studies, Urban Geography*.

PEOPLE, PLACES AND CHANGE
Global Firms in the Industrializing East

The Annenberg
CPB Project

Singapore has emerged as a major world city in the global economy. Its rapidly growing professional services sector exercises control over production and the flow of capital in the world's fastest growing market region—East and Southeast Asia.

Commentator

Singapore is at the heart of the East Asia region. Multinational companies which came to Singapore from Europe and the United States in the 1960s now have their regional headquarters on the island, alongside many of the world's top banks and other financial players.

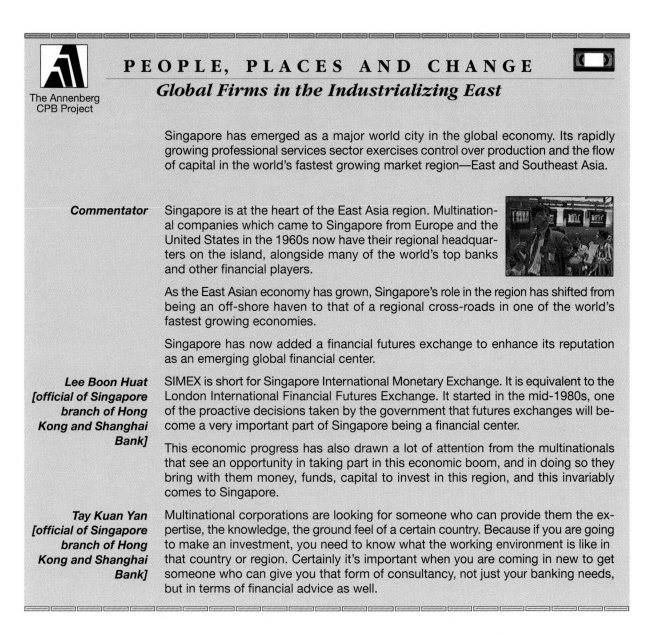

As the East Asian economy has grown, Singapore's role in the region has shifted from being an off-shore haven to that of a regional cross-roads in one of the world's fastest growing economies.

Singapore has now added a financial futures exchange to enhance its reputation as an emerging global financial center.

Lee Boon Huat
[official of Singapore branch of Hong Kong and Shanghai Bank]

SIMEX is short for Singapore International Monetary Exchange. It is equivalent to the London International Financial Futures Exchange. It started in the mid-1980s, one of the proactive decisions taken by the government that futures exchanges will become a very important part of Singapore being a financial center.

This economic progress has also drawn a lot of attention from the multinationals that see an opportunity in taking part in this economic boom, and in doing so they bring with them money, funds, capital to invest in this region, and this invariably comes to Singapore.

Tay Kuan Yan
[official of Singapore branch of Hong Kong and Shanghai Bank]

Multinational corporations are looking for someone who can provide them the expertise, the knowledge, the ground feel of a certain country. Because if you are going to make an investment, you need to know what the working environment is like in that country or region. Certainly it's important when you are coming in new to get someone who can give you that form of consultancy, not just your banking needs, but in terms of financial advice as well.

12

URBAN PATTERNS

KEY ISSUES

1. What activities occur in the central business district?
2. What problems do inner-city residential areas face?
3. What are the causes and consequences of suburbanization?
4. How are different social groups distributed within an urban area?

If you are a football fan, you know that the Detroit Lions actually play their home games at a stadium in Pontiac, Michigan. It is 50 kilometers (30 miles) from downtown Detroit. The New York Giants and New York Jets play their home games in another state altogether, at the New Jersey Meadowlands.

The movement of football clubs out from the center city is just one example of the suburbanization of people and activities in the United States and Canada. More people in these two countries now live in suburbs than in central cities. This changing structure of our cities is a response to conflicting desires. People are moving out of cities to avoid problems, but they still want convenient access to the city's jobs, shops, culture, and recreation.

This chapter examines the causes and consequences of today's evolving urban patterns. For example, how do fans reach the football stadium located in Pontiac, or New Jersey? Typically, they travel by car. But how do people who don't have cars get there? In the old days—when the Lions played in downtown Detroit and the Giants played in New York City—people could use public transportation to reach the stadium. Today, it is inconvenient, if not impossible, for people without cars to attend games.

Attending football games may not be central to your life, but it is just one example of new living patterns. Consider peoples' daily activities, such as working and shopping. Where are jobs and shops today? Increasingly, they are in the suburbs.

THE GINZA, TOKYO. (MIKE YAMASHITA/WEST LIGHT)

Two Families in New Jersey

Ruth Merritt lives in the city of Camden, New Jersey. She is 24 years old, a single parent with three children (ages 7, 2, and 1). Her income, derived from the community's program of aid to families with dependent children, is $235 per month, or $2,820 a year.

The Merritt family lives in a four-room apartment in a row house that was divided some years ago into six dwelling units. The apartment has adequate plumbing and kitchen facilities, but the residents sometimes see rats in the building. The rent is $75 per month, plus an average of $50 per month for electricity and other utilities. Ruth Merritt receives food stamps, but her monthly expenses for food, clothing, and shelter exceed her income. In cold weather, she must sometimes reduce the food budget to pay for heat.

Just 10 kilometers (6 miles) east of Camden, the Johnson family lives in Cherry Hill, New Jersey. William Johnson is a lawyer who commutes to downtown Philadelphia, across the Delaware River from Camden. Diane Johnson works for a nonprofit organization with offices in the suburban community where they live. Their two children attend a recently built school in Cherry Hill.

The Johnson family's dwelling is a detached house with three bedrooms, a living room, dining room, family room, and kitchen. The attached garage contains two cars, one for each parent to get to work. The half-acre lawn surrounding the house provides ample space for the children to play. The Johnsons bought their house 5 years ago for $150,000. The monthly payments for mortgage and utilities are nearly $2,000, but the family's combined annual income of $100,000 is more than adequate to pay the housing costs.

The Merritt and Johnson households illustrate the contrasts that exist today in U.S. urban areas. As you have seen throughout this book, there are dramatic differences in material standards around the world, but the situations described here are based on families living in the same urban area, only a few kilometers apart.

Had these examples been taken from an urban area elsewhere in the world, the spatial patterns might have been reversed. In most of the world, the higher-status Johnsons would live near the center of the city, and the lower-status Merritts would live in the suburbs.

This chapter examines the patterns and problems observed in the modern city. Although different internal structures characterize urban areas in the United States and elsewhere, the problems arising from current spatial trends are quite similar.

The modern city is a complex mosaic of people and activities. Geographers not only describe where different activities are located in a city and where different types of people live; they also try to explain the reasons.

As explained in Chapter 11, urban areas include the central city and surrounding suburbs. The central city includes a central commercial core and inner residential neighborhoods. Suburbs include residences as well as manufacturing and commercial districts. This chapter is organized around the activities occurring in each of these distinctive areas.

KEY ISSUE 1

What Activities Occur in the Central Business District?

- Services
- Consequences of High Land Costs

The center is the best-known and most visually distinctive area of most cities. It is usually one of the oldest districts in a city, often the original site of the settlement. The precise boundary of the central area is not always easily defined. In common usage, it corresponds roughly to the area built up at the time of construction of railroad tracks and terminals in the mid-1800s, especially in Europe.

Services

In most cities, the center is where services, especially retail and office activities, are concentrated. This area is commonly known as *downtown*, but geographers employ a more precise term, the **central business district (CBD)**. The CBD is compact—less than 1 percent of the urban land area—but contains a large percentage of the shops, offices, and public institutions (Figure 12-1).

Retail and office activities are attracted to the CBD because of its accessibility. The center is the easiest part of the city to reach from the rest of the

region and is the focal point of the region's transportation network.

Importance of the CBD for Retailing

Three types of retail services are concentrated in the center because they must be accessible to everyone in the region—shops with a high threshold, shops with a high range, and shops that serve people who work in the center.

Shops with a High Threshold. A shop may be in the center if it has a high *threshold* (defined in Chapter 11 as the minimum number of customers needed to support a service). High-threshold shops, such as department stores, traditionally preferred a central location so that they would be accessible to many customers. Large department stores in the CBD often clustered on both sides of the street on one block. Retailers referred to the intersection nearest such a cluster as the "100 percent corner." Rents were highest there because this location had the highest accessibility for the most customers.

In recent years, many high-threshold shops such as large department stores have closed their downtown branches. CBDs that once boasted three or four stores now have none, or perhaps one struggling survivor. The customers for downtown department stores now consist of downtown office workers, inner-city residents, and tourists. Department stores with high thresholds are now more likely to be in suburban malls.

Shops with a High Range. The second type of shop in the center has a high *range* (a great maximum distance customers are willing to travel to use the service). In general, a high-range shop is very specialized, with customers who patronize it infrequently. High-range shops prefer central locations because their customers are scattered over a wide area. For example, an expensive jewelry or a specialty food shop attracts shoppers from all over the urban area, but each customer visits infrequently.

Some cities have preserved their old downtown markets. These markets feature a large number of stalls, each operated by individual merchants. They may have a high range, because they attract customers who willingly travel far to find more-exotic or higher-quality products. At the same time, inner-city residents may use these markets for their weekly grocery shopping.

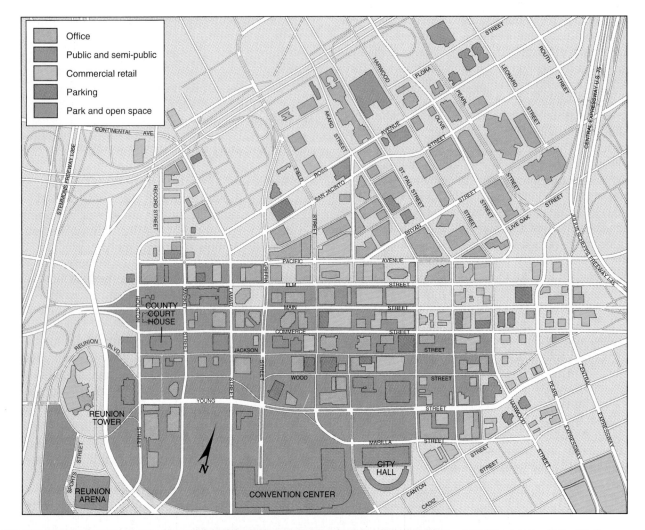

FIGURE 12-1 The CBD of Dallas, Texas. The CBD is dominated by retail and office buildings. Also clustered in the downtown area are public and semipublic buildings, such as City Hall, government office buildings, and the central post office. (The tall needle is the Reunion Towers.) The city's largest indoor arena, the Reunion Arena, is a few blocks to the south (right) of the Tower. (James Blank/FPG International)

High-range shops still can thrive in some CBDs if they combine retailing with recreational activities. People are willing to make a special trip to a specific destination downtown for unusual shops in a dramatic setting, perhaps a central atrium with a fountain or a view of a harbor. But many high-range shops have moved with department stores to suburban shopping malls.

Shops Serving Center Workers. A third type of retail activity in the center serves the many people who work in the center and shop during lunch or working hours. These businesses sell office supplies, computers, and clothing, or offer shoe repair, rapid photocopying, dry cleaning, and so on.

CBDs in cities outside North America are more likely to contain supermarkets, bakeries, butchers, and other food stores. These stores may be open for limited hours in the evenings or on weekends. The 24-hour supermarket is rare outside North America, because of preferences of shopkeepers, government regulations, and long-time shopping habits.

In contrast to the other two types of retailers, shops that appeal to nearby office workers are expanding in the CBD, in part because the number of downtown office workers has increased and in part because downtown offices require more services.

Importance of the CBD for Offices

Offices cluster in the center for accessibility. People in such services as advertising, banking, finance, journalism, and law particularly depend on proximity to colleagues. Lawyers, for example, locate downtown to be near government offices and courts. Services such as temporary secretarial agencies and instant printers locate downtown to be near lawyers, forming a chain of interdependency that continues to draw offices to the center city.

Despite the diffusion of modern telecommunications, many professionals still exchange information with colleagues primarily through face-to-face contact. Financial analysts discuss attractive stocks or impending corporate takeovers. Lawyers meet to settle disputes out of court. Offices are centrally located to facilitate rapid communication of fast-breaking news through spatial proximity. Face-to-face contact also helps to establish a relationship of trust.

A central location also helps businesses that employ workers from a variety of neighborhoods. Top

executives may live in one neighbor... ecutives in another, secretaries in an... todians in another. Only a central loca... accessible to all groups. Firms that nee... cialized employees are most likely to fin... central area, perhaps currently working ...another company downtown.

Consequences of High Land Costs

The center's accessibility produces extreme competition for the limited sites available. As a result, land value in the center is very high. In a rural area, a hectare of land may cost several thousand dollars. In a suburb, it might cost tens of thousands of dollars. But in a large CBD such as New York or London, if a hectare of land were even available, it would cost several hundred million dollars.

Tokyo's CBD probably contains Earth's most expensive land. Transactions have exceeded $250,000 per square meter ($1,000,000,000 per acre). If this page were a parcel of land in Tokyo, it would sell for more than $12,000.

Tokyo's high prices result from a severe shortage of buildable land. Buildings in most areas are legally restricted to less than 10 meters in height (normally three stories) for fear of earthquakes, even though recent earthquakes have demonstrated that modern, well-built skyscrapers are safer than older three-story structures. Further, Japanese tax laws favor retention of agricultural land. Although it is the world's most populous urban area, Tokyo contains 36,000 hectares (90,000 acres) of farmland.

Two distinctive characteristics of any central business district follow from the high land cost. First, land is used more intensively in the center than elsewhere in the city. Second, some activities are excluded from the center because of the high cost of space.

Intensive Land Use

The intensive demand for space gives the CBD a three-dimensional character, pushing it vertically. Compared with other parts of the city, the central area uses more space below and above ground level.

A vast underground network exists beneath most central cities. The typical "underground city" includes multistory parking garages, loading docks for deliveries to offices and shops, and utility lines (water, sewer, phone, electric, and some heating). Subways run beneath the streets of larger central cities. Cities such as Minneapolis, Montréal, and Toronto have built extensive pedestrian passages and shops beneath the center. These underground areas segregate pedestrians from motor vehicles and shield them from harsh winter weather.

Typically, telephone, electric, and cable television wires run beneath the surface in central areas. Not enough space is available in the center for the large number of telephone poles that would be needed for such a dense network, and the wires are unsightly and hazardous.

Skyscrapers. Demand for space in the CBD has also made high-rise structures economically feasible. Downtown skyscrapers give a city one of its most distinctive images and unifying symbols. Suburban houses, shopping malls, and factories look much the same from one city to another, but each city has a unique downtown skyline, resulting from the particular arrangement and architectural styles of its high-rise buildings.

The first skyscrapers were built in Chicago in the 1880s, made possible by two inventions: the elevator and iron-frame building construction. The first high rises caused great inconvenience to neighboring structures, because they blocked light and air movement. The invention of artificial lighting, ventilation, central heating, and air conditioning have helped to solve those problems. Most North American and European cities enacted zoning ordinances early in the twentieth century in part to control the location and height of skyscrapers.

A recent building boom in CBDs of many North American cities is generating problems again. Too many skyscrapers built near each other cause traffic congestion in the narrow streets. Skyscrapers may prevent sunlight from penetrating to the sidewalks and small parcels of open space, and high winds can be channeled through the deep artificial canyons created between buildings. Construction of high rises may also be affected in the future by the need to conserve energy. As the sun and natural air movement are increasingly relied upon again for light and ventilation, the old complaints about high rises may return.

Many recently built skyscrapers are only partially occupied, because private developers overbuilt dur-

ing the 1980s. In other CBDs, tenants have moved to the new skyscrapers, leaving a high percentage of vacancies in the older ones.

Skyscrapers are an interesting example of "vertical geography." The nature of an activity influences which floor it occupies in a typical high rise. Some shop owners demand street-level space to entice the most customers and are willing to pay higher rents. Professional offices are less dependent on walk-in trade and can occupy the higher levels at lower rents. Hotel rooms and apartments may be included in the upper floors of a skyscraper to take advantage of lower noise levels and panoramic views. Residents of the world's highest apartments, on the upper floors of the ninety-seven-story John Hancock Center in Chicago, sometimes are above the clouds. They may telephone the doorman to find out about the weather at street level.

The one large U.S. CBD without skyscrapers is Washington, D.C., where no building is allowed to be higher than the U.S. Capitol dome. Consequent-

In U.S. cities, high-rise buildings cluster in the center, but in European cities such as Paris they cluster in the suburbs, whereas the center contains historic structures. The high-rises in the background are in La Défense, a western suburb of Paris. (Chad Ehlers/Tony Stone Images)

ly, offices in downtown Washington rise no more than thirteen stories. As a result, the typical Washington office building uses more horizontal space—land area—than in other cities. The city's CBD spreads over a much wider area than those in comparable cities.

European CBDs. The central area is less dominated by commercial considerations in Europe than in the United States. In addition to retail and office functions, many European cities display a legacy of low-rise structures and narrow streets, built as long ago as medieval times. Today these buildings are protected from the intrusion of contemporary development. The most prominent structures may be churches and former royal palaces, situated on the most important public squares, at road junctions, or on hilltops. Parks in the center of European cities often were first laid out as private gardens for aristocratic families and later were opened to the public.

Some European cities have tried to preserve their historic core by limiting high-rise buildings and the number of cars. During the early 1970s, several high-rise offices were built in Paris, including Europe's tallest office building (the 210-meter, or 688-foot Tour Montparnasse). The public outcry over this disfigurement of the city's historic skyline was so great that officials reestablished lower height limits. In Rome, officials periodically try to ban private automobiles from the center city, because they cause pollution and congestion and damage ancient monuments.

The central area of Warsaw, Poland, represents an extreme example of preservation. The Nazis completely destroyed Warsaw's medieval core during World War II, but Poland rebuilt the area exactly as it had appeared, working from old photographs and drawings. The reconstruction of central Warsaw served as a powerful symbol of cultural tradition for the Polish people after the upheavals of World War II and the postwar Communist takeover.

Although constructing large new buildings is difficult, many shops and offices still wish to be in the center of European cities. The alternative to new construction is renovation of older buildings. Renovation, however, is even more expensive than new construction and does not always produce enough space to meet the demand. As a result, rents are much higher in the center of European cities than in U.S. cities of comparable size.

Land Uses Excluded from the CBD

High rents and land shortage discourage two principal activities in the central area: manufacturing and residence.

Declining Manufacturing in Central Cities.
The typical modern industry requires a large parcel of land to spread operations among one-story buildings. Suitable land generally is available in suburbs. In central Paris, manufacturing jobs declined from more than 500,000 in the late 1960s to 400,000 around 1980 and 200,000 in the early 1990s. The Citroën automobile factory, situated along the River Seine, barely 1 kilometer from the Eiffel Tower, has been replaced by high-rise offices and apartments. Warehouses on the southeast edge of the central area have also been replaced by office and apartment towers. Slaughterhouses in the northeastern part of central Paris have been replaced by a park and museum complex.

Port cities in North America and Europe have transformed their waterfronts from industry to commercial and recreational activities. Once, ships docked at piers that jutted out into the water, and warehouses lined the waterfront to facilitate loading and unloading of goods. But today's large ocean-going ships are unable to maneuver in the tight, shallow waters of the old inner-city harbors. Consequently, port activities have moved to more modern facilities downstream. Cities have demolished derelict warehouses and rotting piers along their waterfronts and replaced them with new offices, shops, parks, and museums.

Once-rotting downtown waterfronts have become major tourist attractions in both North American cities—including Boston, Toronto, Baltimore, and San Francisco—and European cities such as Barcelona and London. The cities took the lead in clearing the sites and constructing new parks, docks, walkways, museums, and parking lots. They also have built large convention centers to house professional meetings and trade shows. Private developers have added hotels, restaurants, boutiques, and entertainment centers to accommodate tourists and conventioneers.

Declining Residential Use of Central Cities.
Few people live in U.S. CBDs, because offices and

shops can afford to pay higher rents for the scarce space than individuals can. Monthly rents in downtown high-rise office buildings are several dollars per square foot, depending on the city and the quality of the building. Typical apartments in most U.S. cities rent for less than $1 per square foot per month.

The shortage of affordable space is especially critical in Europe, because Europeans prefer living near the center city more than Americans do. Prohibitions on constructing new high rises induce developers to convert older houses into offices.

Abandoned warehouses have been converted into residences in many CBDs. The warehouses may require expensive alterations to meet local code standards for emergency exits and ventilation. City officials welcome the additional downtown residents but regret the permanent loss of industrial space. In reality, manufacturers are highly unlikely to occupy multistory downtown lofts.

Many people used to live downtown. For example, the City of London—the region's 1-square-mile financial center and the site of its earliest settlement—contained 128,000 residents in 1851. The residential population declined to 72,000 in 1871, to 13,000 in 1921, to around 5,000 today. The CBDs of North American cities have witnessed comparable population losses.

People have migrated from central areas for a combination of pull and push factors. First, people have been lured to suburbs, which offer larger homes with private yards and modern schools. Second, people have sought to escape from the dirt, crime, congestion, and poverty of the central city.

Commuting. Because few people dwell in the center city, urban areas are characterized by commuting into the CBD in the morning and out in the evening. The intense concentration of people in the center during working hours strains transportation systems, because a large number of people must reach a small area of land at the same time in the morning and disperse at the same time in the afternoon. As much as 40 percent of all trips made into or out of a CBD may occur during 4 hours of the day, two in the morning and two in the afternoon. **Rush hour**, or *peak hour*, is defined as the four consecutive 15-minute periods that have the heaviest traffic.

In larger cities, public transportation is better suited than cars to moving large numbers of people, be-cause each traveler takes up far less space. But most Americans still prefer to commute by car. One-third of the high-priced CBD land is devoted to streets and parking lots, although multistory and underground garages also are constructed.

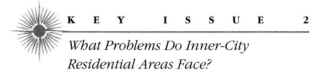

KEY ISSUE 2

What Problems Do Inner-City Residential Areas Face?

- Inner-City Housing
- Problems in Central Cities

Surrounding the CBD are inner-city residential neighborhoods. These areas have acquired other names, including the zone in transition, the gray area, and the twilight zone. In addition to residential areas, the zone in transition also comprises older industries and warehouses. U.S. inner cities contain concentrations of low-income people who face a variety of social and economic problems.

Inner-City Housing

Inner-city neighborhoods contain three main types of housing: older low-quality housing, public housing, and renovated housing.

Low-Quality Housing

Most occupants of inner residential areas in U.S. cities are low-income nonwhites, a pattern that is largely a product of race relations. Many neighborhoods in the United States are racially segregated, with African–Americans or Latinos concentrated in one or two large continuous areas of the inner city and whites living in the suburbs.

Filtering. As low-income and minority families increase in the city, the territory they occupy expands. Neighborhoods can shift from predominantly white middle-class occupants to low-income nonwhites within a few years. Middle-class white families move out of a neighborhood to newer housing farther from the center and sell or rent their houses to lower-income nonwhite families.

Large houses built by wealthy families in the nine-teenth century are subdivided by absentee landlords into smaller dwellings for low-income families. This process of subdivision of houses and occupancy by successive waves of lower-income people is known as **filtering**. The ultimate result of filtering may be abandonment of the dwelling.

Like a car, tape player, or any other object, the better a house is maintained, the longer it will last. Landlords stop maintaining houses when the rent they collect becomes less than the maintenance cost. In such a case, the building soon deteriorates and grows unfit for occupancy. Not even the poorest families will rent the dwelling. This is the point in the filtering process at which the owner may abandon the property, because the value of the structure be-comes less than the cost of taxes. Thousands of va-cant and abandoned houses stand in the inner areas of American cities.

One hundred years ago, low-income inner-city areas in the United States teemed with throngs of re-cent immigrants from Europe. Today, these areas house barely 10 percent of the population of 1900, and less than half of the population of 1960. Schools and shops close because they are no longer needed in inner-city neighborhoods with rapidly declining populations. Through the filtering process, many poor families have moved to less-deteriorated hous-es farther from the center.

Blockbusting and Redlining.

Deterioration in urban neighborhoods is aggravated by blockbusting and redlining. Real estate agents who practice **block-busting** start by convincing white property owners to sell their houses at low prices, preying on their fear that nonwhite families will soon move into the neighborhood. The agent then sells or rents the hous-es to nonwhite families at a considerable profit.

Some banks engage in **redlining**, so-named be-cause they draw lines on a map and refuse to loan money for property within the boundaries. Families who try to fix up houses in the inner city therefore have difficulty borrowing money.

Both blockbusting and redlining are illegal. But en-forcement of laws against them is frequently difficult.

Urban Renewal.

North American and European cities demolished much of their substandard inner-city housing between the 1950s and 1970s through

The zone in transition in many American cities includes extensive areas of vacant and abandoned housing, such as this area of Brooklyn, New York. The population of Brooklyn has declined by about 15 percent since 1950, as people move to neighborhoods and suburban communities farther from the zone of transition. (Geri Engberg/The Stock Market)

urban renewal programs. Under urban renewal, cities identified blighted inner-city neighborhoods, acquired the properties from private owners, relocated the res-idents and businesses, cleared the sites, and built new roads and utilities. The land was then turned over to private developers or to public agencies, such as the board of education or the parks department, to con-struct new buildings. National government grants helped cities pay for urban renewal.

Urban renewal has been criticized for destroying the social cohesion of older neighborhoods and re-ducing the supply of low-cost housing. Because African–Americans constituted a large percentage of the displaced population in U.S. cities, urban renewal was often called "Negro Removal" during the 1960s. Most North American and European cities have turned away from urban renewal since the 1970s, and national governments, including the United States, have stopped funding it.

Public Housing

Many old, substandard houses in European and North American inner cities have been demolished and replaced with public housing. In the United States, **public housing** is reserved for low-income households, who must pay 30 percent of their income for rent. A housing authority, established by the local government, manages the buildings, while the federal government pays the cost of construction and the maintenance, repair, and management costs that are not covered by rent.

In the United States, public housing accounts for only 2 percent of all dwellings, although it may exceed 10 percent in the zone in transition of many cities. In the United Kingdom, more than one-third of all housing is publicly owned, and the percentage is even higher in northern cities such as Liverpool, Manchester, and Glasgow. Private landlords control only a small percentage of housing in the United Kingdom, for the most part confined to central London and resort communities.

Elsewhere in Western Europe, governments typically do not own the housing. Instead, they subsidize construction cost and rent for a large percentage of the privately built housing. Developers of low-cost housing may be either nonprofit organizations, such as church groups and labor unions, or profit-making corporations that agree to build some low-cost housing in exchange for permission to build higher-cost housing elsewhere. The U.S. government has also provided subsidies to private developers, but on a much smaller scale than in Europe.

A number of high-rise public housing projects built in the United States and Europe during the 1950s and early 1960s are now considered unsatisfactory environments for families with children. The elevators are frequently broken, juveniles terrorize other people in the hallways, and drug use and crime rates are high. Some observers claim that the high-rise buildings caused the problem, because too many low-income families are concentrated into a high-density environment. Because of poor conditions, public housing authorities have demolished high-rise public housing projects in recent years in Dallas, Newark, St. Louis, Liverpool in England, Glasgow in Scotland, and other U.S. and European cities.

More recent public housing projects have consisted primarily of two- or three-story apartment buildings and row houses, with high-rise apartments reserved for elderly people. Cities have also experimented with "scattered-site" public housing, in which dwellings are dispersed throughout the city rather than clustered in a large project.

Two high-rise public housing projects in the Clapton Park Estate, in the East End of London, England, are demolished simultaneously. The high-rise buildings (known in England as council tower blocks) will be replaced by town houses with gardens, a more suitable environment for families with children. (Gill Allen/AP/Wide World Photos)

Some neighborhoods in the zone of transition have been renovated by middle class families who wish to live near the central business district in cities such as Boston. (Bill Buchman/Photo Researchers, Inc.)

Decline of Public Housing. In recent years, the U.S. government has stopped funding new public housing altogether. Some federal support is available to renovate older buildings and to help low-income households pay their rent, but the overall level of funding is much lower today than in the late 1970s. As a result, the supply of public housing and other government-subsidized housing diminished by approximately 1 million units between the early 1980s and the early 1990s. But during the same period, the number of households needing low-rent dwellings increased by more than 2 million.

In Britain, the supply of public housing, known as *council estates*, has also declined, because the government has forced local authorities to sell some of the dwellings to the residents. But at the same time, the British have expanded subsidies to nonprofit housing associations, which build housing for groups with special needs, including single mothers, immigrants, the disabled and elderly, as well as the poor.

Renovated Housing

In addition to areas of older low-quality housing and public housing, the third type of inner-city residential area is the high-class neighborhood. Some older neighborhoods never saw decline. They contained some of the city's socially elite, who maintained an enclave of expensive property near the center city. In other cases, inner-city neighborhoods have only recently achieved high status as a result of renovation by the city and private investors.

Some middle-class families are moving back to inner-city neighborhoods, a process known as **gentrification**. Gentrification occurs for several reasons. Some middle-class families are attracted to inner-city neighborhoods by lower prices for larger and more substantially constructed homes. The old houses may possess attractive architectural details such as ornate fireplaces, cornices, high ceilings, and wood trim.

Renovated homes in inner-city neighborhoods also attract middle-class individuals who work downtown. Living here eliminates the strain of commuting on crowded freeways or public transit. Others like the cultural and recreational opportunities increasingly available in central areas. Renovated inner-city housing appeals to persons who have no children, because they are not concerned with the quality of schools.

Renovation of an old house near downtown can be nearly as expensive as buying a new suburban home. Cities encourage young middle-class families to renovate inner-city homes by providing low-cost loans and tax breaks. Public expenditures for renovation have been criticized as subsidies for the middle class at the expense of poor people, who are forced to move out of the revitalized neighborhoods because the rents in the area are suddenly too high for them.

Cities try to reduce the hardship on poor families in two ways:

1. Since 1970, when a family is forced to relocate as a result of public action, U.S. law requires that they be reimbursed both for moving expenses and for rent increases over a 4-year period. Western European countries have similar laws.
2. Cities renovate old houses specifically for lower-income families, through public housing

or other programs. By renting renovated houses, the city also helps to disperse low-income families throughout the city, instead of concentrating them in large inner-city public housing projects.

Problems in Central Cities

Since the 1980s, economic conditions have improved in many North American and European CBDs, primarily because of an unprecedented pace of office construction. Downtowns that were generally considered dead and beyond help as recently as the 1980s are now filled with residents and tourists alike, even during evenings and weekends when offices are closed. The new downtown offices, shops, and recreation facilities provide cities with additional tax revenue for maintaining essential services.

But the animation and prosperity in many CBDs do not extend to surrounding inner-city residential areas. Except for a handful of high-income residents, the inner city is home to people with social and economic problems.

Social Problems of Inner-City Residents

Inner-city residents are increasingly trapped in an unending cycle of economic and social problems and are unable to share in the CBD's revival. They are frequently referred to as a permanent **underclass**.

The underclass suffers from relatively high rates of unemployment, alcoholism, drug addiction, illiteracy, juvenile delinquency, and crime. They live in areas where schools are deteriorated and affordable housing is increasingly difficult to find. Neighborhoods lack adequate police and fire protection, shops, hospitals, clinics, or other health-care facilities.

Lack of Job Skills. The future is especially bleak for the underclass because they are increasingly unable to compete for jobs. Inner-city residents lack the technical skills needed for most jobs, because fewer than half complete high school. The gap between skills demanded by employers and the training possessed by inner-city residents is widening.

In the past, people with limited education could become factory workers or filing clerks, but today those jobs require skills in computing and electronics technology. Meanwhile, inner-city residents don't even have access to the remaining low-skilled jobs, such as custodians and fast-food servers, because these opportunities are increasingly in the distant suburbs.

Despite the importance of education in obtaining jobs, many in the underclass live in an atmosphere that ignores good learning habits, such as regular school attendance and completion of homework. The household may consist of only one parent, who may be forced to choose between working to generate income and staying at home to provide child care.

Trapped in such a hopeless environment, some inner-city residents turn to drugs. Drug use is a problem in suburbs and rural areas as well, but rates of use in recent years have increased most rapidly in the inner cities. Some users turn to crime to obtain money for drugs. Gangs form in inner-city neighborhoods to control lucrative drug distribution. Violence erupts when two gangs fight over the boundaries between their drug distribution areas.

Homeless. An increasing number of the underclass are homeless. Several million Americans sleep in doorways, on heated street grates, and in bus and subway stations. Los Angeles County alone has an estimated 35,000 homeless individuals, attracted by the area's relatively mild climate. Homelessness is an even more serious problem in less developed countries. An estimated 300,000 people in Calcutta sleep, bathe, and eat on sidewalks and traffic islands.

Most people are homeless because they cannot afford housing and have no regular income. Homelessness may have been sparked by family problems or job loss. Roughly one-third of the U.S. homeless, however, are individuals who are unable to cope in society after being released from hospitals or other institutions.

Segregation. Even small cities display strong social distinctions among neighborhoods. A frequently noticed division is between the east and west sides of a city, or between the north and south sides, with one side attracting the higher-income residents and the other left to lower-status and minority families.

A family seeking a new residence usually considers only a few districts, where the residents' social and financial characteristics match their own. Residential areas designed for wealthy families are developed in scenic, attractive areas, possibly a hillside or near a body of water, while flat, dull land closer to industry becomes built up with cheaper housing.

Hundreds of thousands of homeless people sleep on sidewalks and in parks in U.S. cities. An especially large number are attracted to Sunbelt cities with warm climates such as Phoenix, Arizona. (Thomas Ives/ The Stock Market)

In the late 1960s, the National Advisory Commission on Civil Disorders, known as the Kerner Commission, concluded that U.S. cities were divided into two separate and unequal societies, one black and one white. Three decades later, despite serious efforts to integrate and equalize the two, segregation and inequality persist.

African–Americans constitute more than two-thirds of the population in Atlanta, Detroit, Gary, and Washington, and a lesser majority in other large U.S. central cities such as Baltimore, Birmingham, New Orleans, Newark, and Oakland. Within U.S. metropolitan areas, two-thirds of whites live in suburbs and one-third in central cities. The statistic is inverted for African–Americans: two-thirds live in central cities and one-third in suburbs. African–Americans constitute one-fourth of the U.S. central city population but only 7 percent of the suburbs.

Other U.S. metropolitan areas contain large concentrations of Latino residents. Over one-third of the population is Latino in the MSAs (metropolitan statistical areas) or CMSAs (consolidated metropolitan statistical areas) of Albuquerque, Los Angeles, Miami, and several Texas cities, including Corpus Christi, El Paso, and San Antonio. Latinos also constitute over one-sixth of the population of the New York City and San Francisco metropolitan areas. Overall, two-thirds of Latino Americans live in central cities.

Fiscal Problems

The concentration of low-income minority residents in inner neighborhoods of central cities has produced financial problems. These people require city services, but they can pay very little, if any, tax to support the services. Despite higher taxes generated by new CBD projects, central cities face a growing gap between the cost of needed services and the availability of funds to pay for them. The percentage of people below the poverty level living in U.S. central cities increased during the 1980s and is currently more than twice as high as in the suburbs.

Since 1950, overall population has declined more than 40 percent in the central cities of Buffalo, Cleveland, Detroit, and St. Louis, and by more than one-fourth in other cities such as Boston, Cincinnati, Dayton, Jersey City, Louisville, Minneapolis, Newark, and Rochester. The number of tax-paying middle-class families and industries has invariably declined by even higher percentages in these cities.

A city has two choices to close the gap between the cost of services and the funding available from taxes. One alternative is to raise taxes, a move that can drive the remaining wealthier people and industries from the city. The other alternative is to reduce services by closing libraries, eliminating some public transit routes, collecting trash less frequently, and delaying replacement of outdated school equipment. Aside from the hardship imposed on individuals laid off from work, cutbacks in public services also encourage middle-class residents and industries to move from the city.

To avoid this dilemma, cities have increasingly sought funds from state and federal governments. Here is the federal government's contributed share to the budgets of the fifty largest U.S. cities: starting at 1 percent in 1950, it rose to 18 percent in 1980 but then shrank substantially during the 1980s, to 6 percent in 1990. In dollars, federal aid to U.S. cities declined from about $44 billion in 1981 to about $23 billion in 1993, a 66 percent decline when adjusted for inflation. To offset a portion of these lost federal funds, some state governments increased financial assistance to cities. The declining level of outside financial support has intensified the fiscal crisis faced by cities as a result of shifting land-use patterns.

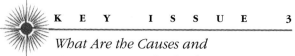

K E Y I S S U E 3

What Are the Causes and Consequences of Suburbanization?

- Attraction of Suburbs
- Changes in Transportation Systems
- Suburbanization of Businesses

Some inner-city neighborhoods are attracting middle-class families, but this movement is quite small compared with the flood of suburbanization. The contemporary city is surrounded by growing residential suburbs, made possible by better transportation. In the suburbs dwell families who prefer lower density than is possible near the central area. To serve these suburban residents, commercial activities have grown.

Attractions of Suburbs

Public opinion polls in the United States and Western Europe show people's strong desire for suburban living. In most polls, more than 90 percent of respondents prefer the suburbs to the zone in transition.

Suburbs offer varied attractions: a detached single-family dwelling rather than a row house or apartment, private land surrounding the house, space to park cars, and a greater opportunity for home own-

ership. The suburban house provides space and privacy, a daily retreat from the stress of urban living.

Families with children are especially attracted to suburbs, which offer more space for play and protection from the high crime rates and heavy traffic that characterize inner-city life. As incomes have risen in the twentieth century, first in the United States and more recently in Western Europe, more families can afford to buy suburban homes.

The suburban population has grown much faster than the overall population, especially in the United States. According to the Bureau of the Census, it has increased from 20 percent in 1950 to 60 percent today. To put it another way, since 1950, the U.S. population has increased by around 100 million people. During that time, population increased by around 135 million in suburbs and declined by 35 million in central cities and rural areas.

The Density Gradient

As you travel outward from the center of a city, you can watch the decline in the density at which people live. Inner-city apartments or row houses may pack as many as 250 dwellings on a hectare of land (100 dwellings per acre). Older suburbs have larger row houses, semidetached houses, and individual houses on small lots, at a density of about ten houses per hectare (four houses per acre). A detached house typically sits on a lot of one-quarter to one-half hectare (one-half to one acre) in new suburbs and a lot of one hectare (2.5 acres) or greater on the fringe of the built-up area.

This density change in an urban area is called the **density gradient**. According to the density gradient, the number of houses per unit of land diminishes as distance from the center city increases.

Changes in Density Gradient. Two changes have affected the density gradient in recent years. First, the number of people living in the center has decreased. The density gradient thus has a gap in the center where few live.

Second is the trend toward less density difference within urban areas. The number of people living on a hectare of land has decreased in the central residential areas through population decline and abandonment of old housing. At the same time, density has increased on the periphery through construction of apartment and row house projects and diffusion of suburbs across a larger area (Figure 12-2).

In European cities, the density gradient has also been affected by low-income high-rise apartments in the suburbs and by stricter control over construction of detached houses on large lots. The result of the two changes is to flatten the density gradient and reduce the extremes of inner and outer areas traditionally found within cities.

The Cost of Suburban Sprawl

U.S. suburbs are characterized by **sprawl**, which is the progressive spread of development over the landscape. When private developers select new housing sites, they seek cheap land that can be easily prepared for construction—land often not con-

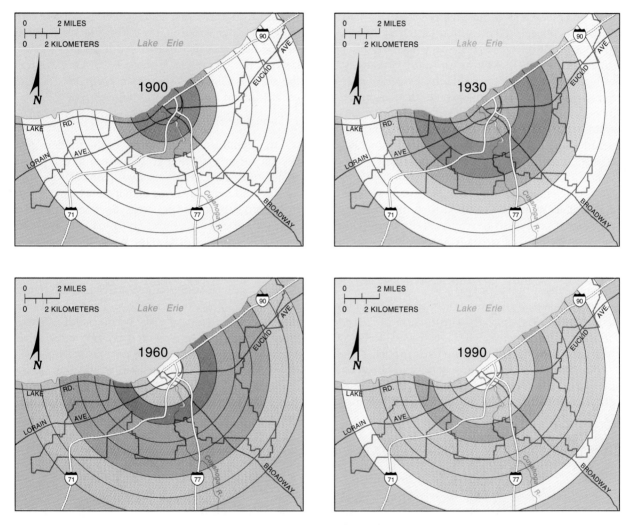

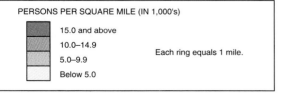

PERSONS PER SQUARE MILE (IN 1,000's)

- 15.0 and above
- 10.0–14.9
- 5.0–9.9
- Below 5.0

Each ring equals 1 mile.

FIGURE 12-2 Cleveland density gradient. The density gradient has changed during the twentieth century. In 1900, population was highly clustered in and near the CBD. In 1930 and 1960, the population was spreading, leaving the original core less dense. By 1990, population was distributed over a much larger area, the variation in the density among different rings was much less, and the area's lowest densities existed in the rings near the CBD. The current boundary of the city of Cleveland is shown. (Adapted from Avery M. Guest, "Population Suburbanization in American Metropolitan Areas, 1940–1970," *Geographical Analysis* 7 (July 1975): 267–83, table 4. Used by permission of the publisher.)

tiguous to the existing built-up area. Sprawl is also fostered by the desire of many families to own large tracts of land.

Suburban Development Process. As long as demand for single-family detached houses remains high, land on the fringe of urbanized areas must be converted from open space to residential land use. The current system for developing land on urban fringes is inefficient in the United States.

Land is not transformed immediately from farms to housing developments in the United States. Instead, developers buy farms for future construction of houses by individual builders. Developers frequently reject land adjacent to built-up areas in favor of detached isolated sites, depending on the price and physical attributes of the alternatives. The rural-urban fringe in U.S. cities therefore looks like Swiss cheese, with pockets of development and gaps of open space.

Urban sprawl has some undesirable traits. Roads and utilities must be extended to connect isolated new developments to nearby built-up areas. Either the cost of these new roads and utilities is either funded by taxes or the services are installed by the developer, who passes the cost on to new residents through higher house prices.

Sprawl also wastes land. Some prime agricultural land may be lost through construction of isolated housing developments, while other sites lie fallow, with speculators waiting for the most profitable time to build homes on them. In reality, sprawl has little impact on the total farmland in the United States, but it does reduce the ability of city dwellers to get

to the country for recreation, and it can affect the supply of local dairy products and vegetables. The low-density suburb also wastes energy, especially because the automobile is required for most trips.

The supply of land for construction of new housing is more severely restricted in European urban areas. Officials attack sprawl by designating areas of mandatory open space. London, Birmingham, and several other British cities are surrounded by **greenbelts**, or rings of open space. New housing is built either in older suburbs inside the greenbelts or in planned extensions to small towns and new towns beyond the greenbelts (Figure 12-3). Restriction of the supply of land on the urban periphery, however, has driven up house prices in Europe.

Suburban Segregation

One significant characteristic of the modern residential suburb is the high degree of two types of segregation. First, residents are separated from commercial and manufacturing activities, which are confined to compact, distinct areas. Second, housing in a given suburban community is usually built for people of a single social class, with others excluded by virtue of the cost, size, or location of the housing.

The homogeneous suburb is a twentieth-century phenomenon. In older cities, activities and classes were more likely to be separated vertically rather than horizontally. In a typical urban building, shops were on the street level, with the shop owner or another well-to-do family living on one or two floors above the shop. Poorer people would live on the higher levels or in the basement, the least attractive parts of the building. The basement was dark and

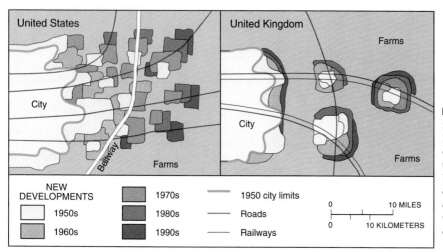

FIGURE 12-3 Suburban development in the United States and the United Kingdom. The United States is characterized by much more sprawl than the United Kingdom. In the U.K., new housing is likely to be concentrated in new towns or planned extensions of existing small towns, whereas in the United States, growth occurs in discontinuous projects.

damp, and before the elevator was invented, the higher levels could be reached only by climbing many flights of stairs. Rich families lived in houses with space available in the basement or attic to accommodate servants.

Once cities spread out over much larger areas, the old pattern of vertical separation was replaced by territorial segregation. Large sections of the city were developed with houses of similar interior dimension, lot size, and cost, appealing to people with similar incomes and lifestyles.

Zoning ordinances, developed in Europe and North America in the early decades of the twentieth century, encouraged spatial separation. They prevented mixing of land uses within the same district. In particular, single-family houses, apartments, industry, and commerce were kept apart, because the location of one activity near another was considered unhealthy and inefficient.

The strongest criticism of U.S. residential suburbs is that low-income and minority people are unable to live in them because of the high cost of the housing and the unfriendliness of established residents. Suburban communities discourage the entry of lower-income and minority individuals because of fear that property values will decline if the high-status composition of the neighborhood is altered. Legal devices, such as requiring each house to sit on a large lot and the prohibition of apartments, prevent low-income families from living in many suburbs.

School Busing. The segregation of residential communities by race has led to a difficult situation in many school systems. Since 1954, when the U.S. Supreme Court ruled that racially segregated school systems are inherently unequal, cities have been faced with the need to improve racial balance in their schools. But the goal of integration has conflicted with the strong desire of many parents and educators that children should live within walking distance of school. As long as neighborhoods have a homogeneous population, it is impossible to achieve both goals.

Some school districts have tried to promote integration by busing students from their homes to schools elsewhere in the city. Busing has been unpopular, but in some communities no other system has been found to integrate schools. In many communities, white parents have chosen to send their children to private schools rather than have them attend integrated public schools. Ironically, because the private school is frequently farther away than the public school, children are bused anyway.

Changes in Transportation Systems

Urban sprawl makes people dependent on vehicular transportation for access to work, shopping, and leisure activities. People do not travel aimlessly: their trips have a precise point of origin, destination, and purpose. More than half of all trips are work-related—commuting between work and home, business travel, or deliveries. Shopping and other personal business and social journeys each account for approximately one-fourth of all trips.

Historically, the growth of suburbs was constrained by transportation problems. People lived in crowded cities because they had to be within walking distance of shops and places of employment. The invention of the railroad in the nineteenth century enabled people to live in suburbs and work in the central city. Cities then built street railways—frequently known as trolleys, streetcars, or trams—and underground railways (subways) to accommodate commuters.

Many so-called *streetcar suburbs* built in the nineteenth century still exist and retain unique visual identities. They consist of houses and shops clustered near a station or former streetcar stop at a much higher density than is found in newer suburbs.

The Automobile

The suburban explosion in the twentieth century has relied on automobiles rather than railroads, especially in the United States. In the nineteenth century, rail and trolley lines restricted suburban development to narrow ribbons within walking distance of the stations. Automobiles have permitted large-scale development of suburbs at greater distances from the center, in the gaps between the rail lines. Automobile drivers have much greater flexibility in the choice of residence than was ever before possible.

Automobile ownership is nearly universal among American households, with the exception of some poor families, older individuals, and people living in the center of large cities such as New York. More than 95 percent of all trips within U.S. cities are made by car, compared with fewer than 5 percent by bus or rail. Outside the big cities, public transportation service is extremely rare or nonexistent.

The U.S. government has encouraged the use of cars by paying 90 percent of the cost of limited-ac-

(Top) The boundary between urban and rural areas is much sharper in European cities, such as Agrigento, Italy (on the island of Sicily). (Martha Bates/Stock Boston) (Bottom) In contrast, suburbs outside U.S. cities, such as Palmdale, California, may be discontinuous and sprawling. (Robert Reiff/FPG International)

cess high-speed interstate highways, which stretch for 70,000 kilometers (44,000 miles) across the country. The use of cars is also supported by policies that limit the price of fuel to less than one-half the level found in Western Europe. A few years ago, Senator Daniel Patrick Moynihan, a former Harvard professor, quipped that the United States has a national urban growth policy—the interstate highway system. He was referring to the dominant role of new expressway construction in fostering decentralization of U.S. cities.

The automobile is an important user of land in the city. An average city allocates about one-fourth of its land to roads and parking lots. Valuable land in the central city is devoted to parking automobiles, although expensive underground and multistory parking structures can reduce the amount of ground-level space needed. Modern six-lane freeways cut a 23-meter (75-foot) path through the heart of cities, and elaborate interchanges consume even more space. European and Japanese cities have been especially disrupted by attempts to insert new roads and parking areas in or near the medieval central areas.

Technological improvements may help motorists elude congested traffic areas. Not far into the future, this scenario may become commonplace: at the beginning of a journey, the driver indicates the starting and destination points to the car's computer. A screen displays a map, stored on CD-ROM, showing the best route to avoid traffic tie-ups. The computer is alerted of traffic conditions by sensors in the wheels or by radio signals, either from roadside transmitters or by satellite. When the automobile enters a high-speed freeway, the computer controls its speed and the spacing between it and other vehicles. Diffusion of such technology reflects the continuing preference of most people in MDCs to continue using private automobiles rather than switch to public transportation.

Public Transit

Automobiles have costs beyond their purchase and operation: delays imposed on others, increased need for highway maintenance, construction of new highways, and pollution. Most people overlook these important costs because they place higher value on the privacy and flexibility of schedule that the car provides.

Public transportation is cheaper, less polluting, and more energy-efficient than the automobile. It also is particularly suited to rapidly bringing a large number of people into a small area. Consequently, its use is increasingly confined in the United States to rush-hour commuting by workers in the CBD. A bus can accommodate thirty people in the amount of space occupied by one automobile; a double-track rapid transit line can transport the same number of people as sixteen lanes of urban freeway.

In North America, public transportation has been the major casualty of commitment to the automobile. Ridership on U.S. public transportation declined from 23 billion per year in the late 1940s to 7 billion in the early 1990s. At the end of World War I, U.S. cities had 50,000 kilometers (30,000 miles) of street railways and trolleys that carried 14 billion passengers a year, but only a few hundred kilometers of track remain. The number of U.S. and Canadian cities with trolley service declined from approximately 50 in 1950 to 8 in the 1960s. You can still ride the trolley in Boston, Cleveland, Newark, New Orleans, Philadelphia, Pittsburgh, San Francisco, and Toronto.

Buses offered a more flexible service than trolleys because they were not restricted to fixed tracks. General Motors acquired many of the privately owned streetcar companies and replaced the trolleys with buses that the company made. Bus ridership, however, has declined from a peak of 11 billion riders per year in the late 1940s to 6 billion in the 1990s. Commuter railroad service, like trolleys and buses, has also been drastically reduced in most U.S. cities.

New Rapid Transit Lines. The one exception to the downward trend in public transportation is the rapid transit line. Such services are now known to transportation planners as either *fixed heavy rail* (subways) or *fixed light rail* (streetcars).

Cities such as Boston and Chicago have attracted new passengers through extension of subway lines and modernization of existing service. Chicago has been a pioneer in the construction of heavy rail rapid transit lines in the median strips of expressways. Entirely new subway systems have been built in recent years in U.S. cities, including Atlanta, Baltimore, Miami, San Francisco, and Washington.

The federal government has permitted Boston, New York, and other cities to use funds originally allocated for interstate highways to modernize rapid transit service instead. New York's subway cars, once covered with graffiti have been cleaned, so that passengers can ride in a more hospitable environment. As a result of these improvements, subway ridership in the United States has increased 2 percent per year since 1980.

The trolley—now known by the more elegant term of *fixed light rail transit*—is making a modest comeback in North America. Once relegated almost exclusively as a tourist attraction in New Orleans and San Francisco, trolley lines have been built or are under construction in Baltimore, Buffalo, Calgary, Edmonton, Los Angeles, Portland (Oregon), Sacramento, St. Louis, San Diego, and San Jose. But new construction in all ten cities amounted to only approximately 200 kilometers (130 miles) during the 1980s and early 1990s.

California, the state that most symbolizes the automobile-oriented American culture, leads in construction of new fixed light rail transit lines. San Diego has added more kilometers than any other city, although Los Angeles will have the most extensive new system when completed. Los Angeles had a rail network exceeding 1,600 kilometers (1,000 miles) as recently as the late 1940s, but the lines were abandoned when freeways were built to accommodate rising automobile usage. In San Diego, one line that runs from the center south to the Mexican border has been irreverently dubbed the "Tijuana trolley" because it is heavily used by residents of nearby Tijuana, Mexico.

Service versus Cost. People who are too poor to own an automobile may still not be able to reach places of employment by public transportation. Low-income people tend to live in inner-city neighborhoods, but the job opportunities, especially those requiring minimal training and skill, are in suburban areas not well served by public transportation. Inner-city neighborhoods have high unemployment rates at the same time that suburban firms have difficulty attracting workers. In some cities, governments and employers subsidize vans to carry low-income inner-city residents to suburban jobs.

Despite modest recent successes, most public transportation systems are caught in a vicious circle, because fares do not cover operating costs. As patronage declines and expenses rise, the fares are increased; passengers use the service less, so service

is reduced and fares are increased even more. Public expenditures to subsidize construction and operating costs have increased, but the United States does not fully recognize that public transportation is a vital utility deserving of subsidy to the degree long assumed by European governments.

Public Transit in Other Countries. Even in developed Western European countries and Japan, where automobile ownership rates are high, extensive networks of bus, tram, and subway lines have been maintained, and funds for new construction have been provided in recent years (Figure 12-4). Since the late 1960s, London has opened 27 kilometers (17 miles) of subways, including two new lines, plus 18 kilometers (11 miles) in light rail transit lines to serve the docklands area, which has been transformed from industrial to residential and office uses. During the same period, Paris has built 65 kilometers (40 miles) of new subway lines, including a new system, known as the Réseau Express Régional (R.E.R.) to serve outer suburbs.

Smaller cities have shared the construction boom. In France alone, new subway lines have been built since the 1970s in Lille, Lyon, and Marseille, and hundreds of kilometers of entirely new tracks have been laid between the country's major cities to operate a high-speed train known as the TGV (*Train à Grande Vitesse*). Growth in the suburbs has stimulated nonresidential construction, including suburban shops, industry, and offices.

Suburbanization of Businesses

Businesses as well as people have moved to suburbs. Manufacturers have selected peripheral locations because land costs are lower. Service providers have moved to the suburbs because most of their customers are there.

Suburbanization of Retailing

Suburban residential growth has fostered change in traditional retailing patterns. Historically, urban residents bought food and other daily necessities at small neighborhood shops in the midst of housing areas and they shopped in the CBD for other products. But, since the end of World War II, downtown sales have not increased, whereas suburban sales have risen at an annual rate of 5 percent.

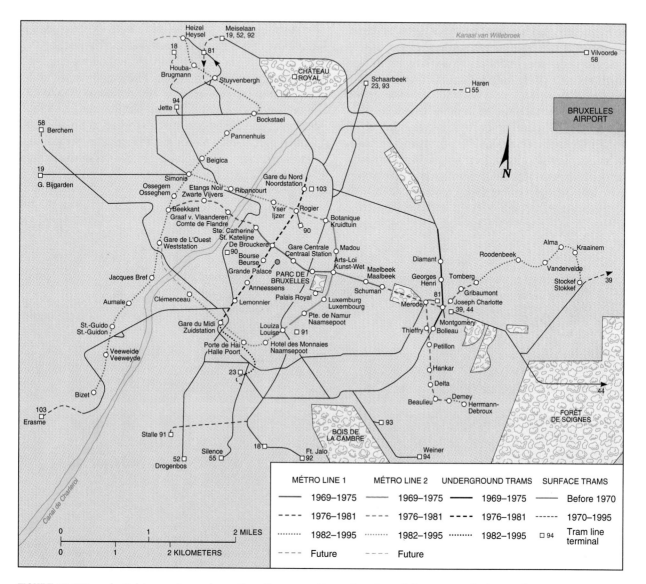

FIGURE 12-4 Brussels, Belgium, métro and tram lines. European cities such as Brussels have invested substantially to improve public transportation in recent years. Brussels provides a good example of a public transport system that integrates heavy rail (métro Line 1 and 2) with light rail (trams). Trams initially used métro tunnels, but the tunnels were large enough to convert to heavy rail lines as funds became available.

Downtown sales have stagnated because suburban residents who live far from the CBD won't make the long journey there. At the same time, small corner shops do not exist in the midst of newer residential suburbs. The low density of residential construction discourages people from walking to stores, and restrictive zoning practices often exclude shops from residential areas.

Shopping Malls. Instead, retailing has been increasingly concentrated in planned suburban shopping malls of varying sizes. Corner shops have been replaced by supermarkets in small shopping centers. Larger malls contain department stores and specialty shops traditionally reserved for the CBD. Generous parking lots surround the stores. Shopping malls require as many as 40 hectares (100 acres) of land and are frequently near key road junctions, such as the interchange of two interstate highways (Figure 12-5).

Some shopping malls are elaborate multilevel structures exceeding 100,000 square meters (1 million square feet), with more than 100 stores arranged along covered walkways. Malls have become centers for activities in suburban areas that lack other types of community facilities. Retired people go to malls for safe, vigorous walking exercises, or they sit on the benches to watch the passing scene. Teenagers arrive after school to meet their friends. Concerts and exhibitions are frequently set up in the malls.

A shopping mall is built by a developer, who buys the land, builds the structures, and leases space to individual merchants. Typically, a merchant's rent is a percentage of sales revenue. The key to a successful large shopping mall is the inclusion of one or more *anchors*, usually large department stores. Typically, consumers go to a mall to shop at an anchor, and while there, patronize the smaller shops. In smaller shopping centers, the anchor is frequently a supermarket or discount store.

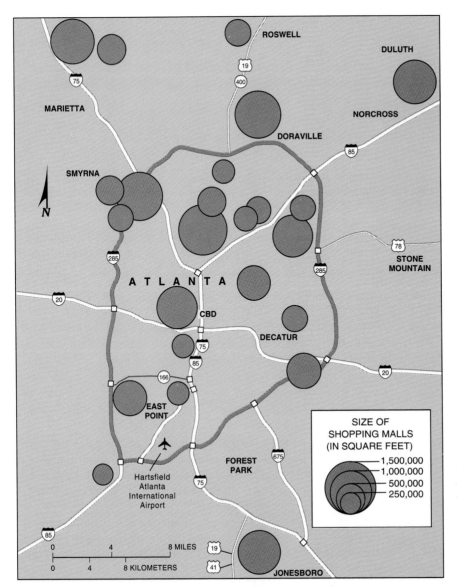

FIGURE 12-5 Major retail centers in Atlanta. Most shopping malls in the Atlanta metropolitan area, as elsewhere in North America, are in the suburbs, not the inner city. The optimal location for a large shopping mall is near an interchange on an interstate highway "beltway", such as I-285, which encircles Atlanta.

Quincy Market, along with the adjacent Fanueil Hall, in downtown Boston, was the city's market center in the eighteenth century. The renovated buildings attract customers from throughout the metropolitan Boston area, as well as tourists. (Geri Engberg/The Stock Market)

Restructured Retailing in the CBD. While retail activities expand in the suburbs, CBDs fight for survival. The total volume of sales in downtown areas has been stable, but the pattern of demand has changed. Large department stores have difficulty attracting their old customers, whereas smaller shops that cater to the special needs of the downtown labor force are surviving. Patrons of downtown shops tend increasingly to be downtown employees who shop during the lunch hour.

Many cities have attempted to revitalize retailing in the CBD and older neighborhoods. One popular method is to ban motor vehicles from busy shopping streets. By converting streets to pedestrian-only walkways, cities emulate one of the most attractive attributes of large shopping malls. Shopping streets reserved for pedestrians are widespread in northern Europe, including the Netherlands, Germany, and Scandinavian countries.

Entirely new large shopping malls have been built in several downtown areas in North America in recent years. In Boston, the eighteenth-century market, known as Faneuil Hall, was transformed from a derelict area into a modern shopping center of more than 150 stores, covering 34,000 square meters (362,000 square feet). Philadelphia's Gallery at Market East, a downtown four-level shopping center of 125,000 square meters (1,348,000 square feet), has more than 200 stores. It is anchored by three large department stores and provides direct access to a subway station and multistory parking garage.

Harbor Place in Baltimore (13,000 square meters, or 135,000 square feet) includes two shopping pavilions with about seventy-five stores integrated into a collection of waterfront museums, tourist attractions, hotels, and cultural facilities. These downtown malls attract suburban shoppers as well as out-of-town tourists because they offer, in addition to retail shops, unique recreation and entertainment experiences.

Decentralization of Factories and Offices

Factories and warehouses have migrated to suburbia for more space, cheaper land, and better truck access. Modern factories and warehouses demand more land for efficient operation because conveyor belts, forklift trucks, loading docks, and machinery are spread over a single level. Suburban locations facilitate truck shipments with good access to main highways and no central-city traffic congestion. Industries increasingly receive inputs and distribute products by truck.

Offices that do not require face-to-face contact increasingly are moving to suburbs, where rents are much lower than in the CBD. Executives can drive on uncongested roads to their offices from their homes in nearby suburbs and park their cars without charge.

For other employees, however, suburban office locations can pose a hardship. Secretaries, custodians, and other lower-status office workers may not have cars, and public transportation may not serve the site. Other office workers may miss the stimulation and animation of a central location, particularly at lunch time.

K E Y   I S S U E   4

How Are Different Social Groups Distributed within an Urban Area?

- Internal Social Structure of Cities
- Use of the Models outside North America

People are not distributed randomly within an urban area. They concentrate in particular neighborhoods, depending on their characteristics. Geographers describe where people with particular characteristics are likely to live within an urban area and offer explanations for why these patterns occur.

Internal Social Structure of Cities

Sociologists, economists, and geographers have developed three models to help to explain where different types of people tend to live in an urban area: the concentric zone, sector, and multiple nuclei models.

Three Models of Social Structure

The three models describing the internal social structure of cities were all developed in Chicago, a city on a flat prairie. Except for Lake Michigan to the east, few physical features have interrupted the region's growth. Chicago includes a CBD, known as the Loop because elevated railway lines loop around it. Surrounding the Loop are residential suburbs to the south, west, and north. The three models were later applied to cities elsewhere in the United States and in other countries.

The Concentric Zone Model. The concentric zone model was the first to explain the distribution of different social groups within urban areas. It was created in 1923 by sociologist E. W. Burgess. According to the **concentric zone model**, a city grows outward from a central area in a series of concentric rings, like the growth rings of a tree. The precise size and width of the rings vary from one city to another, but the same basic types of rings appear in all cities in the same order (Figure 12-6).

The innermost of the five zones is the CBD, where nonresidential activities are concentrated. The CBD is surrounded by the second ring, the zone of tran-

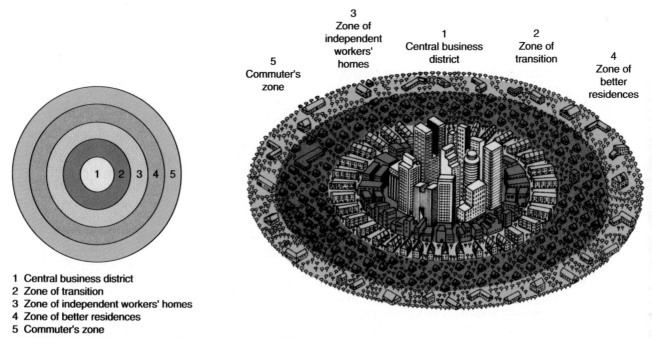

1 Central business district
2 Zone of transition
3 Zone of independent workers' homes
4 Zone of better residences
5 Commuter's zone

FIGURE 12-6 Concentric zone model. According to the model, a city grows in a series of rings that surround the CBD.

sition, which contains industry and poorer-quality housing. Immigrants to the city first live in this zone in small dwelling units, frequently created by subdividing larger houses into apartments. The zone also contains rooming houses for single individuals.

The third ring, the zone of independent workers' homes, contains modest older houses occupied by stable, working-class families. The fourth zone has newer and more spacious houses for middle-class families. Finally, Burgess identified a commuters' zone, beyond the continuous built-up area of the city. Some people who work in the center nonetheless choose to live in small villages that have become dormitory towns for commuters.

The Sector Model. A second theory of urban structure, the **sector model**, was developed in 1939 by land economist Homer Hoyt (Figure 12-7). According to Hoyt, the city develops in a series of sectors, not rings. Certain areas of the city are more attractive for various activities, originally because of an environmental factor or even by mere chance. As a city grows, activities expand outward in a wedge, or sector, from the center. Once a district with high-class housing is established, the most expensive new housing is built on the outer edge of that district, farther out from the center. The best housing is therefore found in a corridor extending from downtown to the outer edge of the city. Industrial and retailing activities develop in other sectors, usually along good transportation lines.

To some extent, the sector model is a refinement of the concentric zone model rather than a radical restatement. Hoyt mapped the highest-rent areas for a number of U.S. cities at different times and showed that the highest social class district usually remained in the same sector, although it moved farther out along that sector over time.

Hoyt and Burgess both claimed that social patterns in Chicago supported their model. According to Burgess, Chicago's CBD was surrounded by a series of rings, broken only by Lake Michigan on the east. Hoyt argued that the best housing in Chicago developed north from the CBD along Lake Michigan, while industry located along major rail lines and roads to the south, southwest, and northwest.

The Multiple Nuclei Model. Geographers C. D. Harris and E. L. Ullman developed the multiple nuclei model in 1945. According to the **multiple nuclei model**, a city is a complex structure that includes more than one center around which activities revolve. Examples of these nodes include a port, neighborhood business center, university, airport, and park (Figure 12-8).

The multiple nuclei theory states that some activities are attracted to particular nodes while others try to avoid them. For example, a university node may attract well-educated residents, pizzerias, and bookstores, whereas an airport may attract hotels and warehouses. On the other hand, incompatible land-use activities will avoid clustering in the same loca-

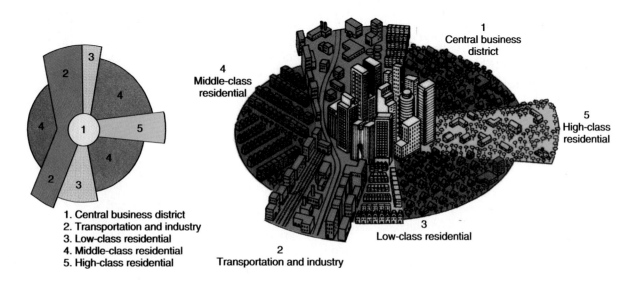

1. Central business district
2. Transportation and industry
3. Low-class residential
4. Middle-class residential
5. High-class residential

FIGURE 12-7 Sector model. According to the model, a city grows in a series of wedges, or corridors, which extend out from the CBD.

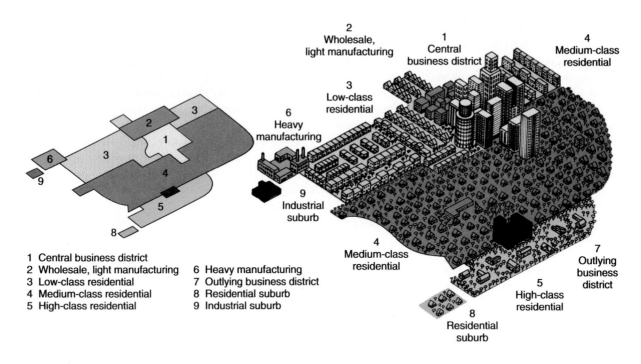

1 Central business district
2 Wholesale, light manufacturing
3 Low-class residential
4 Medium-class residential
5 High-class residential
6 Heavy manufacturing
7 Outlying business district
8 Residential suburb
9 Industrial suburb

FIGURE 12-8 Multiple nuclei model. According to the model, a city consists of a collection of individual nodes, or centers, around which different types of people and activities cluster.

tions. Heavy industry and high-class housing, for example, rarely exist in the same neighborhood.

Geographic Applications of the Models

The three models help us understand where people with different social characteristics tend to live within an urban area. They can also help to explain why certain types of people tend to live in particular places.

Effective use of the models depends on the availability of data at the scale of individual neighborhoods. In the United States and many other countries, that information comes from a national census. U.S. urban areas are divided into **census tracts**, which contain approximately 5,000 residents and correspond where possible to neighborhood boundaries. Every decade, the U.S. Bureau of the Census publishes data summarizing the characteristics of the residents living in each tract. Examples of information the bureau publishes include the number of nonwhites, the median income of all families, and the percentage of adults who finished high school.

Social Area Analysis. The spatial distribution of any of these social characteristics can be plotted on a map of the community's census tracts. Computers are invaluable in this analysis, because they permit rapid creation of maps and storage of voluminous data about each census tract. Social scientists can compare the distributions of characteristics and create an overall picture of where various types of people tend to live. This kind of study is known as *social area analysis.*

None of the three models by itself completely explains why different types of people live in distinctive parts of the city. Critics point out that the models are too simple and fail to consider the variety of reasons that lead people to select particular residential locations. Because the three models are all based on conditions that existed in U.S. cities between the two world wars, critics also question their relevance to contemporary urban patterns in the United States or in other countries.

But if the models are combined, rather than considered independently, they do help geographers explain where different types of people live in a city. People tend to live in certain locations depending on their particular personal characteristics. This does not mean that everyone with the same characteristics must live in the same neighborhood, but the models say that most people prefer to live near others having similar characteristics.

Consider two families with the same income and ethnic background. One family includes married parents with young children and the other is an unmarried couple with no children. The concentric zone model suggests that the married household is much more likely to live in an outer ring and the unmarried one in an inner ring (Figure 12-9).

The sector theory suggests that, given two families of the same age with the same number of children, the family with the higher income will not live in the same sector of the city as the poorer one (Figure 12-10).

The multiple nuclei theory suggests that people with the same ethnic or racial background are likely to live near each other (Figure 12-11).

Putting the three models together, we can identify, for example, the neighborhood in which a childless, high-income, Asian American family is most likely to live.

The dozens of social characteristics mapped for an urban area can be combined into a generalized drawing showing the city's main social areas. The three models complement each other in explaining where people live, because elements of all three models are present in an urban area. For example, the distribution of African–Americans in Baltimore City combines the concentric zone, sector, and multiple nuclei theories (Figure 12-12).

Consistent with the concentric zone model, African–Americans are clustered in the inner city, surrounded by a zone that is racially mixed and a large outer ring that is virtually all white.

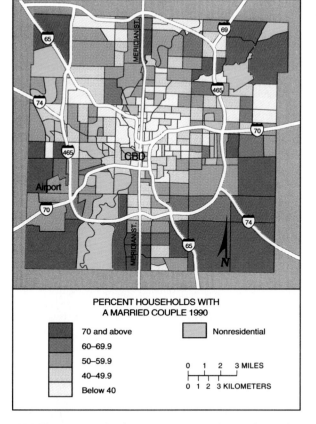

PERCENT HOUSEHOLDS WITH A MARRIED COUPLE 1990

- 70 and above
- 60–69.9
- 50–59.9
- 40–49.9
- Below 40
- Nonresidential

0 1 2 3 MILES
0 1 2 3 KILOMETERS

FIGURE 12-9 Example of concentric zone model in Indianapolis: distribution of married couples. The percentage of households with a married couple is less near the CBD and greater in the outer rings of the city.

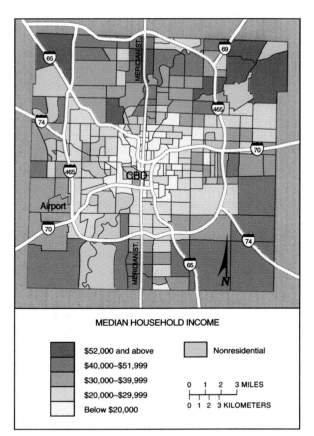

MEDIAN HOUSEHOLD INCOME

- $52,000 and above
- $40,000–$51,999
- $30,000–$39,999
- $20,000–$29,999
- Below $20,000
- Nonresidential

0 1 2 3 MILES
0 1 2 3 KILOMETERS

FIGURE 12-10 Example of sector model in Indianapolis: distribution of high-income households. The median household income is the highest in a sector to the north, which extends beyond the city limits to the adjacent county.

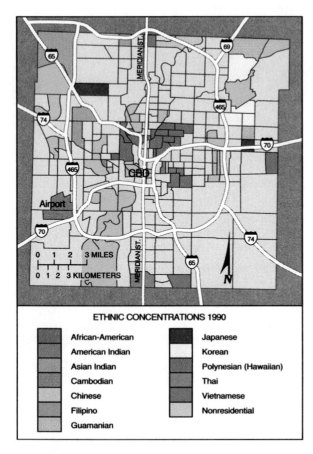

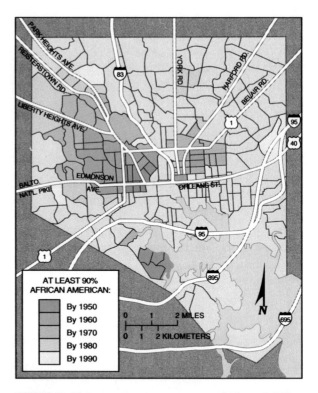

FIGURE 12-11 Example of multiple nuclei model in Indianapolis: distribution of minorities. The black concentration consists of census tracts that are 90 percent or more African–American. The other clusters are tracts that contain at least 5 percent of the total Indianapolis population of that ethnic group.

FIGURE 12-12 Concentric zone, sector, or multiple nuclei? The distribution of African-Americans in Baltimore reveals elements of all three models of the internal structure of cities.

The sector model also helps to explain racial patterns in the city, because a comparison of the current pattern with the past pattern shows that black neighborhoods are expanding in sectors to the northwest and north along several radial roads.

The multiple nuclei model is also useful, because Baltimore's African–American population is concentrated in three neighborhoods—east, west, and south of the CBD. Historically, two independent centers of black culture developed in Baltimore on the east and west sides. Even today, few blacks move between the two sides. The south-side concentration dates from the 1940s, when the city began to build several thousand public housing units on formerly vacant land.

Distribution of Social Problems. Geographic analysis helps us understand factors underlying urban social problems. For example, the ten loca-

tions in the Dayton urban area with the highest number of arrests on felony charges for drug violations were clustered just west of the CBD (Figure 12-13). Social area analysis reveals that, clustered in the inner-west area of Dayton are census tracts that contain relatively high levels of low-income and African–American households.

At first glance, this pattern seems to confirm a stereotype and is the kind of finding that is widely presented misleadingly by the media. But the higher incidence of arrests in low-income African–American areas does not necessarily mean that drug *usage* is higher or that African–Americans are more involved in drug trafficking than whites. Some studies have shown that, among male high school students, rates of drug use may actually be higher among whites.

The real explanation is this: in high-density inner-city areas, people are likely to sell drugs while standing on street corners, under the clear view of neighborhood residents, who may call police. In contrast, drug sales in low-density automobile-oriented suburbs occur discreetly behind closed doors, and arrests may require elaborate undercover operations.

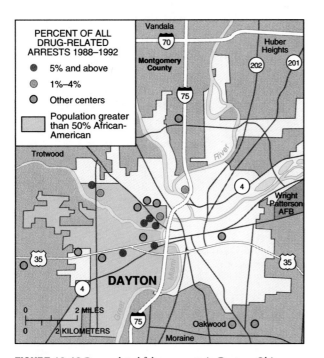

FIGURE 12-13 Drug-related felony arrests in Dayton, Ohio. The ten locations in the Dayton urban area that have the highest numbers of arrests are clustered in the predominantly low-income, African–American, inner-west side of the city.

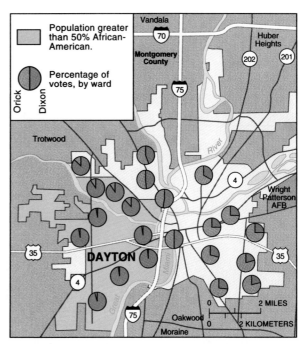

FIGURE 12-14 Race and voting in Dayton. In the 1989 mayoral election, the winner was an African–American who carried every ward on the west side, in some cases with more than 95 percent of the vote. These wards are predominantly black. The losing candidate, who was white, carried every ward on the east side. Compare this figure with Figures 11-13, 11-16, and 12-13. Many inner-city areas suffer from a high incidence of social problems and lack of services.

Segregation by race and ethnicity also explains voting patterns in many American urban areas. The winning candidate for mayor of Dayton in 1991 gained a majority of the votes in every ward on the predominantly black west side and lost every ward on the predominantly white east side. He was African–American, and his opponent was white (Figure 12-14).

Use of the Models Outside North America

The three models may describe the spatial distribution of social classes in the United States, but American urban areas differ from those elsewhere in the world. These differences do not invalidate the models. But they do point out that social groups in other countries may not have the same *reasons* for selecting particular neighborhoods within their cities.

European Cities

As in the United States, wealthier people in European cities cluster along a sector extending out from the CBD. In Paris, for example, the rich moved to the southwestern hills to be near the royal palace (the Louvre beginning in the twelfth century, and the Palace of Versailles from the sixteenth century until the French Revolution in 1789). The preference of the wealthy to cluster in the southwest was reinforced in the nineteenth century during the industrial revolution. Factories were built to the south, east, and north along the Seine and Marne river valleys, but relatively few were built on the southwestern hills (Figure 12-15). Similar high-class sectors developed in other European cities, typically on higher elevation and near royal palaces.

In contrast to the distribution in most U.S. cities, wealthy Europeans still live in the inner rings of the high-class sector, not just in the suburbs. A central location provides proximity to the region's best shops, restaurants, cafes, and cultural facilities. Wealthy people are also attracted by the opportunity to occupy elegant residences in carefully restored, beautiful old buildings.

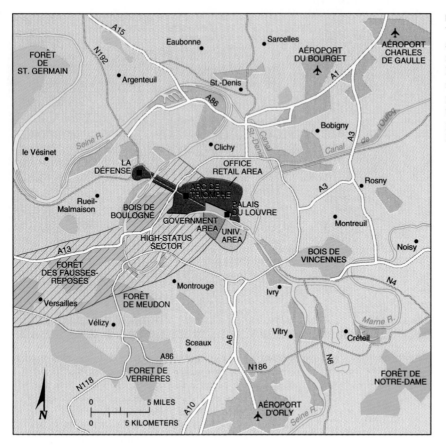

FIGURE 12-15 Social areas in Paris. Wealthy people moved in a southwestern sector, near the king's residences, first in the Louvre and later at Versailles. The eastern neighborhoods of Paris once housed poorer families, but in recent years these have been gentrified, and poorer people have moved to suburban high-rise apartments.

By living in high-density, centrally located town-houses and apartments, wealthy people in Europe do not have large private yards and must go to public parks for open space. To meet the desire for large tracts of privately owned land, some wealthy Europeans purchase abandoned farm buildings in clustered rural settlements for use as second homes on weekends and holidays. Some of the worst traffic jams in Paris occur on summer Sunday nights, when families return from their weekend homes. A trip from the weekend home to the city that normally takes 1 hour can take 4 hours on Sunday night.

In the past, poorer people also lived in the center of European cities. Before the invention of electricity in the nineteenth century, social segregation was vertical: richer people lived on the first or second floors, while poorer people occupied the dark, dank basements, or they climbed many flights of stairs to reach the attics. As the city expanded during the industrial revolution, housing for poorer people was constructed in sectors near the factories and away from the rich.

Today, poorer people are less likely to live in European inner-city neighborhoods. Poor-quality housing has been renovated for wealthy people or demolished and replaced by offices or luxury apartment buildings. Building and zoning codes prohibit anyone from living in basements, and upper floors have become attractive for wealthy people once elevators are installed.

Poorer people have been relegated to the outskirts of European cities (Figure 12-16). Vast suburbs containing dozens of high-rise apartment buildings house the poorer people displaced from the inner city. European suburban residents face the prospect of long commutes by public transportation to reach jobs and other downtown amenities. Shops, schools, and other services are worse than in inner neighborhoods, and the suburbs are centers for crime, violence, and drug dealing. Because the housing is mostly in high-rise buildings, people lack large private yards. Many residents of these dreary suburbs are persons of color or recent immigrants from Africa or Asia who face discrimination and prejudice by "native" Europeans.

European officials encouraged the construction of high-density suburbs to help preserve the countryside from development and avoid the inefficient sprawl that characterizes American suburbs (refer to Figure 12-3). And tourists are attracted to the historic, lively centers of European cities. But these policies have resulted in the clustering of people with social and economic problems in remote suburbs rarely seen by wealthier people.

Less Developed Countries

As in Europe, the rich live near the center of cities in LDCs, as well as in a sector extending from the center, whereas the poor are accommodated in the suburbs. The similarity between European and LDC cities is not a coincidence: past European colonial policies have left a heavy mark on the development of cities in many less developed countries. In fact, most cities in less developed countries have passed through three stages of development—before European colonization, during the European colonial period, and since independence.

Pre-Colonial Cities. Before the Europeans established colonies, few cities existed in Africa, Asia, and Latin America, and most people lived in rural settlements. The principal cities in Latin America were located in Mexico and the Andean highlands of northwestern South America (see Geography in Action box). In Africa, cities could be found along the west coast, Egypt's Nile River valley, and Islamic empires in the north and east (extending into Southwest Asia). Cities were also built in South and East Asia, especially India, China, and Japan.

Cities were often laid out surrounding a religious core, such as a mosque in Muslim regions. The center of Islamic cities also had a bazaar, or marketplace, that served as the commercial core. Government buildings and the homes of wealthy families surrounded the mosque and bazaar. Narrow, winding streets led from the core to other quarters. Families with less wealth and lower status located farther from the core, and recent migrants to the city lived on the edge.

Commercial activities were arranged in a concentric and hierarchical pattern: higher-status busi-

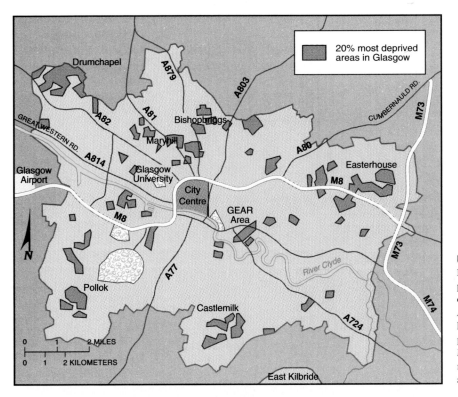

FIGURE 12-16 Glasgow, Scotland. Deprived neighborhoods are primarily in the outer areas, just opposite of the case in U.S. cities. Areas of social deprivation contain high concentrations of unemployed people receiving public assistance. Most of these areas consist of massive housing projects built after World War II.

Three Eras in Mexico City

Mexico City, the Western Hemisphere's largest metropolitan area, displays the influence of three main eras of urban development typical of less developed countries.

The Aztec City (A.D. 1325–1521)

The Aztecs migrated from an unknown location in southwestern Mexico and settled west of present-day downtown Mexico City on a hill known as Chapultepec ("the hill of the grasshopper"). Forced by other people to leave the hill, the Aztecs first migrated a few kilometers south, near the present-day site of the University of Mexico, and then in 1325 to a marshy 10-square-kilometer (4-square-mile) island in Lake Texcoco (Figure 1). They named the city Tenochtitlán.

At first, Tenochtitlán consisted of a small temple and a few huts of thatch and mud. Over the next two centuries, the Aztecs conquered the neighboring peoples and extended their control through much of present-day Mexico. As their wealth and power grew, the Aztecs built elaborate stone houses and temples in Tenochtitlán.

The node of Aztec religious life in Tenochtitlán was the Great Temple, a massive multi-colored structure containing two shrines, one for the rain god (painted blue) and one for

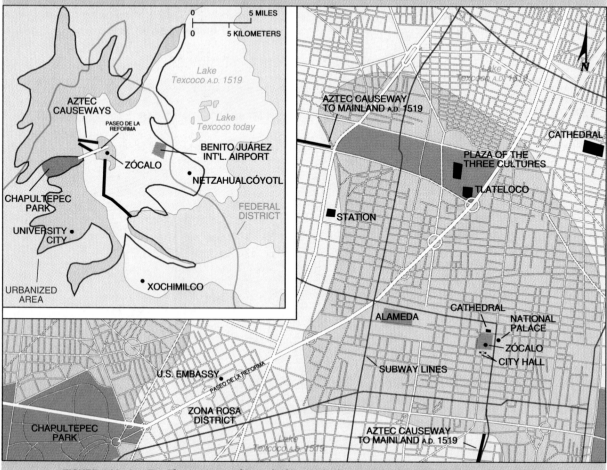

FIGURE 1 Mexico City. The Aztec city of Tenochtitlán was built on an island in Lake Texcoco. The elite live in a sector to the west, while poorer people live on landfill in the former lakebed.

the god of war (painted blood red). The main market center, Tlatelolco, was at the north end of the island.

Most food, merchandise, and building materials crossed from the mainland to the island by canoe, barge, or other boat. The island itself was laced with canals to facilitate pickup and delivery of people and goods. Three causeways with drawbridges linked Tenochtitlán to the mainland and helped to control flooding. An aqueduct brought fresh water from Chapultepec.

The Spanish Colonial City (1521–1821)

When 400 Spanish soldiers under the leadership of Hernando Cortés reached Tenochtitlán in 1519, they were shocked to find a teeming city of more than 500,000 people, probably the largest in the world at that time. After a 2-year siege, the Spanish conquered Tenochtitlán with the aid of 100,000 natives who believed Cortés to be the reincarnation of a former ruler-priest.

The Spanish destroyed Tenochtitlán and dispersed or killed most of the inhabitants. Cortés ordered the surviving Aztecs to move out of the center and divided up the land among his soldiers. The population declined to 30,000. The city, renamed Mexico City, was rebuilt in accordance with Spanish preferences.

A main square, called the Zócalo, was constructed in the center of the island, on the site of the Aztecs' sacred precinct. The Spanish reconstructed the streets in a grid pattern, with the main ones extending from the Zócalo. A Roman Catholic cathedral was built on the north side of the square, near the site of the demolished Great Temple, and the National Palace was built on the east side, on the site of the Aztec emperor Montezuma's destroyed palace. The Spanish placed a church and monastery on the site of the Tlatelolco market.

The Independent City (1821–Present)

Mexico City grew slowly during the three centuries of colonial rule, to about 100,000 people at the time of independence in 1821. Although again the most populous city in the Western Hemisphere, Mexico City had been five times larger when Cortés conquered it.

Although no longer a colony of Spain, Mexico remained under strong European influence during the nineteenth century. The Mexican emperor Maximilian (emperor from 1864 to 1867), who was the brother of Francis Joseph I of Austria, designed a fourteen-lane tree-lined boulevard for Mexico City patterned after the Champs-Elysées in Paris. The boulevard (now known as the Paseo de la Reforma) extended 3 kilometers (2 miles) southwestward from the center to Chapultepec.

The Reforma between downtown and Chapultepec became the spine of an elite sector, as shown in the generalized model of Latin American cities (Figure 12-19). During the regime of Porfirio Díaz (president of Mexico, 1877–1880 and 1884–1911), the wealthy built pretentious *palacios* (palaces) along the Reforma.

Physical factors influenced the movement of wealthy people toward the west along the Reforma. Because elevation was higher than elsewhere in the city, sewage flowed eastward and northward away from Chapultepec. Prevailing winds from the northeast stirred dust storms from the dried-up bottom of Lake Texcoco to the northeast.

In 1903, most of Lake Texcoco was drained by a gigantic canal and tunnel project, allowing the city to expand northward and eastward. But the lakebed was a less desirable residential location than the west side, because of the dust storms stirred by prevailing winds.

As Mexico City's population has grown rapidly during the twentieth century, the social patterns inherited from the nineteenth century have been reinforced. The wealthy push out farther to the west along the spine of the Reforma, replacing the *palacios* with high-rise apartment buildings, offices, and American franchise stores. The poorest people occupy squatter settlements on the dried lakebed and in the inaccessible mountains surrounding the city.

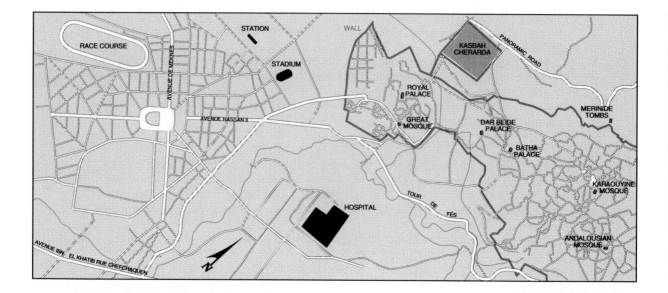

FIGURE 12-17 Layout of Fez, Morocco. The French laid out an entirely new district in the southeast, separate and distinct from the existing city to the northwest (left), characterized by narrow, winding streets, and high density (right). (Craig Aurness/Woodfin Camp & Associates, left; Joseph Nettis/Stock Boston, right)

nesses directly related to religious practices (such as selling religious books, incense, and candles) were located closest to the mosque. In the next ring were secular businesses, such as leather works, tailors, rug shops, and jewelers. In the next ring were sellers of food products, then blacksmiths, basket makers, and potters. One quarter would be reserved for Jews, a second for Christians, and a third for foreigners.

Colonial Cities. When Europeans gained control of Africa, Asia, and Latin America, they expanded existing cities to provide colonial services, such as administration, military command, and international trade, as well as housing for Europeans who settled in the colony. Existing native towns were either left to one side or demolished because they were totally at variance with European ideas.

Fez, Morocco, consists of two separate and distinct towns, one built by the French colonists and the other existing before the French gained control (Figure 12-17). Similarly, the British built New Delhi near the existing city of Delhi, India. On the other hand, the French colonial city of Saigon, Vietnam (now Ho Minh City), was built by completely demolishing the existing city without leaving a trace (Figure 12-18).

Compared with the cities that existed before them, the European districts typically contain wider streets and public squares, larger houses surrounded by gardens, and much lower density. In contrast, the old quarters have narrow, winding streets, little open space, and cramped residences. Colonial cities followed standardized plans. All Spanish cities in Latin America, for example, were built according to the Laws of the Indies, drafted in 1573. The laws explicitly outlined how colonial cities were to be constructed: a gridiron street plan centered on a church and central plaza, walls around individual houses, and neighborhoods centered around smaller plazas with parish churches or monasteries.

Cities Since Independence. After independence, cities became the focal points of change in less developed countries. The rapid population growth of cities in LDCs was documented in Chapter 11. Millions have migrated to the cities in search of work.

Ernest Griffin and Larry Ford have shown that in Latin American cities, wealthy people push out from the center in a well-defined elite residential sector. The elite sector forms on either side of a narrow spine that contains offices, shops, and amenities attractive to wealthy people, such as restaurants, theaters, parks, and zoos (Figure 12-19). The rich are also attracted to the center and spine, because services such as water and electricity are more readily available and reliable there.

For example, in Brazil, Rio de Janeiro's high-income people are clustered in the center of the city and to the south, while low-income people are in

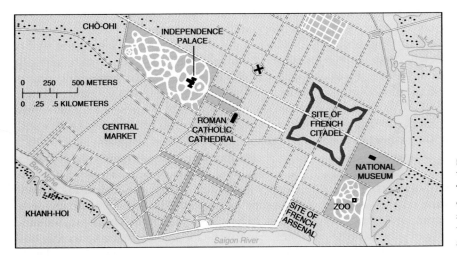

FIGURE 12-18 Layout of Saigon, Vietnam (now Ho Chi Minh City). The French demolished the existing city and replaced it with one built according to colonial principles, with wide boulevards and public squares.

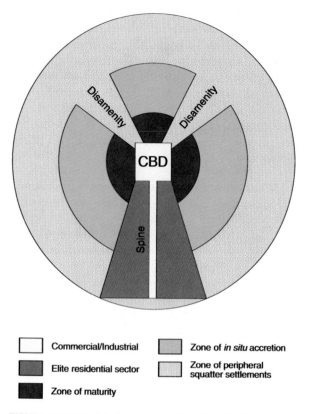

Commercial/Industrial

Elite residential sector

Zone of maturity

Zone of *in situ* accretion

Zone of peripheral squatter settlements

FIGURE 12-19 Model of a Latin American city. Wealthy people live in the inner city and a sector extending along a commercial spine. (Adapted from Ernest Griffin and Larry Ford, "A Model of Latin American City Structure," *Geographical Review* 70 (1980): 406.)

the northern suburbs (Figure 12-20). The distribution of income groups coincides with other social characteristics, such as the percent of households with a telephone, automobile, or television. High-income groups are clustered near the center in part because of greater access to services, such as electricity and city sewers (Figure 12-21).

Physical geography also influences the distribution of social classes within Rio. The original site of the city was along the west shore of Guanabara Bay, a protected harbor. Residents were attracted to the neighborhoods immediately south of the central area, such as Copacabana and Ipanema, to enjoy spectacular views of the Atlantic Ocean and access to beaches. On the other hand, low-income households clustered along the northern edge of the city, where steep mountains restricted construction of other

types of buildings. Development on the east side of Guanabara Bay was restricted until a bridge was constructed in the 1970s.

Squatter Settlements. LDCs are unable to house the rapidly growing population of poor caused by overall population increase and migration from rural areas for job opportunities. Because of the housing shortage, a large percentage of poor immigrants to urban areas in LDCs live in squatter (or informal) settlements. **Squatter settlements** are known by a variety of names, including *barrios*, *barriadas*, and *favelas* in Latin America; *bidonvilles* in North Africa; *bustees* in India; *gecekondu* in Turkey; *kampongs* in Malaysia; and *barung-barong* in the Philippines.

A squatter settlement is typically initiated by a group of people who move together onto land outside the city that is owned either by a private individual or (more frequently) by the government. People move literally overnight with all their possessions, which usually are so few that they can easily be carried. The leaders of the invasion allocate small parcels of the seized land to each participating family.

At first, squatters do little more than camp on the land or sleep in the street. In severe weather, they may take shelter in markets and warehouses. Families then erect primitive shelters with scavenged cardboard, wood boxes, sackcloth, and crushed beverage cans. As they find new bits of material, they add them to their shacks. After a few years, they may build a tin roof and partition the space into rooms, and the structure acquires a more permanent appearance.

Squatter settlements have few services because neither the city nor the residents can afford them. Latrines are usually designated by the settlement's leaders, and water is carried from a central well or dispensed from a truck. The settlements generally lack schools, paved roads, telephones, and sewers. Electricity service may be stolen by running a wire from the nearest line. In the absence of bus service or available private cars, a resident may have to walk 2 hours to reach a place of employment.

To improve their housing conditions, squatters have two basic choices. One alternative is to move illegally into better-quality, vacant housing close to the center of the city. The second alternative is to rent slum housing legally from a landlord. Squatters rarely have the financial means to move directly from a squatter settlement into decent housing on legally owned land.

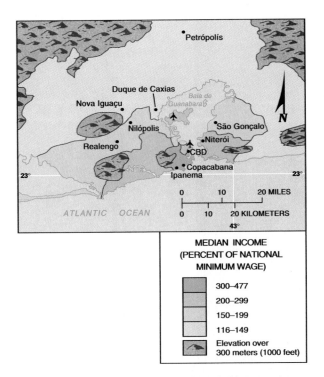

FIGURE 12-20 High- and low-income households in Rio de Janeiro, Brazil. The highest income areas are near the CBD and in a spine along the ocean, whereas low-income people are more likely to live in peripheral areas.

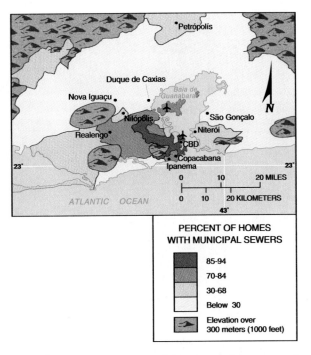

FIGURE 12-21 Sewers in Rio. High-income people are attracted to central areas in LDC cities such as Rio because municipal sewers and other services are more widely available there than in peripheral areas.

The percentage of people living in squatter settlements, slums, and other illegal housing ranges from 32 percent in São Paulo, Brazil, to 85 percent in Addis Ababa, Ethiopia, according to a U.N. study. The United Nations estimates that more than half of the residents live in some form of informal housing in Lusaka, Zambia; Ankara, Turkey; Bogotá, Colombia; Dar es Salaam, Tanzania; and Luanda, Angola (Table 12-1).

Governments in LDCs face a difficult choice regarding squatter settlements. If the government sends in the police or army to raze the settlement, it risks sparking a violent confrontation. On the other hand, if the government decides that improving and legalizing squatter settlements is cheaper than building the necessary new apartment buildings, it may encourage other poor rural people to migrate to the city to live as squatters.

Immigrants to New York and London have lived in squalid conditions, but an expanding economy has at least provided them with jobs, even if rather menial and poorly paid. An adequate supply of jobs is simply not available in Mexico City, São Paulo, and the other large urban settlements of today's LDCs.

Squatter settlements are erected in sight of modern high-rises occupied by middle-class families in Bombay, India. (Viviane Moos/The Stock Market)

TABLE 12-1

Population living in informal settlements

City	Population (in millions)	Percentage in Squatter Settlements
Addis Ababa, Ethiopia	1.7	85
Luanda, Angola	1.1	70
Dar es Salaam, Tanzania	1.4	60
Bogotá, Colombia	6.2	59
Ankara, Turkey	3.0	51
Lusaka, Zambia	1.0	50
Tunis, Tunisia	0.8	45
Manila, Philippines	10.6	40
Mexico City, Mexico	21.6	40
Karachi, Pakistan	8.2	37
Caracas, Venezuela	3.2	34
Lima, Peru	7.0	33
Nairobi, Kenya	1.2	33
São Paulo, Brazil	19.4	32

Source: United Nations Center for Human Settlements, *Land for Human Settlements*, Nairobi, Kenya: UN CHS, 1984, p. 9; in Gill-Chin Lim, "Housing Policy for the Urban Poor in Developing Countries," *Journal of the American Planning Association* (Spring 1987): 176–85, at 178.

Summary   Here is a review of the key issues in this chapter.

1.   What activities occur in the central business district?

Downtown is dominated by service activities, especially retailing and offices. Competition for limited space in the center causes high land values. As a result, land is used more intensively in the center, and manufacturing and residential uses are excluded.

2.   What problems do inner-city residential areas face?

Surrounding the CBD of U.S. cities are inner residential areas containing older low-quality housing and public housing as well as pockets of high-status renovated housing. Cities lack financial resources to meet the needs of their low-income inner-city residents.

3.   What are the causes and consequences of suburbanization?

The suburban lifestyle as exemplified by the detached, single-family house with surrounding yard attracts most people. Transportation improvements, most notably the railroad in the nineteenth century and the automobile in the twentieth century, have facilitated the sprawl of urban areas. Among the negative consequences of large-scale sprawl are segregation and inefficiency.

4.   How are different social groups distributed within an urban area?

Three models have been developed in the United States to explain where various types of people live in urban areas: the concentric zone, sector, and multiple nuclei models. None fully explains the internal structure of the city, but the three combined present a useful framework for understanding the distribution of social and economic groups within an urban area. With modifications, the models also apply to cities in Europe and less developed countries.

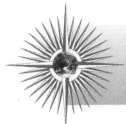

CASE STUDY REVISITED
Contrasts in the City

What is the future for cities? As this chapter has shown, contradictory trends are at work simultaneously. Why does one inner-city neighborhood become a slum and another a high-class district? Why does one city attract new shoppers and visitors while another languishes?

The Camden, New Jersey, urban area displays the strong contrasts that characterize American urban areas. The central city of Camden houses an isolated underclass, while suburban Camden County prospers. The population of the city of Camden has declined from 117,000 in 1960 to less than 90,000 today. Nearly 85 percent of the city's residents are African–American and Latino, and the white population has declined from 90,000 in 1960 to 10,000 today. Only 1 percent of the remaining residents have annual incomes of more than $50,000, compared with 20 percent in the rest of the country and 10 percent among all black households.

More than 40 percent of Camden's residents are under 18. This age distribution is closer to the level found in LDCs than to that in the rest of the United States. Job prospects are not promising for these young people, because more than half have left school without obtaining a high school diploma. In the past, Camden's youths could find jobs in factories that produced Campbell's soups, Esterbrook pens, and RCA Victor records, radios, and televisions, but the city has lost 90 percent of its industrial jobs. The Esterbrook and Campbell factories in Camden are closed, although Campbell's corporate offices remain; General Electric operates the former RCA factory but with a labor force at only 15 percent of the level during the 1960s. Camden's unemployment rate is more than twice the national average.

As Camden's population and industries decline, few shops have enough customers to remain open. The city once had thirteen movie theaters, but none are left. The murder rate soared after gangs carved up the city into districts during the mid-1980s to control cocaine trafficking.

Meanwhile, Camden County (excluding the city) has grown from 275,000 in 1960 to about 420,000 in 1990. Cherry Hill has more than 70,000 residents today, compared with fewer than 10,000 in 1960, and will probably surpass Camden as the largest city in the county before the end of the decade. About 85 percent of Cherry Hill's high school graduates go on to college.

A place like Cherry Hill is now known as an **edge city**, a large node of office and retail activities on the edge of an urban area. An edge city is spread out in a ribbon along boulevards and interstate highways at the edge of a metropolitan area on land that was farmed until a couple of decades ago. Edge cities originated as suburban communities for people who worked in the central city, and then shopping malls were built to be near the residents. Edge cities represent a new stage in urban development, because they are nodes where offices, factories, and warehouses, not just residences and shops, are clustered.

Despite its rapid population growth and trained labor force, an edge city like Cherry Hill has become both a residential area that commuters leave and an employment center that attracts other commuters. Cherry Hill has attracted so many new jobs that a major obstacle to further economic growth is a shortage of qualified workers. But many inner-city Camden residents lack transport to reach the jobs or the skills to hold the jobs or both. Camden's mismatch among locations of people, jobs, resources, and services exemplifies the urban crisis throughout the United States, as well as in other countries. Geographers help us understand why these patterns arise and what can be done about them.

Key Terms

Blockbusting A process by which real estate agents convince white property owners to sell their houses at low prices because of fear that nonwhite families will soon move into the neighborhood.

Census tract An area delineated by the U.S. Bureau of the Census for which statistics are published; in urbanized areas, census tracts correspond roughly to neighborhoods.

Central Business District (CBD) The area of the city where retail and office activities are clustered.

Concentric zone model A model of the internal structure of cities in which social groups are spatially arranged in a series of rings.

Density gradient The change in density in an urban area from the center to the periphery.

Edge city A large node of office and retail activities on the edge of an urban area.

Filtering A process of change in the use of a house, ranging from single-family owner occupancy to abandonment.

Gentrification A process of converting an urban neighborhood from a predominantly low-income renter area to a predominantly middle-class owner-occupied area.

Greenbelt A ring of land maintained as parks, agriculture, or other types of open space to limit the sprawl of an urban area.

Multiple nuclei model A model of the internal structure of cities in which social groups are arranged around a collection of nodes of activities.

Public housing Housing owned by the government; in the United States, it is rented to low-income residents, and the rents are set at 30 percent of the families' incomes.

Redlining A process by which banks draw lines on a map and refuse to lend money to purchase or improve property within the boundaries.

Rush (or **peak**) **hour** The four consecutive 15-minute periods in the morning and evening with the heaviest volumes of traffic.

Sector model A model of the internal structure of cities in which social groups are arranged around a series of sectors, or wedges, radiating out from the CBD.

Sprawl Development of new housing sites at relatively low density and at locations that are not contiguous to the existing built-up area.

Squatter settlement An area within a city in a less developed country in which people illegally establish residences on land they do not own or rent and erect homemade structures.

Underclass A group in society prevented from participating in the material benefits of a more developed society because of a variety of social and economic characteristics.

Zoning ordinance A law that limits the permitted uses of land and maximum density of development in a community.

Thinking Geographically

1. Compare Toronto and Detroit. How do the CBDs and the inner residential areas compare in the two cities? What might account for these differences?

2. Draw a sketch of your community or neighborhood. In accordance with Kevin Lynch's *The Image of the City* (see Further Readings), place five types of information on the map: districts (homogeneous areas), edges (boundaries that separate districts), paths (lines of communication), nodes (central points of interaction), and landmarks (prominent objects on the landscape). How clear an image does your community have for you?

3. To Jane Jacobs (see Further Readings), an attractive urban environment is one that is animated with an intermingling of a variety of people and activities, such as found in many New York City neighborhoods. What are the attractions and drawbacks to living in such environments?

4. Land-use activities in Communist cities were allocated by government rather than private market decisions. To what extent would the absence of a private-sector urban land market affect the form and structure of socialist cities? What impacts may Eastern European cities experience with the switch to market economies?

5. Officials of rapidly growing cities in LDCs discourage the construction of houses that do not meet international standards for sanitation and construction methods. Also discouraged are privately owned transportation services, because the vehicles generally lack decent tires, brakes, and other safety features. Yet the residents prefer substandard housing to no housing, and they prefer unsafe transportation to no transportation. What would be the advantages and problems for a city if health and safety standards for housing, transportation, and other services were relaxed?

Further Readings

Baldasarre, Mark. *Trouble in Paradise: The Suburban Transformation in America.* New York: Columbia University Press, 1986.

Berry, Brian J. L., and John D. Kasarda. *Contemporary Urban Ecology.* New York: Macmillan, 1977.

Bourne, Larry S., ed. *Internal Structure of the City*, 2d ed. New York: Oxford University Press, 1982.

Bratt, Rachel G. *Rebuilding a Low-Income Housing Policy.* Philadelphia: Temple University Press, 1990.

Brunn, Stanley D., and Jack L. Williams, eds. *Cities of the World: World Regional Urban Development.* New York: Harper and Row, 1983.

Cervero, Robert. *America's Suburban Centers: The Land Use-Transportation Link.* Boston: Unwin and Hyman, 1989.

Clawson, Marion, and Peter Hall. *Planning and Urban Growth.* Baltimore: The Johns Hopkins University Press, 1973.

Clay, Grady. *Real Places: An Unconventional Guide to America's Generic Landscape.* Chicago: University of Chicago Press, 1994.

Cybriwsky, Roman. *Tokyo—The Changing Profile of an Urban Giant.* Boston: G. K. Hall, 1991.

Drakalis-Smith, David. *The Third World City.* London: Methuen, 1987.

Ford, Larry R. "Reading the Skylines of American Cities." *Geographical Review* 82 (April 1992): 180–200.

Frieden, Bernard J., and Lynne B. Sagalyn. *Downtown Inc.: How America Rebuilds Cities.* Cambridge, MA: MIT Press, 1989.

Garreau, Joel. *Edge City: Life on the New Frontier.* New York: Doubleday, 1991.

Golany, Gideon, ed. *International Urban Growth Policies: New-Town Contributions.* New York: Wiley, 1978.

Gos, John. "The 'Magic of the Mall': An Analysis of Form, Function, and Meaning in the Contemporary Retail Built Environment." *Annals of the Association of American Geographers* 83 (March 1993): 18–47.

Griffin, Ernest, and Larry Ford. "A Model of Latin American City Structure." *Geographical Review* 70 (October 1980): 387–422.

Guest, Avery M. "Population Suburbanization in American Metropolitan Areas, 1940–1970." *Geographical Analysis* 7 (July 1976): 267–83.

Harris, Chauncey D., and Edward L. Ullman. "The Nature of Cities." *Annals of the American Academy of Political and Social Science* 143 (1945): 7–17.

Hart, John Fraser, ed. *Our Changing Cities.* Baltimore: Johns Hopkins University Press, 1991.

Herzog, Lawrence A. *Where North Meets South: Cities, Space, and Politics on the U.S.-Mexico Border.* Austin: University of Texas, Center for Mexican-American Studies, 1990.

Hoyt, Homer. *The Structure and Growth of Residential Neighborhoods.* Washington, D.C.: Federal Housing Administration, 1939.

Jacobs, Allan B. *Looking at Cities.* Cambridge, MA: Harvard University Press, 1985.

Jacobs, Jane. *Death and Life of Great American Cities.* New York: Random House, 1961.

Johnston, R. J. *City and Society: An Outline for Urban Geography.* London: Hutchinson Education, 1984.

Jones, Kenneth G., and James W. Simmons. *The Retail Environment.* London and New York: Routledge, 1990.

Knox, Paul L. "The Restless Urban Landscape: Economic and Sociocultural Change and the Transformation of Metropolitan Washington, D.C." *Annals of the Association of American Geographers* 81 (June 1991): 181–209.

Lawrence, Henry W. "The Greening of the Squares of London: Transformation of Urban Landscapes and Ideals." *Annals of the Association of American Geographers* 83 (March 1993): 90–118.

Ley, David. "Alternative Explanations for Inner-City Gentrification: A Canadian Assessment." *Annals of the Association of American Geographers* 76 (December 1986): 521–35.

————. *A Social Geography of the City.* New York: Harper and Row, 1983.

Lowder, Stella. *Inside Third World Cities.* London: Routledge, 1988.

Lynch, Kevin. *The Image of the City.* Cambridge, MA: MIT Press, 1960.

Mayer, Harold M., and Charles R. Hayes. *Land Uses in American Cities.* Champaign, IL: Park Press, 1983.

Park, Robert E., Ernest W. Burgess, and Roderick D. McKenzie, eds. *The City.* Chicago: University of Chicago Press, 1925.

Short, John. *The Humane City.* New York and Oxford: Basil Blackwell, 1989.

U. S. National Advisory Commission on Civil Disorders, Otto Kerner, chairman. *Report.* New York: Dutton, 1968.

Vance, James E., Jr. *The Continuing City: Urban Morphology in Western Civilization.* Baltimore: The Johns Hopkins University Press, 1990.

White, Paul. *The West European City: A Social Geography.* London: Longman, 1984.

Whyte, William H. *City: Rediscovering the Center.* New York: Doubleday, 1988.

Also consult these journals: *Environment and Planning, Journal of the American Planning Association, Journal of Housing, Journal of Urban Economics, Land Economics, Planning, Urban Geography, Urban Land, Urban Studies.*

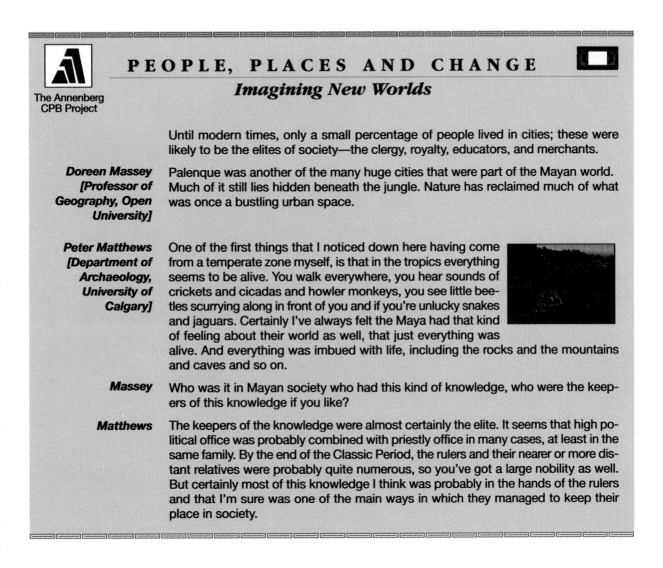

PEOPLE, PLACES AND CHANGE
Imagining New Worlds

The Annenberg
CPB Project

Until modern times, only a small percentage of people lived in cities; these were likely to be the elites of society—the clergy, royalty, educators, and merchants.

**Doreen Massey
[Professor of
Geography, Open
University]**

Palenque was another of the many huge cities that were part of the Mayan world. Much of it still lies hidden beneath the jungle. Nature has reclaimed much of what was once a bustling urban space.

**Peter Matthews
[Department of
Archaeology,
University of
Calgary]**

One of the first things that I noticed down here having come from a temperate zone myself, is that in the tropics everything seems to be alive. You walk everywhere, you hear sounds of crickets and cicadas and howler monkeys, you see little beetles scurrying along in front of you and if you're unlucky snakes and jaguars. Certainly I've always felt the Maya had that kind of feeling about their world as well, that just everything was alive. And everything was imbued with life, including the rocks and the mountains and caves and so on.

Massey

Who was it in Mayan society who had this kind of knowledge, who were the keepers of this knowledge if you like?

Matthews

The keepers of the knowledge were almost certainly the elite. It seems that high political office was probably combined with priestly office in many cases, at least in the same family. By the end of the Classic Period, the rulers and their nearer or more distant relatives were probably quite numerous, so you've got a large nobility as well. But certainly most of this knowledge I think was probably in the hands of the rulers and that I'm sure was one of the main ways in which they managed to keep their place in society.

13

RESOURCE PROBLEMS

When you finish drinking a soda, do you pitch it in the trash or place it in a recycling bin? In winter, if you feel cold, do you put on a sweater, or do you turn up the thermostat? Do you normally eat with disposable plates, cups, and plastic utensils, or do you use washable ceramic and stainless steel products? When you leave a room, do you turn off the lights and television? When you or your family last bought a car, did you select a model on the basis of its high fuel efficiency?

People have always transformed Earth's land, water, and air for their benefit. But human actions in recent years have gone far beyond the impact of the past. The magnitude of transformations is disproportionately shared by North Americans; with only one-twentieth of Earth's population, North Americans consume one-fourth of the world's energy and generate one-fourth of many pollutants. Elsewhere in the world, 2 billion people live without clean water or sewers. One billion live in cities

KEY ISSUES

1. As we deplete fossil fuels, what alternatives can replace them?
2. What are the solutions to pollution?
3. How can we expand the global food supply?

with unsafe sulfur dioxide levels.

Future generations will pay the price if we continue to mismanage Earth's resources. Our shortsightedness could lead to shortages of energy to heat homes and operate motor vehicles. Our carelessness has already led to unsafe drinking water and toxic air in some places. Our inefficiency could lead to shortages of food.

Humans once believed that Earth's resources were infinite, or at least so vast that human actions could never harm or deplete them. But warnings from scientists, geographers, and governments are making clear that resource consumption is indeed a problem. Earth Day 1970 alerted the world to the magnitude of damage that people have done to the environment. A quarter-century later, we have learned much about the processes that produce environmental problems and about the long-term consequences of environmental mismanagement.

SMOKEY MOUNTAINS RUBBISH DUMP, PHILIPPINES. (NIGEL DICKINSON/TONY STONE IMAGES)

Pollution in Mexico City

Eight-year-old Carlos and 9-year-old Maria, residents of Mexico City, did not go to school today. Neither did many of their classmates. And many of their teachers failed to report for work. These people did not leave their homes, because they feared that breathing outside air in Mexico City would be too dangerous.

For much of the year, a stationary cloud hangs over Mexico City, producing a gray-brown fog that irritates the eyes and burns the throat. Residents report frequent conjunctivitis and other eye disorders, skin rashes, bronchitis, other respiratory diseases, and increased susceptibility to heart attacks. The health benefits of outdoor sports such as soccer and running are outweighed by the health risks of breathing the air. Pregnant women are cautioned that living in Mexico City increases risk to fetal health.

This severe air pollution partly results from Mexico City's setting: it rests in a basin some 2,250 meters (about 7,400 feet) above sea level, surrounded by a semicircle of volcanic peaks as high as 5,545 meters (16,900 feet). This giant bowl is open only to the north. Prevailing winds from the north enter the basin and back polluted air against the surrounding mountains. Consequently, emissions from cars and factories are trapped close to the ground in a stationary cloud, especially in the winter, when the climate is cool and dry and winds are calm.

Because the city is at a high altitude, the level of available oxygen is low. Consequently, fossil fuels burn less completely than at lower altitudes, and burning them produces more carbon monoxide and ozone.

Three-fourths of the emissions come from burning fuels in more than 2 million motor vehicles. Natural phenomena (such as fires) and industrial sources account for much of the remainder of the air pollution. Many larger industries are concentrated in the northern part of the valley, so their emissions are blown across the city by prevailing winds.

Mexico City has banned cars from a fifty-square-block central area, and motorists are not allowed to use their cars one day each week, depending on the last digit of the license plate. Cars must now have catalytic converters and use unleaded fuel, and older buses and taxicabs have been removed from service. These measures, however, are offset by an increase in vehicles in this rapidly growing city of more than 16 million inhabitants. Vehicles are essential to economic development: they allow people to get to work and businesses to deliver goods.

The government closed a major employer, the PEMEX oil refinery, located in the northwestern portion of Mexico City, because it was responsible for 7 percent of the city's air pollution. The closure hurt Mexico's economy, not only because jobs were lost, but also because the country had to import some fuel to replace the loss of the refinery's production.

Air pollution is not Mexico City's only environmental problem. Inadequately treated sewage flows into nearby rivers, and 30 percent of the city's homes are not even connected to the sewer system. Solid waste is deposited at large municipal dumps, where 17,000 people known as *pepenadores* survive by picking through rubbish and, in many cases, actually living at the dump. Dust from fecal matter in unsewered areas increases skin and eye infections.

Rapid population growth increases the pressure the city faces to expand economic opportunities and material benefits for the people, regardless of environmental impact. Stricter enforcement of pollution controls would require shutting down many businesses and eliminating jobs.

Plants and animals live in harmony with their environment, but people often do not. Geographers study this troubled relationship between human actions and the physical environment in which we live. From our perspective, Earth offers a large menu of resources available for our use. A **resource** is a substance in the environment that is useful to people, is economically and technologically feasible to access, and is socially acceptable to use. A resource could be food, water, soil, plants, animals, minerals, and even air.

The problem is that most resources are limited, and Earth has a tremendous number of consumers. Geographers observe three major misuses of resources:

1. We deplete scarce resources, especially petroleum, natural gas, and coal, for energy production.
2. We destroy resources such as air, water, and soil by polluting them.
3. We fail to efficiently use resources, especially the global food supply.

These three misuses are the basic themes of this chapter.

As discussed in Chapter 1, human geographers see people and activities becoming more globalized—human actions involve the entire world and result in making something worldwide in scope. People are plugged into a global culture, economy, and environment, and the world has become more uniform, integrated, and interdependent.

Nowhere is the globalization trend more pronounced than in the study of resources. The global economy depends on the availability of natural resources to produce the goods and services that people demand. The global uniformity in cultural preferences means that people in different places value similar natural resources (although not everyone has the same access to them). In a global environment, misuse of a resource in one location affects the well-being of people everywhere.

To study resource problems, we depend on all elements of globalization. As geographers, we understand that our energy problems derive from depletion of resources and from differences in how resources and consumers are distributed across Earth's surface. We see that the pollution problem comes from the concentration of substances that harm the physical environment in particular regions. We find that the food supply problem is related in part to identifying the limits of a region's physical environment and in part to the regional distributions of food production and need.

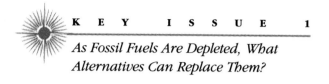

K E Y   I S S U E   1

As Fossil Fuels Are Depleted, What Alternatives Can Replace Them?

- Fossil Fuels
- Alternative Energy Sources

We depend on abundant, low-cost energy to run our industries, transport ourselves, and keep our homes comfortable, but we are depleting the global supply of some energy resources. More developed countries want to preserve current standards of living, and less developed countries are struggling to attain a better standard. Tremendous energy resources are needed, so as we deplete our current sources of energy we must develop alternative ones.

Historically, people relied on power supplied by themselves or by animals, known as **animate power.** Energy from burning wood or flowing water later supplemented animate power. Since the industrial revolution began in the late 1700s, humans have expanded their use of **inanimate power**, generated from machines. Humans have found the technology to harness the great potential energy stored in resources such as coal, oil, gas, and uranium.

Fossil Fuels

Three of Earth's substances provide more than 80 percent of the world's energy and over 90 percent of North America's energy: oil, natural gas, and coal (Figure 13-1). In developed countries, the remainder comes primarily from nuclear, solar, hydroelectric, and geothermal power. Burning wood provides much of the remaining energy in less developed societies.

In the past, the most important energy source worldwide was **biomass fuel**, such as wood, plant material, and animal waste. Biomass fuel is burned directly or converted to charcoal, alcohol, or methane gas. Biomass remains the most important source of fuel in some LDCs, but during the past 200 years MDCs have converted to other energy sources.

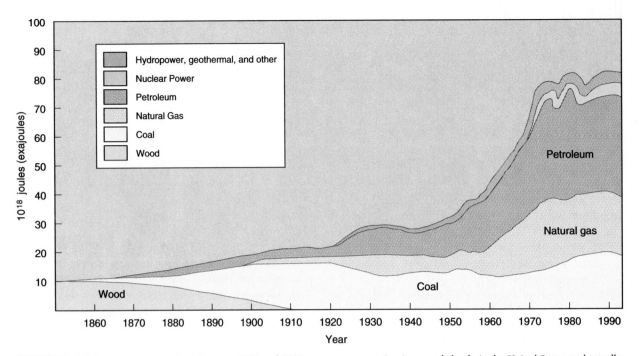

FIGURE 13-1 U.S. energy consumption. Between 1850 and 1950, energy consumption increased slowly in the United States, and actually declined on a per capita basis. Energy savings were achieved through substitution of fossil fuels for wood. U.S. energy consumption increased rapidly between the 1950s and early 1970s. Since then it has increased at a much slower rate, as a result of conservation.

As a consequence of the industrial revolution, coal supplanted wood as the leading energy source in the late 1800s in North America and Western Europe. Petroleum was first pumped in 1859, but it was not an important resource until the diffusion of automobiles in the twentieth century. Natural gas was originally burned off as a waste product of oil drilling but now heats millions of homes.

Energy is used in three principal places: businesses, homes, and transportation. For U.S. businesses, the main energy resource is coal, followed by natural gas and then oil. Some businesses directly burn coal in their own furnaces. Others rely on electricity, mostly generated at coal-burning power plants. At home, energy is used primarily to heat living space and water. Natural gas is the most common source, followed by petroleum (heating oil and kerosene). Almost all transportation systems operate on petroleum products, including automobiles, trucks, buses, airplanes, and most railroads. Only subways, streetcars, and some trains run on coal-generated electricity.

Petroleum, natural gas, and coal are known as fossil fuels. A **fossil fuel** is the residue of plants and an-

imals that were buried millions of years ago. As sediment accumulated over these remains, intense pressure and chemical reactions slowly converted them into the fossil fuels we use today. When we burn these substances today, we are releasing energy originally stored in plants and animals millions of years ago.

Two characteristics of fossil fuels cause great concern for the future:

1. *The supply of fossil fuels is finite.* Once the present supply of fossil fuels is consumed, it is gone, and we must look to other resources for our energy. (Technically, fossil fuels are continually being formed, but the process takes millions of years, so humans must regard the current supply as essentially finite.)

2. *Fossil fuels are distributed unevenly around the globe.* Some regions enjoy a generous supply of fossil fuels, while others have little, and fossil fuels are not consumed in the same regions where they are produced.

Finiteness of Fossil Fuels

To understand Earth's resources, we distinguish between those that are renewable and those that are not. **Renewable energy** is replaced continually, or at least within a human lifespan: solar energy, hydroelectric, geothermal, fusion, and wind are examples. Renewable energy has an essentially unlimited supply and is not depleted when used by people. **Nonrenewable energy** forms so slowly that for practical purposes it cannot be renewed: the fossil fuels, as well as nuclear energy, are examples.

As nonrenewable energy sources, the three main fossil fuels, once burned, are used up for all time. The world faces an energy problem in part because we are rapidly depleting the remaining supply of the three fossil fuels, especially petroleum. Because of dwindling supplies of fossil fuels, most of the buildings in which we live, work, and study will have to be heated another way. Cars, trucks, and buses will have to operate on some other energy source. The many plastic objects that we use, which are made from petroleum, will have to be made with other materials.

We can use other resources for heat, fuel, and manufacturing, but they are likely to be more expensive and less convenient to use than fossil fuels. And converting from fossil fuels will likely disrupt our daily lives and cause us hardship.

Remaining Supply of Fossil Fuels. How much of the fossil fuel supply remains? Despite the critical importance of this question for the future, no one can answer it precisely. Because petroleum, natural gas, and coal are deposited beneath Earth's surface, considerable technology and skill are required to locate these substances and estimate their volume.

The amount of energy remaining in deposits that have been discovered is called a **proven reserve.** Proven reserves can be measured with reasonable accuracy—about 1 trillion barrels of petroleum, about 140 trillion cubic meters of natural gas, and about 1 quadrillion metric tons of coal.

But how many deposits in the world have not yet been discovered? The energy in undiscovered deposits that are *thought* to exist is a **potential reserve.** When a *potential* reserve is actually discovered, it is reclassified as a *proven* reserve. The World Energy Council estimates potential oil reserves of about 0.5 trillion barrels, with the largest fields

thought to lie beneath the South China Sea and northwestern China.

To determine when remaining reserves of an energy source will be depleted, we must know the *rate* at which the resource is being consumed. At the current world petroleum consumption rate of about 25 billion barrels a year, Earth's proven petroleum reserves of 1 trillion barrels will last 40 years.

New petroleum deposits are being discovered each year and added to the inventory of proven reserves (thus extending the number of years of remaining supply), but petroleum is being consumed at a more rapid rate than it is being found, and world demand is increasing by more than 1 percent per year. Unless substantial new proven reserves are found—or consumption decreases sharply—the world's petroleum reserves will be depleted sometime in the twenty-first century.

Similarly, at current rates of use, the world's proven reserves of natural gas will last for about 80 years. Proven reserves of natural gas are less extensive than petroleum reserves, but the remaining supply is projected to last longer because the world currently uses much more oil than gas. If energy users switched from petroleum to natural gas, however, then the proven reserves of petroleum would last longer and natural gas would be depleted more quickly.

For coal, the immediate future is less grim. At current consumption, proven coal reserves can last at least several hundred years. Today, about 55 percent of U.S. electricity comes from power plants that burn coal.

Extraction of Remaining Reserves. Although scientists differ on the volume of potential reserves, they agree that extracting proven reserves will grow harder. When it was first exploited, petroleum "gushed" from wells drilled into rock layers saturated with it. Coal was quarried in open pits.

But now, extraction is harder. Sometimes pumping is not sufficient to remove petroleum, so water or carbon dioxide has to be forced into wells to push out the remaining resource. Oil companies have reduced their expenditures for new drilling by about two-thirds since the early 1980s. Coal mining continues in some thick, high-quality coal seams, both in open pits and underground, but already more mining is being done in thinner, poorer-quality coal deposits.

The problem of removing the last reserves from a proven field is comparable to wringing out a soaked towel. It is easy to quickly remove the main volume of water, but squeezing out the last percent requires more time and patience, and perhaps special technology.

The largest, most accessible deposits of petroleum, natural gas, and coal already have been exploited. Newly discovered reserves generally are smaller and more remote, such as beneath the sea floor, where extraction is costly. Exploration cost has increased because methods are more elaborate and the probability of finding new reserves is less.

Unconventional sources of petroleum and natural gas are being studied and developed, such as *oil shale* and *tar sands (sandstones)*. Oil shale is a "rock that burns" because of its tarlike content. Tar sandstones are saturated with a thick petroleum. They are called *unconventional* because methods currently used to extract resources won't recover these—instead, the rocks must be "cooked" to melt out their petroleum. These are also known as unconventional sources because we currently do not have economically feasible, environmentally sound technology to extract them.

Utah, Wyoming, and Colorado contain more than ten times the petroleum reserves of Saudi Arabia, but as oil shale. The cost of conventional oil resources must increase dramatically before these unconventional sources will become profitable. Even then, the adverse environmental impacts of using these sources are likely to be high.

Uneven Distribution of Fossil Fuels

Geographers observe two important inequalities in the global distribution of fossil fuels:

1. Some regions have abundant reserves, whereas others have little.
2. Consumption of fossil fuels is much higher in some regions than in others.

Given the centrality of fossil fuels in a society's economy and culture, unequal possession and consumption of fossil fuels have been major sources of global instability in the world.

Location of Reserves. Why do some regions have abundant reserves of one or more fossil fuels, but other regions have little? This partly reflects how fossil fuels form.

Coal forms in tropical locations, in lush, swampy areas rich in plants. As a result of the slow movement of Earth's drifting continents, the tropical swamps of 250 million years ago have relocated to the mid-latitudes. Today's main reserves of coal are in mid-latitude countries, rather than in the tropics. The United States and Russia each have about 25 percent of proven coal reserves, other European countries about 15 percent, and China about 10 percent (Figure 13-2). Australia, India, and South Africa have most of the remainder.

Similarly, today's sources of oil and natural gas formed millions of years ago from sediment deposited on the sea floor. Some oil and natural gas reserves still lie beneath such seas as the Persian Gulf and the North Sea, but other reserves are located beneath land that was under water millions of years ago, when sea level was higher.

Nearly two-thirds of the world's oil reserves are in five Middle Eastern countries—about 25 percent in Saudi Arabia and more than 5 percent each in Kuwait, Iran, Iraq, and the United Arab Emirates. Mexico and Venezuela have the most extensive proven reserves in the Western Hemisphere. The United States currently accounts for about one-sixth of the world's annual production of petroleum, but the country possesses about 2 percent of the proven reserves (Figure 13-3).

Countries once part of the Soviet Union, especially Russia, Turkmenistan, and Uzbekistan, possess more than one-third of the world's proven natural gas reserves. The United States currently produces about one-fourth of the world's natural gas, but its proven reserves are extremely limited (Figure 13-4).

Taken as a group, developed countries historically have possessed a disproportionately high percentage of the world's fossil fuel reserves. Europe's nineteenth century industrial development depended on its abundant coal fields, and extensive coal and petroleum supplies helped the United States to become the leading industrial power of the twentieth century. A handful of less developed countries in Africa, Asia, and Latin America have extensive reserves of one or another of the fossil fuels, but most have little.

During the nineteenth and twentieth centuries, developed countries produced most of the world's fossil fuels. But in the twenty-first century, this dominance is likely to end. Many of Europe's coal mines have closed in recent years, because either the coal

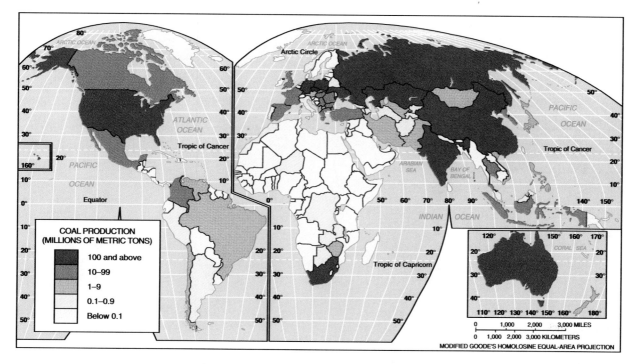

FIGURE 13-2 Coal production and proven reserves. China, the United States, and Russia are the largest producers and have the largest proven reserves of coal.

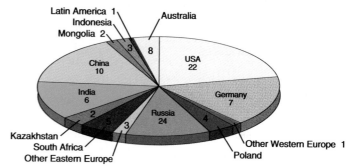

was exhausted or the remaining supply was too expensive to extract, and the region's petroleum and natural gas (in the North Sea) account for small percentages of worldwide reserves. The United States still has extensive coal reserves, but its petroleum and natural gas reserves are being depleted rapidly. Japan has never had significant fossil fuel reserves.

Most of the world's proven reserves (and probably potential reserves) are in a few Asian countries, especially China, the Middle East, and former Soviet Union republics. How these reserves are divided up between more developed and less developed countries (as well as among LDCs) is a critical issue for the world community in the twenty-first century.

Consumption of Fossil Fuels. The global pattern of fossil fuel consumption—like production—will shift in the twenty-first century. Developed countries, with about one-fourth of the world's population, currently consume about three-fourths of the world's energy. Annual per capita consumption of fossil fuels is about 5,000 kilograms in Western Europe and 10,000 kilograms in the United States and Canada (Figure 13-5). This high consumption by a modest percentage

of the world's population supports a lifestyle rich in food, goods, services, comfort, education, and travel. In comparison, per capita consumption is about 800 kilograms in China, 300 in South and Southeast Asia, and below 100 in other LDCs.

The sharp regional difference in fossil fuel consumption has two geographic consequences for the future:

• As they promote economic development and cope with high population growth, LDCs will consume much more energy. As a result of increased demand in LDCs, global consumption of petroleum is expected to increase by about 50 percent during the next two decades, while

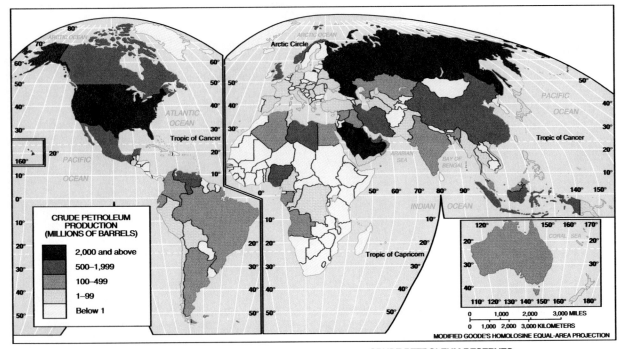

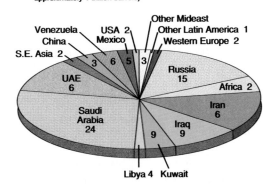

FIGURE 13-3 Petroleum production and proven reserves. Saudi Arabia is the largest producer and has the largest proven reserves of petroleum. The United States is a major producer but has limited reserves.

coal and natural gas consumption are expected to double. The share of world energy consumed by LDCs will increase from about 25 percent today to 40 percent by 2010 and 60 percent by 2020.

• Because MDCs consume more energy than they produce, they must import more fossil fuels, especially petroleum, from LDCs. The United States and Western Europe import more than half their petroleum, and Japan more than 90 percent. Because of economic development and population growth in the LDCs, however, the developed countries will face more competition in obtaining the world's remaining supplies of fossil fuels.

Control of World Petroleum

The sharpest conflicts over energy will be centered on the world's limited proven reserves of petroleum. The United States produced more petroleum than it consumed during the first half of the twentieth century. Beginning in the 1950s, the large transnational companies then in control of in-

ternational petroleum distribution determined that extracting domestic petroleum was more expensive than importing it from the Middle East. U.S. petroleum imports have increased from 14 percent of total consumption in 1954 to more than 50 percent today. European countries and Japan have always depended on foreign petroleum because of limited domestic supplies.

MDCs import most of their petroleum from the Middle East, where most of the world's proven reserves are concentrated. U.S. and Western European transnational companies originally exploited Middle Eastern petroleum fields and sold the petroleum at a low price to consumers in MDCs. At first, Western companies set oil prices and paid the Middle Eastern governments only a small percentage of their oil prof-

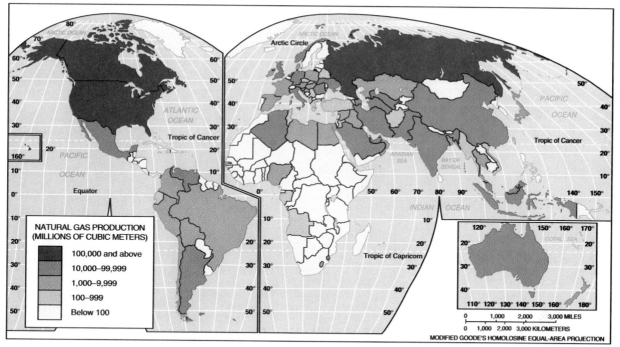

FIGURE 13-4 Natural gas production and proven reserves. Russia is the largest producer and has the largest proven reserves of natural gas. Again, the United States is a major producer but has limited reserves.

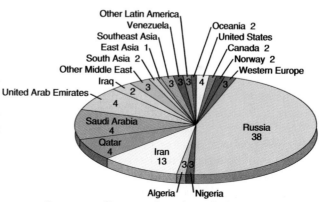

NATURAL GAS RESERVES
(Percentage of world reserves totalling approximately 5 quadrillion cubic meters)

its. But government policies changed in the petroleum-producing countries, especially during the 1970s. Foreign-owned petroleum fields were either nationalized or more tightly controlled, and prices were set by governments rather than by petroleum companies.

OPEC Policies During the 1970s. Several LDCs possessing substantial petroleum reserves created the Organization of Petroleum Exporting Countries (OPEC) in 1960. Arab OPEC members in the Middle East are Algeria, Iraq, Kuwait, Libya, Qatar, Saudi Arabia, and the United Arab Emirates. Another Middle East OPEC member, Iran, is not Arab. OPEC countries elsewhere in the world include Indonesia, Gabon, Nigeria, and Venezuela. Ecuador was a member until 1993.

OPEC's Arab members were angry at North American and Western European countries for supporting Israel during that nation's 1973 war with the Arab states of Egypt, Jordan, and Syria. So, during the winter of 1973–1974, they flexed their new economic muscle with a boycott—Arab OPEC states refused to sell petroleum to the nations that had supported Israel.

Soon, gasoline supplies dwindled in MDCs. Each U.S. gasoline station was rationed a small quantity of fuel, which ran out early in the day. Long lines formed at gas stations, and some motorists waited all night for fuel. Gasoline was rationed by license plate number (cars with licenses ending in an odd number could buy only on odd-numbered days). European countries took more drastic action—the Netherlands, for example, banned all but emergency motor vehicle travel on Sundays.

OPEC lifted the boycott in 1974 but raised petroleum prices from $3 to more than $35 per barrel by 1981. Prices at U.S. gas pumps rose from an average of 39¢ in 1973 to $1.38 per gallon in 1981. Thus did OPEC force a massive increase in oil cost for West-

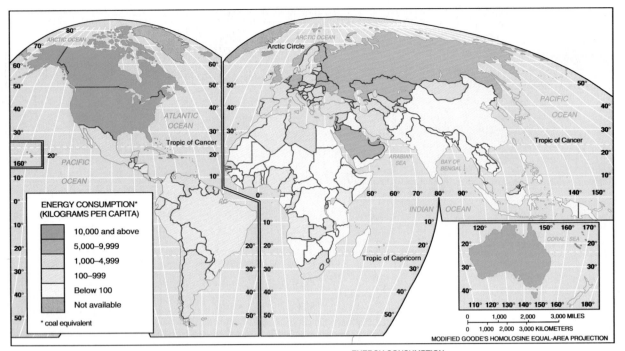

FIGURE 13-5 Per capita fossil fuel consumption. More developed countries consume much more fossil fuel per capita than less developed countries. The United States, with 5 percent of the world's population, consumes about 25 percent of the world's energy.

ern countries. To import oil, U.S. consumers spent $3 billion in 1970, but $80 billion in 1980.

The rapid escalation in petroleum prices caused severe economic problems in MDCs during the 1970s. Production of steel, motor vehicles, and other energy-dependent industries plummeted in the United States in the wake of the 1973–1974 boycott and have never regained their pre-boycott levels (recall Figure 10-20, which shows declining steel production in developed countries since the 1970s). Soaring energy costs forced many manufacturers out of business, and the survivors had to restructure their operations to regain international competitiveness.

LDCs were hurt even more. They depended on low-cost petroleum imports to spur industrial growth. Their fertilizer costs shot up, because many fertilizers are derived from oil. North American and Western European states cushioned themselves by creating a profitable return path for money that was going to OPEC: they encouraged OPEC countries to invest in American and European real estate, banks, and other safe and profitable investments. Comparable investment opportunities were limited in less developed countries.

ENERGY CONSUMPTION
(Percentage of world consumption totalling approximately 11 billion metric tons, coal equivalent)

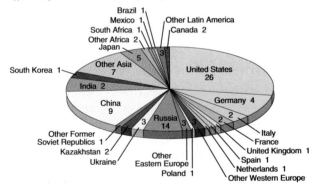

Recent Trends. Internal conflicts have weakened OPEC's influence in the 1980s and 1990s. Iraq warred with Iran, and Libya grew more radical, supporting terrorists. By not acting together, individual OPEC members produced more petroleum than the world demanded, and MDCs stockpiled some of the surplus as protection against another boycott. The price plummeted from over $30 to below $10 per barrel during the 1980s. During the 1991 Gulf War, the price rose briefly to about $40, then settled at about $20, less than the price before the 1973–1974 boycott, with accounting for inflation.

Conservation measures in developed countries have also dampened demand for petroleum in developed countries. The average car sold in the United States got less than 16 miles per gallon in 1975,

The Organization of Petroleum Exporting Countries refused to sell petroleum to North American and Western European countries for a few months during the winter of 1973-74 to protest Western countries support for Israel in the October 1973 war. Motorists in the United States, such as these in Los Angeles, waited in long lines to purchase gas. Note that the cars are in line to enter the Shell station in the background: the Exxon station in the foreground is closed because it already ran out of its day's allotment of fuel. In 1973, Americans regarded Exxon's posted price of 74¢ for a gallon of regular gas to be outrageously high. (Craig Aurness/Woodfin Camp & Associates)

compared with 28 miles per gallon in 1993. But the savings have been offset by increases in the number of vehicles and the number of miles that vehicles are being driven.

The United States has reduced petroleum imports from Arab OPEC countries by one-third since the 1970s, and only about 10 percent of total U.S. petroleum consumption now comes from these countries, mostly Saudi Arabia. Instead, the United States imports more petroleum from firm allies located in the Western Hemisphere, especially Venezuela, Canada, and Mexico. Europeans and Japanese have also decreased dependency on Arab OPEC countries. But the Middle East remains the world's principal source of petroleum (Figure 13-6), and given the global distribution of proven reserves, the Middle East is likely to account for an even higher share of trade in the future.

The world will not literally run out of petroleum during the twenty-first century. But at some point extracting the remaining petroleum reserves will prove so expensive and environmentally damaging that use of alternative energy sources will accelerate, and dependency on petroleum will diminish. The issues for the world are whether dwindling petroleum reserves are handled wisely and other energy sources are substituted peacefully. Given the massive growth in petroleum consumption expected

in countries such as China and India, the United States and other developed countries may have little influence over when prices rise and supplies decline.

Problems with Coal

Coal could substitute for petroleum during the next couple of centuries, especially in the United States, which possesses large proven coal reserves (see Figure 13-2). But problems hinder expanded use of coal: air pollution, mine safety, land subsidence and erosion, economics, and use as automotive fuel. Here is a look at each of these problems.

Air Pollution. Uncontrolled burning of coal releases several pollutants into the atmosphere: sulfur oxides, hydrocarbons, carbon dioxide, and particulates ("soot"). Many communities suffered from coal-polluted air earlier in this century and encouraged their industries to switch to cleaner-burning natural gas and oil. The U.S. Clean Air Act now requires utilities to use better-quality coal or to install "scrubbers" on smokestacks.

These methods can work; Pittsburgh, Pennsylvania, once noted for terrible air pollution when coal was burned for steel mills and glass factories, today has remarkably clean air. But coal-fired power plants still pump copious amounts of carbon dioxide into the atmosphere.

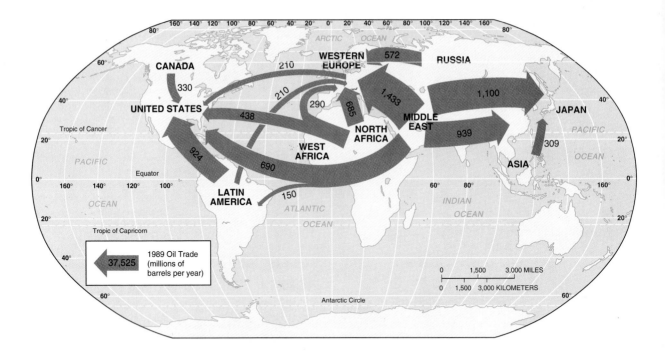

FIGURE 13-6 World petroleum trade. Because petroleum is not produced in the same countries where it is consumed, 11 billion barrels a year are carried by tankers from one country to another. More petroleum is transported internationally than the next three commodities combined (iron ore, coal, and grain), when figured by weight. The photograph shows an oil field in China, which has large petroleum reserves. (Xinhua/Gamma Liasion, Inc.)

Mine Safety. Mining was once an especially dangerous occupation. Before safety regulations were instituted, one thousand miners died annually in the United States, especially in underground mines. Strictly enforced U.S. mine safety laws, improved mine ventilation, intensive safety programs, automation of mining, and a smaller work force have made the American coal industry much safer today. Annual U.S. mine mortality now is below 100. But that figure could rise if mining operations expanded, and miners still are susceptible to black lung disease, for which the U.S. government pays several billion dollars per year in compensation.

Subsidence and Erosion. Both surface mining and underground mining can cause environmental damage. Acid may pollute water by draining into streams, and subsidence of the ground may damage buildings. Removing trees and other surface vegetation may cause soil erosion. In the United States, the mining industry is highly regulated, and most companies today have a good record of "cleaning up after themselves." But less-sensitive mining practices in the past have left a legacy of environmental damage.

Economics. Although heavy, bulky, and expensive to transport, coal must be shipped long distances, because most of the factories and power plants using it are far from the coal fields. Ironically, the principal methods of transporting coal—barge, rail, or truck—are all powered by petroleum. A considerable amount of energy thus is expended to mine and transport coal so that it can be used to generate energy somewhere else.

Using Coal to Power Motor Vehicles. Since motor vehicles appeared about a century ago, petroleum has been the basis for modern transportation. To substitute for petroleum, coal must be adapted for motor vehicles. The simplest way is to generate electricity by burning coal and use the electricity to charge batteries in electric vehicles.

The use of electric vehicles is expanding in developed countries, primarily to reduce air pollution rather than to conserve petroleum. California and several East Coast states require that by the year 2002, 10 percent of all new vehicles must generate "zero emissions"—essentially electric vehicles, given current technology.

In opinion polls, consumers express a willingness to pay a premium for the sake of saving energy and reducing pollution. The major U.S. carmakers—General Motors, Ford, and Chrysler—claim that few consumers are ready to incur the additional cost and inconvenience of an electric vehicle. For the next several decades, electric vehicles may remain much more expensive to purchase and operate than gasoline-powered ones, and they must be recharged every couple of hundred miles. If gasoline becomes hard to find, however, then small electric vehicles may look more attractive to consumers, and large gasoline-powered vehicles will be limited to specialized tasks—or consigned to museums.

Alternative Energy Sources

Coal-generated electricity can reduce the impact of depleted petroleum reserves over the next centu-

ry or two. But coal, like petroleum, is a nonrenewable fossil fuel that will eventually be depleted. It offers little hope to countries that lack substantial coal reserves. In the long run, energy problems can be solved only by converting to renewable resources. Recall that a renewable energy source has an essentially unlimited supply and is not depleted when used by people.

Two types of renewable energy sources—nuclear and solar—figure most prominently in current energy planning. Other alternatives to fossil fuels may become more important in the future.

Nuclear Energy

The big advantage of nuclear power is the large amount of energy that is released from a small amount of material. One kilogram of enriched nuclear fuel contains more than 2 million times the energy in 1 kilogram of coal.

Nuclear power now operates in about 430 reactors worldwide, supplying one-third of all electricity in Western Europe, including five-sixths in Lithuania, three-fourths in France, more than one-half in Belgium and Slovakia, and between one-fourth and one-half in Bulgaria, Czech Republic, Finland, France, Germany, Hungary, Slovenia, Spain, Sweden, Switzerland, Ukraine, and the United Kingdom. Elsewhere, Japan (which has virtually no fossil fuels), South Korea, and Taiwan also rely on nuclear-generated electricity (Figure 13-7).

The United States and Canada use less nuclear energy, in part because of more abundant coal reserves. Nuclear power generates approximately 20 percent of North American electricity as a whole, although New England draws most of its electricity from nuclear power (Figure 13-8).

Nuclear power presents serious problems. These include potential accidents, radioactive waste, generation of plutonium (which can be used to make bombs), a limited uranium supply and uneven geographic distribution, and cost.

Potential Accidents. A nuclear power plant produces electricity from energy released when uranium atoms are split in a controlled environment, a process called **fission**. One product of all nuclear reactions is **radioactive waste,** certain types of which are lethal to people exposed to it. Elaborate safety precautions are taken to prevent nuclear fuel from leaking from a power plant.

Nuclear power plants cannot explode, like a nuclear bomb, because the quantities of uranium are too small and they cannot be brought together fast enough. But it *is* possible to have a runaway reaction, which overheats the reactor, causing a *meltdown,* possible steam explosions, and scattering of radioactive material into the atmosphere. This happened in 1986 at Chernobyl, then in the Soviet Union and now in the north of Ukraine, near the Belarus border.

The Soviet Union reported at the time that the Chernobyl accident caused thirty-one deaths, including two at the accident site itself and twenty-nine elsewhere. These people were exposed to severe radiation and burns. Most scientists dismiss these figures as unrealistically low, because hundreds of thousands of residents and cleanup workers were exposed to high levels of radiation. For example, officials in Belarus, where 70 percent of the fallout hit, report that cancer cases increased 45 percent in the districts closest to the plant during the first 5 years after the accident.

The impact of the Chernobyl accident extended through Europe. Most European governments temporarily banned the sale of milk and fresh vegetables, which were contaminated with radioactive fallout. Half of the eventual victims may be residents of European countries other than Ukraine and Belarus.

American nuclear plants are designed with strong, thick containment buildings surrounding the reactors. But nuclear plants built by the former Soviet Union lack containment buildings and often have defective parts. At a Soviet-built plant in East Germany, eleven of twelve cooling pumps were disabled by a fire and power failure. Had the twelfth pump failed, a meltdown, with its inevitable release of strong radioactive materials, likely would have killed the 50,000 inhabitants of the nearby city of Greifswald. This 1975 accident went unreported for 15 years, making the case for all nuclear plants to be open for inspection.

Radioactive Waste. When nuclear fuel fissions, the waste is highly radioactive and lethal, and it remains so for many years. Plutonium can be harvested from it for making nuclear weapons. Pipes, concrete, and water near the fissioning fuel also become "hot" with radioactivity.

No one has yet devised permanent storage for radioactive waste. The waste cannot be burned or chemically treated—it must be isolated for several

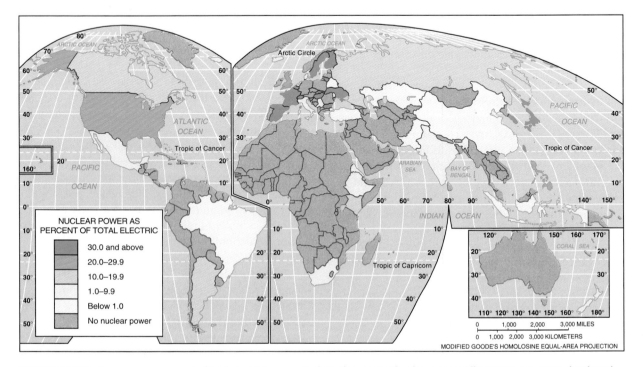

FIGURE 13-7 Nuclear power as percent of total electricity generated. Nuclear power has been especially attractive to more developed countries in Europe that lack abundant reserves of either petroleum or coal.

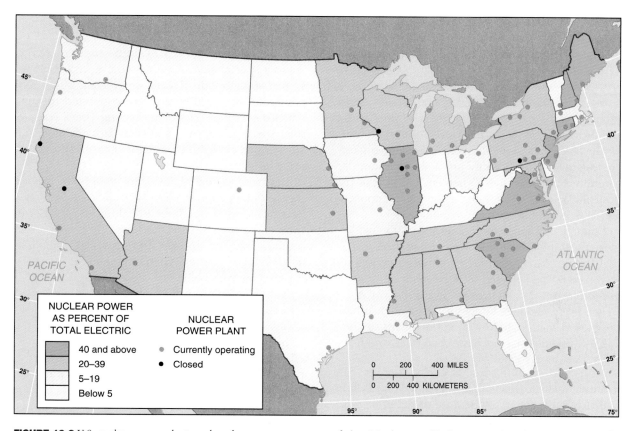

FIGURE 13-8 U.S. nuclear power plants and nuclear power as percent of electricity by state. Nuclear power is an important source of electricity in some northeastern and midwestern states. At a number of locations, more than one nuclear plant has been built.

thousand years until it loses its radioactivity. Spent fuel in the United States is stored "temporarily" in cooling tanks at nuclear power plants, but these tanks are nearly full.

The United States is Earth's fourth largest country in land area, yet it has failed to find a suitable underground storage site, because of worry about groundwater contamination. Proposals abound: burial at sea, in abandoned mines, or in deep layers of rock salt, or rocketing it into the sun. But the universal response is *NIMBY*, which stands for "not in my back yard." No community wants a storage facility near it.

The time required for radioactive waste to decay to a safe level is far longer than any country or civilization has ever existed. What government, army, or other human institution will survive for several thousand years to safeguard the stored waste?

Generation of Plutonium. Nuclear power has been used in warfare twice, in 1945, when two nu-

clear bombs were dropped on Hiroshima and Nagasaki, Japan, ending World War II. Since then, the Soviet Union (now Russia), the United Kingdom, France, and China have tested nuclear weapons, and several other countries are actively developing them, although they have not stated so publicly. No government has dared to use them in war, because leaders have recognized that a full-scale nuclear war could terminate human civilization.

But the black market could provide terrorists with enough plutonium to construct nuclear weapons. Plutonium is more lethal than uranium and could cause more deaths and injuries in an accident. It also is easier to fashion into a bomb.

A few years ago, a Princeton University student wrote a term paper outlining how to make a nuclear weapon. Most of his information came from an encyclopedia and a few unclassified government documents. More chilling is the fact that after publicity about his paper, several organizations and foreign governments contacted him for assistance in making a bomb.

Limited Uranium Supply. Like fossil fuels, proven uranium reserves are limited—about 60 years at current rates of use. And they are not distributed uniformly around the world—two-thirds of the world's proven uranium reserves are in Australia, the United States, South Africa, and Canada. (Russia and China probably rank among world leaders in production and proven reserves, but their levels are unknown).

The chemical composition of natural uranium further aggravates the scarcity problem. Uranium ore naturally contains only 0.7 percent U-235 (the fissionable isotope of uranium), and a greater concentration is needed for power generation.

Uranium is a nonrenewable resource—the world's reserves of minable uranium ore are limited, just as coal and petroleum reserves are. Proven uranium reserves could be depleted in three more decades. A **breeder reactor** turns uranium into a renewable resource by generating plutonium, also a nuclear fuel. But the risks associated with plutonium are so great that few breeder reactors have been built, and none are in the United States.

Cost. Nuclear power plants cost several billion dollars to build, primarily because of elaborate safety measures. Without double and triple backup systems, nuclear energy would be too dangerous to use. Uranium is mined in one place, refined in another, and used in still another. The complexities of safe transportation add cost. As a result, the cost of generating electricity is much higher from nuclear plants than from coal-burning plants.

The future of nuclear power has been seriously hurt by the combination of high risks and costs. Most countries in North America and Western Europe have curtailed construction of new plants. Sweden, which received nearly half of its electricity from nuclear power in the 1980s plans to abandon its nuclear power plants completely by the year 2010. Even in France, where over 70 percent of electricity is generated from nuclear power, public opposition inhibits new development. Nuclear power will decline in other countries as older nuclear plants are closed and not replaced.

Solar Energy

Solar energy is free, does not damage the environment or cause pollution, and is quite safe, unlike nuclear energy or mining coal. The sun's remaining life is estimated at 5 billion years, so solar energy is the ultimate renewable source. There are two general approaches to harnessing solar energy: passive and active.

Passive solar energy systems capture energy without special devices. When you sit by a window so that sunlight falls directly on you, the sun's rays penetrate the window and are converted to heat when they strike your skin, making you a passive solar energy collector. If you wear dark clothing, you are warmed even more, because dark objects absorb more energy.

Passive solar energy systems use similar principles—south-facing windows and dark surfaces—to heat homes and buildings on sunny days. Passive solar energy can also be generated by placing on a south-facing roof an insulated glass box container filled with air or water. When heated, the air or water is piped into the home.

Active solar energy systems collect solar energy and convert it either to heat energy or to electricity (either indirectly or directly).

In *heat* conversion, solar radiation is concentrated with large reflectors and lenses to heat water or rocks. These store the energy for use at night and on cloudy days.

In *indirect electric* conversion, solar radiation is first converted to heat, then to electricity. The sun's rays are concentrated by reflectors onto a pipe filled with synthetic oil. The heat from the oil-filled pipe generates steam to run turbines. Several of these plants serve a quarter-million people in California's Mojave Desert.

In *direct electric* conversion, solar radiation is captured with **photovoltaic cells,** which convert light energy to electrical energy. Each cell generates a small electrical current, but large numbers of them wired together produce significant amounts of electricity. Solar-generated electricity is now used in spacecraft, light-powered calculators, and at remote sites where conventional power is unavailable. The cost of cells must drop and their efficiency must improve for use of solar power to expand.

Solar power can be generated at a central power station, as we now receive most of our power. But solar power also makes feasible individual home systems. An installation costing several thousand dollars provides a solar energy system that provides virtually all household heat and electricity. This high initial cost is offset by very low monthly operating costs, so the system is economical for consumers who remain in the same house for a number of years. Individual solar energy users do not face ris-

Cities throughout the United States, including Denver, have built fixed light rail transit systems in recent years in an attempt to lure commuters out of their cars. Light rail lines are less expensive than subways to construct, because the tracks can be laid on city streets or along the rights-of-way of old railroads, whereas subways involve digging tunnels. (Mirris Best/Uniphoto)

ing electric bills from utilities that pass on their cost of purchasing fossil fuels and constructing facilities.

The United States, Israel, and Japan lead in solar use at home, mostly for heating water. Solar energy will become more attractive as other energy sources become more expensive. A bright future for solar energy is indicated, for petroleum companies now own the major U.S. manufacturers of photovoltaic cells.

Back in the 1950s, government policy in the United States and the Soviet Union was instrumental in developing peacetime use for nuclear energy. Similarly, the speed with which solar energy diffuses in the years ahead depends on the extent of government support. Tax credits for home solar systems and solar-generated electric cars would reduce their cost and encourage consumers to buy them.

Other Energy Sources

Other energy sources include hydroelectric, geothermal, biomass, and fusion. The first three currently are used but offer limited prospects for expansion. Fusion is not a practical source at this time, but may be in the future.

Hydroelectric Power. Water has been a source of mechanical power since before recorded history. It turned water wheels, and the rotational motion was used to grind grain, saw timber, pump water, and operate machines. Over the last hundred years, the energy of moving water has been used to generate electricity, called **hydroelectric power**.

Hydroelectric power is the world's second most popular source of electricity, after coal, supplying about a fourth of worldwide demand. The United States, though, obtains only about 3 percent of its energy through hydroelectric power, and little growth is anticipated, because few acceptable sites to build new dams remain.

Hydroelectric power has drawbacks. Dams may flood formerly usable land, cause erosion, and upset ecosystems. Political problems can result from building dams on rivers that flow through more than one country. Turkey's recently built dam on the Euphrates River was strongly opposed by Syria and Iraq, through which the river also passes. The new dam diverts too much water from the river and makes its water saltier.

Geothermal Energy. Earth's interior is hot from natural nuclear reactions. Toward the surface, heat is especially pronounced in volcanic areas. The hot rocks may encounter groundwater, producing heated water or steam that can be tapped by wells. Energy from this hot water or steam is called **geothermal energy**.

Harnessing geothermal energy is most feasible at the rifts along Earth's surface where crustal plates meet. These rifts also are the sites of many earthquakes and volcanoes. Geothermal energy is being tapped in several locations, including California, Italy, New Zealand, and Japan, and other rift sites are being explored. Iceland and Indonesia make extensive use of this resource. Ironically, in Iceland, an island named for its glaciers, nearly all homes and businesses in the capital of Reykjavik are heated with geothermal steam.

Biomass. Forms of biomass, such as sugar cane, corn, and soybeans, can be processed into motor vehicle fuels. Brazil in particular makes extensive use of biomass to fuel its cars and trucks. Potential for increasing the use of biomass for fuel is limited for several reasons. Burning biomass may be inefficient, because the energy used to *produce* the crops may be as much as the energy *supplied* by the crops. When wood is burned for fuel instead of being left in the forest, the fertility of the forest may be reduced. The most important limitation on using biomass for energy is that it already serves other essential purposes: providing much of Earth's food, clothing, and shelter.

Nuclear Fusion. Some nuclear power problems could be solved with nuclear **fusion,** which is the fusing of hydrogen atoms to form helium. Fusion releases spectacular amounts of energy—a gnat-sized amount of hydrogen releases the energy of thousands of tons of coal. But fusion can occur only at very high temperatures (millions of degrees). Such high temperatures have been briefly achieved in hydrogen bomb tests, but not on a sustained basis in a power-plant reactor, given present technology.

Alternatives such as fusion do not offer immediate solutions to energy shortages in the twenty-first century, but they may become more practical if the price of current energy sources substantially rises. Earth is not running out of energy resources, but the era of dependency on nonrenewable fossil fuels for energy will constitute a remarkably short period of human history.

KEY ISSUE 2

What Are the Solutions to Pollution?

- Sources of Pollution
- Alternatives for Reducing Pollution

In our consideration of resources, consumption was half of the equation—waste disposal is the other half. All of the materials we use eventually are returned to the atmosphere, bodies of water, or land, through burning, rinsing, or discarding. Not all human actions harm the environment, for every ecosystem can accept some waste. When we wash household cleaners and chemicals into a river, the river may dilute them until their concentration is insignificant. But when more waste is added than an ecosystem can accommodate, we have **pollution.** Pollution levels generally are greater where people are concentrated. The actions of many people in a small area are likely to exceed the capacity of the environment to absorb the waste.

When we discard something, we never really eliminate that product; we simply put it somewhere else. It may cause pollution, depending on where we place it. Natural processes may transport pollutants from one part of the environment to another. Discharges to the air often turn up in rivers, and wastes dumped in landfills can produce gases that leak to the atmosphere.

To better understand the causes of pollution, Blair Bower of Resources for the Future, a nonprofit research organization, asks us to consider a dairy cow as an analog of a factory, with inputs, processing, and outputs. We can think of a dairy cow as a factory that uses two main inputs—feed and water—to produce a desired output or product—milk (Figure 13-9).

Like a factory, a cow can pollute the environment. Pollution may result because a cow (like a factory) generates some unintended waste byproducts along

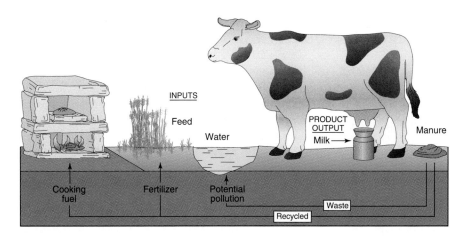

FIGURE 13-9 A dairy cow model for understanding pollution. The cow has inputs (feed and water) and a product (milk). Manure is a waste that can be recycled, in this case perhaps as fertilizer, or it may wash into the stream and become pollution.

with the desired product. In the case of a cow, it is manure. One of two things can happen to the waste: either it is collected and reused or it is discarded into the environment. The waste may or may not constitute pollution. It is a pollutant if the level discharged into the environment exceeds the capacity of the environment to accept it.

The waste created by dairy cows is discharged into the environment in some societies and reused in others. In South Asia, dried manure is reused for fuel, and in many societies it is used for fertilizer. Farmers in developed countries allow the manure to lie on the ground, because collecting and treating it are more expensive than purchasing commercial fertilizer. If the amount discharged by the cow exceeds the capacity of the field and nearby river to absorb it, the manure constitutes pollution.

Not all pollution is caused by humans. Natural pollution occurs when volcanoes erupt, spewing vast quantities of ash, cinders, sulfur gases, and steam into the atmosphere. Erosion from floods can clog streams with silt. Our focus here, however, is on the pollution that we cause.

In the following sections, we look at air, water, and land pollution. Each has distinctive characteristics that illustrate the close connection between human activities and environmental quality.

Sources of Pollution

When we discard something, we do not eliminate the material, but merely place it back into one of our three basic resources: air, water, or land. We will now look at how we pollute each.

Air Pollution

At ground level, Earth's average atmosphere comprises about 78 percent nitrogen, 21 percent oxygen, and less than 1 percent argon. The remaining 0.04 percent includes several *trace gases,* some of which are critical. **Air pollution** is a concentration of trace substances at a greater level than occurs in average air.

The most common air pollutants are carbon monoxide, sulfur dioxide, nitrogen oxides, hydrocarbons, and solid particulates. Concentrations of these trace gases in the air can damage property and adversely affect the health of people, other animals, and plants.

Three human activities generate most air pollution: motor vehicles, industry, and power plants. In all three cases, pollution results from the burning of fossil fuels. Burning gasoline or diesel oil in cars, trucks, buses, and motorcycles produces carbon monoxide, hydrocarbons, nitrogen oxides, and other pollutants. Factories and power plants produce sulfur dioxides and solid particulates, primarily from burning coal.

Air pollution concerns geographers at three scales—global, regional, and local:

Global scale. Air pollution may damage the atmosphere's *ozone* layer and contribute to *global warming.*

Regional scale. Air pollution may damage a region's vegetation and water supply through *acid deposition.*

Local scale. Air pollution is especially severe in local areas where emission sources are concentrated, such as urban areas.

We can examine distinctive problems associated with air pollution at each scale.

Global-Scale Concerns: Global Warming. Human actions, especially the burning of fossil fuels, may be causing Earth's temperature to rise. Earth is warmed by sunlight that passes through the atmosphere, strikes the surface, and is converted to heat. When the heat tries to pass back through the atmosphere to space, some gets through and some is trapped. This process keeps Earth's temperatures moderate and allows life to flourish on the planet.

A concentration of trace gases in the atmosphere can block or delay the return of some of the heat leaving the surface heading for space, thereby raising Earth's surface temperature. When fossil fuels are burned, one of the trace gases, carbon dioxide, is discharged into the atmosphere.

Plants and oceans absorb much of this discharge, but increased burning of fossil fuel during the past 200 years has caused the level of carbon dioxide in the atmosphere to rise by more than one-fourth, according to the U.N. Intergovernmental Panel on Climate Change. And the lingering effects of past emissions will cause the increase to continue even if fossil-fuel burning is reduced immediately. Carbon dioxide is also increasing in the atmosphere from the burning and rotting of trees cut in the rain forests.

During the past century, the average temperature of Earth's surface has increased by 1 degree Celsius (2 degrees Fahrenheit). This increase may or not have been caused by the buildup of carbon dioxide. Unless carbon dioxide emissions are sharply curtailed in the near future, however, average temperatures at the surface of Earth will increase by several degrees over the next century, according to the U.N. panel. This rise in temperature would be comparable to the increase over the past 20,000 years, since the end of the last Ice Age.

The anticipated increase in Earth's temperature, caused as carbon dioxide traps some of the radiation emitted by the surface, is called the **greenhouse ef-**fect. The term *greenhouse effect* is somewhat misleading, because a greenhouse does not work in the same way as trace gases in the atmosphere. In a real greenhouse, the interior gets very warm when the windows remain closed on a sunny day. The sun's light energy passes through the glass into the greenhouse and is converted to heat, while the heat trapped inside the building is unable to escape through the glass. Although an imprecise analogy, *greenhouse effect* has been a widely adopted term to evoke the anticipated warming of Earth's surface when trace gases block some of the heat trying to escape into space.

Regardless of what it is called, global warming of only a few degrees could melt the polar ice caps and raise the level of the oceans many meters. Coastal cities such as New York, Los Angeles, Rio de Janeiro, and Hong Kong would flood. Global patterns of precipitation could shift—some deserts could receive more rainfall, but currently productive agricultural regions, such as the U.S. Midwest, could become too dry for farming. Humans can adapt to a warmer planet, but the shifts in coastlines and precipitation patterns could require massive migration and be accompanied by political disputes.

Global-Scale Concerns: Ozone and CFCs. Earth's atmosphere has zones with distinct characteristics. The stratosphere, the zone between 15 and 50 kilometers (9 to 30 miles) above Earth's surface, contains a concentration of **ozone** gas. The ozone layer absorbs dangerous ultraviolet (UV) rays from the sun. Were it not for the ozone in the stratosphere, UV rays would damage plants, cause skin cancer, and disrupt food chains.

Earth's protective ozone layer is threatened by pollutants called **CFCs (*chlorofluorocarbons*).** CFCs such as *Freon* were widely used as coolants in refrigerators and air conditioners. When they leak from these appliances, the CFCs are carried into the stratosphere, where they break down Earth's protective layer of ozone gas. The 1987 Montréal Protocol called for developed countries to stop using CFCs by 2000 and for LDCs to stop by 2010.

Regional-Scale Concerns: Acid Deposition. Industrialized, densely populated regions in Europe and eastern North America are especially affected by **acid deposition**. Sulfur oxides and nitrogen oxides, emitted by burning fossil fuels, enter the atmosphere,

Acid precipitation has killed a large percentage of the trees in many central European forests, including this one in the Czech Republic. Communist policies encouraged the construction of factories and power plants without pollution control devices. (Jerry Bergman/Gamma Liaison)

where they combine with oxygen and water. Tiny droplets of sulfuric acid and nitric acid form and return to Earth's surface as acid deposition. When dissolved in water, the acids may fall as **acid precipitation**—rain, snow, or fog. The acids may also be deposited in dust. Before they reach the surface, these acidic droplets may be carried hundreds of kilometers by winds.

Acid precipitation has damaged lakes, killing fish and plants. Aquatic life has been eliminated completely from 4 percent of the lakes in the eastern United States and Canada. Another 5 percent of the lakes in the eastern United States and 20 percent in eastern Canada have acidity levels that threaten some species.

On land, concentrations of acid in the soil can injure plants by depriving them of nutrients and can harm soil worms and insects. Acid precipitation has contributed to the decline of the red spruce tree at higher elevations. Buildings and monuments made of marble and limestone have suffered corrosion from acid rain; engravings on old marble tombstones may be illegible as a result.

Since the 1970s, the United States has reduced sulfur dioxide emissions significantly. Many Western European countries cut theirs in half, largely by reducing coal use. Despite this progress, acid precipitation continues to damage forests and lakes.

Governments are reluctant to impose the high cost of controls on their industries and consumers.

Geographers are particularly interested in the effects of acid precipitation because the worst damage is not experienced at the same location as the emission of the pollutants. Within the United States, the major generators of acid deposition are in Ohio and other industrial states along the southern Great Lakes. However, the severest effects of acid rain are felt in several areas farther east (Figure 13-10 left).

The problem of acid precipitation is compounded by the fact that pollutants emitted in one country cause adverse impacts in another. Acid rain falling in Ontario, Canada, for example, can be traced to emissions from coal-burning power plants in the U.S. Great Lakes. Government officials at the source of the pollution may be reluctant to impose strong controls on the offending factories because they fear damaging the local economy.

Eastern Europe has suffered especially severely from acid precipitation, a legacy of Communist policies that encouraged the construction of factories and power plants without pollution control devices. Destruction of forests is widespread because of acid rain emitted from Eastern Europe's major industrial region (southeastern Germany, southern Poland, and northern Czech Republic). Affected by acid precipi-

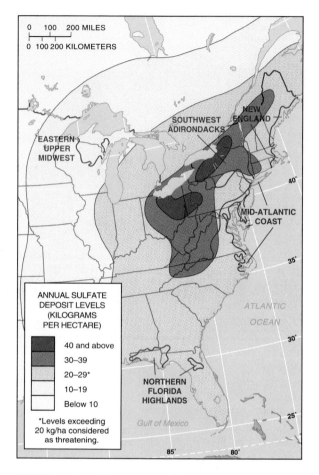

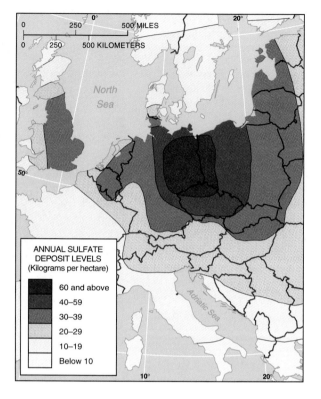

FIGURE 13-10 Acid precipitation. The most severe adverse effects from acid precipitation do not occur where the pollutants are emitted into the air, because they are carried away by wind and then are deposited at a distance. (left) Because of prevailing wind patterns across North America, damage is generally found to the east of the emissions. (right) Precipitation levels in eastern Germany are higher than anywhere in the United States, although elsewhere in central Europe levels are comparable to those in the eastern United States.

tation more than any other European state, the Czech Republic has suffered severe damage in more than 80 percent of the Bohemian Forest and more than one-third of its other forests (Figure 13-10 right).

The destruction of trees has harmed Eastern Europe's seasonal water flow. In dense forests, snow used to melt slowly and trickle into rivers. Now, on the barren sites, it melts and drains quickly, causing flooding in the spring and water shortages in the summer. Perhaps the severest impact is on human life. One-third of the residents of St. Petersburg, Russia's second-largest city, suffer from upper respiratory tract ailments as a result of the intense air pollution. A 40-year-old man living in Poland's polluted southern industrial area has a life expectancy 10 years less than his father had at the same age. Poland is esti-

mated to have between 20,000 and 50,000 additional deaths per year due to pollution.

Local-Scale Concerns: Urban Air Pollution.
The air above cities may be especially polluted because a large number of factories, motor vehicles, and other polluters emit residuals in a concentrated area. Weather conditions may make it difficult for the emissions to dissipate.

Urban air pollution has three basic components:

1. *Carbon monoxide.* Proper burning in power plants and vehicles produces carbon *di*oxide, but improper combustion produces carbon *mon*oxide. Breathing carbon monoxide reduces the oxygen level in blood, impairs vi-

sion and alertness, and threatens those with breathing problems.

2. *Hydrocarbons* also result from improper fuel combustion, as well as evaporation of paint solvents. Hydrocarbons and nitrogen oxides in the presence of sunlight form **photo-chemical smog,** which causes respiratory problems, stinging in the eyes, and an ugly haze over cities.

3. *Particulates* include dust and smoke particles. The dark plume of smoke from a factory stack and the exhaust of a diesel truck are examples of particulates being emitted.

The severity of air pollution resulting from emissions of carbon monoxide, hydrocarbons, and particulates depends on the weather. The worst urban air pollution occurs when winds are slight, skies are clear, and a temperature inversion exists. When the wind blows, it disperses pollutants, and when it is calm pollutants build. Sunlight provides the energy for the formation of smog. Air is normally cooler at higher elevations, but during temperature inversions—in which air is warmer at higher elevations—pollutants are trapped near the ground.

According to the U.S. Environmental Protection Agency, the worst U.S. city for concentrations of carbon monoxide and second worst for particulates is Denver, where residents call the smog "the brown cloud." The Rocky Mountains help trap the gases and produce a permanent temperature inversion. Ironically, the beautiful view of the mountains, which attracted so many migrants to Denver, is often obscured by smog.

The problem is not confined to MDCs. Santiago, Chile, nestled between the Pacific Ocean and the Andes Mountains, suffers severe smog problems. Motor vehicles are also responsible for much of the pollution in Santiago, especially particulates from burning diesel fuel, combined with dust kicked up from dirt streets. Mexico City's serious air pollution problem is discussed in the case study that opens this chapter.

Progress in controlling urban air pollution is mixed. Air has improved in developed countries where strict clean air regulations are enforced. Changes in automobile engines, manufacturing processes, and electrical generation all have helped. For example, in the two decades since the U.S. gov-

ernment has required catalytic converters on motor vehicles, carbon monoxide emissions have been reduced by more than three-fourths, nitrogen oxide and hydrocarbon emissions by more than 95 percent. But more people are driving more, offsetting gains made by emission controls. Limited emission controls in less developed countries are contributing to severe urban air pollution.

Water Pollution

Water serves many human purposes. People must drink water to survive, and we cook and bathe with water. The typical U.S. urban resident consumes 680 liters (180 gallons) of water per day for drinking, cooking, and bathing. Water provides a location for boating, swimming, fishing, and other recreational activities. People consume fish and other aquatic life. These uses depend on fresh, clean, unpolluted water.

Clean water is not always available, because people also use water for purposes that pollute it. Manufacturers use water each year to process food and manufacture goods. People discharge waste down the drain and into water. Farmers let waste wash away into water. When all of these uses are included, the average American consumes nearly 10,000 liters (2,400 gallons) of water per day. By polluting water, humans harm the health of aquatic life and the health of land-based life (including ourselves).

Pollution is widespread, because it is easy to dump waste into a river and let the water carry it downstream where it becomes someone else's problem. Water can decompose some waste without adverse impact on other activities, but the volume exceeds the capacity of many rivers and lakes to accommodate it.

Pollution Sources. Three main sources generate most of the water pollution:

Water-using industries. Industries such as steel, chemicals, paper products, and food processing are major water polluters. Each requires a large amount of water in the manufacturing process and generates a lot of wastewater. Food processors, for example, wash pesticides and chemicals from fruit and vegetables. They also use water to remove skins, stems, and other parts. Water can also be polluted by industrial accidents, such as petroleum spills from

Mexico City suffers from a combination of circumstances that all lead to significant air pollution problems. The city lies in a mountain basin that limits dispersion of pollutants. Automobiles are numerous, traffic is heavy, and there are few emission controls. In the early 1990s the problem reached crisis proportions, and a pollution control effort is now underway. (Tom McHugh/Photo Researchers, Inc.)

ocean tankers and leaks from underground tanks at gasoline stations.

Municipal sewage. In more developed countries, sewers carry wastewater from sinks, bathtubs, and toilets to a municipal treatment plant, where most—but not all—of the pollutants are removed. The treated wastewater is then typically dumped back into a river or lake. In LDCs, sewer systems are rare, and wastewater usually drains untreated into rivers and lakes.

Agriculture. Fertilizers and pesticides spread on fields to increase agricultural productivity are carried into rivers and lakes by the irrigation system or natural runoff. Expanded use of these products may help to avoid a global food crisis, yet they destroy aquatic life by polluting rivers.

These three sources of pollution can be divided into *point sources* and *nonpoint sources.* Point-source pollution enters a stream at a specific location, whereas nonpoint-source pollution comes from a large diffuse area. Manufacturers and municipal sewage systems tend to pollute through point sources, such as a pipe from a wastewater treatment plant. Farmers tend to pollute through nonpoint

sources, such as by permitting fertilizer to wash from a field during a storm. Point-source pollutants are usually smaller in quantity and much easier to control. Nonpoint sources usually pollute in greater quantities and are much harder to control.

Impact on Aquatic Life. Polluted water can harm aquatic life. Aquatic plants and animals consume oxygen, but so does the decomposing organic waste that humans dump in the water. The oxygen consumed by the decomposing organic waste constitutes the **biochemical oxygen demand (BOD).** If too much waste is discharged into the water, the water becomes oxygen-starved, and fish die.

This condition is typical when water becomes loaded with municipal sewage or industrial waste. The sewage and industrial pollutants consume so much oxygen that the water can become unlivable for normal plants and animals, creating a "dead" stream or lake. Similarly, when runoff carries fertilizer from farm fields into streams or lakes, the fertilizer nourishes excessive aquatic plant production—a "pond scum" of algae—that consumes too much oxygen. Either type of pollution unbalances the normal oxygen level, threatening aquatic plants and animals.

Some of the residuals may become concentrated in the fish, making them unsafe for human consumption. For example, salmon from the Great Lakes became unfit to eat because of high concentrations of the pesticide DDT, which washed into streams from farm fields.

Many factories and power plants use water for cooling and then discharge the warm water back into the river or lake. The warm water may not be polluted with chemicals, but it raises the temperature of the body of water it enters. Fish adapted to cold water, such as salmon and trout, may not be able to survive in the warmer water.

Wastewater and Disease. Since passage of the U.S. Clean Water Act and equivalent laws in other developed countries, most treatment plants meet high water-quality standards. Improved treatment procedures have resulted in cleaner rivers and lakes in developed countries (see Geography in Action box).

Although less developed countries generate less wastewater per person than more developed countries, they have less capacity to treat their wastewater. In LDCs, sewage often flows untreated directly into rivers. The drinking water, usually removed from the same rivers, may be inadequately treated, as well. And in squatter settlements on the edge of rapidly growing cities, running water and sewers may be totally lacking.

The combination of untreated water and poor sanitation makes drinking water deadly in LDCs. Waterborne diseases such as cholera, typhoid, and dysentery are major causes of death.

Land Pollution

When we consume a product, we also consume an unwanted byproduct—a glass, metal, paper, or plastic box, wrapper, or container in which the product is packaged. About 2 kilograms (4 pounds) of solid waste per person is generated daily in the United States, including about 60 percent from residences and 40 percent from businesses.

Paper products, such as corrugated cardboard and newspapers, account for the largest percentage of solid waste in the United States, especially among residences and retailers (Figure 13-11). Food products and rubbish from yards, such as grass clipping and leaves, are other important sources of solid

waste. Manufacturers discard large quantities of metal and concrete, as well as paper.

Some consumers demonstrate obvious unconcern for the environment by discarding waste along roadsides and sidewalks, where they cause visual pollution. But even consumers who carefully dispose of solid waste are contributing to a major pollution problem. A particularly severe threat is posed by the careless discharge of toxic waste.

About five-sixths of the solid waste generated in the United States is discharged into the environment in two ways: *landfills* and *incineration*. The remainder is *recycled*.

Sanitary Landfills. The **sanitary landfill** is by far the most common strategy for disposal of solid waste in the United States: over 70 percent of the country's waste is trucked to landfills and buried under soil. This strategy is opposite our disposal of gaseous and liquid wastes: we *disperse* air and water pollutants into the atmosphere, rivers, and eventually the ocean, but we *concentrate* solid waste in thousands of landfills.

Concentration would seem to eliminate solid waste pollution, but it may only hide it—temporarily. Chemicals released by the decomposing solid waste can leak from the landfill into groundwater. This leakage can contaminate water wells, soil, and nearby streams.

Eventually, landfills fill up. To preserve landfill space, many communities prohibit discarding bulky yard waste such as grass clippings, weeds, and leaves. Many communities have closed their landfills. Few new ones are being built, because landfills can contaminate groundwater and devalue property, and no one wants to live near one—the *NIMBY* principle at work again.

Some communities now pay to use landfills elsewhere. San Francisco trucks solid waste to Altamont, California, 100 kilometers (60 miles) away. Passaic County, New Jersey, hauls waste 400 kilometers (250 miles) west to Johnstown, Pennsylvania. New Jersey and New York are the two states that regularly try to dispose of their solid waste by transporting it out of state (Figure 13-12).

New York's problem of transporting solid waste long distances generated an absurd situation in 1987. The town of Islip, New York, sold its solid waste to a private individual who planned to transport the waste to Morehead City, North Carolina, and convert it to methane gas. The 3.1 million kilograms

Two Pollution Stories: Aral Sea and Thames River

Water quality is improving in North America and Western Europe while deteriorating in Africa, Asia, Eastern Europe, and Latin America. Developed countries possess the wealth and technology to clean up polluted rivers and lakes—and their citizens are more willing to spend money for the cleanup. Elsewhere in the world, industrialization may take a higher priority than clean water.

Cleanup of the Thames River

Western European and North American communities have successfully cleaned up lakes and streams. One dramatic example is the River Thames, which passes through London. Before the industrial revolution, the Thames was a major food source for Londoners. Some apprentice workers even went on strike in the early 1800s because their masters fed them too much fish. During the industrial revolution, the Thames became the principal location for dumping waste. The fish died, and the water grew unsafe to drink. The river became so dark, murky, and smelly that novelist Charles Dickens called the Thames "London's Styx," after the underworld river that the dead had to cross in Greek mythology.

In the late 1960s, the British government began a massive cleanup to restore the Thames to health. Regulations prohibited industrial dumping, and sewage systems were modernized to improve treatment. In 1982, a salmon was caught in the Thames, just upstream from London. This event was remarkable because it was the first salmon caught in the river since 1833. Salmon are particularly sensitive to pollution, and for nearly 150 years the Thames was too polluted for salmon to survive.

To demonstrate the success of the cleanup operation, the Thames Water Authority has released 50,000 young salmon, known as parr, into the river each year since 1979. When they are approximately 2 years old, the salmon, then known as smolts, migrate from the river to the sea, where they spend 1 to 3 years. The salmon then return to the river to spawn upstream. Several dozen of the 50,000 salmon released into the river in 1979 were the first to be caught in 1982.

Actually, the first salmon may have been caught several days earlier. An Englishman produced a salmon allegedly taken from the Thames and claimed the prize offered to the person who caught the first one. But government authorities tested his salmon and ruled that it had come from the man's freezer, not from the Thames.

Destruction of the Aral Sea

One of the world's most extreme instances of water pollution is the Aral Sea in Kazakhstan and Uzbekistan. Once the world's fourth-largest lake, the Aral has lost nearly half of its water since 1960. Carp, sturgeon, and other fish species have disappeared, the last fish dying in 1983. Large ships lie aground in salt flats that were once the lake bed, outside of abandoned fishing villages that now lie tens of kilometers from the rapidly receding shore (Figure 1).

The Aral Sea died after the Soviet Union diverted its tributary rivers, the Amu Dar'ya and the Syr Dar'ya, to irrigate cotton fields. This diversion not only sharply reduced the lake's source of freshwater input but also accelerated pollution as chemicals sprayed on the fields flowed into the sea. Ironically, the cotton now is withering because winds pick up salt from the exposed lake bed and deposit it on the fields!

Worse, most households in the surrounding Karakalpak region of Kazakhstan obtain their water directly from polluted ditches, rather than through pipes from treatment plants. Two-thirds of these households now suffer from liver disorders, typhoid, or cancer of the esophagus.

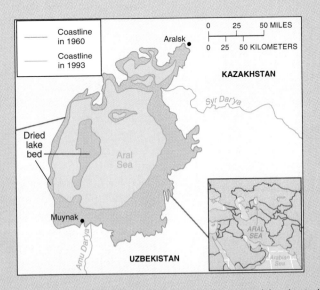

FIGURE 1 The Aral Sea. Once the world's fourth-largest freshwater lake, the Aral Sea has declined in area by nearly one-half since 1960. The principal cause was diversion of two rivers, the Amu Dar'ya and the Syr Dar'ya, to irrigate cotton fields. (Louchine Ugoniok/Sygma)

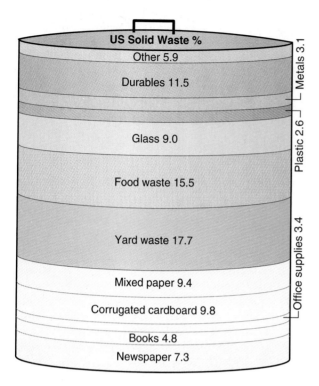

US Solid Waste %

Other 5.9

Durables 11.5

⌐ Metals 3.1

Glass 9.0

Plastic 2.6 ⌐

Food waste 15.5

Yard waste 17.7

Office supplies 3.4 ⌐

Mixed paper 9.4

Corrugated cardboard 9.8

Books 4.8

Newspaper 7.3

FIGURE 13-11 Sources of solid waste. Paper products account for the largest percentage of U.S. solid waste, followed by food products and yard rubbish. Plastics and metals are comparatively small percentages of solid waste.

(3,100 tons) of refuse were trucked to Long Island City and transferred to a barge, named the *Mobro,* for the journey to North Carolina. But officials in Morehead City obtained a court injunction prohibiting the unloading of refuse there.

The *Mobro* then continued farther south, but communities in Alabama, Mississippi, Louisiana, Texas, and Florida all refused to accept it. After Mexico, Belize, and the Bahamas also turned it away, the barge returned to New York, after nearly 2 months and a 9,000-kilometer (5,500-mile) journey. Four months later, the trash was burned in New York City, and the ashes were trucked back to Islip, where the trash had started its journey 6 months earlier.

Incineration. Burning the trash reduces its bulk by about three-fourths, and the remaining ash demands far less landfill space. Incineration also provides energy—the incinerator's heat can boil water to produce steam heat or to operate a turbine that generates electricity. More than 100 incinerators now burn about 10 percent of the trash in the United States. Given the anticipated shortage of space in landfills, the percentage of solid waste that is burned is likely to increase.

However, solid waste, a mixture of many materials, may burn inefficiently. Burning releases some toxins into the air, and some remain in the ash. Thus, solving one pollution problem may increase another pollution problem.

Recycling Solid Waste. As with other residuals, recycling is the only alternative to preventing solid waste from being discharged into a landfill or incinerator. Recycling of solid waste addresses problems of both pollution and resource depletion. Recycling not only reduces the need for landfills and incinerators, it also reuses natural resources that already have been extracted.

Most U.S. communities have instituted some form of mandatory recycling. Newspapers, glass, plastic, and metals are separated from the solid waste destined for the landfill or incinerator. The trash collector sends newspaper to paper mills, "tin" (actually steel) cans to steel-producing minimills, aluminum cans to recycling companies, and glass to bottlers. To encourage recycling, some communities haul recyclables for free or a small fee and charge a high fee to pick up nonrecyclables. In other places, citizens are fined for failing to comply.

Recycling has steadily increased in the United States, from 7 percent of all solid waste in 1970 to 10 percent in 1980, 17 percent in 1990, and 22 percent in 1994. The percentage of recovered materials varies widely by product; 97 percent of discarded auto batteries are recycled, compared with only 2 percent of plastics.

Toxic Pollutants. Disposing of toxic wastes is especially difficult. If poisonous industrial residuals are not carefully placed in protective containers, the chemicals may leach into the soil and contaminate groundwater or escape into the atmosphere. Breathing air or consuming water contaminated with toxic wastes can cause cancer, mutations, chronic ailments, and even immediate death.

Toxic wastes include heavy metals (including mercury, cadmium, and zinc), PCB oils from electrical equipment, cyanides, strong solvents, acids, and caustics. Burial of wastes was once believed to be sufficient to handle the disposal problem, but many of the burial sites have leaked.

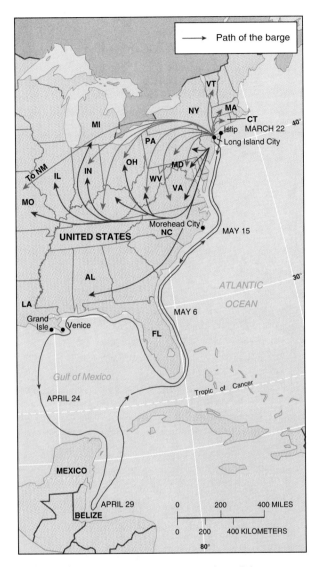

FIGURE 13-12 New York and New Jersey ship solid waste out of state. New York's problem of solid waste disposal was dramatized by the 1987 odyssey of the barge *Mobro*. The city of Islip, New York, lacking space in its landfill for solid waste, hired a company to remove the waste by barge. The waste was to be converted to methane gas near Morehead City, North Carolina, but that state prohibited the *Mobro* from landing. The barge was towed into the Gulf of Mexico but was refused landing rights by Alabama, Florida, Louisiana, and Texas, as well as by Belize and Mexico. Finally, after a 2-month, 9,000-kilometer (5,500-mile) journey, the *Mobro* returned to the New York area. Four months later, the waste was unloaded and burned.

One of the most notorious is Love Canal, near Niagara Falls, New York. During the 1930s, the Hooker Chemicals and Plastic Company buried toxic wastes in metal drums. A school and several hundred homes were built on the site in 1953. Erosion eventually exposed the metal drums, and in 1976 they began to give off a strong stench and slime oozed from them. Residents reported a high incidence of liver ailments, nervous disorders, and other health problems. After four babies were born with birth defects on the same block, New York State officials relocated most of the families and began an expensive cleanup effort. Love Canal is not unique. Toxic wastes have been improperly disposed of at thousands of dumps.

Each company in the United States that releases chemicals classified as toxic by the U.S. Environmental Protection Agency (EPA) must report the amounts that they release. About 2.5 billion kilograms (6 billion pounds) of toxic chemicals are discharged in the United States. About one-fourth of the discharges are by ten companies (DuPont, Monsanto, American Cyanimid, B.P. America, Renco Holdings, 3M, Vulcan Materials, General Motors, Eastman Kodak, and Phelps Dodge).

The EPA ranks U.S. counties on the amount of toxic pollutants (Figure 13-13) they discharge. Counties with relatively high levels of toxic discharges are clustered in the Northeast and Midwest—essentially the U.S. manufacturing belt (refer to Figure 10-4).

As toxic-waste disposal sites become increasingly hard to find, some European and North American firms have tried to transport their waste to West Africa, often unscrupulously. Some firms have signed contracts with West African countries, while others have found isolated locations to dump waste without official consent.

Alternatives for Reducing Pollution

Burning fossil fuels, dumping wastewater, and throwing away paper may or may not constitute pollution. Pollution occurs when the amount of the waste discharged into the environment exceeds the capacity of the air, water, or land to absorb it.

If the amount of a discharge exceeds the capacity of the environment, then only two basic alternatives can reduce pollution: the amount of waste discharged into the environment must be reduced, or the capacity of the environment to accept discharges must be expanded. The merits of the two alternatives are examined here.

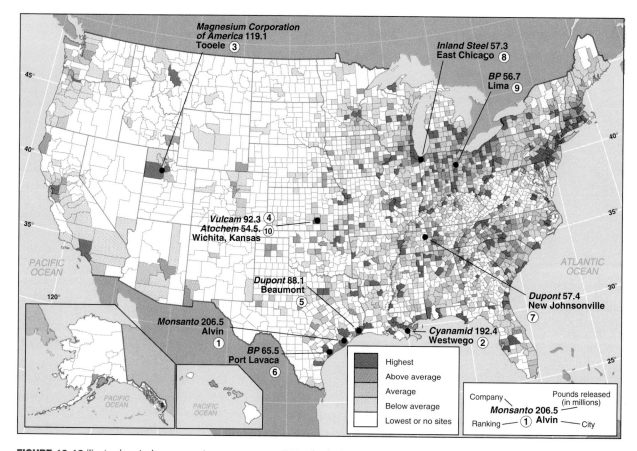

FIGURE 13-13 Toxic chemical concentrations per county, 1989. The highest concentrations are in the northeast and southern Great Lakes regions, where the country's manufacturers are clustered.

Reducing Pollution by Reducing Discharges

Pollution can be prevented by reducing the amount of waste discharged into the environment. Two strategies can reduce discharges:

Strategy 1: Reduce the amount of waste created.
Strategy 2: Recycle the waste.

In the analogy of a polluter to a dairy cow (Figure 13-9), a farmer can reduce a cow's discharge of manure onto the ground in two basic ways. One is to reduce the amount of the waste (manure) the cow generates, either by changing the inputs into the production system (the feed) or by reducing demand for the product (eat less meat or dairy products). The other is to recycle the waste by collecting the manure and using it as fertilizer or fuel rather than letting it accumulate on the ground. These alternatives may not be practical, but they illustrate the variety of strategies available to reduce the discharge of waste into the environment.

Strategy 1: Reduce the amount of waste created. Pollution would be reduced if less waste were generated. Waste can be reduced in two ways:

a. **Change the mix of inputs.** What goes into a production system affects what comes out—as product and as waste. The mix of various inputs can be adjusted to produce a higher ratio of product to waste. For example, gasoline for motor vehicles once contained lead. But most of the lead was discharged through the exhaust pipe and contributed to air pollution. To reduce the generation of lead—once a significant waste—automakers modified engines so that they operate on unleaded instead of leaded gasoline.

A garbage scow is pulled to land in New Jersey, within sight of the New York skyline. (Ray Ellis/Photo Researchers, Inc.)

b. Reduce demand for the product. If consumers purchase smaller quantities of a product, then the production system is down-sized. Factories produce less of the product—or shut down altogether. The creation of fewer products would result in the production of less waste, as well. If consumers drive less, then they will use less gasoline and therefore generate less pollution.

Strategy 2: Recycle the waste. Once waste is discharged into the environment, the only possible strategy for preventing it from accumulating is to recycle more of it. Recycling can take two forms:

a. Reuse the waste in the same production system. For example, a cow's manure can be used as fertilizer to grow more cattle feed, which generates more milk and manure. Or, rather than discharging wastewater into a river, a food processor can treat the water for reuse in production.

b. Reuse the waste in a different production process. For example, the cow's manure can be used for another purpose, such as fuel for heating or cooking. The vegetable pulp produced as an unwanted byproduct of food processing can be used to make pet food.

Increasing Environmental Capacity

The second way to handle pollution is to increase the capacity of the environment to accept the discharges. We can increase environmental capacity to accept waste by using two strategies:

Strategy 1: Make more efficient use of the environment.

Strategy 2: Transform the waste and discharge it into a different part of the environment.

The dairy farmer can make more effective use of the environment in two basic ways. First, the farmer can disperse the cow manure over a wider land area, either by allowing the cow to roam over a larger area or by spreading the manure onto large fields. Second, the manure can be converted from a solid to a gas by burning it, or it can be washed into a nearby stream.

Strategy 1: Use the Environment More Efficiently. The capacity of air, water, and land to accept waste is not fixed but varies among places and at different times. Adding a particular amount of wastewater to a stream may or may not constitute pollution, depending on the flow of the water. A deep, fast-flowing river has a greater capacity to absorb wastewater than a shallow, slow-moving one. Wastewater can be stored when the river level is low and released when the river is high.

Recycling of solid waste requires sorting and separating different types of materials. One approach is to collect them together and separate them at a centralized facility like this one. Alternatively, they can be separated at the source (school, home, or work) and transported separately to reprocessing facilities. (Palmer/Kane/The Stock Market)

The same is true for air: exhaust released into a brisk wind is quickly dispersed, whereas exhaust released into stagnant air during a temperature inversion quickly accumulates to irritating levels. Industries and utilities reduce local air pollution by building taller smokestacks, which better disperse gases at greater heights. Air quality may also be improved by staggering workers' hours so pollution from cars is spread more evenly through the day.

Strategy 2: Transform and Discharge the Waste into a Different Part of the Environment.

The other way to increase environmental capacity is to transform the waste so that it is discharged into something that has the capacity to assimilate it. Matter can be transformed among gaseous, liquid, and solid states and discharged into air, water, or land.

For example, a coal-burning plant discharges gases into the atmosphere, causing *air* pollution. To reduce air pollution, manufacturers install wet scrubbers to wash particulates from the gas before it is released to the atmosphere. Wet scrubbers capture the particulates in *water*, which then can be discharged into a stream. If the stream is polluted by the discharge, then the wastewater can be cleaned in a settling basin where the particulates drop out. This process transforms the residue into a solid waste for disposal on *land*.

A Coking Plant: Using All Reduction Strategies

A coking plant provides an example of applying all four pollution reduction strategies—the two ways to reduce discharges and the two ways to increase environmental capacity (Figure 13-14). The main input into a coking plant is a mixture of coal types, and the intended product is coke, which becomes an input in steel production. The coal is placed in a blast furnace and cooked at very high temperatures to form coke. Four unwanted byproducts result: gases, tars, oils, and heat.

Discharging heat into the environment can cause air pollution. To reduce air pollution from the heat, a coking plant increases the capacity of the environment to accept discharges in two ways. First, the hot coke is taken to a quench station and doused with water to cool it. This process transforms the residual (hot gas) into a liquid (dirty water) as well as another gas (steam). In this way, the waste is transformed and discharged into different parts of the environment. Then the steam is discharged into the environment from a tall smokestack, an example of making more efficient use of whatever initially receives the discharge (air).

The coking plant also minimizes pollution by reducing discharges. The dirty water produced at the quench station is reused to cool more hot coke, an example of recycling in the same production process. Meanwhile, the three unwanted byproducts from the blast furnace (other than heat)—gases, tars, and oils—are captured and sold to other companies for recycling in other processes. The other alternative for reducing discharges—changing the mix of coal used as inputs—is also employed, because the amount of gases emitted by the burning of coke varies depending on the mix of coal.

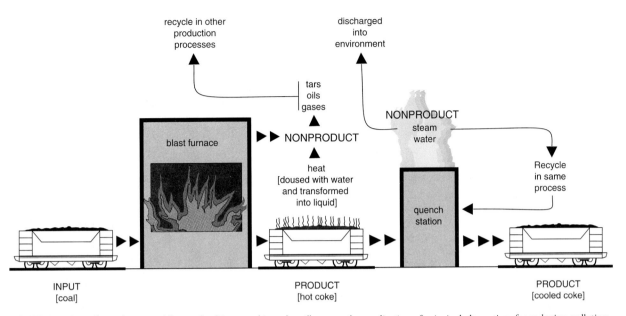

FIGURE 13-14 A coking plant. Used for steelmaking, a coking plant illustrates the application of principal alternatives for reducing pollution:
1. Reduce discharges of waste
   a. Reduce waste (by purchasing cleaner-burning coal)
   b. Recycle discharge (by reusing quenching water)
2. Increase environmental capacity
   a. Use current environment more efficiently (use taller smokestack for discharging steam)
   b. Discharge elsewhere into environment (transform heat into liquid and gaseous residuals)

Comparing Pollution Reduction Strategies

Relying on an increase in the capacity of the environment to accept discharges is risky. Because we do not always know the environment's capacity to assimilate a particular waste, we are likely to exceed it at times. Recent history is filled with examples of wastes discharged into the environment with the belief that they would be dispersed or isolated safely: CFCs in the stratosphere, garbage offshore, and toxic chemicals beneath Love Canal.

Dispersed wastes may remain harmful. Tall smokestacks built to reduce sulfur dioxide discharges around coal-burning industries and metal smelters were successful at dispersing sulfur over a larger area. But the result of the dispersal was that acid precipitation (containing sulfur) fell hundreds of kilometers away, polluting vegetation and lakes over a wide area.

Many pollutants are mobile. They often transfer from air to soil or from soil to water. A pollutant such as sulfur dioxide might exist at tolerable levels in the air, but it damages trees when it accumulates in the soil. In view of the many uncertainties associated with increasing environmental capacity, reducing discharges into the environment (by either changing the production process or recycling) is usually the preferred alternative.

Although the environment has the capacity to accept some discharges, consumers must learn to use this environmental capacity most efficiently. At the same time, consumers must learn to waste less, either by reducing the consumption of products that result in waste or by recycling more. With careful management, we can enjoy the benefits of both industrial development and a cleaner, safer environment.

However, environmental improvements in the more developed countries of North America and Western Europe are likely to be offset in the twenty-first century by increased pollution in less developed countries. According to Grossman and Krueger, a rising level of economic development generates increased pollution, at least until a country reaches a GDP of around $5,000 per person (Figure 13-15). Because GDP per capita in less developed countries averages only about $1,000, development in these countries is likely to cause more pollution. In the early stages of industrialization, pollution control devices are unpopular luxuries that make cars, other consumer goods, and factory construction more expensive.

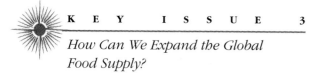

How Can We Expand the Global Food Supply?

- Alternative Strategies to Increase Food Supply
- Africa's Food Supply Crisis

Instead of depleting and destroying resources, we can use them more efficiently. One dramatic example is our better use of Earth to provide food.

Returning to the problem of overpopulation raised in Chapter 2, we concluded that the solutions are to reduce population growth and to expand the capacity of Earth to support life. The ratio of population to food supply has become more favorable in many LDCs, especially in Asia, where population growth has slowed and the food supply has grown. The challenge in these regions is to continue recent progress by further expanding food resources.

In other less developed regions, especially Sub-Saharan Africa, the problem is getting worse. Food supply must be expanded quickly for Africa's burgeoning population.

Alternative Strategies to Increase Food Supply

Four strategies can increase the food supply:

- Expand the land area used for agriculture
- Increase the productivity of land now used for agriculture
- Identify new food sources
- Increase exports from other countries

We will now examine each alternative.

Expand Agricultural Land

Historically, world food production increased primarily by expanding agricultural land. When the world's population began to increase more rapidly in the late 1700s and 1800s, pioneers could migrate to

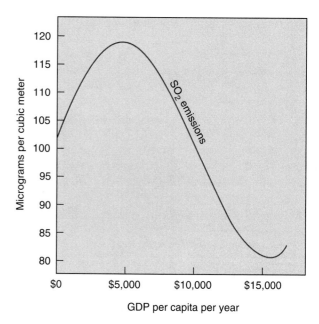

FIGURE 13-15 Pollution compared with a country's wealth. As a country's GDP per capita increases, discharge of sulfur dioxide increases, until GDP reaches about $5,000. Then, discharges tend to decrease, as a country begins to spend money on pollution control devices.

uninhabited territory and cultivate the land. Sparsely inhabited land suitable for agriculture was available in western North America, central Russia, and Argentina's pampas. People believed that good agricultural land would always be available for willing pioneers.

Today, few scientists believe that further expansion of agricultural land can feed the growing world population. Since around 1950, Earth's population has increased faster than agricultural land expansion.

At first glance, new agricultural land appears to be available, because only 11 percent of the world's land area is currently cultivated. In fact, growth is possible in North America, where some arable land is not cultivated for economic reasons, and the tropics of Africa and South America offer some hope for less developed new agricultural land. However, prospects for expanding the percentage of cultivated land are poor in much of Europe, Asia, and Africa.

In some regions, farmland is abandoned for lack of water. Especially in semiarid regions, human actions are causing land to deteriorate to a desertlike condition, a process called **desertification** (more precisely, *semiarid land degradation*). Semiarid lands that can support only a handful of pastoral nomads are overused because of rapid population growth. Excessive crop planting, animal grazing, and tree cutting exhaust the soil's nutrients and preclude agriculture. The United Nations estimates that desertification removes 27 million hectares (104,000 square miles) of land from agricultural production each year, an area roughly equivalent to Colorado (Figure 13-16).

Excessive water threatens other agricultural areas, especially drier lands that receive water from human-built irrigation systems. If the irrigated land has inadequate drainage, the underground water level rises to the point where roots become waterlogged. The United Nations estimates that 10 percent of all irrigated land is waterlogged, mostly in Asia and South America. If the water is salty, it may damage plants. The ancient civilization of Mesopotamia may have collapsed in part because of waterlogging and excessive salinity in their agricultural lands near the Tigris and Euphrates rivers.

Urbanization may also contribute to reducing agricultural land. As urban areas grow in population and land area, farms on the periphery are replaced by homes, roads, shops, and other urban land uses. In North America, farms outside urban areas are left idle until the speculators who own them can sell them at a profit to builders and developers, who convert the land to urban uses.

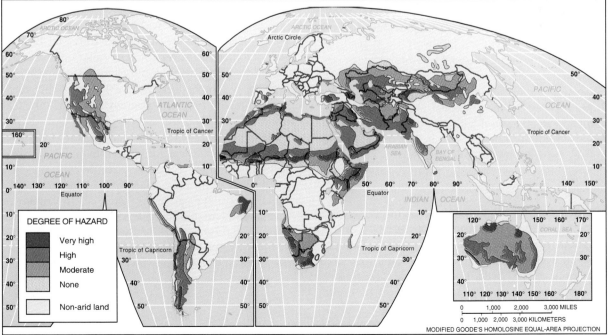

FIGURE 13-16 Desertification (semiarid land degradation). The severest problems are in northern Africa, central Australia, and the southwestern parts of Africa, Asia, North America, and South America. (Steve McCurry/Magnum Photos, Inc.)

Increase Productivity

During the 1960s, population began to grow faster than agricultural land expanded, especially in LDCs. At the time, many experts forecast massive global famine within a decade. These dire predictions have not come true, however, because new agricultural practices have permitted farmers worldwide to achieve much greater yields from the same amount of land.

The Green Revolution. The invention and rapid diffusion of more-productive agricultural techniques during the 1970s and 1980s is called the **green revolution**. The green revolution involves two main practices: the introduction of new higher-yield seeds and the greater use of fertilizers. Because of the green revolution, agricultural productivity at a global scale has increased faster than population growth.

During the 1950s, scientists began an intensive series of experiments to develop a higher-yield form of wheat. A decade later, the "miracle wheat seed" was ready. Shorter and stiffer than traditional breeds, the new wheat was less sensitive to variation in day length, responded better to fertilizers, and matured faster. The Rockefeller and Ford Foundations sponsored many of the studies, and the program's director, Dr. Norman Borlaug, won the Nobel Peace Prize in 1970.

The International Rice Research Institute, established in the Philippines by the Rockefeller and Ford Foundations, worked to create a miracle rice seed. During the 1960s, their scientists introduced a hybrid of Indonesian rice and Taiwan dwarf rice that was hardier and increased yields. More recently, scientists have developed new high-yield maize (corn).

The new miracle seeds were diffused rapidly around the world. India's wheat production, for example, more than doubled in 5 years. After importing 10 million tons of wheat per year in the mid-1960s, India by 1971 had a surplus of several million tons. Other Asian and Latin American countries recorded similar productivity increases.

Need for Fertilizer and Machinery. To take full advantage of the new miracle seeds, farmers must use more fertilizer and machinery. Farmers have known for thousands of years that application of manure, bones, and ashes somehow increases, or at least maintains, the fertility of the land. Not until the nineteenth century did scientists identify nitrogen, phosphorus, and potassium (potash) as the critical elements in these substances that improved fertility. Today, these three elements form the basis for fertilizers—products that farmers apply on their fields to enrich the soil by restoring lost nutrients.

Nitrogen, the most important fertilizer, is a ubiquitous substance. Europeans most commonly produce a fertilizer known as urea, which contains 46 percent nitrogen. In North America, nitrogen is available as ammonia gas, which is 82 percent nitrogen but more awkward than urea to transport and store.

Both urea and ammonia gas combine nitrogen and hydrogen. The problem is that the cheapest way to produce both types of nitrogen-based fertilizers is to obtain hydrogen from natural gas or petroleum. As fossil fuel prices increase, so do the prices for nitrogen-based fertilizers, which then become too expensive for many farmers in LDCs.

In contrast with nitrogen, phosphorus and potash reserves are not distributed uniformly across Earth's surface. Two-thirds of the world's proven phosphate rock reserves are clustered in Morocco and the United States. Proven potash reserves are concentrated in Canada, Germany, Russia, and Ukraine.

Farmers need tractors, irrigation pumps, and other machinery to make most effective use of the new miracle seeds. In LDCs, farmers cannot afford such equipment, nor, in view of high energy costs, can they buy fuel to operate the equipment. To maintain the green revolution, governments in LDCs must allocate scarce funds for subsidizing the cost of seeds, fertilizers, and machinery.

The green revolution did not stop with miracle seeds. Scientists have continued to create higher-yield hybrids that are adapted to environmental conditions in specific regions. Thanks to the green revolution, Dutch scientists calculate that the maximum annual crop yield currently has reached 6,000 kilograms of grain per hectare (5,000 pounds per acre) in parts of Asia and Latin America. This, however, still is far lower than the maximum possible yields of 15,000 kilograms per hectare (13,000 pounds per acre) in Asia and 20,000 kilograms per hectare (18,000 pounds per acre) in Latin America. The green revolution was largely responsible for preventing a food crisis in these regions during the 1970s and 1980s, but will these scientific breakthroughs continue in the 1990s?

Identify New Food Sources

The third alternative for increasing the world's food supply is to develop new food sources. Three strategies being considered are to cultivate the oceans, to develop higher-protein cereals, and to improve palatability of rarely consumed foods.

Cultivating the Oceans. At first glance, increased use of food from the sea is attractive. Oceans are vast, covering nearly three-fourths of Earth's surface and lying near most population concentrations. But, historically, the sea has provided only a small percentage of world food supply. About two-thirds of the fish caught from the ocean is consumed directly, while the remainder is converted to fish meal and fed to poultry and hogs.

Hope grew during the 1950s and 1960s that increased fish consumption could meet the needs of a rapidly growing global population. Indeed, the world's annual fish catch increased about five times, from 22 million tons in 1954 to more than 100 million tons in 1991. However, the population of some fish species has declined because they have been harvested faster than they can reproduce. Overfishing has been particularly acute in the North Atlantic and Pacific oceans. The U.S. National Marine Fisheries Service estimates that 65 of 153 species of fish that it monitors off the Atlantic and Pacific coasts are overfished.

The Law of the Sea gives many countries control of fishing within 200 miles (320 kilometers) of the coast. Participating countries have the right to seize foreign fishing boats that venture into the so-called exclusive economic zone.

Peru has been especially sensitive to the overfishing problem after the country's catch of anchovies, its most important fish, declined by more than 75 percent between 1970 and 1973. To prevent further overfishing, the government nationalized its fish meal production industry, but the Peruvian experience demonstrates that the ocean is not a limitless source of fish.

Higher-Protein Cereals. A second possible new food source is higher-protein cereal grains. People in more developed countries obtain protein by consuming meat, but people in less developed countries generally rely on wheat, corn, and rice, which lack certain proteins. Scientists are experimenting with hybrids of the world's major cereals that have higher protein content.

People can also obtain needed nutrition by consuming foods that are fortified during processing with vitamins, minerals, and protein-carrying amino acids. This approach achieves better nutrition without changing food consumption habits. However, fortification has limited application in LDCs, where most people grow their own food rather than buy processed food.

Improving Palatability of Rarely Consumed Foods. To fulfill basic nutritional needs, people consume types of food adapted to their community's climate, soil, and other physical characteristics. People also select foods on the basis of religious values, taboos, and other social customs that are unrelated to nutritional or environmental factors. A third way to make more effective use of existing global resources is to encourage consumption of foods that are avoided for social reasons.

A prominent example of an underused food resource in North America is the soybean. Although the soybean is one of the region's leading crops, most of the output is processed into animal feed, in part because many North Americans avoid consuming tofu, sprouts, and other recognizable soybean products. However, burgers, franks, oils, and other products that don't look like soybeans are more widely accepted in North America. New food products have been created in LDCs as well. In Asia, for example, high-protein beverages made from seeds resemble popular soft drinks.

Krill (a term for a group of small crustaceans) could be an important source of food from the oceans. The krill population has increased rapidly in recent years, because overhunting has reduced the number of whales that eat krill. About 1 million tons of krill are currently harvested, most of which goes to Russia and Eastern Europe to feed chickens and livestock. The harvest could be substantially increased for human food with new processing methods, because krill deteriorates rapidly. But krill doesn't taste very good.

Increase Exports from Countries with Surpluses

The fourth alternative for increasing the world's food supply is to export more food from countries that produce surpluses. The three top export grains are wheat, maize (corn), and rice. Few countries are major exporters of food, but increased production in these countries could cover the gap elsewhere.

Before World War II, Western Europe was the only major grain importing region. Before their independence, colonies of Western European countries supplied food to their parent states. Asia became a net grain importer in the 1950s, Africa and Eastern Europe in the 1960s, and Latin America in the 1970s. Population increases in these regions largely accounted for the need to import grain. By 1980, North America was the only major exporting region in the world.

In response to the increasing global demand for food imports, the United States passed Public Law 480, the Agricultural, Trade, and Assistance Act of 1954 (frequently referred to as "P.L. 480"). Title I of the act provided for the sale of grain at low interest rates, and Title II gave grants to needy groups of people.

The largest beneficiary of U.S. food aid has been India. In 1966 and 1967, when the monsoon rains failed, 60 million Indians were fed entirely by U.S. grain. At the height of the rescue, 600 ships filled with grain sailed to India, the largest maritime maneuver since the Allied invasion of Normandy on D-Day, June 6, 1944. During those years, the United States allocated 20 percent of its wheat crop to feed India's population.

The United States remains the largest grain exporter and accounts for nearly two-thirds of all corn and soybean exports, one-third of wheat, and one-fifth of rice. Since 1980, however, the United States has decreased its grain exports, while other countries have increased theirs. Thailand replaced the United States as the leading rice exporter. Other Asian countries such as Pakistan, Vietnam, and India account for most of the remaining rice exports. Australia and France have joined the United States and Canada as major wheat exporters (Figure 13-17).

Russia is by far the leading grain importer and ranks at or near the top in wheat, corn, and rice. Russia and Japan together account for one-half of the world's corn imports, while Russia and China together account for one-fourth of the wheat imports. Asian countries account for nearly all of the rice imports.

Africa's Food Supply Crisis

Some countries that previously depended on imported grain have become self-sufficient in recent years. Higher productivity generated by the green revolution is primarily responsible for reducing dependency on imports, especially in Asia. India no longer ranks as a major wheat importer, and China no longer imports rice. As long as population growth continues to decline and agricultural productivity continues to increase, the large population concentrations of Asia can maintain the delicate balance between population and resources.

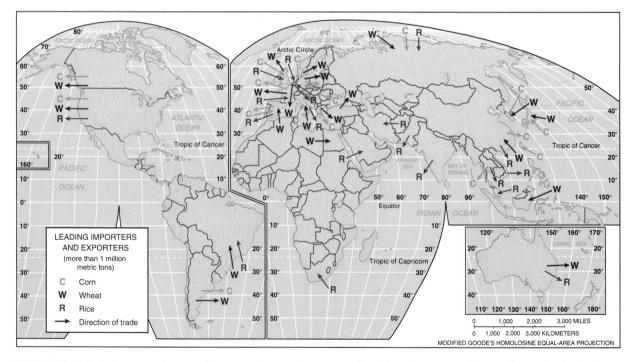

FIGURE 13-17 Grain imports and exports. Most countries must import more food than they export. The United States has by far the largest excess of food exports compared with imports. Argentina, Australia, Canada, and France are the other leading food exporters.

Animals, such as the blue wildebeest and impala, cluster at a water hole in Africa. The dry lands of Africa can support limited populations, but the number of people and animals has exceeded the region's supply of food and water. (Leonard Lee Ruff II/Photo Researchers, Inc.)

In contrast, Sub-Saharan Africa is losing the race to keep food production ahead of population growth. The U.N. Food and Agricultural Organization estimates that 70 percent of Africans have too little to eat. Widespread famine exists in half of the African countries. By all estimates, the problems will grow worse.

Production of most food crops is lower today in Africa than in the 1960s. At the same time, population is increasing more rapidly than in any other world region. As a result, food production per person declined during the 1970s and 1980s in all but a few of the region's countries, in several cases by more than 20 percent. At current population growth rates, by the year 2000, agriculture in Sub-Saharan Africa will be able to feed little more than half of the region's population.

The problem is particularly severe in the Horn of Africa, including Somalia, Ethiopia, and Sudan. Also facing severe food shortages are countries in the Sahel region, a 400- to 550-kilometer (250- to 350-mile) belt in West Africa that marks the southern border of the Sahara (Figure 13-18). The most severely affected countries in the Sahel are Gambia, Senegal, Mali, Mauritania, Burkina Faso, Niger, and Chad.

Traditionally, this region supported limited agriculture. Pastoral nomads moved their herds frequently, permitting vegetation to regenerate. Farmers grew groundnuts for export and used the receipts to import rice. With rapid population growth, herd size increased beyond the capacity of the land to support them. Animals overgrazed the limited vegetation and clustered at scarce water sources. Many died of hunger.

Farmers overplanted, exhausting soil nutrients, and reduced fallow time, during which unplanted fields can recover. Soil erosion increased after most of the remaining trees were cut for wood and charcoal, used for urban cooking and heating. Productivity declined further after several unusual drought years in the 1970s, 1980s, and 1990s.

Government policies have aggravated the food shortage crisis. To make food affordable for urban residents, governments keep agricultural prices low. Constrained by price controls, farmers are unable to sell their commodities at a profit and therefore have little incentive to increase productivity.

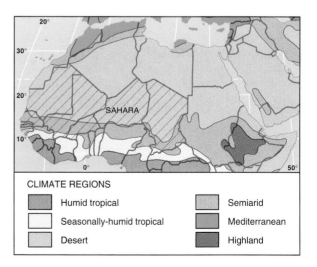

CLIMATE REGIONS

- Humid tropical
- Seasonally-humid tropical
- Desert
- Semiarid
- Mediterranean
- Highland

FIGURE 13-18 The Sahel and Horn of Africa face severe food supply problems. The Sahel lies south of the drylands of the Sahara.

Summary

We have examined problems of depletion, degradation, and inefficient use of Earth's resources. The distribution of resources, as well as patterns of use and abuse, vary locally. But actions with regard to resources in one region can affect people everywhere. Here again are the key issues in Chapter 13.

1. As we deplete fossil fuels, what alternatives can replace them?

As we consume fossil fuel resources to produce energy, we are depleting Earth's supply. Consumption of fossil fuels, as well as remaining supplies, are distributed unevenly across Earth. Over the coming decades, we must turn to renewable energy sources. At this time, however, renewable energy sources are more expensive than fossil fuels.

2. What are the solutions to pollution?

Human beings are damaging and destroying Earth's resources through pollution. Pollution is the discharge of waste at a rate that exceeds the environment's capacity to absorb it. Pollutants are discharged into the atmosphere, water, and onto land. We can reduce pollution only by decreasing the amount of waste we generate or by increasing the environment's capacity to accept it.

3. How can we expand the global food supply?

We fail to make full use of Earth's resources to feed Earth's rapidly growing population. Four alternatives exist to increasing the food supply: expand the amount of cultivated land, increase productivity of land now used for agriculture, develop new food sources, and expand exports from productive countries. Because of increased productivity, most regions are generating enough food to feed their populations. The exception is Sub-Saharan Africa, where the gap between food supply and population size is growing wider.

C A S E   S T U D Y   R E V I S I T E D
Future Directions

Some scientists believe that further depletion and destruction of Earth's resources will lead to disaster in the near future. A quarter of a century ago, a group of scientists known as the Club of Rome presented a particularly influential statement of this position in a report titled *The Limits to Growth*. According to these scientists, many of whom were professors at the Massachusetts Institute of Technology, the combination of population growth, resource depletion, and unrestricted use of industrial technology will disrupt the world's ecology and economy and lead to mass starvation, widespread suffering, and destruction of the physical environment.

In a recent update, the authors argued that environmental destruction is proceeding at a more rapid rate than they had originally thought. If a new set of attitudes and policies toward environmental protection is not in place within 20 years, the environment will be permanently damaged and people's standard of living will fall.

The threat of irreparable global environmental damage is heightened by confrontation between more developed and less developed regions. MDCs have achieved wealth in part by using large percentages of the world's resources and discharging large percentages of the world's pollutants. Now, LDCs are being asked to promote economic development with greater sensitivity to the environment than today's more developed countries showed in the past. People in more developed countries are increasingly willing to allocate some of their wealth to clean up the environment. Subsistence farmers in less developed countries cannot afford to invest in environmental protection.

Most geographers recognize that unrestricted industrial and demographic growth will have negative consequences, but they do not believe that the dire predictions of *The Limits to Growth* are inevitable. Human actions have depleted some resources, but substitutes may be available. Although pollution degrades the physical environment, industrial growth can be compatible with environmental protection. Demand for food is increasing, but human actions are also expanding the capacity of Earth to provide food.

Geographers emphasize that each resource in the physical environment has a distinctive capacity for accommodating human activities. Just as a good farmer knows how many animals can be fed on a parcel of land, a scientist can pinpoint the constraints that resources place on population density or economic development in a particular region. With knowledge of these constraints, we will be able to maintain agricultural and industrial development in the future.

Future generations can maintain agricultural and industrial development without depleting and abusing resources, but they must move toward sustainable development. **Sustainable development** is the level of development that can be maintained in a country without depleting resources to the extent that future generations will be unable to achieve a comparable level of development. A 1987 report by a U.N. commission on Environment and Development defined sustainable development as "development that meets the needs of the present without compromising the ability of future generations to meet their own needs."

The concept of sustainable development is based on the current practice of sustained yield management of renewable resources, such as forests and fisheries. In some places, the amount of timber cut down in a forest or the number of fish removed from a body of water is controlled at a level that does not reduce future supplies.

In recent years, the World Bank and other international development agencies have embraced the concept of sustainable development. Planning for development involves consideration of many more environmental and social issues today than was the case in the past. However, one important recommendation of the U.N. report has not been implemented: increased international cooperation to reduce the gap between more developed and less developed countries

Similarly, food supply can be expanded without damaging Earth's resources if farmers adopt sustainable agriculture. **Sustainable agriculture** is the application of farming methods that preserve long-term productivity of land and minimize pollution of the soil, groundwater, and streams that drain the land. In most cases, sustainable agriculture means rotating soil-restoring crops with cash crops and reducing inputs of fertilizer and pesticides.

Farmers practicing sustainable agriculture typically generate lower revenues than conventional farmers, but they also have lower costs. On balance, sustainable agriculture may enjoy greater net benefits when costs are subtracted from revenues, especially if long-term environmental costs are included. It remains the world's best hope for increased long-term productivity in LDCs, consistent with sound environmental management.

Key Terms

Acid deposition Sulfur oxides and nitrogen oxides, emitted by burning fossil fuels, enter the atmosphere—where they combine with oxygen and water to form sulfuric acid and nitric acid—and return to Earth's surface.

Acid precipitation Conversion of sulfur oxides and nitrogen oxides to acids that return to Earth as rain, snow, or fog.

Active solar energy system Solar energy system that collects energy through the use of mechanical devices such as photovoltaic cells or flatplate collectors.

Air pollution Concentration of trace substances, such as carbon monoxide, sulfur dioxide, nitrogen oxides, hydrocarbons, and solid particulates, at a greater level than occurs in average air.

Animate power Power supplied by people or animals.

Biochemical oxygen demand (BOD) Amount of oxygen required by aquatic bacteria to decompose a given load of organic waste, a measure of water pollution.

Biomass fuel Fuel derived from plant material and animal waste.

Breeder reactor A nuclear power plant that creates its own fuel from plutonium.

Chlorofluorocarbon (CFC) A gas used as a solvent, a propellant in aerosols, and a refrigerant, and in plastic foams and fire extinguishers.

Desertification Degradation of land, especially in semiarid areas, primarily because of human actions such as excessive crop planting, animal grazing, and tree cutting.

Fission The splitting of an atomic nucleus to release energy.

Fossil fuel Energy source formed from the residue of plants and animals buried millions of years ago.

Fusion Creation of energy by joining the nuclei of two hydrogen atoms to form helium.

Geothermal energy Energy from steam or hot water produced from hot or molten underground rocks.

Green revolution Rapid diffusion of new agricultural technology, especially new high-yield seeds and fertilizers.

Greenhouse effect Anticipated increase in Earth's temperature, caused as carbon dioxide (emitted by burning fossil fuels) traps some of the radiation emitted by the surface.

Hydroelectric power Power generated from moving water.

Inanimate power Power supplied by machines.

Nonrenewable energy A source of energy that is a finite supply capable of being exhausted.

Ozone A gas that absorbs ultraviolet solar radiation; found in the stratosphere, a zone between 15 and 50 kilometers (9 to 30 miles) above Earth's surface.

Passive solar energy system Solar energy system that collects energy without the use of mechanical devices.

Photochemical smog An atmospheric condition in which sunlight causes nitrogen oxides and hydrocarbons to react in the atmosphere, forming other pollutants.

Photovoltaic cell Solar energy cells, usually made from silicon, that collect solar rays to generate electricity.

Pollution Addition of more waste than an ecosystem can accommodate.

Potential reserve The amount of energy in deposits not yet identified but thought to exist.

Proven reserve The amount of a resource remaining in discovered deposits.

Radioactive waste Particles from a nuclear reaction that emit radiation; contact with such particles may be harmful or lethal to people, and therefore the waste must be safely stored for thousands of years.

Renewable energy A resource that has a theoretically unlimited supply and is not depleted when used by people.

Resource A substance in the environment that is useful to people, is economically and technologically feasible to access, and is socially acceptable to use.

Sanitary landfill A place to deposit solid waste, where a layer of earth is bulldozed over garbage each day to reduce emissions of gases and odors from the decaying trash, minimize fires, and discourage vermin.

Sustainable agriculture Farming methods that preserve long-term productivity of land and minimize pollution, typically by rotating soil-restoring crops with cash crops and reducing inputs of fertilizer and pesticides.

Sustainable development The level of development that can be maintained in a country without depleting resources to the extent that future generations will be unable to achieve a comparable level of development.

Thinking Geographically

1. What steps has your community taken to recycle solid waste and to conserve energy?

2. U.S. automakers must meet a standard for Corporate Average Fuel Efficiency (CAFE). This means that the average miles per gallon achieved by all models of a company's American-made cars must meet a government-mandated level. If they do not, the company must pay a stiff fine. Should the United States raise the CAFE standard to conserve fuel and reduce air pollution, even if the result is a loss of American jobs? Explain.

3. A recent study compared paper and polystyrene foam drinking cups. Conventional wisdom is that foam cups are bad for the environment, because they are made from petroleum and don't degrade in landfills. However, the manufacture of a paper cup consumes 36 times as much electricity and generates 580 times as much wastewater. Further, as they degrade in landfills, paper cups release methane gas, a contributor to the greenhouse effect. Which types of cups should companies such as McDonald's be encouraged to use? Why?

4. Pollution is a byproduct of producing almost anything. How can more developed countries, which historically have been responsible for generating the most pollution, encourage less developed countries to seek to minimize the adverse effects of pollution as they improve their levels of development?

5. Malthus argued 200 years ago that overpopulation was inevitable, because population increased geometrically, while food supply increased arithmetically. Was Malthus correct? Why, or why not?

Further Readings

Beach, Timothy, and P. Gershmehl. "Soil Erosion, T Values, and Sustainability: A Review and Exercise." *Journal of Geography* 92 (January–February 1993): 16–22.

Bower, Blair T., and Daniel J. Basta. *Residuals-Environmental Quality Management: Applying the Concept.* Baltimore: The Johns Hopkins University Center for Metropolitan Planning and Research, 1973.

Brown, Lester R., et al. *State of the World.* New York: W. W. Norton, annually since 1984.

Brown, Lester R., and Pamela Shaw. *Six Steps to a Sustainable Society.* Worldwatch Paper 48. Washington, D.C.: Worldwatch Institute, March 1982.

Brown, Lester R., and Edward C. Wolf. *Reversing Africa's Decline.* Worldwatch Paper 65. Washington, D.C.: Worldwatch Institute, 1985.

Bugliarello, George, Ariel Alexandre, John Barnes, and Charles Wakstein. *The Impact of Noise Pollution.* New York: Pergamon Press, 1976.

Calzonetti, Frank J., and Barry D. Solomon. *Geographical Dimensions of Energy.* Dordrecht, Netherlands: D. Reidel, 1985.

Chakravarti, A. K. "Green Revolution in India." *Annals of the Association of American Geographers* 63 (September 1973): 319–30.

Clements, Donald W. "Recent Trends in the Geography of Coal." *Annals of the Association of American Geographers* 67 (March 1977): 109–25.

Cole, H. S. D., Christopher Freeman, Marie Jahoda, and K. L. R. Pavitt. *Models of Doom: A Critique of "The Limits to Growth."* New York: Universe Books, 1972.

Commoner, Barry. *Making Peace with the Planet.* New York: The New Press, 1990.

_____. *The Poverty of Power.* New York: Knopf, 1976.

Costanza, Robert, and H. E. Daly. "Natural Capital and Sustainable Development." *Conservation Biology* 6 (March 1992): 37–46.

Cuff, David, and William J. Young. *The United States Energy Atlas,* 2d ed. New York: Free Press, 1984.

Cusack, David F., ed. *Agroclimate Information for Development: Reviving the Green Revolution.* Boulder, CO: Westview Press, 1983.

Cutter, Susan L., Hilary Lambert Renwick, and William H. Renwick. *Exploitation, Conservation, Preservation: A Geographic Perspective on Natural Resource Use.* 2d ed. New York: Wiley, 1991.

Dakers, Sonya. *Sustainable Agriculture: Future Dimensions.* Ottawa: Library of Parliament, Research Branch, 1992.

de Freitas, C. R. "The Greenhouse Crisis: Myths and Misconceptions." *Area* 23 (March 1991): 11–18.

Dodd, Jerrold L. "Desertification and Degradation in Sub-Saharan Africa: The Role of Livestock." *BioScience* 44 (January 1994): 28–34.

Ehrlich, Anne H., and Paul R. Ehrlich. *The Earth.* New York: Franklin Watts, 1987.

Elsom, Derek. *Atmospheric Pollution: A Global Problem,* 2d ed. Cambridge, MA: Blackwell, 1992.

Falkenmark, Malin, and Carl Widstrand. "Population and Water Resources: A Delicate Balance." *Population Bulletin* 47, no. 3. Washington, D.C.: Population Reference Bureau, November 1992.

Flavin, Christopher. *Electricity's Future: The Shift to Efficiency and Small-Scale Power.* Worldwatch Paper 61. Washington, D.C.: Worldwatch Institute, November 1984.

_____. *Nuclear Power: The Market Test.* Worldwatch Paper 57. Washington, D.C.: Worldwatch Institute, December 1983.

_____. *World Oil: Coping with the Dangers of Success.* Worldwatch Paper 66. Washington, D.C.: Worldwatch Institute, July 1985

Francis, Charles A., ed. *Sustainable Agriculture in Temperate Zones.* New York: Wiley, 1990.

Greenberg, M. R.. R. Anderson, and G. W. Page. *Environmental Impact Statements.* Washington, D.C.: Association of American Geographers, 1978.

Grigg, David. *The World Food Problem 1950–1980.* New York: Basil Blackwell, 1985.

Hammer, W. M., "Krill—Untapped Bounty from the Sea" *National Geographic* 165 (May 1984): 626–43.

James, Peter. *The Future of Coal.* 2d ed. London: Macmillan, 1984.

Kates, Robert W., Christoph Hohenemser, and Jeanne X. Kasperson, eds. *Perilous Progress: Technology as Hazard.* Boulder, CO: Westview, 1984.

Knight, C. G., and P. Wilcox. *Triumph or Triage? The World Food Problem in Geographical Perspective.* Washington, D.C.: Association of American Geographers, 1975.

Meadows, Donnela H., Dennis L. Meadows, and Jorgen Randers. *Beyond the Limits.* Post Mills, VT: Chelsea Green Publishing, 1992.

Meadows, Donnela H., Dennis L. Meadows, Jorgen Randers, and William W. Behrens III. *The Limits to Growth,* 2d ed. New York: Universe Books, 1973.

Mounfield, P. R. "Nuclear Power in Western Europe: Geographical Patterns and Political Problems." *Geography* 70 (October 1985): 315–27.

Murdock, Steve H., F. Larry Leistritz, and Rita R. Hamm, eds. *Nuclear Waste: Socioeconomic Dimensions of Long-Term Storage.* Boulder, CO: Westview Press, 1983.

National Geographic. *Energy: Special Report.* Washington, D.C.: National Geographic Society, 1981.

National Research Council, Board on Radioactive Waste Management, Panel on Social and Economic Aspects of Radioactive Waste Management. *Social and Economic Aspects of Radioactive Waste Disposal: Considerations for Institutional Management.* Washington, D.C.: National Academy Press, 1984.

Openshaw, Stan. *Nuclear Power: Siting and Safety.* London: Routledge and Kegan Paul, 1986.

Pasqualetti, Martin J., and K. David Pijawka, eds. *Nuclear Power: Assessing and Managing Hazardous Technology.* Boulder, CO: Westview Press, 1984.

Pierce, John T. *The Food Resource.* New York: Longman Scientific and Technical, 1990.

Pollack, Cynthia. *Decommissioning: Nuclear Power's Missing Link.* Worldwatch Paper 69. Washington, D.C.: Worldwatch Institute, April 1986.

Postel, Sandra. *Air Pollution, Acid Rain, and the Future of Forests.* Worldwatch Paper 58. Washington, D.C.: Worldwatch Institute, March 1984.

_____. *Conserving Water: The Untapped Alternative.* Worldwatch Paper 67. Washington, D.C.: Worldwatch Institute, September 1985.

Pryde, Philip R. *Environmental Management in the Soviet Union.* Cambridge, England: Cambridge University Press, 1991.

Schmandt, Jurgen, and Hilliard Roderick, eds. *Acid Rain and Friendly Neighbors: The Policy Dispute between Canada and the U.S.* Durham, NC: Duke University Press, 1985.

Sills, David L., C. P. Wolf, and Vivien B. Shelanski, eds. *Accident at Three Mile Island: The Human Dimensions.* Boulder, CO: Westview Press, 1982.

Turner, B. L., II, Robert W. Kates, and William C. Clark. *The Earth as Transformed by Human Action.* Cambridge, England: Cambridge University Press, 1990.

U.S. Congress, Office of Technology Assessment. *Acid Rain and Transported Air Pollutants: Implications for Public Policy.* Washington, D.C.: U.S. Government Printing Office, 1984.

World Commission on Environment and Development. *Food 2000: Global Policies for Sustainable Agriculture.* London: Zed Books, 1987.

_____. *Our Common Future.* London: Oxford University Press, 1987.

Also consult these journals: *Ecological Economics; Ecologist, Energy Journal, Energy Policy, Environment, Environmental Management, Environmental Pollution, Journal of Environmental Management, Worldwatch.*

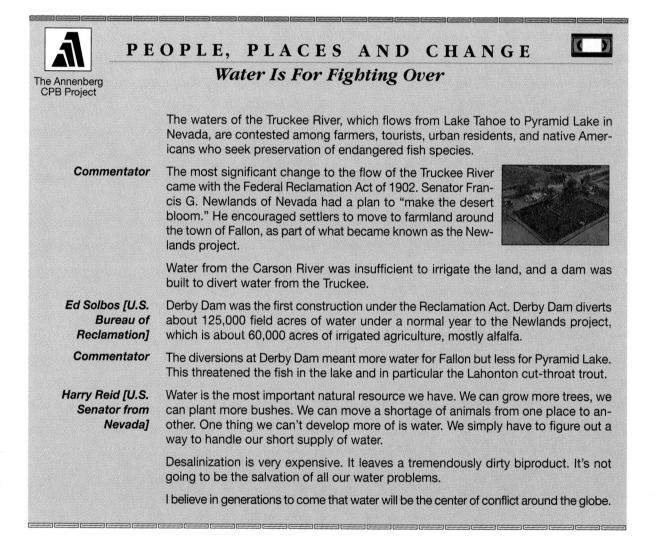

The Annenberg CPB Project

PEOPLE, PLACES AND CHANGE
Water Is For Fighting Over

The waters of the Truckee River, which flows from Lake Tahoe to Pyramid Lake in Nevada, are contested among farmers, tourists, urban residents, and native Americans who seek preservation of endangered fish species.

Commentator

The most significant change to the flow of the Truckee River came with the Federal Reclamation Act of 1902. Senator Francis G. Newlands of Nevada had a plan to "make the desert bloom." He encouraged settlers to move to farmland around the town of Fallon, as part of what became known as the Newlands project.

Water from the Carson River was insufficient to irrigate the land, and a dam was built to divert water from the Truckee.

Ed Solbos [U.S. Bureau of Reclamation]

Derby Dam was the first construction under the Reclamation Act. Derby Dam diverts about 125,000 field acres of water under a normal year to the Newlands project, which is about 60,000 acres of irrigated agriculture, mostly alfalfa.

Commentator

The diversions at Derby Dam meant more water for Fallon but less for Pyramid Lake. This threatened the fish in the lake and in particular the Lahonton cut-throat trout.

Harry Reid [U.S. Senator from Nevada]

Water is the most important natural resource we have. We can grow more trees, we can plant more bushes. We can move a shortage of animals from one place to another. One thing we can't develop more of is water. We simply have to figure out a way to handle our short supply of water.

Desalinization is very expensive. It leaves a tremendously dirty biproduct. It's not going to be the salvation of all our water problems.

I believe in generations to come that water will be the center of conflict around the globe.

CONCLUSION
CAREERS IN GEOGRAPHY

An increasing number of students recognize that geographic education is practical as well as stimulating. Employment opportunities are expanding for students trained in geography, especially in teaching, government service, and business.

Teaching. As of 1995, a doctorate in geography was offered at fifty-five U.S. and twenty-three Canadian universities, and the master's was the highest available degree at ninety-one U.S. and five Canadian universities. Traditionally, most trained geographers became teachers in high schools, colleges, or universities.

A career as a geography teacher is promising, because schools throughout North America are expanding the amount of geography in the curriculum. Educators increasingly recognize geography's role in teaching students about global diversity.

Some university geography departments have emphasized good teaching over research; others are increasingly concerned with research. The Association of American Geographers includes several dozen specialty groups organized around research themes, including agricultural, industrial, medical, and transportation geography.

Government. Some geographers find employment with cities, states, provinces, and other units of local government. Typically, these opportunities are found in departments of planning, transportation, parks and recreation, economic development, housing, or other similarly titled government agencies. Geographers may be hired to conduct studies of local economic, social, and physical patterns; to prepare information through maps and reports; and to help to plan the community's future.

Many national government agencies also employ geographers. In the United States, the Bureau of the Census in the Department of Commerce has a geography division that studies and reports on changing national population trends. Other U.S. government agencies that employ geographers include the Department of Defense Mapping Agency, the Soil Conservation Service and the Geological Survey in the Department of Interior, and the National Aeronautics and Space Administration.

Geographers contribute their knowledge of the location of activities, the patterns underlying the distribution of various activities, and the interpretation of information from maps. For example, in the 1940s the British government hired the geographer L. Dudley Stamp to conduct a land-use study of the entire country. Stamp identified the country's best agricultural land and contributed to the development of laws that strictly protected valuable land from urban development.

In recent years, geographers have been hired by government agencies because of their ability to interpret data generated from satellite imagery. Geographers also increasingly display information and interpret information through computer-generated maps.

Another career area for geographers is government foreign service, especially if they have expertise about other parts of the world. The tradition of geographic service in foreign affairs strengthened after World War I. The American geographer Isaiah Bowman advised President Woodrow Wilson on redrawing the map of Europe after the war, so that national boundaries more closely conformed to cultural patterns. At approximately the same time, the British geographer Halford J. Mackinder advised the British government on military strategy. He argued that the world's heartland, Eastern Europe, was surrounded by a rim of maritime powers. The key to Mackinder's international military strategy was understanding the relationship of the location of countries to their opportunity to exercise either land or naval power.

Business.

An increasing number of American geographers are finding jobs with private companies. The list of possibilities is long, but here are some common examples.

- Developers hire geographers to find the best locations for new shopping centers.
- Real estate firms hire geographers to assess the value of properties.
- Supermarket chains, department stores, and other retailers hire geographers to determine the potential market for new stores.
- Banks hire geographers to assess the probability that a loan applicant has planned a successful development.
- Distributors and wholesalers hire geographers to find ways to minimize transportation costs.
- Transnational corporations hire geographers to predict the behavior of consumers and officials in other countries.
- Manufacturers hire geographers to identify new sources of raw materials and markets.
- Utility companies hire geographers to determine future demand at different locations for gas, electricity, and other services.

For more information on careers in geography, contact the Association of American Geographers in Washington, D.C., or the National Council for Geographic Education at Indiana University of Pennsylvania.

Woody Allen's Final Word to the Graduates

This book is supposed to end with a word about the future to the graduates of the class. Woody Allen is not a geographer, but his speech to graduates has captured effectively some of the interrelationships among various human actions and the physical environment, which form the core of human geography.

More than any other time in history, mankind faces a crossroads. One path leads to despair and utter hopelessness. The other,

to total extinction. Let us pray we have the wisdom to choose correctly....

Science is something we depend on all the time. If I develop a pain in the chest I must take an X-ray. But what if the radiation from the X ray causes me deeper problems? Before I know it, I'm going in for surgery. Naturally, while they're giving me oxygen an intern decides to light up a cigarette. The next thing you know I'm rocketing over the World Trade Center in bed clothes....

At no other time in history has man been so afraid to cut into his veal chop for fear that it will explode. Violence breeds more violence and it is predicted that...kidnapping will be the dominant mode of social interaction. Overpopulation will exacerbate problems to the breaking point. Figures tell us that there are already more people on earth than we need to move even the heaviest piano. If we do not call a halt to breeding, by the year 2000 there will be no room to serve dinner unless one is willing to set the table on the heads of strangers. Then they must not move for an hour while we eat. Of course energy will be in short supply and each car owner will be allowed only enough gasoline to back up a few inches....

Summing up, it is clear the future holds great opportunities. It also holds pitfalls. The trick will be to avoid the pitfalls, seize the opportunities, and get back home by six o'clock.*

Human geographers do not know how to solve all of the world's problems of population growth, cultural and political conflict, economic development, and abuse of resources. This course has tried to expose you to the need to understand differences among human actions in different regions, the interdependencies between people and the environment, and other geographic perspectives on world problems. Above all, this book's aim is to heighten your sense of global awareness, that is, an understanding that our comfort—if not survival—requires greater knowledge of Earth's human and physical processes.

APPENDIX
MAP SCALE AND PROJECTIONS

Phillip C. Muercke

Unaided, our human senses provide a limited view of our surroundings. To overcome these limitations, people have developed powerful vehicles of thought and communication, such as language, mathematics, and graphics. Each of these tools is based on elaborate rules, each has an information bias, and each may distort its message, often in subtle ways. Consequently, to use these aids effectively, we must understand their rules, biases, and distortions. The same is true for the special form of graphics we call maps: we must master the logic behind the mapping process before we can use maps effectively.

A fundamental issue in cartography—the science and art of making maps—is the vast difference between the size and geometry of what is being mapped—the real world, we will call it—and that of the map itself. *Scale* and *projection* are the basic cartographic concepts that help us understand this difference and its effects.

Map Scale

Our senses are dwarfed by the immensity of our planet—we can sense directly only our local surroundings. Thus, we cannot possibly look at our whole state or country at one time, even though we may be able to see the entire street where we live. Cartography helps us expand what we can see at one time by letting us view the scene from some distant vantage point. The greater the imaginary distance is between that point and what we are looking at the larger the area the map can cover, but the smaller the features on the map will appear. This reduction is defined by the *map scale,* the ratio of the distance on the map to the distance on Earth. You need to know about map scale for two reasons: (1) so you can convert measurements on a map into meaningful real-world measures and (2) so you can know how abstract the cartographic representation is.

Real-world measures. A map can provide a useful substitute for the real world for many analytic purposes. With the scale of a map, for instance, we can compute the actual size of mapped features (length, area, or volume). These calculations are helped by three expressions of map scale: a word statement, a graphic scale, and a representative fraction.

A *word statement* of a map scale compares *X* units on the map with *Y* units on Earth, often abbreviated "*X* units to *Y* units." For example, the expression "1 inch equals 10 miles" means that 1 inch on the map represents 10 miles on Earth (Figure A-1). Because the map is normally smaller than the area that has been mapped, the ground unit is always the larger number. Both units are expressed in meaningful terms, such as inches and miles or centimeters and kilometers. Word statements are not intended for precise calculations but give the map user a rough idea of size and distance.

A *graphic scale,* such as a bar graph, is concrete. It therefore overcomes the need to visualize inches and miles required by use of a word statement of scale (see Figure A-1). A graphic scale permits direct visual comparison of feature sizes and the distances between features. No ruler is required; any measuring aid will do. It needs only to be compared with the scaled bar: if the length of one toothpick is equal to 2 miles on the ground and the map distance equals the length of four toothpicks, then the ground distance is 4 times 2, or 8 miles.

Graphic scales are especially convenient in this age of copying machines, when we are more likely to be working with a copy than with the original map. If a map is reduced or enlarged as it is copied, the graphic scale will change in proportion to the change in the size of the map and thus will remain accurate.

The third form of map scale is the *representative fraction (RF)*. An RF defines the ratio between the distance on the map and the distance on Earth in fractional terms, such as 1/633,600 (also written 1:633,600). The numerator of the fraction always refers to the distance on the map, and the denominator always refers to the real distance on Earth. No units of measurement are given, because any unit can be used, but the two numbers must be expressed in the *same* units. Because map distances are extremely small relative to the size of Earth, it makes sense to use small units, such as inches or centimeters. Thus, the RF 1:633,600 might be read as "1 inch on the map to 633,600 inches on Earth."

Herein lies a problem with the RF. Meaningful map-distance units imply a denominator so large that it is

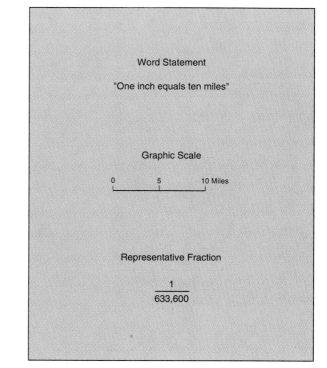

FIGURE A-1 Common expressions of map scale.

impossible to visualize. Thus, in practice, reading the map scale involves an additional step of converting the denominator to a meaningful ground measure, such as miles or kilometers. The unwieldy 633,600 becomes the more manageable 10 miles when divided by the number of inches in a mile (63,360).

On the plus side, the RF is good for calculations. In particular, the ground distance between points can easily be determined from a map with an RF. One simply multiplies the distance between the points on the map by the denominator of the RF. Thus, a distance of 5 inches on a map with an RF of 1/126,720 would signify a ground distance of 5 × 126,720, which equals 633,600. Because all units are inches and there are 63,360 inches in a mile, the ground distance is 633,600 ÷ 63,360, or 10 miles. Computation of area is equally straightforward with an RF. Computer manipulation and analysis of maps are based on the RF form of map scale.

Guides to generalization. Scales also help map users visualize the nature of the symbolic relation between the map and the real world. It is convenient here to think of maps as falling into three broad scale categories (Figure A-2). Do not be confused by the use of the words large and small in this context; just

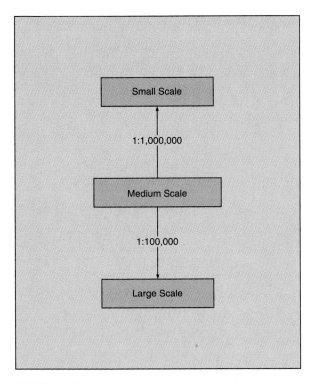

FIGURE A-2 The scale gradient can be divided into three broad categories.

remember that the larger the denominator, the smaller the scale ratio, and the larger the area that is shown on the map. Scale ratios greater than 1:100,000, such as the 1:24,000 scale of U.S. Geological Survey topographic quadrangles, are large-scale maps. Although these maps can cover only a local area, they can be drawn to rather rigid standards of accuracy. Thus, they are useful for a wide range of applications that require detailed and accurate maps, including zoning, navigation, and construction.

At the other extreme are maps with scale ratios of less than 1:1,000,000, such as maps of the world that are published in atlases. These are small-scale maps. Because they cover large areas, the symbols on them must be highly abstract. They are therefore best suited to general reference or planning, when detail is not important. Medium- or intermediate-scale maps have scales between 1:100,000 and 1:1,000,000. They are good for regional reference and planning purposes.

Another important aspect of map scale is to give us some notion of geometric accuracy. The fundamental problem is one of presenting Earth's curved surface on a flat sheet. The greater the expanse of the real world shown on a map, the less accurate is the geometry of that map. Figure A-3 shows why. If

a curve is represented by straight line segments, short segments (X) are more similar to the curve than are long segments (Y). Similarly, if a plane is placed in contact with a sphere, the difference between the two surfaces is slight where they touch (A) but grows rapidly with increasing distance (B) from the point of contact. In view of the large diameter and slight local curvature of Earth, distances are well represented on large-scale maps (those with small denominators, for example, 24,000) but will be increasingly poorly represented at smaller scales (those with large denominators, for example, 1,000,000). This close relationship between map scale and map geometry brings us to the topic of map projections.

Map Projections

The spherical surface of Earth is shown on flat maps by means of *map projections*. The process of "flattening" Earth is essentially a problem in geometry that has captured the attention of the best mathematical minds for centuries. Yet no one has found a perfect solution: there is no known way to avoid spatial distortion of one kind or another. Many map projections have been devised, but only a few have become standard.

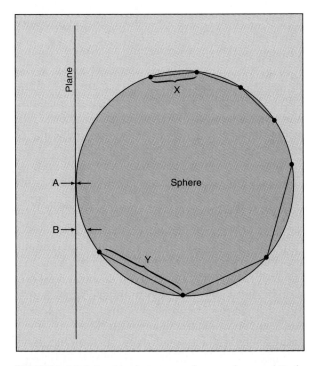

FIGURE A-3 Relationships between surfaces on the round Earth and a flat map.

Because a single flat map cannot preserve all aspects of Earth's surface geometry, a mapmaker must be careful to match the projection with the task at hand. Mapping something that involves distance, for example, requires a projection in which distance is not distorted. In addition, a map user should be able to recognize which aspects of a map's geometry are accurate and which are distortions caused by a particular projection process. Fortunately, this task is not too difficult.

It is helpful to think of the creation of a projection as a two-step process (Figure A-4). First, our immense planet is reduced to a small globe with a scale equal to that of the desired flat map. All spatial properties on the globe remain true to those on the real Earth. Second, the globe is flattened. This cannot be done without distortion, so it is accomplished in such a way that the resulting map exhibits certain desirable spatial properties.

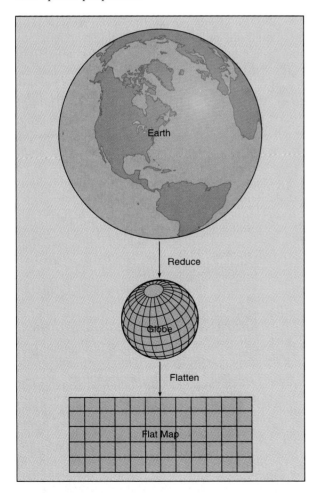

FIGURE A-4 The two-step process of creating a projection.

Perspective models.

Early map projections were sometimes created with the aid of perspective methods, but this approach has changed. In the modern electronic age, projections are normally developed by strictly mathematical means and are plotted out or displayed on computer-driven graphics devices. The concept of perspective is still useful, however, in visualizing what map projections do. Thus, projection methods are often illustrated by using strategically located light sources to cast shadows on a projection surface from a latitude-longitude net inscribed on a transparent globe.

The success of the perspective approach depends on finding a projection surface that is flat or that can be flattened without distortion. The cone, cylinder, and plane possess these attributes and serve as models for three general classes of map projections: *conic, cylindrical,* and *planar* (or azimuthal). Figure A-5 shows these three classes, as well as a fourth, a false cylindrical class with an oval shape. Although the *oval* class is not of perspective origin, it appears to combine properties of the cylindrical and planar classes (Figure A-6).

The relationship between the projection surface and the model at the point or line of contact is critical because distortion of spatial properties on the projection is symmetrical about, and increases with distance from, that point or line. This condition is illustrated for the cylindrical and planar classes of projections in Figure A-7. If the point or line of contact is changed to some other position on the globe, the distortion pattern will be recentered on the new position but will retain the same symmetrical form. Thus, centering a projection on the area of interest on Earth's surface can minimize the effects of projection distortion. And recognizing the general projection shape, associating it with a perspective model, and recalling the characteristic distortion pat-

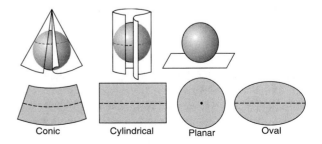

FIGURE A-5 General classes of map projections (Courtesy of ACSM.)

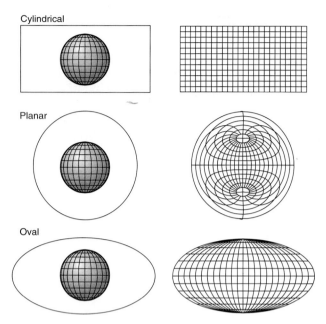

Cylindrical

Planar

Oval

FIGURE A-6 The visual properties of cylindrical and planar projections combined in oval projections (Courtesy of ACSM.)

tern will provide the information necessary to compensate for projection distortion.

Preserved properties. A map projection can truthfully depict the geometry of Earth's surface only if it preserves the spatial attributes of distance, direction, area, shape, and proximity. This task can be readily accomplished on a globe, but it is not possible on a flap map. To preserve area, for example, a mapmaker must stretch or shear shapes (consider what happens when you flatten an orange). Thus, area and shape cannot be preserved on the same map.

If both direction and distance from a point are depicted, area must be distorted. Similarly, if area and direction from a point are depicted, distance must be distorted. Because Earth's surface is continuous in all directions from every point, distortions of proximity relationships must occur on all map projections. The trick is to place these discontinuities where they will have the least impact on the spatial relationships in which the map user is interested.

We must be careful when we use spatial terms because the properties they refer to can be confusing. The geometry of the familiar plane is very different from that of a sphere; yet when we refer to a flat map, we are in fact making reference to the spherical Earth that was mapped. A shape-preserving projection, for example, is truthful to local shapes—such as the right-angle crossing of latitude and longitude lines—but cannot preserve shapes at continental or global levels.

A distance-preserving projection can preserve distance from one point on the map in all directions, or from a number of points in several directions, but distance cannot be preserved in the general sense that area can be preserved. Direction also can be preserved generally from a single point, or in several directions from a number of points, but not from all points simultaneously. Thus, a shape, distance, or direction-preserving projection is truthful to these properties only in part.

Partial truths are not the only consequence of transforming a sphere into a flat surface. Some projections exploit this transformation by expressing

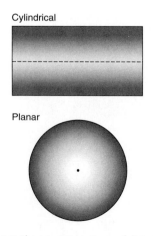

Cylindrical

Planar

FIGURE A-7 Characteristic patterns of distortion for the cylindrical and planar projection classes. Here, darker shading implies greater distortion (Courtesy of ACSM.)

traits that are of considerable value for specific applications. One of these is the famous shape-preserving *Mercator projection* (Figure A-8). This cylindrical projection was derived mathematically in the 1500s so that compass bearings (called *rhumb* lines) between any two points on Earth would plot as straight lines on the map. This trait let navigators plan, plot, and follow courses between origin and destination, but it was achieved at the expense of extreme areal distortion toward the margins of the projection (see Antarctica in Figure A-8). Although the Mercator projection is admirably suited for its intended purpose, its widespread—and inappropriate—use for nonnavigational purposes has drawn a great deal of criticism.

The *gnomonic projection* is also useful for navigation. It is a planar projection with the valuable characteristic of showing the shortest (or great circle) route between any two points on Earth as straight lines. Long-distance navigators first plot the great circle course between origin and destination on a gnomonic projection (Figure A-9, top). Next they transfer the straight line to a Mercator projection, where it normally appears as a curve (Figure A-9, bottom). Finally, using straight-line segments, they construct an approximation of this course on the Mercator projection. Navigating the shortest course between origin and destination then involves following the

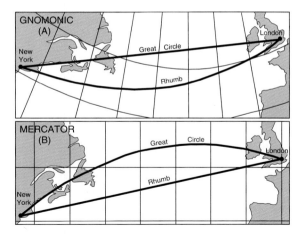

FIGURE A-9 A gnomonic projection (A) and a Mercator projection (B), both of value to long-distance navigators.

straight segments of the course and making directional corrections between segments. Like the Mercator projection, the specialized gnomonic projection distorts other spatial properties so severely that it should not be used for any purpose other than navigation or communications.

Projections used in textbooks. Although a map projection cannot be free of distortion, it can represent one or several spatial properties of Earth's surface accurately if other properties are sacrificed. The two projections used for world maps throughout this text illustrate this point well. Goode's homolosine projection, shown in the center of Figure A-10, belongs to the oval category. It shows area accurately, although it gives the impression that Earth's surface has been torn, peeled, and flattened. The interruptions in Figure A-10 have been placed in the major oceans, giving continuity to the land masses. Ocean areas could be featured instead by placing the interruptions in the continents.

Obviously, this type of interrupted projection severely distorts proximity relationships. Consequently, in different locations the properties of distance, direction, and shape are also distorted to varying degrees. The distortion pattern mimics that of cylindrical projections, with the equatorial zone the most faithfully represented (Figure A-11).

An alternative to special-property projections such as the equal-area Goode's homolosine is the compromise projection. In this case, no special property is achieved at the expense of others, and distortion

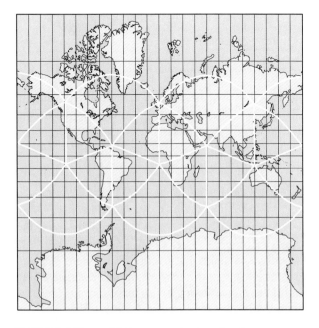

FIGURE A-8 The useful Mercator projection, showing extreme area distortion in the higher latitudes (Courtesy of ACSM.)

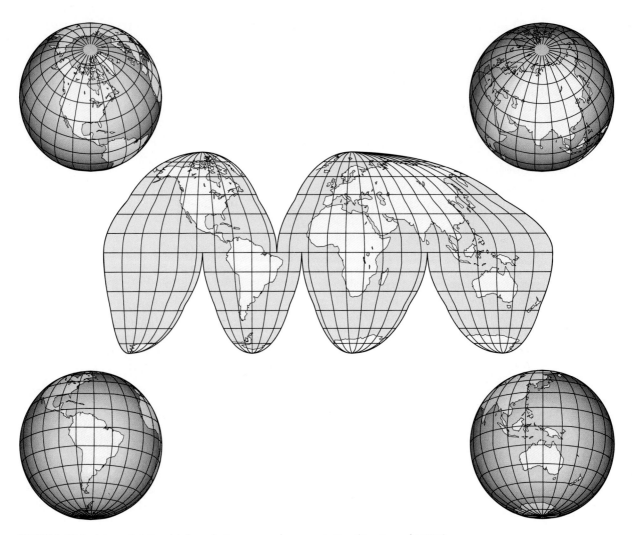

FIGURE A-10 An interrupted Goode's homolosine, an equal-area projection (Courtesy of ACSM.)

is rather evenly distributed among the various properties, instead of being focused on one or several properties. The *Robinson projection,* which is also used in this text, falls into this category (Figure A-12).

The oval Robinson projection has a global feel, somewhat like that of Goode's homolosine. But it shows the North Pole and the South Pole as lines that are slightly more than half the length of the equator, thus exaggerating distances and areas near the poles. Areas look larger than they really are in the high latitudes (near the poles) and smaller than they really are in the low latitudes (near the equator). In addition, not all latitude and longitude lines intersect at right angles, as they do on the real Earth, so we know that the Robinson projection does not preserve direction or shape either. However, it has fewer

interruptions than Goode's homolosine projection, so it preserves proximity better. Overall, the Robinson projection does a good job of representing spatial relationships, especially in the low to middle latitudes and along the central meridian.

Scale and Projections in Modern Geography

Computers have drastically changed the way in which maps are made and used. In the pre-electronic age, maps were so laborious, time-consuming, and expensive to make that relatively few were created. Frustrated, geographers and other scientists often found themselves trying to use maps for purposes not intended by the map designers. But today, anyone with access to computer mapping facilities can create projections in a flash. Thus, projections are being increasingly tailored to specific needs, and more scientists are doing their own mapping, rather than having someone else guess what they need in a map.

Computer mapping creates opportunities that go far beyond the construction of projections, of course. Once maps and related geographic data are entered into computers, many types of analysis can be carried out involving map scales and projections. Distances, areas, and volumes can be computed; searches can be conducted; information from different maps can be combined; optimal routes can be selected; facilities can be allocated to the most suitable sites; and so forth. The term used to describe these processes is *geographical information system,* or *GIS.*

Within a GIS, projections provide the mechanism for linking data from different sources, and scale provides the basis for size calculations of all sorts. Mastery of both projection and scale becomes the user's responsibility, because the map user is also the mapmaker. Now more than ever, effective geography depends on knowledge of the close association between scale and projection.

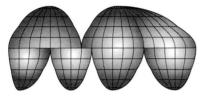

FIGURE A-11 The distortion pattern of the interrupted Goode's homolosine projection, which mimics that of cylindrical projections (Courtesy of ACSM.)

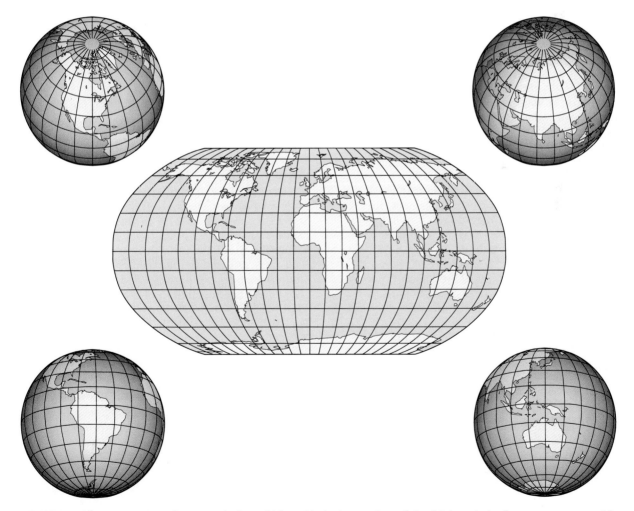

FIGURE A-12 The compromise Robinson projection, which avoids the interruptions of Goode's homolosine but preserves no special properties (Courtesy of ACSM.)

CREDITS

FIGURE 1-3 Adapted from David Lewis, *The Voyaging Stars* (New York: W.W. Norton, 1978), drawing page 120.

FIGURE 1-10 Adapted from Stanley D. Brunn, "Sunbelt USA," *Focus* 36 (Spring 1986): 35. Used by permission of The American Geographical Society.

FIGURE 4-1 Adapted from A. Meillet and M. Cohen, *Les langues du monde*, 1952 (Paris: Centre National de la Recherche Scientifique), carte XIB.

FIGURE 4-4 Adapted from *Encyclopaedia Britannica*, 15th edition (1987), 22: 660.

FIGURE 4-5 and **4-6** Adapted from Antoine Meillet and Marcel Cohen, *Les langues du monde* 1952.

FIGURE 4-7 Adapted from A. K. Ramanujan and Colin Masica, "A Phonological Typology of the Indian Liguistic Area," *Current Trends in Linguistics* 5 (1969): 561, with permission of Mouton de Gruyter, a division of Walter de Gruyter & Co.

FIGURE 4-8 Reprinted from George Cardona, Henry M. Hoenigswald, and Alfred Senn, "Indo-European and Indo-Europeans," in *Proto-Indo-European Culture* by Marija Gimbutas, University of Pennsylvania Press, Philadelphia, 1970.

FIGURE 4-9 Adapted from Colin Renfrew, "The Origins of Indo-Eruopean Languages," *Scientific American*, October 1989, map, p. 112.

FIGURE 4-11 Adapted from *Encyclopaedia Britannica*, 15th edition, 1987, 22:766 and 769.

FIGURE 4-12 Adapted from *Encyclopaedia Britannica*, 15th edition, 1987, 29:907.

FIGURE 4-15 Adapted from *Children's Games in Street and Playground* by Iona and Peter Opie. Iona and Peter Opie 1969. Published by Oxford University Press 1969.

FIGURE 4-16 Adapted from Hans Kurath, *A Word Geography of the Eastern United States* (Ann Arbor: University of Michigan Press), 1949, Figure 3.

FIGURE 4-17 Adapted from David H. Kaplan, "Population and Politics in a Plural Society: The Changing Geography of Canada's Linguistic Groups," *Annals of the Association of American Geographers*, March 1994, Figure 3.

FIGURE IN BOX 4-1 Adapted from *Encyclopaedia Britannica*, 15th edition (1987), 28:358.

FIGURE IN BOX 4-2 Adapted from *Encyclopaedia Britannica*, 15th edition (1987) 23:346.

FIGURE 5-1 Adapted from D. Sopher, *Geography of Religions* (Englewood Cliffs, NJ.: Prentice Hall), 1967.

FIGURE 5-3 From W. Shepherd, *Historical Atlas*, by permission of Barnes & Noble Books.

FIGURE 5-4 Adapted from Jan and Mel Thompson, *The R. E. Atlas: World Religions in Maps and Notes* (Sevenoaks, England: Hodder & Stoughton), 1986, p. 44; by permission of the publisher.

FIGURE 5-6 Adapted from Douglas W. Johnson, Paul R. Picard, and Bernard Quinn, *Churches and Church Membership in the United States* (Bethesda, MD; Glenmary Research Center), 1971.

FIGURE 5-7, 5-8, 5-9, 5-10, 5-11 From Ismail Ragi al Farugi and David E. Sopher, *Historical Atlas of the Religions of the World* (New York: Macmillan), 1974.

FIGURE 5-16 Adapted from *Encyclopaedia Britannica*, 15th edition (1987), 28:181.

FIGURE 6-1 Adapted from John F. Rooney, Jr., Wilbur Zelinsky, and Dean R. Louder, eds., *This Remarkable Continent: An Atlas of United States and Canadian Society and Culture* (College Station, TX: Texas A&M University Press), 1982, page 244, figure 11-13, George O. Carney.

FIGURE 6-3 Reproduced by permission from the *Annals of the Association of American Geographers*, Volume 68, 1978, p. 262, figure 11, W. K. Crowley.

FIGURE 6-4 Reproduced by permissions from the *Annals of the Association of American Geographers*, Volume 66, 1976, p. 490, figure 2; P. P. Karan and E. E. Mather.

FIGURE 6-6 Adapted from Jean-Paul Bourdier and Nezar Alsayyad, *Dwellings, Settlements, and Tradition* (Lanham, MD: University Press of America, 1989).

FIGURE 6-7 Adapted from Robert W. McColl, "By Their Dwellings Shall We Know Them: Home and Setting Among China's Inner Asian Ethnic Groups," *Focus*, Winter 1989, photos pp. 6 and 7, and Ronald G. Knapp, *China's Traditional Rural Architecture: A Cultural Geography of the Common House* (Honolulu: University of Hawaii Press, 1986), plate 2, p. 114.

FIGURE 6-8 and **6-9** Kniffen, Fred B. "Folk-Housing: Key to Diffusion." *Annals of the Association of American Geographers,* 55 (December 1965): p. 549-77.

FIGURE 6-10 Adapted from Virginia McAlester and Lee McAlester, *A Field Guide to American Houses* (New York: Alfred A. Knopf, 1984)

FIGURE 6-11 Adapted from John A. Jakle, Robert W. Bastian, and Douglas K. Meyer, *Common Houses in America's Small Towns* (Athens: The University of Georgia Press, 1989).

FIGURE 6-12 Adapted from John F. Rooney, Jr., and Paul L. Butt, "Beer, Bourbon, and Boone's Farm: A Geographical Examination of Alcoholic Drink in the United States," in *Journal of Popular Culture*, Vol. 11 (1968) 4:842-48. Reprinted with the permission of the editor.

FIGURE 6-13 Adapted from Barbara A. Shortridge and James R. Shortridge, "Consumption of Fresh Produce in the Metropolitan United States," *Geographical Review*, Vol. 79 (1989) 1: p.86, Table IV. Used by permission of the American Geographical Society.

FIGURE 6-16 Adapted from John F. Rooney, Jr., "American Golf Courses: A Regional Analysis of Supply," *Sport Place International*, Vol. 3 (1989) 1/2: pp. 6-8, figures 3, 4, and 6.

FIGURE 7-20 Adapted from George P. Murdock, *Africa: Its Peoples and Their Cultural History* (New York: McGraw Hill, 1959).

FIGURE 8-12 Adapted from Edward B. Espenshade, Jr., editor, *Goode's World Atlas,* 18th ed. (Chicago: Rand McNally, 1990), map p. 201.

FIGURE 9-3 Reproduced by permission from the *Annals of the Association of American Geographers*, Vol. 26, 1936, p. 241, figure 1; D. Whittlesey.

FIGURE 10-2 From Peter A. Gould, "Spatial Diffusion" (Washington, D.C.: *Association of American Geographers*) Resource Publication in Geography, No. 4, 1969, page 52 (including figure 57). Reprinted by permission.

FIGURE 11-6 Adapted from Leonardo Benevolo, *The History of the City* (Cambridge, MA: MIT Press), 1980, figures 31, 33, and 36.

FIGURE 11-15 From Walter Christaller, *Die Zentralen Orte in Sudeutschland as found in The Central Places in Southern Germany*, a translation by Carlisle W. Baskin (Englewood Cliffs, N.J.: Prentice Hall, 1966). Used by permission.

FIGURE 11-18 Adapted from J. Clark Archer and Ellen R. White, "Service Classification of American Cities," *Urban Geography*, Vol 5 (1985): 122-151.

FIGURE 11-19 Adapted from Paul Knox, *Urbanization: An Introduction to Urban Geography* (Englewood Cliffs, NJ: Prentice Hall, 1994), p. 61.

FIGURE 11-20 Adapted from Paul Knox, *Urbanization: An Introduction to Urban Geography* (Englewood Cliffs, NJ: Prentice Hall, 1994), p. 64.

FIGURE 12-3 From Marion Clawson and Peter Hall, *Planning and Urban Growth* (Baltimore: The Johns Hopkins University Press), 1973, p. 131. Published for Resources for the Future, Inc. by the Johns Hopkins University Press.

FIGURE 12-17 Adapted from Leonardo Benevolo, *The History of the City* (Cambridge: MIT Press, 1980), map pp. 828-29.

FIGURE 13-9 From Blair T. Bower and Daniel J. Basta, *Residuals-Environmental Quality Management: Applying the Concept* (Baltimore: The Johns Hopkins University Center for Metropolitan Planning and Research), 1973, p.3.

FIGURE 13-10 Adapted from William K. Stevens, "Study of Acid Rain Uncovers a Threat to Far Wider Area," *The New York Times*, January 16, 1990, p. 21, map.

FIGURE 13-12 Adapted from Peter Passell, "The Garbage Problem: It May Be Politics, Not Nature," *The New York Times*, February 26, 1991, p. B5, map; and Philip S. Gutis, "New York Begins Getting Rid of the Trash No One Wanted," *The New York Times*, May 18, 1987, p. 12, map.

FIGURE 13-13 Adapted from "The Nation's Polluters—Who Emits What, and Where," *The New York Times*, October 13, 1991, p. 10, map.

FIGURE 13-15 Adapted from Edward Carr, "Power to the People," *The Economist*, June 18, 1994, chart, p. 15

SELECTED MAP INDEX

INDEX